D1539911

AN ANNOTATED SECONDARY BIBLIOGRAPHY SERIES ON ENGLISH LITERATURE IN TRANSITION

1880–1920

W. EUGENE DAVIS

GENERAL EDITOR

JOSEPH CONRAD

THOMAS HARDY

E. M. FORSTER

JOHN GALSWORTHY

GEORGE GISSING

D. H. LAWRENCE

H. G. WELLS

WALTER PATER

G. B. SHAW

CONTRIBUTORS

Jean-Claude Almaric   *Université Paul Valéry,
Montpellier, France*
Gordon N. Bergquist   *Creighton University*
Werner Bies   *University of Trier, Germany*
Arthur L. Colby   *Arizona State University*
Richard Farr Dietrich   *University of South Florida*
Lidia W. Haberman   *Arizona State University*
David F. Holden   *University of Tennessee*
Gale K. Larson   *California State University, Northridge*
Masahiko Masumoto   *Nagoya University, Japan*
Janice Mouton   *Loyola University of Chicago*
Lisë B. Pedersen   *McNeese State University, Louisiana*
Asela Rodriguez de Laguna   *Rutgers University*
Karl-Heinz Schoeps   *University of Illinois*
Susan Stone-Blackburn   *University of Calgary, Canada*
David Welsh   *London, England*

ASSOCIATE CONTRIBUTORS

Vladimir T. Borovansky   *Arizona State University*
Susan Brewer   *Phoenix, Arizona*
Rodica Jackson   *Tempe, Arizona*
Eugene Steele   *University of Jos, Nigeria*
Bronislava Volek   *Indiana University*
Stella Wachsler   *Baltimore, Maryland*

G. B. Shaw

AN ANNOTATED BIBLIOGRAPHY OF WRITINGS ABOUT HIM

VOLUME III: 1957–1978

COMPILED AND EDITED BY

DONALD C. HABERMAN

NORTHERN ILLINOIS UNIVERSITY PRESS

DEKALB, ILLINOIS 1986

Donald C. Haberman is professor of English at Arizona State University, Tempe, where his areas of special interest are drama and modern British literature. The recipient of a Yale Ph.D., he has also taught at Lafayette College and the University of Montana. He is the author of *The Plays of Thornton Wilder, A Critical Study* and has also written articles on Ford Madox Ford, Marcel Proust, Stéphane Mallarmé, James Joyce, Plautus, and Waugh.

Library of Congress Cataloging-in-Publication Data

Haberman, Donald
G. B. Shaw: an annotated bibliography
of writings about him.
(Annotated secondary bibliography series on
English literature in transition, 1880–1920)
Includes indexes.
1. Shaw, Bernard, 1856–1950—Bibliography.
I. Title.   II. Series.
Z8814.5.H33   1986   [PR5366]   016.822'912   86-12477
ISBN 0-87580-111-0 (v. 3)

Publication of this book was assisted by
a grant from the Mellan Foundation

Preface

The ideal aim of this volume (one of three) of a bibliography of writings about George Bernard Shaw was completeness. Reality, of course, intruded, and I have had to settle for something less. The 2,677 entries include abstracts of a variety of writings: reviews; general appreciations; bibliographies; biographies; critical books and articles; chapters in books; histories of politics, the theater, and science; doctoral dissertations; letters to the editors of journals and newspapers as well as news items; introductions to Shaw's work in English and in translation; explications in anthologies; "case books"; and even dramatizations. I hope, though undoubtedly in vain, that I have not missed any significant piece of writing about Shaw for the period 1957 to 1978. Included are abstracts of writing that will seem trivial or foolish to the ordinary Shaw scholar. But partly because of Shaw's wide-ranging interests, I felt that any single judgment of the value of a piece of writing, based, just for example, on my own interest in Shaw as a writer and man of the theater, was obviously too narrow. The very variety of approaches to Shaw makes me believe that what may appear nonsensical to some users of this bibliography will be of interest to some others. Though approximately 1,000 abstracts were culled as being either repetitive or too slight, I have erred on the side of inclusion rather than exclusion.

I have tried to make the bibliographical information exact. Some items that seemed significant but were not obtainable are included without abstracts and are labeled in brackets: "Not seen." The abstracts represent through summary, paraphrase, and quotation the voice of the original author as closely as human judgment permits. All efforts to clarify, explain, or interpret the author's intentions have been resisted. Editorial and critical comments are bracketed. For those items easily found on the shelves of most college and university libraries, the abstracts are generally briefer than importance or size might warrant; I do not pretend to provide a substitite for reading the original item, only a guide to what may be found there.

I have put entries under the date of first publication and have provided data on reprintings, revisions, and translations, insofar as I could determine this information. When the original could not be located, the entry is still under the date of first publication, but I have indicated that it is the reprinted text that has been abstracted. The text of abstracts is followed by five indexes to simplify and broaden the usefulness of the bibliography.

Some of the limitations of this bibliography are by choice. With very few exceptions--usually when there was some unusual comment on Shaw or his work--reviews of secondary works are not included. Also not included are undergraduate honors theses and M.A. theses. Ph.D. dissertations are listed without abstracts but with references to DISSERTATION ABSTRACTS INTERNATIONAL, or similar series, when applicable. If possible, I have provided abstracts for foreign dissertations, especially if they have been published. Since productions of Shaw plays for the period covered by this bibliography are obviously revivals, I have chosen to abstract reviews only of productions in New York, London and some important English provincial cities, and Canada, plus some arbitrarily selected representative foreign-language productions. Reviews of films of Shaw plays have been severely limited.

I expected to encounter the greatest difficulty with the foreign-language items, though I was not prepared for the great number in Japanese and Russian. Especially for the writing about Shaw in Russian, items frequently could not be located, and also I feel certain there are additional ones I did not learn about. Because of the great range in quality as well as the great number, the Japanese items are representative. In addition, a few items in the languages of India and a rather large number of items in Hebrew came to my attention too late to locate and prepare abstracts. Still, I feel secure in the coverage of foreign-language writing about Shaw, owing to the exceptional efforts of the Interlibrary Loan staff of the Arizona State University Library, the cooperation of the National Libraries especially of Czechoslovakia, Hungary, and Romania, and most prominently the extraordinary diligence and work of Jean-Claude Amalric, Werner Bies, Susan Brewer, Masahito Masumoto, Asela Rodríguez-de Laguna, Karl-Heinz Schoeps, and David Welch.

Although a supplement to this work is beyond my expectation, I should be grateful to hear from any students of Shaw who might provide either correction or additional significant Shaviana.

PREFACE

ACKNOWLEDGMENTS

It is difficult for me adequately to convey the great sense of debt I owe to all who have helped in preparing this volume. The contributors are credited on a separate page, but I wish specifically to acknowledge and praise their industry, their professional judgment and knowledge, and their skill and care.

Among many others who have aided in crucial ways are Daniel Brink (Arizona State University), Marianna Brose (Arizona State University), Charles Carpenter (State University of New York at Binghamton), James Cradler (Illinois State University), Mario Currelli (University of Pisa, Italy), R. Derolez (Rijksuniversiteit-Gent), Steffi Gross (Haifa, Israel), Jacob Lamberts (Arizona State University), and Eugene Steele (University of Jos, Nigeria).

I want also to thank several undergraduate and graduate students: Chris Cox and Linda Schoen (University of South Florida), Christian Gollub (University of Illinois), Sofia Haberman (Yale University), Diane A. Facinelli (Arizona State University), Alice C. Patterson (Arizona State University), and Patrick Welch (Arizona State University).

Without the imaginative persistence and exceptional professional knowledge and competence of Jane E. Conrow, who was head of Interlibrary Loan Services of the Library at Arizona State University, and Bobbie Graham, Jewel Hayden, and their staff, this bibliography would have been literally impossible. I am grateful to the New York Public Library, especially the Library at Lincoln Center, and, in particular, Monty Arnold, as well as to the New York University Library.

Wilfred A. Ferrell, Marvin A. Fisher, and Nicholas A. Salerno, chairmen of the English Department at Arizona State University, helpfully provided graduate asisstants as well as encouragement. The Arizona State University Grants Committee twice supported my work with Summer Faculty Grants-in-Aid, for which I am grateful. Gwen Stowe and LaVeda Musser and the Arizona State University Word Processing Center helped to prepare the manuscript.

Few bibliographers labor unaided by the efforts of earlier workers. Of the many bibliographies that have contributed to this volume, I am compelled to mention the Continuing Check-list of the *Shaw Review*; the *Modern Drama* annual bibliography; "Shaw in the Hispanic World: A Bibliography," in *Modern Drama*, by Asela Rodríguez-Seda [Rodriguez de Laguna]; and Paul F. Breed and Florence M. Sniderman, *Dramatic Criticism Index*.

Finally, I owe the genesis of this work to the late Helmut E. Gerber. But I am thankful to him for much more: his constant guidance, expert knowledge, and kind and good-humored encouragement.

Contents

A Selective Checklist

OF THE WORKS OF G. B. SHAW

I. COLLECTED EDITION

Standard Edition of the Works of Bernard Shaw. Lond and
   NY, 1930-1950

II. PLAYS AND SCREENPLAYS

*The Bodley Head Bernard Shaw. Collected Plays with Their
   Prefaces*, ed by Dan H. Laurence. Lond, 1970-1974.
The Collected Screenplays of Bernard Shaw, ed by Bernard
   Dukore. Athens, Georgia, 1980.
"Why She Would Not." London Magazine III (Aug 1956), pp.
   11-20.

III. FICTION

Cashel Byron's Profession. Carbondale and Edwardsville,
   Illinois, 1968.
An Unfinished Novel, ed by Stanley Weintraub. Lond and
   NY, 1958.
Immaturity. Lond, 1931.
The Irrational Knot. NY, 1926.
Love among the Artists. NY, 1916.
Short Stories, Scraps and Shavings. NY, 1934.
An Unsocial Socialist. NY, 1905.

IV. ESSAYS

Advice to a Young Critic, ed by E. J. West. NY, 1955.
Bernard Shaw: The Road to Equality: Ten Unpublished

Lectures and Essays, 1884-1918, ed by Louis Crompton. Boston, 1971.

Bernard Shaw's Nondramatic Literary Criticism, ed by Stanley Weintraub. Lincoln, Nebraska, 1972.

Collected Music Criticism of George Bernard Shaw, 4 vols. NY, 1974.

G. B. S. on Music. Harmondsworth, 1962.

How to Become a Musical Critic, ed by Dan H. Laurence. Lond and NY, 1962.

The Matter with Ireland, ed by David Grene and Dan H. Laurence. Lond and NY, 1962.

My Dear Dorothea. NY, 1957.

On Language, ed by Abraham Tauber. NY, 1963.

Platform and Pulpit, ed by Dan H. Laurence. NY, 1961.

"Preface" to THREE PLAYS BY BRIEUX. NY, 1911.

The Rationalization of Russia, ed by H. M. Geduld. Bloomington, Indiana, 1964.

The Religious Speeches of Bernard Shaw, ed by Warren Sylvester Smith. University Park, Pennsylvania, 1964.

Selected Non-Dramatic Writings of Bernard Shaw, ed by Dan H. Laurence. Boston, 1965.

Shaw on Language, ed by A. Tauber. Lond, 1965.

Shaw on Religion, ed by Warren Sylvester Smith. Lond and NY, 1967.

Shaw's Music: The Complete Musical Criticism in Three Volumes, ed by Dan H. Laurence. NY, 1981.

Shaw on Theatre, ed by E. J. West. NY, 1958.

V. AUTOBIOGRAPHY

Shaw. An Autobiography 1856-1898, selected from his writings by Stanley Weintraub. Lond and NY, 1969.

Shaw. An Autobiography 1898-1950, selected from his writings by Stanley Weintraub. Lond and NY, 1970.

Sixteen Self Sketches. NY, 1949.

VI. LETTERS

Separate collections of Shaw's letters to: Alma Murray, Florence Farr, Ellen Terry, Mrs. Patrick Campbell, Granville Barker, Golding Bright, and Molly Tompkins.

Bernard Shaw: Collected Letters, vol I 1874-1897; vol II 1898-1910, ed by Dan H. Laurence. Lond and NY, 1965.

Acronyms of Secondary Works

BDDTG—Blätter Des Deutschen Theatres in Gootingen

BNYPL—Bulletin of the New York Public Library

CShav—California Shavian

DA—Dissertation Abstracts

DAI—Dissertation Abstracts International

DAID—Dissertations on Anglo-Irish Drama

DRAMA—Drama, The Quarterly Theatre Review

DramS—Drama Survey

ETJ—Educational Theatre Journal

FF—Fabian Feminist, Bernard Shaw and Women

ISh—Independent Shavian

List—Listener

McNamee—Dissertations in English and American Literature

MD—Modern Drama

N&Q—Notes and Queries

NS&Nation—New Statesman and Nation

NStat—New Statesman

NY—New Yorker

NYHT—New York Herald Tribune

NYT--New York Times

NYTMag--New York Times Magazine

P&P--Plays and Players

QQ--Queen's Quarterly

Reg--Regional

Shav--Shavian

ShawB--Shaw Bulletin

ShawR--Shaw Review

ShawSB--Shaw Society Bulletin

Spec--Spectator

SRL--Saturday Review of Literature

TAM--Theater Arts Monthly

TH--Theater Heute

TLS--Times Literary Supplement

TWCIMB--Twentieth Century Interpretations of Major Barbara

Introduction

An account of the secondary material on Bernard Shaw for the years 1957 through 1978 must to a great extent be a disorderly affair. Although critical attention is steady, in fact, steadily increasing, a clear picture of the critical view of Shaw's achievement is difficult to discern. It is just about as difficult to find a clear explanation for this situation.

The beginning year for this bibliography is almost entirely arbitrary, though it does mark the beginning of the second hundred years since Shaw's birth in 1856. Shaw lived almost until the centennial of his birth, and although his major writing was done by ten years before his death in 1950, he did not quite put down his pen until he was safely dead. He lived too long to be easily categorized in a time slot. Is he a Victorian? Edwardian? modern? Or all three? The fifty-year period of Shaw's major dramatic writing was also a time of violent and swift changes in human assumptions, and since Shaw responded to these changes, no neat intellectual categories exist for him either. Too many ideas, events, activities interested him, and he was not shy about expressing his views with authority. In turn the religious writer, the philosopher, the political or social historian, the economist, the biologist have all responded to Shaw and each from his own perspective. If Shaw's dramatic achievement seems to be most important, it is certainly not his only achievement, and also it cannot be separated from his other activities. Simply, Shaw is too big and too various to be easily evaluated.

Shaw felt that he and Shakespeare divided the world of English drama between them. If there is little critical quarrel with Shaw's claim, it is not because there is anything like agreement that Shaw is a creditable rival to Shakespeare in the comprehensiveness of his art or human understanding. The situation is for many readers and playgoers one of *faute de mieux*. To many the field of English drama seems empty except for Shakespeare, and

Shaw's presence somewhere on the edge is acknowledged only because of the sheer quantity of production, energy, and attention-getting antics. Even among Shaw's admirers nothing like unanimity of opinion is to be found about the nature of his success as a writer; about his views on important issues; even about which plays ought to be recognized as masterpieces.

The plays are performed regularly, in Great Britain, the United States, Canada, Germany, and the Socialist countries of Eastern Europe, including the Soviet Union. Clive Barnes finally confessed what was apparent to his readers, that he does not like Shaw, and at the time of his tenure as drama critic for the New York *Times* during the late sixties and early seventies, any New York production of Shaw without a star admired by Barnes was a financial risk. Since Barnes has been replaced on the *Times*, the situation has changed; such is the power of one man to determine what the Broadway (and off-Broadway) audience will not see. There are successful summer theater festivals, most notably for this period the one at Niagara-on-the-Lake in Canada. *Heartbreak House* and *Saint Joan* and perhaps *Man and Superman* seem to be the favorites of literary critics and audiences alike. *Mrs. Warren's Profession, Candida, Major Barbara,* and *Pygmalion* (apart from MY FAIR LADY) are a very close second, and probably even among the front runners in terms of production. *Arms and the Man, The Devil's Disciple, Caesar and Cleopatra, Captain Brassbound's Conversion, The Doctor's Dilemma, Misalliance, Androcles and the Lion, The Apple Cart,* and *The Millionairess* are under constant critical scrutiny and also appear regularly on the stage. There is increasing interest in *In Good King Charles's Golden Days* both as a valuable literary work and as an amusing play, but somehow it does not appear to be able to capture firm support. *Back to Methuselah* is the most problematic. Many readers especially, though adventuresome productions have been mounted, have struggled to justify Shaw's high estimate of this jumbo work. Just as many critics have explanations for its failure.

Shaw's success as a playwright is the justification for the more than special interest in most of his other activities. During this same period there has been sporadic and sometimes comic attention paid to his ideas about food, photography, the alphabet, and typography and printing. More seriously his measure as a novelist has been considered. His music criticism has been collected and is acknowledged to be a model of excellence. His importance as a critic--theoretical, in his books on Ibsen and Wagner, and practical, in his theater reviews--is firmly established. He is a major figure in the history of Socialist politics. There is some uncertainty about his importance as a religious thinker, and also controversy about his philosophical biology. The recent efforts at re-evaluation of the position of women has given prominence to still another facet of Shaw, though there is some disagreement about whether he is a saint or a false prophet for the women's movement.

It is no surprise, then, that opinion is unsettled, that few writers on Shaw have the courage, the knowledge, or the energy to attempt more than a very partial evaluation. A. C. Ward's BERNARD SHAW (1957) is the first trustworthy and positive general evaluation of Shaw for this period. Bronisława Bałutowa's DRAMAT BERNARDA SHAW (The Plays of Bernard Shaw, 1957) is one of the best examples of the generally high level of writing about Shaw in Polish. After World War II, in all the countries of Eastern Europe the official Socialist line is taken. Bałutowa does not distort Shaw, and the book is a valuable representative of the Continental attitudes toward Shaw's dramatic work. Julian B. Kaye in BERNARD SHAW AND THE NINETEENTH CENTURY TRADITION (1958) provides one of the first thorough examinations of Shaw's intellectual debts to his immediate past. Zdeněk Vančura's UMĚNI G. B. SHAW (The Art of G. B. Shaw, 1958) is a serious general evaluation of Shaw, which is marred somewhat by its emphasis on Socialist ideology; but it is valuable for the information and bibliography about Shaw's work in Czechoslovakia. It is significant also as a Socialist work consciously different from Balutowa's in its emphasis on Shaw's developing ideas.

In 1959 Harold Clurman's important production of *Heartbreak House* opened in New York. The SHAW BULLETIN announced and consolidated its success by becoming the SHAW REVIEW. Two important bibliographies were published: Earl Farley and Marvin Carlson's "George Bernard Shaw: A Selected Bibliography (1954 - 1955)" and Lawrence C. Keough's "George Bernard Shaw, 1946 - 1955: A Selected Bibliography." Miklós Almási's chapter on Shaw in A MODERN DRÁMA ÚTJAIN (Along the Byways of Modern Drama, 1961) is further evidence of the generally superior attempts at this time in Eastern Europe to see Shaw entire. In "Another Look at Bernard Shaw" (1961) Frederick P. W. McDowell assessed both Shaw's reputation and some of the critical trends, concluding that in spite of much unenthusiastic criticism of Shaw's plays, the late work especially, the plays are popular in the theater.

In 1962, in line with the rebellious times, Robert Brustein argued in THE THEATRE OF REVOLT that Shaw was more revolutionary than artist. But in the same year John Gassner, with less eagerness to be fashionable, reconciled Shaw's pedagogical elements with the histrionic. Richard

C. Ohmann's SHAW: THE STYLE AND THE MAN is the first serious linguistic analysis of Shaw, and it remains a model. It also marks the beginning of the appearance of many thoughtful book-length studies of Shaw.

Marcell Benedek's G. B. SHAW (1963) is a solid study in Hungarian that delicately steps around the Socialist bias of his government. Martin Meisell's exceptional book SHAW AND THE NINETEENTH CENTURY THEATER shows Shaw's exploitation of the theatrical genres of the nineteenth century. In this same year appeared Homer Edwards Woodbridge's GEORGE BERNARD SHAW: CREATIVE ARTIST, which traces Shaw's entire development, and J. I. M. Stewart included Shaw in his volume of the Oxford History of English Literature, EIGHT MODERN WRITERS. Barbara Bellow Watson, tuning in to one of the major social developments of the sixties, analyzed and acknowledged Shaw's attempt to raise the consciousness of his audience to the plight of women in A SHAVIAN GUIDE TO THE INTELLIGENT WOMAN.

Publication during the middle sixties seemed to pause for assessment and consolidation. R. J. Kaufmann edited an anthology by many hands, G. B. SHAW: A COLLECTION OF CRITICAL ESSAYS (1965). The same year Dan H. Laurence, the major editor of Shaw's works, issued BERNARD SHAW: COLLECTED LETTERS, 1875 - 1897, and also SELECTED NON-DRAMATIC WRITINGS OF BERNARD SHAW. The papers from the Shaw meeting in conjunction with the play festival at Niagara-on-the-Lake, including solid but unadventuresome essays by R. B. Parker, Stanley Weintraub, Boyd Neel, and Robert F. Whitman, were edited by Norman Rosenblood and published as SHAW SEMINAR PAPERS - 65 (1966). Harold Fromm's BERNARD SHAW AND THE THEATER IN THE NINETIES: A STUDY OF SHAW'S DRAMATIC CRITICISM (1967) considered at length and in detail the role of Shaw as a drama critic and its relation to his later practice as a playwright. Continuing along Richard Ohmann's path of language analysis, Fred Mayne with a narrower focus illuminated the relationship between Shaw's use of wit and his didactic purpose in THE WIT AND SATIRE OF BERNARD SHAW (1967). Stanley Weintraub promoted another aspect of Shaw's career, the writing of novels, by issuing his edition of Cashel Byron's Profession (1968).

Romania, like Poland and Hungary, had mounted Shaw's plays on the stage regularly; G. B. SHAW IN ROMÂNIA (1968) by Ileana Berlogea surveys Romanian productions and criticism, paying particular attention to Candida and to the important Romanian critic Radu Lupan. Although Russian criticism has been constant, the years 1968 - 1970, for reasons that must remain mysterious to us in the West, witnessed the first great wave in a flood of writing about Shaw that continues to the present.

INTRODUCTION

Charles A. Carpenter, who is also important to Shaw as a bibliographer for MODERN DRAMA, concentrated on the beginning of Shaw's career as a dramatist in BERNARD SHAW AND THE ART OF DESTROYING IDEALS: THE EARLY PLAYS (1969), and showed that Shaw did not so much marshal a coherent argument as expose the idealistic illusions of his contemporary society. R. F. Dietrich, looking even earlier in Shaw's development as a writer, did a full scale workout on Shaw's attempts at fiction in PORTRAIT OF THE ARTIST AS A YOUNG SUPERMAN: A STUDY OF SHAW'S NOVELS (1969). Both Louis Crompton in SHAW THE DRAMATIST (1969) and Colin Wilson in BERNARD SHAW: A REASSESSMENT (1969) attempt not without some success the impossible, a broad survey of Shaw that is not also too general, Crompton concentrating on the dramatist and Wilson on the thinker.

Shaw wrote no autobiography, and Stanley Weintraub, a tireless promoter of Shaw's reputation, stepped in to provide what Shaw neglected; from a pastiche of Shaw's writing, he constructed first in SHAW: AN AUTOBIOGRAPHY, 1856 - 1898 (1969) and then in SHAW: AN AUTOBIOGRAPHY, 1898 - 1950 (1970), a coherent "patchwork self-portrait."

Shaw, of course, is important to the history of Socialism, especially in Great Britain. James W. Hulse places Shaw in the context of this history as well as of his fellow Socialists in REVOLUTIONISTS IN LONDON: A STUDY OF FIVE UNORTHODOX SOCIALISTS (1970). Shaw's plays have formed a part of the reading for Hungarian secondary school students since long before the Socialist revolution there; they have taken a lively role in the very active Hungarian theater as well. Géza Hegedüs in G. B. SHAW BILAGA (The World of G. B. Shaw, 1970) surveys the role of Shaw in Hungary and also provides a critical overview of Shaw's achievement. An indicator of Shaw's importance to American students is the appearance (1970) of Warren Sylvester Smith's Norton Critical Edition of BERNARD SHAW'S PLAYS, which combines texts of four plays and three critical essays for each play.

Two works in German criticism stand out for 1971: Friedhelm Denninghaus's DIE DRAMATISCHE KONZEPTION GEORGE BERNARD SHAWS (George Bernard Shaw's Dramatic Concept) and Dietrich Schwanitz's GEORGE BERNARD SHAW. Denninghaus sees Shaw's dramas as socially determined from the Marxist point of view, which has made his work significant for Shaw's Communist audience, and in fact the book was translated and published in Russia. Schwanitz has a broader view and emphasizes Shaw as a modern dramatist, showing Shaw's artistic strategies as attempts to deal with a chaotic world.

Elsie B. Adams put Shaw in an intellectual context that is generally neglected or considered controversial, when it is considered at all, in BERNARD SHAW AND THE AESTHETES (1971). Earl Dean Bevan's A CONCORDANCE TO THE PLAYS OF BERNARD SHAW (1971) simply by its appearance acknowledges Shaw as a giant of some sort.

1972 seems a dry year for Shaw scholarship except for Dan H. Laurence's second volume of the correspondence: BERNARD SHAW: COLLECTED LETTERS, 1898 - 1910. But 1973 was more lively. It was this year that Clive Barnes, reviewing *Don Juan in Hell*, confessed that he did not feel that Shaw was "one of the great dramatists of the century." Bernard F. Dukore, who had already examined Shaw's experience as a practical man of the theater in BERNARD SHAW, DIRECTOR (1971), published a complementary book, BERNARD SHAW, PLAYWRIGHT: ASPECTS OF SHAVIAN THEORY AND PRACTICE, which acknowledges Shaw's attention to stagecraft but is really in the camp of those who view Shaw's art as deriving from doctrine. Charles A. Berst's BERNARD SHAW AND THE ART OF DRAMA surveys Shaw's middle plays, stressing Shaw's self-conscious dramaturgy and concluding that his best work is dramatic poetry. The particular focus of Paul A. Hummert's BERNARD SHAW'S MARXIAN ROMANCE is Shaw's dependence on Marxist economics, which he humanized, as he searched by means of his plays for a better world. Maurice Valency in THE CART AND THE TRUMPET comes as close as anybody in writing about Shaw whole. He covers Shaw's entire career, including his intellectual, social, and historical milieus; he does not neglect Shaw's aesthetic or his conscious skill as a writer; he uses Shaw's biography where it is most illuminating; he makes judgments. Perhaps it is petty carping to note that Valency sounds rather tired and hurried at the end; the book is nevertheless exceptional and indispensable.

Continuing the stream of notable books is Karl-Heinz Schoeps's BERTOLT BRECHT AND BERNARD SHAW (1974), which documents an interesting relationship in the history of modern playwriting. J. L. Wisenthal's THE MARRIAGE OF CONTRARIES (1974) is limited to the important middle period; he reads the plays from the thesis that Shaw saw the world in terms of contraries and presented what he saw in sets of complementary characters. Unlike many studies with a specific thesis, Wisenthal's book is illuminating and generous. BERNARD SHAW: A PSYCHOLOGICAL STUDY (1975) by Daniel Dervin is a sensitive Freudian examination of the plays that is readable and free from cant. Andrew K. Kennedy's chapter on Shaw in SIX CHARACTERS IN SEARCH OF A LANGUAGE is another important study of Shaw's language, but it stresses Shaw's verbal theatricality, providing a close examination of the plays as plays, not as evidence to support a theory.

The second half of the seventies begins with several valuable but somewhat narrower perspectives on Shaw. An attempt to provide a handy overview of the range of attitudes toward Shaw during his lifetime is SHAW, THE CRITICAL HERITAGE (1976), edited by T. F. Evans. SHAW'S MORAL VISION (1976) by Alfred A. Turco, Jr., takes Shaw's ethical views as a means to evaluate the plays. Jean-Claude Amalric's BERNARD SHAW: DU RÉFORMATEUE VICTORIEN AU PROPHETE EDOUARDIENN (Bernard Shaw: From Victorian Reformer to Edwardian Prophet, 1977) is a detailed examination of the development of Shaw's ideas. It is also the major work on Shaw published in France, where Shaw has generally not been appreciated. The sections concerned with *Heartbreak House* in Thomas R. Whitaker's FIELDS OF PLAY IN MODERN DRAMA (1977) provide a refreshingly new way to understand Shaw's linguistic comedy and characterization. FABIAN FEMINIST: BERNARD SHAW AND WOMEN, edited by Rodelle Weintraub, acknowledges the current interest in the position and role of women; much of it is reprinted from the special issue of the SHAW REVIEW in 1974.

Daniel J. Leary shows that Shaw can be put through the latest critical apparatus in "Shaw versus Shakespeare: the Refinishing of CYMBELINE" (1978). Leary demonstrates Shaw's use of Harold Bloom's strategems from his study of the anxiety of influence in *Cymbeline Refinished* as a paradigm of all Shaw's work.

It should be remembered that the works included in this brief survey exist in a vast sea of writing about Shaw. It is worthwhile to note in particular the quantity of scholarship in Japanese, which is periodically surveyed by Masahiko Masumoto.

If a pattern exists in this fluid mass, unless it is simply liveliness and disagreement (but without much variety), I cannot see it. Shaw is the great British playwright, perhaps more accurately, one of the Great British *events*, of the first half of the twentieth century, but what that might mean or what value might lie in it has not yet emerged clearly. Furthermore, little of the writing about Shaw is in its nature startling or exciting. There are some exceptions: the work of Andrew K. Kennedy, J. L. Wisenthal, Maurice Valency, Friederich Denninghaus, Thomas R. Whitaker, and Daniel Dervin among them. Almost all the writers on Shaw put his work in the traditional (and useful) contexts of biography, cultural and intellectual history, or simply explanation. Our understanding of Shaw has not reached the point where his writing has brought into being its own kind of critical standards and perception. And it is not possible yet to determine certainly whether or not it will ever command or support this sort of attention. So in spite of the quantity, there is little variety; the overwhelming sense is that the preliminary work is still in process.

For Lidia, Sofia, and Alice

G. B. Shaw

AN ANNOTATED BIBLIOGRAPHY

OF WRITINGS ABOUT HIM

VOLUME III

The Bibliography

1957

---

1 Adania, Alf. "Ultima Piesâ a lui Bernard Shaw" (Last Plays of Bernard Shaw), ROMÂNIA LIBERÂ, 2 June 1957.
Until the end of his life Shaw remained the adversary of the bourgeoisie and capitalism. [In Romanian.]

2 Anderson Imbert, Enrique. "Se mos murio Bernard Shaw" (Bernard Shaw Died in US), LOS GRANDES LIBROS DE OCCIDENTE (Buenos Aires: Andrea, 1957), pp. 164-75.
[A eulogy to Shaw on his death. Anderson Imbert tells of his first literary encounter with Shaw and of the resulting impact on his political thought.] [In Spanish.]

3 Atkinson, Brooks. "Theatre: Capital Arena," NYT, 1 April 1957, p. 21.
Man of Destiny at the Arena Stage in Washington offers impudent insights into the cupidity of Napoleon and an adventuress.

4 Auden, W. H. "Crying Spoils the Appearance," NY, XXXIII (7 Sept 1957), 130-32.
Along with Shaw's early art criticism, *My Dear Dorothea* (1956) reveals that Shaw's brilliant style matured early. Other than differences in construction, his later plays and prefaces are of the same maturity and style. Shaw's cynical but cheerful advice to Dorothea to act in her own self-interests and rely on her intellect, individuality, and independence arises from his view of childhood being a lonely, loveless time. The Shavian *jeu d'esprit* which makes Shaw's works immortal appears to spring from a comic version of stoic suffering.

1

5 Bab, Julius. "Bernard Shaw und die Kritiker des *Androklus*" (Bernard Shaw and the Critics of *Androcles*), BDDTG, VIII (1957-58), 38-40.
[Discusses the Christian ideas in Shaw's play and blames all critics who are not able to discover them.] [In German.]

6 Bałutowa, Bronisława. DRAMAT BERNARDA SHAW (The Plays of Bernard Shaw) (Lodz: Zakład im. Ossolinskich [Łodzkie Tow. Naukowe. Prace Wydziatu], 1957).
[This book attempts to provide for the Polish reader "indispensable information" about Shaw, detailed examination of his plays, and interpretation of ideas that are exotic to the non-specialist.] Table of Contents: I. Life and Artistic Production. II. Misunderstanding of Shaw [Survey of productions of Shaw's plays with critical and popular response, emphasizing especially continental history, Polish in particular.] The production of *Candida* (Lwow, 1906) inaugurated Shaw's popularity in Poland. It was favorably noticed by critics and much spoken of, opening the way for further productions. But Shaw's plays also aroused some uneasiness. The translations by Sobieniewski were often inadequate. III. Intellectualism of Bernard Shaw. IV. Didacticism of Bernard Shaw. V. Comic Drama of Bernard Shaw. VI. Value of Shaw's Drama. Shaw is really a post-Victorian writer not a contemporary one. If only his early plays [up through *Saint Joan*] are considered, Shaw must be regarded not only as one of the greatest playwrights of England, but of the world. Shaw's work is faulty in several respects: artificiality in constructing conflicts, the intellectualization of positive heroes, the construction of characters, and elimination of love motives. His attitude to art was on the whole somewhat contemptuous. It is difficult to assess the extent of Shaw's influence. [Contains woodcut of Shaw by M. Pikov, chronology of Shaw's works, and bibliography. Excellent consideration of Shaw and his work in the content of his time and especially valuable for its continental point of view.] [In Polish.]

7 Barber, George S. "Shaw's Contributions to Music Criticism," PMLA, LXXII (Dec 1957), 1005-18.
Shaw's music criticism deserves to be taken seriously. Incorruptible himself, Shaw attacked the commercialization of the opera house and concert house in the hands of the impresario. Eager to relate art to life, Shaw pointed out the deleterious effect on both artists and their music of

the capitalist system. The remedy was in a public endow-
ment of music. Shaw's concern for making the best music
available to the public "was motivated by the belief that
music was the highest and most powerful educational
force." Shaw's attack on the corrupting impresario was
seconded by his rebuke of the musically ignorant editor
who allowed worthless criticism to be perpetrated on the
public. Shaw further argued that, since criticism is
inevitably subjective, the critic should not pretend
otherwise. Finally, Shaw felt the duty of the critic was
to fight for excellence in performance and composition by
magnifying faults and praising virtues.

8 Barrett, William. "A Plausible Irishman,"
PARTISAN REVIEW, XXIV (Winter 1957), 101-5.
Shaw gives his audience a feeling of purpose in his plays
which they desire. His middlebrow journalistic style
appeals to them while presenting the aging, but to them
daring, ideas of Continental authors. Moreover, "as Shaw
is able to circumvent his lack of great comic imagination,
he is almost able . . . to get around his most serious
limitation, an almost total lack of poetry" by giving the
actors a chance to achieve poetry through their craft.
Finally, while a Shaw revival will not do any good for the
American theater, his warm human contact will not do any
harm.

9 Batson, Eric J. "Shaw's First Book," SHAVIAN,
VIII (1957), 20-21.
My Dear Dorothea was the first of Shaw's assaults on the
female mind. It is addressed to the incipient Intelligent
Woman.

10 Bennett, Mark. "G.B.S.'s Advice to Children of
All Ages," ShawB, II (May 1957), 17-18.
My Dear Dorothea is full of wicked counsel from the young
experimental philosopher.

11 Bennett, Mark. "The Permanent, Portable *Saint
Joan*," ShawB, II (Jan 1957), 19-20.
[Review of the RCA Victor recording of the Cambridge Drama
Festival production of *Saint Joan*, starring Siobhan
McKenna.] The first recording of a Shaw play in its
entirety, although slightly abridged, lacks the visual
dimension; "the play on record emerges as the intellectual
drama Shaw conceived it to be."

3

12 Bentley, Eric [Russell]. "Appendix to the Second Edition (1957): Shaw and the Actors," BERNARD SHAW: 1856-1950 (NY: New Directions, 1957), pp. 220-32. Shaw plays are far from naturalism, though we have difficulty realizing it. Modern drama begins with Shaw the actor. He demanded heroic actors. Perhaps only in the actresses, Florence Farr, Elizabeth Robbins, and Janet Achurch, do Ibsen and Shaw meet. Mrs. Patrick Campbell and Ellen Terry formed Shaw's notion of what women could be. The problem of acting Shaw is to render the long speeches. His plays demand the grand style supported by rigorous training in artistic sensitivity, a synthesis of grandeur and naturalness.

13 "Biographer's Blunders Corrected: G.B.S. on Edward McNulty's GEORGE BERNARD SHAW AS A BOY," Shaw B, II (Sept 1957), 7.
[A brief biography of Shaw's boyhood companion, Matthew Edward McNulty, and a summary of Shaw's emendations of McNulty's memoir, GEORGE BERNARD SHAW.]

14 Bogdan, Mihai. "George Bernard Shaw: Teatru" (George Bernard Shaw: Theater), STEAUA, IX (1957), 98-99.
[Essay-review of Petru Comarnescu's Romanian translations of *Widowers' Houses, Man and Superman, The Doctor's Dilemma, Saint Joan, Major Barbara,* and *Pygmalion.*] Shaw introduced the Ibsen theater of ideas on the English stage, although he had no rigorous philosophic system of his own. His success on the Romanian stage is possible only because of magnificent translations like Petru Comarnescu's one of *Pygmalion.* [In Romanian.]

15 Carrington, Norman Thomas. NOTES ON G. BERNARD SHAW: PYGMALION (Lond: Brodie [Notes on Chosen English Texts], [1957]).
[Biography, explanatory notes, and study questions. Not seen.]

16 Casserly, C. J. "Living at Shaw's Corner," List, LVIII (10 Oct 1957), 561-62.
Shaw's Corner reflects a Fabian decor, institutional browns and beiges. One cannot live in this "shrine" without feeling the presence of Shaw himself. Shaw knew the sinner gets more publicity than the saint, and he, as well as his home, are getting their fair share.

17 Cathey, Kenneth Clay. "George Bernard Shaw's Drama of Ideas," DA, XVII (1957), 2606. Unpublished dissertation, Vanderbilt University, 1957.

18 "The Centenary in the Theatre," SHAVIAN, VIII (1957), 22-24.
[Reviews of numerous Shaw plays recently produced.]

19 Collins, P. A. W. "Shaw on Shakespeare," SHAKE-SPEARE QUARTERLY, VIII (Winter 1957), 1-13.
Much of Shaw's Shakespeare criticism was merely a cunning ploy in his campaign for the New Drama. It is as a critic of Shakespearian performances that Shaw is at his best. He favored Poel's revival of Elizabethan staging over Irving's Lyceum mutilations. It was Shakespeare's "word music" Shaw praised, not Shakespeare's content. Despite some incidental insights, Shaw was incapable of responding to poetic drama. Nevertheless, the irritated reader should not overlook his originality. His remarks about Shakespeare lead one halfway towards a truth. The trick is not following Shaw too far and arriving at a falsehood.

20 Costello, Donald P. "G. B. S. the Movie Critic," QUARTERLY OF FILM, RADIO AND TELEVISION, XI (1957), 256-75.
Shaw saw the cinema as a greater invention than printing because it was able to reach the poor, ignorant, and mentally lazy. He considered films from two points of view: as art forms and as a form of mass communication. As an art form the cinema was limited by the pursuit of profit and the need to please everyone. As mass communication, Shaw saw movies as "moral levelers." He appreciated their use as cheap entertainment and education for the poor and uncultured, but he feared what the democratic impulse would do to their moral standard. Shaw recognized cinema as the perfect medium for fantasy because of its greater ability to create the illusion of reality. With the advent of talking pictures, he no longer perceived any difference between drama and cinema except for the film's increased magnification and intensification.

21 Couchman, Gordon W. "Here Was a Caesar: Shaw's Comedy Today," PMLA, LXXII (March 1957), 272-85.
Caesar and Cleopatra was, in its first productions, hailed as "opera bouffe," "burlesque," and "extravaganza," which

incensed the Shaw who was temporarily pretending to be a
dramatic realist (for semantic reasons having to do with
his assault upon the "romantic" theater of his predecessors), but the play must at least be considered a fantasy.
The principal proof is in the frequent discrepancies between Shaw's treatment of his characters and the accounts
of historians. Especially interesting in this regard is
Shaw's further idealization of the character of Caesar as
he took it from the already idealized version in Mommsen's
HISTORY OF ROME, in view of Shaw's claim that he took
Caesar's story "without alteration from Mommsen." The
paradox is that, in humanizing Caesar, Shaw went to the
one source calculated to make him seem superhuman and then
either overlooked or ignored those touches of realism or
self-interest that even Mommsen was compelled to acknowledge.

22 Dębnicki, Antoni and Ryszard Gorski. "Bernard
Shaw na Scenach Polskich: Okres Pierwszy 1903-1913"
(Bernard Shaw in Polish Theaters: First Period
1903-1913), PAMIĘTNIK TEATRALNY, II (1957), 227-42.
Since the 1940's there has been no season without at least
a few Shaw plays in Polish theaters. In February of 1903
Shaw was performed first on the Continent in Vienna and
Berlin and only a few months later in Poland. Although
the problems of the plays after the World War have become
historic (though not completely), because they are easy to
understand with vivid action and skillful dramaturgy the
plays still amuse and force the audience to think. The
intelligent bourgeois audience earlier was interested in
the personalities of the characters but did not consider
the sick system they represented or else felt the problems
were exotic for Poland. For example, *Fanny's First Play*
has three aims: 1) to deride the English bourgoisie, 2)
to attack English police brutality, and 3) to expose
English critics. When the play opened in Krakow in 1907,
the review stressed the production, the acting, and the
entertaining comedy. The critical and public reception of
Shaw in Lwow, unlike Krakow and Warsaw, was cool. But in
this ten year period between 1903 and 1913 the Polish
theater and audience adapted to Shaw. Between 1914 and
1939 in Warsaw 20 of Shaw's plays were performed.
Although *Candida* was given 17 times, its success could not
compete with the musical adaptation of *Arms and the Man*.
Today's public prefers PARISIAN LIFE (LA VIE PARISIENNE?)
to *Saint Joan*. [Table of productions, with casts and
reviews, in Warsaw, Lwow, Poznan, Krakow, Wilno, Kalisz,
and other places of: *The Devil's Disciple, Arms and the
Man, Candida, You Never Can Tell, Mrs. Warren's Profes-*

sion, The Philanderer, The Doctor's Dilemma, The Man of Destiny, Major Barbara, Fanny's First Play, and *Misalliance.*] [In Polish.]

23 Dent, A. "Mounting Satisfaction," ILLUSTRATED LONDON NEWS, CCXXX (13 July 1957), 281-82.
Otto Preminger's film of *Saint Joan* gives us little more than a couple of sips out of Shaw's great overflowing goblet of a play.

24 "Discussion on Bernard Shaw between Alec Clunes, Lionel Hale and Wolf Mankowitz," WORLD THEATRE (Brussels), VI (Spring 1957), 27-42.
AC: The plays of the major period are being performed; revival of the late plays is unwise. WM: There is a difference between Shaw's reputation with the public, which is wide, and with the newspapers, which is critical, a healthy thing. AC: In the revaluating of Shaw, *Saint Joan* is staying at the top; *Heartbreak House* is still topical. *Androcles and the Lion, Arms and the Man,* and *Man and Superman* have not lost their validity. LH: Some of the small comedies are surviving, too. WM: Shaw's being a propagandist did not spoil him for working in the theater. LH: (Moans). WM: But some plays like *The Doctor's Dilemma* have lost their point in the Welfare State. AC: Shaw was profoundly religious. WM: To me, Shaw is the antithesis of metaphysical religious argument. AC: There is an enormous sense of mystery in Shaw. WM: Shaw did not understand women's irrationality. Candida is an unconvincing character in an unconvincing situation. AC: Shaw had ample equipment for understanding the irrationality of women. WM: His characters are never in a directly sexual situation. All the managers are women. He could not accept that he was only a man and that he must die. AC: His admiration for dictators came from his own saintly nature. [Parallel text in French.]

25 Dower, Margaret Winifred. "The Political and Social Thinking of George Bernard Shaw," DA, XVII (1957), 1580-1581. Unpublished dissertation, Boston University, 1957.

26 Elder, Eleanor. "GBS on the Art of Rehearsal," SHAVIAN, XI (1957), 20-21.

[Account of how the sister of Shaw's secretary, Ann Elder, was allowed to publishs in THE ARTS LEAGUE ANNUAL BULLETIN a Shaw letter to Edward McNulty on theater production.]

27 Eyrignoux, L. "Le Centenaire de la naissance de Bernard Shaw" (The Centenary of Bernard Shaw's Birth), ETUDES ANGLAISES, X (April–June 1957), 123–27.

Because of the originality of Shaw's mind and because he was heretical in so many areas, his reputation has suffered. Though some of his plays are outmoded and not all of the later plays are very good, the dialogue of his great plays is so brilliant that his will remain among the great names of English drama. [In French.]

28 Falkenberg, Hans-Geert. "Randnotizen zum *Androklus*" (Marginal Notes on *Androcle*), BDDTG, VIII (1957–58), 48–49.

[Brief notes on the genesis of the play, the British first night, the German first night and the early German reception.] [In German.]

29 F[alkenberg], H[ans-]G[eert]. "Sieben Tage nach dem Tode Shaws"' (Seven Years after Shaw's Death), BDDTG, VIII (1957–58), 50–51.

[A few rather slight notes on the reception of Shaw's works between 1950 and 1957. Mentions a few articles and some first nights.] [In German.]

30 Fielden, John. "Shaw's *Saint Joan* as Tragedy," TWENTIETH CENTURY LITERATURE, III (1957), 59–67; rptd in STUDENTS' SOURCES FOR SHAKESPEARE'S HAMLET, SHAW'S SAINT JOAN, CONRAD'S HEART OF DARKNESS, comp by Roy Bentley (Agincourt, Ontario: Book Society of Canada, 1966), pp. 65–74; in StJFYA.

Saint Joan has the elements of a classical tragedy. One such element is a divinity or force which shapes men's lives, whether God or the Life Force. Like the Greeks, Shaw too places his tragic action in the context of an ultimately meaningful existence, in his case the progressive nature of Creative Evolution. Shaw does not present Joan as being a saint in the sense of flawless or otherworldly but as a person honored with the title "saint" in reward for heroic action. Her tragic flaw is the hubris that changes her from a humble, selfless warrior of the Life Force into the bored, demanding, self-righteous, proud figure of Act V. She becomes a scapegoat, paying for social and religious change. Traditional pity and terror are evoked at her trial and, as proper in classical tragedy, her flaming death takes place off stage.

31 "A Film about Shaw," SHAVIAN, VIII (1957), 27-28. [Reviews a film about Shaw made by Triangle Films and produced by Theodora Olenbert.]

32 Fiske, Irving. "My Correspondence with GBS," SHAVIAN, XI (1957), 12-15.
Shaw heartily approved of Fiske's translating HAMLET into modern English, though he wondered how Shakespeare's intentional vulgarities would be handled. Shaw declared Fiske's essay, BERNARD SHAW'S DEBT TO WILLIAM BLAKE, (1951) to be "the one I would have published and circulated as widely as if I had written it myself.

33 Fremantle, Anne. "Shaw and Religion," COMMONWEAL, LXVII (1957), 249-51.
Even those biographer-contemporaries of Shaw--Henderson and Ervine--whose works are opinionated, moralizing, and editorial, must agree with Chesterton that Shaw was an intensely religious person. He rejected the exclusive, confining religion of his childhood because of his life-long concern with the essentials of religion and his impatience with non-essentials. He attended church to contact the Godhead within. The saintly seriousness of his hard crystalline intellect never gave his principles a rest, never allowed his wit to become merely a sense of humor. Henderson and Ervine miss the point about Shaw's view of Jesus and of man's highest possibility, the intellectual love of Truth.

34 Fried, Vilém. "Tečka za Bernardem Shawem?" (The End of Bernard Shaw?), KULTURNÍ ZAJÍMAVOSTI, VI (1957), 246-52.
Shaw's paradoxes are only illusory; he points a way to the future, suggesting much, though he failed to think his ideas through. His need as dramatist to imitate class differences in pronunciation brought him to alphabet reform. English orthography is uniquely antiquated among modern literary languages. [Describes Shaw's ideas and arguments for the new alphabet as well as the difficulties over the alphabet bequest in Shaw's will.] [In Czechoslovak.]

35 Galinsky, Hans. "G. B. Shaw als Gegenstand der Kritik und Quelle dramatischer Anregung für T. S. Eliot" (G. B. Shaw as Object of Criticism and Source of Dramatic Inspiration for T. S. Eliot), GERMANISCH-ROMANISCHE MONATSSCHRIFT, Neue Folge VII (April 1957), 146-64.
Although Shaw and T. S. Eliot represent different trends of modern drama, they can be seen together under several aspects: both came from English speaking areas outside England to give new impulses to English drama, both revitalized the old tradition of the religious play with *Saint Joan* and MURDER IN THE CATHEDRAL, both were moralists, both shared a lifelong preoccupation with Shakespeare. As a detailed study of Eliot's lecture POETRY AND DRAMA (1950) and his DIALOGUE ON DRAMATIC POETRY (1928) reveals, there is a further aspect: the influence of Shaw's prose on Eliot. Despite critical remarks about Shaw, Eliot already acknowledged the quality of Shaw's prose in his DIALOGUE. In his lecture he outright admitted to influence. There are numerous differences between *Joan* and *MURDER IN THE CATHEDRAL*. But the platform prose and the transposition from historical to modern times in MURDER IN THE CATHEDRAL are strongly reminiscent of *Joan*; they have a similar purpose: "to shock the audience out of their complacency" (Eliot). Whether the final chorus of MURDER IN THE CATHEDRAL is also influenced by *Joan* is questionable but by no means improbable, as a close examination shows. [In German.]

36 "G. B. S. v. ABC," TIME, LXIX (4 March 1957), 71. [A summary of the alphabet trust case, pointing out the reasons for the court test of Shaw's Will.]

37 Gertz, Elmer. "One Hundred Years of Shaw," MANUSCRIPTS, IX (1957), 74-76.
[A report by the first president of the Chicago Chapter of the Shaw Society of America on Chicago's centennial tribute to Shaw. Mostly a listing of the Shaviana of the exhibition in the Bernard Shaw Room of the Hotel Sherman, but also an account of the events of the celebration.]

38 Gilroy, Harry. "Shaw Play Stirs Ire of Berliners," NYT, 31 March 1957, I, p. 81.
[Reports a controversy over a proposed West German theater company's performance of *Major Barbara* in an East German city.]

39 González Lanuza, Eduardo. "Bernard Shaw y Sócrates" (Bernard Shaw and Socrates), LA GACETA, XVI (12 May 1957) 513.
[A comparison of the ideas and their influence on their time and society of Shaw and Socrates.] [In Spanish.]

40 Gordon, John D. "Bernard Shaw: 1856-1950. An Exhibition from the Berg collection," BNYPL, LXI (March 1957), 117-38; (April 1957), 192-207; (May 1957), 250-59; also printed as a separate pamphlet by the New York Public Library.
[Descriptive catalog of material by and about Shaw exhibited in the New York Public Library.]

41 Gordon, John D. "New in the Berg Collection: 1952-1956. Part II - Concluded," BNYPL, LXI (July 1957), items 53-57, 359-60.
[Listing and description of Shaw material: Autograph notebook; Presentation copy of *Three Plays for Puritans*; Letters to Siegfried Trebitsch and Floryan Sobieniowski; Presentation copy of *Saint Joan*.]

42 Grendon, Felix. "*The Apple Cart*," ShawB, II (Jan 1957), 16-19.
[A review of Maurice Evan's production of *The Apple Cart*. Largely a plot summary.]

43 Grendon, Felix. "A Shaw Evening at the Grolier Club: THE FASCINATING FOUNDLING and *Why She Would Not*," ShawB, II (May 1957), 21-22.
[A review of the two play productions, it explains the British juridical customs that THE FASCINATING FOUNDLING is based on.]

44 Groshong, James W. "G. B. S. and Germany, the Major Aspects," Unpublished Dissertation, Stanford University, 1957. [Listed in McNamee.]

45 Han, Tien. "Bernard Shaw: Master of Realist Drama," ShawB, II (Sept 1957), 11-15.
[A Peking tribute to Ibsen and Shaw by the Chairman of the Chinese Union of Stage Artists at "A Meeting in Commemoration of Great Figures of World Culture" in July of 1956.]

Shaw began, as Lenin said, as "a good man fallen among Fabians," but after a period of disillusionment with bourgeois reform he found the correct path in revolutionary communism.

46 Harmon, Lord Chief Justice Charles. "On the Will of Bernard Shaw" (1957); rptd in THE LAW AS LITERATURE: AN ANTHOLOGY OF GREAT WRITING IN AND ABOUT THE LAW (Lond: Bodley Head, 1961); GEORGE BERNARD SHAW ON LANGUAGE, ed by Abraham Tauber (Lond: Peter Owen, 1963), pp. 171-73.
[Harmon's decision against the alphabet trusts in Shaw's Will.]

47 Helsztynski, Stanisław. "Bernard Shaw: W Setną Rocznicę Urodzin 1856-1956" (Bernard Shaw: On the Hundredth Anniversary of His Birth 1856-1956), KWARTALNIK NEOFILOLOGICZNY, IV (1957), 15-29.
Unlike Robertson, Jones, and Pinero, Shaw rejected the opinion of Victorian society, making the theater a platform of social protest. Not since Shakespeare and the Elizabethan audience had the English theater been so strong a social institution. The neglect of his parents freed Shaw from tradition. The vacuum in his education was filled with nature (Dalkey countryside), music (thanks to his mother and Lee), and art from the Dublin Art Gallery. [Biographical sketch, with some emphasis on the role of Marx and Darwin in Shaw's thought, and a survey of his plays.] When Shaw counselled, at the expense of Polish territory, peace with Hitler after Germany's invasion of Poland, he lacked common sense. The personality of a dictator always acted more on his imagination than the destiny of people and society. Shaw's plays will survive on their artistic value, their beauty, their moral passion, and their genial poetic expression. His plays present living people. [In Polish.]

48 Houston, Penelope. "*Saint Joan*," SHAVIAN, XI (1957), 17-19.
[Report of several reviews of the Otto Preminger film of *Saint Joan*.]

49 Humphreys, Hubert. "My Last Great Adventure," SHAVIAN, XI (1957), 10-12.
[During a trip to South Africa, at a speaking engagement

in Durban, Humphreys encountered great enthusiasm for Shaw.]

50 Innes, Hanley Tullah. THE STRANGE TRIANGLE OF
G.B.S. (Bost: Bruce Humphries, 1957).
[A fictionalized treatment of the relationship between Shaw and the Charringtons, Mrs. Charrington being the actress Janet Achurch. Shaw plays Marchbanks to her Candida. Advertised as "the story of his true, secret love."]

51 Jěrabek, Dušan. "Dvě premiery Mahenovy činohry"
(Two First Nights at the Mahen Theater, Brno)
DIVADLO (Prague) VIII: 2 (1957), 149-52.
Shaw based *Caesar and Cleopatra* on problems of contemporary life, contrasting the conventional ideas of past history with the morality of the ruling class of Victorian England, building a new empire on foundations similar to those of Rome. But Caesar should not be depicted as a historical figure, though the producer tries to keep the balance between the historical framework and its present-day relevance. [In Czech.]

52 Johnson, Edgar. "Dickens and Shaw: Critics of
Society," VIRGINIA QUARTERLY REVIEW, XXXIII (1957),
66-79.
Shaw's description of Dicken's work as a bible for him is testimony to his deep regard for Dickens the writer. Shaw ascribed the style of his early novels to Dickens, but the resemblance between the two is not merely one of style; it is also of temperament and moral conviction. Both loved slapstick, farce, and wild horseplay, and there are many parallels in their creation of humorous characters and situations, but both dedicated their art to the betterment of mankind. Shaw describes himself as well as Dickens when he cites Dicken's unrestrained use of humor to lampoon bigots, monomaniacs, sophists, and that Victorian social structure which for both men became the source of much of mankind's suffering.

53 Jones, Howard Mumford. "Shaw as a Victorian,"
VICTORIAN STUDIES, I (1957), 165-72.
Shaw grew up in the middle of the Victorian era, and his ideas were formed by nineteenth century men such as Marx and Morris. His works, too, are based on Victorian types; his plays owe a great deal to the well-made play and to

Victorian farce comedy, and *My Dear Dorothea* is a heavy-handed example of Victorian topsy-turvy. Biographically, Shaw is well covered, but scholarship has yet to research his source materials.

54 Jordan, John. "Shaw's *Heartbreak House*," THRESHOLD, I (1957), 50-56.
On the most obvious level a political allegory, *Heartbreak House* is so poetically resonant that its allegory extends to other levels as well. Principally its allegory is of the perennial human condition, Captain Shotover being an Everyman who relearns primal truths about life on the Ark and introduces them to Ellie Dunn. Together they enact the need to struggle against facile illusions, the means being "heartbreak," not as "a luxurious sense of sorrow, but rather an arid plain, profitable only if accepted and integrated into the pattern of experience."

55 Kelling, Lucile. "Archibald Henderson: A Selected Bibliography of His Writings on Shaw, Drama and Theatre," ShawB, II (May 1957), 3-8.
[A selected list of Henderson's writings, prefaced by a summary of what has been left out.]

56 Kerr, Walter. PIECES AT EIGHT (NY: Simon & Schuster, 1957), pp. 105-7, 112-13, 117-20.
[Comments on *Don Juan in Hell and MY FAIR LADY*.] Shaw must be measured against the standard of Congreve, Sheridan and Wilde.

57 Knorr, Heinz. "George Bernard Shaw und seine 'Helden'" (George Bernard Shaw and his 'Heroes'), DIE VOLKSBÜHNE, VII (1957), 234-36.
In his desire to entertain and to instruct, Shaw belongs to a long line of dramatists from the baroque period and Schiller to Hauptmann and Brecht. His artistic means are irony, satire and wit. His play *Arms and the Man* is a good example. [In German.]

58 Laing, Allan M. "The Seance," SHAVIAN, VIII (1957), 25-26.
[A brief playlet in which Shaw speaks through a medium his opinion of Stephen Winsten's JESTING APOSTLE (1956).]

59 Lambert, J. W. "Plays in performance," DRAMA,
ns, XLIV (Spring 1957), 22.
Avis Bunnage was full-blooded in *Captain Brassbound's
Conversion.* Tyrone Power easily dominated as Dick Dudgeon
in *The Devil's Disciple.*

60 Laurence, Dan. "Ed. Note," Reg, I (Dec 1957), 8.
[A letter commenting on whether Shaw had ever studied
Logic.]

61 "Law Report. January 16. Mr. Bernard Shaw's
Will: Plan for a New Alphabet," TIMES (Lond) (17
Jan 1957), 12.
[A report of the opening of the "alphabet trust" litiga-
tion before Mr. Justice Harman.]

62 "Law Report, February 20," TIMES (Lond) (21 Feb
1957), 13.
[A full report of judgment read by Mr. Justice Harman in
the case *In re Shaw's Will Trusts: Public Trustee v. Day
and others.*]

63 Low, David. LOW'S AUTOBIOGRAPHY. (NY: Simon &
Schuster, 1957), pp. 137-39.
[The cartoonist's memoirs include portraits of Shaw in
both caricature and anecdote.]

64 Lutter, Tibor. "George Bernard Shaw," ANNALES
SCIENTIARUM BUDAPESTINENSIS (SECTIO PHILOLOGICA)
(Budapest), I (1957), 137-46.
Shaw is chiefly remembered in Hungary as a humorous
writer, yet he was also profoundly serious. He was one of
the great iconoclasts of form. His plots are generally
poor, but the central interest in his plays is the dialogue and moral lesson. He used a new dramatic rhythm,
with the division into acts often rhapsodical, marking off
episodes rather than forming dramatic units. His plays
are problem plays, but he refused to give any positive
solutions, leaving the moral lesson to be drawn by the
audience. His plays originate in the tradition of moralities. His politics formed an essential part of his
dramatic art, and his ideal was Realism: to Shaw, Romanticism denoted cant, prejudice, lies, and false sentiment.

65 McDermott, William F. "Shavian Self-Portraits," CLEVELAND PLAIN DEALER, 24 Feb 1957; rptd in THE BEST OF McDERMOTT (Cleveland and NY: World Publishing Company, 1959), pp. 67-69.
It is only partly true that the characters in Shaw's plays are echoes of himself.

66 McDowell, Frederick P. W. "Victorian Shaw," VICTORIAN NEWSLETTER, XI (1957), 16-19.
A reading of the two recent biographies of Shaw--by Ervine and Henderson--impresses upon the reader the extent to which Shaw was shaped and influenced by Victorian ideas. Beneath his surface iconoclasm, which looks beyond the Victorian Age, Shaw was yet of this period in his affirmations, his ethical seriousness, and his moral idealism.

67 McDowell, Frederick P. W. "The World, God, and World Bettering: Shaw's *Buoyant Billions*," BOSTON UNIVERSITY STUDIES IN ENGLISH, III (1957), 167-76.
Buoyant Billions demonstrates the continuity of Shaw's intellectual life. It proves that Shaw's final views are, in essence, incremental elaborations of, or adroit variations upon, the ideas broached in the germinal plays of his prime. In this late play Shaw treats once again his favorite concern--the problem of rightful leadership--and arrives at more or less the same synthesis of idealism and realism, vision and power, that had been the conclusion of *Major Barbara*, and with the understanding that a religious comprehension of life is vital to the synthesis of leadership qualities.

68 McNulty, Edward. "George Bernard Shaw as a Boy," ShawB, II (Sept 1957), 8-10.
[McNulty's brief account of his boyhood friendship with Shaw.] McNulty and Shaw were rival caricaturists; as cricketers they broke Catholic chapel windows, as thespians they acted Hamlet (Shaw was Ophelia); they haunted art galleries, violated "No Trespassing" signs on communistic principles, parted with the supernaturalism of Christianity at the same age (13), and exchanged literary efforts (Shaw's first serious one being "Strawberrinos, or, The Haunted Winebin"). Shaw did not care for a literary career, was unable to afford the study of art, and so announced that he would start a new religion. McNulty was horrified and insisted that Shaw become famous in literature.

69 "Major Barbara," TAM, XLI (Jan 1957), 21-22.
A revival of Shaw's timeless comedy is well adapted to the
Martin Beck Theatre as presented by Robert L. Joseph and
directed by Charles Laughton. A combination of effective
scenery, creditable characters, and skillful directing
render this production memorable and authentically
Shavian.

70 Melchinger, Siegfried. DRAMA ZWISCHEN SHAW UND
BRECHT: EIN LEITFADEN DURCH DAS ZEITGENÖSSISCHE
SCHAUSPIEL (Drama between Shaw and Brecht: A Guide
through Contemporary Drama) (Bremen: Carl
Schunemann Verlag, 1957; 5th ed 1963).
[The book contains a survey and analysis of modern drama,
documents to the theory of contemporary theater (including
a passage from Shaw's Preface to *Plays for Puritans*), a
glossary of terms pertaining to the theory of modern
theater, brief articles on modern playwrights, and a table
of first performances from 1900 to 1963.] Shaw believes
he can change the world through theater by appealing to
reason; he speaks truths in the disguise of a fool. [In
German.]

71 Mikhailova, I., and E. Tabatchikova. "Letopis'
teatral'noi zhizni Leningrada 1917-1956" (Chronicle
of Theatrical Life in Leningrad 1917-56), TEATR I
ZHIZN (Theater and Life) (Leningrad-Moscow:
Iskusstvo, 1957), pp. 406, 410, 419.
Pygmalion was produced at the Pushkin Theater, Leningrad,
on 22 June 1945: *Mrs. Warren's Profession* in 1948, and
The Devil's Disciple by the Great Gorky Dramatic Theater
in May, 1956. [In Russian.]

72 Miller, Henry. "An American's Point of View re
THE STRANGE TRIANGLE OF G.B.S.--A Rebuttal," ShawB,
II (May 1957), 15-16.
[Miller disagrees with the review, Ozy (Pseud). "THE
STRANGE TRIANGLE OF G.B.S.," Shaw B, II (Jan 1957), 20-21,
panning Tullah Innes Hanby's biographical novel about
Shaw.] A biographical novel, if written with sincerity,
offers a truer, more significant portrait than a bio-
graphical study based exclusively on facts and documents.
Hanley's delineation of the indefatigable workhorse and
ineffectual lover, though a women's intuitive view of
Shaw, has a ring of truth which no amount of argument and
factual evidence will ever successfully down.

73 Miserocchi, Manlio. "Attraverso il Centenario di G. B. Shaw Quello di O. Wilde" (The Centennial of O. Wilde through That of G. B. Shaw), NUOVA ANTOLOGIA, XCII (1957), 377-86.
The centennial of Shaw's birth is talked about not because of his birth but because of his will, which has ended in court due to the absurd clause of imposing a new alphabet on the English. Wilde's centennial went unobserved, except as it emerged through Shaw's. [Anecdotes of Miserocchi's meeting of Shaw and brief survey of their critical appreciation of each other.] [In Italian.]

74 *My Fair Lady*, ILLUSTRATED LONDON NEWS, CCXXX (29 June 1957), 1079.
[A report of the Broadway success of MY FAIR LADY. Consists mainly of scenes from the musical.]

75 O'Donnell, Norbert F. "Ibsen and Shaw: The Tragic and the Tragic-Comic," THEATRE ANNUAL, XV (1957-58), 15-27.
Ibsen's social dramas did influence Shaw--both condemn by implication socially induced attitudes which produce automatic behavior and the suppression of the truly human--but still there are sharp differences of technique and theme between Ibsen and Shaw. Ibsen's method was essentially the implicit method of a determined naturalism that created a modern tragedy; Shaw's method was one of brilliant explicitness that created a modern comedy or tragi-comedy. In the thematic realm, Ibsen, while by no means unaware of the social forces which play upon his characters, was most deeply interested in a subjective world of personal relationships; whereas Shaw, decidedly aware of the corruption of personal relationships by institutions, was preoccupied with the objective world of social forces in whose perspective he saw the individual problems of his characters. [Compares *Candida* with *A DOLL'S HOUSE*, *Major Barbara* with *ROSMERSHOLM*, and *The Apple Cart* with *THE MASTERBUILDER*.] When any of Ibsen's heroes are concerned with public affairs, the concern always seems to be a relatively meaningless reflection of their private struggles, whereas Shaw's heroic figures are always engaged in the effort to impose the results of their relatively untroubled private reflections on a world which is to one degree or another unyielding. Shaw's heroes know nothing of the tragic personal guilt that shapes the lives of Ibsen's characters.

76 O'Donnell, Norbert F. "Shaw, Bunyan, and
Puritanism," PMLA, LXXII (June 1957), 520-33.
Chesterton's notion that Shaw was a Puritan is incorrect;
the famous Shavian 'puritanism' was merely one of the many
masks which Shaw held between himself and a world which he
meant to irritate, entertain, and instruct. As a polemicist Shaw used names abstractly, as symbols of general
vices or virtues, and thus "Bunyan" served nicely as a
stalking horse against the London theater, which was
characterized by inanity and prurience, and against Shakespeare, representative of the outmoded, pre-modern
theater. Shaw obviously reinterpreted the Bunyan of his
youth in the light of his understanding of such writers as
Schopenhauer and Marx, Nietzsche and ibsen, and in
transforming the simple tinker into a modern artist-
philosopher Shaw was deliberately anachronistic. There
was no such seventeenth-century Nietzsche, no such seventeenth-century Ibsen as he describes. Yet anyone who
shares to any degree Shaw's view of life must feel that he
has a point. True puritan though he was, Bunyan *did* have
a place in the struggle between human vitality and the
artificial system of morality which went on in the
seventeenth-century as it does today. In calling attention to this fact, Shaw may have made as valuable a
contribution in his way to an understanding of the universality of Bunyan as many a critic who has striven imagina-
tively to live Bunyan's life and to think Bunyan's
thoughts.

77 Oppel, Horst. "Der Einfluss der englischen
Literatur auf die deutsche" (The influence of
English Literature on German literature), DEUTSCHE
PHILOLOGIE IM AUFRISS (German Philology in Outline),
ed by Wolfgang Stammler (Berlin: Erich Schmidt,
1957 and 1962), cols. 201-308.
Shaw, Galsworthy and the Scandinavians were the most
important playwrights of our century. Shaw's popularity
with the German audience is due to *Pygmalion*. [In
German.]

78 Ozy (Pseud). "Theatre Notes: Good King Charles
Off-Broadway," ShawB, II (May 1957), 19-20.
In Good King Charles's Golden Days at the Downtown Theatre
is a surprisingly impressive production.

79 Pécsi, Antal. "Shaw és a film" (Shaw and the
Movies), NAGYVILÁG (Budapest), II (1957), 895-98.

[Review on the occasion of the revival of the 1938 film of *Pygmalion*.] Shaw recognized that the movies were the most persuasive art. He appeared often in the movies, most notably eulogizing Lenin on the occasion of his visit to the USSR in 1931. [In Hungarian.]

80 Perrine, Laurence. "Shaw's *Arms and the Man*," EXPLICATOR, XV(1957), Item 54.
The major thematic conflict of *Arms and the Man* is between realism (Bluntschli) and romantic idealism (Sergius), with realism carrying the field and winning the girl. While Raina becomes a realist when her romantic illusions are punctured, Sergius only becomes disillusioned with reality. Sergius blames human nature for failing to live up to his unrealistic ideals, which he uses to screen himself from reality.

81 "Poland's Long Connection with Shaw's Plays," TIMES (Lond), 31 Dec 1956, 3.
[An account of Shavian productions in Poland since 1914.]

82 Povedano, Enrique. "Bernard Shaw y la horma de su zapato" (Bernard Shaw and the Mold of His Shoe), TEATRO, XXII (April-June 1957), 78.
[Anecdote in Spanish.]

83 Purdom, C. B. (ed). BERNARD SHAW'S LETTERS TO GRANVILLE BARKER (NY: Theatre Arts Books; Lond: Phoenix House, 1957).
[A collection of Shaw's correspondence from 1900 to 1943, mostly to Granville Barker. Concerned with practical stage work, they reveal a Shaw who was extremely knowledgeable about and vitally interested in the details of producing the new drama, of Barker and others as well as of his own. Helpfully annotated by Purdom with a connective narrative, they chronicle the period of Shaw's most intense involvement in the theater, coinciding with Barker's blossoming as a Shavian actor, and with Barker's collaborations as producer-director with such managements as the Stage Society, Vedrenne, Frohman, and finally with his wife, Lillah McCarthy, in repertory.]

84 Quigly, Isabel. "A Poor Maid," Spec, CXCVIII (28 June 1957), 847.

The Preminger film of *Saint Joan* is uneven, caught between film and stage play. It is well-acted by Gielgud and the rest, but rendered mediocre by the totally inadequate performance of Jean Seberg as the Maid. The result is not quite Shaw and not quite anything else.

85 R., G. "Teatro: *Armas y el hombre*" (Theater: *Arms and the Man*), CULTURA PERUANA, XVII (Jan 1957), n.p.
The performance of *Arms and the Man* by the Talía Group was received with enough enthusiasm by the public. [In Spanish.]

86 Rattray, Dr. R. F. "Shaw as the Sorcerer's Apprentice," SHAVIAN, XI (1957), 9-12.
Shaw had second thoughts about some of the Socialist policies he helped to bring about, but once the demon had been let out, the sorcerer's apprentice could not get him back into the bottle.

87 Rice, Elmer. "Extemporaneous Remarks," ShawB, II (Jan 1957), 5-7.
[Rice describes the tremendous impact reading Shaw had on him as a young man and testifies to Shaw's effectiveness in the theater.]

88 Rockman, Robert E. "Dickens and Shaw: Another Parallel," ShawB, II (Jan 1957), 8-10.
[Illustrates similarities in plot and characterization between Dickens's LITTLE DORRITT and *Widowers' Houses.*]

89 Rose, Clarkson. "Shaw and 'Twinkle,'" SHAVIAN, XI (1957), 16-17.
[An anecdote of Rose's meeting with Shaw at the Glyndebourne Festival, where Shaw's *Geneva* was playing opposite Rose's WITH A TWINKLE IN MY EYE. Shaw was much taken by the cyclorama used in Rose's pantomime.]

90 Rypins, Stanley. "Bernard Shaw Remembered," VIRGINIA QUARTERLY REVIEW, XXXIII (Winter 1957), 80-92.
[A centenary tribute to Shaw in the form of personal recollections of five or six meetings Rypins had with Shaw from 1914 on.] Although Shaw was a very good listener,

especially responsive to intelligent questions, our first meeting left me feeling depressed because Shaw's mental agility and effortless superiority were so overwhelming. On another occasion, I found Shaw a great, wholesome, natural boy, with a brain beyond his years; if as unaffected and amiable with others as always with me, it's no wonder people like him. [Contains an account of Shaw's visit to New York in 1933 that contradicts certain embroidered accounts of others.]

91 "*Saint Joan*," ILLUSTRATED LONDON NEWS, CCXXX (1 June 1957), 908-9.
[A reporting of the world premiere of the Otto Preminger movie. Consists mainly of scenes from the film.]

92 Schellenberger, Johannes. "George Bernard Shaws Dramen sind nicht nur auf der Bühne wirksam. Zum Erscheinen seiner 'Dramatischen Werke'" (G. B. S.'s Plays Are Not Only Effective on Stage. A Comment on the Publication of His Dramatic Works), DER BIBLIO-THEKAR, XI (July 1957), 699-703.
In the German Democratic Republic, Shaw was somewhat pushed aside by Bertolt Brecht after 1945. But his plays are not out of date. Because of their epic quality, they are also good and healthy reading. Shaw never considered art for art's sake. Despite all witticisms he is a social critic. [Article occasioned by the publication of 4 vols of plays and prefaces with introduction by Hans Mayer in Aufbau-Verlag, Berlin, 1956.] [In German.]

93 Schlauch, Margaret. "Postacie Symboliczne i Technika Symboliki u Shawa" (Symbolic Form and Symbolic Technique in Shaw), KWARTALNIK NEOFILOLOG-ICZNY, IV (1957), 30-40; trans as "Symbolic Figures and the Symbolic Technique of George Bernard Shaw," SCIENCE & SOCIETY, XXI (1957), 210-21.
Shaw criticism in the years preceding the hundredth anniversary of his birth has emphasized his intellectual achievement. Marxist critics in particular call attention to his role in exposing the importance of the role of class conditions in all aspects of life. The poetic side of Shaw received less attention. Shaw used rhapsodic style and myth, but especially symbolic characters. One of the symbolic techniques is to create characters who remain individual but possess symbolic meaning. A faster way is direct allegory, adapted from the Old French Romance, Dante, Milton and Bunyan. Opera, especially

Mozart and Wagner, showed Shaw the way to adapt this old technique to contemporary terms. But Shaw did not borrow; he developed independently. Unlike Ibsen, who was imbued with the mythology of his native land, Shaw rejected Irish myth, as the single satiric reference to Cathleen ni Hoolihan in *John Bull's Other Island* suggests. He was too much a realist to create myths under the dictation of Jung's "racial unconscious." Shaw did create heroes, as shown in *Caesar and Cleopatra, The Devil's Disciple, Androcles and the Lion,* and *Saint Joan,* but in order to expose the bourgeois parliamentary system. Possibly Shaw learned the technique of hero or anti-hero from Ibsen's PEER GYNT. Another symbolic character type is the Mother-Goddess - Lady Cicely Waynefleet, Candida, and Mrs. George - to demonstrate his sympathy for women's equality and as an allegoric means for his Life-Force theory, more clearly articulated in *Man and Superman* and *Back to Methuselah.* The major difference between Shaw and Ibsen is Shaw's emphasis on life. Ibsen was fatalistic. But Shaw and Ibsen were both dissatisfied with the social reality. *Major Barbara* and *Geneva* describe the problem of complete destruction by war. Especially in our time of "megadeath," Shaw's optimism and philosophy of biological vitalism is an inspiration. [In Polish.]

94 Schlegelmilch, Wolfgang. "Shaw und die Äbtissin" (Shaw and the Abbess), HOCHLAND, LI (Aug 1957), 589-91).
Hugo von Hofmannsthal's criticism that Shaw lacked the necessary deep religious commitment to be a guarantor of the cultural unity of Enrope in times of turmoil is justified--as Shaw's letters to Abbess Laurentia McLachlan show. [In German.]

95 "Shavian News Notes," ShawB, II (Jan 1957), 3-4.
[Reports controversy over whether stage, radio and television performances of *Pygmalion* have been restricted in order to allow a clear field for MY FAIR LADY; a series of dramatic readings of Shaw's plays by the Chicago Chapter; a successful arena stage production of *Heartbreak House,* directed by Warren S. Smith, at Pennsylvania State University; a performance by the New York Chapter of *Why She Would Not,* directed by Zara Shadow; the televising of the Maurice Evans' production of *Man and Superman;* exhibits of Shaviana at the New York Public library and at the University of North Carolina.]

96 "Shavian News Notes," ShawB, II (May 1957), 13-14.
[Reports the litigation over Shaw's Will concerning the phonetic-alphabet behest; the scheduled premiere of the Otto Preminger-Graham Greene screen version of *Saint Joan* in France; two more film treatments of Shaw's plays—*The Devil's Disciple* and *Candida*; an off-Broadway production of *O'Flaherty V.C.* and *Press Cuttings*; controversy in West Berlin over whether a proposed production of *Major Barbara* in Leipzig would aid the cause of communism; Colin Wilson's work on a book on major religious figures of the modern era, which will culminate with a chapter on Shaw.]

97 "Shavian News Notes," ShawB, II (Sept 1957), 10, 25.
[Reports a list of Shaw's plays on the summer circuit; 28 bound volumes of Shavian page proof discovered at Ayot St. Lawrence; the sale of Shaw's love letters to Alice Lockett (1883-85); further openings of the *Saint Joan* film; NYT estimate that a million-and-a-half people saw Shaw plays during the centenary year; prospect of a pre-Broadway tour of an adaptation of *Back to Methuselah*.]

98 "Shaw and the Actor," TAM, XLI (March 1957), 29-30, 88-89.
Rex Harrison believes Shaw wrote himself as Higgins, probably unconsciously, and he, as an actor, tried to imitate Shaw's manner. Harrison's advice to young actors is always to play Shaw, not as a classic, but as a contemporary, because the vitality of his plays is in their sense of relevance to the present moment. Siobhan McKenna sees Shaw as a very religious man whose genuine love of the common people is manifested in his portrayal of Joan. Joan is a practical saint, and her spiritual quality is not ascetic. Her great achievement was not in fulfilling God's will but in asserting her own will to freedom when her voices deserted her. Shaw is a poetic dramatist, whose plays should be played more realistically and less didactically, and whose flow of words in dialogue is both passionate and artful.

99 "Shaw's Guide for Children," NYT Mag, 10 March 1957, pp. 12, 20, 22.
[Excerpts from *My Dear Dorothea*, with illustrations by Clare Winston.]

100 "Shaw-Testament: Vierzehn Buchstaben zuwenig" (Shaw's Testament: Fourteen Letters Missing), DER SPIEGEL (Hamburg), XI (6 March 1957), pp. 61-62.
In its extravagance Shaw's testament resembles his plays. [On Shaw's wish to promote a research project in order to set up an alphabet of 40 letters.] [In German.]

101 Silverman,   Albert H.   "Bernard Shaw's Shakespeare Criticism," PMLA, LXXII (Sept 1957), 722-736.
Shaw's criticism of Shakespeare is to be explained not merely in terms of Shaw's position vis-a-vis the Victorian theater but also straightforwardly as dogma consistent with his antitragic, antiromantic criticism of art and life.   To counteract the view that Shaw was merely opposingn an old tradition with a new, or the view that Shaw's criticism of shakespeare and the Elizabethan dramatists was an unhistorical and peculiarly modern judgment, one need only note how frequently Shaw's ideas were anticipated by Ben Jonson.   More often than not, Shaw judges Shakespeare not by modern standards but by the standards of Shakespeare's own epoch.

102 Smith, J. Percy. "GBS on HAMLET," SHAVIAN, VIII (1957), 14-17.
Though Shaw thought HAMLET outdated by its revenge code, he believed it to be a genuine problem play.   It states the problem of justifying actions that are motivated, not by reason, but by Schopenhauer's Immanent Will (or Shaw's Life Force).   Shakespeare had an intuition of the Schopenhauerian solution to Hamlet's problem, but was, in Shaw's words, incompetent to think out the revolt of his feeling against ready-made morality.

103 Smith, Warren S[ylvester].   "The Nun and the Dramatist," ShawB, II (Sept 1957), 21-23.
[A review of IN A GREAT TRADITION: TRIBUTE TO DAME LAURENTIA MCLACHLAN, ABBESS OF STANBROOK (1956).]   In Shaw, the Abbess faced not so much an unbeliever as a man with a rival religion.   The conflict between them was like that of "The Religion of Tradition vs. The Religion of Heresy."

104 Smoker, Barbara.   "A Financier Meets His Match," SHAVIAN, XI (1957), 22-23.

Edward Lowdness Westropp, in a book on millionaires called THE WAY TO FORTUNE, writes of dealings he had with Shaw over a certain crematorium company they both owned shares in. Shaw egged Westropp on to harrass the management to make their business more profitable and efficient.

105 Smoker, Barbara. "In Court," Reg, I (Aug 1957), 8.
Since I officially represented both the Shaw Society and the Phonetic Alphabet Association at the hearing on Shaw's will, I was allowed to attend in the body of the court, and I advised Counsel for the Attorney-General.

106 Smoker, Barbara. "The £&d of G. B. S.," NStat, LIII (23 Feb 1957), 227-28.
At the time of the Chancery Division of the High Court of Justice's judgment on Shaw's bequest for the propagation of a new alphabet, most people were amazed to learn his estate was penniless. Shaw was his own publisher and never parted with the copyrights of his major works, not even after his death. The Estate Duty Office and Public Trustee assessed the copyrights far in excess of what was expected. The effect was to increase the net estate and that in turn increased the death duty. However, the estate is almost out of debt, ironically due to the American musical MY FAIR LADY based on Shaw's *Pygmalion*.

107 Smoker, Barbara. "Shaw and the Abbess," SHAVIAN, VIII (1957), 19-20.
[Review of IN A GREAT TRADITION: A TRIBUTE TO DAME LAURENTIA MCLACHLAN.] Shaw's correspondence with the Abbess of Stanbrook was another of his "paper courtships," but on a plane in which souls are wooed, not bodies.

108 Smoker, Barbara. "Shaw and the Alphabet," NStat, LIII (26 Jan 1957), 94, 96.
[An account of Shaw's will regarding his wish to reform the alphabet, which argues Shaw's case for it.] Shaw wanted not an expansion of an old alphabet, but a completely new alphabet.

109 Smoker, Barbara. "Silk Worms Save Shaw Museum," Reg, I (Dec 1957), 7-8.
Shaw did not endow his house and garden, and since the National Trust was unwilling to lose money, a silk worm

farm was moved to the property. Now bus-loads of school children, taken to see the silk worms, "do" Shaw's home at the same time.

110 Spencer, Terence James. "The Dramatic Principles of George Bernard Shaw." (DA, XVIII (1958), 594.) Unpublished dissertation, Stanford University, 1957. ([Listed in DAID.])

111 Stamm, Rudolf. ENGLISCHE LITERATUR (English Literature)(Bern: A. Francke, 1957), pp. 241, 340, 345, 396-97, 398-400.
[A survey of Shaw research. Introduces the most important books on Shaw.] [In German.]

112 Stamm, Rudolf. "George Bernard Shaw and Shakespeare's CYMBELINE," orig. publ. 1957, place unknown; rptd in STUDIES IN HONOR OF T. W. BALDWIN, ed, by Don Cameron Allen (Urbana: U of Illinois P, 1958), 254-66; rptd in THE SHAPING POWERS AT WORK (Heidelberg: Winter, 1967), 130-45.
Many of Shaw's outbursts against Shakespeare should be understood simply as attacks on established art by a growing artist trying to create a taste for his own style, and certainly the modern realistic theater and Shakespeare's plays were incompatible. Still, Shaw loved and reverenced Shakespeare's creations. His correspondence with Ellen Terry brought him into contact with preparations for Sir Henry Irving's 1896 production of CYMBELINE, which Shaw reviewed for SATURDAY REVIEW. He complimented Ellen Terry for her interpretation of Imogen--which followed the line he had recommended to her in his letters: to eliminate the "odious Mrs. Grundyish" part of Imogen. Shaw's approach to Shakespeare was limited by his classical taste. "He was unable to conceive of the plays as organic wholes; he had hardly anything useful to say on their complete meaning and esthetic quality, but he was a shrewd interpreter of . . . details of speeches, of characters, and of situations. Above all, he had the born dramatist's flair for the theatrical physiognomy of the plays." Shaw could not resist the temptation to improve on Shakespeare with CYMBELINE REFINISHED, an "esthetic impossibility" which has no connection with the fairy-tale quality of the play as a whole, but his foreward comes closer to justifying Shakespeare's original fifth act than his own version.

113 Starr, William T. "Romain Rolland and George Bernard Shaw," ShawB, II (Sept 1957), 3-6.
Shaw and Rolland were poles apart, except in their love for music and their iconoclastic attitude. Shaw was the witty anti-Romantic and Rolland the very embodiment of Don Quixote and his seriousness. Nevertheless, they had admiration for each other and corresponded for some years, especially during World War I. Shaw frequently disappointed Rolland by not taking more militant stands on important issues.

114 Steinhardt, Maxwell. "Laughton's Version of *Major Barbara*," ShawB, II (Jan 1957), 15-16.
[Review of a current production of *Major Barbara* at the Morosco Theatre in New York, directed by Charles Laughton.] Cornelia Otis Skinner performs satisfactorily as Lady Britomart, but Charles Laughton's Undershaft is a parody of the Shavian intention.

115 Sundaram, P. S. "Bernard Shaw," JOURNAL OF THE KARNATAK UNIVERSITY (India), 1 June 1957, 8-16.
Shaw is the greatest English man-of-letters since Shakespeare. His real greatness, like Gandhi's, was in his moral courage.

116 "The Talk of the Town," NY, XXXIII (2 March 1957), 26-27.
[Includes reminiscences of Shaw by Dame Sybil Thorndike and her husband, Sir Lewis Casson.]

117 Tauber, Abraham. "MY FAIR LADY and G.B.S.," WORD STUDY, XXXIII (1957), 1-4.
Behind Shaw's satirical thrust in *Pygmalion* lay a genuine interest in phonetics, as attested to by his granting money in his Will for the establishment of a new phonetic alphabet. For the sake of both greater economy and furthering social equality, Shaw sought an enlarged alphabet that would make English a more efficient and learnable language and thus more likely as an international language. Ironically, although Shaw's Will was overturned in court, the success of MY FAIR LADY and the entire Shaw literary heritage have caused his estate to grow in value to make the support of phonetic reform a possibility once again. But Shaw's real purpose in all this may simply have been to publicize the need for such reform, and in this he has been extremely successful.

118 Tenschert, Joachim. "Unannehmlichkeiten des Theaters. *Die heilige Johanna* von Shaw in der Volksbühne Berlin" (Discomforts of the Theater, Shaw's *Saint Joan* at the Volksbühne Berlin), THEATER DER ZEIT, XII (March 1957), 40-43.
The Volksbuhne production of Shaw's *Saint Joan* [in 1956] was almost a total disaster because it did not present the clarity of style and thought of this masterful play nor its social, political and historical implications which are so aptly described in Shaw's preface to the play. [In German.]

119 Trilling, Ossia. "Mysteriet omkring Bernard Shaws sidste stykke: *Hvorfor Hun Idde Vilde*" (The Mystery Surrounding Bernard Shaw's Last Play: *Why She Would Not*), DET DANSKE MAGASIN, V (1957), 20-25.
Both the Public Trustee, as Shaw's executor, and the Society of Authors, as his literary agents, have behaved strangely with regard to his last play, *Why She Would Not*. [History of the manuscript of *Would Not*]. Now that the play has been published, the Public Trustee has a duty, in the interest of literary history, to release the names of the literary advisers who could be presumptuous enough to make an arbitrary decision to attempt to suppress Shaw's play and who could believe that Shaw's standing was so insecure that it could be damaged by a short play written in his old age. Both external and internal evidence refutes their claim that the play is unfinished, and the play itself is evidence of the strong and vigorous spirit that Shaw retained until at least five months before his death, despite his 94 years. [In Danish.]

120 Veilleux, Jere Shanor. "An Analysis of the Rhetorical Situation and Rhetorical Character Types in Selected Plays of George Bernard Shaw," DA, XVII (1957), 2089. Unpublished Dissertation, University of Minnesota, 1957.

121 Vocadlo, Otakar. "Shaw in Bohemia," SHAVIAN, X (1957), 14-17.
[A detailed account of Shaw's popularity and influence in Czechoslovakia.]

122 Ward, A. C. BERNARD SHAW. (Lond: Longmans, Green [Writers and Their Work], 1957).

GEORGE BERNARD SHAW

[A brief biography, containing standard information, with an appendix of first performances of Shaw's principal plays.] Shaw was for modern Britain what Socrates was for ancient Greece, the Good Man of his time, whose ironic pose was too frequently misunderstood. Far from being a merely destructive critic of society, Shaw still satisfies a hunger for affirmations in an age of denials. He is being rediscovered in the 50's as an extremely relevant playwright, and as a wit and humorist who could contemplate disaster with moral courage and spiritual buoyancy.

123 Weintraub, Stanley. "Bernard Shaw, Charles Lever, and *Immaturity*," ShawB, II (Jan 1957), 11-15. The hero of *Immaturity* is apparently an amalgam of the hero of Charles Lever's A DAY'S RIDE; A LIFE'S ROMANCE (1863) and of the immature Shaw. Both Shaw and Lever deal in, as Shaw puts it, "the tragi-comic irony of the conflict between real life and the romantic imagination."

124 Weintraub, Stanley. "Bernard Shaw, Novelist," DA, XVII (1957), 369-70. Unpublished dissertation, Pennsylvania State University, 1956.

125 Weintraub, Stanley. "The Garnetts, the Fabians, and the Paradox Club," ShawB, II (May 1957), 9-12. [An account of Shaw's relationship with Edward Garnett and his wife-to-be, the Russian translator Constance Black, whom Shaw said he would have married if he could have afforded it.] Constance's bringing Edward along to Fabian meetings resulted in his writing a Peacockian novel called THE PARADOX CLUB (1888), in which a satiric treatment of the Fabians serves as a frame for Garnett's recreation of the romance of Constance and himself. Shaw is supposedly represented by a character named Martell.

126 Weintraub, Stanley. "'Humors' Names in Shaw's Prentice Novels," NAMES, V (Dec 1957), 222-25. Shaw was interested in the connotative power of nomenclature from the start, developed the technique of naming characters as he developed as a novelist, and then transferred his skill to the drama.

127 West, E. J. "G.B.S. and the Rival Queens--Duse and Bernhardt," QUARTERLY JOURNAL OF SPEECH, XLIII (1957), 265-73.
The appearance of Sarah Bernhardt and Eleanora Duse in London in 1895 at the same time and in many of the same parts resulted in the interesting phenomenon of comparative reviews by an impressionist, William Archer, and an analyst, Shaw. While Shaw looked in the theater for the vivid presentation of thought, however artificial the means, Archer preferred the creation of an illusion through verismilitude. Shaw approved of Duse because, without the compelling beauty and charm that made Bernhardt great, she transformed herself from a plain woman to compelling focus of attention with her art. On the other hand, Shaw felt Bernhardt never acted anyone but herself, providing emotional outbursts on cue, in a somewhat forced manner. Archer thought Bernhardt the greater actress and Duse nothing but an exhibitionist of herself.

128 Whitebait, William. *Saint Joan*, NStat, LIII (29 June 1957), 839.
[The adaptation of Shaw's *Saint Joan* by Graham Greene and produced by Otto Preminger.] A classy, rather null film that leaves out Shaw's main argument--that Joan was a Protestant. Jean Seberg as Joan is appealing but not enough self-reliant.

129 Whittemore, Reed. "Shaw's Abstract Clarity," TULANE DRAMA REVIEW II (Nov 1957), 46-57.
Shaw was "a walking contradiction; for all the time that he insisted he dealt with hard facts he dealt, on the contrary, with ideas." His realism is abstract, a creation of the mind, for in fact he was a moonshiner. Shaw constantly *talked* about the need for realism and constantly *wrote* theatrically, unrealistically. He simultaneously ridiculed illusions and constructed illusions with loving care.

130 Woodward, Mary K. "Otto Preminger at the New York Regional Group's May Meeting," Reg, I (Aug 1957), 1, 5.
[Otto Preminger's explanation of his film version of *Saint Joan* with some comment.]

1958

131 Albert, Sidney P. "The Mood of Barbara," Reg, II (Oct 1958), 8.
Both "Major" and "Barbara" have meanings connected with the syllogism in traditional logic. They imply that the essence of the plot development is the undermining of Barbara's way of life by exposing the weaknesses of her major premise. This educational process Barbara undergoes sets the formal structure of the play.

132 Allen, Douglas. "Drama among the Mormons," TAM, XLII (Dec 1958); rptd "Shaw among the Mormons," SHAVIAN, XV (June 1959), 10-12.
[*Pygmalion* as performed in one Salt Lake City Mormon Ward.]

133 Allsop, Kenneth. "What a Corner for Shaw to Be in . . . ," DAILY MAIL, 15 March 1958; rptd in SHAVIAN, XII (May 1958) 19-20.
It is ridiculous for the reputation of our greatest dramatist since Shakespeare to depend on "the ballyhoo and frou-frou" of MY FAIR LADY. Shaw, who was about to subside into that twilight where we British keep our classics, is suddenly the rage sage.

134 Altrincham, Lord. "Reflections on *The Apple Cart*," NATIONAL AND ENGLISH REVIEW, CLI (July 1958), 18-23.
Shaw was an authoritarian in mind, a libertarian at heart. *The Apple Cart* reflects the contradictions in his political attitudes. In it Shaw has made democracy seem ridiculous; the national leaders behave like quarrelsome children, and by contrast the King is a tolerant and resourceful adult. He triumphs, but--and here Shaw's emotions came to terms with his intellect--he does so within the limits of the Constitution. King Edward VIII might have profited from Magnus' example; had he refused the title offered him, he might have eventually become Prime Minister, for Magnus' scheme is quite workable. Shaw's ideal monarch is too much identified with England and too little with the Commonwealth to be entirely appropriate to the present age.

135 Atkinson, Brooks. "Theatre: Shavian Prose,"
   NYT, 27 March 1958, p. 41.
Back to Methuselah is not exhilarating, and reducing its
length has not lightened its spirits.

136 Atkinson, Brooks.   "Shaw Said 'Fathead,'" NYT,
   24 Aug 1958, II, p. 1.
Clive Bell's aestheticism offended Shaw's puritanism, so
that he called Bell a "fathead" and a "voluptuary."
[Comments on SHAW ON THE THEATRE ed by E. J. West (1958)
and SEVEN ONE-ACT PLAYS (Penguin, 1958), "two interesting
items that have disturbed the peace of summer."]

137 Barnes, Kenneth R. WELCOME, GOOD FRIENDS: THE
   AUTOBIOGRAPHY OF KENNETH R. BARNES, ed by Phillis
   Hartnoll (Lond: Peter Davies, 1958).
[Barnes records his reaction to Shaw as a new sort of
theatrical experience: first doubt as to the credibility
of Shaw's characters, then suspicion that motives in life
might resemble those of Shaw's characters more closely
than most people cared to admit. One chapter is devoted
to his long friendship with Shaw from 1912, when Shaw
joined the Council of the Academy of Dramatic Art, until
Shaw's death.   Shaw's part in the affairs of the R.A.D.A.
is recorded: his generosity in times of financial
trouble, his insistence on including women on the Council,
his attention to rehearsals of his plays by Academy
students, his authorship of *The R.A.D.A. Graduates'
Keepsake and Collector*, containing advice to young actors.
Barnes includes a long letter from Shaw offering advice on
his play THE LETTER OF THE LAW which, Barnes thought,
showed clearly Shaw's "powers of concentration, and the
extent to which his kind heart motivated the workings of
his keen brain."]

138 Bentley, Eric [Russell].   "My Fair Lady,"
   SHAVIAN, XIII (Sept 1958), 3; rptd in MD, I (Sept
   1958), 135-36.
MY FAIR LADY is un-Shavian in spirit. Higgins, once an
eccentric professor, becomes just an average man, and
while the original ending was human reality, the romantic
ending is a facile daydream, returning to that very
romance and melodrama which Shaw spent all his energies
getting away from.

139 Bierman, Judah, James Hart, and Stanley Johnson. THE DRAMATIC EXPERIENCE (Englewood Cliffs, NJ: Prentice-Hall, 1958), pp. 260-62.
[A drama anthology which includes *Caesar and Cleopatra* with an introduction discussing the play as comedy.] The comedy is primarily in the conflict of characters, and Caesar is the "comic seer" who reveals that "it is our vanities and prejudices, disguised as inviolable social conventions, that keep us running in darkness instead of walking in light." Caesar interacts with Cleopatra, the silly girl who must learn about power, with Britannus, the prototype of pious British morality, and with the Egyptian court, the corrupt world, to reveal the follies of each. Caesar has many brillant sides but little depth, for comic characters must be treated externally.

140 Blissett, William. "Bernard Shaw: Imperfect Wagnerite," UNIVERSITY OF TORONTO QUARTERLY, XXVII (Jan 1958), 185-99.
Wagner's impact on literature was enormous, and Shaw is foremost among his champions and interpreters. Yet Shaw saw Wagner's music as the culmination of the nineteenth century, not the Art-Work of the Future, and he confessed that he did not care for the pure ritual of PARSIFAL. He championed Wagner the social thinker and the musician. Shaw's Wagnerism is part of and limited by his religion of the Life Force. Life, not love, is Shaw's religion; here, he and Wagner part company, though defiance of the old by the young, on Siegfried's pattern, plays a significant part in Shaw's drama. Shaw does not make use of Wagner's Leitmotif system, nor do his characters belong to the realm of myth. Shaw did not build on Wagner's most distinctive achievement, nor did he share many of his gravest failings; Shaw's art is classical.

141 Blow, Sydney. THROUGH STAGE DOORS (Edinburgh and Lond: W & R Chambers, 1958), pp. 203-4.
[A second-hand account of Shaw's unchivalrous treatment of his wife is included, as well as Shaw's refusal of Blow's request to write a one act play of half an hour, saying he impressed audiences by the length of his plays.]

142 Boas, Robert. "Death of a Shavian Dustman," DRAMA, ns, L (Autumn 1958), 36-37.
Though most of the characters in MY FAIR LADY are very similar to their prototypes in *Pygmalion*, Alfred Doolittle becomes simply a conventional cockney comic. Shaw's

inspired working-class philosopher is lost, sacrificed to realism. The greatest loss is in the transformation of the last act where Shaw's hilarious comedy of the *déclassé* proletarian evaporates, and only a cockney working man come into money and going on the razzle remains.

143 Bright, Mary Chavelita Dunne [George Egerton]. A LEAF FROM THE YELLOW BOOK: THE CORRESPONDENCE OF GEORGE EGERTON, ed by Terence de Vere White (Lond: Richards P, 1958).
[Two letters from Shaw containing detailed advice on two of George Egerton's plays are included, and her judgment on Shaw as "the most sterilizing influence on the theatre . . . in fifty years" is recorded.]

144 Brome, Vincent. SIX STUDIES IN QUARRELLING (Lond: Cresset Press, 1958).
[Shaw is central in three of the six studies.] Chap 1: "Shaw versus Wells." Though Wells and Shaw were friends, both were aggressive and argumentative. They first quarrelled over the policies of the Fabian Society, which Wells attacked for its complacent gradualism. Later they disagreed about politics and about vivisection, Pavlov and science in general, which Shaw attacked and Wells defended. Finally, science and the Life Force were the two poles of the quarrel, according to Shaw; this is supported by passages from *Back to Methuselah* and Wells's THE CONQUEST OF TIME. Chap 2: "Shaw and Wells versus Henry Arthur Jones." Shaw's lack of reverence for Shakespeare, his plays' lack of form and particularly his lack of patriotism during the war all provoked attacks from Jones. Shaw was gracious and generous to Jones, generally overlooking his attacks rather than furthering the feud. Chap 5: "G. K. Chesterton versus Bernard Shaw." Like Jones, Chesterton opposed Shaw's antipatriotic stand during World War I. Economics was another basis for quarrels. Religion was perhaps the most central difference between the two; Chesterton found Shaw's belief that we were "not very successful attempts at God" and that "there would never be a God unless we made one" particularly outrageous. Nonetheless, the two remained on good terms. [More successful at depicting personalities of quarrellers than at clarification of issues. Partially documented.]

145 "Bruder Bernhard" (Brother Bernhard), DER SPIEGEL (Hamburg), XII (26 March 1958), 56-61.

[An account of Shaw's friendship with the Abbess Laurentia of the Stanbrook Abbey. The title is chosen because Shaw signed his letters to the abbess "Brother John."] [In German.]

146 Byrne, John, and Geoffrey Johnson. "Introduction," THREE MODERN PLAYS (Lond: Methuen, 1958), pp. 9-12.
Village Wooing was conceived in terms of an operatic duet. The play exhibits in miniature most of Shaw's pet theories and the characteristics of his style. More concerned with revolutionary thought than with individuals, Shaw makes his characters vividly animated abstract ideas. It may be a caricature of Shaw's own literary self. Though the play is largely talk, it is first-class dramatic entertainment; Shaw's intellectual audacity, his wit, his humor, his irony, his brilliance of epigram and paradox, his infectious tomfoolery and exploitation of anticlimax do hold the audience.

147 Carrington, Norman Thomas. NOTES ON G. BERNARD SHAW: CAESAR AND CLEOPATRA (Lond: Brodie [Notes on Chosen English Texts], [1958]).
[Biography, explanatory notes, and study questions. Not seen.]

148 Carrington, Norman Thomas. NOTES ON G. BERNARD SHAW: SAINT JOAN (Lond: Brodie [Notes on Chosen English Texts], [1958]).
[Biography, explanatory notes, and study questions. Note seen.]

149 Daiches, David. THE PRESENT AGE IN BRITISH LITERATURE (Bloomington: Indiana U P, 1958), pp. 106, 149, 152, 153, 163, 164, 172, 174, 178, 213, 326.
Though Shaw had a gift for standing the popular view on its head, he was not important as a dramatic innovator; structurally and thematically he kept to the well-made play. "Detailed psychological stage directions put the burden of conveying meaning on to the actor and producer and help to perpetuate that very dominance of the drama by the theatre that Shaw began by deploring." *Saint Joan* was not meant to be a tragedy; it is given humor, vitality and conviction by Shaw's interpretation of events in modern terms, by his refusal to be awed by historical or

religious dogma. Towards the end of the play, when the comic element fades, Shaw falls back on standard romanticism for emotional effect.

150 Debnicki, Antoni. "Earliest Shavian Productions in Poland," SHAVIAN, XIII (Sept 1958), 14-16.
The first Shaw play to be staged in Poland was *The Devil's Disciple* in 1903. The City Theater of Cracow produced twelve Shaw plays between 1903 and 1912, and many other theaters, even small provincial ones, produced Shaw. Generally, the critics responded more favorably than the public. After a decade Polish actors became more adept at acting Shaw's plays, and they became more popular; after Shakespeare, Shaw was the English dramatist most often staged.

151 Denham, Reginald. STARS IN MY HAIR (NY: Crown, 1958), pp. 42, 79, 111-12, 145, 169, 175.
The Oxford Playhouse opened in 1923 with *Heartbreak House*. "The grand old man himself came to rehearsal, if you can call it such. He acted all the parts from memory and played the audience as well, laughing uproariously at the comedy lines. Hardly anybody in the cast spoke at all." Shaw came to the last performance; in consequence, the actors overplayed, the audience politely overlaughed, and in response to insistent calls for 'Author' afterwards, Shaw declared it one of the most depressing evenings he had ever spent in the theater. He thought he had written a quiet, thoughtful, semi-tragic play, but it appeared to have been regarded as a bedroom farce.

152 Eckstein, Harry. THE ENGLISH HEALTH SERVICE (Cambridge, Mass.:   Harvard U P, 1958), pp. 77, 103, 104, 169, 227.
Nowhere are the Fabians's suspicions of the medical profession more evident than in *The Doctor's Dilemma* and its preface. Shaw was reconciled only to the Medical Officer of Health, a salaried civil servant, "because he had no selfish stake in the public's diseases and was concerned with their most important cause, environment." Shaw's naïveté in believing that there would be no place in a proper society for surgeries and hospitals is now apparent, but there was some truth in his belief in the relationship between the incidence of disease and social stratification.

153 Edwards, Oliver. "Visit to London," TIMES (Lond), 14 Aug 1958; rptd in SHAVIAN, XIV (Feb 1959), 9-11.
Shaw gave the money from his Nobel Prize to establish the Anglo-Swedish Literary Foundation. The money was to encourage the translation and publication of Swedish works for English readers. The first to benefit from this was August Strindberg, who with his wife Freda Uhl, visited London around the turn of the century.

154 Étienne, Fernand. GEORGE BERNARD SHAW (Bruges [?]: Desclée De Brouwer [Ontmoetingen (Encounters)], 1958).
[A short monograph covering Shaw's life and major works. Bibliography.] [In Dutch.]

155 Evans, T. F. "Granville-Barker: Shavian Disciple," ShawB, II (May 1958), 1-19.
Shaw called Barker's plays "superb," "masterpieces," but his fame as a dramatist now has faded almost completely. Barker's plays recall Shaw's in their use of detailed psychological stage directions and in their cerebral quality; Barker is above all a dramatist of ideas. But there is in his plays none of the high spirited tomfoolery of Shaw's plays. Shaw used melodramatic devices and "seasoned his discussion of ideas with comic interludes, pantomime and any other diversion that his inventive genius could conceive. For Barker these tricks were illegitimate; he appealed entirely to the mind." Shaw lacked Barker's delicacy and restraint and so could be "cruder, more ridiculous, sometimes cheaper, often sillier—and yet achieve results, which Barker could not."

156 Evans, T. F. "Shaw and the Play of Ideas," SHAVIAN XII (May 1958) 24-26.
Though Shaw's great contribution to the English drama is said to be the play of ideas, Robertson, Pinero and Henry Arthur Jones wrote plays of roughly this kind before Shaw. Nonetheless, Shaw is an improvement in dealing with matters other than sexual adventures and in treating serious ideas humorously. In view of the absence of great tragedy in contemporary drama, dramatists might be well advised to treat contemporary problems along Shavian lines.

157 Ewen, David. COMPLETE BOOK OF THE AMERICAN
MUSICAL THEATRE (NY: Holt, Rinehart & Winston,
1958), pp. 196-98.
Shaw vigorously opposed turning his plays into musicals,
but after his death Lerner and Loewe obtained the rights
to create a musical version of *Pygmalion*. To make a big
musical of the play, they had only to add what happened
offstage in the play. The few additions and Lerner's
lyrics were so Shavian in spirit and style that it is
often difficult to tell where Shaw left off and Lerner
began.

158 Fay, Gerard. THE ABBEY THEATRE, CRADLE OF
GENIUS (Lond: Hollis & Carter; NY: Macmillan;
Dublin: Clonmore & Reynolds, 1958), pp. 55, 67, 74,
75, 110, 119, 138, 144.
Shaw said that Ireland's National Theatre would not
produce *John Bull's Other Island* because it would outrage
the Irish Nationalists, but really the reason was the
difficulty of casting it; Dublin offered a small choice,
and there was no one suitable for Broadbent. Shaw
naturally ridiculed the ardent Irish nationalism which
prompted attacks on Synge's PLAYBOY for depicting an
Irishman who attempted to murder his father. A burst of
publicity almost equal to PLAYBOY'S was brought on by the
Abbey's decision to produce *The Shewing-up of Blanco
Posnet*, which had been banned in England, but the play was
presented successfully.

159 Fehse, Willi. "Der Dolmetsch Bernard Shaws"
(Bernard Shaw's Interpreter), WELTSTIMMEN, XXVII
(1958), 182-83.
Siegfried Trebitsch was a dedicated and capable translator
of Shaw's work and a poet in his own right. [In German.]

160 Gassner, John. "Broadway in Review," ETJ, X
(1958), 244-45.
Curiously, in Arnold Moss's one-night version of *Back to
Methuselah* Shaw seemed more loquacious than in the uncut
version. This is not surprising; prolixity is a matter of
thinness, the result of hastily presented ideas. The bare
bones of the argument are not especially interesting; Shaw
is "robbed of his mystery by having his tongue curbed."
He is at his best when he is "rationally irrational,
circuitously direct, and engrossed by both sides of an
argument."

161 Gelb, Phillip, et al. "Ideas and the Theatre: A G.B.S. Symposium," ShawB, II (Sept 1958), 15-20.
[Abridged transcript of a broadcast tape, presenting ten prominent writers and critics with Phillip Gelb as moderator, debating Shaw's success as a social propagandist.]

162 Gibbs, Wolcott. "Life Everlasting," NY, XXXIV (5 April 1958), 56-58.
Arnold Moss's drastically edited *Back to Methuselah* retains the tone of Shaw's original version; in both "the Master [is] willful, arch, self-conscious, and generally exasperating."

163 Glicksberg, Charles I. "The Modern Playwright and the Absolute: The Decline of Tragedy," QQ, LXV (Autumn 1958), 459-71.
Though *Heartbreak House* presents a heart-rending picture of Europe, Shaw did not altogether despair. The inhabitants of Heartbreak House have lost the capacity to love and have no controlling sense of purpose. Shotover's reference to the laws of God remind us that Shaw was essentially a visionary, for all his rationalist criticism of the Church.

164 Groshong, James Willard. "G. B. S. and Germany: The Major Aspects," DA, XVIII (1958), 588. Unpublished dissertation, Stanford University, 1957.

165 Heidicke, Manfred. "G.B.S. oder K.P.? *Der Mann des Schicksals* und *Blanco Posnets Erweckung* von George Bernard Shaw in den Kammerspielen Berlin" (G.B.S. or K.P.? *The Man of Destiny* and *The Shewing-up of Blanco Posnet* in the kammerspiele Berlin), THEATER DER ZEIT, XIII (July 1958), 50-53.
The production of *The Man of Destiny* was more Karl Paryla, the director and principal actor, than Shaw. *The Shewing-up of Blanco Posnet* is meaningless for a modern (East) German audience. [In German.]

166 Holland, Norman. "Shavian Encounter," SHAVIAN, XII (May, 1958), 29.
[Impressions of Shaw on meeting him in 1932.]

167 Inglis, Brian. "Well, Would He?" Spec, 2 May
1958, p. 555.
Would Shaw have objected to MY FAIR LADY? Marriage
between Higgins and Eliza is not in keeping with the
Freudian spirit of *Pygmalion*. Higgins, like Shaw, would
never grow out of his mother fixation. (Surprisingly,
when Shaw and Freud met, Shaw accepted Freud's explanation
that Shaw's mother fixation was no less real for being
unconscious.) But Pascal, who was able to cajole Shaw
into a romanticized film version of *Pygmalion*, would no
doubt have been able to arrange a Shavian benediction for
MY FAIR LADY as well.

168 Jones, Frank. "Unpublished Shaw; Grammar and
Communism," TIMES EDUCATIONAL SUPPLEMENT, No. 2248
(20 June 1958), p. 1041.
My letter to Shaw in 1928 protesting his use of
"whomsoever" when the nominative case was called for began
a brief exchange of letters with him. He defended his
usage on the dubious ground that it introduced no
ambiguity. Shaw thought that schools and schoolmasters
had not changed since his day and that the effect of the
education described in THE DIARY OF A COMMUNIST SCHOOLBOY
must be less demeaning than that of English schools.

169 Kaye, Julian B. BERNARD SHAW AND THE
NINETEENTH-CENTURY TRADITION (Norman: U of Oklahoma
P, 1958); pp. 132-52 rptd BERNARD SHAW'S PLAYS, ed
by Warren Sylvester Smith (1970).
In Shaw we find a living record of the reaction of a
nineteenth-century mind to the confusion and instability
of our own age. Shaw's *Weltanschauung* was formed by the
nineteenth-century and fixed by the time of the outbreak
of World War I; to recognize this is to understand the
many wrong answers he gave to twentieth-century questions.
Despite Shaw's reactions against romanticism, Carlyle was
a molder of Shavian thought in his opposition to *laissez
faire*, his admiration for the great man, his Puritanism,
and his conception of the role of God in history. In both
Heartbreak House and *On the Rocks* Shaw employs Carlyle's
political metaphor of the ship in need of the best
possible pilot. *Major Barbara* shows the influence of
Ruskin's UNTO THIS LAST, as do *Intelligent Woman's Guide
to Socialism and Capitalism* and *Everybody's Political
What's What*. Shaw appreciated too Dickens's attack on the
inhumanity of Classical political economy in HARD TIMES.
Shaw followed Mill's opposition to revolutionary
Socialism, and he also adopted the demand for protection

of unpopular ideas made in ON LIBERTY. Comte is probably the ultimate source of Shaw's relativism. Shaw adopts Arnold's conservatism in attempting to preserve valuable insights of Christianity by separating them from false theology. Butler was a conservative influence of Shaw's economic thinking, and Bergson stimulated Shaw both as artist and as philosopher. Schopenhauer's overthrow of rationalism allowed Shaw to develop his philosophy of Creative Evolution. As a religious radical, an artist-prophet, and a man who hated cruelty, punishment, and revenge, Blake influenced Shaw. Shaw and Shelley shared fundamentally ethical rather than theological religious convictions. Henry George aroused Shaw's interest in economic problems, but Shaw was soon converted to Marx and then to Jevons, for he rejected Marx's theory of class struggle. Shaw used Marx's prostitution metaphor for capitalism in *Mrs. Warren's Profession*. *Barbara* rejects the metaphor and criticizes Marxism as a way of understanding historical change. The Preface of *Androcles and the Lion* uses Bellamy's arguments to support equality of income as one of Jesus's tenets, and the eugenic argument for equality of income in *The Revolutionist's Handbook* is also Bellamy's. Ibsen's suspicion of political democracy, his moral relativism, his pragmatism, and meliorism influenced Shaw's conception of the superman and the Life-Force. Wagner appealed to Shaw both as a revolutionist and as an artist, though he abhorred Wagner's pessimism, amorism, nationalism, and the asceticism of his old age. Whenever his synthesis of nineteenth-century ideas was relevant to the situation, his judgment was sound; when it was not, he often seemed naive or perverse.

170 Kerr, Walter. "First Night Report," NYHT, 27 March 1958.
Back to Methuselah needs to be more or less than a joke.

171 Kirov, T. "Kriticheskiiat realizum na Bernard Shou" (Shaw's Critical Realism), TEATUR (Sofia), No 2 (1958), 37-43.
[Not seen.] [In Bulgarian.]

172 Komatsu, Motoya. "Shaw no Shakaihihan to Tojojinbutsu" (Shaw's Social Criticism and Characters), AKITA DAIGAKU GAKUGEIGAKUBU KENKYUKIYO (Akita), (Jinbunkagaku) No. 8 (Feb 1958), pp. 81-94.
Shaw's intention in his proposition of the Life Force is not to build up a systematic philosophy but to create a

frame of reference for his social criticism. [In Japanese.]

173 Kornbluth, Martin L. "Shaw and Restoration Comedy." ShawB, II (Jan 1958), 9-17.
Despite Shaw's general Puritanical condemnation of Restoration dramatists, his plays are remarkably similar to theirs. Like theirs, Shaw's plays are essentially comedies of manners; common characteristics are: brilliant talk rather than action; indoor settings with the outdoors just another place, not depicting forces of nature; many primarily 'humours' characters who lack deep emotion; the relationship of the sexes depicted largely as a war of wits; cynicism apparent in iconoclasm, lack of respect for idealists, and anti-romantic treatment of emotions. There are also similarities in plots. Of course, comedies of manners have similar characteristics regardless of the century, but Shaw seems to have been conscious of Restoration comedy as a model.

174 Laing, Allan M. "G. B. S. Repeats Himself," SHAVIAN XII (May 1958) 26-28.
[Dialogue of imaginary television interview of Shaw on the subject of censorship in which "S" reaffirms his opposition to censorship and the basic reasons for it, citing the Preface to *The Shewing-up of Blanco Posnet*.]

175 Lambert, J. W. "Plays in Performance," DRAMA, ns LI (Winter 1958), 16-17.
In *Major Barbara* Shaw used with superficial brilliance characters from a wide range of society, not observed with scientific accuracy, but possessing a truth of their own. Joan Plowright as Barbara did not sound born and bred in Knightsbridge. [Photograph.]

176 Landau, Jacob M. STUDIES IN THE ARAB THEATER AND CINEMA (Phila: U of Pennsylvania P, 1958); rptd "Shaw in Arabia," ISh, V (Fall 1966), 9.
[Bibliography of translated plays includes: *The Apple Cart, Caesar and Cleopatra, The Devil's Disciple, The Doctor's Dilemma, Geneva, The Man of Destiny,* and *Saint Joan.*]

177 Leary, Daniel James. "The Superman and Structure in George Bernard Shaw's Plays: A Study in Dialectic Action," DA, XIX (1959), 2081. Unpublished dissertation, Syracuse University, 1958.

178 "The Love Letters of Bernard Shaw," ESQUIRE, XLIX (April 1958), 63-65.
[Shaw's letters to Alice Lockett (Sept 1883-Oct 1885). The editor's note describes her as "the object of his first--and most desperately romantic--passion" and connects the end of their correspondence with the start of Shaw's first affair, with Jenny Patterson.]

179 Lowe, Robert Liddell. "Two Shaw Letters," MODERN LANGUAGE REVIEW, LIII (Oct 1958), 548-50.
Two previously unpublished letters from Shaw to Percy William Bunting, editor of the CONTEMPORARY REVIEW, shed light on Shaw's career as a journalist.

180 Lüdecke, Henry. "Bernard Shaw und sein Werk" (Bernard Shaw and His Work), UNIVERSITAS, XIII (1958), 137-50.
Shaw's personality is transparent in all his works. Women play a most important role in his life and work ("the nobility of Shaw's personality shines brightest in his women"). His religion is best illustrated in his Caesar, "a political Jesus" and charity (caritas) personified. [In German.]

181 Lupis-Vukic, J. F. "Shaw's 1929 Program for Easing World Tensions--and How It Originated," Shaw B, II (Jan 1958), 1-4.
During his 1929 visit to Yugoslavia, Shaw left a statement for the press which was censored and remained unpublished. But his statement on some international questions, on mixed nationalities, on generals and politicians during wartime may still represent a sound political view today. [Shaw's statement, which also includes a defense of authors rendered helpless by inadequate copyright laws, is reproduced.]

182 Matlaw, Myron. "The Denouement of *Pygmalion*," MD, I (May 1958), 29-34.
Shaw chose the title of *Pygmalion* to emphasize the centrality of Higgins and the story of the creation of human life. (Contrast MY FAIR LADY, with its emphasis on Eliza and the Cinderella theme.) In *Pygmalion* Eliza

personifies the potential of a human being, while Higgins
is the lifegiver, Shaw's ideal hero: childlike (as are
other Shaw heroes such as Caesar and Joan), unsentimental,
devoid of sensuality, witty, preoccupied with a particular
application of intellectual or philosophical questions
which is generally misunderstood by others. Higgins
transforms Eliza from subhuman to human, but "marrying
Eliza would be preposterous for Higgins, a Superman with
the vitality of a soul and a "Miltonic mind" . . . who
lives on an entirely different plane."

183 Matlaw, Myron. "Will Higgins Marry Eliza?"
SHAVIAN XII (May 1958) 14-19.
The epilogue of *Pygmalion* is dramatically inevitable; it
is the ending of the film which is capricious. A
comparison of myth and play suggests that Shaw chose the
title because both are stories of creation of human life,
though the endings and the natures of the artists differ.
It is not the transformation of Eliza but the conflict
between Higgins, the artist-philosopher representative of
the Life Force, and Eliza, representative of middle-class
morality, which is central. Higgins is the ideal Shaw
hero, the life-giver, a Superman embodying a life force
divorced from human social and sensual drives. Eliza is
to him rather as Cleopatra is to Caesar; it is unthinkable
that he should marry her.

184 Mehus, Donald V. "George Bernard Shaw als
Muziekcriticus" (George Bernard Shaw as a Music
Critic), DE VLAAMSE GIDS, XLII (Nov 1958), 653-56;
trans and rptd "Bernard Shaw als Musikkritiker,"
ÖSTERREICHISCHE MUSIKZEITSCHRIFT, XV (Nov 1960),
514-17; ISh, XV (Winter/Spring 1977), 22-23.
Shaw's music reviews betray a considerable knowledge of
and understanding for music. They are well written, and
many of them are still valid and worth reading today. [In
Dutch, German and English.]

185 Miller, Arthur, interviewed by Phillip Gelb.
"Morality and Modern Drama," ETJ, X (Oct 1958), 190-
202.
Miller: With occasional exceptions, usually women, Shaw's
characters are not realistic, nor does he mean them to be.
"You always know it's Shaw speaking no matter what side of
the argument is being set forth, and that is part of the
charm." He was observing issues rather than psychology.
Gelb: Shaw was writing real people with real motives;

they just speak more eloquently, more intellectually than real people. Miller: Shaw was impatient with the insignificant part of real people, so he stripped it all away. What remains may be valid, but it is not real in the naturalistic sense. Shaw's people never get off the subject; he is following not psychology but theme.

186 Millett, Fred B. "Contemporary British Literature," CONTEMPORARY LITERARY SCHOLARSHIP: A CRITICAL REVIEW, ed by Lewis Leary (NY: Appleton-Century-Crofts, 1958), 187-200.
Although the quantity of commentary on Shaw is abundant, if not overpowering, the quality is not impressive. No really searching study of Shaw's complex and sometimes contradictory ideas and their origins has yet been made.

187 Montes, Jorge. "Celluloide *Santa Juana*" (Celluloid *Saint Joan*), ATLÁNTIDA (Argentina), XLI (April 1958), 90.
Otto Preminger's *Saint Joan* followed Shaw carefully and intelligently. [In Spanish.]

188 Moss, Arnold. "Classic or Potboiler?" NYT, 23 March 1958, II, pp. 1, 3.
The "plot" of *Back to Methuselah* is "you get what you want because you want it badly enough to keep trying for it until it comes along." Its reaffirmation of hope for the future of mankind inspired me to devise a marketable condensation by "arranging, eliminating, inserting and transposing the pertinent material of the five-play cycle, of the 30,000 word preface and the 1944 postscript, without adding a single word of my own authorship," tying scenes together with a Shaw character speaking words from the text. As a result, more people are paying more money to see *Methuselah*, hitherto notoriously uncommercial, than any other play by or devised from Shaw, except MY FAIR LADY.

189 Musulin, Stella. "Der Freidenker und die Nonne" (The Freethinker and the Nun), WORT UND WAHRHEIT, XIII, (May 1958), 398-400.
Shaw's letters to Abbess Laurentia McLachlan, now available in a German translation, reveal his true and undistorted feelings and opinions. [In German.]

190 Nethercot, Arthur H. "*Major Barbara*: Rebuttal and Addendum," ShawB, II (May 1958), 20-21.
[A reply to Ozy, "The Dramatist's Dilemma," ShawB, 1958.]
The article overlooks the possibility that Cusins may introduce his own "true morality" into the firm when he takes it over. Also, Undershaft's name has significance: St. Andrew was the patron saint of gunpowder makers. There is a church of St. Andrew Undershaft in London which took its name from a famous maypole, a fertility symbol.

191 Nichols, Beverley. THE SWEET AND TWENTIES (Lond: Weidenfeld & Nicolson, 1958), pp. 59-65.
Apart from *Saint Joan*, Shaw never wrote a line of great poetry, nor created a single character who lives when he steps off the stage. [A DAILY NEWS article Shaw wrote on the Carpentier-Dempsey fight and a scrap of dialogue from THE WILD OAT by Sydney Blow Shaw wrote, which satirizes himself and Hall Caine, are included.]

192 Nickson, Joseph R. "The Art and Politics of the Later Plays of Bernard Shaw," Unpublished Dissertation, University of Southern California, 1958. [Listed in McNamee.]

193 O'Donnell, Norbert F. "Harmony and Discord in *Good King Charles*," ShawB, II (Jan 1958), 5-8.
The first act of *In Good King Charles's Golden Days* is perhaps the purest intellectual discussion in Shaw's drama. Engaged in the discussion are representatives of different philosophical perspectives: Newton, the scientific rationalist; Fox, the religious mystic; Kneller, the aesthetic intuitionist; Charles, the pragmatist. The revelation of the possibility of a degree of harmony in the first act is ironically contrasted with the discord prevailing in the world of political action in the second act. Shaw's late plays show our culture on the brink of disasters; *King Charles* is a dramatic reflection on the tolerance apparent in the world of intellectual discussion and ironically absent in the world of political and social action.

194 Ozy [pseud]. "The Dramatist's Dilemma: An Interpretation of *Major Barbara*," ShawB, II (Jan 1958), 18-24.
The contradiction between Shaw the realist and Shaw the idealist is evident in his characterization of Undershaft.

"Undershaft, an instrument of the Death Force, battered his way into the play and laid waste to . . . the humbugs of our deadly virtues," in accord with Shaw's realism. But he grew into a frightening giant that threatened to block his creator's purpose: the propagation of his belief that the Life Force is helping the human race evolve toward perfection. With Undershaft's challenge to Cusins: "Dare you make war on war? Here are the means . . . , " Shaw the idealist demolishes his creation, transforming Undershaft from the Prince of Darkness into an angel of light.

195 Park, Bruce R. "A Mote in the Critic's Eye: Bernard Shaw and Comedy," TEXAS STUDIES IN ENGLISH, XXXVII (1958), 195-210, rptd R. J. Kaufman (ed), G. B. SHAW: A COLLECTION OF CRITICAL ESSAYS (1965).
The lack of serious criticism of Shaw's work reveals a constriction in the vision of modern criticism: it has no way to value Shaw's kind of literature. Shaw wanted to be thought of as a poet, but his definition differs from that of modern criticism. The traditional terms with which modern critics define poetry were to Shaw merely terms for the decorations which differentiated verse from prose, the organic form of language. Critics are more interested in the art of poetry than of drama, or if they do study drama, they concentrate on tragedy rather than comedy. Shaw's Platonic rationalizing is also less to the taste of modern criticism than is mythicizing.

196 Pearson, Hesketh, "My Uninvited Collaborator G B S," HORIZON, I (Nov 1958), 18-22, 134-37.
Shaw was unceasingly generous with help and advice for the biography undertaken in 1938, but he classified as silly gossip some anecdotes which were verified by a number of witnesses. When the book was finished, Shaw spent a year correcting and adding to it. [A sample page of corrected manuscript is reproduced here.] Among the "trivialities" Shaw thought should be left out of the biography were his accounts of the opening of *Overruled* on a bill with one-act plays of Pinero and Barrie, his indignity at being the victim of a kidney-stone despite his careful diet, and his one-sided relationship with Erica Cotterill. At the publisher's insistence, additional material was cut, including Shaw's identification of himself and Stella Campbell with Magnus and Orinthia in *The Apple Cart.* Shaw repudiated any claim to the conception or authorship or profits of the biography, but on the flyleaf of the

author's copy, under the signature, he wrote "Also his humble collaborator G. Bernard Shaw."

197 Pearson, Hesketh. "A Shavian Musical," SHAVIAN, XIII (Sept 1958), 4-6.
Shaw would have been exasperated by MY FAIR LADY. He approved of neither THE CHOCOLATE SOLDIER, the musical version of *Arms and the Man*, nor a proposed musical version of *Captain Brassbound's Conversion*. In general, he thought his work better suited to grand opera than to musical comedy. Though he granted that plots were anybody's property, his philosophy was important; he did not want his work parodied and its meaning destroyed.

198 Pitman, Sir James. "My Fair Ladies-and Gentlemen," Insert in the playbills at the London production of MY FAIR LADY, 1958-59; rptd in GEORGE BERNARD SHAW ON LANGUAGE, ed by Abraham Tauber (NY: Philosophical Library, 1963; Lond: Peter Owen, 1965), pp. 179-83.
[Brief Survey of Shaw's efforts at alphabet reform.]

199 Poirier, Philip P. THE ADVENT OF THE BRITISH LABOUR PARTY (Lond: Allen & Unwin; NY: Columbia U P, 1958), pp. 25, 26, 29, 32-36, 42, 46, 58, 78, 88, 104, 105, 106, 107, 109, 110-11, 125, 146, 161, 223, 226, 268.
Shaw and Webb's 1893 manifesto attacking the Liberals and calling for formation of a labor party marked a shift in Fabian policy from relying on their influence on the Liberals to identifying with a movement "over which they had little control and which they only vaguely understood." Shaw claimed to have been very influential in organizing the Independent Labour Party, but there is no evidence to corroborate his claim; he was in fact regarded with suspicion, though he did have a share in drawing up the list of Socialist objectives in the I.L.P. programme.

200 Pollock, Sir John. CURTAIN UP (Lond: Peter Davies, 1958), pp. 17, 57, 71, 81-83, 88, 127, 139, 140.
Due to Shaw's influence "theatrical diversions without any subject or with a subject distorted, broken or quite lost in the vagaries of its development have worked towards the

debasement of dramatic taste." Moreover, in Shaw's hands, historical drama was "silly, captious or claptrap."

201 Popkin, Henry. "The Drama," CONTEMPORARY LITERARY SCHOLARSHIP: A CRITICAL REVIEW, ed by Lewis Leary (NY: Appleton-Century-Crofts, 1958), 289-337.
Shaw is the most written-about literary man of our time. [Evaluates works on Shaw.]

202 Reichart, Walter A. "Gerhart Hauptmann, War Propaganda, and George Bernard Shaw," GERMANIC REVIEW, XXXIII (Oct 1958), 176-80.
Though Hauptmann's wartime writings were singularly free from the hatred and acrimony of his compatriots, he could not free himself from national prejudice. Shaw, on the other hand, "never lost his Olympian calm and viewed the spectacle of European self-destruction with almost inhuman objectivity," dismissing reports of English and German atrocities alike as worthless propaganda. Shaw and Hauptmann respected each other's work, and Shaw defended Hauptmann when he was under attack for staying in Germany during the Hitler regime.

203 "Return of Ulysses," TIMES EDUCATIONAL SUPPLEMENT, Sept 12, 1958; rptd in SHAVIAN, XV (June 1959), 5-7.
"*Major Barbara* is a better and more enduring play than they had imagined . . . ."

204 Rouché, Jacques. "Portraits: G. Bernard Shaw," REVUE D'HISTOIRE DU THÉÂTRE, X (1958), 300-3.
M. and Mme. Hamon translated Shaw's works and promoted his interests in France. Shaw disliked the 1908 Theatre des Arts production of *Candida* which made him dubious about permitting them to do *Man and Superman*. Productions of *Arms and the Man* and particularly *Mrs. Warren's Profession* in 1911 and 1912, however, were successful. [In French.]

205 Rudman, Harry W. "Shaw's *Saint Joan* and Motion Picture Censorship," ShawB, II (Sept 1958), 1-14.
Otto Preminger's movie of *Saint Joan* is a failure, because it is the sort of eviscerated version of the play which Shaw refused to allow in 1936 because of censorship. Disappointingly, Shaw finally accepted the principle of

censorship as a necessary evil but rejected its particular application as incompetent and unofficial. Preminger's 1956 film, screenplay by Graham Greene, omits all references to Protestantism, removing Shaw's theme of Joan as a Protestant, presumably in anticipation of probable censorship.

206 "Shavian Dead Letter File," ShawB, II (May 1958), 23-24.
[Ephemeral Shaviana from booksellers' catalogues, including Shaw comments on his diet, financial advice to a floundering theater, dealings with his literary agents and his response to a request that he revise the Prayer Book.]

207 "Shaw in China," SHAVIAN, XII (May 1958), 30-31.
[Summary of R. J. Minney's impressions of the Shaw Centenary celebrations in China.] *Mrs. Warren's Profession* is popular, despite the lack of brothels, because of the emergence of Chinese women from long subjection. Most Shaw plays have been translated; his progressive ideas appeal to the Chinese. [Includes an anecdote about Shaw's visit to China in 1933.]

208 Shenfield, M[argaret]. "Shaw as a Music Critic," MUSIC & LETTERS, XXXIX (Oct 1958), 378-84.
Shaw's writings on music are readable even for those who have little knowledge of or interest in music. His use of irony, paradox and striking words or phrases creates a mood of comic detachment. Shaw does not describe music; he criticizes it. Reason is the basic criterion for Shaw's judgments; he demands organic coherence, the organization of all elements of the music to support a purpose.

209 Shields, Jean Louise. "Shaw's Women Characters: An Analysis and a Survey of Influences from Life," DA, XIX (1959), 2347. Unpublished dissertation, Indiana University, 1958.

210 Shirvell, James. "THE CHOCOLATE SOLDIER, An Episode," SHAVIAN, XII (May 1958) 21-24.
[Recounts his 1940 experience of arranging to perform THE CHOCOLATE SOLDIER in London and receiving a letter from Shaw announcing that the libretto infringed on his copyright in *Arms and the Man*. But on discovering

Shirvell's financial plight and finding that the English version of the operatta was not offensive, as the original German had been, Shaw licensed the run of THE CHOCOLATE SOLDIER, charging only one shilling per performance.]

211 Simon, Louis. SHAW ON EDUCATION (NY: Columbia UP, 1958).
Socialism and evolution were the two pillars of Shaw's thought about education, man, and society. Theater was a major constituent of the educative process, a means of destroying stereotyped concepts of life to improve morals and behavior. Forced instruction seemed a complete waste of time; it kept Shaw from the natural education offered by books, pictures, music, nature, and friendships. Shaw's recourse to eugenic breeding followed disillusion-ment with education as a means of improving human nature. But instruction in facts was an improvement on ignorance, he felt; he clearly still had hopes for education when he wrote *Man and Superman*. *Back to Methuselah* illustrates the desirable educational process, in which the Ancients put up with the taunts of the young and allow them com-plete freedom of thought to grow into recognition of the truth of the Ancients' teachings. The plays offer no practical or consistent method for realizing growth; they are allegories designed to convey the urgent need for growth. *Misalliance*, which cannot be safely interpreted for Shaw's commentary on education without its preface, may dramatize the tragedy of a society which respects neither leisure nor opportunities for self-improvement. Shaw would make compulsory a technical education: reading and writing, a knowledge of moral, religious and intellec-tual concepts, science, including political science; these things are necessary to the individual's functioning in society. The liberal education, which cannot be taught by compulsion, would be optional. In addition to developing his ideas about general education, Shaw addressed himself specifically to the education of society's rulers, doctors, and actors and to the rehabilitation--or educa-tion--of criminals.

212 Smirnov, B. A. "Dramaturgiía Bernarda Shou," (Dramaturgy of Bernard Shaw), UCHENYE ZAPISKI LENINGRADSKOGO PED. INST. (Leningrad), CLXXXIV (1958), 299-325.
[Not seen.] [In Russian.]

213 Smoker, Barbara, "Shaw's Alphabet Bequest,"
SHAVIAN XII (May 1958) 9-13.
A competition is under way to produce the best phonetic
alphabet for English in accordance with Shaw's will.
Though the panel of adjudicators is too small, with some
important areas of expertise not represented, and though
Shaw was too sanguine in his reliance on appeal to reason
of adults and not knowledgeable enough to suggest the best
possible alphabet himself, a more phonetic alphabet will
eventually emerge.

214 Smoker, Barbara. "Was Shaw an Original
Thinker?," Reg, I (May 1958), 5.
Even Shaw never claimed that his ideas were original. He
selected from a wide range of ideas at hand those which
fitted his general outlook and brought these ideas within
the popular grasp. Better to receive them second hand
from Shaw, invested with exuberant vitality, than to be
bored stiff by the original source.

215 Smoker, Barbara. "What Is Wrong with the ABC?"
Reg, II (Oct 1958), 3.
Shaw was seriously concerned with the defects of our
alphabet, the most important one being the insufficiency
of letters.

216 Sos, E. *"Az ördög cimborája"* (*The Devil's
Disciple*), MAGYAR NEMZET (Budapest), 24 Dec 1958.
[Not seen.] [In Hungarian.]

217 Spector, Samuel Hardy. "The Social and Educational Philosophy of George Bernard Shaw," DA, XVIII
(1958), 2169. Unpublished dissertation, Wayne State
University, 1958.

218 Stamm, Rudolf. "George Bernard Shaw and
Shakespeare's CYMBELINE," STUDIES IN HONOR OF T. W.
BALDWIN, ed by Don Cameron Allen (Urbana: U of
Illinois P, 1958), pp. 254-66.
[See item 112.]

219 Stamm, Rudolf. "Shaw und Shakespeare,"
SHAKESPEARE JAHRBUCH, XCIV (1958), 9-28; rptd in
ZWISCHEN VISION UND WIRKLICHKEIT (Between Vision and

Reality) by Rudolf Stamm (Bern, München: Francke, 1964), pp. 91-119.
Shaw was a neo-classicist who was preoccupied with Shakespeare throughout his life. His judgments of the great Elizabethan poet are often colored by propagandistic purposes. He neglected the wealth of Shakespearian imagery, his adaptation of CYMBELINE is "jejeune," and his views on Shakespearian blank verse are questionable. But he also gave many fruitful impulses to modern Shakespearian research: he saw Shakespeare primarily as a dramatist, not as a philosopher; he pointed out the importance of Shakespeare's "problem plays," and he did not view Shakespeare's characters as independent psychological case studies. [In German.]

220 Stokes, E. E. Jr. "Bernard Shaw and Economics," SOUTHWESTERN SOCIAL SCIENCE QUARTERLY, XXXIX (Dec 1958), 242-48.
In all Shaw's work his economic point of view is pervasive. Shaw's economic thought was influenced by George, Marx, Ricardo, Jevons, Mill, Benthane, Cairnes, Proudhon and Lassalle, as well as Ruskin, Morris and Butler. His major economic works, two essays in *Fabian Essays in Socialism* (1889), *The Intelligent Woman's Guide to Socialism and Capitalism* (1928), and *Everybody's Political What's What?* (1944) show the changes in his thought during his lifetime, though he is consistent in fundamentals. These works show that Shaw's economic thought is solidly in the British tradition, incorporating the ideals of gradualness, orderly constitutional change, and "gentlemanliness." His ideas were seldom really original, but independent, incisive, stimulating, free of rigid dogma and false reverence. He summed up in himself the whole complex of intellectual forces and cross-currents of his time; "his was perhaps the last 'universal mind.'"

221 Sutherland, James. ENGLISH SATIRE (Cambridge: U P, 1958), pp. 1, 4, 16-17, 18, 42, 134, 145, 150-52.
Many of the shortcomings of men Shaw exposes are inescapable parts of the human condition, but it is in the nature of satire to simplify and exaggerate. Shaw's unfailing good nature, his gaiety and charm are rare in satire; they humanized his reforming zeal and gained him the attention of playgoers. His satires helped to change the thinking of several generations.

222 Thoma, Friedrich M. "George Bernard Shaw," URANIA (Leipzig/Jena), XXI (Nov 1958), 402-6.
Throughout his life, Shaw, "the critical realist of the capitalist bourgeoisie," attacked the foundations of capitalism and fought for a better future. Shaw never was a Marxist; he was more interested in the ethical side of Marx's DAS KAPITAL than in its economic aspects. He fell under the fateful influence of Sidney Webb and the Fabians, but he also sympathized with communism and the Soviet Union. [In German.]

223 Vančura, Zdeněk. "Dramaticka Výstavba Shawowy *Svaté Jany*" (The Dramatic Structure of Shaw's *Saint Joan*), ČASOPIS PRO MODERNÍ FILOLOGII, XL (1958), 1-18; rptd in UMĚNÍ G. B. SHAW (Prague: Československý Spisovatel, 1958).
Shaw's claim to objectivity in *Saint Joan* cannot be taken seriously. Dramatic action is interrupted by discussion, which forms the central purpose of the play. Shaw quarrels with history and historians to criticize the present. His methods of playing down the dramatic action are 1) burlesque, 2) patterning the plot in such a way that it resembles fairy tale or myth rather than reality, and 3) anachronism. Joan's ideal strength is that she is a force making the future; her weakness is her failure to perform what her "voices" told her to do. In the sixth act Joan is simply a human Everyman, which is why Shaw needed the Epilogue--to re-assess her role in history. [In Czechoslovak, with summary in English.]

224 Vančura, Zdeněk. UMĚNÍ G. B. SHAW (The Art of G. B. Shaw), (Prague: Cs. Spisovatel, 1958).
Shaw is politician, artist, reformer, and critic, but primarily an artist who created a new theatrical technique, that of interrupted action and multiform paradox. This technique appears as early as *My Dear Dorothea* and it is prior to Shaw's awareness of Nietzsche, Ibsen, or Bergson. The basic components of the plays are ideological motifs, not characters, which are merely contrastive. Shaw's language lacks poetry; there is too much philosophy and intellectualism. But his greatness does not lie in his phiosophy; it is in his ethos, his social criticism, and his destruction of prejudices. His thesis is contradictory, containing heterogeneous opinions and producing paradox. His idea of the Superman is pessimistic; he is the heir of Romanticism. Shaw is a voluntaristic, ethical activist, a partisan of tolerance, an idealistic individualist but a collective reformer, and

a political activist. Much of his work today is out-of-date and incomprehensible. My approach to Shaw's art is genetic not analytical or isolated, like that of B. Balutowa, PRACE POLONISTYCZNE (1952). [Contains bibliography of Shaw's work in Czechoslovak translation. Vancura emphasizes the ideological aspects of Shaw]. [In Czechoslovak.]

225 Veilleux, Jere. "Shavian Drama: A Dialectical Convention for the Modern Theater," TWENTIETH CENTURY LITERATURE, III (Jan 1958), 170-76.
The source of Shaw's greatest appeal may in fact begin at the very point where most of Shaw's critics dismiss him: with the words "rhetoric" and "dialectic." His presentation of rhetorical situations in which the problem is seen from a comic angle within a dramatic action results in a dialectical author-audience relationship. Shaw's characters are often rhetoricians of various types: the natural rhetorician, the master rhetorician or the professional rhetorician. *John Bull's Other Island* is the clearest example of Shaw's dialectical convention, with Doyle, Keegan and Broadbent the three types of rhetoricians who interact in a discussion of Ireland's problems. Also in *Candida, Saint Joan, Man and Superman, Major Barbara,* and *Heartbreak House* Shaw creates successful drama of the rhetorical convention.

226 Ward, A. C. "Introduction" and "Notes" to *The Devil's Disciple* (Lond: Longmans, Green & Co., 1958), pp. 105-42.
[A "General Introduction" to Shaw, largely biographical, is included.] *The Devil's Disciple* exhibits Shaw's technique of captivating his audiences by offering them something familiar, while at the same time striving to improve their taste and opinions. The play is melodrama with a difference; "physical action is subordinated to mental and spiritual conflict between those who--though 'bad' by conventional standards--act in conformity with their own sincere principles of right behaviour." This is a play for Puritans in its absence of sensuality but also in its portrayal of Puritans as Shaw saw them, in all their "soul-destroying intolerance, their blinding spiritual arrogance, their rejection of the Creator's gifts of beauty and joy." Shaw brought mind back into the English drama and religion as well, recapturing for the stage its intellectual and moral birthright.

227 Ward, A. C. "Introduction" and "Notes" to *Major Barbara* (Lond: Longmans, Green & Co., 1958), pp. 143-200.
[A "General Introduction" to Shaw, largely biographical, is included.] *Major Barbara* offended the orthodox in 1905, but it is a deeply religious play. To them religion was a comfort, but to Shaw it was a life-changing force. To him the Enemy was not the Devil but Poverty; its source, human, not supernatural. Shaw appears to defend wholesale destruction, for Undeshaft's arguments seem to triumph over Barbara's. In fact, Shaw is arguing simply that poverty is a destroyer still worse than armaments.

228 Weales, Gerald Clifford. "Religion in Modern English Drama," DA, XIX (1958), 142. Dissertation, Columbia University, 1958; pub under same title (1961).

229 Webster, Margaret. "Soliloquy on Methuselah Shaw," TAM, XLII (April 1958), 70-72.
[Written by the director of Arnold Moss's cut-to-one-evening version of *Back to Methuselah* during its tour en route to Broadway.] Shaw would probably have taken no interest in the struggle to bring the living theater to the great, unreached American audience. But when all the long stretches of political caricature, topical jokes, social satire and economic comment are stripped from *Methuselah*, the remainder is so staggering, so timely, that it is well worth while to do the play.

230 Weintraub, Stanley. "Introduction," AN UNFINISHED NOVEL by Bernard Shaw (Lond: Constable; NY: Dodd, Mead, 1958), pp. 3-32.
Shaw produced a novel a year between 1897 and 1883. *Immaturity*, "reminiscent of Dickens and anticipatory of Gissing," was an autobiographical portrait, but more, had it been published when it was written, it might have tempered the gloomy realism that was coming into vogue. *The Irrational Knot* was dominated by Shaw's iconoclastic attacks on marriage, about which he knew little, and publishers' readers found its morality perverse and crude. *Love among the Artists* reflects in its composer-hero Shaw's confidence in his talent and his bitterness at remaining unrecognized. *Cashel Byron's Profession* is "replete with comic absurdity of incident in the best tradition of the later plays," with Socialism "daubed in" as an afterthought. *An Unsocial Socialist*, his last

completed novel, "broke down under the weight of its incongruities." Shaw then directed his writing energies into other channels, but in May 1887 be began another novel, which he stopped working on in June. Shaw returned briefly to the new novel in January 1888, but his enthusiasm for it had gone, and he abandoned it entirely. The fragment shows signs that Shaw was ready to compromise to gain popular appeal; it includes the popular profession of medicine, a personable hero, a stage villain and unsatisfactorily married females eager for the hero's attention. The villain and his attractive wife resemble Hubert Bland and his wife enough that Shaw's friendship with them might have suffered if the novel had been completed, but it is more likely that Shaw abandoned it because its conventional plot was unsuited to his virtuoso manner.

231 Weintraub, Stanley. "'Shaw's Divine Comedy': Addendum," Shaw B, II (May 1958), 21-22. [Intended as addendum to "*Major Barbara*, Shaw's Divine Comedy," PMLA, LXXI (March 1956), 61-74.]
Andrew Undershaft's name "calls attention to the religious import of the play." He is named for the Church of St. Andrew Undershaft, in which an interesting conflict over the profane symbol of the maypole is recorded. The name, then, ironically recalls the old conflict between bleak, negative orthodoxy and the small-scale but positive juxtaposition of divine and materialistic happiness. The problem reasserts itself in Undershaft's suggestion that Barbara try her hand on his men, whose "souls are hungry because their bodies are full."

232 West, E. J. "Introduction," SHAW ON THEATRE (NY: Hill and Wang, 1958), pp. IX-XI; rptd "On Printed Plays," TAM, XLII (Aug 1958), 14.
To the innate gifts of the good critic, Shaw added the practical self-education in public speaking, literary, art and music criticism, playwriting and stage managing.

233 Williams, Raymond. CULTURE AND SOCIETY 1780-1950 (Lond: Chatto & Windus; Toronto: Clarke, Irwin, 1958), pp. 179-84.
Shaw felt that every class of society as it now exists, from the ruling class to the working class, was bad. It would do no good, then, to give the power to *any* class; regeneration will have to be done *for* mankind, and Shaw counted on the aristocracy of intellect. Shaw, though drawn to the concept of evolution, aligned himself with

Fabian gradualism, thus bringing together two formerly separate traditions. A loss of faith in democracy combined with the Fabian social model of evolution brought Shaw finally to the idea of an evolution of humanity beyond man.

234 Williamson, Audrey. "Wagner and Shaw: a Dramatic Comparison," MUSIC REVIEW, XIX (1958), 186-91.
Shaw was strongly influenced by music in his youth, as Wagner was by drama. The two shared a common bond as artists, though Shaw had no use for Wagner's romanticism and little for his presentation of sexual relationships. They had in common Socialism, the Superman idea and the dramatic conception of the "wise Ancient." Shaw and Wagner, finally, were united in the creative instinct and the questing process of the intellect.

235 Wilson, E. Edwin, Jr. "Shaw's Shakespearean Criticism." Unpublished dissertation, Yale University, 1958. [Listed in DAID.]

1959

---

236 Arnot, R. Page. "Shaw in His Sixties," SHAVIAN, XV (June 1959), 12-13.
After leaving the Fabian Executive in 1912, Shaw was still quite active writing his *Common Sense about the War*, chairing the Labour Research Department, and taking a political stand against the war.

237 Atkinson, Brooks. "Chekhov and Shaw," NYT, 4 Oct 1959, II, p. 1.
The Shewing-up of Blanco Posnet can be enjoyed on its own as melodrama, but it is also an extension of the religious theory of the Life Force of *Man and Superman*. It is hard to believe this pot boiler shocked Tolstoy and the British censor.

238 Atkinson, Brooks. "Comedy of Futility," NYT, 25 Oct 1959, II, p. 1.

Although the principles of *Heartbreak House* are high, the achievements are limited. As a writer in the Chekhov manner, Shaw was too intellectual and he always had a plan. *Heartbreak* is most interesting in the last act when Shaw the prophet takes over. The comedy of manners drifts off too frequently into tedious jocosity. Shaw is too direct.

239 Atkinson, Brooks. "Introduction," MAN AND SUPERMAN by Bernard Shaw (NY: Bantam Books, 1959). [Not seen.]

240 Atkinson, Brooks. "Maurice Evans Stars in Comedy Revival," NYT, 19 Oct 1959, p. 37.
The first two acts of *Heartbreak House* are "prolix and inconclusive," but the last act is still relevant today. As performed in the Billy Rose Theater, it is "only moderately interesting."

241 Balch, Jack. "The Openings: *Heartbreak House*," TAM, XLIII (Dec 1959), 85, 88.
Heartbreak House at the Billy Rose Theater is a well-directed, star-studded comedy.

242 Batson, Eric J. "Shaw in Metrocolor," SHAVIAN, XV (June 1959), 3-5.
Shaw and film adaptions of his works do not always agree. The Metro-Goldwyn-Mayer film of *The Doctor's Dilemma* is certainly by far the best Shaw film since before 1950.

243 Batson, Eric J. and Stanley Weintraub. "Eliza's Prototypes," TLS, LVIII, (13 Nov 1959), 668.
Ethel Turner's THE CHILD OF THE CHILDREN is not a likely source for Shaw's *Pygmalion*.

244 Block, Toni. "Shaw's Women," MD, II (Sept 1959), 133-38.
Jenny Patterson, May Morris, Ellen Terry, Stella Campbell, Charlotte Payne-Townshend, "the Ibsen Women" and numerous female relatives -- all representative of Shaw's predilection for strong women -- were his source for the women in his dramas.

245 Blomfield, Richard.   "Dr. Mabel Palmer on GBS"
SHAVIAN, XVI (Oct 1959), 8-9.
Shaw was shy, kind, generous, courteous, gentle, with an
"acute sensibility to social evils."

246 Bond, George Robert.   "The Method of Iconoclasm
in George Bernard Shaw," DA, XX (1959), 1780.
Unpublished dissertation, University of Michigan,
1959.

247 Brecht, Bertolt.   "Ovation for Shaw," trans from
German by Gerhard H. W. Zuther, MD, II (Sept 1959),
184-87; rptd Kaufmann, R. J. (ed) G. B. SHAW: A
COLLECTION OF CRITICAL ESSAYS (1965).
Shaw is a terrorist and his strongest weapon is humor.   He
appeals to the intellect and takes delight in upsetting
habitual prejudices and traditional concepts.   His
literary activities do not separate him from life, and he
believes that man is capable of infinite improvement.

248 Brome, Vincent.   FRANK HARRIS: THE LIFE AND
LOVES OF A SCOUNDREL (Lond: Cassell; NY: Thomas
Yoseloff, 1959), pp. 3, 4-5, 57, 76, 80, 86, 89, 90,
92-97, 107-8, 120, 126, 127, 140, 149, 156, 157,
160-63, 181, 182, 185, 191, 196-201, 211-14, 221-22,
224-26.
[Shaw's role in the biography of Harris.]

249 Brown, John Mason.   "G B S, Headmaster to the
Universe," in THE SATURDAY REVIEW GALLERY, ed by
Jerome Beatty, Jr. and the eds of THE SATURDAY
REVIEW (NY: Simon & Schuster, 1959), pp. 283-91.
"Shaw was not only a genius; he was an event."   He had an
extraordinary mind and a vast variety of interests.   His
inconsistencies are part of his greatness.   He was "a
modern Plato who could not resist also being Puck and
Pantaloon."   Shaw the artist is more important than Shaw
the polemicist.   He was honest and "essentially good,
kindly, clean, and gentle."

250 Brunstein, Robert.   "Theater: This Man Is
Dangerous," NEW REPUBLIC, CXLI, (2 Nov 1959), 20-21.
Shaw's *Heartbreak House*, a play full of bitterness, is
misstaged as a comedy at the Billy Rose Theater.

251 Bullough, Geoffrey. "Bernard Shaw, the Dramatist: A Centenary Tribute," CAIRO STUDIES IN ENGLISH, 1959, pp. 59-75.
Shaw revived the English theater and made the theatergoer think. His characters are more intellectual than emotional; his antiromantic comedy is in line with the classical comedy from Plautus to Meredith. He saw in Shakespeare a realistic author possessing intelligence and a great sense of humor who, unfortunately, pandered to public taste--hence the romanticism and unrealities in plays like AS YOU LIKE IT. Shaw's social awareness was deeper and more intense than Ibsen's, as shown in *Widowers' Houses* and *Mrs. Warren's Profession*. With *Man and Superman* the emphasis of Shaw's doctrine shifted from social legislation to eugenic amelioration. Another change in emphasis occurred in his maturest comedy, *Back to Methuselah*; social legislation and eugenics are not sufficient, a prolonged life span is necessary for real progress. Women are the central figures in the process of evolution. Joan, a realist and an individualist, is the first "Modern Woman." She was ahead of her time and was burned as a deadly enemy to society. *Superman, Methuselah* and *Saint Joan* are Shaw's Bible. Later plays fall off in quality but are not a volte-face in opinion. [A lucid and concise assessment of Shaw's life and work.]

252 Burton, H. M. "Introduction," BERNARD SHAW: A PROSE ANTHOLOGY, by George Bernard Shaw (Lond: Longmans & Constable, 1959; rptd. Greenwich, Conn: Fawcett Publications, 1965), pp. 13-18.
Shaw wrote "simple direct prose which meant only what it seemed to mean."

253 Büttner, Ludwig. "Einführung" (Introduction), EUROPÄISCHE DRAMEN VON IBSEN BIS ZUCKMAYER: DARGESTELLT AN EINZEL-INTERPRETATIONEN (European Plays from Ibsen to Zuckmayer: Presented in Individual Interpretations) (Frankfurt/M.: Moritz Diesterweg Å1959 or 1960; rptd 1961 and 196-), pp. 7-16.
Shaw is an antiromantic and satiric writer. His place is within the naturalistic movement. [In German.]

254 Collis, John Stewart. HAVELOCK ELLIS: ARTIST OF LIFE; A STUDY OF HIS LIFE AND WORK (NY: William Sloane Associates, 1959), pp. 31, 52, 62-63, 95, 128, 129, 162, 179, 203-5, 211.

[Shaw and scientific natural history, the Nordic spirit and the Celtic Movement, *Saint Joan*, and the Superman contrasted with Ellis.]

255 Corrigan, Robert W. "*Heartbreak House*: Shaw's Elegy for Europe," ShawR, II (1959), 2-6.
"There has been a radical change in the intervening years between *Major Barbara* and *Heartbreak House*. Man has lost faith in himself and without faith there can no truth."

256 Dent, Alan. "Shaw and Welles and Asquith," ILLUSTRATED LONDON NEWS, CCXXXIV (2 May 1959), 764.
The Doctor's Dilemma, directed by Anthony Asquith, "is the most satisfying Shavian film since *Pygmalion*."

257 Dickson, Ronald J. "The Diabolonian Character in Shaw's Plays," UNIVERSITY OF KANSAS CITY REVIEW, XXVI (Dec 1959), 145-51.
Shaw had to persuade his audience to divest itself of traditional attitudes toward the devil and society. He wanted the diabolonian character to be admired not scorned. For the audience to accept such a character it had to "entertain precepts of Shavian, rather than conventional, morality." Examples of this type of character are seen in *The Devil's Disciple* (Dick Dudgeon), *Man and Superman* (Don Juan and Tanner), and *Major Barbara* (Undershaft). The diabolonian characters adhere to their beliefs throughout the plays, even though these beliefs may go against traditional accepted societal norms. The "most fully-developed Shavian example" of the diabolonian is Undershaft.

258 Driver, Tom F. "Drama: Lost in Its Stars," CHRISTIAN CENTURY, LXXVI, (18 Nov 1959), 1345.
Shaw's *Heartbreak House* is still relevant today. But in the sumptuous production at the Billy Rose Theater, Shaw's bitter message gets lost in the galaxy of star actors and director Clurman's emphasis on comedy.

259 Ellmann, Richard. JAMES JOYCE (NY: Oxford UP, 1959), pp. 3, 55, 110, 153, 294-95, 299, 411, 429, 454, 457-58, 480, 522, 526, 578, 587-89, 599, 672-73, 736, 782, 788, 791.

Joyce reviewed the premiere of the *Shewing-up of Blanco Posnet* at the Abbey Theatre for PICCOLO DELLA SERA unfavorably. Shaw found EXILES obscene and protested its being on the program of the Stage Society. There were royalty complications about the English Players performance of *Mrs. Warren's Profession* that involved Joyce. Shaw later mellowed toward Joyce and attended the performance of EXILES and recognized ULYSSES as a masterpiece, though he refused to sign a protest against Samuel Roth's unauthorized republication of it.

260 Ervine, St. John. "George Bernard Shaw (1856-1950)," DICTIONARY OF NATIONAL BIOGRAPHY 1941-1950 (Lond: Oxford U P 1959), pp. 773-82.
[Brief biography.] Shaw's novels were unsuccessful because he had little talent for narrative. Most important at this time was "his conquest of himself." His music criticism is written in "excellent and understandable prose." *Widowers' Houses* is "ramshackle," but full of vitality. *The Philanderer* is Shaw's "worst play." After poor beginnings Shaw finally succeeded as a playwright. His life with his wife was "entirely felicitous." *Man and Superman* is Shaw's "most brilliant comedy." In World War I, his popularity suffered. After the great success of *Saint Joan*, Shaw was "beyond question the most famous living dramatist in the world," except in France. The old Shaw became increasingly careless about form. His great work ended with *Joan*. Shaw outlived his friends and his time. He was essentially a religious-minded man; his faith was in creative evolution. "His socialism was no more than a desire for an orderly community . . . . He was essentially aristocratic and individualistic in temper."

261 Evans, Maurice. "Some Reminiscences of Shaw," TAM, XLIII (Nov 1959), 17.
[Evans's personal encounters with Shaw. A few Shavian remarks on acting, playwriting and *Man and Superman*.]

262 Farley, Earl, and Marvin Carlson. "George Bernard Shaw: A Selected Bibliography (1945-1955) Part One: Books," MD, II (Sept 1959), 188-202.
[A "selected" listing of books and parts thereof on and by Shaw.]

263 Farley, Earl, and Marvin Carlson. "George
Bernard Shaw: A Selected Bibliography (1945-1955)
Part II: Periodicals," MD, II (Dec 1959), 295-325.
[The first section (pp. 295-318) lists general articles on
and by Shaw. The second (pp. 318-323) lists articles on
specific plays, which are organized alphabetically by play
title.]

264 Farmer, Henry George. BERNARD SHAW'S SISTER AND
HER FRIENDS: A NEW ANGLE ON G.B.S. (Leiden: E. J.
Brill, 1959).
There is no evidence that Lucy Carr Shaw was "cold and
unloving" towards her brother as alleged in Ervine's book,
BERNARD SHAW: HIS LIFE, WORK AND FRIENDS, (1956), and by
G B S himself in his *Sixteen Self Sketches*. Janey
Drysdale, a good friend of Lucy's, reported that Lucy was
warm hearted and often mentioned brother George with
affection. Lucy's German friend and nurse Eva M.
Schneider also recalled that "Lucy was very fond of him
and proud of him." Other "delightful impressions of Lucy"
can be found in Georgina Sime's BRAVE SPIRITS (1952). As
reviews from ERA show, Lucy was also an accomplished
actress and not "wooden on stage" as Ervine claims. Shaw
deliberately distorted his relations with his family and
thus misled several of his biographers. [Informative
study of Lucy and her career but somewhat querulous and
repetitive.]

265 "Filming *The Doctor's Dilemma*" SHAVIAN, XVI (Oct
1959), 28-29.
"By far the most worthy Shaw film production for a long
while."

266 Fisher, F. G.   "Ibsen and His Background,"
ANGLO-WELSH REVIEW, X (1959), 42-47.
Shaw, who said so much about Ibsen that still seems
irrefutable, provides an explanation of the processes and
influences at work in his mind.

267 Frederick, Moritia-Leah.   "Shelley, Shaw and the
Vegetable Kingdom," Reg, II (Aug 1959), 3.
Shaw and Shelley both were vegetarians as an extension of
their moral beliefs to all living beings.

268 Funke, Lewis. *"Buoyant Billions* is Part of Double Bill," NYT, 27 May 1959, p. 32.
Buoyant Billions and curtain raiser *Overruled* at the Provincetown Playhouse are well staged, but the material is minor.

269 Geduld, H[arry] M. *"Back to Methuselah* and the Birmingham Repertory Company," MD, II (Sept 1959), 115-29.
Shaw took an active part in the rehearsals and preparations of the Birmingham Repertory Company's production of *Back to Methuselah*. Although Shaw himself did not approve of certain aspects of the production, it was considered an artistic and critical success.

270 Geduld, Harry M. "Mozart, Masons and Methuselah," Reg, II (Aug 1959), 7.
[Comparison of *The Tragedy of the Elderly Gentleman* with THE MAGIC FLUTE.]

271 Gibbon, Monk. THE MASTERPIECE AND THE MAN: YEATS AS I KNEW HIM (NY: Macmillan Company, 1959), pp. 29, 39, 150, 159, 160, 214.
[Shaw's role in the attempt to found with Yeats an Irish Academy of *Belles Lettres.*]

272 Goodman, Henry. *"The Devil's Disciple* and *The Doctor's Dilemma,"* FILM QUARTERLY, XIII (Winter 1959), 56-58.
The recent film versions of *The Devil's Disciple* and *The Doctor's Dilemma* are "not very worthwhile movie fare and . . . considerably more dubious Shaw."

273 Gordon, John D. "New in the Berg Collection: 1957-1958 (Part II-Conclusion)," BNYPL, LXIII (April 1959), 209-11.
[Description of Shaw autograph manuscripts and letters, corrected proofs, and presentation copies.]

274 Grazhdanskaîa, Zoîa Tikhonovna. *"P'esy dlîa puritan* B. Shou" (B. Shaw's *Three Plays for Puritans*), UCHENYE ZAPISKI MOSKOVSKOGO OBLASTNOGO PEDA-GOGICHESKOGO INSTITUTA LXXVIII (TRUDY KAFEDRY ZARU-BEZHNOI LITERATURY) (Moscow) No 6 (1959), 255-86.

In the preface to his *Three Plays for Puritans*, Shaw declares war on any kind of "romanticism" (powerful feelings, fantasy, love), but the plays themselves are a different matter. The hidden lyricism in *Mrs. Warren's Profession* and *Candida* is to be felt even more strongly in the "Puritan" plays; there is as well a wide range of human feelings, including love. The most important aspect of the three plays is, however, their anti-war stance, especially the condemnation of British colonialism, which had begun in *Arms and the Man*. Most Western scholars and critics take Shaw's Napoleon and Caesar as "positive, realistic heroes," but Soviet literary scholarship, e.g. Balashev in his Preface to Shaw's *Selected Works* (2 vols., Moscow, 1956), rightly regards Caesar as a repulsive warmonger (which is confirmed by the text). Nor should we draw a parallel with Caesar in Shaw and the imperialistic usurpers in Africa at the end of the nineteenth century. In *Captain Brassbound's Conversion* Shaw sought to oppose bloodshed with the goodness of the individual during the British aggression which was hanging over Africa and threatening all mankind. Shaw himself may have been disappointed in his own play, with its unreality and poor results. [In Russian.]

275 Grazhdanskaĭa, Zoĭa Tikhonovna. "Vliĭanie Velikoi Oktĭabr'skoi Sot͡zialisticheskoi Revoliŭtsii na tvorchestvo Bernarda Shou" (Influence of the Great October Socialist Revolution on the Works of Bernard Shaw), UCHENYE ZAPISKI MOSKOVSKOGO OBLASTNOGO PEDAGOGICHESKOGO INSTITUTA LXXVIII (TRUDY KAFEDRY ZARUBEZHNOI LITERATURY) (Moscow), No 6 (1959), 287-315.
Shaw hailed the October (1917) Revolution as the salvation of mankind, though he failed to understand the scientific theory of the proletarian revolution and the construction of Socialism. For us in the Soviet Union, Shaw is primarily a dramatist, not a sociologist or philosopher. The post-Revolutionary period and its ideas are not directly reflected in his plays, so it is not surprising that British and American, and even some Soviet, critics try not to refer to the influence of the Revolution (except in his journalism). In this connection, two questions arise: the undoubted intensification of critical and satirical tendencies in his work after 1917, and the superiority of these works to those of the earlier period which, even in Soviet criticism, are sometimes considered better. His post-1917 plays attack all aspects of bourgeois democracy and have a political aspect (the "political extravaganzas"). His paradoxes become espe-

cially open, and everything is caricatured. However, it must be said that some plays of the later period (except *Saint Joan* and *The Apple Cart*) are artistically weak. *Heartbreak House* is a transitional work. *Annajanska* stresses the doom of monarchy, although its farcical nature does not correspond to its grandiose theme. *Back to Methuselah* is a half serious, half ironic presentation of Shaw's idealistic philosophy of "Creative Evolution" and is contradictory in content and form, since it does not take the October Revolution into account and is ideologically and artistically weak. The choice of Saint Joan for a play provides evidence that Shaw sought to depict a heroic and national figure, nor was it mere chance that persuaded other major progressive writers of the early twentieth century to look for democratic movements in the gloom of the capitalist world. Shaw's interest was also partly due to the revolutionary events in Ireland (1916-1921), and in *Saint Joan*, he expressed the tragedy of his own native country. Joan, modest and pure, fights all kinds of moral decay in the Army, and Shaw depicts her correctly as the leader of peasant masses liberating their country from foreign usurpers. *The Apple Cart* characterizes the British political system during a period of world crisis. During the thirties Shaw was very different from the author of *Plays Pleasant and Unpleasant*, but contemporary imperialism demanded farcical and fantastic treatment, and this "second Shaw" was indebted to the October (1917) Revolution. [In Russian.]

276 Grevenius, Herbert. SHAW REBELLEN: HANDBOOK TILL RADIO-TEATERNS 1959-60 (Shaw the Rebel: Handbook to Radio-Theater 1959-60) (Stockholm: Sveriges Radio, 1959).
[This book is a source of information rather than an argument with a thesis. It includes a biography, plot summaries and critical analyses of almost all the plays, and information about the production and critical reception of the plays. A long penultimate chapter deals with the history of Shaw's works in Sweden, and a shorter last chapter provides the history of his works in the rest of the world and on the radio and in film. A 30 page appendix includes a calendar of Shaw's life and times; a list of all the plays with the dates of their writing and the date and place of first production; a list of all the productions in Sweden, with date, place, principal actors, and sometimes director; and a bibliography of works by and about Shaw available in Swedish.] [In Swedish.]

277 Häusermann, H. W. "W. J. Turner and Bernard Shaw: A Disagreement," ENGLISH MISCELLANY, X (1959), 293-327.
W. J. Turner, pioneer of expressionistic drama in England, aspired to become the successor of Shaw in the theater. Throughout his life he was associated with and similar to Shaw in one way or another. He was a member of the Fabian Society. He was a music critic. He read Socialist literature. In 1913 he went to Germany where Shaw's plays were extremely popular. As editor of the DAILY HERALD Turner approached Shaw with the possibility of writing some short reviews for the paper. Shaw refused, as the rumor that the DAILY HERALD was accepting a large sum of money from the Russians in order to support the Socialist cause in England was not to his liking. Their heated disagreement in letter form resulted in Turner's critical assessment of Shaw the writer. Turner admitted that Shaw was the best dramatist in England at the time, but that he was not equal to Pirandello. While Shaw was an inventive and masterful writer, his plays were spoiled by "intellectual tyranny."

278 Hassall, Christopher. EDWARD MARSH: PATRON OF THE ARTS (Lond: Longmans; A BIOGRAPHY OF EDWARD MARSH, NY: Harcourt, Brace and Company, 1959), pp. 42, 148, 152, 207, 213, 245, 262, 395, 575, 581-82.
[Marsh's views, often unfavorable, of *Widowers' Houses, The Shewing-up of Blanco Posnet, Misalliance, Androcles and the Lion,* and *The Doctor's Dilemma.* Shaw's and Marsh's quarrel over pronunciation.]

279 "*Heartbreak House* Revisited." NYTMag, 20 Sept 1959, p. 86.
[Photographs of the Harold Clurman production of *Heartbreak House.*]

280 Henderson, Archibald. "Shaw and America: The End of a Century," MD, II (Sept 1959), 173-77.
That Shaw was already in vogue in the United States in 1904 and is much more in vogue in 1959 can be demonstrated from several angles. The Shaw Society of America not only issues the SHAW REVIEW but also lends exhibits of Shaviana to public and private organizations and gives readings and plays. Theater groups such as the New York Theatre Guild, the Hedgerow Theatre, the First Drama Quartette, and numerous small theaters on the "Straw Hat Trail" have presented Shaw's plays so that all but six of his plays

have been produced in the United States. In addition Shaw's works are being filmed and televised, adapted for the Broadway stage (MY FAIR LADY), and issued on records. There are numerous collectors of Shaviana as well as regular Shaw festivals. Articles, books, and dissertations appear frequently. But "Shaw's success has been too complete . . . . He is predestined to sink into unending forgetfulness."

281 Henríquez Ureña, Pedro. "Tres escritores ingleses: Oscar Wilde, Pinero, Bernard Shaw" (Three English Writers: Oscar Wilde, Pinero, Bernard Shaw), OBRA CRÍTICA (Mexico) (1959), 7-16.
Shaw is a polemicist, an aggressive writer of daring ideas, who discusses human problems in a ridiculous way in *You Never Can Tell*, through melodrama in *The Devil's Disciple*, and with philosophical humor in *Man and Superman*. *Candida* is one of Shaw's most beautiful comedies. [Probably the first article in Spanish by a Latin American about Shaw, 1903.] [In Spanish.]

282 Hewitt, Barnard. THEATRE U.S.A., 1665 to 1957 (NY, Toronto, Lond: McGraw-Hill Book Company, 1959), pp. 291-93, 317-19.
[Shaw on the New York stage.]

283 Hill, Eldon C. "Shaw's 'Biographer-in-Chief'," MD, II, (Sept 1959), 164-72.
Archibald Henderson, the American whom Shaw authorized as his "biographer-in-chief," was trained as a mathematician but developed an interest in modern drama while still a student. In addition to his numerous articles on mathematics, Henderson contributed notably in countless books, articles and essays to the field of modern drama. While his dramatic criticism focused on Shaw, Henderson wrote on such dramatists as Strindberg, Ibsen, Maeterlinck, Schnitzler, and Wilde. Henderson was not only Shaw's designated biographer but also a close friend for over 40 years. Shaw praised Henderson's efforts as a biographer, stating that "Henderson collected me, and thereby advanced my standing very materially."

284 Hovey, Richard B. JOHN JAY CHAPMAN (NY: Columbia UP, 1959), pp. 116, 144, 194-95, 203, 217.
Chapman shocked like Shaw, but he thought Shaw "crude."

285 Howard, Leslie Ruth. A QUITE REMARKABLE FATHER
(NY: Harcourt, Brace and Company, 1959), pp. 6, 21,
23, 44, 244, 246-52.
[The events surrounding the filming of *Pygmalion*.]

286 Hummert, Paul A. "Bernard Shaw's Marxist
Utopias," ShawR, II (Sept 1959), 7-26.
Shaw set three of his plays (*Back to Methuselah, The
Simpleton of the Unexpected Isles,* and *Farfetched Fables*)
in the future. In each of them two Shavian themes
prevail: creative evolution and Marxist Communism. Shaw
was disillusioned with the Fabian method of Socialism and
turned to the philosophy of Marx who denounced Darwin's
doctrine of natural selection. This doctrine, according
to Shaw, was closely linked with capitalism. the real
basis for creative evolution was not natural but
purposeful selection through the human will (the
Lamarckian theory). Shaw noted that Russia was the first
country to apply this theory to politics. By 1948 Fabian
and Marxist had become one and the same for Shaw.

287 Hummert, Paul A. "Bernard Shaw's *On The Rocks*,"
DRAMA CRITIQUE, II (Feb 1959), 34-41.
On the Rocks is a poor play and is dominated by Marxist
philosophy and profound cynicism.

288 Irvine, William. "Shaw and America," MD, II
(Sept 1959), 160-61.
"Shaw's criticism of the United States, delightful and
pointed as it is, is not among his greatest achievements."

289 Irving, Laurence. "Eliza's Prototypes," TLS,
LVIII (20 Nov 1959), 677.
The male lead in Louis N. Parker's play THE MAN IN THE
STREET is Doolittle in embryo.

290 Joseph, Bertram. THE TRAGIC ACTOR (Lond:
Routledge and Kegan Paul, 1959), pp. 34-35, 365-67,
378, 387-89.
[Shaw's comments on the actors Barry Sullivan, Henry
Irving, and Johnston Forbes-Robertson.]

291 Kalmar, Jack. "Shaw on Art," MD, II (Sept
1959), 147-50.

Shaw respects the pre-Raphaelite painters (Edward Burne-Jones and Holman Hunt for example) who fulfill his ideal in art. He also supported the Impressionists (Whistler for example) because they succeeded in creating more adherence to actual visual impression than their studio predecessors had with all their attention to detail. To Shaw, whose norm was essentially that of the eighteenth century, faithfulness to nature as moral norm typified the end of art. Shaw defended experimentation but did not write about abstract art probably because it tended too much toward art for its own sake, the triumph of design and pattern over moral intent and content to satisfy the Puritan spirit. He praised Japanese art, William Morris and the arts and crafts movement. Man, in whatever field of expression, must "strive towards perfection." [The article is followed by 4 reprints of Shaw criticism from the *World*.]

> **292** Keough, Lawrence C. "George Bernard Shaw, 1946-1955: A Selected Bibliography," BULLETIN OF BIBLIOGRAPHY, XXII, (Sept-Dec 1959), 224-26 (part I). [Part II in XXIII, (Jan-April 1960), 20-24; part III in XXIII, (May-Aug 1960), 36-41.]

"The purpose of this bibliography is to list all the Shaviana in print for the ten year period from 1946-1955."

> **293** Kerr, Walter. "First Night Report: *Heartbreak House*," NYHT, 19 Oct 1959, 12.

Shaw's dire warnings in *Heartbreak House* are not convincing because his characters are too attractive and eloquent. The production of this play at the Billy Rose Theater is uneven but worthwhile.

> **294** Kesten, Hermann. MEINE FREUNDE DIE POETEN (My Friends the Poets) (Munich: Kurt Desch, 1959), pp. 40, 114, 206, 486, 523, 530, 532.

[Briefly compares Shaw with the German authors Alfred Döblin and Heinrich Heine and with Mark Twain.] [In German.]

> **295** King, Carlyle. "G. B. S. on Literature. The Author as Critic," QQ, LXVI (Spring 1959), 135-45.

Shaw as critic of books was comparatively restrained. He took aesthetic considerations for granted, was against art for art's sake, and held that literature must have social utility. He felt that criticism was more difficult than authorship.   Shaw's limitations are apparent in his comments on poetry.

296 King, Walter N. "The Rhetoric of *Candida*," MD, II (Sept 1959), 71-83.
If the key to the interpretation of *Candida* exists, it lies in the rhetoric of the play. The play is a "neatly wrought verbal fabric" and to neglect the verbal patterning is to pass by an essential clue to the play's meaning. The real conflict in the play is between two rhetoricians, Morell and Marchbanks, both of whom misunderstand the nature of the woman primarily because neither understands himself or the rhetoric each esteems. Morell's final rhetorical bid for Candida misjudges her. He has yet to learn what Marchbanks already knows, that love must be asked for. Marchbanks's plea is the ironic complement of Morell's. The poet's strength is in understanding the need to ask for love, but he fails to estimate the degree of Candida's domesticity and hence susceptibility to Morell's bid. The secret, as Shaw states in *Sixteen Self Sketches*, is "that domestic life is not the poet's destiny." Morell's Candida is closer to the real Candida, whereas Marchbanks's Candida is an ideal and a romantic illusion. She represents "the intuitive wisdom of vitality resisting system."

297 Kornbluth, Martin L. "Two Fallen Women: Paula Tanqueray and Kitty Warren," SHAVIAN, XIV (Feb 1959), 14-15.
Shaw and Pinero treat the problem of a misspent life with similar means but do not carry it to the same end.

298 Kozelka, Paul. A GLOSSARY TO THE PLAYS OF BERNARD SHAW (NY: Bureau of Publications, Teachers' College, Columbia U, 1959).
"This glossary was prepared for students of the theatre to help them understand certain words and expressions which are uniquely Shavian or peculiarly British."

299 Laing, Allan M. "'A Night to Remember,'" SHAVIAN, XIV (Feb 1959), 11-13.
[Summary of an "almost forgotten exchange" on the Titanic disaster between Shaw and Conan Doyle.]

300 Laurence, Dan H. "Genesis of a Dramatic Critic," MD, II (Sept 1959), 178-83.
Shaw frequently went to Dublin's Royal Theatre and wrote verse drama, one called *Strawberrinos; or, the Haunted Winebin* and an incomplete Passion Play. He also ghost-wrote music criticism for Vandeleur Lee. He continued through July, 1877, to write criticism, "capsule biographies, news notes, and occasional editorial attacks" for the HORNET. He wrote articles, essays, fiction, only to have them rejected. Archer's intervention for Shaw caused his change of fortune. Archer got him jobs with the PALL MALL GAZETTE and the WORLD. Shaw began to write for the MANCHESTER GUARDIAN, the DRAMATIC REVIEW, the MAGAZINE OF MUSIC, and EPOCH (New York). In addition, he joined the Fabians, lectured, went to London theaters, and wrote copiously. "No journalistic assignment was beneath his dignity, too difficult, or too inconsequential to receive the full Shavian treatment." Shaw's goal was "to attain really exhaustive literary expression." Thus his SATURDAY REVIEW articles were "the apex of Shaw's journalistic career."

301 Lewis, Theophilus. "Theater," AMERICA, CI (13 June 1959), 438.
Shaw's *Buoyant Billions* is beautifully performed at the Provincetown Playhouse. Shaw in decline is better than most contemporary playwrights.

302 Lewis, Theophilus. "Theater," AMERICA, CII (14 Nov 1959), 218.
In the production of Shaw's *Heartbreak House* at the Billy Rose Theater "the impending disaster imminent in the drama is obscured by emphasis on humor."

303 McDowell, Frederick P. W. "The External against the Expedient: Structure and Theme in Shaw's *The Apple Cart*," MD, II (Sept 1959), 99-113.
In *The Apple Cart* Shaw was concerned with "an analysis of ideal personal distinction." He tried to demonstrate that King Magnus was as great as his name implied. The structural germ of the play is the preliminary conversation between Sempronius and Pamphilius. The king's superiority is established through the discussion of the personality of Sempronius's father. Magnus's greatness is further revealed through his dealings with Boanerges, through his rival Proteus's acknowledgment of his powers, and in his encounters with various members of

his cabinet. The latter part in Act II again pairs the classic rivals Magnus and Proteus "in parallel sequence with the concluding passages of Act I." At the end of the play "Magnus is solemn at the thought of a world where all peoples melt into one another, where true distinction tends to disappear as a result of faces which make for standardization." Although the interlude between the two acts has been considered irrelevant to the play, it is not so, either structurally or philosophically. It must be considered a pivot upon which the two main parts of the play rest. The interlude "alleviates the monotony inherent in two acts parallel in organization." *Cart* is one of the more satisfying of Shaw's lesser known works, in that it contains thematic suggestiveness, technical dexterity, dialectical skill and good-natured wit and satire.

304 McKee, Irving. "Bernard Shaw's Beginnings on the London Stage," PMLA, LXXIV (Sept 1959), 470-81.
Two of Shaw's early plays, *Widowers' Houses* and *Arms and the Man*, were written to save the Independent Theatre and the Avenue Theatre respectively. The former play was a failure. The latter was "uproariously funny, keenly satiric, and excellently acted." It was performed not only in London but in America and Germany as well. *Candida*, written shortly after *Arms* was not performed for three years. Janet Achurch, the most important woman in Shaw's adult life before his marriage, was the first to play the title role, but the play was not a success in England. It had a much greater success abroad. *The Man of Destiny: A Trifle* and *You Never Can Tell: A Pleasant Play in Four Acts* preceeded Shaw's eighth play *The Devil's Disciple*. It achieved great success in New York with Richard Mansfield in the role of Dick Dudgeon. The play was not performed in England until 1899. It had a favorable although reserved reception. By 1907 it was a great success in England as well as on the continent.

305 Malcolm, Donald. "Off Broadway: Arrears," NY, XXXV (21 March 1959), 102-3.
Shaw's *Widowers' Houses*, at the Downtown Theater, is "not a very good play." It might have succeeded as an inquiry into slum housing - if the performers had been adequate to the job.

306 Malcolm, Donald. "Off Broadway: Shavian Horse Opera," NY, XXXV (26 Sept 1959), 95-96.

Shaw's *The Shewing-up of Blanco Posnet*, playing at the Provincetown Playhouse, anticipates and burlesques the television Western.

307 Malcolm, Donald. "The Theatre: Off Broadway," NY, XXXV (6 June 1959), 112-14.
Measured against his best plays, Shaw's *Buoyant Billions* "simply doesn't exist." As curtain raiser to the production of this play at the Provincetown Playhouse the producer chose *Overruled*, "a strenuously ingenious Shaw farce."

308 Malcolm, Donald. "The Theatre: Off Broadway," NY, XXXV (13 June 1959), 84-86.
Shaw's *Getting Married* at the Provincetown Playhouse is "fun to watch" but not nearly as good as some other Shaw comedies. A good part of the discussion on divorce is outdated.

309 Matlaw, Myron. "*Heartbreak House Reopened*" Reg, II (Dec 1959), 7.
[Essay-review of Harold Clurman's *Heartbreak House*.] The fault of the play lies with Shaw.

310 Matthews, John F. (ed). GEORGE BERNARD SHAW. DRAMATIC CRITICISM (1895-1898): A SELECTION (NY: Hill & Wang, 1959, rptd, NY: Columbia UP, 1969).
This volume "attempts simply to provide a characteristic self-portrait of Shaw as a dramatic critic, using as his subject the London Theatre of the Nineties."

311 Maurois, Andre. LA VIE DE SIR ALEXANDER FLEMING (Paris and Montreal: Hachette, 1959), pp. 36, 37, 47-49, 78, 88, 92, 205; trans by Gerard Hopkins as THE LIFE OF SIR ALEXANDER FLEMING (Lond: Jonathan Cape; NY: E. P. Dutton, 1959), pp. 40, 41, 51-53, 79, 89, 93, 194.
[Passing references to Shaw including the anecdote describing Shaw's using Sir Almoth Wright as the character source of Colenso Ridgeon in *The Doctor's Dilemma*.] [In French.]

312 Mayne, Fred. "Consonance and Consequence," ENGLISH STUDIES IN AFRICA (Johannesburg), II (1959), 59-72.
Shaw's rhetorical devices "transformed chastening comedy into proselytizing satire." Through them he strove for intellectual conversion, perception, and illumination. His polemical wit was accentuated by rhetorical figures such as alliteration, asssonance, rhythm, and epizeuxis.

313 Mehus, Donald. "Mut zur Subjektivität. Bernard Shaw als Musikkritiker" (Courage to be Subjective. Bernard Shaw as Music Critic), RHEINISCHER MERKUR, (20 March 1959), 7.
Unfortunately, the writings of Shaw, the music critic, are less well known than the works of Shaw, the playwright and social critic. He was steeped in music, and most of his writings on music still rank among the best of this kind. His style is witty, precise and easy to read. He adored Bach, Handel, Haydn, Mozart, Beethoven, and Wagner, but he absoslutely could not stomach Brahms, especially his "Requiem." [In German.]

314 Nethercot, Arthur H. "Bernard Shaw, Ladies and Gentlemen," MD, II (Sept 1959), 84-98.
Shaw's attack on the gentlemanly class is based on the discrepancy between the gentlemanly code and the behavior of those following it. Tanner's aphorism in *The Revolutionist's Handbook* provides a framework for the numerous Shavian gentlemen. The gentleman is 1) unprincipled, but always hiding behind his honor; 2) a consumer who does not produce; 3) a parasite; 4) a sportsman-warrior type or an intellectual cultivated type, both destined to fail; and 5) the enemy of his country. The term gentleman is used in Shavian drama to apply to all classes, and "only the very exceptional Shavian person . . . is unwilling and even eager to admit that he is not a gentleman." Shaw's opinion of ladies "was based on the same premises, though he sometimes treated the sex in a slightly more gentlemanly fashion." Shaw's attitude toward ladies and gentlemen is one of "amused scorn."

315 Nethercot, Arthur H. "The Vivie-Frank Relationship in *Mrs. Warren's Profession*," SHAVIAN, XV (June 1959), 7-9.
"Shaw has taken an 'advanced' position theoretically in regard to incest, just as Ibsen did in *Ghosts*, but has

stopped far short of actually illustrating it in his play."

316 Nickson, Richard. "George Bernard Shaw: British Fascist?" SHAVIAN, XVI (Oct 1959), 9-15. Shaw's letters regarding Gaetano Salvemini, Mussolini, and Fascism reveal that he was neither very ready to get rid of democratic institutions, nor very willing to accept Fascism. Reply: Allen, Geoffrey. "Letter to the Editor," SHAVIAN, II (Feb 1960), 14-15. Richard Nickson too easily whitewashes Shaw's flirtation with Fascism. Counterreply: Nickson, Richard. "GBS: Mosleyite?" SHAVIAN (Sept 1960, 11-14. [A reply to Geoffrey Allen's letter in the Feb. 1960 SHAVIAN which challenged Nickson's article, "G.B.S.: British Fascist?" in the Oct 1959 issue.] Throughout his political life Shaw was a Communist, not a Fascist. He agreed with Mussolini that "liberty under Parliamentary government of the British type is a sham," but he meant that British government represented "nobody except the comfortably off people" who prefer endless talk to actual reform. Shaw objected to Fascism on the grounds that it provided for domination by producers rather than consumers. Shaw's comments on Mosley can be found in the 26 Nov 1943 EXPRESS, where he says it is ridiculous for people to be so frightened of Mosley that they would imprison him and not dare to bring him to trial.

317 Nickson, Richard. "The World Betterer: Shav versus Shav," ShawR, II (Sept 1959), 34-44. "Opinionated though he was . . . Shaw sometimes had to bear the heavy, human load of a mind divided against itself. And sometimes during his nearly century-long quarrel with the world as it was, he quarreled with himself." In *Buoyant Billions* Shaw included an argument between a middle-class businessman and his revolutionist son. The son, when asked his intended profession, states that he wants to be a world betterer. Claiming that he is not the first, but rather following in the steps of such people as Lenin, Stalin, Ruskin, Plato, Luther, and William Morris, the young man attempts to convince the father of his youthful ideology. Although two viewpoints are expressed by two characters, "Bernard Shaw found himself, at odds with Bernard Shaw." Father and son represent the conflict within Shaw.

318 Nolte, William Henry.   "The Literary Criticism of H. L. Mencken," DA, XX (1959) 2296-2297.   Unpublished dissertation, University of Illinois, 1959.

319 O'Donnell, Norbert F.   "Doctor Ridgeon's Deceptive Dilemma," ShawR, II (Jan 1959), 1-5.
Shaw does not share Ridgeon's attitude toward the problem in *The Doctor's Dilemma*.   His aim is a comic critique of the professional attitude which has caused Ridgeon to believe that the dilemma is real.   Dubedat may not be a great artist, as Ridgeon thinks he is.   Ridgeon's lines on self-sacrifice imply that Dubedat's sacrifice of others was selfish and that he was "self-centered rather than an instrument of the Life Force."   Ridgeon misjudges Jennifer.   Both remain to a degree in a world of illusion, but Jennifer is closer to right, defending "the world of vitality and feeling against a rational mind seeking to justify a will infected by self-interest and prejudice." She conveys the play's deepest level of meaning.   Dubedat is a pseudo-Shavian, yet he exposes the pretentions of the doctors and at least poses as a great artist.   The audience is supposed gradually to lose sympathy for Ridgeon. His assumption that he holds the power of life and death and his pride and cruelty cause Jennifer to equate him with the vivisector.   Although Shaw did not object to some political killing (Rufio's murder of Ftateeta), he hated medical killing for experimental purposes.

320 "Old Play on Broadway," TIME, LXXIV (2 Nov 1959), 32.
Heartbreak House on Broadway is "quite marvelous in bits and pieces, but too miscellaneous and uneven as a whole."

321 O'Neill, Michael J.   "Some Shavian Links with Dublin as Recorded in the Holloway Diaries," ShawR, II (May 1959), 2-7.
[The article contains lengthy excerpts from Joseph Holloway's diary THE IMPRESSIONS OF A DUBLIN PLAYGOER (1968; 1970).   Not only do these reveal information concerning the censorship and first production of the English-banned *The Shewing-up of Blanco Posnet*, but they also summarize Shaw's critical remarks during lectures he gave as well as others he attended.]

322 Parker, Robert Allerton, THE TRANSATLANTIC SMITHS (NY: Random House, 1959), pp. xi, 62, 64, 65, 70, 74, 119, 150, 217.
[Shaw's appearance in the biographies of Alys Smith Russell and Logan Pearsall Smith.]

323 Pearson, Hesketh. "Music to Shaw's Ears?" TAM, XLIII, (Jan 1959), 54-56.
Shaw knew what he was talking about when it came to musicals. He did not think much of Gilbert and Sullivan nor of Offenbach. When the celebrated librettist and composer team quarreled, their manager approached Shaw as a successor to Gilbert, and Shaw declined. His attitude toward musical versions of his own work was negative, particularly when it came to THE CHOCOLATE SOLDIER. Although offered royalties, Shaw refused them. His reaction was similar to proposed musical versions of *Captain Brassbound's Conversion* and *The Devil's Disciple*. It may be concluded that Shaw would likewise object to the extraordinary success of MY FAIR LADY.

324 Pécsi, A. "A *Pygmalion* 350. előadásán" (350th Performance of *Pygmalion*), MAGYAR NEMZET (Budapest), 22 Oct 1959. [Not seen.] [In Hungarian.]

325 Pollock, Ellen. "The Lightness in Shaw," MD, II (Sept 1959), 130-32.
[Pollock recounts Shaw's method of directing his plays.] Shaw first read a new play to the company then plotted it and gave individual character analyses. He took notes during rehearsals and delivered them to the actors. [Shaw's kindness and sharp observation are recounted in anecdotes.]

326 Quigly, Isabel. "Cinema: If You Were the Only . . ." Spec, CCIII (11 Sept 1959), 334-35.
"The Hecht-Hill-Lancaster production of *The Devil's Disciple* is all that a film of a Shaw play shouldn't be."

327 Quigly, Isabel. "The Man under St. Paul's," Spec, CCII (1 May 1959), 618.
Shaw's *The Doctor Dilemma* is "transferred to the screen with enormous style by Anatole Grunwald."

328 Rankin, H. D. "Plato and Bernard Shaw, Their
Ideal Communities," HERMATHENA, XCIII (1959), 71-77.
Both Plato and Shaw are fundamentally rationalist; both
dislike enthusiasm; both are distrustful of poetry and
romance; both are temperamentally unsympathetic to the
common man; they are revolted by the vulgarity of his
tastes and wearied by his incorrigible irrationality.
Shaw's ideal community is portrayed in *As Far As Thought
Can Reach*.

329 Rao, E. Nageswara. SHAW THE NOVELIST. A
CRITICAL STUDY OF SHAW'S NARRATIVE FICTION
(Masulipatam and Madras: Triveni Publishers, 1959).
The essence of Shaw's narrative fiction and his plays is
almost the same. The main focus of his first novel,
Immaturity, is the problem of love, marriage, and the
raising of children. That children have their own rights
also plays a role in Shaw's second novel, *The Irrational
Knot*. Its title is to be understood metaphorically as
referring to the problems of marriage. In addition Shaw's
atheism, sympathy for the proletariat, views on art,
religion, abhorrence of all that is ugly and hypocritical
find their expression in this novel. *Love among the
Artists*, Shaw's third novel, breaks from the first two and
starts Shaw on the study of genius. In addition to
dealing with the problem of marriage, the third novel adds
the artistic dimension in all the characters. *Cashel
Byron's Profession* is Shaw's fourth and most popular
novel. While the heroes of the first three novels
possessed intellectual gifts, Byron is not endowed with
any; his only gift is his great physical prowess. Shaw's
adaptation of this novel into the play *The Admirable
Bashville or Constancy Unrewarded* demonstrates that playwriting is a more suitable medium for Shaw than the novel.
An Unsocial Socialist was written after Shaw's conversion
to Marxism. This last novel may be seen as a rough outline of that monumental work, *The Intelligent Woman's
Guide to Socialism and Capitalism*. The structure of the
novels is dramatic. By comparing the novels and the
plays, it becomes apparent that there is no essential
difference between the ideas of the young and the mature
Shaw. That the novels were never very popular stems from
the fact that there is a great deficiency in them. The
emotional nature is lacking. the reader cannot identify
with the characters. There is little depth or profundity.

330 Reed, Robert R. "Boss Mangan, Peer Gynt, and
Heartbreak House," ShawR, II (Jan 1959), 6-12.

"When we brush aside all the misconceptions as to Mangan's character and ask ourselves, in plain language, Who is this misguided individual? What is his basic nature? we are apt to come face to face with the twentieth-century Peer Gynt." There are numerous "close similitudes" which link Boss Mangan to Peer Gynt. Shaw, however, solves the problem of self-realization more adequately than Ibsen did through the character of Ellie Dunn. She is the prototype of what Shaw felt would be "a new generation of Englishman, a generation capable of rebuilding the England that had been brought to wreckage by men of Mangan's caliber."

331 "Return of Billy the Kid," NEWSWEEK, LIV (2 Nov 1959), 97-98.
Shaw's *Heartbreak House* in New York's Billy Rose Theater is "an unmixed pleasure to listen and to watch . . . . Doom can be delightful."

332 Richardson, Joanna. SARAH BERNHARDT (Lond: Max Reinhardt, 1959), pp. 128-29, 139.
[Comment on Shaw criticism of Bernhardt.]

333 "Russia-With and Without Shaw," SHAVIAN, XV (June 1959), 14-16.
[Summary of a 90 minute talk by Dan H. Laurence at the National Book League, 28 Nov 1958. Laurence's experience in Russia-with and without Shaw.]

334 St. John, Christopher. ETHEL SMYTH: A BIOGRAPHY (Lond, NY, and Toronto: Longmans, Green and Co., 1959), pp. 35, 129, 148, 157, 184-87, 278-79.
[Passing references to Shaw, including letters to Ethel Smyth about music.]

335 Sharp, William. "*Getting Married*: New Dramaturgy in Comedy," ETJ, XI (May 1959), 103-09.
Getting Married, one of Shaw's "problem children," is quite often dismissed as "talk" or "debate," since it has not yet convinced producers of its dramatic and theatrical worth. The center of drama is 1. action; 2. character; or 3. thought. Although the first two are underdeveloped in this play to allow for a more complete development of Shavian thought, they are not completely absent.

336 Sharpe, Robert Boies. IRONY IN THE DRAMA (Chapel Hill: U of North Carolina P, 1959), pp. 164-76.
What makes Shaw the comic genius of our time is his power of seeing the synthesis of opposites beyond the antitheses. Shaw had a rich variety of comic ironies at his command. He is self-limited by a violent reaction against romanticism and idealism.

337 "Shaw with Water," TIME, LXXIII (27 April 1959), 53.
Dear Liar, Jerome Kilty's adaptation for the stage of Shaw's letters to Mrs. Patrick Campbell, is very successful on tour and in Atlantic City.

338 Shrive, Norman. "Granville-Barker and Edwardian Thearte" [sic], WATERLOO REVIEW, I (Winter 1959), 34-46.
Granville-Barker's appearance in *Candida* was important to himself, to Shaw, and to the future of English Drama.

339 Smoker, Barbara. "GBS and the ABC," MD, II (Sept 1959), 139-46.
Among Shaw's numerous and various interests were phonetics and the introduction of a modern phonetic alphabet for English. After Shaw's death, his will revealed that he had left the bulk of his estate to the development of this new alphabet. The estate was tied up in court for several years, but finally 8,300 pounds was allotted for the alphabet project. Since Shaw did not design an alphabet of his own, a competition had to be held. The winner of the competition has not yet been chosen. Shaw, as a master craftsman with the written word and an amateur disciple of Henry Sweet in phonetics, was neither suffering from senility nor perpetrating a posthumous joke.

340 Smoker, Barbara M. "The Place of Shaw in the Modern Repertory," SHAVIAN, XIV (Feb 1959), 18-20.
[Summary of a public discussion organized by the English Stage Society at the Royal Court Theatre on 31 August 1958.]

341 Smoker, Barbara. "What Is Wrong with the ABC? (Part II)," Reg, II (March 1959), 6.
Shaw hated the phonetic deficiency of our alphabet.

342 Speckhard, Robert Riedel. "Shaw and Aristophanes: A Study of the Eiron, Agon, Alazon, Doctor/Cook and Sacred Marriage in Shavian Comedy," DA, XIX (1959), 3308. Unpublished dissertation, University of Michigan, 1959.

343 Spencer, T. J. "An Annotated Check-List of Criticism of the Post-*Saint Joan* Plays," ShawR, II (Sept 1959), 45-48.
[The items, arranged alphabetically according to the 20 authors, are followed by a short critical evaluation and commentary.]

344 Steege, Viktor. "George Bernard Shaw: *Die Heilige Johanna*" (George Bernard Shaw: *Saint Joan*), EUROPÄISCHE DRAMEN VON IBSEN BIS ZUCKMAYER: DARGESTELLT AN EINZELINTERPRETATIONEN (European Plays from Ibsen to Zuckmayer: Presented in Individual Interpretations) (Frankfurt/M: Moritz Diesterweg [1959 or 1960; rptd 1961 and 196-]), pp. 87-107.
[A discussion of *Saint Joan* for the use of German teachers of English. Emphasis on the prologue and the epilogue of the play. A comparison between Schiller's romantic JUNGFRAU VON ORLEANS and Shaw's realistic *Saint Joan*. A close reading of selected scenes.] *Saint Joan* treats the difference between "genius" and "average man." On the whole, Siegried Trebitsch's translation of the play is satisfactory, but still there remain some faults. [In German.]

345 Stigler, George J. "Bernard Shaw, Sidney Webb, and the Theory of Fabian Socialism," PROCEEDINGS OF THE AMERICAN PHILOSOPHICAL SOCIETY, CIII, (15 June 1959), 469-75, rptd, in ESSAYS IN THE HISTORY OF ECONOMICS (Chicago and Lond: U of Chicago P, 1965), pp. 268-286.
It is a testimony to his penetration that Shaw found the crucial flaw in Karl Marx's labor theory of value. But his and Sidney Webb's criticism of the capitalistic system resting on the classical theory of the rent of land is vastly overblown. Their criticism turns a minor aspect of capitalism into its major flaw, and it is not based on a thorough knowledge of economics.

346 Strauss, Albrecht B. "Eliza's Prototypes," TLS, LVIII (11 Dec 1959), 725.
Shaw himself refuted the claim that Smollett's PEREGRINE PICKLE was a source for *Pygmalion*.

347 Thorndike, Dame Sybil, and Barbara Jefford. "From THE CENCI to *Saint Joan*," SHAVIAN, XVI (Oct 1959), 24-26.
Dame Sybil: "I remember well playing Beatrice in THE CENCI during the first public performance released by the Lord Chamberlain. It was after that performance that Shaw decided to write *Saint Joan*." Barbara Jefford has "found a new insight into Joan through Beatrice."

348 Thornton-Duesbery, J. P. "The Electric Hedge," N&Q, ns VI (Sept 1959), 338.
A passage in Shaw's *Back to Methuselah*, Part iv, Act 1, is very similar to "As Easy as A. B. C.," the first story in A DIVERSITY OF CREATURES, first published by Kipling in magazine form in 1912.

349 Turner, Ethel S. (Curlewis). THE CHILD OF THE CHILDREN (London, Melbourne and Cape Town: Ward, Lock, 1897; first pub in book form in 1959; with original Victorian illustrations by Frances Ewan and intro by J. B. Wright).
Ethel Turner's children's story which appeared in an issue of THE WINDSOR MAGAZINE for 1897 is a "germ" for *Pygmalion*. The main character of Turner's story is a slum child "Flip" Huggins. A group of upper class children change her name to Eliza, give her new clothes, teach her correct speech, French, and dance, and present her to their parents as Lady Dorothy. But the experiment fails; Flip returns to her family.

350 Tynan, Kenneth. "The Theatre: Ireland Unvanquished," NY, XXXV (31 Oct 1959), 131-32.
Shaw's *Heartbreak House* is "the finest comic writing at present available on Broadway." Shaw's dialogue is too witty and alive to create the impression of an aimless existence.

351 Van Noppen, John J. "Henderson Meets Shaw," APPALACHIAN STATE TEACHERS COLLEGE FACULTY PUBLICATIONS, 1959-60, pp. 3-14.

The relationship between Henderson and Shaw was one of the most remarkable ones in literary history. As a biographer, Henderson ranks with Boswell.

352 Vaughan, Stuart. "Theatre," NATION, CLXXXIX (7 Nov 1959), 338.
The production of Shaw's *Heartbreak House* at New York's Billy Rose Theater is "unclear, unfocused and distressing."

353 Vidal, Gore. "Views and Reviews: Debate in the Moonlight," REPORTER, XXI (26 Nov 1959), 33-35.
In *Heartbreak House* Shaw sets out to show the hollowness of the establishment, but he did not succeed. He "keeps marching into conversational *culs-de-sac*," and his characters are too attractive. The play is not at all a Shavian CHERRY ORCHARD. The production of this play at New York's Billy Rose Theater is, on the whole, quite good.

354 Walker, Roy. "Shakes v Shav," SHAVIAN, XIV (Feb 1959), 7-9.
"On the stage the opposites know how indispensable they are to one another."

355 Weinstein, Leo. THE METAMORPHOSES OF DON JUAN (Stanford: Stanford U P, 1959), pp. 152-54.
Shaw's Treatment of the Don Juan theme led to a dead end from which further developments were practically impossible.

356 Weintraub, Stanley. "The Embryo Playwright in Bernard Shaw's Early Novels," TEXAS STUDIES IN LITERATURE AND LANGUAGE, I (Autumn 1959), 327-55; rptd CShav, IV (Nov-Dec 1963), 2-17.
Structural and ideological relationships between Shaw's novels and his plays abound. For example, Harry Trench of *Widowers' Houses* and Sidney Trefusis of *An Unsocial Socialist* share common sources of wealth and attitudes toward that wealth. In *The Philanderer*, as in *Socialist*, the hero pursues one woman while he is pursued by another of whom he is weary. Shaw's New Woman appears as early as *Immaturity* and *The Irrational Knot*. In *Mrs. Warren's Profession*, Vivie Warren leaves her mother for the same reason Conolly leaves Marian in *Knot*, and Conolly himself

appears to be a "preliminary sketch or an ancestor" of
Dick Dudgeon or Louis Dubedat. Owen Jack, in *Love among
the Artists*, seems to be the first of the "prosaic Shavian
Men of Destiny who, with great goals to pursue, will not
be turned from his purposes by the petty passions and
preoccupations to which ordinary men are subject."
Another major Shavian theme, the "evolutionary appetite,"
links such novels as *Socialist* and *Cashel Byron's
Profession* with *Man and Superman* and *Back to Methuselah*.
Shaw's attitude toward politicians links *Immaturity* with
John Bull's Other Island; his satire of medicine and
doctors links *Socialist* with *The Doctor's Dilemma* and many
other plays. His preoccupation with the nature of the
artist appears first in *Immaturity* and *Knot* before
developing into the thesis of *Knot* and occupying an
important part in many of the plays. [Citations of all
novels, some short fiction, and most major plays.]

357 Weintraub, Stanley, ed. "Shavian Dead Letter
File," ShawR, II (Jan 1959), 16-18.
[Weintraub lists and comments upon short quotes from
numerous and varied letters and cards written by Shaw
concerning some aspect of Shaviana. These items are taken
from booksellers' sales and auction catalogues.]

358 Weintraub, Stanley. *"Un Petit Drame,"* ESQUIRE,
LII (1959), 172-74.
Un Petit Drame is Shaw's first and previously unpublished
play. "Serious fun on several of Bernard Shaw's pet
preoccupations, and probably never intended for publication in his lifetime, its autobiographical interest out-
weighs its questionable literary value. While exorcising
some of the most persistent ghosts in his family cupboard,
the major playwright of our time concocted his first (and
most rudimentary) farce."

359 Wellwarth, George E. "Mrs. Warren Comes to
America, or the Blue-Noses, the Politicians, and the
Procurers," ShawR, II (1959), 8-16.
Mrs. Warren's Profession was written in order to convince
people that prostitution was a highly organized and
profitable international business. The American history
of the play can be described as "curious and eventful."
"The blue-noses unintentionally advertised it and then
demanded its suppression; the politicians used it as a
pawn for their own ends; and the procurers, realizing its
purpose, attacked it violently through the newspapers

which they helped to support with their advertisements." Reviewers of the play either wanted it suppressed or "saw no harm" in it and "definitely did not want it suppressed." Most of the critics were "thrown into a semi-hysterical state by the play." The NEW YORK HERALD was taken to court, charged with "depositing non-mailable matter for mailing and delivery."

360 White, William. "GBS on Joyce's EXILES," TLS, 4 Dec 1959, 709.
Although Richard Ellmann's JAMES JOYCE (1959) states that Shaw found EXILES obscene, this is not the case. Shaw recommended EXILES to the Stage Society.

361 Whitebait, William. "Fairly Jolly Shaw," N Stat, LVIII (12 Sept 1959), 308.
Hecht-Hill-Lancaster film production of *The Devil's Disciple* "is a fair film."

362 Wilson, Colin. "Shaw and Strindberg," SHAVIAN, XV (June 1959), 22-24.
"Strindberg is the necessary antithesis of Shaw. Shaw stands outside his works; he very seldom descends from his mountain-tops. Strindberg and his works are synonymous."

363 Wilson, Colin. THE STATURE OF MAN (Bost: Houghton Mifflin, 1959; rptd. Westport, Connecticut: Greenwood, 1968), pp. 94-96.
Caesar in *Caesar and Cleopatra* is the only serious attempt in twentieth century literature to portray an undefeated hero. Shaw is alone in facing the ultimate religious issue of death.

364 Wilson, J. Dover. "Memories of Harley Granville-Barker and Two of His Friends," in ELISABETHAN AND JACOBEAN STUDIES, PRESENTED TO FRANK PERCY WILSON IN HONOUR OF HIS SEVENTIETH BIRTHDAY, ed by Herbert Davis and Helen Gardner (Oxford: Clarendon, 1959), pp. 327-37.
Cooperation between Granville-Barker and Shaw was of mutual benefit. Shaw never understood Shakespeare but Granville-Barker did. [J.D.W.'s letter to F. P. Wilson contains some interesting tidbits about Granville-Barker, J. M. Barrie and Shaw.]

365 Winsten, Stephen. "GBS on Joyce's EXILES," TLS, 18 Dec 1959, 741.
While Shaw liked EXILES, he suggested that Joyce change some parts of it as "a good obscene act . . . bores me to tears." Richard Ellmann's statement in JAMES JOYCE (1959) -- Shaw found EXILES obscene -- is therefore true and need not be corrected.

366 "With GBS to the Opera," SHAVIAN, XV (June 1959), 9-10.
[Review of Lionel Dunlop's lecture-recital, "With GBS to the Opera."]

367 Wright, J. B. "Introduction," THE CHILD OF THE CHILDREN, by Ethel Turner (Lond, Melbourne and Capetown: Ward, Lock, 1959), pp. 7-9.
The similarities between Ethel Turner's THE CHILD AND THE CHILDREN and *Pygmalion* are significant.

368 Zinner, E. R. "Bernard Shou i russkaia literatura: L. N. Tolstoi, Chekov, Gorkii (Bernard Shaw and Russian Literature: L. N. Tolstoi, Chekov and Gorky), UCHENYE ZAPISKI IRKUTSKOGO PEDAGOGICHES-KOGO INSTYTUTA (Irkutsk), XV (1959), 280-307.
Shaw did not copy, but creatively adopted, the artistic method of his teacher, Tolstoi. Tolstoi's influence helped Shaw work out new democratic views and the way to new forms of comedy most suited to the depiction of contemporary reality and the creative perception of the most vital features of classical eighteenth-century English comedy. Chekov taught Shaw harmonious and artistic expression. For Shaw, Chekov continued and perfected the basic principles of Tolstoi's realistic art and revealed to him the narrowness of traditional dramatic genres. In *Heartbreak House*, Shaw moved from depicting the tragedy of the individual to that of a dying class. Externally, Shaw's characters are not similar to Chekov's, though they talk a great deal while realizing they are uttering empty words. Shaw found the simple truth about life in Gorky, whose works opened to Shaw the way to revolution. Gorky admired Shaw's boldness in the fight against bourgeois morality and realized that Shaw would be useful in the general struggle against the capitalist system. Shaw first saw the Revolution through Gorky's heroes. Shaw's visit to the Soviet Union in 1931 enabled him to define his position towards the Revolution and Socialism, though his way to understanding the Socialist Revolution was not

always direct. He sometimes underwent doubts and recidivism. [In Russian.]

369 Zirkle, Conway. EVOLUTION, MARXIAN BIOLOGY, AND THE SOCIAL SCENE (Phila: U of Pennsylvania P, 1959), pp. 131, 300, 301-2, 304, 337-46, 349, 350.
Shaw's biology was Marxian, and he rejected every biological advance of the past 75 years because they conflicted with his escapist devices and cure-alls. He has done more in his plays to misrepresent science than any other single writer.

1960

---

370 Adler, Jacob H. "Ibsen, Shaw and *Candida*," JOURNAL OF ENGLISH AND GERMANIC PHILOLOGY, LIX (1960), 50-58.
Candida parallels THE WILD DUCK more closely than A DOLL'S HOUSE. Like Gina, Candida is a Philistine who sees her husband as he is--and keeps him. Like Gregers, Marchbanks intrudes on a marriage wanting a truth told which will be no help to the marriage. The husbands in both plays are idealists regarding marriage who magnify the importance of their work. Both wives shield their husbands from unpleasantness. When unpleasant truths do emerge, both Hialmar and Morell will apparently be able to forget the truth and go on as before. Shaw's counterparts to Ibsen's characters are the more likeable or admirable. Marchbanks, for example, is younger and so more forgivable than Gregers; moreover, he is capable of becoming a realist, while Gregers will remain an idealist. Burgess parallels old Ekdal in contributing humor and character revelation.

371 Alvaro, Francisco. "*César y Cleopatra*" (*Caesar and Cleopatra*), EL ESPECTADOR Y LA CRÍTICA (The Spectator and the Critic) (Valladolid: Talleres Gráfico Ceres, 1960), pp. 129-32.
Shaw's plays are aggressive attacks on the bourgeois and puritan principles, but there is little or no action. They are characterized by excessive rhetoric, partiality in defense of the thesis, and failure to follow traditional dramatic technique. However, in any of Shaw's plays one can find sagacity and cleverness and also human values that lift Shaw above his contemporaries. [Includes

diverse and contradictory critical notices of *Caesar and Cleopatra*.] [In Spanish.]

372 Atherton, James S. THE BOOKS AT THE WAKE; A STUDY OF LITERARY ALLUSIONS IN JAMES JOYCE'S *FINNEGANS WAKE* (NY: Viking P, 1960), p. 279.
[Quotes 15 phrases probably alluding to Shaw.]

373 Atkinson, Brooks. "The Theatre: DEAR LIAR," NYT, 18 March 1960, p. 19.
Katherine Cornell and Brian Aherne star in an intelligent adaptation by Jerome Kilty of the letters between Mrs. Pat Campbell and Shaw.

374 Austin, Don De Forest. "The Comic Structure in Five Plays of Bernard Shaw," DA, XX (1960), 4658. Unpublished dissertation, University of Washington, 1960.

375 Ausubel, Herman. IN HARD TIMES; REFORMERS AMONG THE LATE VICTORIANS (NY: Columbia U P, 1960), pp. 33, 92, 95, 104, 110, 118, 147, 154, 155, 156-59, 162, 167, 168, 170, 171, 183, 193, 230, 258.
Socialism was Shaw's salvation in his late twenties and thirties, giving him a sense of success which he was to find only later as a man of letters. Shaw's incredible labors on behalf of the Fabian Society were of personal value; he "ascribed his originality to his refusal to be simply a man of letters and to his determination to be immersed in the life of his times." Particularly valuable was Shaw's development of his wit as a device for attracting attention to important topics. [Brief references throughout to Shaw's opinions in establishing thought of the era and in discussing differences among the Fabians.]

376 Bab, Julius. "Erlebtes mit G. B. S." (Encounters with G. B. S.), ÜBER DEN TAG HINAUS. KRITISCHE BETRACHTUNGEN (Beyond the Day. Critical Observations), ed by Harry Bergholz (Heidelberg, Darmstadt: Verlag Lambert Schneider, 1960), pp. 181-88.
[Julius Bab who, in 1910, wrote the first book about Shaw, discusses his personal relationship with Shaw.] [In German.]

377 Bab, Julius. "G. B. Shaws Anti-Liebeslied" (G. B. Shaw's Anti-Love Song), ÜBER DEN TAG HINAUS. KRITISCHE BETRACHTUNGEN (Beyond the Day. Critical Observations), ed by Harry Bergholz (Heidelberg, Darmstadt: Verlag Lambert Schneider, 1960), pp. 179-81.
Shaw's only lyric poem (Apollodorus's song in *Caesar and Cleopatra*) is an anti-love poem. [In German.]

378 Bagar, Andrej *et al.* PAMÁTNICA SLOVENSKEHO NARODNEHO DIVADLA: SBORNIK (Memorial of the Slovak National Theater: Collection of Essays), (Bratislava: Slovenske vydavatel'stvo krasnej literatury, 1960).
The Slovak National Theater in Bratislava produced *Pygmalion*, *Man and Superman*, and *Mrs. Warren's Profession* in the 1920's, with *Saint Joan* in the '30s and *Superman* again in 1946. [In Slovak.]

379 Barnet, Sylvan, Morton Berman, and William Burto (eds). "The Irish Theater: an Introduction" and "George Bernard Shaw: *John Bull's Other Island*," THE GENIUS OF THE IRISH THEATER (NY: New American Library [Mentor], 1960), pp. 7, 12-15.
John Bull's Other Island was delayed at the Abbey Theatre because Yeats objected to its didacticism. The portrayal of Irish life was not in keeping with the tradition, and Shaw wished to destroy the stage-Irishman.

380 Behrman, S. N. "Profiles: Conversation with Max," NY, XXXV (6 Feb 1960), 45-80; rptd in PORTRAIT OF MAX: AN INTIMATE MEMOIR OF SIR MAX BEERBOHM (NY: Random House, 1960).
There was marked ambivalence in Max's feeling for Shaw; though he admitted he had never had anything but kindness from him, he thought Shaw cold; he admired Shaw's genius while dissenting "from almost any view that he holds about anything." Max admired Shaw but did not like him, loved his comic plays but not the serious ones; Shaw's philosophy, he thought, rested on profound ignorance of human nature.

381 Benedek, Marcell. "G. B. Shaw," in A NYUGATEURÓPAI DRÁMA ÉS SZÍNJÁTSZÁS A XVIII-XX. SZÁZADIG. KIEG. JEGYZET. (Western European Drama and Theatrical Art from the Eighteenth to the

Twentieth Centuries) ed by Miklós Hubay, Judit
Szántó and György Székely (Budapest: Népmüv Int.,
1960).
[Not seen.] [In Hungarian.]

382 Bentley, Eric [Russell]. "The Making of a
Dramatist (1892-1903)," TULANE DRAMA REVIEW, V
(Sept 1960), 3-21; rptd in THEATRE IN THE TWENTIETH
CENTURY, ed by Robert W. Corrigan (NY: Grove Press,
1963), 282-303; in MODERN DRAMA: ESSAYS IN
CRITICISM, ed by Travis Bogard and William I. Oliver
(NY: Oxford UP, 1965), pp. 290-313; in THEATRE OF
WAR, COMMENTS ON 32 OCCASIONS, by Eric Bentley (NY:
Viking Press, 1960, 1972), pp. 3-21; in THE
NINETEENTH CENTURY, ed by Robert W. Corrigan (NY:
Dell Publishing Co. [Laurel British Drama], 1967),
305-29.
Shaw's drama has not yet been seen in perspective; he is
too often considered only a man of ideas or only a
fabulous entertainer. He is both capable of meeting
critics' demands for effective structure to reveal
character in action and for emotional substance in
characters. Though Shaw was reacting against the well-
made-play tradition, he also used it. Both *Arms and the
Man* and *Widowers' Houses* use situations to be found in the
well-made-play; the difference is that Shaw's characters
are individuals; they influence the action instead of
being conventional victims of a coincidental sequence of
incidents. Conversation is more significant than incident
in determining decisive turns in the action. Unlike
Scribe, who wrote for the climax, Shaw was predisposed
toward the anticlimax, but it is the dialectical
interaction between Scribean and anti-Scribean elements in
Shaw which makes his work dramatic. *Man and Superman* is a
good illustration. Characters' emotions are vital in
Shaw, but perhaps they are underrated because Shaw is not
treating the emotions people expect. Strength and
weakness, not love and hate, are at the center of *Candida*,
for example. Desolation more than romantic excitement is
the key emotion, as in Morell or Vivie Warren. Sexuality
is certainly evident in Shaw, but usually our expectations
fall victim to anticlimax, as in *Captain Brassbound's
Conversion* or *The Apple Cart*. The ending of *Pygmalion* is
classical Shaw, with someone "clamourously refusing to
enter the bedroom." It is emotional, but not erotic.
Shaw's later plays suffer from the lack of strong emotions
in characters and from the lack of close structure.

383 Biasio, Laura del Giudice. "Giovanna d'Arco nel Dramma di Schiller ed in Quello di Shaw: Crisi Individuale e Crisi Sociale" (Joan of Arc in the Play by Schiller and the One by Shaw: Individual and Social Crises), ANNUARIO (Yearbook) (Liceo-Ginnasio Statale "G. Palmieri," Lecce) (1960-61), 59-79.

Shaw with his anti-romantic and anti-rational intentions returns Joan to a human figure. Both Schiller and Shaw give Joan a strong sense of duty; in Shaw duty arises according to an inner law of the self, without religious reference. Shaw's Joan is a modern woman, and the question of the source of her spiritual strength, whether from the intellect or from the soul, is posed. Shaw enlarges the personal drama within society in order to warn his contemporaries that strengthening one's faith in an ideal means creating a better social ambience in which to live one's life. [In Italian.]

384 Bogoslovskiĭ, Nikita. "Bravo 'Mei Fer Ledi'!" (Bravo MY FAIR LADY!), KUL'TURA I ZHIZN' (Moscow), 1960, p. 52.

The Hellinger American Theater company production of MY FAIR LADY in Leningrad, Moscow, and Kiev shows that the authors have achieved an organic blend of music, dialogue, songs and dances into a talented, musical and elegant spectacle which gave great satisfaction to all who saw it. [In Russian.]

385 Boroff, David. "Words for Today: By G.B.S." NYTMag, 6 Nov 1960, pp. 27, 132.

He posed as an intellectual playboy, but Shaw was really a benign but stern schoolmaster whose pronouncements still echo today. [A sampling of Shaw. A Beerbohm caricature. Photograph.]

386 Bradbrook, B. R. "Letters to England from Karel Capek," SLAVONIC AND EAST EUROPEAN REVIEW, XXXIX (Dec 1960), 61-72.

In preparing for his trip to England in 1924 Capek expressed a wish to meet Shaw. Shaw, who later wrote of Capek that he was "a prolific and terrific playwright," entertained him at a vegetarian luncheon, but Capek, who greatly admired Shaw, was shy in his company.

387 Brooks, Harold F. "*Pygmalion* and WHEN WE DEAD
AWAKEN," N&Q, VII (Dec 1960), 469-71.
Ibsen's WHEN WE DEAD AWAKEN, with its egotistic sculptor-
hero, is a source for *Pygmalion*. There were other sources
in 1897-9 for Shaw's earliest conception of the play, but
there is no evidence that Shaw had at that stage "thought
out, in terms of human relationship, the corollary of his
heroine's share in her transmutation at the hands of the
hero; nor even that he had associated it, so far, with the
myth of Pygmalion." When he actually wrote the play in
1912, however, there is ample evidence that WHEN WE DEAD
AWAKEN was in his mind.

388 Burns, Edward McNall. IDEAS IN CONFLICT; THE
POLITICAL THEORIES OF THE CONTEMPORARY WORLD (NY:
Norton, 1960), pp. 167, 169, 170-73.
[The Fabians are treated in the "Non-Marxian Socialism"
section.] Shaw was a "rank nonconformist" whose ideas
were often not shared by his colleagues. "Shaw's attitude
toward government was a strange farrago of elitism,
aristocracy, Machiavellianism, and worship of efficiency
and getting things done." [A superficial and sometimes
misleading survey of Shaw's political views.]

389 C., J. "Shaw and America," Reg, III (Aug
1960), 7.
[Report of a talk by Harry Geduld.] America to Shaw,
because of its unbridled capitalism, was the embodiment of
the economic errors he hated.

390 Cerf, Bennett. "No Business like Shaw's
Business," THIS WEEK, 20 March 60, pp. 4-5.
[Shaw anecdotes.]

391 Clarke, Arthur C. "Shaw and the Sound Barrier,"
VIRGINIA QUARTERLY REVIEW, XXXVI (Winter 1960), 72-
77.
Letters exchanged with Shaw in early 1947 on the subject
of aeronautics reveal a good deal of confusion about the
subject on Shaw's part, though this did not diminish his
willingness to pronounce upon it. But Shaw joined the
British Interplanetary Society and remained a member
during the three years before his death, an admirable
effort to keep abreast of the times at his age.

392 Cockerel, Sydney. "Shavian," TLS, 29 July 1960, p. 481.
Shaw adopted the term "Shavian" from a joke told me by William Morris which I repeated to Shaw.

393 Collis, John Stewart. "John Bull's Other Islander," SHAVIAN, II (Sept 1960), 20-23.
[Notes from a talk Collis gave to the Shaw Society.] In *John Bull's Other Island* Kegan reflects Shaw's kindness and compassion. But Shaw was like Larry in being so afraid of the Celtic Twilight mood that he ran away from it in his twenties to go in for Progress, and he makes fun of his Fabian self in Broadbent. Personal meetings with Shaw showed how greatly he failed in his old age; his obsession with money, for instance, was quite sad. But that decline can not detract from the greatness that was his.

394 Collis, Maurice. NANCY ASTOR (N Y: Dutton, 1960), pp. 142 seq., 160 seq., 179, 189, 202, 203, 209, 210, 214.
Shaw's conversation was champagne to Lady Astor, and she also admired him as a genuine reformer. Their relationship was not one of intellect but of spirit; they brought out each other's sense of humor and feeling of well-being. The greater part of *The Apple Cart* was composed at the Astor home, and its proposal for amalgamating England and America is "an exaggerated version of Lady Astor's wish for the two countries to be united in indissoluble friendship." *The Apple Cart* was popularly received in Moscow as a skit on democratic government, which accounted in part for the warmth of Shaw's reception in Russia in 1931. He was welcomed so enthusiastically that his vanity was flattered. Chesterton afterwards accused Shaw, "the great dissipator of illusions," of having become "the victim of the illusion that Russia was the scene of a Socialist victory."

395 Cordell, Richard A. "Shaw in the Classroom," Reg, III (Dec 1960), 910.
Shaw despised the university because he felt education could not be forced, and this bias accounts for his objection to being brought into the classroom. [Brief history of the first college course devoted to Shaw's plays.]

396 Couchman, Gordon W. "Comic Catharsis in *Caesar and Cleopatra*," ShawR, III (Jan 1960) 11-14.

Caesar and Cleopatra has a twofold purpose: to spoof Shakespeare's heroes and heroine and to present a new kind of hero. The Shakespeare spoof can be seen in characterizations, dialogue and situations; for instance, the lighthouse scene in Shaw's play is a comic version of the monument scene in ANTONY AND CLEOPATRA. Though Shaw may appear to be debunking his Caesar, he is only humanizing him in order to emphasize his more truly heroic traits. Shaw's hero may be "somewhat romanticized after Shaw's own fashion, but he is at all events in no danger of becoming a victim either of hubris or selfindulgence." Perhaps Shaw's depiction of Caesar was an attempt to resolve a conflict within himself: the desire for a hero and his sense of the ridiculous in the traditional hero and in his own (and his audience's) inclination to hero-worship. The resolution of this conflict is a kind of catharsis in comedy.

397 Daiches, David. A CRITICAL HISTORY OF ENGLISH LITERATURE, Vol. II (N Y: Ronald P; Lond: Secker & Warburg, 1960), pp. 1104-8.

Shaw's *Quintessence of Ibsenism*, which emphasized the social plays and paid less attention to the more symbolic and poetic ones, reflected Shaw's own view of the drama as a means for presenting entertainingly and provocatively his views on the human experience and the abuses and contradictions of the social order. Typically, he takes the standard pattern of melodrama or comedy, then inverts it by transposing the parts of hero and villain, then inverts it again to show that his hero *is* a hero of a new kind, to encourage his audience to shed their own romantic illusions. Shaw was a Lamarckian evolutionist, but he is least successful as a dramatist when dealing directly with such large themes, as in *Back to Methuselah*. He is for natural vitality and against "that thoughtless, complacent, sentimental society" represented by the average playgoer; the true villain of Shaw's drama is his audience. Like eighteenth century moralists Shaw assumed that generalizations about men in one time and place were valid for all; he lacked the historical imagination to understand Caesar or Joan. Shaw's reliance on complex stage directions suggests that he could not incorporate his total pattern of meaning into dramatic dialogue; he did not attempt to create a new dramatic idiom which could fully express the total dramatic meaning.

398 De Selincourt, Aubrey. SIX GREAT PLAYWRIGHTS
(Lond: Hamish Hamilton, 1960), 161-90.
Shaw's purpose was intellectual rather than artistic. He
sought an explicit and reasoned philosophy of life. The
function of drama was, thus, not merely to entertain but
to make people think. Of course he was a marvelous
entertainer too, for he knew that "a dull sermon saves no
souls." Shaw made war on illusions, romantic morality,
and taught us to see more clearly. But, lacking
imaginative power, he was not a true creator; rather he
was a commentator and critic who threw his comments and
his criticism into brilliant and vivid dramatic form. His
plays are all propagandist and didactic. "Shaw the
playwright was a sort of archangelical schoolmaster,
working on the modern principle of education through
entertainment." His vision was very limited. His
intellectual approach led to over-simplification (as, for
example, the way he attributed all of mankind's
difficulties to stupidity). "Both of the folly and the
grandeur of passion he was unaware . . . . Shaw never
really belonged to this world."

399 Döpfner, Julius. "Shaw und das Gebet" (Shaw and
Prayer), WORT AUS BERLIN by Kardinal Julius Döpfner
(Berlin: Morus Verlag, 1960), pp. 64-66.
Shaw attests to the power of prayer in a letter to Abbess
Laurentia, dated 17 August 1948, in which he describes the
miraculous rescue of Mrs. Gene Tunney. [In German.]

400 Duffin, Henry Charles. "The Bourgeois Moralist
in Shaw," SHAVIAN, II (Feb 1960), 12-14.
Though occasionally capable of poetry, Shaw lacked poetic
vision; he was primarily concerned with conduct, a
"bourgeois moralist." His teaching is most valuable in
its support of ordinary goodness: "Virtue consists not in
abstaining from vice but in not desiring it." "Vice is
waste of life." Even his doctrine of Creative Evolution
affects conduct and reveals Shaw's lack of poetic vision
in its failure to conceive any teleological end to
evolution.

401 Dukore, Bernard. "About *Mrs. Warren's Profession*," Reg, III (Dec 1960), 3, 8.
Mrs. Warren's Profession is still fresh, both because the
Mrs. Warrens are still with us and because society reacts
to her in much the same way the Lord Chamberlain's Reader
of Plays reacted when he refused to license the play.

402 Dunbar, Janet. FLORA ROBSON (Lond: Harrap,
1960), pp. 40, 60-61, 62-63, 226, ["Shavian
Charmer"] 244-50.
Flora loved playing Lady Cicely in *Captain Brassbound's
Conversion*, but Shaw would not permit a West End
production for fear that paying taxes on the profits would
ruin him. Flora's favorite of Shaw's characters was
Captain Shotover in *Heartbreak House*. Shaw told her his
inspiration for Shotover was Lena Ashwell's father, a
retired sea captain who had afterwards been ordained.
[Includes a 1948 letter from Shaw to Flora with advice on
playing Lady Macbeth.]

403 Dunlap, Joseph R. "The Typographical Shaw: G B
S and the Revival of Printing," BNYPL, LXIV (1960),
534-47; rptd in SHAVIAN, II (Feb 1961), 4-15.
Shaw followed William Morris's lead in valuing the
ornamental effect of books. By 1897 Shaw was already
trying to change standard printing practices for emphasis,
contractions and spacing in his published plays. To
achieve blacker pages he chose small type (ten point
Caslon) and distinguished among character names, stage
directions and dialogue by using capitals and italics, not
by spacing. Later Shaw allowed larger type and was
persuaded (to his own shock) that a machine-set page was
actually preferable to a hand-set one. Surprisingly,
Shaw's American publishers deviated significantly from his
typographical preferences, which "may have contributed to
Shaw's astringent views on America." His forays into the
field of typography reflect his self-assurance, and they
helped to improve modern typography.

404 Feldman, Eddy S. "Bernard Shaw's Legacy," C
Shav, I, (March-April 1960), [3 pp.].
[A transcript of the debate in the House of Commons on 16
Dec 1959 initiated by I. J. Pitman on the desirability of
carrying out the intent of Shaw's last will and
testament.]

405 Feldman, Eddy S. "A Note on the Provision for
Alphabet Reform in Shaw's Will," CShav, I (May-June
1960) [6 pp].
Shaw wrote so much that it is not surprising that he saw
the advantages of a more efficient alphabet. He
calculated a 26 percent wastage of paper, ink, wear and
tear on machinery, and compositor's, machinist's and
author's time with our current alphabet. But Shaw's Will,

providing for design and introduction of a new alphabet and publication and circulation of literature in it, was pronounced invalid. The trusts were ruled not charitable because their purpose was neither educational (Shaw cited primarily economic grounds for reform) nor obviously beneficial to the community (Shaw's belief that it was so did not make it so, the Court decided). And one cannot have a trust for the benefit of objects rather than individuals unless it is a charitable trust. So Shaw's wealth went to the residuary legatees, specified by him in anticipation of the Court's ruling, which did provide 8300 pounds to carry out Shaw's wishes. [Extensive notes quote from Shaw's Will, British law, and Court records of the case.]

406 "Four Share Bernard Shaw Alphabet Prize," MANCHESTER GUARDIAN WEEKLY, LXXII (7 Jan 1960), 10. The 500 pound prize from the Shaw estate for a new British alphabet was divided among four "semi-successful" entrants when none of the 467 entries was found to merit final adoption. Work will continue to devise a final alphabet.

407 Frederick, Moritia, "Letter to the Editor" Reg, III (Dec 1960), 7, 8. "Shaw may have been Shelly, [but] he most certainly was Shakespeare." [Comic scholarly essay.]

408 Freedman, Morrris. "Reading Drama," COLORADO QUARTERLY, VIII (Spring 1960), 368-78. Many texts, such as *Misalliance*, play better than they read, yet the text itself must be the ultimate source of thorough understanding. Shaw provides much in the way of stage directions, prefaces and epilogues which cannot be staged, yet sometimes his "heckling of the text" can distort it as much as a production can. The preface to *The Doctor's Dilemma* can mislead; the play itself is more human and humorous. *Candida* and *Pygmalion* are other plays which can be seen more fully through the text alone than through either Shaw's comments on them or particular productions.

409 Fremantle, Anne. THIS LITTLE BAND OF PROPHETS, THE STORY OF THE GENTLE FABIANS (Lond: George Allen & Unwin Ltd, 1959; NY: Macmillan, 1960), passim. [Shaw's role in the history of the Fabian Society.]

410 Gallo, Blas Raul. INTRODUCCION AL TEATRO DE BERNARD SHAW (Introduction of the Theater of Bernard Shaw) (Buenos Aires: Siglo Veinte, 1960).
[Table of contents: I, Desde *La otra isla de John Bull*; II, Un critico con olor a polvora. Shakespeare, Ibsen, Irving . . . y Bernard Shaw. El Humorista. La lucha de los sexos; III, El dramaturgo Mejor que Shakespeare? El espirito del siglo.] There are two modalities in Shaw's drama. The first is a group of plays following traditional forms and influenced by Ibsen: *Widowers' Houses, Mrs. Warren's Profession, Candida,* and *Pygmalion.* In the second group, *Fanny's First Play, Man and Superman,* and *Back to Methuselah.* The action concerns a collision between ideas about intellectual conflict; "the supreme ability resides in the fact that all the characters participate and become the vehicle of his ideas; he manages those ideas with the objective of illuminating a problem, or at least of actualizing it." Shaw's best plays are *Saint Joan* and *Superman* for their profundity and beauty. [In Spanish.]

411 Gassner, John. "Introduction," PLAY-MAKING: A MANUAL OF CRAFTSMANSHIP by William Archer (NY: Dover, 1960), pp. v-xxxi.
[Draws on Shaw's portrait of Archer in his introduction to THREE PLAYS BY WILLIAM ARCHER (1926)]. Shaw's and Archer's feelings for each other were equally warm. Archer was Shaw's mentor both in helping him with his early career and in continually urging him to write plays of sound construction rooted in character, like *Candida.* Shaw disagreed with Archer's preference for the "constructed" play, defending instead an organic view of dramaturgy. One might well consider many of Shaw's plays "constructed," but on musical rather than mechanical principles.

412 Gassner, John. THEATRE AT THE CROSSROADS; PLAYS AND PLAYWRIGHTS OF THE MID-CENTURY AMERICAN STAGE (NY: Holt, Rinehart & Winston, 1960), pp. xvi, 4, 14-15, 20, 26, 31, 36, 49, 55, 114, 115, 195, 196-201.
Though Shaw has come under suspicion in Great Britain, America remains faithful in its "realistic manner and musical-comedy fashion." Regrettably, there is a growing tendency to perform Shaw "loaded down with the ball and chain of realism." "We draw his sting, as if we are resolved to deprive him of his right to be considered one of the world's great satirists, and we subdue his buoyancy

as if it is a quality unbecoming a writer whom we are bent upon investing with the respectability of a classic. We give him character creation instead, even when Shaw had other and (heresy!) more appropriate intentions." [A number of mid-century American productions are mentioned, The Phoenix Theatre's treatment of *The Doctor's Dilemma* and *Saint Joan* in greatest detail.]

413 Geduld, Harry M. "G.B.S. Contradicting Himself," Reg, III (April 1960), 7.
Shaw was seldom inconsistent, and lapses of memory may explain his occasional contradictions. [Brief examination of several of Shaw's inconsistencies.]

414 Geduld, H[arry] M. "On Refusing to Visit America," CShav, I (Sept-Oct 1960) [2 pp.].
Shaw's excuses for not visiting America were many. His real reasons were that he was revolted by America's excesses of capitalism, and he regarded the nation as barbaric for extending the crude moralities and hypocrisies of England. Also, he was an Irishman rebelling against the view of America as the Mecca of the oppressed Irish, and he was a Communist who knew his politics would not be taken seriously in the U.S. [History of the prelude to Shaw's appearance at the Metropolitan Opera House.]

415 Geduld, Harry. "Shaw Collections in the U.S.A." CShav, I (March-April 1960), [1 p.].
The U.S.A. is a Mecca for Shaw scholars. The New York Public Library's Berg collection includes several hundred Shaw-Trebitsch letters and the great Theatre Collection. The Sterling Library at Yale has the files of the Theatre Guild of New York and some of Archibald Henderson's earlier collections. The University of North Carolina and Henderson himself possess comprehensive collections. The Henly Collection, recently acquired by the University of Texas, contains about 5,000 Ms items, including the Mss of fourteen plays and many letters to and from Shaw's celebrated friends.

416 Geduld, H[arry] M., "Shaw's Philosophy and Cosmology," CShav, I (May-June 1960) [8 pp.].
Back to Methuselah contains thoughts on art, illusion and reality, determinism and free will, the body-mind relationship, and youth and age. Shaw envisages in the

creation of the universe four "elementals":   Will
(Lilith), Life, Force, and Matter.   Originally everything
was created as an act of Will; eventually Life will be
supreme of the four.   Though the goal of evolution in
Methuselah is for Life to become "a disembodied vortex in
pure intelligence, *Farfetched Fables* suggests a cyclic
evolutionary movement from embodied to disembodied life
and back again.   Finally, *Methuselah* is philosophically—
though not dramatically—vague and incomplete; it does not
provide a coherent philosophical system.

417 "Georg Bernard Shaw und das sozialkritische
Theater" (George Bernard Shaw and the Theater of
Social Criticism), DRUNK UND PAPIER.   ZENTRALORGAN
DER INDUSTRIEGEWERKSCHAFT DRUCK UND PAPIER, XII (1
Dec 1960), 454.
Shaw was not an ivory tower intellectual; he discussed the
burning social issues of his time.   Most of his plays are
still relevant today.   [In German.]

418 Gerould,   Daniel   Charles.   "The   Critical
Reception of Shaw's Plays in France: 1908-1950."
Unpublished   dissertation,   University   of   Chicago,
1960.   [Listed in McNamee.]

419 Glicksberg, Charles I. LITERATURE AND RELIGION:
A STUDY IN CONFLICT (Dallas: Southern Methodist U
P, 1960)), pp. 117-19.
Though in *Heartbreak House* Shaw indicted England "on the
ground of indifference, cynicism, heartlessness, and
unconscionable cruelty," he believed that civilization
would survive.   Shotover appeals "to universal moral law,
a categorical sense of duty, the laws of God."   Shaw was
essentially religious, dedicated to his purpose, seeking
to transform the theater into a true church.   He differs
basically from contemporary man, who is committed to no
humanistic or transcendent ideal.

420 Goldstone, Richard Henry.   "The Pariah in Modern
American and British Literature: An Illustration of
a Method for Teachers of Literature," DA, XXI
(1960), 893.   Unpublished dissertation, Columbia
University, 1960.

421 Graham, Philip Bruce. "Bernard Shaw's Dramatic Technique, 1892-1924." Unpublished dissertation, Yale, 1960. [Listed in McNamee.]

422 Grevenius, Herbert. "Shaw in Sweden," SHAVIAN, II (Feb 1960), 7-12.
Arms and the Man was the first Shaw play produced in Sweden, quickly followed by six others in 1904-7. Most were very successful, though an unsentimental *Candida* was too unconventional for Swedish taste. [Shaw's visit to Sweden in 1908, including a meeting with Strindberg, is mentioned, and a conversation with a journalist about the fate of his plays in the English-speaking world and English and Irish feelings for art are recorded.] Though Swedish interest in Shaw has fluctuated, his post-war popularity has been greater than ever. Swedish theater has begun to discover in Shaw "a skilled dissector of the human soul."

423 Harrison, G. B. (ed). JULIUS CAESAR IN SHAKESPEARE, SHAW AND THE ANCIENTS (NY: Harcourt Brace [Harbrace Sourcebook], 1960).
[Designed for students' use, the book contains *Caesar and Cleopatra* and Shakespeare's JULIUS CAESAR together with relevant excerpts from Plutarch, Cicero, Julius Caesar, Suetonius and Appian plus topics for writing and research, a list of books for further reading, a chronological table of events in Caesar's life, a glossary and maps.]

424 Hayward, John [?]. "Commentary," BOOK COLLECTOR, IX (Summer 1960), 143.
The British Museum has derived benefits at the rate of 2,000 pounds a month from MY FAIR LADY.

425 Hogan, Robert Goode. THE EXPERIMENTS OF SEAN O'CASEY (NY: St. Martin's P, 1960), pp. 9, 15, 31, 40, 78, 80, 84, 101-2, 132, 138, 143, 173, 176, 178-79, 194, 195, 198-201.
[Shaw is referred to throughout as a kind of measuring rod for dramatic success: Shaw and O'Casey are classed with Shakespeare and Molière as capable of writing a play which was both a literary and a theatrical masterpiece. Shaw's letters to Lady Gregory and O'Casey championing O'Casey in his dispute with the Abbey Theatre over The SILVER TASSIE are included.]

426 Īakubovich, V. "Sud'ba *Pigmaliona* B. Shou" (The Fate of Shaw's *Pygmalion*), UCHENYE ZAPISKI PĪATIGOR-SKII GOD. PED. INST. (Piatigorsk), XXI (1960), 103-24.
[Not seen.] [In Russian.]

427 Janković, Mira. "G. B. Shaw (U Povodu Desete Obljetnice Smrti)" (G. B. Shaw: On the Occasion of the Tenth Anniversary of His Death), ZADARSKA REVIJA, IX (Dec 1960), 432-39.
Early critics of Shaw did not understand the moral meaning in his plays; later critics confined themselves to anecdotes about his eccentricities. Criticism takes sides politically and speaks of "communist" Shaw and "fascist" Shaw. This situation changed after his death. His relationship to language is important. Shaw created a new kind of theater like the Theatre Libre in Paris and the Frei Buehne in Berlin. In his creative synthesis, intellectuality excludes emotions, purposely in reaction to the sentimentality of Victorian drama. *Saint Joan* is the climax of his work. Shaw recalls Shakespeare in his many levels of meaning and because his text is literary as well as theatrical. He took account of his reader by detailed description of scenes and characters and by his prefaces. [In Croatian.]

428 Johnson, Jerah. "Professor Einstein and the Chorus Girl," JOURNAL OF AMERICAN FOLKLORE, LXXIII (July-Sept 1960), 248-49.
Shaw verified the authenticity of the story that a beautiful actress had proposed that with her body and his brain, they could produce the perfect child, and he had replied, "That's all very well . . . but suppose the child had my body and your brain?" The same anecdote is told of Einstein. Though Shaw was willing to take credit for it, the story appears repeatedly through the centuries and can be traced as far back as an Old French manuscript of 1319.

429 Johnson, Maurice. "Charles Surface and Shaw's Heroines," ShawR, III (May 1960), 27-28.
In 1896 Shaw wrote that to bring Sheridan's SCHOOL FOR SCANDAL "up to date, you must make Charles a woman, and Joseph a perfectly sincere moralist." Thus, Charles Surface becomes Candida or Ann Whitefield; like him, they are "philandering, extravagant, and endearing."

430 Johnston, Denis. "Preface," COLLECTED PLAYS
(Lond: Jonathan Cape, 1960), I, 7-9.
I listen to Shaw's advice with becoming respect but
usually try to do the opposite. His claim that good
playwrights should explain themselves in prefaces displays
"his genius for giving cockeyed directives to those of us
who happened to be circling perilously in his orbit." The
fact that Shaw's prefaces bear little relation to the
plays shows that he was wise enough not to follow his own
advice.

431 Keough, Lawrence C. "George Bernard Shaw, 1946-
1955: A Bibliography, Part II" BULLETIN OF BIBLIOG-
RAPHY, XXIII (Jan-April 1960), 20-24.
[Bibliography.]

432 Keough, Lawrence C. "George Bernard Shaw, 1946-
1955: A Bibliography, Part III," BULLETIN OF
BIBLIOGRAPHY, XXIII (May-Aug 1960), 36-41.
[Bibliography.]

433 Kerr, Walter. "First Night Report," NYHT, 18
March 1960.
The sense of combat is distant in DEAR LIAR, Jerome
Kilty's adaptation of the correspondence between Mrs. Pat
Campbell and Shaw.

434 Kilty, Jerome. DEAR LIAR (Lond: Reinhardt; NY:
Dodd, Mead & Co., 1960).
[A comedy in two acts adapted from the correspondence of
Shaw and Mrs. Patrick Campbell. The play takes its two
characters from the beginning of their acquaintance to
the end, for the most part staying very close to the
published correspondence, despite inevitable rearranging
and excerpting. Of interest are both the recreation of
the two personalities and observations on Shaw the
playwright.]

435 Komatsu, Motoya. "Shaw Hito to Chojin Kosatsu"
(On Shaw's *Man and Superman*), AKITA DAIGAKU
GAKUGEIGAKUBU KENKYUKIYO (Akita), No. 10 (March
1960), pp. 37-58.
To interpret *Man and Superman* as chiefly a philosophical
play on the Life Force tends to ignore another important
element of the play. This is a realistic and critical

comedy, and its importance is endorsed by Shaw's attitude in the preface to the play, the meaning of the Life Force, and a consideration of the handling of the characters. The alleged theory of the Life Force is quite incomplete and disappointing as such. However, its importance and relevance become clear when they are understood as the Shavian criticism of reality. [In Japanese.]

436 Kozelka, Paul. "*Heartbreak House* Revived," Shaw R, III (Jan 1960), 38-39.
The production of *Heartbreak House* at the Billy Rose Theatre directed by Harold Clurman is "a high class performance by a high class stock company," but except for the long Act II scene between Ellie and Shotover there is no real development between or within characters. Mangan is inadequately portrayed: the audience laughed at his breaking heart, when, although he "is a fool to the members of the house party . . . the audience should see the tragic figure underneath." The set is also inappropriate. However, "a spectacular production like the present one should arouse new interest in Shaw as a prophet."

437 Krasiński, Edward. "Repertuar teatrow lwowskich za dyrekcji Wilama Horzycy (1932-1937): Wybor," (Repertoire of the Lwow Theaters under the Direction of Wilam Horzyca (1932-1937): a Selection), PAMIĘTNIK TEATRALNY (Warsaw) IX (1960), 12-38.
In 1932, *The Dark Lady of the Sonnets* was produced in Lwow (18 performances that season), and *Misalliance* (26), as well as *Too True to Be Good* (22). In 1933, *Caesar and Cleopatra* was produced (11). In 1934, *Candida* (12) and *Man and Superman* (13) were produced. *Fanny's First Play* (13) was produced in 1935, and in 1936 *Major Barbara* (13) and *Pygmalion* (23). *The Dark Lady* was revived in 1937 (4), and *Mrs. Warren's Profession* (13). [In Polish.]

438 Krause, David. SEAN O'CASEY, THE MAN AND HIS WORKS (NY: Macmillan, 1960), pp. 36, 45, 51, 52, 67, 75, 83, 84, 85, 95, 107, 126, 135, 154, 180, 232, 252, 274, 275, 277, 279-80, 284, 301-2, 311.
[Shaw's role in O'Casey's life and work.]

439 Kronenberger, Louis. "Introduction," ARMS AND THE MAN, A PLEASANT PLAY, by Bernard Shaw (NY: Bantam Books, 1960). [Not seen.]

440 Kulakovskaîa, T. "Eliza Dulitl i Khiggins pouit
. . . " (Eliza Doolittle and Higgins Sing . . .),
TEATRAL'NAÎA ZHIZN' 1960, pp. 10, 19.
The performances of MY FAIR LADY by the American company
and their reception by the Soviet people will help develop
friendly relations between the peoples of both countries.
[In Russian.]

441 Kuosaite, E. "Bernardos Šo i ir jo dramas"
(Bernard Shaw and His Plays), in SVENTOIJI JOANA.
PJESES (*Saint Joan*. Plays), by Bernard Shaw
(Vilnius: 1960), pp. 5-19.
[Not seen.] [In Latvian.]

442 Lambert, J. W. "Plays in Performance," DRAMA,
ns LVII (Summer 1960), 16, 23-24.
Saint Joan, with Barbara Jefford and Alec McCowen, was
done without tricks.

443 Langner, Lawrence. THE PLAY'S THE THING (NY:
Putnam's Sons, 1960, passim.
[This manual on playwriting refers to Shaw for
illustration more often than to any other playwright.]

444 Laurence, Dan H. "G.B.S. and the GAZETTE: a
Bibliographical Study," ShawR, III (Sept 1960), 20-
26.
Only since Shaw's death have records of his various
anonymous contributions, many of them to the PALL MALL
GAZETTE, come to light. Shaw preserved clippings of his
GAZETTE contributions mounted on heavy paper. These
record his "amazingly diverse activities in the middle
eighties." There were 107 book reviews and reports of
meetings of the Browning Society, the New Shakespeare
Society, the Society for Psychical Research, the Fabian
Society and the Royal Society of Literature, as well as
letters on assorted subjects from vegetarianism to haunted
houses, including music, art, drama and political issues.
Shaw's wit is already apparent, but 1888 saw the last of
his regular book reviewing because the books he was
assigned were, for the most part, rubbish.

445 Laurence, Dan H. (ed). "Introduction," *How to
Become a Musical Critic* by Bernard Shaw, (Lond:
Rupert Hart-Davis, 1960).

Music was a profound influence on Shaw from childhood;
this is reflected in the prevalence of music in his
writing. Shaw's first journalistic experience, at 20, was
ghosting for Vandaleur Lee for nearly a year as musical
critic for the HORNET. Even then he had a remarkable
capacity for spotting the weaknesses of a performance.
His criticism for the STAR in the late 1880's and the
WORLD in the 1890's shows added maturity in style; it is
more subtle, more colorful. Shaw knew more than any other
critic of the Italian repertory which dominated the London
musical scene, but he was quick to recognize other musical
values. Though he occasionally blundered, as in
misjudging Brahms, "he wrote with logic, wit, directness,
conscience, courage, and a liveliness of intellect which
was unique in his time and remains so in ours. The
musical journalism he produced is as brilliant as any that
literate man can ever hope to see."

446 Laurence, Dan H. "Shaw and the GUARDIAN,
MANCHESTER GUARDIAN, 28 Nov 1959, rptd Reg, III
(April 1960), 4-6.
William Archer deserves credit for first making a dramatic
critic of Shaw, for when Archer was unable to attend a
first night, he sent Shaw in his place to review the play
for the MANCHESTER GUARDIAN. Though the reviews were
unsigned, Shaw's unpublished diaries and correspondence
with Janet Achurch show that he acted as "substitute
critic" for the GUARDIAN from 1887 to 1891. The most
significant of his reviews [reprinted here] was of Janet
Achurch's June 1889 production of A DOLL'S HOUSE.

447 Laurence, Dan H. "Shaw's *War Issues for
Irishmen*," IRISH BOOK, I (1960), 75-77.
War Issues for Irishmen, written by Shaw to assist the
Irish Recruiting Council in its World War I work, is "one
of Shaw's scarcest and most desirable works, and,
historically, one of his most important." Written in
1918, it was rushed into print and ready to issue when the
Armistice was declared. Shaw ordered the edition pulped,
but at least a dozen author's copies survive.

448 Lauter, Paul. "*Candida* and *Pygmalion*: Shaw's
Subversion of Stereotypes," Shaw R, III (Sept 1960),
14-19.
Audiences refuse to accept criticisms of themselves or
views which make them uncomfortable. Consequently, though
Shaw frequently explained himself in print, he is

persistently misconstrued. Perhaps Shaw deserves to be misunderstood, for the source of the confusion is the fact that he deliberately generates misleading expectations in his audience. Appearing to work in romantic comedy, in both *Pygmalion* and *Candida* Shaw attempts "to defeat the audience's expectations in order to discompose their stereotypes and to establish the position and function of the creative individual in the modern world." Each play provides an apparent hero (or heroine: Eliza and Candida) who fits the sentimental stereotype and a real hero (the artists, Higgins and Marchbanks), with whom we must identify if we think about the play before us.

449 Lawson, John Howard. THEORY AND TECHNIQUE OF PLAYWRITING (NY: Hill & Wang "Drama book," 1960), pp. x, xii, 57, 71, 78, 107-113, 115, 127, 129, 135, 151, 194, 208, 214.
[The material on Shaw is unchanged in this edition, but the new introduction concludes, after a resume of the absurdist trend in theater, "The theatre will be restored to creative life when it returns to the classic function described by Shaw: 'The theatre is a factory of thought, a prompter of conscience, an elucidator of social conduct, an armory against despair and darkness, and a temple of the ascent of man.'"]

450 Lewis, Arthur O., Jr., and Stanley Weintraub. "Bernard Shaw—Aspects and Problems of Research," ShawR, III (May 1960), 18-26.
[Transcript of the first meeting of American Shaw scholars at the Modern Language Association meeting on 28 December 1959, focusing on what has been done and what needs to be done in three areas of Shaw scholarship: Arthur Nethercot dealt with biography, Dan H. Laurence, with bibliography and Frederick P. W. McDowell, with criticism; in addition some discussion of their remarks is recorded.]

451 Longley, Marjorie, Louis Silverstein, and Samuel A. Tower. AMERICA's TASTE 1851-1959: THE CULTURAL EVENTS OF A CENTURY REPORTED BY CONTEMPORARY OBSERVERS IN THE PAGES OF THE NEW YORK TIMES (NY: Simon & Schuster, 1960), pp. 170, 171, 182, 207,245, 313.
[Includes letters and an article about the controversy over Arnold Daly's 1905 production of Shaw's filthy" *Mrs. Warren's Profession*, mention of *Back to Methuselah* among "outstanding broadcasts of 1937," and Brooks Atkinson's

approbation of MY FAIR LADY (1956) as "one of the most literate comedies in the language . . . [of which] Shaw's crackling mind is still the genius."]

452 McCleary, G. F. ON DETECTIVE FICTION AND OTHER THINGS (Lond: Hollis and Carter, 1960); rptd. as "Meetings with Bernard Shaw," ShawR, XVIII (Jan 1975), 33-37.
[A short essay-memoir of the author's meetings with Shaw, including some anecdotes about Shaw and music, particularly that of Mendelssohn and Elgar.]

453 McDowell, Frederick P. W. "Spiritual and Political Reality: Shaw's *The Simpleton of the Unexpected Isles*," MD, III (Sept 1960), 196-210.
In his later plays Shaw lost interest in human beings as individuals and turned instead to speculation on the social and political scene in the form of the symbolic fable. the structural principle at work in these plays is a full analysis of central intellectual themes with variations being adroitly played upon them. Even *Simpleton*, usually regarded as one of the loosest plays structurally, reveals "a careful balancing of masses of material and a clearly wrought parallelism of structure in its two acts." Though from the standpoint of plot the prologue could be dispensed with, it provides an atmosphere of lively fantasy, it adumbrates theme, and it establishes the initial inconsequence of many of its characters. The coda appended to the climactic judgment, in which Pra and Prola discuss what has taken place, balances the prologue in importance. The two centers of interest in the play, the eugenics project and the "judgment," balance each other and are linked by the problem of the nature of political reality.

454 Mann, Thomas, and Karl Kerényi. GESPRÄCH IN BRIEFEN (A Talk in Letters) (Zürich: Rhein-Verlag, 1960), p. 182.
[A reference to Shaw's *Pygmalion* in a letter by Thomas Mann.] [In German.]

455 Matlaw, Myron. "Bernard Shaw and *The Interlude at The Playhouse*," ShawR, III (May, 1960), 9-17.
Interlude at The Playhouse [here reprinted] was written by Shaw for his friends Cyril Maude and Winifred Emery to perform at the grand opening of Maude's theater, The

Playhouse, on 28 January 1907. The playlet was the hit of the evening, and though its authorship was not mentioned in the program, the text was reprinted with Shaw's name in the DAILY MAIL the next day. The playlet gave Maude's wife, who had been too ill to take part in the rest of the program, a role on this important occasion. The *Interlude*, a gem among Shaw's minor dramatic works, includes a comic reference to the Charing Cross station disaster which had killed eight people and entirely wrecked the nearly completed theater, long delaying its opening.

456 Mayer, David. "The Case for Harlequin: A Footnote on Shaw's Dramatic Method," MD, III (May 1960), 60-74.
The Christmas pantomime of nineteenth-century England was "a medley of children's fables, topical satire, farce, music and spectacle," consisting of a dramatized expanded nursery tale, which provided the plot, and a harlequinade, united by a scene which transformed the characters of the fable into those of the harlequinade. Shaw's letters and reviews show that he considered seriously the methods of pantomime. Four early plays are built around variations of the transformation scene and the harlequinade. *The Man of Destiny* contains a simplified transformation when the characters have reached an impasse; the Lady becomes her brother. In *You Never Can Tell* Walter Boon is the instigator of the transformation scene, in which he produces Lawyer Bohun and ultimately resolves the conflict; the harlequinade costumes of the twins contribute to the effect. In *Captain Brassbound's Conversion* Lady Cecily is the fairy queen who transforms the pirate into a gentleman. In *Man and Superman* the third act contains the transformation of the characters into those of the dream scene in hell. Here the conflict is debated on an abstract level and simplified, preparing for the resolution in the last act. Understanding the pantomime source shows the third act to be "inescapably bound to the remainder of the play."

457 Meredith, Charles. "Bernard Shaw: Dear Liar and a Great Silly Dear," CShav, I (Jan 1960) [2 pp.].
Letters can be made to approximate a dramatic script only "by distortion, mutilation and corruption." DEAR LIAR distorts Shaw into a kind of matinee-idol, retaining little of Shaw's solid character and conscience, his purpose, high standards and clarity of vision. A

recording of "a similar mutilation" of the Shaw-Terry letters has been made with Peggy Ashcroft and Cyril Cusack.

458 Meredith, Charles. "Mr. Burt Lancaster," CShav (March-April 1960), I [1 p.].
Burt Lancaster addressed the Shaw Society of California on the adaptation of *The Devil's Disciple* to film, observing that while theater audiences are moved by what they hear, movie audiences respond to what they see, which makes a Shaw play, whose verbal magic constitutes much of its effectiveness, particularly difficult to adapt for the screen. Moreover, Shaw characters, who are more articulate than most mortals, may not be credible to the usual movie audience.

459 Meredith, Charles. "On Readings of Shaw," C Shav, I (May-June 1960) [1 p.].
Moss Hart advises young actors to stay away from Shaw parts because though "he wrote marvelous parts, . . . he cannot be played without style—he becomes dull." This oblique compliment to Shaw reminds us of the appreciation deserved by a number of skilled performers who have recently recreated Shaw's plays for us.

460 Metwally, A. A. "The Influences of Ibsen on Shaw." Unpublished dissertation, Trinity College Dublin, 1960. [Listed in DAID.]

461 Mihályi, G. "*Barbara örnagy*" (*Major Barbara*), NÉPSZABADSÁG (Budapest), 21 Dec 1960.
[Not seen.] [In Hungarian.]

462 Morgan, Margery M. "*Back to Methuselah*: The Poet and the City," ESSAYS AND STUDIES, ns XIII (1960), The English Association (Lond: John Murray, 1960), pp. 82-98; rptd R. J. Kaufmann (ed), G. B. SHAW (1965), pp. 130-42; rptd in THE SHAVIAN PLAYGROUND (Lond: Methuen, 1972), expanded and revised as Ch. 13.
The fable of longevity may delude us into seeing *Back to Methuselah* as a straggling chronicle play, but this Shavian GULLIVER'S TRAVELS is "a hall of mirrors directed upon human nature from many angles and all distorting in

various ways," with *The Tragedy of an Elderly Gentleman* as the emotional centre of the whole. The Elderly Gentleman is the only heroic figure in the cycle, the romantic fool who is the true Shavian hero. The power of *Methuselah* is derived from the Platonic conflict between the rational and the sensual in man, a conflict Shaw felt in himself. Represented most clearly in the relation of the Ancients and the Youths, the antithesis occurs too in the Longlivers and Shortlivers and in Burge and Lubin and the Barnabas brothers. The play is in part political satire which shows the distance between image and actuality which the political idealist ignores. That Shaw's personifications of reason throughout the play lack sympathetic appeal while the romantic fools like Strephon invite compassion is surely part of Shaw's design. The tragedy of the Elderly Gentleman is "counterbalanced by the comedy of *Pygmalion*, with its theme of the destructiveness of pure intellect in the context of human life." Shaw acknowledges that both rational and appetitive faculties are essential to man.

463 Murray, Gilbert, and friends. GILBERT MURRAY: AN UNFINISHED AUTOBIOGRAPHY, ed by Jean Smith and Arnold Toynbee (Lond: Allen & Unwin, 1960), pp. 154-56.
Shaw praised Murray's plays translated from the Greek, describing his ELECTRA as "immense." In *Major Barbara* Barker, who played Adolphus Cusins, a portrait of Murray, was made up exactly like Murray at Shaw's request. Barbara and Lady Britomart "bear a close resemblance to Lady Mary Murray and her mother," and Shaw's correspondence with Murray indicates that he had a hand in the composition of the play. Shaw may have planned *Barbara* "as a Euripidean drama leading to a dilemma of which the only logical solution was the taking over of the armament industry by the proletariat, and then provided an ironic solution through the intervention of the goddess Aphrodite in the form of Barbara's love for Cusins. If so, the idea got lost in the torrent of Undershaft's eloquence in the last act."

464 Nakagawa, Ryoichi. "Gekisakka toshiteno Shaw" (Shaw as Dramatist), EIGO SEINEN (Tokyo), CVI (Nov 1960), 596-98.
Shaw is extremely unpopular in Japan now. What we should do is to forget his voluminous prefaces and approach his plays with no conceived ideas.

465 Nathan, George Jean. THE MAGIC MIRROR, ed by
Thomas Quinn Curtiss (NY: Alfred A. Knopf, 1960).
[Four of Nathan's essays on Shaw, abstracted under date of
first publication: From MATERIA CRITICA (1924); from
TESTAMENT OF A CRITIC (1931); from THE INTIMATE NOTEBOOKS
OF GEORGE JEAN NATHAN (1932); from THE THEATRE BOOK OF THE
YEAR (1945-1946).]

466 Nethercot, Arthur H. THE FIRST FIVE LIVES OF
ANNIE BESANT (Chicago: U of Chicago P, 1960), pp.
10, 25, 43, 66, 128, 159, 205, 207, 218, 222, 226,
292-93, 296, 347, 392, 411-12, 432, 443, 449, 458,
465.
[Shaw figures prominently in Annie Besant's "fourth life"
as a Socialist labor agitator.] Shaw and Mrs. Besant were
on opposite sides in a clash between Socialist and
Freethought groups in their first encounter in May 1884,
but at a January 1885 Dialectical Society meeting, to
everyone's surprise, she supported Shaw in advocating
Socialism and asked him to nominate her for election to
the Fabian Society. Soon afterward Shaw took over the
"Art Corner" in her OUR CORNER magazine, which published
some of his early writing. Shaw and Mrs. Besant were
close friends for a year or two and Fabian comrades until
she dropped the Fabians for the Social Democrats and took
up theosophy in 1889.

467 Nethercot, Arthur H. "What Shaw Really Thought
of Americans," ShawR, III (May 1960), 2-8.
References to Americans and American products sprinkled
through Shaw's plays and prefaces suggest that Shaw can
see little else than a materialistic society in America.
He sees Americans as uncultured and the perfection of
American democracy as "pure poppycock." He thought
America was run by capitalists and Americans were
anachronistic and sentimental. Yet, though Shaw informed
his American listeners of all this in a speech during his
one brief visit to America in 1933, he softened the blow
by claiming that he shared some of their characteristics
himself and had always been fond of Americans.

468 Ohmann, Richard Malin. "Studies in Prose Style:
Arnold, Shaw, Wilde." Dissertation, Harvard Univer-
sity, 1960, published partly as SHAW: THE STYLE AND
THE MAN (1962). [Listed in McNamee.]

469 Pálfy, István. "Az elsö Shaw-bemutató Magyar-orszagon" (The First Shaw Performance in Hungary), ALFÖLD, V (Sept-Oct 1960), 116-19. [Not seen.] [In Hungarian.]

470 Petrić, V. "Realizam i intelektualni simbolizam (Povodom Šoove *Svete Jovanke* i zvedene u Narodnom Pozorištu u Beogradu)" (Realism and Intellectual Symbolism: On the Occasion of Shaw's *Saint Joan* at the National Theater in Belgrade), KNJIŽEVNOST (Belgrade), XXX (1960), 21522.
In *Saint Joan*, Shaw as a superior, modern intellectual, describes far-off historical events. He is a philosopher who has out-grown his philosophical systems. his dialogue can only exist in his audience's intellectual sphere, while his intellectual conversations and symbolism are based purely on thought. [In Serbian.]

471 Pickett, Roy Glenwood. "H. L. Mencken's Rhetorical Battle," DA, XXI (1960), 1570. Unpublished dissertation, State University of Iowa, 1960.

472 Popkin, Henry. "Shaw: Man of (Love) Letters," NYTMag, 25 Dec 1960, p. 14, 27, 28.
Shaw's epistolary wooings gave him an escape from a virtuous marriage. He was lover and creator in his letters to actresses. His shyness is also an explanation for his energetic correspondence. [Descriptions of and excerpts from the letters to Ellen Terry, Mrs. Patrick Campbell and Molly Tompkins. Photographs.]

473 Priestley, J. B. LITERATURE AND WESTERN MAN (NY: Harper & Brothers, 1960), pp. 77, 100, 102, 243, 280, 284, 293, 306, 317, 319, 328, 336, 342, 344-53, 380.
Shaw, the man, and G. B. S., his persona, were distinct and very different beings. the former was "courteous, kind, generous, shy rather than impudent," while the latter "combined inpudent wit with ruthless destructive criticism, showed no reverence for anybody or anything, spared no feelings, pulled down and kicked aside all idols." G. B. S. was not honestly committed to his ideas; he was a clown who existed in the world of debate and intellectual comedy, not in the real physical and emotional world. To the drama the public G. B. S. contributed the power of debate, the wit, the impudence,

the iconoclasm; the private Shaw contributed the characters, the cheerful nonsense, the occasional and unexpected flashes of beauty, tenderness, wisdom. The combination produced the copious, original and vital drama which entitles Shaw to recognition as the greatest comic dramatist since Molière. Rather than developing existing theatrical techniques, Shaw's playwriting methods grew out of his experience in public speaking and his love of opera.

474 Quartermaine, Leon. "Talking about Actors and Acting," ShawR, III (Sept 1960), 6-13.
[Reminiscences by an actor who began his career in the nineties of Henry Irving, Ellen Terry, Mrs. Patrick Campbell, Forbes-Robertson, Granville-Barker and others. He acted the Emperor in *Androcles and the Lion*, when he first met Shaw, who attended rehearsals, though he never interfered with the director. Other Shaw roles included Hector Hushabye in *Heartbreak House*, The Inquisitor in *Saint Joan* and one of the doctors in *The Doctor's Dilemma*.] "I always enjoyed acting in [Shaw's] plays .... He writes such wonderful parts for actors."

475 Reinert, Otto. "Old History and New: Anachronism in *Caesar and Cleopatra*," MD, III (May 1960), 37-41.
Shaw's iconoclasm is vital to his plays, not a burden on them. In *Caesar and Cleopatra* "the anachronisms bring the solemnities of the past down to the trivialities of the present," and in this lies the essence of Shaw's reading of history: Progress is a myth, and where there is no change there can be no anachronism. Though Pompey falls, his spirit prevails over Caesar's. Cleopatra's education is false progress, Caesar fails in his efforts to turn old history into new; ultimately "the play's only anachronism is Caesar himself, the godlike Superman far ahead of his time."

476 Robert, Rudolph. "G. Bernard Shaw, Music Critic," MUSIC JOURNAL, XVIII (Nov-Dec 1960), 18, 72-73.
[A brief summary of the music in Shaw's life, ranging from the musical atmosphere of his boyhood to the success of MY FAIR LADY.]

477 Robinson, Marie J. "Revivals on the New York Stage, 1930-1950, with a Statistical Survey of Their Performances from 1750-1950," 2 Vols., DA, XXI (1960), 1291. Unpublished dissertation, Northwestern University, 1960.

478 Roman, Robert C. "G.B.S. on the Screen," FILMS IN REVIEW, XI (Aug-Sept 1960), 406-18.
In the silent film era Shaw refused to allow any of his plays to be filmed because of the importance of words in his plays, but he was impressed by the potential of talkies and in 1928 appeared himself in a newsreel. Early films of *How He Lied to Her Husband* (1931) and *Arms and the Man* (1932) were little more than filmed stage productions; Shaw would not permit a single cut or change in the plays, and they were not successful. Gabriel Pascal managed to get from Shaw "blanket permission to film his plays," and his *Pygmalion*, for which Shaw did the screenplay, instituted a new era in filming Shaw plays; a number of changes in play and dialogue were made, and the film was a success. *Major Barbara* (1940) and *Caesar and Cleopatra* (1945) followed, again with Shaw doing the screenplay. The film of *Barbara* was more simply written than the play and gave more emphasis to Barbara's romance with Cusins; it was "undeniably an improvement of his original play." Since Shaw's death films of *Androcles and the Lion, Saint Joan, The Doctor's Dilemma* and *The Devil's Disciple* have been variously bungled; none have been worthy of the plays.

479 Scott, Charles. "Genus, Superman; Species, Multiform," ETJ, XII (Dec 1960), 289-94.
Shaw's Superman is defined by Don Juan in *Man and Superman* and in the Epistle Dedicatory to the play, in a 1910 letter from Shaw to Tolstoy and in the Preface to *Major Barbara*. We look in vain through Shaw's plays for the perfect example of a Superman, though Don Juan, Epifania in *The Millionairess*, Undershaft, Barbara and Cusins in *Barbara*, Caesar in *Caesar and Cleopatra* and Joan in *Saint Joan* all approximate the ideal in various ways, by virtue of their usefulness, their leadership abilities, or their dedication to improving life. "There are artists, philosophers, teachers, warriors, saints and bosses, all falling short of the ideal and yet certainly Supermen when compared with the rest of their society." Salvation, Shaw felt, might be found in striving toward the ideal Superman.

480 Sinclair, Upton. MY LIFETIME IN LETTERS
(Columbia, Missouri: U of Missouri P, 1960), pp.
56-71, 174, 176, 183-84, 374.
[Letters between Shaw and Sinclair.]

481 Slonim, Marc. "Four Western Writers on
Tolstoy," RUSSIAN REVIEW, XIX (April 1960), 187-204.
To Shaw Tolstoy was an ally in the war against prudery,
hypocrisy, social conventions, militarism and capitalistic
platitudes. Tolstoy's influence is easily seen in many
Shaw plays. For example, Shaw felt that comparison of
Heartbreak House to Chekhov's CHERRY ORCHARD was unfair
because Tolstoy had dealt with the same subject earlier.
He cited Tolstoy as a writer who faced issues seriously,
without resorting to voluptuous or romantic devices. Like
most of Tolstoy's other interpreters, Shaw failed to face
the problem of Tolstoy's complexity; he saw in him "only
what he liked or needed for strengthening his own position
as a satirist and moralist--and he dismissed rather
lightly all the rest."

482 Smith, J. Percy. "G. B. S. on the Theatre,"
TAMARACK REVIEW, No. 15 (Spring 1960), 73-86.
Though drama criticism is for the most part ephemeral,
Shaw's has deservedly survived. It is perceptive and
stimulating, distinguished by his continual application of
a set of criteria that go far beyond the mechanics of the
play. The theater, like the church, Shaw thought, was
properly a place for intellectual seriousness, not for the
shallow amusement of cheap emotions. The playwright must
deal with the realities of life, and he must have moral
purpose. Shaw called too for courage and gaity in drama.
He required of the actors, the theater's priesthood,
imagination, intelligence and technical perfection.

483 Smith, Warren S. "The Bishop, the Dancer, and
Bernard Shaw," ShawR, III (Jan 1960), 2-10.
Shaw entered into a controversy occasioned by the clergy's
objection to the performance of a French variety artiste
with a long letter to the TIMES on 8 November 1913,
spurred, perhaps, by recent attacks on *Androcles and the
Lion* into another round of his long battle with the
censor. Shaw here went beyond the immediate object of
contention into the wider realm of religion and morality,
comparing the theater to the church both in terms of
possible abuse or morbidity and in terms of the necessity
for freedom: temperance and toleration are desirable in

both. He claimed that there is voluptuous ecstasy, which
makes it impossible to eliminate the one without also
attacking the other. Shaw is apparently unable to
conceive of real lewdness or pornography, though this
blind spot does not necessarily invalidate his argument.
He thought that self-discipline, not the censor, must be
the source of morality. The simple course for censors is
to forbid what is not customary, and nothing but vulgarity
is customary, so Shaw feared, "our souls are to have no
adventures because adventures are dangerous."

484 Smoker, Barbara. "The Chestershaw," Reg, III
(Aug 1960), 1, 3.
[Introducing, tongue-in-cheek, a parallel to the
Shakespearian authorship controversy: who really wrote
the plays attributed to Shaw?] Considering Shaw's scant
education and his asceticism, to suppose that he wrote
such plays as *Man and Superman* and *The Apple Cart* is
ludicrous. Chesterton is a more likely candidate. Or, as
a 1 September 1909 item in the BYSTANDER implies, perhaps
Shaw invented Chesterton as an alter-ego, his outward
antithesis, and the Chesterton-Shaw debates were a simple
mirror trick.

485 Smoker, Barbara. "The Prize-Winning Alphabets,"
CShav, I (Jan-Feb 1960) [3 pp.].
The prize for the best new alphabet for English
incorporating specifications set forth in Shaw's will was
divided among four competitors, as no one of the 467
entries was ideal. Professor P.A.D. McCarthy will try to
co-ordinate the best features of the four alphabets to
obtain a suitable alphabet for use in publishing the bi-
alphabetic edition of *Androcles and the Lion* Shaw's will
provided for.

486 Speaight, Robert. TWENTIETH CENTURY ENCYCLO-
PEDIA OF CATHOLICISM: CHRISTIAN THEATRE (NY:
Hawthorn Books, 1960), CXXIV, 122-24.
Shaw, whose "thought is as puerile as his style and
artistry are superb," wanted, as the Preface to *Major
Barbara* shows, a Christianity without Christ. *Saint Joan*
"is a magnificent and moving play about something which
never really happened," for Shaw juggled the facts.
Nonetheless, the saint's victory over the dramatist makes
it one of the great plays of the Christian theater. Shaw
showed that religion could be as exciting a subject as
politics or adultery, even in the twentieth century.

487 Stambusky, Alan A.   "Bernard Shaw's Farcical
Vision: Comic Perspective in the Traditional Mode,"
DRAMA CRITIQUE, III (May 1960), 80-87.
Shaw was not a theatrical innovator; he wrote, in the
tradition of Aristophanes and Molière, fundamentally uni-
versal comedy which was not bound by a limited society.
Shaw is a social satirist who performs for his age the
same service that Aristophanes and Molière did for theirs.

488 Staud, Géza.   "Bernard Shaw és Hevesi Sándor,
Levelezése (Bernard Shaw and Sandor Hevesi, Correspondence) VILÁGIRODALMI FIGYELÖ, VI (1960), 169-80.
The plays of Shaw were first presented unsuccessfully
during the first decade of this century. Shaw's
theatrical manager, Teleki, chose Hevesi Sandor, a stage
manager and aesthetician, to interpret Shaw for the
Hungarian public. In 1910 Hevesi gained exclusive rights
to translate Shaw. Shaw's letters, kept in the Historical
Museum of Theater, concern translation and copyright of
the plays and testify to the personal relationship between
the two men. [Text of Shaw letters.] [In Hungarian, with
English summary.]

489 Steinhardt, Maxwell. *The Devil's Disciple* on
the Screen," ShawR, III (Jan 1960), 39-41.
The screen version of *The Devil's Disciple*, starring Sir
Laurence Olivier as Burgoyne, Kirk Douglas as Dick Dudgeon
and Burt Lancaster as Anthony Anderson, is "decidedly
third-rate." A number of new scenes have been added which
do not justify the cuts in Shaw's play. The best scenes,
left substantially as Shaw wrote them, are the reading of
the Will, the tea shared by the Andersons and Dick
followed by Dick's arrest, and the court-martial. The
stars must share part of the blame for "this bungled
Devil's Disciple" with the producer and director for
agreeing to participate in "a shameful distortion of a
work of art by one of the world's great dramatists."

490 Stork, Charles Wharton. "Personal Impressions
of Bernard Shaw," VISVABHARATI QUARTERLY, XXVI
(Summer 1960), 45-53.
Shaw shocked us young people deliciously, and we revelled
in his exposures of sham sentiment and sham morality. The
best of his plays reveal the mystical element in Shaw's
character; he was a deeply religious man. *Pygmalion*,
however, contains evidence of charlatanism, the appearance
of substantial drama in what is really mere whimsy.

Shaw's work is "at once profound and trivial, dignified and slapstick, the inspired utterance of a prophet slipping into the cheap tricks of a demagogue and the circus antics of a clown." Finally, Shaw is "best in occasional flashes, he is provocative, not conclusive; stimulating, not sustaining."

491 Styan, J. L. THE ELEMENTS OF DRAMA (Cambridge: Cambridge U P, 1960), pp. 13, 64, 87-88, 89 ff., 99-100, 101 ff., 107, 146 ff., 169, 170 ff., 178, 188, 205, 214, 236, 238, 255, 263.
[Styan frequently chooses Shaw plays to illustrate the principles of drama. The scene from *Saint Joan* between de Baudricourt and his Steward is analyzed in detail in terms of tempo.] A Shaw speech has "a vocal music which corresponds strictly with its logical structure, and it does not tire the listener." *Arms and the Man* is "about *poseurs* and the quality of posing;" both visual and verbal gesture reinforce the theme. The later plays contain lengthy rhetorical speeches, but the "rhetoric arises legitimately from the character, the situation and the subjects." Yet, as the scene between Magnus and Orinthia in *The Apple Cart* shows, Shaw "did not forget the living presence of his actors; the scene is conceived visually as well as verbally."

492 Suenaga, Kuniaki. "G. B. Shaw to Shingekiundo" (G. B. Shaw and the New Drama Movement), EIGO SEINEN (Tokyo), CVI (Nov 1960) 595-96.
[A brief survey of Shaw productions at the Independent Theatre, the Stage Society and the Vedrenne-Barker Management.] [In Japanese.]

493 Tompkins, Peter (ed). "Introduction," TO A YOUNG ACTRESS: THE LETTERS OF BERNARD SHAW TO MOLLY TOMPKINS (NY: Clarkson N. Potter, 1960).
Laurence and Molly Tompkins, a young American couple, went to England to find Shaw, a prophet whom they greatly admired, and to propagate his gospel by designing a Shavian theater and acting in his plays. During their friendship with Shaw, which lasted from 1921 until his death, he sent Molly many letters [here reproduced], counselling her on her personal life as well as "on how to speak and to act, how to dress and make up, how to handle theatrical managers, write a fine hand, paint pictures, write plays, and, above all, master the art of saying a plain 'No!'"

494 Troiani, Osiris. "Shaw o la provocación" (Shaw or the Provocation), FICCIÓN, XXVI (July-Aug 1960), 76-79.
Despite Shaw's belonging to the past because his works are outdated, because his writing lacks poetry, and because of his tendency to didacticism and moralizing, he still attracts readers because of his constant attack on society and his always being provocative. [In Spanish.]

495 Unwin, Sir Stanley. THE TRUTH ABOUT A PUBLISHER (NY: Macmillan; Lond: Allen & Unwin, 1960).
Proofs of H. C. Duffin's QUINTESSENCE OF BERNARD SHAW (1920) were sent to Shaw, who liked the book and returned the proofs heavily annotated. On seeing the agreement between publisher and author, Shaw leaped to the defense of Duffin, who, he thought, was being taken advantage of by "sharks." Subsequent miscellaneous dealings with Shaw were marked by his "courtesy and consideration." [Several letters exchanged by Unwin and Shaw, on subjects ranging from Mrs. Shaw to proposed publication of Shaw's letters and music criticism to Shaw's use of Carpenter's ENGLAND ARISE! IN *On the Rocks* are included.]

496 Urnov, M. "Spory o Shou: Shovian v 1958-1960 godakh," (Quarrels about Shaw: *THE SHAVIAN* 1958-1960), VOPROSY LITERATURY (Moscow), IV (1960), 144-45.
In England, interest in Shaw has greatly decreased since 1956, though it is more lively in the United States. A few TV productions have been given, but there is little of interest in the theater. The Shavians attentively follow the increase in Shaw's popularity in the Peoples' Democracies and the Soviet Union. [In Russian.]

497 Vlokh, I. "Diskusiĩa ĩak kharakterna risa dialogu v p'esakh Shou" (Discussion as a Characteristic of Dialogue in Shaw's Plays), ZBIRNIK ROBIT ASPIRANTIV KAFEDR FILOLOGICHESKIKH NAUK (Lviv) (1960), 83-89.
[Not seen.] [In Ukrainian.]

498 Vrudnii, A. "O nekotorykh osobesnnostiakh satiry Shou" (On Some Characteristics of Shaw's Satire), UCHENYE ZAPISKI FILOLOGICHESKOGO FAKULTETA

GEORGE BERNARD SHAW

KIRGIZSKOGO GOS. UNIVERSITET (Frundze), No 6 (1960), 153-69.
[Not seen.] [In Russian.]

499 Ward, A. C. "Introduction" and "Notes" to *Caesar and Cleopatra: A HISTORY* (Lond: Longmans, Green, 1960); rptd (Don Mills, Ontario: Longmans Canada Ltd., 1967), pp. 135-78.
[A "General Introduction" to Shaw, largely biographical, is included]. Shaw thought Shakespeare's ANTONY AND CLEOPATRA "glamorized and falsified a ruinous code of sensual indulgence and debauchery;" he sought in *Caesar and Cleopatra* to show that passion should be disciplined by reason. His portrait of a kittenish Cleopatra is probably no more accurate historicallly than Shakespeare's, but it served his purpose, "to show a soldier-statesman's attempts to turn a crude and spiteful teenager into a responsible queen and to teach his own colleagues that clemency is the best policy." The principal characters are memorable more as symbols of opposing standards than as individuals, but Rufio, Ftatateeta and Britannus are better individualized. No historical play by another playwright is likely to outlive *Caesar*.

500 Weales, Gerald. "The Edwardian Theater and the Shadow of Shaw," EDWARDIANS AND LATE VICTORIANS, ENGLISH INSTITUTE ESSAYS, 1959, ed by Richard Ellmann (NY: Columbia UP, 1960), pp. 160-87.
Shaw like others faced the future confidently at the turn of the century. Shaw's shadow fell across Edwardian drama in two ways: he determined the idea of the theater, and his brilliance obscured the other playwrights.

501 Weintraub, Stanley. "Apostate Apostle: H. L. Mencken as Shavophile and Shavophobe," ETJ, XII (Oct 1960), 184-190; rptd in CShav III (Sept-Oct 1963), 1-6.
Mencken is, more than any other American critic, responsible for the popular misconception of Shaw as "self-advertising clown and coiner of cheap paradoxes." Mencken was a great Shaw enthusiast at the beginning of his critical career. Later, wanting to replace Shaw as arch-heretic himself, he attacked him. What once appeared to Mencken to be Shaw's most searching and illuminating observations he now described as mere platitudes. He retained some of his admiration for Shaw's writing, but

for its most superficial aspects. Mencken could not understand Shaw well enough to grasp his larger concerns of morality and Socialism. In his later years Mencken mellowed toward Shaw but could not recant, and apparently preferred to forget all about him. Shaw, however, found Mencken a valuable critic.

502 Weintraub, Stanley. "Bernard Shaw, Actor," TAM, XLIV (Oct 1960), 66-67.
In his miniscule career as actor Shaw was cast as Krogstad in a private reading of Ibsen's A DOLL'S HOUSE in 1888 with Eleanor Marx as Nora. In 1897 he appeared in a copyright performance of The Devil's Disciple as Anthony Anderson. In 1908 he was in a copyright performance of Granville-Barker's WASTE, and in the same year he apparently stood in as the Beadle in Getting Married.

503 Weintraub, Stanley. "Ibsen's DOLL'S HOUSE Metaphor Foreshadowed in Victorian Fiction," NINE-TEENTH CENTURY FICTION, XIII (June 1958), 67-69.
In The Irrational Knot Marian foreshadows Ibsen's Nora in speaking of girls' ignorance on the subject of happiness in marriage and in longing to be something other than a fragile ornament in a glass case. Her husband, she says, "would as soon think of submitting any project of his to the judgment of a doll as to mine," and she ultimately rebuffs her husband's attempt at a reconciliation. His anticipation of Ibsen Shaw later cited as evidence that Ibsen was "a representative writer, marching with the world, and not against it, or by himself, as some people suppose."

504 W[eintraub], S[tanley] (ed). "St. Pancras Mani-festo," ShawR, III (Jan 1960), 21-31.
Shaw ran with Sir William Nevill M. Geary for the Borough of St. Pancras in the London County Council in 1904. He supported improvement of Church schools, even if public funds were needed. This apparently lost him the election by alienating the Nonconformists. The manifesto [reprinted here] which was their campaign platform was signed by both Shaw and Geary, but "the language and form of its 15 pages have the ring of Shaw's prefaces."

505 Whiting, George W. "The Cleopatra Rug Scene: Another Source," ShawR, III (Jan 1960), 15-17.

Cleopatra's delivery to Caesar rolled up in a rug does not appear in Mommsen's HISTORY OF ROME, Shaw's primary source for *Caesar and Cleopatra*. Plutarch's life of Julius Caesar is probably Shaw's source for the scene, but he may also have known of Gérome's painting, "Cléopatra aportée à César dans un tapis," which was exhibited in London five years before Shaw's arrival.

506 Whitman, Wanda. "Postscript," Reg, III (Aug 1960), 8.
[An account of Shaw's appearance at the Metropolitan Opera House in 1933.]

507 Wilson, Colin. "Shaw's Existentialism," SHAVIAN, II (Feb 1960), 4-6.
Though other Shaw plays may be greater, wittier, or more philosophically brilliant, *Major Barbara* is the most significant for the thought of the Nineteen-Sixties. In our contemporary "maelstrom of neurosis and futility, the sensitive man of imagination . . . is faced with a need for direction and purpose." *Barbara* deals with salvationism and the tentative, intuitive religion of the poet as responses to this problem. Undershaft and Cusins make plain what was still uncertain in *Man and Superman* and *John Bull's Other Island*: that if the businessman will take any interest in "helping life in its struggle upwards," then the mystics must become businessmen. Shaw failed to develop this theme fully, though he returned to it later in *Heartbreak House*. Its importance is becoming increasingly evident; the play was far ahead of its time.

508 Yamada, Hideo. "Fabianshakaishugi to Teikoku-shugi-Nanasenso omeguru Shaw, Webb, Hobson-" (Fabian Socialism and Imperialism-Shaw, Webb and Hobson on the Boer War-) in SHAKAIKAIKAU ENO TEIGEN (Proposals for Social Reforms), ed by Hiromi Arisawa, Shigeto Tsuru *et al* (Tokyo: Keiso Shobo, 1960), pp. 202-26.
J. A. Hobson in his book IMPERIALISM, A STUDY (1902) branded Fabians as imperialists because the Fabian Society supported the Boer War by publishing *Fabianism and the Empire* drafted by Shaw. The early Fabians were not well prepared to refute Hobson's accusation. In fact, the question of imperialism was not within the field of the early Fabians. It is, as it were, their Achilles' heel.
[In Japanese.]

509 Zograf, N. G., *et al.* OCHERKI ISTORII SOVET-
SKOGO DRAMATICHESKOGO TEATR (Sketches of the History
of the Soviet Russian Theater), II (Moscow:
Akademiia nauk SSSR, 1960), 588-89, 685.
Zubov's production of *Pygmalion* at the Malyi Theater
(Moscow, 1943) emphasized Shaw's basic theme, instead of
producing the play as usual earlier simply as a comedy of
manners with the transformation of a flower-girl into a
society lady. Eliza unmasks the egoism and limited
morality of her Pygmalion. Zubov portrayed Higgins as a
man of strong will and intellect, but also as ruthless,
and the ending revealed that Eliza has conquered him (a
democratic and humanistic ending). The production at the
Theater of Comedy (Leningrad, 1944) was also treated as
powerful satire. Shaw's journalistic afterward was
included, and in it the characters addressed the audience
directly. [In Russian.]

1961

510 Adler, Henry. "Brecht and After," DRAMA, ns
LXIII (Winter 1961), 29-31.
Unlike Brecht's dialectic, Shaw's arguments have a logical
progression, and his wit involves us in laughter at
unexpected leaps of thought.

511 Adler, Henry. "29 Fitzroy Square," SHAVIAN, II
(June, 1961), 12-14.
[A very brief survey of houses lived in by Shaw up to
1898.]

512 Åhman, Sven. "Genier Emellan: Nyfunna brev från
Shaw till Strindberg" (Between Geniuses: Newfound
Letters from Shaw to Strindberg), DAGENS NYHETER
(Stockholm), 1 Oct 1961, pp. 3, 5.
Two letters written by Shaw to Strindberg in March 1910
and recently discovered in the Kungliga Biblioteket (Royal
Library) in Stockholm constitute the first evidence that
these two representatives of the golden age of modern
European drama had any written correspondence with one
another. Another recent chance find is the discovery in
Alfred Kerr's NEW YORK UND LONDON of still another version
of Shaw's oft-repeated story that Strindberg broke off
their 1908 meeting--or a letter or a phone call about the

meeting--with the abrupt announcement that at 2:00 he would become ill. [In Swedish.]

513 Almási, Miklós. A MODERN DRÁMA ÚTJAIN: AZ ÚJABB DRÁMATÖRTÉNET ÉS SHAKESPEARE - I HAGYOMÁNYOK (Along the Byways of Modern Drama: The More Recent History of Drama and the Shakespearean Tradition) (Budapest: Gondolat, 1961), pp. 166-201.
Shaw presents the atypical as typical, so that the audience leaves the theater in a state of agitation. For this reason Shaw needed the prologues and epilogues to explain himself. Shaw is the "ironic closer" of the bourgeois era. His theater is absurd because his characters do wrong especially when they feel they are doing good. He views bourgeois civilization as passionless and worthless in *Saint Joan* and *The Devil's Disciple*. Sentiment is portrayed as a romantic illusion in *Getting Married* and *Candida*. Shaw exposes tragedy as the obverse of comedy--a pose--in *Captain Brassbound's Conversion, Candida, Arms and the Man,* and *The Doctor's Dilemma*. Saint Joan's tragedy stems from her being a heroine of the people, and unlike classic tragedy, she dies because she achieves her goals. The wise are not wise (Tanner and Caesar), but toys of history. Shaw's Prefaces and Epilogues result from Shaw's upsetting the audience's expectations as in *Major Barbara*. He destroyed bourgeois drama, preparing the way for the "new drama." [Illustrations of many productions.] [In Hungarian.]

514 Armand, I. L. "Kharakternye cherti angliiskogo iumora v p'esakh Bernarda Shou" (Characteristic Features of English Humor in Bernard Shaw's Plays), TRUDY TBLISKOGO PEDAGOGICHESKOGO INSTITUTA INOSTRANNYKH IAZIKOV (Tiflis), No. 4 (1961), 51-56.
Shaw uses humor in characterization e.g. speaking names, derived from Ben Jonson, Fielding, Dickens and others. In describing persons, he adopted an ironic or realistic manner (defined as an organic connection between the author's style and the speech of his characters). This method also occurs in stage-directions. Shaw also uses humor of situation, with parody and paradox. These aspects of comedy intensify the vital social questions of the plays. [In Russian.]

515 Barnes, T. R. "Shaw and the London Theatre," THE MODERN AGE (Pelican Guide to English Literature,

vol. 7), ed by Boris Ford (Baltimore: Penguin Books, 1961), pp. 209-20.
Shaw's claim to be in the tradition of Molière is weakened by the loss in the contemporary world of shared language and morals. When he deals with emotion, there is only cliche, but his wit, gaiety, and his passion for justice remain undimmed. He was a pioneer in publishing plays in a form readers could enjoy, and it is only a reader who can grasp the coherence of Shaw's plays.

516 Beatty, C. J. P. "A Shavian Allusion," N & Q, ns VIII (June 1961), 232-33.
In suggesting that Shaw got the name Octavius in *Man and Superman* from Kipling, Dr. Foster has overlooked Shaw's statement in the Preface to the play that he took Octavius unaltered from Mozart. There is an added interest, as my grandfather, Octavius Holmes Beatty, was the younger brother of Pakenham Beatty, who was one of Shaw's oldest and closest friends. My grandfather was known as Tavy in the family and to Shaw also, as is proved by letters from Shaw to members of my family. [See Foster, Brian. "A Shavian Allusion," N & Q, ns VIII (March 1961), 106-7.]

517 Behrman, S. N. "The Paddy Vein," PRAIRIE SCHOONER, XXXV (Spring 1961), 10-13.
[An introduction for a new edition of *You Never Can Tell*, University of Nebraska P, 1961.] No one before or since Shaw has ever made a romantic hero out of a dentist. *You Never Can Tell* is one of the funniest plays ever written. In construction, it is a "well-made play." This was Max Beerbohm's favorite Shaw play. In this play there is a typically Irish impulse to "pure mischief." This "paddy vein" reaches its climax in the third act, in one of his richest comic characters, Bohun the lawyer. C. E. Montague and Max Beerbohm agree with me that Shaw cared about social questions and principles, not about persons. I enjoy familial fun more than the cosmic serious; I am no longer impressed by Shaw's "great" plays, but the emanations from his "paddy vein" delight me as much as ever.

518 Béra, M. A. "G.B.S. ou Bernard Shaw" (G.B.S. or Bernard Shaw), LES LANGUES MODERNES, II (March-April 1961), 43-45.
The success of the Pitoeffs's *Saint Joan* is misleading because the French were responding to nationalist and religious glory. Shaw's plays show us intelligent puppets, and his lucid, self-conscious art alienates him

from us. *Pygmalion* is his masterpiece, emphasizing the power of language itself. [In French.]

519 Bissell, Claude. "The Butlerian Inheritance of G. B. Shaw," DALHOUSIE REVIEW, XLI (Summer 1961), 159-73.
Although Samuel Butler is a minor figure, he exerted a pervasive influence on Shaw. Further, there is a basic similarity in attitudes between the two, especially their admiration for Bunyan. Both recognized the importance of money. Both believed that man was inseparable from the natural processes and at the same time superior to them.

520 Chappelow, Allan (ed). SHAW THE VILLAGER AND HUMAN BEING (Lond: Charles Skilton, 1961; NY: Macmillan, 1962).
["A Biographical Symposium" assembled and narrated by Chappelow. Photographs.]

521 Cherniavs'ka, S. P. "Do pitannîa pro maïster-nost' Bernarda Shou-dramaturga" (On the Question of Bernard Shaw's Mastery as Dramaturg), DOPOVIDI TA POVIDOMENNIA L'VIVS'KII DERZH. UNIVERSITET (Lvov), No 9 (1961), 186-88.
[Not seen.] [In Ukrainian.]

522 Churchill, R. C. "The Comedy of Ideas: Cross-currents in the Fiction and Drama of the Twentieth Century," THE MODERN AGE (Pelican Guide to English Literature, vol 7), ed by Boris Ford (Baltimore: Penguin Books, 1961), pp. 221-30.
While Henry James was trying to make the novel dramatic, Shaw was trying to get the virtues of the novel into drama. Both had a limited success.

523 Clayton, Robert Bovee. "The Salvation Myth in the Drama of George Bernard Shaw." Unpublished dissertation, University of California, 1961. [Listed in DAID.]

524 Clurman, Harold. "Notes for a Production of *Heartbreak House*," TULANE DRAMA REVIEW (Spring 1961), 58-67; rptd in Robert W. Corrigan (ed). LAUREL BRITISH DRAMA: THE TWENTIETH CENTURY (NY:

Dell, 1965), pp. [31]-41; BERNARD SHAW'S PLAYS, ed
by Warren Sylvester Smith (1970); Harold Clurman.
ON DIRECTING (NY: Macmillan; Lond: Collier-
Macmillan, 1972), pp. 229-41.
[The working notes for a New York revival of *Heartbreak
House* in 1959-60, directed by the author. The random
notes emphasize the director's view of the play as crazy
and loony; he also wants to stress the "fun" of the play,
its arch frivolity. He told the actors to disregard
Shaw's remarks about Chekhov and about *Heartbreak* being a
play in the "Russian manner."]

525 Cole, Margaret. THE STORY OF FABIAN SOCIALISM
(Stanford, California: Stanford U P, 1961), passim.
[The only straight history of the Fabian Society since
Pease in 1916; the book aims at being a history, not of
the Fabian Society in isolation, but of Fabian Socialism.
Shaw is mentioned in connection with his work, talks, and
writing for the Society.]

526 Couchman, Gordon W. "ANTONY AND CLEOPATRA and
the Subjective Convention," PMLA, LXXVI (Sept 1961),
420-25.
Shaw's aggressive onslaught on Shakespeare's ANTONY AND
CLEOPATRA, a part of his critical assault on the romantic
theater, is well-known from the Preface to *Three Plays for
Puritans*. Similar though less familiar strictures can be
found in one of his SATURDAY REVIEW articles for 1897, in
reviews in the same year of two performances of ANTONY AND
CLEOPATRA, in an article in the NEW STATESMAN in 1913 on a
revival of *Caesar and Cleopatra*, and in a 1927 interview
in the LIVERPOOL POST. Shaw's *Caesar* is more of a
reaction to Shakespeare's Antony than his Caesar. Shaw's
assault must be understood as polemic, not criticism. But
Shaw is mistaken in accusing Shakespeare of being
infatuated with his romantic hero and heroine. Shaw forgot (or chose to ignore) the comments in the play of such
characters as Scarus and Enobarbus who express about
Antony almost exactly Shaw's view. Shaw has also missed
Shakespeare's depiction of the moral decay of the Roman
world of the time. Shaw thus reveals how completely his
anti-romantic enthusiasms could blind him. "Is it unfair
to say that Shaw was led (or misled) into a degree of
romantic hero-worship of Caesar by his very dislike of the
romantic weakness" of Antony?

527 Crivât, Dana. "George Bernard Shaw, Regizor," (George Bernard Shaw, Stage Director), REVISTA TEATRUL, X (10 Oct 1961), 79-83.
Shaw, unlike Gordon Craig, respected the personalities of actors. [Quotes and paraphrases extensively from Shaw's letters (1921-22) to McNulty and from an essay "Rules for Play Producers" (STRAND 1950). Photograph of Shaw and of a page of *Pygmalion* with Shaw's notes.] [In Romanian.]

528 Davidson, J. A. "A Canadian Sidelight on Bernard Shaw and his Alphabet 'Thing'," QQ, LXVIII (Summer 1961), 280-85.
Shaw's Preface on alphabet reform to THE MIRACULOUS BIRTH OF LANGUAGE by the Canadian scholar, R. A. Wilson, is silly and unconvincing. After a few introductory remarks, Shaw harangues on alphabet reform which has nothing to do with Wilson's theories. The working out of several reformed alphabets, on lines suggested by Shaw, is notably unsuccessful. [The author was a student of Professor Wilson.]

529 Dietrich, Richard Farr. "Shaw and the Passionate Mind," ShawR, IV (May 1961), 2-11.
Most critics have described the ethic of the Shavian hero as "vitalist" and/or "pragmatist." but pragmatism and vitalism would seem to be antithetical. What is called in Shavian ethic, pragmatism, should be better named as *frein vital* (the term is from Irving Babbitt and means a power of vital control over the *elan vital*) or superrational intuition; it is thus not associated with any preconceived rational discipline. These distinctions may be illustrated by looking at three plays; *Caesar and Cleopatra, Saint Joan,* and *The Apple Cart.* The examination of these plays shows that the ethic of the Shavian hero is largely intuitive. If we take reason as a mechincal thing which fixes thought in time and space, then Shaw is not a rationalist; if reason is the highest passion of the mind, acting vitally upon the other passions, then Shaw may be called a rationalist. If Shaw is a pragmatist, then his pragmatism must be clearly distinguished from that of other pragmatists; Shavian pragmatism makes not rational judgments but inspired guesses.

530 Downer, Alan S. "Introduction," THE THEATRE OF BERNARD SHAW, ed by Alan S. Downer, 2 vols (NY: Dodd, Mead, 1961), pp. 1-19.

The ten plays selected have been chosen to indicate the development of Shaw's dramatic technique. Shaw's method involved the inversion of conventional, taken-for-granted plots and moral evaluations; it also involved the creation of the Shavian hero. Shaw's techniques involved the discussion play, in which the hero debates with worthy opponents, and the dramatic parable. In a letter to Downer (21 January 1948) Shaw said that a playwright does not merely hold the mirror up to nature, but interprets the passing show by parables.

531 Drews, Wolfgang. "Notizen über George Bernard Shaw" (Notes on George Bernard Shaw), THEATER UND ZEIT, IX (1961-62), 209-11.
Shaw was a man with many faces. His best plays are *Candida, Caesar and Cleopatra* and *Saint Joan*. [In German.]

532 Du Cann, C.G.L. "The Shaw Marriage," HUMANIST, LXXVI (July 1961), 203-5.
When Shaw saw his wife's correspondence with T. E. Lawrence, he realized that there was a side of her he had never known. The sterility of his marriage proves Shaw false to his proclaimed religion of fecundity. Two letters in the Sept issue, p. 285: Mirian Allen deFord, "an unconsummated marriage is no marriage at all." J.M., "Shaw suffered from some slight . . . physical defect which made him incapable of normal sexual intercourse."

533 Dukore, Bernard F. "The Fabian and the Freudian," SHAVIAN, II (June 1961), 8-11.
If *Mrs. Warren's Profession* were written today, it is possible that the orientation would be more psychological than sociological. This comment is occasioned by a film (made from a psychoanalytical study) GIRL OF THE NIGHT. The film attempts to illuminate the relationship between personality and chosen occupation. The psychoanalytic study concludes that girls often become prostitutes because of an early feeling of rejection by their mothers. Call girls stay at the trade for the same reasons as given by Mrs. Warren in her confrontation with Vivie. Both the psychological and economic arguments are persuasive, but both deal with extremes. If Shaw had studied prostitutes of a different class origin from Mrs. Warren's, he might have given more weight to psychological causes.

534 Dukore, Bernard F. "Shaw and a Chicago Art Theatre," ShawR, IV (Sept 1961), 2-6.
Maurice Browne is thought of as the founder of the little theater movement. The Little Theatre in Chicago, which Browne ran from February 1912 to December 1917, had its destinies indirectly affected by Shaw. A production of *The Philanderer* was their first unqualified financial success. In 1916, the group produced *Mrs. Warren's Profession* in a large theater and, because of disagreements and misunderstandings, were locked out after a week's run. The company's last new production 26 November 1917 was *Candida*.

535 Dunlap, Joseph R. "Arts, Crafts, and a Centennial," Reg, IV (Aug 1961), 9-10.
[Comment on a crafts exhibition at the New Gallery (Lond) and Shaw's review in THE WORLD.]

536 Dunlap, Joseph R. "The Typographical Shaw: GBS and the Revival of Printing," SHAVIAN, II (February 1961), 4-15.
[See Dunlap, Joseph R., 1960.]

537 Dupler, Dorothy. "An Analytical Study of the Use of Rhetorical Devices in Three Selected Plays of George Bernard Shaw: *Saint Joan, Androcles and the Lion*, and *Candida*," DA, XXII (1961), 359. Unpublished dissertation, University of Southern California, 1961. [Abstract in SPEECH MONOGRAPHS, XXXIX (June 1962), 122; excerpt in STUDENTS' SOURCES FOR SHAKESPEARE'S HAMLET, SHAW'S SAINT JOAN, CONRAD'S HEART OF DARKNESS, comp by Roy Bentley (Agincourt, Ontario: Book Society of Canada, 1966), p. 64.]

538 Ford, Boris (ed). THE MODERN AGE (Pelican Guide to English Literature vol 7) (Baltimore, Penguin, 1961), pp. 557-58.
[Very brief career and bibliography. Also references to Shaw in several of the essays in the collection.]

539 Foster, Brian. "A Shavian Allusion," N & Q, ns VIII (March 1961), 106-7.
In Kozelka's GLOSSARY TO THE PLAYS OF BERNARD SHAW (1959) there is no explanation of "ricky-ticky-tavy" as a nickname for Octavius in *Man and Superman*. Shaw evidently

lifted this from a story of the same name in Kipling's
JUNGLE BOOK, where it is the name of a nongoose. Shaw's
purpose in choosing this name is that it continues and
fits the imagery of *Superman* where Ann is likened to a boa
constrictor and where there is supposed to be an opposition between Octavius the mongoose (snake killer) and Ann,
the boa constrictor.

540 Frederick, Moritia. "Was Shaw Shelley's
    Grandson?" Reg, IV (Dec 1961), 4.
[Comic relating of events that suggest Shaw's father was
the illegitimate son of Shelley.]

541 Geduld, H. M. "Bernard Shaw and Adolph Hitler,"
    ShawR, IV (Jan 1961), 11-20.
Shaw's misjudgments about Hitler and his anti-semitism and
concentration camps spring from tired old age and awareness of the "injustices" of Versailles. Shaw's view of
Hitler is not paradoxical; he was simply baffled by anti-
semitism, which he tended to excuse as a temporary political expedient, and by the political importance of racism
to the Nazis. Shaw's "comic-strip analysis of Hitler,"
from the early thirties through the forties, is seen in
newspaper articles and interviews, in *On the Rocks, The
Millionairess,* and (principally) *Geneva* and its Preface.

542 Gillespie, Charles Richard. "A Study of Charac-
    terization in Selected Disquisitory Plays of Bernard
    Shaw," DA, XXI (1961), 2038-39. Unpublished disser-
    tation, State University of Iowa, 1960.

543 Glackens, Ira. "The First American *Candida* and
    Louise Closser Hale," Reg, III (April 1961), 7-9.
[Reminiscence of Louise Hale, Prossy in the first production of *Candida* in America.]

544 Green, Martin. "British Comedy and the British
    Sense of Humor: Shaw, Waugh, and Amis," TEXAS
    QUARTERLY, IV (Autumn 1961), 217-27.
The national sense of humor is acutely class-conscious,
deeply asexual, and generally reactionary and antinatural
in this century. Shaw was not a comic genius, but he was,
up to 1920, the most original creator of comic situations
and effects. He gave shape, for example, still recognizable, to the wife who acquiesces in all to her husband and

then in fact arranges matters her own way. Another of Shaw's inventions is the well-bred deflation of melodrama, as in *Captain Brassbound's Conversion* and *The Man of Destiny*. But Shaw did not have the variety, scope, social vision, or richness which great comedy gets from the tension of differing truths, because he saw and heard things and people too much in relation to himself. There are really only two fully realized characters in Shaw's world: Shaw and Woman. Shaw is especially impoverished in his treatment of English society. Further, Shaw's humor is essentially that of the debating-club maverick. He had a deep revulsion from death, sex, or anything deeply personal; his humor is essentially upper middle class and conservative. Shaw's humor is thus deficient because it is really too intellectual, too interested in making debating points; but this did not prevent him from being socially effective. Shaw's real material was his own *persona* as a public figure; we delight in the variety of masks he assumes.

545 Henson, Janice. "Bernard Shaw's Contribution to the Wagner Controversy in England," Shaw R, IV (Jan 1961), 21-26.
While Shaw's defense of Wagner, in his musical columns and in *The Perfect Wagnerite*, was an important aspect of his musical career, its significance was not that he was among the first to champion Wagner but that he defended and interpreted the Wagnerian spirit. Shaw attempted to take for his own critical use the revolutionary and Socialistic elements of the Wagnerian spirit. Shaw is unable to accept, however, Wagner's view of redemption through love; nor can Shaw overlook the decided political conservatism and the support of Bismarck of Wagner's later years. Therefore, "one cannot speak of Shaw as a 'perfect Wagnerite' without some qualification."

546 Hildeman, Per-Axel. "Shaw and the Anglo-Swedish Literary Foundation," SHAVIAN, II (Feb 1961), 34-37.
Shaw turned his Nobel Prize money over to found the Anglo-Swedish Literary Foundation. The Foundation has sponsored a number of translations of Strindberg, Geijer, Hallstrom, Bergman, Moberg, and Lagerkvist; histories and biographies have also been published. After World War II the Foundation contributed to the rebuilding of the Swedish section of University College, London, Library and has enabled various Swedish artists to visit Britain.

547 Hogan, Patrick G., Jr, and Joseph O. Baylen, "G. Bernard Shaw and W. T. Stead: An Unexplored Relationship," STUDIES IN ENGLISH LITERATURE, 1500-1900, I (Autumn 1961), 123-47.
[This article examines the complexity of the relationship between Shaw and Stead.] Both Shaw and Stead realized the vital role of the New Journalism. Stead appreciated Shaw's genius for self-advertisement, but failed to understand him, especially the deadly serious purpose beneath the humor.

548 Jacobi, Johannes. "Kritik und Information. Hamburg, Das neue Thalia Theater" (Criticism and Information. Hamburg, The New Thalia Theater), T H, II (Jan 1961), 32-33.
[Reviews *Saint Joan* produced by Willy Maertens.] Shaw is very humble towards the heroine of his play. In view of her tragic fate he completely forgets his satirical outlook. [In German.]

549 Kárpáti, Aurél. "Elözetes Utószó G.B.S.-Ról" (Preliminary Postscript on G.B.S.), TEGNAPTÓL MÁIG, VALOGATT IRODALMI TANULMANYOK (From Yesterday to Today, Selected Literary Essays) (Budapest: Szepirodalmi Konyvkiado, 1961), pp. 405-17.
Since the "Liberation" Shaw has become the most popular author on the Hungarian stage. It is therefore surprising that recently some have been critical towards his work. [In Hungarian.]

550 Keunen, J. "Rond *Pygmalion* van G. B. Shaw" (On G. B. Shaw's *Pygamalion*), DIETSCHE WARANDE EN BELFORT, CVI (July-Aug 1961), 392-403.
In direct contrast with the Greek Pygmalion tradition, Shaw's Pygmalion-Higgins does not become enamored of his creation, Eliza Doolittle. Shaw, in fact, fought doggedly against the romantic version of Higgins's relationship with his pupil, especially the early Max Beerbohm Tree interpretation of the role. Shaw's distaste for the concept of romantic love was essentially the same in this play as it was in all of his other man-vs-woman pieces. The play is very much another in the series of Shaw's didactic dramatizations of his theories; in this case, the point is that artistic creations can never be the equal of their creator, a point Shaw had made earlier in *The Dark Lady of the Sonnets*; emotional experiences are merely the raw material of artistic activity, appropriately subject

to deliberate manipulation by the artist-genius. [In Dutch.]

551 Knörrich, Otto. "G.B. Shaw - Mystiker der Ratio" (G.B. Shaw—the Mystic of Rationalism), DIE NEUEREN SPRACHEN, Neue Folge, No. 3 (March 1961), 110-20.
Shaw is one of the great rationalists of Western civilization. Following the tradition of Horaz and the enlightenment, he wants to entertain and instruct at the same time. His boundless belief in the power of reason is also a form of mysticism. In his opposition to any kind of romanticism Shaw went too far. In *Back to Methuselah* he created his religion with the myth of creative evolution. Yet even here we see Shaw's origin in nineteenth century rationalism. Shaw's irony which extends to everything, even himself, makes it difficult to pin him down. It also is an escape from responsibility. [In German.]

552 Krutch, Joseph Wood. "G.B.S. and Intimations of Immortality," TAM, XLV (Feb 1961), 65-67, 77.
Perhaps it is too soon to say, but it seems likely that Shaw's work will last. [Photographs.]

553 L.T., A. "Teatro: SACRIFICIO de Rabindranath Tagore, y *Aurora* de George Bernard Shaw" (Theater: SACRIFICE of Rabindranath Tagore and *Aurora* of Bernard Shaw), CULTURA PERUANA, XX1 (Jan-Feb 1961), n.p.
How He Lied to Her Husband is trivial and unimportant. [In Spanish.]

554 Lambert, J. W. "Plays in Performance," DRAMA, ns LXIII (Winter 1961), 21, 22.
The Shewing-up of Blanco Posnet is a confused and sentimental sketch. In *Androcles and the Lion,* Shaw understands those who, like Christians, are prepared to die for an idea. In *Heartbreak House* he wrote a play about people he could not understand at all. The play speaks superbly for itself. [Photograph.]

555 Laurence, Dan H. "Introduction," PLATFORM AND PULPIT, ed by Dan H. Laurence (NY: Hill & Wang, 1961), pp. ix-xv.
Shaw delivered his first full-fledged oration to the Zetetical Society in 1882. For years he lectured every

Sunday to all sorts of groups. He did not depend for his success on mere oratory, but he did know and could use effectively the techniques of the orator. He preferred open-air lecturing. He claimed that he never spoke without giving offense to many, but he was so affable that even the most hostile audiences were at times disarmed. Though his popularity as a speaker increased, his opinions and advice more often went unheeded. Shaw ascribed this to a defect in his listeners rather than in himself. In the course of his life he probably lectured nearly 2,000 times. In 1933 he bade farewell to the lecture platform and turned to the use of the radio where he came across as a fatherly figure using simple language.

556 Leary, Daniel, and Richard Foster. "Adam and Eve: Evolving Archetypes in *Back to Methuselah*," ShawR, IV (May 1961) 12-23.
In *Back to Methuselah* sex declines with the evolutionary rise of mind; Shaw also suggests the elimination of matter and of limited time and death. These developments depend on four spiritual capacities (desiring, imagining, willing, creating) which have application to each of the five plays. In Play I, the Evolutionary Will in Adam insists that change is more necessary than security. In Play II, Eve's desire that Enoch might have more time to develop is given imaginative form through the scientific theory in the gospel of the brothers Barnabas. In Play III, *The Thing Happens* the Domestic Minister, with her ideal of efficiency in human affairs, must be taken as a sign of evolutionary progress. The next part, *Tragedy of an Elderly Gentleman*, shows Zoo who does not wish to preserve, like Eve, all life, but to select superior forms. The Elderly Gentleman finally comes to realize that his life is important only as a part of something greater; Shaw apparently identifies himself with the Gentleman. In Part V there are no short-livers left, and the discarding of time, sex, and matter has reached its logical end. The pattern in the series of plays has been the movement from desire to imagination to will to creation. In the Ancients man has become Seer and Thinker. "Adam's loss of vision and Cain's death-wish give birth to Eve's desire to go beyond sex. In the final play, the last of the human illusions are destroyed by the Ancients who go beyond art, nature, science, and even religion, in their self-creation."

557 Leer, Norman. "The Two-sided Dictator in Shaw's Later Thought," CShav, II (May-June 1961), n.p.

Shaw's presentation of non-socialist dictators is a combination of "desired assertion and childish egoism," with which Shaw is himself disillusioned. The next stage is religious faith in the Superman, but since this is an ideal, in *Everybody's Political What's What* Shaw suggests a rule by enlightened councils. Even if Shaw does not propose an acceptable answer, he forces a recognition of the problem.

558 Lewis, Arthur O., and Stanley Weintraub, "Bernard Shaw--Ten Years After (1950-1960): A Transcript of the Second MLA Conference of Scholars on Shaw," ShawR, IV (May 1961), 29-32.
[Heavily abridged transcript of remarks of some of the 24 conferees at the second annual gathering of American Shaw scholars.]

559 McDowell, Frederick P. W. "Another Look at Bernard Shaw: A Reassessment of His Dramatic Theory, His Practice and His Achievement," DramS, I (May 1961), 34-53.
Three or four reliable evaluations of Shaw now exist (Bentley, Irvine, Ward, Nethercot); most of the critiques before 1947, except Chesterton's, are of little value. Much of the writing on Shaw is severely critical, not enthusiastic; his late plays particularly suffer, perhaps unduly. Yet he continues to be popular in the theater. He conveys the intricacies of experience and thus often seems contradictory; in *Man and Superman* we not only have universal types but such new types as the parent without illusions and the modern young woman. He reconciles apparent contradictions without resolving them. The lack of appreciation of Shaw's artifice is what still impedes satisfactory criticism of the plays after *Heartbreak House*. He uses startling effects (e.g., the plane crash in *Misalliance*), distortion of characters (his realism is psychological rather than external). Artifice comes also into Shaw's structures. His characters are kept from being merely allegorical by their social and psychological accuracy. The doctrine of the Life Force kept his plays from being illustrations of Fabian tracts. Most commentators agree, however, that Shaw lacked a sense of ingrained evil and of the corruptions of power. The critics do not agree on Shaw's best plays, except for *Saint Joan* and *Heartbreak*.

560 McDowell, Frederick P. W. "Crisis and Unreason: Shaw's *On the Rocks*," ETJ, XIII (Oct 1961), 192-200.
On the Rocks conveys a sense of disintegration in society and of the violence under the "civilized" surfaces of modern life. By the end of the play, Sir Arthur Chavender has realized the instability of government which ignores spiritual values; he comes to the conclusion that a despot may be needed to usher in a new age, and he realizes that he is not the man to carry through the revolution. For comic and aesthetic effect, Shaw utilized the disproportions between the realities of "vital economy" and the accidents which obscure those realities. In Act II, Sir Arthur is converted to a Socialist program; it fails, however, because the various leaders are without principles. Shaw's feeling that strong leadership was what was needed is an undesirable extremity in his political philosophy, but is not without some wisdom as can be seen in the skill with which he has analysed the terrible situation of those years and the force with which he has recreated the aimlessness and confusion of modern man. The play possesses force and meaning for a later troubled generation.

561 Masur, Gerhard. PROPHETS OF YESTERDAY: STUDIES IN EUROPEAN CULTURE 1890-1914 (NY: Macmillan, 1961; rptd Lond: Weidenfeld and Nicolson, 1963; NY: Harper & Row, 1966; trans PROPHETEN VON GESTERN: ZUR EUROPÄISCHEN KULTUR [Frankfurt am Main: S. Fischer, 1965]), pp. 214, 236, 237, 239, 274-86, 288, 378, 395, 397, 412.
The essence of Shaw's thought emanates from the late Victorian and the Edwardian eras. The answers to the questions that arise from his contradictions may be found in the complexities of his youth. He was impatient with democracy. His plays bring to light the economic motivations in human behavior. Shaw differed from Marxism by refusing to accept the underlying thesis of materialism. [Survey of Shaw's economics, Life Force, and views of women.] His struggle for success made him view society as one great conspiracy. His art is a vegetarian's art, which never reaches the depth of human agony. His theses were neither destructive nor anarchic; they were part of European slum clearance.

562 Matlaw, Myron. "*You Never Can Tell* in the Theatre," Reg, IV (Aug 1961), 6-7.
[Stage history of *You Never Can Tell*.]

563 Meisel, Martin. "Shaw and the Nineteenth-Century Theater," DA, XXI (1961), 3788. Published dissertation, Princeton, 1960; pub as SHAW AND THE NINETEENTH CENTURY THEATER (Princeton, New Jersey: Princeton UP, 1963).

564 Mendelssohn, Peter de. THE AGE OF CHURCHILL, HERITAGE AND ADVENTURE, 1874-1911, vol. VI (NY: Alfred A. Knopf, 1961), pp. 87, 188, 236, 321, 327, 549-51.
Shaw was one of Churchill's earliest antipathies, but he ended admiring him as a man of letters.

565 Michaelis, Rolf. "Kritik und Information, Stuttgart" (Criticism and Information, Stuttgart), TH, II (Jan 1961), 35.
[Reviews *Pygmalion* produced by Günther Lüders.] The play is a mixture of a comic fairy tale and a cool demonstration of a scientific experiment. [In German.]

566 Mihelic, Mira. "George Bernard Shaw Covori" (George Bernard Shaw Speaks), GLEDALIŠKI LIST MESTNEGO GLEDALIŠČE (Ljubljana), XII (1961/62), 88-92.
[Not seen.] [In Slovenian.]

567 Mills, John Arvin. "Language and Laughter, A Study of Comic Diction in the Plays of B. Shaw," DA, XXII (1961), 4017-4018. Unpublished dissertation, Indiana University, 1961.

568 Montes, Jorge. "Celluloide: Shaw" (Celluloid: Shaw), ATLÁNTIDA (Argentina), XLIII (Jan 1961), 93.
the film version of *The Doctor's Dilemma* is another proof of the difficult task to recreate the work of an outdated author. [In Spanish.]

569 Morgan, Margery M. A DRAMA OF POLITICAL MAN, A STUDY IN THE PLAYS OF HARLEY GRANVILLE BARKER (Lond: Sidgwick & Jackson, 1961), passim.
[Shaw and Harley Granville-Barker.]

570 Neukirchen, Alfons. "Kritik und Information. Düsseldorf, Shaw, *Androklus und der Löwe*" (Criticism and Information. Dusseldorf, Shaw, *Androcles and the Lion*), TH, II (April 1961), 30.
[Reviews Alfons Neukirchen's production of *Androcles and the Lion*.] Shaw's play is both awkward and outdated. It does not suit the contemporary stage. [In German.]

571 Pallette, Drew B. "An Early Shaw Article on Actors," ShawR, IV (Jan 1961), 27-29.
When Shaw was its music critic, the DRAMATIC REVIEW published, on 19 September 1885, an almost hitherto unknown article by Shaw, "Qualifications of the Complete Actor." This article, employing satire and burlesque, was Shaw's contribution to the then-current debate over whether an actor was to develop his role by spontaneous emotion or by calculated technique. Shaw, a follower of the calculated technique school, urges the beginner to study: Sir Charles Bell, Spencer, Galton, Darwin; all the modern languages; the proceedings of scientific societies; wrestling; the arts and sciences; religious ritual; statistics.

572 Pašteka, Július. "Ideový dramatik--Shaw" (Shaw --Dramatist of Ideas), SLOVENSKY POHL'ED (Brno), LXXVII (1961), 123-24.
All Shaw's works are pamphlets or treatises of genius in dramatic form directed against the morality, the lifestyle and "humanism" of Puritan society. They are permeated with his own political views. All his ideological criticism of society is not philosophical, but cast in the form of dialogue. Fourteen of Shaw's plays are now translated into Slovak (2 volumes, 1956, 1960). Reading them, we see that his personality outdid his work, and he was more significant as a cultural figure than a creative artist. [In Slovak.]

573 Paxson, Omar Martin. "Bernard Shaw's Stage Directions," DA, XXI (1961), 2827. Unpublished dissertation, Northwestern University, 1960.

574 Pearson, Hesketh. BERNARD SHAW: HIS LIFE AND PERSONALITY (Lond: Methuen, 1961; NY: Atheneum, 1963; as BERNARD SHAW: DAS LEBEN-DER MENSCH, trans Otto Schütte (Tübingen: Rainer-Wunderlich, 1965).

[The first combined publication of Pearson's BERNARD SHAW: HIS LIFE AND PERSONALITY (London: Collins, 1942) and his G.B.S.: A POSTSCRIPT (NY: Harper & Brothers, 1950). A few episodes omitted from the original edition have been added.]

575 Pierce, Glenn Quimby, Jr. "Arnold Daly's Productions of Plays by Bernard Shaw," DA, XXI (1961), 3195. Unpublished dissertation, University of Illinois, 1960.

576 Pukhalo, Duman. "Pogovor u knjigi B. Sho *Kandida*" (Post-script to Bernard Shaw's *Candida*) in *Kandida*, by B. Sho (Belgrade: Rad, 1961), 84-92. [Not seen.] [In Serbian.]

577 Pumphrey, Byron. "Shaw as a Dramatic Critic," CShav, II (July-Aug 1961), n.p.
[Survey of Shaw's dramatic criticism, developing from his art and music criticism, and using the letters to Golding Bright as a source for Shaw's methods.]

578 Reinert, Otto. "Comment" and "Bernard Shaw," in DRAMA: AN INTRODUCTORY ANTHOLOGY, ed by Otto Reinert (Bost: Little, Brown, 1961), pp. 361-63, 645-46; "Bernard Shaw" reprinted, with modified list of suggested reading, in DRAMA: AN INTRODUCTORY ANTHOLOGY, ALTERNATE EDITION (Bost and Toronto: Little, Brown, 1964), pp. 880-81 and MODERN DRAMA, ALTERNATE EDITION (Bost and Toronto: Little, Brown, 1966), pp. 617-18.
What is chronicled in *Arms and the Man* is the conversion of Raina and Sergius from romantic idealism to healthy realism. The realism that the play substitutes for idealistic attitudes is not prosaic practical-mindedness; Bluntschli's "incurably romantic disposition" is responsible for almost every single plot development. The most significant dialogue in the play is Raina's remark that Bluntschli is the first man who did not take her seriously and his reply that she really means that he is the first man who *has* taken her seriously. [Appendix includes a brief biographical note on Shaw with a list of suggested reading.]

579 Rypins, Stanley, and Irving McKee. "Influential Women in Bernard Shaw's Life," PMLA, LXXVI (March 1961), 156-57.
[An exchange of four letters occasioned by a statement in McKee's article "Bernard Shaw's Beginnings on the London Stage," PMLA, LXXIV (Sept 1959), 470-481, that "Janet Achurch . . . was by far the most important woman in Shaw's adult life before his marriage in 1898."]

580 Scriabine, Vera. "Past Group Events," Reg, IV (Aug 1961), 7-9.
[Abstracts of talks by Stanley Rypins, "Bernard Shaw: Knight-Errant," and Dan H. Laurence, "Bernard Shaw and Arnold Daly."]

581 S[moker], B[arbara]. "Shaw's Marriage," SHAVIAN, II (Oct 1961), 30-31.
[A brief disagreement with C. G. L. DuCann, "The Shaw Marriage" (1961) and two further letters to the editor.]

582 Soper, Paul. "GBS as a Play Director," STUDIES IN HONOR OF JOHN C. HODGES AND ALWIN THALER [Tennessee Studies in Literature, Special Number], ed by Richard Beale Davis and John Leon Lievsay (Knoxville: U of Tennessee P, 1961, pp. 109-19.
Shaw exerted considerable influence on English stage production, and he paralleled his continental contemporaries, notably Stanislavsky. The key to Shaw's new acting is "the passion and intuition of the artist." He voiced his principles by attacks upon acting error: the rhetorical actor, the *hysterique*, the imitationist, and the personality actor. Shaw had a preference for speech above action. The positive response to those plays which he wrote and directed is the best evidence of his effectiveness.

583 Stanton, Stephen S. "Shaw's Debt to Scribe," PMLA, LXXVI (Dec 1961), 575-85.
It is known that Shaw cared little for Scribe (father of the "well-made" play) or for Scribe's disciple, Sardou. Shaw's first attack in print on Scribe appeared in the Preface to the first edition of *Widowers' Houses*; by 1895 Shaw was already beginning to sound tired as he scoffed at Sardou. In 1946 he took exception to Allardyce Nicoll's claim that Shaw's plays were indebted to the well-made plays he had known as a boy. Shaw used as many of the

tricks and devices of the stagecraft of Scribe as would
help him establish on the stage his early plays. One play
of Scribe's (BATAILLE DE DAMES) is the core of *Candida,*
The Devil's Disciple, Captain Brassbound's Conversion, and
Man and Superman. [Here follows a lengthy, detailed
establishing of parallels between BATAILLE DE DAMES and
Candida in structure and device, as well as similar parallels for *Disciple, Captain Brassbound,* and *Superman.*]
Scribean drama thus contributed greatly to the flowering
of the New Drama of Bernard Shaw. To make this claim is
not to deny Shaw's creative genius; his thought-charged
plays ranged far beyond the clever but tepid entertainments of such plays. But is is significant that Shaw
created an entertaining, yet lethal, satire of Victorian
complacency and sentimentalism through his provocative
adaptation of these tricks.

584 Stokes, E. E., Jr. "Morris and Bernard Shaw,"
JOURNAL OF THE WILLIAM MORRIS SOCIETY, I (Winter,
1961), 13-18; rptd in CShav, IV (July-Aug 1963),
n.p.
The influence on Shaw of William Morris was considerable
and can be seen in the care Shaw took with the physical
appearance of his published works. The principal
importance of the Morris-Shaw relationship, however, lay
in their both being Socialists, although each had come to
Socialism by a different route. Shaw's route was intellectual; Morris's, practical--a response to the ugliness
of his society. They discovered literary interests in
common--Dickens, Ruskin, Shakespeare--but while Shaw was a
Shelleyan, Morris preferred Keats. The two also found
common interests in art and architecture, although not in
music, for which Morris had no concern. Their artistic
relationship was carried on wholly in Morris's terms, and
in this respect, the influence of Morris on Shaw was
major.

585 Thon, Frederick. "And Two for the Money:
Pygmalion and MY FAIR LADY," CShav, II (March-April
1962), n.p.
[Comparison of Shaw's stage and film versions of *Pygmalion*
with MY FAIR LADY.]

586 Thorndike, Dame Sybil. "Foreword," SHAW THE
VILLAGER AND HUMAN BEING, ed by Allan Chappelow

(Lond: Charles Skilton, 1961; NY: Macmillan, 1962), pp. vii-viii.
Shaw had an immense interest in his fellow-beings.

587 Todisco, Alfredo. "Il Nuovo Pigmalione" (The
   New Pygmalion), IL MONDO, XIII (11 April 1961), 14.
Shaw's ideas have lost their bite in England's welfare
state. The great success of MY FAIR LADY is due not to
the pleasant tunes but to the theme of social climbing so
dear to the British public. [In Italian.]

588 Tompkins, Molly (Arthur). SHAW AND MOLLY
   TOMPKINS IN THEIR OWN WORDS, ed by Peter Tompkins
   (NY: Clarkson N. Potter, 1961).
[A linking of the letters of Shaw to Molly Tompkins (first
published as TO A YOUNG ACTRESS: THE LETTERS OF BERNARD
SHAW TO MOLLY TOMPKINS, ed with an introduction by Peter
Tompkins (Clarkson N. Potter, Inc., 1960) with Molly's
tape-recorded reminiscences, by her son. More about
Molly and her husband than about Shaw.]

589 Tynan, Kenneth. CURTAINS, SELECTIONS FROM THE
   DRAMA CRITICISM AND RELATED WRITINGS (NY: Atheneum,
   1961), pp. 8-9, 12, 19, 26-28, 29-30, 38, 40, 47,
   69, 76, 83, 92, 95, 107, 113, 118, 12-24, 135, 150-
   52, 184, 195, 228, 234, 237-38, 254, 266, 281-83,
   284, 351, 399, 427, 456, 460.
[A collection of reviews from 1951-1961, including those
of Shaw's plays (*Caesar and Cleopatra, The Millionairess,
Don Juan in Hell, Saint Joan* and MY FAIR LADY), on the
British and American stages.]

590 Urbascheck, Bruno. "Kritik und Information.
Kassel: Shaw, *Frau Warrens Gerwerbe*" (Criticism and
Information. Kassel: Shaw, *Mrs. Warren's Profes-
sion*), TH, II (June 1961), 27.
[A review of Otto Kurth's production of *Mrs. Warren's
Profession* at the Kassel Theater.] In Shaw's attitude
towards prostitution his hard Irish mentality is proved.
[In German.]

591 "Vom Briefwechsel zum Theaterstück. Notizen und
Aufführungsfotos zu Jerome Kiltys GELIEBTER LÜGNER"
(From Correspondence to Play. Notes and Photographs

Relating to Jerome Kilty's DEAR LIAR), TH, II (Nov 1961), 53-55.
[Briefly explains the genesis of Jerome Kilty's play DEAR LIAR, A COMEDY OF LETTERS. ADAPTED BY J. KILTY FROM THE CORRESPONDENCE OF BERNARD SHAW AND MRS. PATRICK CAMPBELL (Lond: Max Reinhardt, 1960). The notes introduce the German translation which is printed in the same issue of the journal, pp. I-XII.]

592 Weales, Gerald. RELIGION IN MODERN ENGLISH DRAMA (Phila: U of Pennsylvania P, 1961), pp. 55-79.
[Mentions Shaw, especially as critic of religious plays.] Shaw never accepted the basic tenets of orthodox Christianity but was willing to use Christian phrases to declare his own beliefs and to find practical, political, and social theories in the Gospels. He found the cross the most offensive element in Christianity. *The Devil's Disciple* says do not mask your behavior by dressing it in the doctrine of God or the Devil. In *Caesar and Cleopatra* there is the first indication of the idea of Creative Evolution, which is first specifically presented in *Man and Superman*. In *John Bull's Other Island*, Father Keegan's hell is a world of selfish gain, his heaven a kind of Socialistic vision. *Major Barbara* is Shaw's most perfect study of a religious personality; its major insistence is that no soul can be saved in a hungry body. This is his most important religious play. In *The Shewing-up of Blanco Posnet* the theme of the man who revolts and runs away from God only to be snapped back against his will is as old as Jonah--only the God is Shavian. *Androcles and the Lion* is a fable of any infant religion or political creed facing its oppressor; Ferrovius and Lavinia are more nearly Shavian regligious figures than is Androcles. *Back to Methuselah* is Shaw's most extensive presentation of Creative Evolution. The play is not to be taken literally, and Shaw faces the practical difficulties of every writer who tries to conceive of some sort of heaven. *Saint Joan* presents a natural genius, like Shaw's Caesar; one half of Joan is an embodiment of the Life Force, the other half a shrewd peasant girl. The prevailing tone of the plays after *Methuselah* is despair; the religious version of these largely political plays is *Too True to Be Good*. In *The Simpleton of the Unexpected Isles* Shaw presents a Judgment Day in which the mature world involves not the uplifting of the weak, but their erasure. *Barbara* and *Joan* are two of the most moving religious plays in the language. And in *Superman* Shaw came close to providing a

mythology for his own religion, without the ponderousness that marked *Methuselah.*

593 Webster, Grant. "Smollett and Shaw: A Note on a Source for *Heartbreak House*," ShawR, IV (Sept 1961), 16-17.
The device in *Heartbreak House* of the nautical setting may have originated in Smollett's PEREGRINE PICKLE. Shaw almost certainly read the novel before the play was written. *Heartbreak* follows PEREGRINE PICKLE in its general setting, in an expressed distrust of women, and in the characters of the heroes, Commodore Trunnion and Captain Shotover. The physical characteristics of the two, however, do not match.

594 Weisert, John J. "Clothes Make the Man," ShawR, IV (Jan 1961), 30-31.
Beginning about 1872, Dr. Gustav Jaeger, a Swabian zoologist, developed a rationale of human physiology based on these rules: wear Sanitary Woolen Clothing; sleep in and on wool; keep the bedroom window open at night. The human body gives off noxious emanations partly through the skin; wool, but not materials made from dead vegetable matter such as cotton and linen, can facilitate the evaporation of water from the skin. Shaw was an enthusiastic Jaegerite, but with reservations.

595 Wendt, Ernst. "Kritik und Information. Hamburg: Shaw, *Man kann nie wissen*" (Criticism and Information. Hamburg: Shaw, *You Never Can Tell*), TH, II (March 1961), 36.
[A review of Edward Rothe's production of *You Never Can Tell* at the Hamburger kammerspiele.] The play is very feeble, its problems are outdated, and the solution is a *tour de force.* [In German.]

596 West, E. J. "Disciple and Master: Shaw and Mozart," SHAVIAN, II (Feb 1961), 16-23.
[A brief record of Shaw's tributes over the years to Mozart, the composer and musician. There is no attempt to compare or contrast Shaw and Mozart.]

597 White, William. "Irish Antithesis: Shaw and Joyce," SHAVIAN, II (Feb 1961), 24-34.

[Shaw and Joyce never met, but this is an account of their "relationship," in which Shaw shows himself kinder and more generous.

598 Whitman, Wanda. "[Notes]," Reg, IV (Aug 1961), 5.
When the Black Girl in the *Adventures of the Black Girl in Her Search for God* settles down with the red-bearded gentleman, Shaw is not establishing a correspondence with an episode in his own life, but expressing the poliltical meaning found in *Peace Conference Hints*: "Nations which cannot intermarry without a strong sense of miscegenation will hardly arrive at laws or verdicts by the same process of reasoning."

599 Wilson, Edwin. "Introduction" and "Headnotes," SHAW ON SHAKESPEARE: AN ANTHOLOGY OF BERNARD SHAW'S WRITINGS ON THE PLAYS AND PRODUCTION OF SHAKESPEARE (NY: E. P. Dutton, 1961), pp. ix-xxii.
Shaw's assets as a Shakespearean critic are his knowledge of Shakespeare and Shakespearean criticism, his own dramatic ability, his critical faculty, and his brilliant prose style. He has prejudices as well: his predilection for the drama of Ibsen, his own essentially anti-tragic view of life, and his puritanism. Oddly his view that form is separable from and less important than content puts him on Shakespeare's side, because he could praise Shakespeare's art. Shaw is best as a critic of production. His criticism gives insight into himself.

600 Zeltmann, William. "Shaw, Farleigh and a Collection, ShawR, IV (May 1961), 24, 26-28.
The collaboration between John Farleigh, who illustrated *The Adventures of the Black Girl in Her Search for God*, and Shaw began with a letter from Shaw on 8 May 1932; in later letters Shaw supplied Farleigh with advice, word pictures and a dozen sketches and water colors. Farleigh comments that Shaw's drawing was vigorous and direct; it had an intellectual clarity. We are reminded that Henderson remarked that Shaw studied art as a lad and that the language of the artist might be better used to discuss him.

1962

601 Abbott, Anthony Sternsen. "Shaw and Christianity." Unpublished dissertation, Harvard University, 1962.
[Listed in DAID.]

602 Atkinson, Brooks. "Critic at Large: Shaw,
Despite Acts of Heartlessness, Showed a Real Concern
for Mankind," NYT, 24 July 1962, p. 24.
Was Shaw heartless? There is evidence on both sides.
Death stimulated Shaw's sense of humor. He was insensitive to the moods of others, and his political sentiments
could be inhuman. But there are also numerous incidents
of his personal kindliness and generosity. The motive for
his many years of devotion to Socialism was certainly the
welfare of mankind. He often said heartless things, but
he did not do them.

603 Atkinson, Brooks. "To G.B.S. the Idea Was the
Thing," NEW YORK TIMES BOOK REVIEW, 6 May 1962, pp.
1, 36-37.
[A review of the six volume COMPLETE PLAYS WITH PREFACES
(1962).] At the age of 93, Shaw could no longer write
plays, but he was still a formidable polemicist, alert to
political problems. He was a political animal who believed art should be didactic. He did not play tricks
with language or waste time on literary flourishes; ideas
were his obsession. He had no taste for debauches except
of intellectual argument; *Back to Methuselah* is the most
obvious of these. He could not be deliberately superficial. When he tried to be jocose, he became flat;
horseplay for the mob was not his forte. These volumes
make clear that Shaw was preoccupied with Shakespeare.
But as a polemicist, he was closer to Bunyan. Shaw and
Shakespeare were not at all alike, but they do complement
each other; Shakespeare was the master of verse, Shaw of
prose.

604 Austin, Don. "Dramatic Structure in *Caesar and
Cleopatra*," C Shav, III (Sept-Oct 1962), n.p.
Caesar and Cleopatra illuminates Cleopatra's growing
awareness of Caesar's greatness. Each of the first four

acts juxtaposes Cleopatra's world with Caesar's. Act V is a general reconciliation. Darkness and light serve as structural commentary as do pomp and ritual, though the ritualistic elements are undercut with irony to dramatize Cleopatra's change.

605 Batson, Eric. "Review-article on Beaverbrook, Shaw, and Jesus," CShav, III (Sept-Oct 1962), n.p.
There are some remarkable similarities and differences on the subject of Jesus between Shaw and Lord Beaverbrook in his THE DIVINE PROPAGANDIST.

606 Baylen, Joseph O. "George Bernard Shaw and the Socialist League, Some Unpublished Letters, "INTER-NATIONAL REVIEW OF SOCIAL HISTORY, VII (1962), 426-40.
Shaw cooperated with the Socialist League's attempts to educate the working class more out of respect for William Morris and the conviction that education must precede any change in the structure of society than agreement with Morris's rejection of Parliament. [Tests of Shaw communications to the Secretaries of the Socialist League.]

607 Baylen, Joseph O., and Patrick G. Hogan, Jr. "Shaw's Advice to Stead on the 'New Journalism'," JOURNALISM QUARTERLY, XXXIX (Winter 1962), 90-91.
While Shaw was a member of the literary staff of the PALL MALL GAZETTE, on two occasions he enlightened his editor, W. T. Stead, on what he thought should be the method and purpose of the "New Journalism" which Stead had launched at the PMG in February 1883. In a letter in the PMG in February, 1886, Shaw commended Stead for his revelations about the white slave traffic but said that the PMG was still a capitalist paper, which concentrated upon a study of men in power, not on principles. Shaw replied to a letter by John Ruskin (in a letter never published in the PMG) that Stead's paper was the only one with a chance of influencing someone; the PMG had earned this unique position from "its memorable resolution to attack social abuses with the terrible weapon of truth-telling." This was a plea for Stead to make his "New Journalism" even more outspoken in the struggle for social justice.

608 Bennett, Kenneth Chisholm, Jr. "George Bernard Shaw's Philosophy of Art," DA, XXII (1962), 3197. Unpublished dissertation, Indiana University, 1962.

609 Bernd, Daniel Walter. "The Dramatic Theory of G. B. Shaw," DA, XXIII (1962), 2910-11. Unpublished dissertation, University of Nebraska, 1962.

610 Briant, Keith. PASSIONATE PARADOX, THE LIFE OF MARIE STOPES (NY: W. W. Norton, 1962), pp. 171-84, 194-95, 206-9, 212-13, 228, 234.
Shaw's influence on the life of Marie Stopes stretched over 30 years, though he refused to become entangled as her active supporter. [Long quotation from Shaw about his mother and his childhood. The relationship among Stopes, Shaw, and Lord Alfred Douglas is examined.]

611 Brien, Alan. "A Clean, Well-lighted Mind," SPEC, 16 Feb 1962, pp. 211-12.
[A review, mixed with general remarks on Shaw, of SHAW ON SHAKESPEARE, ed by Edwin Wilson (1961); BERNARD SHAW: PLATFORM AND PULPIT, ed by Dan H. Laurence (1961); SHAW THE VILLAGER AND HUMAN BEING, ed by Allan Chapelow (1962).]

Shaw totally misunderstood Shakespeare, whose characters did not speak so as to reveal their moral, political, and social opinions. His devotion to common sense can be seen in his distrust of passion, his distaste for strong emotion, and his suspicion of sexual desire. Shaw applied the standards of common sense to politics as to poetry; his opponents either wilfully refused to understand or else they did not have the necessary information. In principle Shaw was a pacifist, but not in particular instances. He was almost always wrong on questions of practical politics. He was a yes-or-no thinker.

612 Brown, Alison. "The George Bernard Shaw Papers," CShav, III (Nov-Dec 1962), n.p.
[Description of copyright and non-copyright material in the Shaw papers of the British Museum.]

613 Brustein, Robert. THE THEATRE OF REVOLT, AN APPROACH TO MODERN DRAMA (Bost: Little, Brown, 1962, 1964), pp. 4, 6, 8-10, 12, 14, 17-28, 183-227,

231-33, 238n, 252, 283-85, 316, 321-22, 325, 345;
pp. 203-227 rptd in R. J. Kaufmann (ed), G. B. SHAW:
A COLLECTION OF CRITICAL ESSAYS (1965).
Shaw is Romantic in identifying himself with his heroes.
Shaw's rebels are both hopeful and longwinded. His drama
is messianic. [*Man and Superman* and *Back to Methuselah*.]
The drama itself is rhetorical; its significance lies less
in its content than in its stance. The hero's doctrine,
because the hero is abandoned by the playwright before the
play's end, is rarely realized, though *Methuselah* is an
exception. Although social revolt characterizes most of
Shaw, his political ideology is compromised in his plays;
in fact, it remains outside them.

Shaw was an artist as well as an ideologist, a literary
rebel and a social reformer, and this dualism must be
taken into account by any serious critic. He is sometimes
driven by his evangelical fervor into visionary wishful-
thinking of the most extreme sort, where conflict
subordinated to argument does not result in a masterpiece.
[*Methuselah* and *Too True to Be Good*.]

Shaw ignores what is most depressing in nineteenth-century
thought and in the end exhibits the emptiness of the
Victorian progressive temper. "The negative power of
Shaw's rebellion in *Heartbreak House* brings the play
closer to an authentic art of revolt than anything in the
Shavian canon." [Compares Shaw with Brecht, Pirandello
and O'Neill.]

614 Bullough, Geoffrey. "Literary Relations of
Shaw's Mrs. Warren," PHILOLOGICAL QUARTERLY, XLI
(Jan 1962), 339-58; rptd CShav, III (July-Aug 1962),
n.p.
Janet Achurch told Shaw the story of YVETTE by de
Maupassant; it came to form one of the bases for *MRS.
WARREN'S PROFESSION*. "To explore the relationship between
YVETTE, Mrs. Warren, and MRS. DAINTREE'S DAUGHTER [a play
by Achurch also based on YVETTE] throws light on Shaw's
mind and on the . . . ways in which the same situation
could inspire three writers." Shaw regarded Maupassant's
tale as "ultra-romantic," but he underestimated its actual
realism. Mrs. Warren is conceived in a blend of sympathy
and satire. Shaw brings out the grossness of her life
more than de Maupassant does. Mrs. Warren's standards are
those of the respectable, while the Marquise is openly
happy in her shady world. For Shaw, Mrs. Warren exemplifies the economic basis of morals and class-distinctions.
Vivie is unlike Yvette, who was a "womanly woman." Shaw

was helped in his delineation of her as a well-known type of University woman, by his acquaintance with 22-year-old Arabella Susan Lawrence, then in Fabian circles.

Mrs. Warren is like the Marquise in her early background, her realization of the value of savings, her moral obliquity. Her defense in her vindication scene is roughly the same as the Marquise's. This defense is a natural outcome of a similar defense in *Cashel Byron's Profession* (hence the title of the play).

Miss Achurch's play, MRS. DAINTREE'S DAUGHTER, is significant as perhaps the first play in which Shaw's dramatic influence made itself felt.

615 Burgaft, E. M. "Dvoĭnoĭ aspekt dramaturgii Bernarda Shou" (Dual Aspect of Bernard Shaw's Dramaturgy), UCHENYE ZAPISKI UL'IANSKOGO PED. INST. (Ulianovsk), XVII (1962), 123-52.
[Not seen.] [In Russian.]

616 Calvin, Judith S. "The GBSence of Giraudoux," ShawR, V (Jan 1962), 21-35.
Shaw and Giraudoux probably never met, and there is no evidence that either was familiar with the other's works, yet traces of Shavian thought permeate Giraudoux's plays. The most evident areas of comparison are: *Saint Joan* and ONDINE; the ideal woman theme; Father Keegan and Countess Aurelia, the super-sane lunatics; and the historical plays. In addition, traces of Shaw's Life Force and original morality are seen most predominantly in JUDITH (1931) and THE ENCHANTED (1933).

617 Carlson, Marvin Albert. "The Théâtre Libre, The Freie Bühne, The Independent Theatre, A Comparative Study," DA, XXII (1962), 2504. Unpublished dissertation, Cornell University, 1961.

618 C[astello], G[iulio] C[esare]. "Shaw, George Bernard," in ENCICLOPEDIA DELLO SPETTACOLO, VOL VIII (Roma: Casa Editrice le Maschere, 1962), pp. 1920-33.
[Survey of Shaw's life and work. Photographs of productions.] [In Italian.]

619 Cherry, D. R. "The Fabianism of Shaw," QQ, LXIX (Spring 1962), 83-93.
Many admirers of Shaw's plays ignore the less subtle propaganda of his Socialist pamphlets and thus fail to understand the basis of his political position. Since Shaw defines fine art as "the subtlest . . . the most effective instrument of moral propaganda" it is necessary to understand the propaganda of his pamphlets. A constant theme in Shaw was the immorality of capitalism. In economics, Shaw rejected Marx and followed Jevons. Shaw attempts to describe modern industrial capitalism through an analysis of land use and the development of an agricultural economy. His study of economics stood him in good stead when he came to write his early plays. In the eighties Shaw's essays were largely concerned with economics, in the nineties with the political stratregy of Socialism. Shaw patiently demonstrated to Socialists that their hope lay in using the State as an instrument of reform. His first solution was permeation, his second a plan for a political party pledged to Socialist principles. Romantic Socialism was always anathema to Shaw. Years of executive and committee work gave Shaw the right to criticize the democratic process, and we should therefore take him seriously when he points out weaknesses. Shaw's major contribution to Socialism was not a shocking radicalism, but his insistence on Socialism's moral superiority to capitalism.

620 Cherry, D. R. "Shaw's Novels," DALHOUSIE REVIEW, XLII (Winter 1962-63), 459-71.
The Irrational Knot and *Cashel Byron's Profession* should find readers who are scholars or Socialists as well as readers who are neither. Even with encouragement it is unlikely that Shaw could have become a successful novelist. He was out of sympathy with realism. The novels are most useful as a source of the ideas of the later plays.

621 Diakonova, Nina. "Shaw in the Soviet Union," SOVIET LITERATURE, No. 11 (1962), 153-56.
[Survey of the mutual interest of Shaw and the Soviet Union.]

622 Duerksen, Roland A. "Shelleyan Ideas in Victorian Literature," DA, XXII (March 1962), 3198-99.
Dissertation, published as SHELLEYAN IDEAS IN

VICTORIAN LITERATURE (The Hague: Mouton, 1966).
[Chapter VII "Shelley and Shaw," PMLA (1963).]

623 Eaton, Peter.   "Shaw and Shaviana," BOOK COLLEC-
TOR, XI (Autumn 1962), 349-50.
The author, a bookseller, acquired the entire stock of a
pamphlet by Shaw, *Are We Heading for War*. He has acquired
various presentation copies of Shaw's plays, and he
bought the books Shaw left behind when he left Fitzroy
Square. He also acquired 20 sheets of love poems from GBS
to Ellen Terry.

624 "The Exuberant Anarchist," TLS (9 Feb 1962), p.
88.
[Remarks occasioned by a review of PLATFORM AND PULPIT, ed
by Dan H. Laurence (1961) and of SHAW ON SHAKESPEARE, ed
by Edwin Wilson (1961).]

From 1880 to 1933, Shaw spoke on any occasion and on every
conceivable subject. His political gospel derived from
George, Ruskin, and Marx. His value lay in prying open
minds and demolishing prejudices by ridicule. The causes
he espoused were much the same as those propagated in his
plays. Shaw's life-long attack on Shakespeare suggests
that he was never quite sure he had defeated Shakespeare.
Shaw was perhaps not taken seriously as a Shakespeare
critic because he was the victim of his own bombast.
Shaw's attacks have had no lasting effect on Shakespearian
stage practice, but we should recognize Shaw's claim to be
the successor of Shakespeare.

625 Forster, E[dward] M[organ].   "Letter" LETTERS TO
T. E. LAWRENCE, ed by A. W. Lawrence (Lond: Jona-
than Cape, 1962), p. 101.
Shaw was pleasant.

626 Fridberg, L. M.   "K voprosu o perdache iazykovoi
kharateristiki personazhei na materiale analyza
p'ecy B. Shou *Pigmalion*" (On the Question of
Transferring the Linguistic Character in the Speech
of Characters in B. Shaw's *Pygmalion*), UCHENYE
ZAPISKI TASHKENT GOS. PED. INST. (Tashkent), VI
(1962), 375-95.
[Not seen.] [In Georgian and Russian.]

627 Fromm, Harold. "Bernard Shaw and the Theaters in the Nineties," DA, XXIII (1962), 1364-65. Unpublished dissertation, University of Wisconsin, 1962.

628 Garnett, Edward. "Letter," LETTERS TO T. E. LAWRENCE, ed by A. W. Lawrence (Lond: Jonathon Cape, 1962), p. 101.
Don't show Shaw THE MINT, if people are not to talk of it, as it will suit his reforming.

629 Gassner, John. "Bernard Shaw and the Making of the Modern Mind," COLLEGE ENGLISH, XXIII (April 1962), 517-25; rptd BERNARD SHAW'S PLAYS, ed by Warren Sylvester Smith (1970).
Shaw's achievement as a literary and dramatic genius lay in his ability to reconcile his pedagogical and histrionic inclinations.

Dramatic Criticism: Shaw clearly saw that Pinero's fashionable realism was only a pretense. The majority of Shaw's contemporaries were interested in "well-made" plays; Shaw was only interested if they were provocative dramas of ideas. Shaw was the champion, not of Ibsen's provincial realism, but of his "play of ideas"—and looked forward to the art of such as O'Casey, Pirandello, Giraudoux, and Brecht.

Estheticism: Though he defended Art against Philistine attacks, he rejected art for art's sake.

Feminism: Shaw is an ardent feminist, yet can satirize feminist fads and extravagances.

Social Reform: Shaw saw clearly the unreliability of social progress and the failure of parliamentary democracy. He wanted to believe in saviour-heroes; in his view of Mussolini, Hitler, and Stalin he is typical of the divided and self-betrayed modern mind. Shaw was also tripped up by his faith in collectivism. He demonstrated an exaggerated trust in economics. Shaw is most a man of the twentieth century in his trust in the desirability and inevitability of progress and in his impatience with delay in gradualist reform.

630 Geduld, H[arry] M. "Bernard Shaw, Vestryman and Borough Councillor," CShav, III (May-June 1962), n.p., rptd SHAVIAN, II (June 1964), 7-13.

[History of Shaw's term of office as Vestryman and Councillor of St. Pancras (1897-1903), including references to and excerpts from the Vestry and Council MINUTES.]

631 Geduld, H[arry] M. "The Textual Problem in Shaw," ShawR, V (May 1962), 54-60.
A number of Shaw scholars question whether the implementation of a Shaw variorum is premature or even necessary. The author's difficulties with a textual survey of *Back to Methuselah* give evidence of the problems involved. [Here follows a summary of the survey, highly detailed, of the various editions, impressions, additions to the dialogue by Shaw.] The conclusion is that there is sufficient justification for a variorum.

632 Grazhdanskaĭa, Zoĭâ Tikhonovna. "Dramaturgiĭâ B. Shou mezhdu 1905 i 1914 godami" (Shaw's Dramaturgy between 1905 and 1914), UCHENYE ZAPISKI MOSKOVSKOGO OBL PED. INSTITUTA (Moscow), III (1962), 5-7.
[Not seen.] [In Russian.]

633 Grunwald, Henry Anatole. "The Disappearance of Don Juan," HORIZON, IV (Jan 1962), 56-65.
Man and Superman is the last major work in which Don Juan appears. Jack Tanner is unable to conquer women and unable to carry out his rebellion against God.

634 Huss, Roy. "Max the 'Incomparable' on G. B. S. the 'Irrepressible,'" ShawR, V (Jan 1962), 10-20.
The uncertainty of Beerbohm's reaction to the early Shaw was probably an attempt to cope with an unprecedented talent. Beerbohm judged that Shaw was not influenced by Ibsen in dramatic method or purpose; he also felt that Shaw's comic originality surmounted the Ibsen influence. Beerbohm seems to have attacked Shaw on three main points: 1) His characters were lifeless and artificial when judged by the standards of modern realism. 2) Shavian philosophy was an eccentric personal idealism. 3) Most importantly, Beerbohm saw serious defects in Shaw's mixture of forms and his loosening of form or substitution of rhetorical forms that were nondramatic. He welcomed Shaw's abandonment of a predominantly serious tone in his early plays, because he felt that frivolity negated seriousness. Beerbohm complained also that Shaw was often a writer of

discussions, Platonic dialogues, or debates--but not drama. He was right in seeing *Getting Married* and *Misalliance* as a "symposium," but he has misunderstood the nature of Shaw's use of the comic *agon*, in which the underlying pattern is: intelligent flexibility, mistakenly thought to be inadequate, defeating private or social inflexibility, erroneously felt to be adequate. In 1905, Beerbohm recanted all his previous statements about Shaw and admitted that a play, judged poor when read, turned out truly dramatic on the stage. Max attacked *Man and Superman* on all three of his grounds but still found in the play a compensating freshness and skill. He most applauded the play as "a complete expression of the most distinct personality in current literature." He also enjoyed *You Never Can Tell* for its revelation of the author's delightfully contradictory temperament.

635 James, Eugene Nelson. "The Critic as Dramatist: George Bernard Shaw, 1895-1898," ShawR, V (Sept 1962), 97-108.

In his dramatic reviews from 1895 to 1898, Shaw attacked four sorts of plays: the high society farce, the pseudo-religious play, the woman-with-a-past story, and the sentimental romance. Shaw gives in his reviews indications as to how the plays *should* have been written. His Prefaces (cf. those to *Plays: Pleasant and Unpleasant* and *Three Plays for Puritans*) give some hints that in his own dramatic practice he was trying to write better plays on the same four formulae; he may also have been trying to correct his contemporaries by example. Shaw's version of the high-society IMPORTANCE OF BEING EARNEST is *You Never Can Tell*. *The Devil's Disciple* is Shaw's religious play, analogous to Jones' MICHAEL AND HIS LOST ANGEL. *Caesar and Cleopatra* is Shaw's "rewrite" of THE SECOND MRS. TANQUERAY, presenting Cleopatra as a *real* version of the "ill-tempered sensual woman." The sentimental romance, THE LITTLE MINISTER, by Barrie, is answered by *Captain Brassbound's Conversion*, though the resemblances between the two are not so clear as in the other plays. In Shaw's play we have a serious treatment of the theme of finding a trustworthy leader and characters who are humanly and naturally inconsistent, not following romantic presuppositions.

636 John, Augustus. "Letter," LETTERS TO T. E. LAWRENCE, ed by A. W. Lawrence (Lond: Jonathan Cape, 1962), pp. 119-20.

I hear you are Shaw's son.

637 Jones, A. R. "George Bernard Shaw," CONTEMPOR-
ARY THEATRE, ed by John Russell Brown and Bernard
Harris (Lond: Edward Arnold [Stratford-upon-Avon
Studies], 1962), pp. 57-75.
One wonders why modern playwrights such as Osborne,
Wesker, or Arden, who are interested in using the theater
as a vehicle for social and political ideas, reject the
example of Shaw. Shaw carried on his fight almost single-
handedly against the social and theatrical Establishment.
Technically, he strove for the ability to manipulate the
discussion of a moral problem within the framework of
naturalistic drama. In *Plays Unpleasant* Shaw gets around
his inability to construct a plot by using and parodying
the plot of the well-made play. He was only partly
successful in that ideas moved the characters rather than
arising from the dramatic conflict. These plays have an
artificial and contrived quality, which does not entirely
carry dramatic conviction. In *Arms and the Man* discussion
more interpenetrates the action. Shaw was clearly trying
to find a dramatic form in which discussion and drama
would coalesce. But by parodying his precursors' plays,
though his own were superior, he produced nothing
different in kind. In *Man of Destiny* and *Caesar and
Cleopatra*, Shaw begins to take an interest in the extraordinary man, who is developed in *Man and Superman*. In
ideas, character, and plot, Shaw does not challenge the
conventions head-on, but he attempts to widen the range of
possibilities. He is engaged in reform, not revolution.
His most thorough-going analysis of society is *Major
Barbara*, which is an indictment of religious and political
idealism for neglecting the social realities of power.

As a dramatist, Shaw is in the tradition of Goldsmith,
Sheridan, and Wilde, moving with superb skill in the
conventions of the comedy of manners. *Pygmalion* is a
Victorian success story. In *Heartbreak House* he expresses
his romantic dissatisfactions. His admiration for
dictators shows the extent of his disillusion with
society. Shaw's prose style is to be highly praised.
[Examples from *Devil's Disciple*, *Barbara*, and *Candida*.]
Shaw extended the comedy of manners by introducing social
and political ideas; he insisted on drama as a serious art
form.

638 Kantorovich, I. B. "*Dom, gde pazbivaiutsia
serdtsa i krizis fabianizma Shou*" (*Heartbreak House*
and the Crisis of Fabianism in Shaw), UCHENYE ZAPI-

SKI PERMSKOGO UNIVERSITETA (Perm), XXIII (1962), 26-39.
[Not seen.] [In Russian.]

639 Kerr, Walter. "First Night Report," NYHT, 21 Feb 1962, n. p.
The Old Vic's current production of *Saint Joan* invites the audience to examine the ironic comedy and the heroic content separately.

640 Kim, C. K. "Bernard Shaw on Education," ENGLISH LANGUAGE AND LITERATURE (Korea), XI (June 1962), 130-46.
Because Shaw used social deviance and immorality, it is possible to conclude that he has a social activist philosophy for his drama. In the character Lexy in *Candida* and Tanner in *Man and Superman* Shaw slanders college education. Cleopatra and Eliza have a successful education through experience. So, too, has Percival in *Misalliance*. [Brief decription of the Life Force.] Shaw's own formal education was horrible. The perfect education is achieved when the Life Force, through effort and will, develops through experience. [In Korean.]

641 King, Seth S. "The Millions Roll In," NYTMag, 18 Feb 1962, pp. 27-28, 30.
Shaw deliberately cultivated a reputation for rapacity and meanness and refused to concede that he had any aptitude for making money. When he died, however, he left an estate of $1,028,252, and in the eleven years since his death, his works, principally *Pygmalion* as the basis for MY FAIR LADY, have brought in more than 2.1 million. Though Shaw tried to make his Will fool-proof and litigation-proof, it was seven years before the beneficiaries started getting their money because of (successful) challenges to the "alphabet trust." Meanwhile Shaw remains popular on stage and screen, and the money keeps coming in.

642 Klein, John W. "Shaw and Brieux--An Enigma," DRAMA, ns LXVII (Winter 1962), 33-35.
The idolatry of Shaw and Mrs. Shaw for Brieux, Shaw's intellectual inferior, is strange. Shaw tended to overlook the fact that French drama between the Renaissance and the Moderns is not so poor as English. There is little evidence that Brieux's ideas influenced

Shaw. It was his puritanical earnestness that must have attracted him. Shaw had to disregard Brieux's jingoism.

643 Knight, G. Wilson. "Shaw," THE GOLDEN LABY-RINTH: A STUDY OF BRITISH DRAMA (Lond: Phoenix House, 1962), pp. 342-54; rptd in R. J. Kaufmann (ed), G. B. SHAW: A COLLECTION OF CRITICAL ESSAYS (1965), pp. 119-29.
Shaw is a critic, humorist, and visionary, related to Marx, Goethe, Lamarck, Wagner, Ibsen, and Nietzsche. He regards self-deception as more dangerous than criminality. He has sympathy with energies, and his thought ranges widely; he brings comedy to bear on subjects usually reserved for tragedy. His considered philosophy is evolutionary, the Life Force, which is particularly strong in women. This is the context in which we must understand Shaw's dramatic Socialism--which contains strong aristocratic sympathies as seen in *Captain Brassbound's Conversion, Misalliance, On the Rocks,* and *The Apple Cart.* In these plays we see the necessity of the interdependence of aristocracy and democracy. Similarly, power must be bisexual, as in *Man and Superman, Candida,* and Lady Cicely. Accordingly, Shaw presents a number of part-feminine men: Dubedat, the boy Bentley in *Misalliance,* Marchbanks, the Dauphin. Integration conditions male leadership; the firmest realization of this is Caesar in *Caesar and Cleopatra.* Shaw likes soldiers (Bluntschli, Private Meek); they are often associated with religion (Major Barbara, Anthony Anderson, the Roman captain in *Androcles and the Lion.)* The approach to the character may be mystical: Mrs. George in *Getting Married,* Keegan, Captain Shotover, Saint Joan. This other-worldly metaphysic often follows in its method the teachings of Spiritualism in the hearing of voices or receiving of messages. Shaw's dramas are shot through with comedy. Vengeful retaliation is repudiated, as in the Gunner in *Misalliance* and the avenging pirate in *Captain Brassbound;* he also repudiates both the Crucifixion and Hell. Superficialities of all sorts are also overturned. Shaw relies on comic surprise to replace the tensions and expectations of tragedy. The comic surprises come from "the inexhaustable stores of futurity." Such humor is never cruel. Shaw's prose style may be bare, but his drama is colorful as seen in rich costumes and the wide variety of often exotic settings.

644 Kocztur, Gizella. "G. B. Shaw," in UNIVERSAL
HANDBOOK OF WORLD LITERATURE (Budapest: Tanköny-
vkiado, 1962), pp. 116-32.
[Not seen.] [In Hungarian.]

645 Komatsu, Motoya. "Saint Joan Kosatsu" (On *Saint
Joan*), AKITA DAIGAKU GAKUGEIGAKUBU KENKYUKIYO
(Akita), (Jinbunkagaku) No. 12 (March 1962), pp. 14-
27.
What Shaw tries to depict in *Saint Joan* is the process of
the individual clashing against the social order. [In
Japanese.]

646 Lapan, Maureen Thérèse. "An Analysis of
Selected Plays of George Bernard Shaw as Media for
the Examination of 'Closed Areas' of Contemporary
Society by Secondary-School Students," DA, XXIII
(1962), 1557-58. Unpublished dissertation, University of Connecticut, 1962.

647 Laurence, Dan H., and David H. Greene.
"Introduction," THE MATTER WITH IRELAND, ed by Dan
H. Laurence and David H. Greene (NY: Hill & Wang,
1962), pp. ix-xv.
Shaw lived in Ireland for only 20 of his 94 years, and it
is remarkable how objective, temperate, and wise Shaw
could be in the midst of the rabid partisanship on the
"Irish Question." It is also surprising to learn just how
concerned Shaw was about the problems of his native
country. Shaw was always ready with good advice and
guidance for those who traveled the road of Home Rule,
though he himself did not. Over 60 years he addressed
himself to virtually every important question in Ireland's
political and social life: he defended Home Rule; he
renounced Irish nationalism *per se*; he thought that
partition was evil; he had little sympathy for the
artificial revival of Gaelic; he was unhappy about Irish
literary censorship; he believed that Ireland was wrong to
remain neutral in World War II; he was eloquent in
defending individual Irishmen of courage and good
conscience.

648 Lawrence, D[avid] H[erbert]. THE COLLECTED
LETTERS OF D. H. LAWRENCE, 2 Vols, ed by Harry T.
Moore (NY: Viking P, 1962), pp. 12, 42, 44, 182,
205, 877, 979-80.

"Do not think because I rave at Bernard Shaw I don't like him."

649 L[azar?], M[agda]. "George Bernard Shaw,"
"Shaw: Szerelmi Házasság" (Shaw: Marriage Founded
on Love [*Getting Married* or *Misalliance*?]), "Shaw:
Candida," "Shaw: Az Ör dög, Cimborája" (Shaw: *The
Devil's Disciple*), "Shaw: Warrenné Mestersége"
(Shaw: *Mrs. Warren's Profession*), "Shaw: Sosem
Lehet Tudni" (Shaw: *You Never Can Tell*), "Shaw:
Ember és Felsöbbrendü Ember (Shaw: *Man and Super-
man*), "Shaw: Pygmalion," and "Shaw: Szent Johanna"
(Shaw: *Saint Joan*) in Vajda, Gyorgy Mihaly, ed,
SZÍNHÁZI KALAUZ (Theatrical Leader) (Budapest:
Gondolat Kiado, 1962), pp. 727-47.
[Short biography with critical synopses of the plays.]
[In Hungarian.]

650 Leary, Daniel J. "The Moral Dialectic in *Caesar
and Cleopatra*," ShawR, V (May 1962), 42-53.
In *Caesar and Cleopatra* where "blurring" between opposites
occurs, "it is due not to 'trickery' but to artistic and
philosophic integrity," and where dissociation occurs,
there is actually a meaningful tension between opposites.
[The approach is by a sustaining reference to Bergson's
THE TWO SOURCES OF MORALITY AND RELIGION to set out Shaw's
view of human psychology, and by applying to Shaw's
dramatic structuring and characterization a theory of
"dialectic action."

651 Lecky, Eleazer. "Lecky on Shaw on Shakespeare,"
CShav, III (July-Aug 1962), n.p.
"Although his criticism of Shakespeare lacks comprehen-
siveness, it is the best criticism of Shakespeare in
performance that we are likely to get." [Essay-review of
SHAW ON SHAKESPEARE by Edwin Wilson (1961).]

652 Lewis, Allan. "The Drama of Discussion--George
Bernard Shaw," THE CONTEMPORARY THEATRE: THE SIG-
NIFICANT PLAYWRIGHTS OF OUR TIME (NY: Crown Publishers, 1962), pp. 80-111.
Widowers' Houses, though a failure in its initial
presentation, showed the three factors of wit, Socialism,
and discussion which Shaw was to contribute to the modern
theater.   Whereas Ibsen was interested in the moral
rehabilitation of man, Shaw dealt with economic conditions

that alter human nature, as in *Widowers' Houses* and *Mrs. Warren's Profession*. *Candida* shows a growing perfection in Shaw's use of discussion and inversion. *Man and Superman* is actually a sparkling debate between the passion for Truth and the Passion for Motherhood; the discussion is clearest in the Don Juan Interlude. In *Major Barbara* Shaw is concerned with the nonsense that surrounds the virtue of poverty in modern industrial society. *Heartbreak House*, the best of Shaw's disquisitory plays, is typical of the decade of disillusion for Shaw, 1910-1920. The making of Shaw the rebel came mainly from Wagner, Ibsen, and Marx; the Fabian belief in proper action in the proper direction by proper people drew Shaw to the concept of the unique individual. Shaw is most successful when he arranges the conflict of ideas in the form of a musical composition, as in *Heartbreak, Barbara,* and *Saint Joan*; he proves that it is futile to say that discussion cannot be drama. Shaw could create memorable characters, but they are less important than the ideas they represent. In most modern drama, characters do not know what they want, but in *Heartbreak* the characters are fully aware. In the drama of discussion, there can be no heroes or villains; therefore, Shaw leans over backward to show the virtues of the villain. Shaw rarely realized the fusion of art and message, but he did in *Heartbreak* and *Joan*.

653 McBriar, A. M. FABIAN SOCIALISM AND ENGLISH POLITICS 1884-1918 (Cambridge: Cambridge UP, 1962), passim.
[Shaw and Fabian doctrine.]

654 Manning, Frederick. "Letters," in LETTERS TO T. E. LAWRENCE, ed by A. W. Lawrence (Lond: Jonathan Cape, 1962), pp. 142, 143, 144.
Shaw is a sophist too Protean to be refuted cursorily. [Some discussion of Lawrence as the model for Private Meek in *Too True to Be Good*.]

655 Manolescu, Ion. AMINTIRI (Memories) (Bucureşti: Editura Meridiane: 1962), pp. 134, 244.
[Manolescu, Romanian actor-director, discusses C. I. Nottara's performance in *The Doctor's Dilemma* and Paul Gusty's stage directions for *Misalliance*.] [In Romanian.]

656 Mayer, Hans. "Der Dramatiker Bernard Shaw" (Bernard Shaw, the Dramatist), ANSICHTEN ZUR LITERATUR DER ZEIT (Reinbek bei Hamburg: Rowohlt, 1962), pp. 119-32; rptd in NEUE DEUTSCHE HEFTE, LXXXIX (Sept-Oct 1962), 91-110, and "George Bernard Shaw," ENGLISCHE DICHTER DER MODERNE. IHR LEBEN UND WERK (Modern English Writers. Their Life and Work), ed by Rudolf Sühnel and Dieter Riesner (Berlin: Erich Schmidt Verlag, 1971), pp. 165-79.

Unlike Goethe and Thomas Mann, Shaw never saw himself in a historic light since the structure of the society he attacked never changed. There are two common misinterpretations of Shaw: Shaw as a mere clown, and Shaw as a mere Fabian social critic. He was always a social critic and a sensitive artist. His new drama contains many musical and epic elements. His characters are full of contradictions; there is no organic development. Characteristic of Shaw's drama are characters - mostly female - who serve as commentators representing the author's view. [In German.]

657 Meisel, Martin. "Political Extravaganza," THEATRE SURVEY, III (1962), 19-31.

The Political Extravaganza did not die in the nineteenth century. It is the dominant mode of Shaw's last period from *Back to Methuselah* on.

658 Meredith, Charles. "Towards a Shaw Theatre," CShav, III (Nov-Dec 1962), n.p.

Shaw would head the list of playwrights to be produced by a doctrinal theater, for a Shaw Theater is the most needed by a world in disastrous confusion.

659 Morgan, Margery M. "Bernard Shaw on the Tightrope," MD, IV (Feb 1962), 343-54.

Shaw's *Misalliance* and Granville Barker's THE MADRAS HOUSE (July 1910) are truly companion pieces. The principal themes treated in Barker's opening pages are religion, food, commerce, women, talk, and revolution. Shaw uses all of these. The first physical gestures of the two plays are also related. Shaw has also borrowed from Euripides' THE BACCHAE. But there is no room for the tragic catastrophe of Euripides in *Misalliance*. The most prominent misalliance is beast and God. Nietzsche has said that humanity is a tightrope between beast and superman. In one sense, the elements of Shaw's play were thought out in Barker's dense and introvert drama.

Misalliance is founded in burlesque but has a kind of beauty in the rhythm of its development, its energy, and the significance of its recurring images.

660 Morgan, Margery M. "Two Varieties of Political Drama: *The Apple Cart* and Granville Barker's HIS MAJESTY," SHAVIAN, II (April 1962), 9-16.
One of the sources of *The Apple Cart* was a political satire, KING JOHN OF JINGALO (1912) by Laurence Housman. In 1928 Shaw was reminded of this work by the publication of Granville Barker's HIS MAJESTY, a play with some features of Housman's work. Barker's play took five years to write and is much more ambitious in scale and conception than *Cart*; it has never been professionally performed. Similar identities in Shaw's and Barker's plays are obscured by differences of method: Shaw's play is *opera bouffe*, Barker's is tragi-comedy. *Cart* is important for its penetrating exposure of the divorce between power and the functions of government. The "Mozartian overture" to Shaw's play is based on many of the same *leitmotifs* as Barker's; king as a metaphysical not political conception; the difference between a formal and a meaningful symbolism; the metaphor of the world-theater; the motif of faith; the distinction between the actual nature and the potentiality of the mob. The difference in emphasis makes Shaw and Barker distinct; Shaw is more abstract and more concerned with political institutions, Barker more subjective.

661 Newman, Ernest. TESTAMENT OF MUSIC (Lond: Putnam, 1962), pp. xv, 115-62, 268, 298.
[Shaw-Newman controversy over Strauss; letters to the NATION, 1910-1914.] The fault of *Man and Superman* is that Shaw insists that we take it seriously rather than accept it simply as an amusing comedy. It would be too bad if some future literary historian, drawing only on the many attacks on him, should conclude that Shaw was never understood in his lifetime.

662 Nicoll, Allardyce. THE THEATRE AND DRAMATIC THEORY (NY: Barnes & Noble, 1962), pp. 56, 58, 74, 153-54.
[Shaw used as an example of dramatic technique.]

663 Nucete Sarde, J. "Bernard Shaw: su teatro y su mejor personaje" (Bernard Shaw: His Theater and His Finest Character), REVISTA NACIONAL DE CULTURA (Venezuela), XXIV (1962), 21-33.
Shaw possessed an unbreakable resolution to be, at every moment and in every circumstance of his life, always himself. He was his own best dramatic creation. [In Spanish.]

664 O'Donnell, Norbert F. "The Conflict of Wills in Shaw's Tragicomedy," MD, IV (Feb 1962), 413-25; rptd in R. J. Kaufmann (ed), G. B. SHAW: A COLLECTION OF CRITICAL ESSAYS (1965).
Shaw's plays portray life in which will is the key to human motives and relationships. Intimidation by another is the worst thing that can happen to someone. The best thing is the sense of assurance which comes from insight into another's motives and thus gives an ability to control the outcome of the conflict of wills. The strife of wills occurs in Shaw between 1) parents and children—they are never emotionally bound together in Shaw's drama, 2) lovers, e.g. *Captain Brassbound's Conversion, Man and Superman,* and 3) married couples such as Hector and Hesione Hushabye. The conflict of wills results in several sorts of moments of true feeling: 1) nakedness, e.g., Eliza's defeat when she first comes to Higgins' house, Mangan's reaction to the frankness at Heartbreak House, Mrs. Warren, the anguished Elderly Gentleman; 2) disillusionment, e.g., Eliza throwing the slipper, Captain Brassbound, Major Barbara, Ellie Dunn, the Preacher in *Too True to Be Good*; 3) conversion, e.g., Eliza, Brassbound, Barbara. When Shaw preserves some feeling for individuals in their struggle to assert their wills, he is a tragedian; when he regards them with amused detachment, he is a comedian. His usual attitude is detached amusement.

665 Ohmann, Richard M. SHAW: THE STYLE AND THE MAN (Middletown, Connecticut: Wesleyan UP, 1962); Chap. III rptd in R. J. Kauffmann (ed), G. B. SHAW: A COLLECTION OF CRITICAL ESSAYS (1965); Edward P. J. Corbett (ed) RHETORICAL ANALYSIS OF LITERARY WORKS (1969), pp. 204-13.
Shaw is the most impressive writer of expository English prose in this century. Shaw employs the following Modes of Order: 1) Collections of Things, 2) Likenesses, 3) Luck or Cunning, and 4) Similarity and Exaggeration. Shaw's iconoclasm is only superficially paradoxical. Change can imply: 1) A change of contiguity order (rather

than of similarity patterns), or 2) a succession of fixed states. To a large extent, Shaw's ethic is one of discontinuity, of experimentation, of progress. The dialogues in Shaw's plays reflect his refusal to sanction the conventional. Although Shaw denies the possibility of style for its own sake, he rewrote and polished assiduously. Furthermore, he uses language with low predictability (high "entropy" or randomness) and low redundancy (i.e., he exploits surprise in syntax as well as sense).

The Posture of Genius: 1) Along with Shaw the man of genius there is Shaw the antagonist. 2) Shaw confronts the opposition not with one argument but with ten. 3) Shaw's plays have few villains. He does not present all sides in his work. He voices his opposition's argument, then rejects it by stating his own position. 4) Shaw stands as a realist in the midst of the rest of the world's illusions. His language reflects his contempt for lies and hypocrisy.

Social Socialist and Unphilosophical Philosopher: 1) Shaw's usual supposed audience is the intelligent, generally uninformed or misinformed reader. He writes to convince or to agitate. 2) His optimism makes him believe in an ultimately tidy universe. 3) Shaw also argues from real or imagined peoples' points of view, especially using indirect quotations assigned to real, imagined, or indefinite people. [A most valuable study.]

666 Okumura, Saburo. "Kagami to Gui-*Major Barbara* Shiron" (Mirror and Parable--on *Major Barbara*), KAGAWA DAIGAKU GAKUGEIGAKUBU KENKYUHOKOKU (Takamatsu), Part I, No. 15 (May 1962), pp. 1-32.
The necessity of a political system that will unite the three elements which exist now independently from each other represented by Andrew Undershaft, Barbara and Cusins is the parable of *Major Barbara*. [In Japanese.]

667 Palfy, Istvan. "B. Shaw Magyarorszagon 1913-1919" (B. Shaw in Hungary 1913-1919). Unpublished dissertation, Library of Kossuth University, Debrecen, Hungary, 1962.
[In Hungarian.]

668 Pearson, Hesketh. "Bernard Shaw," LIVES OF THE WITS (Lond: Heinemann; NY: Harper & Row, 1962), pp. 248-68.

[Brief biography of Shaw. Attributes the application to Shaw of Oscar Wilde's description of Harrowden as one of those men "who have no enemies but are thoroughly disliked by their friends" to Shaw himself.]

669 Perdeck, A. BERNARD SHAW (Den Haag: Krauseman [Kopstukken Uit De Twintigste Eeuw] (Masterpieces of the Twentiethh Century), 1962).
[Discusses Shaw and the Netherlands; Shaw's attitude toward war; Shaw and Russia. *Saint Joan*. The Life Force.] [In Dutch.]

670 Peteler, Patricia Marjorie. "The Social and Symbolical Drama of the English Language Theatre 1929-1949," DA, XXII (1962), 4441-42. Unpublished dissertation, University of Utah, 1961.

671 Pietch, Frances. "The Relationship between Music and Literature in the Victorian Period: Studies in Browning, Hardy and Shaw," DA, XXII (1962), 2386-67. Unpublished dissertation, Northwestern University, 1961.

672 Pilecki, Gerard Anthony. "Shaw's *Geneva*: A Critical Study of the Evolution of the Text in Relation to Shaw's Political Thought and Dramatic Practice," DA, XXII (Jan 1962), 2399. Dissertation, Cornell University, 1961, published under the same title (The Hague: Mouton & Co.; NY: Humanities Press [Studies in English Literature, vol. VIII], 1965).

673 Reidinger, Otto. "Ethelbert Stauffer und George Bernard Shaw. *Major Barbara* in theologischer Auslegung" (Ethelbert Stauffer and George Bernard Shaw. *Major Barbara* in theological Interpretation), MONATSSCHRIFT FÜR PASTORALTHEOLOGIE, LI (1962), 360-67.
Stauffer is mistaken when he interprets St. Matthew 20, 1-15 (the simile of the householder and the laborers in his vineyard) as an allegory of a social program in the sense of Andrew Undershaft's social ideas. To claim that anyone who fights poverty fights for the cause of Jesus is to overlook the brutalities of communism. [In German.]

674 Sainer, Arthur. "DEAR LIAR: Adapted and directed by Jerome Kilty from the Correspondence between George Bernard Shaw and Mrs. Patrick Campbell, presented by Frank Gero at the Theatre Marquee," VILLAGE VOICE (NY), 22 March 1962; rptd in Arthur Sainer, THE SLEEPWALKER AND THE ASSASSIN, A VIEW OF THE CONTEMPORARY THEATRE (NY: Bridgehead Books, 1964), pp. 44-45.
Shaw, in "Hell," writes to Mrs. Patrick Campbell, "Elsewhere," generally approving of DEAR LIAR and especially of this revival. [The attempted cleverness of this review is an insult to Shaw.]

675 Salazar Chapela, E. "El alfabeto de Bernard Shaw" (Bernard Shaw's Alphabet), ATLÁNTIDA (Argentina), XLV (Aug 1962), 20, 64.
[Discussion of Shaw's alphabet reform.] [In Spanish.]

676 Salovac, Ivo. "G. B. Shaw u Hrvatskog" (G. B. Shaw in Croatian), FILOLOGIJA (Zagreb), III (1962), 259-72.
[Bibliography for 1906-1956: section A (72 items: interviews, obituaries, etc.), B (152 items: productions in Croatia), C (7 items: plays not produced in Croatia, but noticed elsewhere), and D (36 items: Shaw's works in Croatian).] [In Croatian.]

677 Scriabine, Vera. "Past Group Events," Reg, IV (April 1962), 6-8.
[Abstracts of talks given by Gordon N. Ray, "Bernard Shaw and H. G. Wells: A Turbulent Friendship," Judith Spink and David Shapiro, "Shaw in American Education."]

678 Seidel, Christian. "Die Entwicklung Eines Fabiers, George Bernard Shaw," (The Development of a Fabian: George Bernard Shaw). Unpublished dissertation, München University, 1962.
[Listed in DAID.] [In German.]

679 Sharp, Sister M. Corona, O. S. U. "The Theme of Masks in *Geneva*," ShawR, V (Sept 1962), 82-91.
Several critics (Bentley, Krim, Nethercot, Perruchot) have noted the use of masks by Shaw. Here "mask" is used as disguise, traditionally a comic device. To the usual idea of disguise, Shaw adds the notion of an unconscious pose;

the stripping down of masked characters forms the basis of his later political plays. In *Geneva,* the dialectic structure, the juxtaposition of the ideas represented by the various characters, forms the vehicle for the theme of masks, which moves on three levels: 1) the catchwords and ambitions of each character are his personal mask; 2) the characters themselves are masks of human beings; 3) the whole political game is a giant mask. The power of words proves negative in three ways: words conceal character; words also expose; words can spark verbal feuds. On the second level the politician masks the individual, one indication of which is the names, often really only a classification (the Jew, the Bishop, etc.). The names also indicate concepts and national traits; the patriot is the one who identifies himself with his country's bias. The characters in the play show intellectual pretension and ignorance of self. This second level dehumanization of the characters opens out to the third level of masks: the political game is finally shown as *only* a game. But after all the unmasking, what is left? One view is that this shows the sense of the ridiculous in the teeth of despair. In plays other than *Geneva* (*Candida, Man and Superman, Saint Joan*) when the masks are stripped, there remains a wholeness of dramatic character. But in *Geneva,* the basic humanity is lacking.

680 "Shaw's Alphabet: Ploys Unpleasant?" ECONO-MIST, CCV (24 Nov 1962), 754.
[A review of the Shaw Alphabet Edition of *Androcles and the Lion.*] There are many practical difficulties with and objections to this alphabet; the only claim for it that can be substantiated is that it saves space.

681 Shenfield, Margaret. BERNARD SHAW: A PICTORIAL BIOGRAPHY (NY: The Viking Press [Studio Book]: 1962); trans into French by M. Matignon (Paris: Hachette, 1967). [Biography with many illustra-tions.]

682 Solomon, Stanley J. "Theme and Structure in *Getting Married,*" ShawR, V (Sept 1962), 92-96.
Many critics see *Getting Married* as a play without action, but the structure of the play is more ingenious than the sub-title "A disquisitory Play" would suggest. The play in fact contains a considerable amount of action and five fully developed plots. Shaw actually underplays certain farcical possibilities in order to direct the laughter

toward the institution satirized; he chooses to emphasize theme to avoid turning the play into "low" comedy. The situations, however, are the means of presenting the thematic material. All five plots are concerned with the problems of marriage in modern civilization; these are tied together by family relationships and interpentration. The theme seems to be that, as difficult as the marriage system is, it is the best thing man has yet devised. Thus it is structurally necessary for Shaw to "vindicate" marriage, for he concentrates his attack on the unreasonable qualities of human nature. There is an air of happy ending about the play, but the final arrangements are not all that satisfactory.

683 "Sprache-Shaw Alphabet: Piep" (Language-Shaw Alphabet: Peep), DER SPIEGEL, XVI (5 Dec 1962), 128-29.
[Brief report of Bernard Shaw – Kingsley Read's Peep-tot-kick alphabet and Peter MacCarthy's transcription of Shaw's *Androcles and the Lion* into this alphabet.] [In German.]

684 Steen, Marguerite. A PRIDE OF TERRYS (Lond: Longmans, Green, 1962), pp. 159, 218, 219-20, 231-33, 244, 265, 282-83, 300, 307, 326.
[Shaw and the Terrys.]

685 Stokes, E. E., Jr. "Sydney Carlyle Cockerell: 1867-1962," ShawR, V (Sept 1962), 109-11.
[Obituary of an intimate associate of Shaw, who introduced T. E. Lawrence and Dame Laurentia McLachlan to the Shaws.]

686 Stresau, Hermann. GEORGE BERNARD SHAW IN SELBSTZEUGNISSEN UND BILDDOKUMENTEN (A Portrait of GBS with Autobiographical Remarks and Illustrations) (Reinbek bei Hamburg: Rowohlt, 1962; rptd 1965, 1967, 1973); excerpt rptd as "Shaw und die Million-ärin" (Shaw and the Millionairess), BDDTG, No 331 (1969/70).
Decisive influences on Shaw were his loveless upbringing, Henry George, Karl Marx, Richard Wagner and Charles Darwin. In Wagner he saw more the musical than the political revolutionary. Important stations on his way as a dramatist were *Man and Superman* and *Back to Methuselah*. *Methuselah* is his most important play but artistically *Heartbreak House* and *Saint Joan* are his best plays.

Heartbreak must be read in the original in order to recognize that its structure is shaped by Mozart's music. There are no villains in Shaw's plays; dramatic conflicts arise from clashes between characters who can see clearly and those whose vision is obscured by ideological prejudices. Shaw never was a true democrat. His aristocratic communism made sense only in the abstract; applied to reality it got entangled in a network of contradictions. [Stresau's book attempts to give an overview of Shaw's life and work, using many quotes from Shaw's writings, and illustrations. Appended are a chronology, samples of critical appreciations of Shaw, and a bibliography.] [In German.]

687 Styan, J. L. THE DARK COMEDY: THE DEVELOPMENT OF MODERN COMIC TRAGEDY (Cambridge: Cambridge UP, 1962), pp. 139-46, passim.
It was Shaw's avowed intention to disturb us. He allows us no romance and no tragedy. We are deceived into the pleasure of suffering tragic feelings only in order to be shown our self-indulgence by the sudden return to farcical fantasy. Shaw takes an Irish delight in refusing us comfort. Shaw's scenes are built as contrasts of attitudes to life in which neither side is necessarily right. Shaw the politician and the philosopher have bothered us too long; Shaw the dramatist has scarcely been noted. Shaw's plays are most alive when, though static in action, they are intensely disturbing in the mind.

688 Takami, Yukio. "Bernard Shaw Saiko" (Bernard Shaw, a Reconsideration), OBERON (Tokyo), VI (June 1962), 13-23.
Shaw's dramas have not appeared on the Japanese stage for many years mainly because 1) they contain too many non-dramatic elements, 2) they are nothing but ironical talk, and 3) his ideas do not appeal to us any more. [In Japanese.]

689 Taubman, Howard. "Theatre: Old Vic Presents *Saint Joan*," NYHT, 21 Feb 1962.
Saint Joan is likely Shaw's finest play.

690 Torn, Jesse. "A Figleaf in Her Bonnet: a Scene and a Preface," ShawR, V (May 1962), 61-68.

[A Preface and the last scene of a dramatization of the love affair of Shaw and Mrs. Patrick Campbell (Off-Broadway, 1961)]

691 Ujhelyi, J. "Brecht és Shaw" (Brecht and Shaw) ALFÖLD (Budapest), XIII (1962), 72-75.
[Not seen.] [In Hungarian.]

692 Weintraub, Stanley. "Shaw's Mommsenite Caesar," ANGLO-GERMAN AND AMERICAN-GERMAN CROSSCURRENTS, II, ed by Philip Allison Shelley and Arthur O. Lewis, Jr. (Chapel Hill: U of North Carolina P, 1962), pp. 257-72.
Theodor Mommsen, the German historian, "played Plutarch to the author of one of the great historical dramas of the modern English stage."

693 Weisert, John J. "Shaw in Central Europe before 1914," ANGLO-GERMAN AND AMERICAN-GERMAN CROSS-CURRENTS, II, ed by Philip Allison Shelley and Arthur O. Lewis, Jr. (Chapel Hill: U of North Carolina P, 1962), pp. 273-302.
[A history of Shaw in the German-speaking lands before World War I.]

1963

694 Abel, Lionel. METATHEATRE: A NEW VIEW OF DRAMATIC FORM (NY: Hill and Wang, 1963), pp. 106-07.
Brecht and Shaw, whose political and social views were similar, may be compared. For Shaw, life was no dream, yet this is what some of his finest works say, e.g. *Pygmalion*. *Don Juan in Hell* is a "thoroughgoing metaplay." The play may argue that life is not a dream and must be taken seriously, yet it deals with characters and a setting that are wholly illusory. Brecht may be said to have gone one step further than Shaw: Don Juan says he will go to heaven; Brecht assumed he was already there.

695 Anikst, A. A. "Predislovie" (Foreword), in BERNARD SHOU O DRAME I TEATRE (Shaw on Drama and Theater), ed by A. A. Anikst and S. Kornilovaîa (Moscow: Izd. Innostranoi Literatury, 1963). [Not seen.] [In Russian.]

696 Anniah Gowda, H. H. THE REVIVAL OF ENGLISH POETIC DRAMA (New Delhi: Orient Longman, 1963; enlgd ed, 1972), pp. 54, 58, 62, 63, 90, 93, 169, 171, 221, 280.
Although Shaw's plays are in prose, they have some of the features of poetic plays: extravagance and a poetic ring. Shaw wrote *The Admirable Bashville* in blank verse to ridicule verse drama. James Elroy Flecker's DON JUAN is a mixture of romantic yearning and ill-digested Shavianism.

697 Atkinson, Brooks. "Critic at Large," NYT, 9 April 1963, p. 28.
The meeting of Shaw and T. E. Lawrence, both egoists, produced the wittiest parts of *Too True to Be Good*. David Wayne as Meek and Cyril Richard as his commanding officer make a brilliant vaudeville act of it. Shaw was never deceived by Lawrence's humbug.

698 Auchincloss, Katherine L. "Shaw and the Commissars: The Lenin Years," ShawR, VI (May 1963), 51-59.
Among British Socialists, Shaw had the least to say about the early years of the Soviet experiment. He turned down Hearst's suggestion that he go to Russia and record his observations. However, between 1917 and 1924, Shaw did write close to 60 articles on various subjects for Hearst; eight of these articles were on Soviet Russia. The general theme of these articles, as of Shaw's other political writings of the period, is that of the inadequacies of the democracies during and after the war. His charges caused great resentment against Shaw, and the eight articles themselves provide interesting insights into Shaw's feelings about his country and the allies, the Soviet Union, and various other matters during this period in his life.

699 Ayling, Robert. "GBS and the Timid Tailors,"
SHAVIAN, II (Oct 1963), 14-16.
While *Androcles and the Lion* was in production at the
Abbey Theatre, Dublin, in November 1919, the theater's
manager, Lennox Robinson, received a letter from the
secretary of a local branch of the Amalgamated Society of
Tailors. The letter objected to the depiction of the
tailor and urged that the part be eliminated from the
play. Robinson forwarded the letter to Shaw, who replied
expressing surprise that there could be objection to his
sympathetic portrayal of a tailor when tailors were traditionally treated as comic figures in drama. Shaw's letter
was sent on to the tailors, who apologized by way of a
letter to Robinson, to Shaw. Shaw, in turn, forgave the
tailors.

700 Barth, Max. "Das Shaw-Alfabet" (The Shaw-
Alphabet), FORM UND TECHNIK, XIV (1963), 37-39.
Shaw's alphabet, designed by Kingsley Read, is supposed to
save space and time in reading and writing. But since it
is based on spoken English, it presents great difficulties
to foreigners. [In German.]

701 Barzun, Jacques. "Shaw against the Alphabet,"
ISh, I (April 1963), 1, 3-5.
Only Shaw's views on language and spelling are unworthy of
his intelligence. Shaw's argument for reform is a saving
of money. Pronunciation spelling would be more anarchic
than the present system because of the variety of
speaking. Shaw preaches the simplification of grammar in
a complicated language that contradicts his argument.
Shaw's saving of money is also a foolish argument, because
everything would have to be reprinted in the new alphabet.
English would not be easier for foreigners, since they
would have to learn a new alphabet. Shaw actually wanted
"to get rid of the past, to give a part of mankind a fresh
start by isolating it from its own history."

702 Batson, Eric. "The Religion of Bernard Shaw,"
ARYAN PATH, XXXIV (March 1963), 113-18.
Of his three favorite subjects--religion, politics, and
sex--Shaw's most favorite was religion. To be religious,
for Shaw, was to feel oneself the instrument of some high
purpose in the universe. By the usual standards the
religious Shaw was heterodox, heretical, certainly
unconventional. This is what accounts for his importance
as a religious writer. Shaw was essentially a mystic;

reason was finally an inadequate faculty. Despite his own phase of Shelleyan atheism, Shaw rejected atheism as too negative and agnosticism as simply atheism without conviction. Ibsen taught Shaw that revelation is continuous. His view of orthodox religions was essentially Marxist, yet behind the gods and religions created by human cultures was an imperfect God who was evolving with the universe. Shaw's "purposive religious philosophy is above all the religion of a free soul."

703 Bender, William. *"Mrs. Warren's Profession,"* NYHT, 25 April 1963.
Mrs. Warren's Profession seems tame.

704 Benedek, Marcell. G. B. SHAW (Budapest: Gondolat, 1963).
[Solid standard biography and comment on works with only sparing use of the Socialist rule.] I. Shaw's youth. II. Shaw the critic. III. Shaw the Socialist. IV. Private life [Mostly limited to Ellen Terry]. V. Family affairs. VI. The struggle for the stage. VII. *Plays Pleasant and Unpleasant.* VIII. *Three Plays for Puritans.* IX. *Man and Superman.* X. *Back to Methuselah.* XI. *Saint Joan.* XII. Plays of old age. XIII. Epilogue. Shaw, though not a misanthrope, did not like people. Because his life was free from suffering, his work lacks sympathy. XIV. Bibliography [Useful for published works in Hungarian, premieres of plays in Budapest, and Shaviana in Hungarian. [In Hungarian.]

705 Benedek, Marcell. "George Bernard Shaw," in KÖNYV ÉS SZÍNHÁZ (Book and Theater) (Budapest: Szépirodalmi Könyvkiadó, 1963), pp. 443-61.
[Brief survey of Shaw's theatrical work.] Shaw is the greatest dramatist of the first half of the twentieth century. He achieved his success while disregarding the tenets of contemporary dramaturgy. He brought polemic drama to its zenith. [In Hungarian.]

706 Berstl, Julius. ODYSSEE EINES THEATERMENSCHEN (The Odyssey of a Theater Fan) (Berlin: Arani, 1963), pp. 37, 40, 42-44, 45, 46, 47, 57, 65, 86, 90, 93, 96, 99, 135, 137, 156, 161, 175, 210, 220.
[A survey of the Berlin theaters during the first half of the twentieth century.] The directors Barnowsky and

Reinhardt helped Shaw to gain his high reputation with the German public. [In German.]

707 Black, Matthew W. "Shaw to Arliss," ShawR, VI
(Jan 1963), 28-29.
In September 1941, having pleaded guilty of failing to list his American and Canadian securities with the Inland Revenue, actor George Arliss was fined. On the 27th, Shaw wrote a letter "characteristic . . . in its paradoxical wit," in which he pointed out to Arliss that he should have pleaded not guilty, since his failure to list the securities proceeded from no guilty intention.

708 Bridges, Adam W. "The Unquenchable Mr. Grein,"
DRAMA, ns LXXI (Winter 1963), 32-35.
Jacob Thomas Grein, the displaced son of a Dutch mercantile family from Amsterdam, was the impresario who, with Archer as chief translator and Shaw as chief propagandist, brought the plays of Ibsen to England.

709 Brockway, Fenner. OUTSIDE THE RIGHT (Lond:
George Allen & Unwin, 1963).
[Appreciation and reminiscence of Shaw; reproduction of a Shaw "lost play"; photograph; facsimile of Shaw postcard; Appendix consisting of Shaw correspondence with Brockway concerning the police seizure in London of all copies of Brockway's one-act play THE DEVIL'S BUSINESS.]

710 Brooks, Harold F. and Jean R. "Dickens in
Shaw," DICKENSIAN, LIX (May, 1963), 93-99.
Shaw was thoroughly grounded in Dickens. In 40 volumes of Shaw there are over 300 allusions to Dickens or his works and mention of almost 130 characters from every novel. The greatest number of allusions are to PICKWICK PAPERS and BLEAK HOUSE. In the drama, Shaw's debt to Dickens is both specific (situations, characters, phrases) and general (dramatic and comic method). Like Dickens, Shaw enjoyed making up appropriate, often comically so, names for his characters. He also learned negative lessons from Dickens, rejecting the plot mechanisms Dickens inherited from the theatrical tradition. It is in the area of social criticism that, finally, Shaw and Dickens are most closely allied and in which Shaw's genuine love for Dickens can be most clearly seen.

711 Byers, William Franklin. "The Nineteenth Century English Farce and Its Influence on George Bernard Shaw," DA, XXIV (1963), 4693. Unpublished dissertation, Columbia University, 1963.

712 Byrom, Michael. "What Was Shaw?," SHAVIAN, II (Oct 1963), 17-19.
Shaw was abnormal, therefore interesting. Superficially an egotist, he seemed guilty of pride. Yet he was a humble man, who saw himself as the instrument of the life-force and was contemptuous of the world and its institutions. Thus, Shaw would seem to have been "a religious mystic masquerading as a socialist and popular playwright." But mystics do not attain worldly success, and the contradictions in Shaw are the result of his idealism having been interfered with by things transient. Shaw's greatness of achievement as a man of the world ultimately limits his spiritual stature.

713 Cantieri, Giovanni. "Dos *Juanas de Arco*" (Two *Saint Joans*), PRIMER ACTO (Spain), XLVI (1963), 51.
The performance of *Saint Joan* by the Escuela de Arte Dramático Adriá Gual lacked poetry and is saved only by Joan's irony. [In Spanish.]

714 Carpenter, Charles Albert, Jr. "Bernard Shaw's Development as a Dramatic Artist, 1884-1899," DA, XXIV (1963), 295. Unpublished dissertation, Cornell, 1963.

715 Cline, Catherine Ann. RECRUITS TO LABOUR (Syracuse: Syracuse UP, 1963), pp. 25, 30, 51, 57-58.
Webb's and Shaw's *To Your Tents, Oh Israel* (1893) announced the Fabian Society's failure to influence the Liberal government and the need to form an independent labor party.

716 Collar, Georges. "Beckett, Shaw y dos actores ingleses" (Beckett, Shaw and Two English Actors), CUADERNOS DEL SUR, XIII (Aug 1963), 738-39.
DEAR LIAR is brilliant. [In Spanish.]

717 Costello, Donald P. "George Bernard Shaw and the Motion Picture. His Theory and Practice. [Listed in Lawrence F. McNamee, DISSERTATIONS IN ENGLISHS AND AMERICAN LITERATURE (NY & Lond: R. R. Bowker, 1968), p. 535. Published dissertation, University of Chicago, 1963; pub as THE SERPENT'S EYE. SHAW AND THE CINEMA, 1965.

718 Crompton, Louis. "Shaw's Challenge to Liberalism," PRAIRIE SCHOONER, XXXVII (1963), 229-44; rptd as "*Major Barbara*: Shaw's Challenge to Liberalism," in Bernice Slate (ed), LITERATURE AND SOCIETY (1964), pp. 121-41; R. J. Kaufmann (ed), G. B. SHAW: A COLLECTION OF CRITICAL ESSAYS (1965).
Major Barbara raises the question of whether art is to be seen as autonomous or as something to be judged in terms of some ulterior standard. In terms of theme, mood, and dramatic structure, it is to be grouped with *Man and Superman* and *John Bull's Other Island*. Each presents us with a high-minded idealist who is then made the object of comedy, the contradictions in his nature being thus exposed. In *Barbara*, this character is Lady Britomart. It is in Cusins that we see the ideal embodiment of liberalism. In the crisis precipitated by the clash between Undershaft and Barbara, it is Cusins who hails the seemingly diabolical Undershaft as the new Dionysos of a Bergsonian "dynamic religion" that Cusins had previously thought he saw in Barbara's Salvation Army. Undershaft, then, has caused the confusion among Shaw critics. Undershaft's ruthlessness is not disguised by any conviction of moral superiority, and his genuine virtues are not muddled by blindness to economic realities. Cusins and Barbara are hard put to accept Undershaft's position that might does make right. Cusins is forced to accept Undershaft's view, even if it means losing Barbara, and Barbara faces the realities of her father's position, which is clearly that of Shaw as well.

719 Demaray, John G. "Bernard Shaw and C. E. M. Joad: The Adventures of Two Puritans in Their Search for God," PMLA, LXXVIII (June 1963), 262-70.
Joad was Shaw's principal academic apologist, and his MATTER, LIFE AND VALUE was written to formalize Shaw's philosophy. He revered Shaw as second only to Plato. Although as a systematized philosophy it is of little significance today, Shaw—and Joad—"united the vitalism of Nietzsche, the rationalism of Descartes, and the evolutionary theories of the nineteenth century into the

best of all possible Puritan compromises." [Details the
parallel "spiritual pilgrimages" that led to Joad's
ultimate faith in God and Shaw's in intelligence for the
saving of mankind.]

720 Doromby, K.   "*Genf*, 1938" (*Geneva*, 1938) VIGILIA
(Budapest), XXVII (1963), 55-56.
[Not seen.] [In Hungarian.]

721 DuCann, C. G. L. THE LOVES OF GEORGE BERNARD
SHAW (NY: Funk & Wagnalls; Lond: Arthur Barker,
1963).
Although neither a rake nor a libertine, Shaw was
nevertheless a philanderer. Apparently continent until
the age of 29, he then embarked on a series of romantic
affairs, some sexually consummated and some not, with a
vast number of women including Alice Lockett, Jenny
Patterson, Florence Farr, Annie Besant, May Morris,
Eleanor Marx, Edith Nesbit, Ellen Terry, Mrs. Patrick
Campbell, and many others.   His marriage to Charlotte
Payne-Townshend was, of course, unconsummated. It is
necessary that one know about, if not understand, "the
foibles, the follies and the faults of this great, unusual
man." [Often speculative; often irritatingly coy in
tone.]

722 Dudek,   Louis.   "Art,   Entertainment   and
Religion," QQ, LXX (Autumn 1963), 413-30.
Shaw is among those writers of the nineteenth century and
today who "look for new affirmations and new bearings"
instead of returning to abandoned religious sources.

723 Duerksen, Roland A. "Shelley and Shaw," PMLA,
LXVIII (March 1963), 114-27; rptd as Chap VII in
Roland A. Duerksen, SHELLEYAN IDEAS IN VICTORIAN
LITERATURE (The Hague: Mouton, 1966).
Shelley was by "the sheer logic of his poetry" a major
influence on the development of Shaw's thoughts on man and
society.   Shaw admired Shelley the thinker more than
Shelley the poet, and he most appreciated those poems
which were essentially didactic, like political
statements. He criticized THE CENCI because its social
criticism was weakened by the demands of its poetic form.
While disagreeing with Shelley's faith in love as a
solution for human problems, Shaw nevertheless regarded
him as a superman, leading others to become social

prophets. Just as Shelley himself can be seen in the character of Marchbanks, so certain obvious links can be seen between, for example, THE WITCH OF ATLAS and *Captain Brassbound's Conversion*, OZYMANDIAS and Part V of *Back to Methuselah*, and AN ESSAY ON CHRISTIANITY and *Androcles and the Lion*.

724 Dukore, Bernard F. "Shaw Improves Shaw," MD, VI (May, 1963), 26-31.
The sometimes enormous differences between early editions of Shaw's early plays and the texts of the Standard Edition can be seen by comparing the 1904 version of *How He Lied to Her Husband* with that of the Standard Edition (1931). The deletions are all references to *Candida*, of which Shaw originally saw *Lied* as a spoof. He seems to have realized that the humorous allusions to *Candida* would be lost on post-1931 audiences.

725 Dukore, Bernard F. "Toward an Interpretation of *Major Barbara*," ShawR, VI (May 1963), 62-70.
Shaw's description of Andrew Undershaft as the hero of *Major Barbara* has caused great confusion among the critics. An examination of the changes made in the text from the first edition (1907) to the Standard Edition (1931) will help determine Shaw's attitudes towards the importance of Undershaft, Cusins, and Barbara. The revisions of the play can finally be seen either as refinement of details or more specific direction for interpretation. The changes make Cusins and Barbara, particularly the latter, more important; Undershaft, consequently, becomes less so, and his cruelty is revealed. The play ends in anticipation of Cusins, literally, and Barbara replacing Undershaft and, in a sense, defeating him.

726 Dunbar, Janet. MRS. G.B.S., A PORTRAIT (NY and Evanston: Harper & Row, 1963).
[In two parts: Charlotte Townshend's life before meeting Shaw, and her life after meeting Shaw, on 29 January 1896; an appendix deals with the controversy generated by her Will; photographs. Scattered references, undocumented and in excerpts from various letters, to the writings of Shaw are inconsequential.]

727 Dunlap, Joseph R. "A Note on Shaw's 'Formula'
and Pre-Kelmscott Printing," ISh, II (Winter
1963/64), 20.
[A comparison of the look of Shaw's page with Morris's, to
show Shaw did not model his books on Morris's ROOTS OF THE
MOUNTAINS.]

728 "An English Academy of Letters: A Correspondence of 1897," ShawR, VI (Jan 1963), 13-26.
Near the end of 1897, the ACADEMY, an English weekly,
proposed the formation of an English Academy of Letters,
suggesting criteria for the composition and membership of
such an Academy and naming 40 prominent Britons as
suitable members. Shaw was not named, and only one of the
letters (from H. G. Wells) generated by the proposal
suggested Shaw should be on the list.

Shaw himself was interested in the formation of an English
Academy and wrote to the weekly that the Academy "should
consist exclusively of men of letters," whom he defines as
those "who write for the sake of writing," not simply to
inform or persuade. He suggested further names to be
added to the ACADEMY's list and some to be deleted. In a
letter a week later, written at the ACADEMY's request, he
amplified his suggestions for the membership of an English
Academy.

729 Esterow, Milton. "Theater," NYT, 25 April 1963,
p. 39.
The revival of *Mrs. Warren's Profession* is a bore.

730 Feldman, Eddy S. "A New Alphabet Known as
'Shavian'," Œhav, IV (March-April 1963), n.p.
[Background of Shaw's interest in alphabet reform, and
reproduction of the phonetic alphabet devised by Mr.
Kingsley Read and used for the transliteration, in
accordance with Shaw's will, of *Androcles and the Lion*,
which was published on 22 November 1962 by Penguin Books.]

731 Feron, James. "Editor's Refusal to Submit Work
Stops Publication of Shaw Diary," NYT, 24 Nov 1963,
p. 22.
Professor Stanley Rypins's effort to publish his
transcription of a Shaw diary written in shorthand between
1885 and 1897 and bequeathed to the London School of
Economics has failed because of Rypins's refusal to submit

the transcription to the Shaw estate's trustees for approval.

732 Freeman, John. LITERATURE AND LOCALITY, THE LITERARY TOPOGRAPHY OF BRITAIN AND IRELAND (Lond: Cassell & Company, 1963), pp. 44, 140, 312-13, 320, 323.
[Guide to locations associated with Shaw.]

733 Fried, Vilém. "V Stopách Shawovy Závěti: Neboli o Nejnovějších Úvahách o Anglickém Pravopise" (The Aftermath of Shaw's Will: Recent Reflections on English Spelling), PHILOLOGICA PRAGENSIA, VI (1963), 90-100.
This paper sets out to inform the Czech reader of recent proposals for reforming English spelling, with an account of the fate of Shaw's New English Alphabet. [In Czechoslovak with an English summary.]

734 Gassner, John. "Shaw on Shakespeare," ISh, II (Fall 1963), 1, 3-5; (Winter, 1963/64), 13, 15, 23-24.
Shaw's criticism was useful in encouraging adequate and discouraging inadequate stage productions of Shakespeare. But Shaw came to be known as Shakespeare's most formidable enemy. First, because he often identified what a character said with Shakespeare's own views. He also measured the plays against the needs of the theater to deal with modern times. He preferred the discursive mode to the poetic. But Shaw and Shakespeare are closer "on the ground of common aspirations for humanity than Shaw was apt to realize."

735 "G. B. Shaw i muzika" (G.B. Shaw and Music), TELEGRAM (Zagreb), IV (1963), 174.
[Not seen.] [In Croatian.]

736 Geduld, Harry M. "Bernard Shaw and Leo Tolstoy," CShav, IV (March-April 1963), n.p.
Tolstoy anticipated many of Shaw's ideas, and Shaw openly acknowledged his debt to Tolstoy. The similarities between Tolstoy and Shaw are most striking in the areas of religion; economic theory; attitudes towards Darwin and his followers, experimental science, Western philosophical thought; and teleology. With respect to fundamental

morality, however, their positions were virtually opposite. Finally, Tolstoy and Shaw shared personal eccentricities in such matters as diet, dress, attitude toward the medical profession, and music. The two corresponded but never met.

737 Geduld, Harry M. "Bernard Shaw and Leo Tolstoy, II--The Shavian Critique of Tolstoy," C Shav, IV (May-June, 1963), n.p.
Shaw's essay, *Tolstoy on Art*, a critique of Tolstoy's WHAT IS ART?, is ostensibly an attack on the use of art for religious or political propaganda. In fact, however, the essay expresses Shaw's conviction that Tolstoy was really a crypto-Socialist who could not go all the way in his beliefs because of class loyalty. A second essay, *Tolstoy: Tragedian or Comedian?*, considers Tolstoy's dramatic writing.

738 Geduld, H[arry] M. "The Comprehensionist," SHAVIAN, II (Oct 1963), 22-26.
Frederick J. Wilson was a social reformer, pamphleteer, and crank whose ideas, nevertheless, influenced the young Shaw long before Shaw had heard of Henry George, Socialism, or the philosophy of Nietzsche.

739 Geduld, Harry M. "The Premiere of the Pentateuch," CShav, IV (Jan-Feb, 1963), n.p.
Back to Methuselah had its world premiere in 1922 by the Theatre Guild of New York, which had also presented *Heartbreak House* in its world premiere in 1920 and whose activities Shaw had first been informed of by St. John Ervine in 1919. Shaw took interest in the technical aspects of both productions and was typically adamant about there being no cuts made in his texts. On a London visit, Langner persuaded Shaw to cut Part IV, but this proved not greatly to prolong the run of the play.

740 Gerould, Daniel Charles. "George Bernard Shaw's Criticism of Ibsen," COMPARATIVE LITERATURE, XV (1963), 130-45.
Until now, critical estimate of Shaw's writing on Ibsen has been mostly unfavorable. Even Ibsen himself on one occasion decried Shaw's calling him a Socialist, or social critic. *The Quintessence of Ibsenism* was largely regarded as a misrepresentation. Shaw's critical views of Ibsen were constantly changing and reflect his own growth as an artist, not a constant misinterpretation of Ibsen.

741 Gershkovich, A. A. SOVREMENNYĬ VENGERSKIĬ TEATR (Contemporary Hungarian Theater) (Moscow: Izd. Akademiĭ nauk, 1963).
In 1945, *The Shewing-up of Blanco Posnet* was produced by E. Gellert at the "Free" Theater, Budapest, on 6 July, and *Saint John* at the National Theater (Budapest) on 19 October. In 1946, *Pygmalion* was produced at the "Magyar" Theater on 2 April, *Heartbreak House* at the "Madach" Theater on 20 April. Gellert's production of *Androcles and the Lion* at the National Theater, 1 May 1947, was followed by another production of *Pygmalion* at the "Belvaroszi" Theater, 7 September, and with another production at the "Belvaroszi" Theater, 29 September 1948. *Mrs. Warren's Profession* was produced at the National Theater (Filial), 4 May 1948, and again at the "Maior" Theater, 12 October 1951 (another production at the same theater, 7 March 1957). Gellert's production of *Pygmalion* at the National Theater, 1953, was hailed as "a classic of the Hungarian 'realist' theater." *Caesar and Cleopatra* was produced at the "Madach" Theater, 6 January 1955, and *Joan* at the "National Army" Theater (formerly the "Vigsinkaz" Theater) on 25 November 1955. On 21 December 1955, *The Devil's Disciple* was produced at the "Madach" Theater. [In Russian.]

742 Gilenson, Boris. "Shaw in the Soviet Union," SHAVIAN, II (Oct 1963), 11-13.
[Note by a Russian on Shaw's continuing popularity in the Soviet Union from his first communication with Lenin to the present.]

743 Gordon, John D. "New in the Berg Collection: 1959-61," BNYPL, LXVII (Dec 1963), 625-38.
[Account of "Pamphlets and books; autograph manuscripts, including an early synopsis of *Man and Superman*; typescripts; and some autograph letters" in the Berg Collection.]

744 Hales, John, "Shaw's Comedy," DA, XXIV (1963), 3324. Unpublished dissertation, University of Texas, 1963.

745 Harris, Harold J. "Shaw, Chekhov, and Two Great Ladies of the Theater," ShawR, VI (Sept 1963), 96-99.

In commenting on Bernhardt and Duse, Chekhov and Shaw
revealed remarkably similar theories of drama.

746 Hermann, István. "Tanner John házassága" (John
Tanner's Native Land) ÉLET ÉS IRODALOM (Budapest),
VII (1963), 7-8; rptd A SZÉMELYISÉG NYOMÁBAN:
DRAMÁI KALAUZ (Budapest: Magvetö, 1972), pp. 418-
28; see also pp. 405-17.
[Not seen.] [In Hungarian.]

747 Himmelstein, Morgan Yale. DRAMA WAS A WEAPON
(New Brunswick, NJ: Rutgers U P, 1963), pp. 106-35.
Shaw was denounced by the Communists for promoting Fascist
tyranny and for slandering the proletariat. *Androcles and
the Lion* was approved by the left-wing critics because of
its universal theme of the oppression of minorities.
Heartbreak House was not well received by the Communist
Party because of the play's failure to offer simple
answers to complex questions. *The Simpleton of the
Unexpected Isles*, which failed after 40 performances in
1935, denied that the future was predictable and
scientifically achievable and was largely overlooked by
the Marxist press. Shaw's *Geneva* was one of four plays of
social significance which were produced by Chekhov Theatre
Productions and which failed during the 1939-40 season.

748 Hogan, Patrick G., Jr., and Joseph O. Baylen.
"Shaw, W. T. Stead, and the 'International Peace
Crusade,' 1898-99," ShawR, VI (May 1963), 60-61.
Stead issued a call for an "International Peace Crusade"
in response to Nicholas II's 1898 proposal for an arms
reduction conference. Like other Socialists and radicals,
Shaw mistrusted Russia and the Tsar's motives, and he
deplored Stead's enthusiasm for the conference in a letter
to Sir Arthur Conan Doyle. Stead later reported Shaw's
alternative proposal for an international tribune to
settle disputes rather than mere arms reduction. Shaw's
idea was more nearly realized than Stead's in the Hague
Conferences of 1899 and 1907.

749 Hogan, Patrick G., Jr., and Joseph O. Baylen.
"An Unpublished Letter from Shaw to Archer," N&Q, X
(1963), 267-68.
Although recognizing Shaw's promise in his contributions
to the PALL MALL GAZETTE, William T. Stead, its editor

from 1883-90, seems never to have had any personal contact with him in that period. A letter dated 18 March 1885 from Shaw to William Archer indicates that the latter had attempted to arrange a meeting with Stead which in fact never took place. This is a further example of Archer's efforts to promote the welfare of the young Shaw.

750 Holt, Charles Loyd. "The Musical Dramaturgy of Bernard Shaw," DA, XXV (1963), 1892. Unpublished dissertation, Wayne State University, 1963.

751 Hübner, Walter. DAS ENGLISCHE LITERATURWERK. THEORIE UND PRAXIS DER INTERPRETATION (The English Literary Work. Theory and Practice of Interpretation) (Heidelberg: Quelle & Meyer, 1963), pp. 149, 157.
[Discusses Shaw's prose style in *The Intelligent Woman's Guide to Socialism and Capitalism* (1929).] Shaw is witty, committed to reality, and didactic. [In German.]

752 Ivanov, Blagoja. "Bernard Sho: *Pigmalion*," (Bernard Shaw: *Pygmalion*), KULTUREN ZHIVOT (Skopje) VIII (1963), 34.
The production of *Pygmalion* at the Skopje National Theater stresses Shaw's irony, his amusing and individual humor, permeated with feeling and sarcasm, revealing the complexity of human emotions. [In Macedonian.]

753 Kerr, Alison. BERNARD SHAW, AN EXHIBITION OF BOOKS AND MANUSCRIPTS FROM THE COLLECTION PRESENTED BY MR. BERNARD BURGUNDER, CORNELL, 1918 (Ithaca, NY: Cornell University Library, 1963).
[The catalogue of an exhibition drawn from the Burgunder collection; includes proofs, first editions, autograph letters, miscellaneous Shaw-related items, some quite peripheral.]

754 Kerr, Walter. "*Too True to Be Good*," NYHT, 13 Mar 1963, n.p.
Too True to Be Good is not a good play.

755 Klein, John X. "Applause and the Dramatist," DRAMA, LXXI (Winter 1963), 30-32.

Shaw was an outstanding exception among the well-known dramatists of his time in his delight in appearing on stage to thank the actors and audiences of his plays. He remained discreetly out of sight, however, on the evening of 18 October 1921, the disasterous opening night of *Heartbreak House*, and it was perhaps at his prompting that the manager announced that the play had put its author to sleep (as it had, in fact, Arnold Bennett).

756 Kostić, Dušan. "G. B. Shaw - 'Uomo Virtuoso'" (G. B. Shaw the Virtuoso), ZVUK (Sarajevo), LVI (1963), 12-17.
Even in his early music reviews (discussing works by Hubert Parry and Villiers Stanford) Shaw shows his characteristic sarcasm, contempt for things English, hatred of old-fashioned ideas, and impatience with academicism, Brahms, Schubert, and Schumann. He remains England's finest music critic. [In Croatian.]

757 Kovać, Mirko. "Bernard Shaw: *Davolov učenik*" (Bernard Shaw: *The Devil's Disciple*), BORBA (Belgrade), XXIII (1963), 285.
[Not seen.] [In Serbian.]

758 Kumor, Stanisława. "Epizod Polski w Twórczósci Bernarda Shaw" (Polish Episodes in Bernard Shaw's Creative Life), KWARTALNIK NEOFILOLOGICZNY (Neophilological Quarterly), X (April 1963), 375-85.
Shaw apparently considered the Poles not sufficiently mature for independence. In an interview for KRYTYKA (Kracow, 1906), he gave the impression that Poland was a nation of "heroes" and musicians. Perhaps this is a false impression resulting from language difficulties: he received the questions in French; he answered in English; the final copy was a translation into Polish. He disapproved of the new independent Poland because its borders were military and not ethnic and because its government was not Socialist. In 1939 Shaw surprised the public by not condemning the German invasion but blaming it on the policy of the great powers. After the war he believed Poland's only hope was federation with the U.S.S.R. [In Polish.]

759 Kuŋziŋš, Kārlis. LATYSHSKIĬ TEATR: OCHERK ISTORIĬ (Latvian Theater: A Sketch of Its History), (Moscow: "Iskusstvo," 1963).

The Devil's Disciple was produced in Latvian at the New Riga Theater in the 1913/14 season. In 1922, *Candida* was included in the repertoire of the Travelling Theater, a company organized by the Latvian Theater Society. The company performed in towns and villages throughout Latvia. [In Russian.]

760 Lambert, J. W. "Plays in Performance," DRAMA, ns. LXVIII (Spring 1963), 20-27.
Misalliance is never rightly considered one of Shaw's major works, but it is hugely enjoyable and dances with irresistible *elan*.

761 Lambert, J. W. "Plays in Performance," DRAMA, ns. LXX (Autumn 1963), 16-26.
The Doctor's Dilemma was butchered, but the performances were fresh. [Photograph.]

762 Lambert, J. W. "Plays in Performance," DRAMA, ns. LXXI (Winter 1963), 18-26.
Joan Plowright is a rounded but hedge-sparrow Joan in *Saint Joan*.

763 Langner, Lawrence, G.B.S. AND THE LUNATIC (NY: Atheneum, 1963; Lond: Hutchinson, 1964).
[Reminiscences by Langner of his association, as director of the Theatre Guild, with Shaw, in the course of which were produced the world premieres of *Heartbreak House, Back to Methuselah, Saint Joan, Too True to Be Good, The Simpleton of the Unexpected Isles,* and *The Millionairess*. All told, a total of 25 Shaw plays was produced by Langner with the Theatre Guild and at the Westport County Playhouse. Separate chapters on major Theatre Guild productions of Shaw (including MY FAIR LADY). Anecdotes. Copious citation of letters from Shaw to Langner regarding productions.]

764 Lausch, Anne N. "The Road to Rome by Way of Alexandria and Tavazzano," ShawR, VI (Jan 1963), 2-12.
Robert Sherwood's THE ROAD TO ROME was widely and favorably compared by the critics with *Caesar and Cleopatra*. There are also obvious points of resemblance between the Sherwood play and *The Man of Destiny*.

765 Lausch, Anne N. "Robert Sherwood's *Heartbreak House*," ShawR, VI (May 1963), 42-50.
In its despair about the world situation, THE PETRIFIED FOREST is Robert Sherwood's *Heartbreak House*.

766 Leary, Daniel J. "Shaw's Use of Stylized Characters and Speech in *Man and Superman*," MD, V (Feb 1963), 477-90; rptd CShav, IV (May-June, 1963), n.p.
Shaw saw wooden puppets as the primitive form of real actors. The characteristic features of puppets, their symbolic costumes, their fixed stares, their caricature of human action result, according to Shaw, in an intensity which reduces real humans to insignificance. In *Man and Superman*, Shaw sought to intensify his characters to the point where, in addition to being seen as real human characters, they could also be seen as puppets manipulated by the Life Force, characters both possessed of wavering human frailty and driven beyond their personal wishes by an impersonal will. The stylistic devices Shaw used to intensify his characters include the familiar word in an unfamiliar context, thus altering the original value of the word, the juxtaposition of opposites, such as "the immoral man of integrity," the juxtaposition of the trivial and the grand, and long, rhetorical speeches patterned after operatic arias, with the statement of a major theme and its repetition through variations for a cumulative dramatic effect.

767 Liebert, Herman W. "The Colgate Bequest," YALE UNIVERSITY LIBRARY GAZETTE, XXXVII Jan 1963), 106-08.
Among the bequests by Henry A. Colgate to Yale are 33 Shaw items, including proofs of several works, privately printed editions, inscribed copies, and a typescript, corrected in Shaw's hand, of the prologue to *Caesar and Cleopatra*.

768 McDowell, Frederick P. W. "Heaven, Hell, and Turn-of-the-Century, London: Reflections upon Shaw's *Man and Superman*," DramS, II (1963), 245-68.
Man and Superman cannot be properly understood without the Hell Scene in Act III being recognized as the center of the play. For Shaw, Heaven and Hell differ only with respect to one's state of mind; Hell is what one experiences when one's spiritual health is poor, and one need not be dead to experience it. Shaw's Devil makes it

clear that this world is itself a Hell. The characters of the Hell Scene are not the exact counterparts of the characters of the rest of the play, but they and the scene itself serve as withering commentary on the smug late-Victorian society of Roebuck Ramsden.

769 Maloney, Henry B. "*Pygmalion*: A Study Guide," CLEARING HOUSE, XXXVII (Jan 1963), 317-18.
Pygmalion is still vital after 50 years as attested by the success of the 1938 film and of MY FAIR LADY. It is especially timely because of its concern with such matters as linguistics, phonetics, the aural-oral method of studying a second language, and the effectiveness of certain teaching approaches. [Written in anticipation of the February 6 "Hallmark Hall of Fame" production of *Pygmalion* with Julie Harris; seven "Study Questions" are suggested.]

770 Mason, Michael. "Captain Brassbound and Governor Eyre," SHAVIAN, II (Oct 1963), 20-22.
[Some historical material concerning Governor Edward John Eyre of Jamaica and the Morant Bay Rising on which *Captain Brassbound's Conversion* is based.]

771 Matsubara, Tadashi. "Bernard Shaw," EIBUNGAKU (The English Literature Society of Waseda University, Tokyo), No. 24 (Nov 1963), 26-34.
Shaw had that "higher dramatic gift of sympathy with character—of the power of seeing the world from the point of view of others instead of merely describing or judging them from one's point of view" which Shaw once claimed A. W. Pinero lacked. This, however, might be both a strong and weak point, for it could mean that Shaw did not feel any strong and positive sympathy with any characters. Shaw was not obsessed with the so-called disease of self-confession, a rare case among modern writers. Probably that made it possible for him to become a classical writer of comedy. [In Japanese.]

772 Matsubara, Tadashi. "Gokai sareteiru Bernard Shaw" (The Misunderstood Bernard Shaw), KUMO (Tokyo) No. 1 (March 1963), 34-37.
There are two unfortunate reasons why none of Shaw's plays have been put on the professional stage for more than 30 years in Japan. First, most translations are defective in rendering Shaw's wonderful English into Japanese;

secondly, Shaw has been regarded only as a writer of problem plays or a mere propagandist. It is high time that we understood his true stature as Britain's greatest prose playwright. [In Japanese.]

773 Mayne, Fred. "The Real and the Ideal: Irony in Shaw," SOUTHERN REVIEW [Adelaide, Australia], I (1963), 15-26.
The end-product of Shaw's irony is irresolution; for Shaw, there is no ideal that can survive attack by the ironic real. Because Shaw was writing to a general audience, it is especially unlikely that verbal irony be found in the plays; what does occur is so heavy-handed as to be undistinguishable from sarcasm or so underscored that it can not be missed. Yet Shaw's ironists see the complex realities that are missing in the simple worlds of his romantic characters. Shaw's less successful ironists, like King Magnus in *The Apple Cart* and Lady Cicely in *Captain Brassbound's Conversion*, exhibit too much ironic detachment. The ultimate irony in Shaw is achieved by the bridging of the gap, by madness, the destruction of the real, between the real and the ideal.

774 Mazov, Ivan. "Bernard Shaw: *Pigmalion*," NOVA MAKEDONIJA (Skopje), XX (1963), 5853.
[Not seen.] [In Macedonian.]

775 Meisel, Martin. SHAW AND THE NINETEENTH-CENTURY THEATER (Princeton, NJ: Princeton UP, 1963); rptd 1968; part rptd in Rose Zimbardo (ed), TCIMB; pp. 38-61 rptd in Warren Sylvester Smith (ed), BERNARD SHAW'S PLAYS (1970).
Unlike his predecessors, Shaw did not write serious drama in the form of five-act, blank verse tragedy; instead he chose to adapt the conventions and techniques of nineteenth-century popular theater for his purposes. Shaw's drama is in the mainstream of English dramatic history. Working with the materials of popular drama, Shaw adapted "an inherited dramatic rhetoric of the passions to a rhetorical drama of ideas." [Considers Shaw's use of the various nineteenth century genres and traditions of the theater, as well as acting style, ranging throughout Shaw's works. An exceptionally important, interesting and useful book.]

776 Mendelsohn, Michael J. "The Heartbreak Houses of Shaw and Chekov," Shaw R, VI (Sept 1963), 89-95; rptd in BERNARD SHAW'S PLAYS, ed by Warren Sylvester Smith (1970).

As a description of a European society whose days are numbered, Heartbreak House is as pessimistic as Eliot's WASTELAND or as anything in Hemingway. It can be readily understood by considering its points of comparison with Chekov's CHERRY ORCHARD: the apparent absence of plot, pecularities of dialogue, tone, characters, and theme. The critical attacks on *Heartbreak* for being tedious or fatuous or inconclusive may have occurred because the play was ahead of its time; we can appreciate it now because its Chekovian undertones ring all too true in the ears of the 1960's.

777 Meredith, Charles H. "What Are the Facts--Who Are Responsible?" CShav, IV (March-April, 1963), n.p.

[Relevance of Shaw's views on subsidized theater, censorship, and related matters to legislative efforts to advance the cause of the performing arts in California and in the United States as a whole.]

778 Mix, Katherine Lyon. "Max on Shaw," Shaw R, VI (Sept 1963), 100-04.

Shaw preceded Max Beerbohm as drama critic of SATURDAY REVIEW, and the "incomparable Max" (Shaw's description) never again was able to free himself of preoccupation with Shaw. Shaw appears more in Beerbohm's caricatures than anyone else. Although capable of censuring Shaw for what he detected to be pride, Beerbohm was also given to high praise of Shaw's intellect. This ambivalence remained. [Anecodtes detailing Beerbohm's reactions to Shaw on various occasions.]

779 Monleón, José. "El Teatro Nacional Ingles: Shakespeare y Bernard Shaw" (The English National Theatre: Shakespeare and Shaw), PRIMER ACTO (Spain), XLVIII (Dec 1963), 4-8.

[Essay-review of *Saint Joan* at the Old Vic.] The confrontation between Joan and the Inquisitor is one of Shaw's most brilliant scenes. [In Spanish.]

780 Moore, Harry T. "Preface," GEORGE BERNARD SHAW, CREATIVE ARTIST by Homer E. Woodbridge (Carbondale: Southern Illinois UP [Crosscurrents/Modern Critiques], 1963), pp. v - xii.
Shaw looms as one of the important literary figures of the age.

781 Morgan, Margery M. "The English Theatre," TLS, 23 Aug 1963, p. 645.
If Shaw contributed nothing to the cause of English acting by demanding of his actors that they make no further effort than what was demanded of the already established mid-nineteenth-century romantic manner, the same should not be said of Granville-Barker, too easily dismissed as a mere imitator of Shaw and furtherer of the narrow view of Ibsen as social reformer.

782 "Napoleón o el destino del hombre "(Napoleon or the Man of Destiny), PRIMERA PLANA, XLI (26 Nov 1963), 8.
The presentation of *The Man of Destiny* in Buenos Aires is a comedia deliciosa. [In Spanish.]

783 Nethercot, Arthur H. "Foreword," THE RELIGIOUS SPEECHES OF BERNARD SHAW, ed by Warren Sylvester Smith (University Park, Pennsylvania: Pennsylvania State U P, 1963; NY: McGraw-Hill, 1965), pp. vii-ix.
This collection of speeches will correct the mistaken idea that Shaw was not religious, although his idea of religion was an unorthodox one. Some have called Shaw a mystic, some a cynic; in fact, he was both. These lectures leave no doubt as to his mysticism. Ideas on religion expressed in these speeches occur in the later plays and prefaces.

784 Nethercot, Arthur H. THE LAST FOUR LIVES OF ANNIE BESANT (Chicago: U of Chicago P; Toronto: U of Toronto P; Lond: Rupert Hart-Davis, 1963).
[Scattered references to Annie Besant's friendship with Shaw.]

785 Nichols, Marie Hochmuth. "George Bernard Shaw: Rhetorician and Public Speaker," RHETORIC AND CRITICISM (Baton Rouge: Louisiana State U P, 1963), pp. 109-29.

Shaw believed strongly in the usefulness of public discussion; only from controversy can commitment be generated. His manner of speaking, however controversial, arose from a carefully developed theory of rhetoric. Through his membership in various societies, Shaw nurtured a delight in and skill at debate that was lifelong and which manifested itself in virtually all of his activities. The first real attention Shaw gained was as a contentious and brilliant debater, and the principal activity of his life, at least until his retirement from the platform in 1941, was the writing and delivery of speeches on every conceivable topic. The themes of the prefaces to many of the plays are anticipated in Shaw's speeches. Even the famous *Quintessence of Ibsenism* was first delivered as a public lecture. His rhetorical techniques included the ploy of arousing his audience by insulting them. He often used analogy, paradox, hyperbole, bits of dialogue, and exaggeration in his speeches and believed that speeches should contain "ideas" not "information." His chaffing wit was a lifelong characteristic, but it was tempered by a graciousness evident even when he was being most outrageous. His effectiveness as a speaker was due also to his voice and delivery. *How* English was spoken was a passionate concern, and he was especially interested in the mechanics of voice production. He also knew and practiced effective gestures. He denied, however, having ever studied any of the well-known manuals on speaking. It is a mistake, too, to assume his speeches were always great successes, and he was not consistently popular with the same groups or classes of people. Shaw made speeches because he knew how, and because he hoped, through them, to make the world a better place.

786 O'Donovan, John. "Shaw and Ireland," SHAVIAN, II (Oct 1963), 33-35.
There were many reasons for the Irish dislike of Shaw, yet no Irish writer evinced more concern for Ireland than did Shaw, as is made clear by David H. Green's THE MATTER WITH IRELAND (1962), previously uncollected pieces by Shaw.

787 Okumura, Saburo. "Rekishi to Kigekiseishin - *Saint Joan* Shiron-" (History and Comic Spirit -on *Saint Joan*-), KAGAWA DAIGAKU GAKUGEIGAKUBU KENKYUHO- KOKU (Takamatsu), Part I, No. 16 (Jan 1963), 51-83.
Shaw criticizes human beings who cannot understand Joan, and at the same time his criticism is directed to Joan too, who fails to make herself understandable to others.

This is a play of Joan's disillusion. The famous concluding speech of Joan at the end of Epilogue is a cry of despair. Apparently Shaw has recognized his own image in Joan: both of them have suffered bitter disillusion more than once. [In Japanese.]

788 Okumura, Saburo. "Victoriacho no Shicho to Shaw no Chojin oyobi Seimeiryoku no Shiso" (Victorian Thought and Shaw's Idea of the Superman and the Life Force), KAGAWA DAIGAKU GAKUGEIGAKUBU KENKYUHOKOKU (Takamatsu), Part I, No. 17 (June 1963), 1-41.
Shaw is never an optimist as many critics claim; he is a staunch disbeliever in progress. He also opposes pessimistic views of life. His ideas of the Superman and the Life Force are fruits of his strong opposition to Victorian ideas on progress and pessimism. The key word to Shaw's ideas on the Superman and the Life Force would be 'endeavor.' The saying "Do the likeliest and God will do the best" explains well Shaw's basic attitude. He opposes the Victorian idea of progress, because it tends to make light of or ignore the necessity of human endeavor. He also strongly criticizes the pessimistic view because it nullifies any human efforts. [In Japanese.]

789 Omerov, I. M. "Kritika imperializma i voiny v tvorchestve B. Shou" (Criticism of Imperialism and War in Shaw's Works), UCHENYE ZAPISKI AZERBAIZHAN-SKII GOS. UNIVERSITET (Baku), No 5 (1963), 45-53.
[Not seen.] [In Azerbaijani.]

790 Oppel, Horst. "George Bernard Shaw: *Mrs. Warren's Profession*," DAS MODERNE ENGLISCHE DRAMA: INTERPRETATIONEN (Modern English Drama: Interpretations), ed by Horst Oppel (Berlin: Erich Schmidt Verlag, 1963; 2nd revd ed 1966; 3rd revd ed 1976), pp. 11-25.
Mrs. Warren's Profession's structure is in contrast with classical five-act drama and drawing room comedy. There is careful selection of characters, and no simple division in good and bad; it is a well balanced masterpiece. The core of the play is Mrs. Warren's life story at the end of Act II. Shaw's main criticism is directed against "fashionable morality." But if Vivie is indeed a "new woman," the question arises: What is gained if she can only see life as it is at the expense of all beauty and romance? [In German.]

791 Otten, Kurt. "George Bernard Shaw: *Pygmalion*," DAS MODERNE ENGLISCHE DRAMA: INTERPRETATIONEN (Modern English Drama: Interpretations), ed. by Horst Oppel (Berlin: Erich Schmidt verlap, 1963; 2nd revd ed 1966; 3rd revd ed 1976), pp. 126-48.
Although *Pygmalion* has become the darling of audiences everywhere, it has remained a wallflower in literary criticism. However, one outstanding interpretation--that of Eric Bentley from 1957--provided most valuable groundwork for this analysis.

Shaw's *Pygmalion* is a rich and complex play. The theme of social advancement is connected with the problems of education. These problems stem from the conflicts between knowledge and culture [*Bildung*], spontaneity and mimesis. Other issues in the play are the gentleman ideal, the relationships of language, intellect and individuality to each other, the dualism between body and soul, the schism between social conventions and individual morality as well as the battle between the sexes. All this is presented in such an entertaining way that the readers and spectators only gradually realize the didactic purposes of the play. [In German.]

792 Palfy, Istvan. "George Bernard Shaw's Reception in Hungary, the Early Years, 1903-1914," ANGOL FILO-LOGIAI TANULMANYOK (Hungarian Studies in English), I (1963), 25-41.
[History of Shaw's extraordinary popularity in Hungary. Summary in Hungarian.]

793 Pálfy, István. "George Bernard Shaw's Reception in Hungary, 1914-1939," ANGOL FILOLOGIAI TANULMANYOK (Hungarian Studies in English), II (1963), 93-104.
Shaw's political writings and statements about the War were noticed in Budapest dailies and periodicals and translated into Hungarian. Little of Shaw's was produced or translated until the Revolution (October 1918), when *Pygmalion* was successfully revived. During the Hungarian Socialist Republic (March-August, 1919), the theaters were nationalized, and *Candida* and *Mrs. Warren's Profession* were produced in Budapest, remaining in the repertoire until the 1920/21 season. Shaw's collected works in translation were published 1923-25. By 1926, Shaw was recognized as one of the greatest dramatists and thinkers of the period. He was attacked by the extreme right. Shaw's letter to Karel Čapek (*Lidove noviny*, Prague, 31 Oct 1928) on the national minorities in Czechoslovakia and

Hungary infuriated the chauvinistic upper classes in Hungary, and Shaw's letter in the right-wing newspaper UJ NEMZEVEDEK made things worse. Nothing of Shaw's was produced for two years, except *Saint Joan*, which was intended as a manifesto against the ruling upper class and right-wing politics. [Summary in Hungarian.]

794 Papajewski, Helmut. "George Bernard Shaw: *Saint Joan*," DAS MODERNE ENGLISCHE DRAMA: INTERPRETATIONEN (Modern English Drama: Interpretations), ed by Horst Oppel (Berlin: Erich Schmidt Verlag 1963; 2nd revd ed 1966; 3rd rev ed 1976), pp. 164-80.
Through her canonization Joan is effectively silenced as an agent of the progressive life force. Thus her protestantism ("the supremacy of private judgment") and her nationalism (in the 15th century a progressive force in the liberation of the lower classes) are rendered ineffective. The basic issue of the play is: How can the faith in the progressive life force be restored after the disillusionment of World War I? [In German.]

795 Parker, Francine. "An Analysis of Shaw's *Saint Joan* in Preparation for Directing Scenes IV and V," CShav, IV (Sept-Oct 1963), 8.
What Shaw says in *Saint Joan* is more important than the validity of his historical interpretation. The play is tragedy, without austerity.

796 Pastalosky, Rosa. GEORGE BERNARD SHAW: SU IDEARIO POLITICO, FILOSOFICO Y SOCIAL (George Bernard Shaw: His Political, Philosophical and Social Ideology) (Santa Fé, Argentina: Castellvi, 1963).
[Brief biography of Shaw. He is placed in the literary milieu of his time.] Although a representative of the dramatist of ideas Shaw differs in the cerebral nature of his works. The action frequently adheres to traditional forms, but Shaw's is a drama of disquisition and polemic. His major philosophical work is *Back to Methuselah*, and his economic and political ideas are best seen in *John Bull's Other Island*. The influence of Marx can be found in his Socialism in three fundamental principles: 1) the abolition of private enterprise and the absorption of basic industry by the state; 2) the elimination of the class structure; and 3) the requirement that everyone should perform equal work. Shaw differed from Marx in

advocating absolute equality of salary. Though Shaw was a revolutionary, he loved tradition and order. He fought against private capital but also denounced the rebellion of the masses to achieve progress. His Socialism was not scientific but ethical and moral. Shaw had no faith in the common man and rejected Marx's dictatorship of the proletariat. He was very far from Marx in his wish that the world be governed by a superman. Though Shaw was original in philosophy, politics, and economics, he was cautiously conservative and traditional in social and moral areas. [In Spanish.]

797 Pavlovic, Luka. "Bernard Shaw: *Davolov Učenik* (Bernard Shaw: *The Devil's Disciple*) OSLOBODENJE (Sarajevo), XX (1963), 5577.
[Not seen.] [In Croation.]

798 Pitman, Sir James. "Comments on the Decision *in re* Shaw's Will," GEORGE BERNARD SHAW ON LANGUAGE, ed by Abraham Tauber (NY: Philosophical Library, 1963; Lond: Peter Owen, 1965), pp. 174-78.
The writer disagrees with the interpretation of Shaw's intentions as expressed in the Will. The Will quite clearly provided for the establishment of an educational trust and, probably, described a limited and certain objective to be achieved.

799 Pitman, Sir James. "Foreword," GEORGE BERNARD SHAW ON LANGUAGE, ed by Abraham Tauber (NY: Philosophical Library, 1963; Lond: Peter Owen, 1965), pp. 11-16.
Shaw warned about the difficulties to be faced by anyone who, like himself, clearly saw the need for alphabet and spelling reform. Shaw predicted the opposition to his Will, yet welcomed the publicity such opposition would give his ideas. He predicted that the Will would stand if supported by the Society, which it did. And once accepted, Shaw accurately predicted, the Will's specific provisions would be accepted as well.

800 Pitman, Sir James. "On the Shaw and Initial Teaching Alphabets," in GEORGE BERNARD SHAW ON LANGUAGE (NY: Philosophical Library, 1963; Lond: Peter Owen, 1965), pp. 191-98.
[Describes the differences between Shaw's system and the Pitman Initial Teaching Alphabet, and recounts Shaw's

effort to convince Pitman of the practicality, as well as
the logic, of a non-romanic system.]

801 Plotinsky, Melvin Lloyd. "The Play of the Mind.
A Study of Bernard Shaw's Dramatic Apprenticeship,"
AMERICAN DOCTORAL DISSERTATIONS, p. 127. Unpub-
lished dissertation, Harvard University, 1963.

802 "Primeira Publicação do Nôvo Alfabeto de George
Bernard Shaw," REVISTA DE TEATRO (Rio de Janeiro),
No. 333 (May-June, 1963), 35.
[Review of the new alphabet edition of *Androcles and the
Lion*.] [In Portugese.]

803 Purdom, Charles Benjamin. A GUIDE TO THE PLAYS
OF BERNARD SHAW (Lond: Methuen; NY: Collier, 1963;
rptd 1964).
[In three major sections--"The Man," "The Dramatist," and
"The Plays." The first section, a biographical sketch,
concludes with the assertion that "Everywhere he looked he
saw comic significance, and as a dramatist he holds
eternal converse with Aristophanes, Shakespeare and
Molière," from which point of view Purdom's consideration
proceeds. A "Note on Biographies" follows. The second
section briefly considers five topics--"The Comic Genius,"
"Better than Shakespeare?," "Themes," "The Characters,"
and "The Prefaces" and is followed by "A Note on Printing
the Plays." The third section includes an outline of the
nature, plot, and characters of each play in chronological
order, and for each play, a comment on "Production" and "A
Note on Productions," where applicable. Useful handbook.]

804 Quinn, Michael. "Form and Intention: A
Negative View of *Arms and the Man*," CRITICAL QUAR-
TERLY, V (1963), 148-54.
Critical assessment of Shaw is made difficult by the
confusion, encouraged by himself, between the polemical
author of the Prefaces and the successful dramatist.
Despite the popularity of *Saint Joan*, Shaw was essentially
a comic dramatist, and his effort to develop a native
comic form can be seen reflected in *Arms and the Man*, his
first popular success. Love and war are two concerns
which are too often regarded as romantic ideals, and *Arms*
is an attack on both. It fails to succeed as a polemic
because no real debate between opposing positions occurs
in the play, partly because the characters are only

superficially motivated. The play cannot be seen as a
serious comedy in the neo-classical tradition because of
its form, which is, paradoxically, essentially that of the
well-made play as Shaw defined it. The play is directed
not to a satiric attack on human folly but merely to a
happy ending. This disparity between dramatic intention
and actualization is no more than evidence of Shaw's
awareness of theatrical reality; at the time *Arms* was
written audiences wanted entertainment, not lectures.
Arms is high comedy, but it is not the chastening attack
on idealism that its Preface says it should be.

805 Sainer, Arthur, "*Mrs. Warren's Profession*: The
Play by George Bernard Shaw, Presented by and at the
Showboat Theatre. Directed by Andy Milligan,"
VILLAGE VOICE (NY), 2 May 1963; rptd in Arthur
Sainer, THE SLEEPWALKER AND THE ASSASSIN, A VIEW OF
THE CONTEMPORARY THEATRE (NY: Bridgehead Books,
1964), p. 78.
"I have nothing good to say about the current production."

806 "Santa Juana" (Saint Joan), PRIMER ACTO (Argentina), XLVIII (1963), 11-14.
[Discussion of plays about St. Joan.] His model was a
mature woman, organizer of schools for the Fabian Society,
Mary Hankinson. [In Spanish.]

807 Saroyan, William. NOT DYING (NY: Harcourt
Brace & World, 1963; Lond: Cassell, 1966), pp. 214-
15.
Shaw was a "saint whose religion was intelligence."

808 Scherer, Gunther. "Das *Shaw Alphabet* und das
Initial Teaching Alphabet. Zu neueren Bemühungen um
die englische Rechtschreibung" (The Shaw Alphabet
and the Initial Teaching Alphabet. New Efforts for
English Orthography), FESTSCHRIFT FÜR WALTER HÜBNER,
ed by Dieter Riesner and Helmut Gneuss (Berlin:
Erich Schmidt, 1963), pp. 51-60.
Shaw's "Proposed British Alphabet" may have various economic advantages in the long run, but it is very unlikely
that it will succeed. [In German.]

809 Schroeder, J. G. "Brecht, Büchner y Shaw,"
PRIMER ACTO (Spain) XLVII (1963), 50-51.

The Agrupación Dramática of Barcelona together with the Escuela de Arte Dramática Adrian Gual presented during the 1963 season Shaw's *Saint Joan* in various localities and to different classes of people ranging from the very poor to the very rich. [In Spanish.]

810 "Shaw mira a Napoleón" (Shaw Looks at Napoleon), PRIMERA PLANA (Argentina), XI (12 Nov 1963), 57.
[Review of *The Man of Destiny* performed in Buenos Aires.] Shaw enjoys destroying myths. In this play he portrays Napoleon in human ways in a witty comedy. [In Spanish.]

811 Smith, Warren S[ylvester]. "Moncure Daniel Conway at South Place Chapel," CHRISTIAN CENTURY, LXXX (16 Jan 1963), 77-80.
Moncure Daniel Conway, American Unitarian and abolitionist, minister of South Place Chapel, Finsbury, London, and a familiar spokesman for the London religious left wing, like Shaw regarded evolution as beneficent. Shaw admired Conway, and his preface to *Androcles and the Lion* closely parallels Conway's CHRISTIANITY (1876). Their views of Jesus were similar.

812 Smith, Warren S[ylvester]. "The Religion of Bernard Shaw," CHRISTIAN CENTURY, LXXX (16 Oct 1963), 1266-69.
After arriving in London in 1876, Shaw stayed aloof from both religious and atheistic groups. Eventually, he came to realize he was developing a religion of his own. In *Man and Superman, John Bull's Other Island,* and *Major Barbara,* we find Shaw to have become a truly religious figure. His views were that religion is necessary, that institutional religions are all unsatisfactory, that true religion is mystical and practical, that God is a blind Life Force with a will both of its own and perhaps in all living things, and that we are needed to carry out the Life Force's purposes. Shaw was effective because he was able to appear both orthodox and radical at the same time and would deplore any effort to mute this in his plays in order to exploit merely their entertainment value.

813 Smith, Warren Sylvester (ed). THE RELIGIOUS SPEECHES OF BERNARD SHAW. With a foreword by Arthur H. Nethercot (University Park, Pennsylvania: Pennsylvania State U P, 1963; NY: McGraw-Hill, 1965).

[General introduction. Brief, identifying headnote to each speech. Notes. No index.]

814 Smith, Warren Sylvester. "Shaw's Kinship to Quakers," FRIENDS JOURNAL, 1 Oct 1963, pp. 416-17. Shaw claimed kinship with Friends because he believed in inner light, because he believed the Life Force works through men, and because he rejected a priesthood and the doctrine of man's depravity.

815 Smoker, Barbara. "Review Article: Simpler than ABC," CShav, IV (May-June 1963), n.p. [Account of the devising by Kingsley Read of a new alphabet which was approved by Shaw in 1942, although not mentioned in his Will, and which, after the compromise settlement of the Will in 1957, was one of four winners in the contest to design a Shaw Alphabet. After efforts to coordinate the four alphabets failed, the Read design was adopted and is here extensively described. The two editions of *Androcles and the Lion*, the ordinary Penguin edition and the Public Trustee's Edition printed in the Shaw Alphabet are described. Smoker, who is General Secretary of the Shaw Society, London, concludes that it is "just possible" that Read's system is "the alphabet of the future."]

816 Spink, Judith B. "The Image of the Artist in the Plays of Bernard Shaw," ShawR, VI (Sept 1963), 82-88. Figures of the artist in the plays of Shaw are "conspicuously less of heroic stature and more of biting satire" than one might expect. Shaw's Socialism accounts for the change in his attitude toward art in early and later work. The change is apparent in the difference between Owen Jack (lonely, a social failure) and Trefusis (a social success, an "*anti*-artist"). The prototype of the weak minor artist (Chichester Erskine, Octavius in *Man and Superman*, the "pale gentleman" of *A Village Wooing*) is Adrian Herbert, in *Love among the Artists*, who "exemplifies the man of feeling but of no force whatsoever." Ibsen and Wagner provided images of the contemporary artist for Shaw; each was a great artist to the extent that he was a great propagandist. Marchbanks embodies the popular idea of the artistic temperament. He can be compared with the real-life Lord Alfred Douglas. Octavius, of *Superman*, is even "more decisively condemned" by Shaw in his rejection by Ann, but Tanner's description of the artist is not of a Shaw hero either, but of a compulsive, driven, "semi-criminal." Louis Dubedat is another version of the popular, respectable person's view of the artist. The character of the artist in Shaw's plays contains "more of the fool and knave than of the sane and honest man," since Shaw the artist could not himself have been further removed "from either the bohemian mode of existence, or from the life of literary cliches." In *As Far As Thought Can Reach*, art is finally reduced to being an occupation for children that in the future will be superfluous. Meanwhile, Shaw used art only because "it still served the purposes of humanity."

817 Stewart, J. I. M. EIGHT MODERN WRITERS (Oxford: Clarendon [OXFORD HISTORY OF ENGLISH LITERATURE XII], 1963), pp. 122-83; rptd in StJFYA, pp. 197-200.

[Life and works of Shaw through 1935.] The "Augustan purity" of Shaw's writing was "sharpened and quickened by the practice of debate" and enhanced by a wit "unexcelled in the English language." The discovery of his "moral passion" Shaw believed to have been the great event of his adolescence. The plays were written to sell Shaw's ideas; the prefaces were written to sell the plays, to give the reader more than he would get in the theater. Shaw's claim that solely for art's sake he "would not face the toil of writing a single sentence" cannot be true, "for the art of the plays is elaborated not to give us something more persuasive than the prefaces but simply something more delightful." In *Widowers' Houses*, Shaw dissipates the central irony by the unsympathetic, comic portrayal of the two protagonists. *The Philanderer* "is closer to the line of Shaw's true develoment" than *Mrs. Warren's Profession*. Because Shaw's knowledge of clergymen was better than his knowledge of poets, *Candida*'s Morell is more convincing than Marchbanks. Believing that ultimately life imitates art, Shaw saw real Caesars appearing in the world. We cannot believe that the Octavius of *Man and Superman* is a poet; he is "the merest sentimental cipher," without even the conventional posturing as a poet of Marchbanks. "The long and excrescent" third act of *Superman* makes the play a drama of ideas and explores "the operatic rather than the intellectual boundaries of drama." In *Major Barbara*, Undershaft's contention that it is more moral to do evil than to exist where the doing of evil is hard to avoid is "demonstrably untenable," his arguments are hard to follow, and the play lacks coherence. In *The Doctor's Dilemma*, Dubedat is done better by the doctors than by

Shaw. The "paradox of the morally imbecile genius destroys itself in the making." Shaw found the character "boring." In *Pygmalion*, Eliza is the antithesis of Galatea since she becomes an artifact; the play's moral lesson is that it is "inhuman to treat any human being as a means to an end."

818 Tauber, Abraham (ed). GEORGE BERNARD SHAW ON LANGUAGE (NY: Philosophical Library, 1963; Lond: Peter Owen, 1965).
[An anthology of materials mostly by and some about Shaw on the subject of alphabet and spelling reform, with a brief introduction on the history of Shaw's interest in such reform, an epilogue noting that the spirit of Shaw's intentions is being carried on, and introductory notes to each item or group of items. Illustrations.] Contents, abstracted under date of first appearance: Pitman, Sir James, "Foreword" (1963); Harman, Lord Justice Charles, "On the Will of Bernard Shaw" (1957); Pitman, Sir James, "Comments on the Decision *in re* Shaw's Will" (1963); Pitman, Sir James, "My Fair Ladies--and Gentlemen" (1958); and Pitman, Sir James, "On Shaw and Initial Teaching Alphabets" (1963). Not abstracted: Pitman, Sir James, "Introduction," SHAW ALPHABET EDITION OF ANDROCLES AND THE LION (1962).

819 Taubman, Howard. "Shaw's 13 Unpublished Diaries Shed Light on Start of Career," NYT, 17 Nov 1963, pp. 1, 80.
Shaw kept diaries in Pitman shorthand for the years 1885-97 which have been seen by none of his biographers.

820 Taubman, Howard. "*Too True to Be Good*," NYT, 13 Mar 1963, p. 8.
Too True to Be Good, even cut, is wordy and thin, but is is also exhilarating.

821 Trewin, J[ohn] C[ourtenay]. THE BIRMINGHAM REPERTORY THEATRE (Lond: Barrie and Rockliff, 1963), pp. 2, 9, 11, 14, 18, 24-25, 30, 32, 41-42, 47, 63, 68-70, 72-77, 79, 83-84, 90, 93-94, 98, 100-08, 111n, 115-17, 118, 125, 127, 135, 140, 143, 156, 159n, 160, 163-65, 181.
[History of the Birmingham Repertory Theatre with descriptions of productions of Shaw plays. Shaw's message on the company's Silver Jubilee. Photographs. Tables.]

822 "Un drama siempre actual: Juana de Arco en la
vision de Bernard Shaw" (A Realistic Play: Joan of
Arc According to Bernard Shaw), PRIMERA PLANA
(Argentina), XL (13 Aug 1963), 44.
The director and actors obviously think that Shaw is as
timeless as Shakespeare and Lope de Vega. Parts of Shaw's
Preface were inserted in the play. [In Spanish.]

823 Valency, Maurice. THE FLOWER AND THE CASTLE
(NY: Macmillan; Lond: Collier-Macmillan, 1963),
pp. 79, 90, 92, 111, 113, 116, 123, 169, 177, 217,
219, 311, 386, 397, 399-400, 402.
The revelatory technique of Shaw simply involves a substitution of stereotypes. Shaw's scientific natural history
is not much more than the bourgeois revolt against literary values. Shaw's *Quintessence of Ibsenism* did more harm
than good; he was actually explaining Brieux and Becque,
not expounding Ibsen. Unlike Shaw, Ibsen was a poet.

824 Watson, Barbara B. "A Shavian Guide to the
Intelligent Woman." Published dissertation Columbia
University, 1963; pub under the same title (1964).

825 Weintraub, Stanley. "How History Gets Rewrit-
ten: Lawrence of Arabia in the Theatre," DramS, II
(Spring 1963), 269-75.
[Anecdotes relating to Lawrence's connection with Shaw.]

826 Weintraub, Stanley. PRIVATE SHAW AND PUBLIC
SHAW (NY: George Braziller, 1963).
[This "dual portrait" of Shaw and T. E. Lawrence covers
the period from their first meeting, on 25 March 1922, to
Lawrence's death, on 13 May 1935. Weintraub sees Lawrence
as having replaced Granville Barker in the lives of Shaw
and Mrs. Shaw as a kind of surrogate son. Many of
Lawrence's character traits were reflected in Shaw's
characters, in plays written both before and after meeting
Lawrence, and Lawrence is "caricatured" as Private
Napoleon Alexander Trotsky Meek in *Too True to Be Good*.]

827 Whitman, Wanda. "Shaw and Shakespeare on Saint
Joan," ISh, II (1963), 6.
The nature of Shaw's feud with Shakespeare, often over-
simplified, is seen in their different views of Joan.

828 Whittemore, Reed. "The Fascination of the Abomination--Wells, Shaw, Ford, Conrad," THE FASCINATION OF THE ABOMINATION: POEMS, STORIES, AND ESSAYS (NY: Macmillan Company; Lond: Collier-Macmillan, 1963), pp. 129-66.

Among Wells, Ford, Conrad and Shaw, Shaw probably retained a pre-War literary temperament. Shaw insisted on "facts" (as opposed to fictions); his is a simple dualism. His most realist characters are committed to the present, to the facts of their own time. For Shaw it would follow that journalism is the highest form of literature. Yet the supposed clarity and simplicity of Shaw are not really so dependent on hard facts. Shaw's reputation is not, then, as a playwright of facts but as a playwright of ideas. His view of daily affairs was god-like, not that of the journalist. His fictional characters behave like fictional characters. [On the way to arriving at this conclusion, Whittemore makes a bizarre comparison between Conrad's HEART OF DARKNESS and Shaw's *Major Barbara*, particularly between Kurtz and Barbara herself.]

829 Williamson, Audrey. BERNARD SHAW: MAN AND ARTIST (NY: Crowell-Collier, 1963); as BERNARD SHAW: MAN AND WRITER (Lond: Collier-Macmillan, 1963).

[An introduction to the life and works of Shaw. The biography adds nothing new; the criticism is not particularly penetrating. Quotes Shaw on music; comments on affinities between Shaw and Wagner; compares Shaw with Ibsen; usual comments on major plays.]

830 Wilson, Edmund. "Meetings with Max Beerbohm," ENCOUNTER, XXI (Dec 1963), 16-22.

Beerbohm thought Shaw's alphabet "an absurd and outrageous idea" and apparently thought Shaw had invented a new alphabet to be imposed by law. He obviously disliked Shaw for his egoism and for his unpleasant personal appearance. Yet he had some left-handed praise for Shaw, as for his debating skill. He disfigured his copy of Henderson's Shaw biography, perhaps because he hated the idea that Shaw had become a great man.

831 Woodbridge, Homer Edwards. GEORGE BERNARD SHAW: CREATIVE ARTIST. With a preface by Harry T. Moore (Carbondale: Southern Illinois U P [Cross-currents/Modern Critiques], 1963).

In the five novels written before Shaw turned to drama, he is more interested in characters and their interactions than in propaganda. As a whole, Shaw's novels reveal him as a rebel against tradition, an observer of human nature, an artist and critic, a reformer, and a comic. In *Widowers' Houses*, Shaw's satire fails because he put the social criticism in the mouth of Sartorius, "an obviously insincere and rascally person." In *Mrs. Warren's Profession* Shaw's imagination got the better of his intention and "consequently he produces his first masterpiece." *Candida*'s plot parallels that of Shakesperian romantic comedy with its high and low comedy groups, its title character a Rosalind, its Burgess a Dogberry. *How He Lied to Her Husband* is not a parody but a burlesque of *Candida*. *Caesar and Cleopatra* is like a Shakesperian chronicle play. *Man and Superman* uses an "Elizabethan formula," a double plot with two heroines and two love stories. The Preface to *Major Barbara* attacks in all directions but is not particularly enlightening about the play, which is more propagandistic than earlier days. The play's thinking is muddled and its characters not credible. The "dilemma" of *The Doctor's Dilemma* "is really trumped up to give the audience a little suspense." *Cymbeline Refinished* improves Shakespeare's plot, but the character changes are not so felicitous. Shaw's imaginative and intellectual powers were in conflict, thus many of the Prefaces are irrelevant to their plays. *Heartbreak House* is in intention at least a morality play. *Saint Joan* is a saint play, and it is the sunset of Shaw's genius. *Back to Methuselah* is a miracle play. Shaw knew and said that "great plays do not originate in the philosopher's ratiocinations or the reformer's zeal." He is a greater artist than thinker.

1964

---

832 Armstrong, William A. "Bernard Shaw and Forbes-Robertson's HAMLET," SHAKESPEARE QUARTERLY, XV (1964), 27-31.
[Reconstruction from two letters by Shaw to Ellen Terry, from Shaw's review in the SATURDAY REVIEW of the production and from the reviews of other dramatic critics, of Shaw's suggestions, originally on "four pages of foolscap, closely written," for Forbes-Robertson's 1897 production of HAMLET.]

833 Ayling, Ronald. "The Ten Birthplaces of *Saint Joan*: A Letter from G.B.S.," Shaw R, VIII (Jan 1964), 24.
A radio quiz program in 1943 accepted "Glengarriff" as the place of composition of *Saint Joan*. The editor of the KILKENNY PEOPLE, citing Hesketh Pearson, wrote a letter to the IRISH INDEPENDENT claiming the play was actually written in Parknasilla. Shaw responded with a subsequent letter to the INDEPENDENT. [Letter naming ten places where play was composed.]

834 Barr, Alan Philip. "Bernard Shaw as a Religious Dramatist," DA, XXV (1964), 1902-03. Unpublished dissertation, University of Rochester, 1964.

835 Baxter, Kay M. SPEAK WHAT WE FEEL (Lond: SCM Press, 1964); CONTEMPORARY THEATRE AND THE CHRISTIAN FAITH (NY: Abingdon P, 1965).
Ibsen, Shaw, and Claudel are three figures of the recent theatrical past who dealt with religious themes. Ibsen's passion for truth made him a model for Shaw. Although Shaw's contribution to the contemporary theater is currently undervalued, the drama of the first half of the twentieth century would be considerably poorer without his 52 plays. His certainties, however, even if Lilith's final speech in *Back to Methuselah* seems in touch with current astronomical thinking, have been undercut by subsequent events. In the Preface to *Androcles and the Lion*, Shaw attacked the church for its failure to progress with modern science. But by the time he wrote *Too True to Be Good*, even Shaw himself was no longer certain of the inevitability of evolutionary progress or of the absence of chance in the universe. Shaw continued to preach, but without conviction.

836 Bentley, Eric. THE LIFE OF THE DRAMA (NY: Atheneum, 1964; reprinted NY: Atheneum; London, Methuen, 1965, pp. 11, 24, 35, 49, 54, 55, 69, 73, 79, 87, 103, 127-32, 133, 141, 158, 167-68, 184, 185, 197, 212-13, 228, 250, 254, 257, 319, 322, 338.
Shaw railed against plot but often used intricate ones. He claimed that plays developed naturally and were not constructed. He acknowledged his dependence on character types. In Shaw's famous discussion scenes the dialogue is not all perfected. The theater's chief preacher of recent times is Shaw. Only he has been able to get away with

setting characters on a stage and just letting them talk, because of the wit, paradox, complexity of ideas, and muliplicity of levels in the situations. Shaw at his best wrote no mere thesis play. He tells us that the actor is the least hypocritical of men because he admits he's acting; he urges us to find adequate masks. In both prefaces and plays, Shaw attacks melodrama, because he hated the morals of melodrama.

837 Bernstein, Melvin H. JOHN JAY CHAPMAN (NY: Twayne [TUSAS 70], 1964), pp. 84, 95-97.
[Chapman's puritanical dislike of Shaw.]

838 Besant, Lloyd. "Shaw's Women Characters," DA, XXV (1964), 2661-62. Unpublished dissertation, University of Wisconsin, 1964.

839 Blau, Herbert. THE IMPOSSIBLE THEATER, A MANIFESTO (NY: Macmillan; Lond: Collier-Macmillan, 1964), pp. 210-13.
[Notes on the 1963 San Francisco production of *Major Barbara* by The Actor's Workshop.]

840 Blunt, Wilfred. THE LIFE OF SYDNEY CARLYLE COCKERELL (Lond: Hamish Hamilton, 1964); as COCK-ERELL: SYDNEY CARLYLE COCKERELL, FRIEND OF RUSKIN AND WILLIAM MORRIS AND DIRECTOR OF THE FITZWILLIAM MUSEUM, CAMBRIDGE (NY: Alfred A. Knopf, 1965).
[Passing references to and anecdotes of Cockerell's lifelong friendship with Shaw.]

841 Bosworth, R. F. "Shaw Recordings at the B.B.C.," ShawR, VII (May 1964), 42-46.
[Discography of ten recordings of Shaw's voice preserved in the record library of the B.B.C. and dated from 11 July 1932 to 12 Nov 1947.]

842 Brooks, Cleanth, John T. Purser, and Robert Penn Warren. "Discussion," AN APPROACH TO LITERATURE, 4th ed. (NY: Appleton, Century, Crofts, 1964), pp. 619-22.
Our appreciation of *Saint Joan* is not dependent on our believing Shaw's double thesis that Joan was one of the first Protestant martyrs and one of the first apostles of

Nationalism. In the play, as opposed to the Preface, Shaw the artist, not the propagandist, is dominant. Joan's final speech is a statement of the thesis that persons like her are hard to live with, which runs throughout the play, although the play is too complex to allow us to see her statement as a summation. By playing down the supernatural and depicting Joan's "miracles" as accidents Shaw may have been attempting to secularize Joan, but in so doing, he highlights her good sense. Shaw's treatment of the miraculous in *Saint Joan* is one way in which the meaning of Joan's life is revealed.

843 Brown, Ivor. "Bardolatry Year," DRAMA, ns LXXII (Spring 1964), 28-32.
[Shaw's notorious tirade against Shakespeare in his review of Irving's 1896 production of CYMBELINE is "not very convincingly justified" in a letter from Shaw to Brown.]

844 Brown, Jack R. "Two Notes on Shaw's *Advice to a Young Critic: You Can Never Tell* and *Arms and the Man*," ShawR, VII (Jan 1964), 25-27.
In his edition of *Advice to a Young Critic*, Shaw's letters to Golding Bright, E. J. West is unable to explain Shaw's rebuking Bright for claiming that Mrs. Patrick Campbell was to play the mother, not the sister, of Winifred Emery in *You Never Can Tell*. In a letter from Shaw to Ellen Terry, however, it can be seen that Mrs. Patrick Campbell was indeed considered for the role of Gloria, although this came to nothing, thus West's confusion. Also, West is unable to explain Shaw's reference to Bright's booing, at the first night of *Arms and the Man*, what he took as an improper allusion to the Royal Family. There are, however, some lines in Act III spoken by Sergius and Louka where such an allusion might have been perceived.

845 Brown, T. J. "English Literary Autographs L: George Bernard Shaw, 1856-1950," BOOK COLLECTOR, XIII (1964), 195.
[Two examples of Shaw's handwriting, with analysis.]

846 Bryden, Ronald. "Brecht and Shaw," NStat, LXVII (19 June 1964), 966-67; rpt CShav, V (July-Aug 1964), 4-5.

Tony Richardson's production of Brecht's SAINT JOAN OF THE STOCKYARDS provides sufficient evidence that the play is a masterpiece. It is a "deliberate conflation" of Shaw's *Saint Joan* and *Major Barbara*. Shaw's importance to Brecht lay in the fact that Shaw had invented a theater of revolution. Brecht was Shaw's St. Paul. However, ST. JOAN OF THE STOCKYARDS has "a colour, a consistent theatricality" that is not found in Shaw.

847 Carpenter, Charles A., Jr. "Shaw's Cross-section of Anti-Shavian Opinion," Shaw R, VII (Sept 1964), 78-86.
The very success of Shaw's plays on the London stage became an obstacle in the way of other avant-garde dramatists. Shaw's solution to the problem was first to remove most of his plays from production and then to smooth the way for other new playwrights by satirizing the anti-Shavian and anti-new drama bias in popular and journalistic criticism. This he did in *Fanny's First Play*.

848 Cavallini, Graziano. IBSEN SHAW PIRANDELLO. ANALISI DELLA FUNZIONE SOCIO-PEDAGOGICA DEL TEATRO (Ibsen Shaw Pirandello. Analysis of the Socio-Pedagogic Function of the Theater) (Milano: Litografia D. Cislaghi [Biblioteca di Studi e Testi Universitari 8], 1964), pp. 7-13, 41-68, 113-15.
Shaw affirms that theater does not make drama but vice versa. The theater of Ibsen, Pirandello and Shaw has both propaganda and artistic elements, though the second one is predominant in Shaw. Shaw's first goal is to reach the conscience of the public by attacking its common sense (unlike Molière). He denounces in conventional ideals the mask which hides social injustice. *Widowers' Houses* attacks the immorality of wealth. The dramatic conflict of *Mrs. Warren's Profession* is between dependence and the struggle to be oneself. *The Philanderer* exposes the relationships between men and women and is a transition to *Plays Pleasant*, which contrasts the real with the ideal. *Candida* fails as drama because it does not provide catharsis. *Back to Methuselah* contrasts reality with illusion. Shaw's Life Force cannot be explained by Schopenhauer or Nietzsche. The true value of Shaw's work lies in the discovery by the individual, in the development of humanity, of the force and reason of

personal affirmation. Like Marx, Shaw believes in continuous revolution, revealing the collapse in modern theater of a fixed objective reality. [In Italian.]

849 Cecil, David. MAX (Lond: Constable, 1964; Bost: Houghton Mifflin, 1965), pp. 70, 92, 163-64, 166, 167, 180, 187, 201, 242, 248, 261, 262, 270, 320, 326, 328, 354, 364, 370-72, 374, 409, 462, 470, 472, 485, 490.
Beerbohn said Wilde was the better companion but Shaw was the better character. The so-called Decadents of the 'nineties were worth little compared with such contemporaries as Shaw. Beerbohm did not suppose Shaw to be actually close to the truth of things. There are no references in his notebooks to Shaw, of whom Beerbohm saw much in the 'nineties. In his SATURDAY REVIEW pieces Beerbohm praised Shaw. As a frequent guest of the *haute bourgeoisie*, Beerbohm enlarged his knowledge of Shaw and others. London came to be for Beerbohm the capital of the England of others, like Shaw, not of himself. For all his admiration of Shaw, Beerbohm was not uncritical and was often hostile.

850 Chaplin, Charles. MY AUTOBIOGRAPHY (NY: Simon & Schuster, 1964), pp. 94, 272-73, 338, 339, 343, 345, 435.
[Anecdotes. Photograph with Shaw.]

851 Clunes, Alec. THE BRITISH THEATRE (Lond: Cassell, 1964; NY: A. S. Barnes [The Arts of Man], 1965), pp. 72, 130, 141, 143, 146-52, 155, 156, 157-60, 161, 162, 166, 179.
In decrying poverty as a social evil, Shaw was anticipated by George Farquhar. In the nineteenth century the best critical writing was achieved at the beginning of the century only by Hazlitt and at the end by Shaw. In the 90's, in *The Quintessence of Ibsenism* and in his drama criticism, Shaw set Ibsen as the critical standard for judging the drama of the time. Shaw the iconoclast paradoxically put Ellen Terry on a pedestal; he tried to make a New Woman of her, but she, in effect, unmade him. Like a number of men of the twentieth-century theater, Shaw wrote for purposes other than to make money (although he did do that, too); he wrote for the good of mankind. Shaw demonstrated that, unlike those of Ibsen, reform plays need not be gloomy. He had learned from his public-speaking experiences that an audience's interest could be

maintained by making it laugh. His consequent popularity thus freed the theater from those critics who contended it was an unsuitable forum for social reform. Critics insisted that the plays were all talk and no action, that they were plotless, yet they do reveal patterns that can be best described in terms of music. Shaw's method of promoting reform in the plays was to turn conventionally held ideas of what is right or desirable inside-out. His principal contribution to the theater was not his technical innovations but his popularization of drama with serious social purpose. Strindberg's THE FATHER and Shaw's *Candida* are Ibsen's A DOLL'S HOUSE with a man as the doll. [Illustrations.]

852 Cohn, Ruby. "Hell on the Twentieth-Century Stage," WISCONSIN STUDIES IN CONTEMPORARY LITERA-TURE, V (Winter-Spring 1964), 48-53.
[Contrasts modern depictions of Hell with those of medieval and Renaissance drama, and compares Shaw's Hell Scene, Act III of *Man and Superman*, with Satre's HUIS CLOS and the "infernal Epilogue" of Frisch's BIEDERMANN UND DIE BRANDTSTIFTER.]

853 Cordell, Richard A. "Shaw in the College Classroom," ISh, III (Fall 1964), 1-3.
Shaw was wrong about collegians detesting his plays. He provides a one-man liberal education and an appreciation of good writing; he is a great dramatist; he wrote so much himself there is no need of secondary sources.

854 Corrigan, Robert W. "George Bernard Shaw," THE MODERN THEATRE (NY: Macmillan, 1964), 878-79; rptd in MASTERPIECES OF THE MODERN ENGLISH THEATRE (NY: Collier Books, Macmillan, 1967), p. 110.
Shaw created the modern comedy of ideas. He was not so much an original thinker as he was an articulate stage magician. Readers sometimes get so involved with the intellectual intricacies that they forget he is a master craftsman of the theater, who uses the conventions of realism for ends radically different from those of the traditional realist.

855 Delacorte, Valerie. "G.B.S. in Filmland," ESQUIRE, LXII (Dec 1964), 150-51, 153, 288-92.
[Amusing account, by Gabriel Pascal's widow, of Pascal's initial meeting with Shaw, his subsequently obtaining the

film rights to *Pygmalion*, the filming of *Pygmalion* and other Shaw plays under Shaw's supervision, and the ultimate success, two years after Pascal's death, of MY FAIR LADY.]

856 Dukore, Bernard F. "Brecht's Shavian Saint," QUARTERLY JOURNAL OF SPEECH, L (April 1964), 136-39; rptd CShav, V (July-Aug 1964), 1-4
A number of parallels can be drawn between Brecht's SAINT JOAN OF THE STOCKYARDS and Shaw's *Saint Joan* which suggest strongly that the Brecht play is more indebted to *Saint Joan* than, as many critics have insisted, to *Major Barbara*.

857 Durbin, James H., Jr. "Ayot St. Lawrence and the Middle Border," CORANTO, I (Spring 1964), 3-13.
[Excerpts from and comments on 12 essentially inconsequential Shaw postcards, two Shaw letters, a note from Charlotte Shaw, and several Shaw photographs among the Hamlin Garland papers in the American Literature Collection of the University of Southern California Library.]

858 Evans, T. F. "Shaw in 1914," SHAVIAN, II (June 1964), 17-25.
[Shaw's "activities and utterances" during the Great War of 1914-18.]

859 Feldman, Eddy S. "George Bernard Shaw: Friend of Libraries," CORANTO, I (Spring 1964), 14-23; rptd CShav, V (May-June 1964), 12-17.
In many ways, not the least his bequests to the British Museum, the National Gallery of Ireland, and the Royal Academy of Dramatic Art, Shaw demonstrated his love of libraries.

860 Fricker, Robert. DAS MODERNE ENGLISCHE DRAMA (Modern English Drama) (Göttingen: Vandenhoeck & Ruprecht, 1964; 1974), pp. 11-24.
Shaw was a reformer of English theater. He is a modern classic, whose dramatic work outlived his theoretical pronouncements. The structure of his plays can be reduced to a few basic patterns, and his characters are variations of a few basic types. But these limitations are due to the social message Shaw wants to convey with his plays. His later plays are weak, but his ten greatest plays live

on because of Shaw's comic genius and his masterly dialogue, the vitality of his characters and his dramatic dialectics. [Fricker's book deals with several modern British playwrights. In his chapter on Shaw, he provides a brief interpretation of a few selected plays.] [In German.]

861 Gassner, John. "Shaw on Ibsen and the Drama of Ideas," IDEAS AND THE DRAMA: SELECTED PAPERS FROM THE ENGLISH INSTITUTE, ed by John Gassner (NY and Lond: Columbia U P, 1964), pp. 71-100.
It has long been an article of faith that Ibsen created the drama of ideas and that Shaw was his chief apostle. This is an oversimplification, however, and the idea that the *Quintessence of Ibsenism* is really the "Quintessence of Shavianism" more accurately describes the situation where Shaw himself was the principal contributor to the concept of drama of ideas. Shaw's concern with Ibsen passed through three stages. During the first two he secured Ibsen's place in England; in the third, he described this acceptance of Ibsen as the principal event in the shaping of modern drama. [Gassner proceeds to analyze the *Quintessence*, demonstrating that while, as exposition of Ibsen, Shaw's discussions are sometimes distortions or misrepresentations of the plays, the work, especially its summation, does define the concept of drama of ideas as written by such modern playwrights as Satre, Brecht, Duerrenmatt, and, of course, Shaw himself.]

862 Gassner, John, and Ralph G. Allen. THEATRE AND DRAMA IN THE MAKING (Bost: Houghton Mifflin, 1964), pp. 511-12, 549, 571-72, 678, 681, 783, 684n, 770-71, 776, 823, 824, 827, 828, 955, 960, 967-71, 983, 984, 1053, 1054, 1057.
Shaw shared William Archer's distaste for the earlier dramatic conventions and wished to appeal not to emotion but to intellect. He often criticized Shakespeare's artificiality but believed Shakespeare should be performed as written. *The Devil's Disciple* is an example of the "well-made" play. While Shaw's *The Quintessence of Ibsenism* served as the rallying point for Ibsen's defenders, neither Shaw nor the others really saw beneath the surfaces of Ibsen's plays. Shaw made theater communicate on the highest intellectual level; he was a master of dialogue; Eliot's MURDER IN THE CATHEDRAL and FAMILY REUNION owe much to Shaw and Coward. Shaw followed the way of comedy as a response to the human condition. The "new

realism" of Ibsen and Shaw had a great impact on the American theater.

863 Geduld, Harry M. "Introduction," THE RATIONALI-ZATION OF RUSSIA BY BERNARD SHAW, ed by Harry M. Geduld (Bloomington: Indiana UP, 1964), pp. 9-32.
The Rationalization of Russia was begun and abandoned in South Africa in 1932, the year after Shaw's only trip to Russia, while Mrs. Shaw was confined to her bed for several weeks following an automobile accident. *The Black Girl in Her Search for God* was completed during the same forced stay in South Africa. The work may be seen as a sketch of ideas which are reflected in the political Prefaces of the 1930's and are echoed in *On the Rocks, Too True to Be Good,* and *The Simpleton of the Unexpected Isles.* It is a witty attack on European capitalism and the corruptions of Western society and a spirited defense of Soviet Communism. "It is unthinkable that Shavian prose of such brilliance and vitality should remain in the obscurity of an unpublished manuscript." Shaw's visit to Russia in 1931 confirmed his high opinions of the Soviet system. Had *The Rationalization* been completed, it would presumably have included an account of Shaw's trip. [In the absence of such an account or a travel diary, Geduld devotes the remainder of his introduction to a reconstruction, from various secondary sources, of Shaw's trip, made in the company of, among others, Nancy Astor. If accurately reconstructed, the trip was not without its comic aspects. Photographs.]

864 Geduld, H[arry] M. "The Lineage of Lilith," Shaw R, VII (May 1964), 58-61.
The character of Lilith, who appears only once, just before the final curtain, in *Back to Methuselah,* can be traced to her origins in Assyrian legend, Biblical and Talmudic literature, medieval superstition, and the works of Goethe, Shelley, and Rossetti.

865 Geduld, H[arry] M. "Place and Treatment of Persons in *Back to Methuselah,*" CShav, V (Nov-Dec 1964), 1-12.
There is no Shavian formula for characterization in his plays; the issues of a play determine the range of character. The characters are sufficient to carry the themes.

866 Geduld, H[arry] M. "Shaw's Philosophy as Expounded in *Back to Methuselah*," CShav, V (Sept-Oct 1964), 11-19.
In extracting philosophy from *Back to Methuselah*, ideas of art, illusion and reality, determinism and free will, the body-mind relationship, and youth and age can be distinguished.

867 Geduld, H[arry] M. "Sources and Influences of Shaw's Pentateuch," C Shav, V (May-June 1964), 1-10.
Back to Methuselah is the first example of Utopian literature in play form. Shaw adopted the time-span of mediaeval mystery cycles. In presenting his vision of the future, Shaw's major innovations are biological, political, and ethical, and his only device is the television. He presents the conventions of his future world by conflict of characters: the knowledgeable confronting the perplexed. Shaw created not only a credible world of the future, but one that develops. [Reference to other Utopian writers, notably Swift, Butler, and Marx.]

868 Gerould, Daniel C. *"Saint Joan* in Paris," ShawR, VII (Jan 1964), 11-23; rptd StJFYA.
Until 28 April 1925, all efforts to establish Shaw in France as a major modern dramatist had failed, then the production of *Saint Joan* was an unqualified and lasting success. *Joan* has remained the one Shaw play not regarded as so essentially a satire of British society as to be incomprehensible to the French.

869 Hart-Davis, Rupert (ed). LETTERS TO REGGIE TURNER (Lond: Rupert Hart-Davis, 1964); as MAX BEERBOHM'S LETTERS TO REGGIE TURNER (Phila and NY: J. B. Lippincott, 1965).
[Several references to Shaw and an amusing anecdote (letter dated 14 April 1914) concerning Shaw's having agreed to pose for a wax effigy for Madame Tussaud's.]

870 Hentschel, Irene. "Producing for Shaw and Priestly," DRAMA, ns LXXV (Winter 1964), 32-34.
[Reminiscences of producing Shaw plays.]

871 Hobsbawm, E. J. LABOURING MEN: STUDIES IN THE HISTORY OF LABOUR (Lond: Weidenfeld and Nicolson,

1964; rptd Garden City, NY: Basic Books, 1967); 247, ["The Fabians Reconsidered"] 250-69.
In a Hampstead discussion group of which Shaw was a part and in which Marx's CAPITAL was discussed, much of the FABIAN ESSAYS matured. The Fabian alternative to Marxist economics, as outlined by Shaw in the FABIAN ESSAYS, had little effect on other British non-Marxist Socialist groups. That Shaw was an enthusiastic supporter of Soviet Communism was not inconsistent with his earlier thought. The Fabian concern for what to do with tainted money is reflected in Shaw's *Widowers' Houses*. Shaw was among the group of writers and journalists, men and women, who comprised half of the middle-class membership of the Fabian Society and played a key role in Fabian theory. Shaw realized that an appeal to self-interest would not be an adequate attraction to Socialism.

872 Kantorovich, I. "Na zare i na zakate (Shekspir i Shou)" (At Dawn and Dusk/Shakespeare and Shaw/), URAL, no. 4 (1964), 159-63.
After the Romantic drama of Byron and Shelley, no significantly original play was written in England until the end of the nineteenth century. The low ideological standard of the English theater was also evident in productions of Shakespeare and was reflected in Shaw's attitude to him. Shaw read Tolstoi's essay on Shakespeare and the drama, with which he disagreed. The Socialist Revolution of October 1917 struck a blow at Fabianism and led to a new stage in Shaw's development. [In Russian.]

873 Kerr, Walter F. "*Man and Superman*," NYHT, 7 Dec 1964.
With the "Don Juan in Hell" sequence, *Man and Superman* becomes a "tremendous Trifle."

874 Laurence, Dan H. (ed). "The Roger Casement Trial," MASSACHUSETTS REVIEW, V (Winter 1964), 311-14; rptd. in Skelton, Robin and David R. Clark. IRISH RENAISSANCE: A GATHERING OF ESSAYS, MEMOIRS AND LETTERS FROM THE MASSACHUSETTS REVIEW (Dublin: Dolmen P, 1965), pp. 94-97.
[Texts of statement from Shaw (1934) concerning Roger Casement and of letter from Gertrude Bannister (Parry) thanking Shaw for his support of Casement, with note.]

875 McDowell, Frederick P. W. "Review Article: *The Rationalization of Russia*," ISh, III (Fall 1964), 4-5.
Shaw's *Rationalization of Russia* is a mood piece and not noteworthy for coherence. Its disillusionment derives from parliament's failure to bring about a revolutionary society. He sees the deficiencies of the middle class and seems to approve of "liquidation" of social drones. It is not first-rate, but it "fills the contours of our knowledge about Shaw's temperament and ideas."

876 McKee, Irving. "Shaw's *Saint Joan* and the American Critics," SHAVIAN, II (1964), 13-16.
The New York critics of *Saint Joan* at its world premiere in 1923, with the exception of Ludwig Lewisohn, were essentially negative, as were those, excepting John Mason Brown, of the revival 12 years later. From the time of the second revival, in 1939, however, critics have uniformly treated the play as a classic.

877 McVeigh, Hugh. "When the Abbey Theatre Did Battle with the Castle," IRISH DIGEST, LXXXI (Oct 1964), 50-52.
The Abbey Theatre in 1909 prepared for August production *The Shewing-up of Blanco Posnet*, which had been banned in England by the Lord Chamberlain. The Irish censor warned that some of the play's expressions might be considered blasphemous. The play was performed as scheduled to an enthusiastic reception; the government took no action.

878 Martínez Herrera, A. "El socialismo de Bernard Shaw" (The Socialism of Bernard Shaw), DE GOLPE Y PORROZO (At One Fell Blow) (La Habana: 1964), pp. 21-29.,
[Not seen.] [In Spanish.]

879 Martínez Ruiz, Florencio. "Pigmalión," RESEÑA (Spain), V (Dec 1964), 377-78.
[Review of *Pygmalion* production in a translation by Mendez Herrea, which was not liked because it catered to the taste of the common people.] [In Spanish.]

880 Mason, W. H. *ST. JOAN* (G. BERNARD SHAW) (NY: Barnes & Noble, 1964).

[A study guide "designed primarily for the school, college, and university student" and consisting of three parts: I—a biographical sketch and background of the play; II—an analysis of the play's six scenes and epilogue; III—an estimate of the play's dramatic achievement. Study questions and a very brief bibliography.]

881 Masumoto, Masahiko. "Shaw in Japan—A Preliminary Report," ISh, III (Winter 1964/65), 15.
[Survey of Shaw translations in Japan.]

882 Matlaw, Myron. "Shaw, Farleigh, and the Black Girl," ISh, II (Spring 1964), insert.
[The story of John Farleigh's illustrations for *The Adventures of the Black Girl in Her Search for God*, illustrated with Shaw's sketches and Farleigh's work.]

883 Maulnier, Thierry. "De Bernard Shaw à Jean Schlumberger," LA REVUE DE PARIS, LXXI (May 1964), 132-35.
Shaw's Joan is only partially the true Joan, but the Joan of this Irish Voltaire is mysterious and irritating. His *Saint Joan* belongs to the great theater repertoire of the first half of the twentieth century. The translation of Georges Neveux is elegant. [Review of the Théâtre Montparnasse production of *Saint Joan*, starring Danielle Delorme.] [In French.]

884 May, Frederick. ["Introductory Note"] "Bernard Shaw's *Saint Joan*," by Luigi Pirandello, SHAVIAN, II (Feb 1964), 6-12.
Shaw expressed his regard for Pirandello, especially for SIX CHARACTERS IN SEARCH OF AN AUTHOR.

885 Mayne, Fred. "Types and Contrasts in Shaw," ENGLISH STUDIES IN AFRICA, VII (Sept 1964), 187-94.
Although Shaw's characters can readily be classified as either realists or idealists, or wits and butts, this is not to say that Shaw's characters are mere types. Shaw's genius was such that he recognized and embodied in his characters the complexities and contradictions inherent in all human natures.

886 Meisel, Martin. "Cleopatra and 'The Flight into Egypt,'" Shaw R, VII (May 1964), 62-63.
The Sphinx scene of *Caesar and Cleopatra* seems to have been suggested by Shaw's memory of a reproduction of Luc Olivier Merson's painting "Repos en Égypte." This is only one instance of scenes in Shaw apparently suggested by pictures he had once seen.

887 Méléra, Marguerite Yerta. "Introduction," BERNARD SHAW ET LES FEMMES (Bernard Shaw and Women), by C. G. L. DuCann, trans by Marguerite Yerta Méléra (Paris: La Palatine, 1964), pp. 9-24. [Originally published as THE LOVES OF BERNARD SHAW (1963).]
Shaw's relations with women are not spoken of often. He began modestly in his relations, but once started, advanced quickly. He modelled himself as always on Dickens, but he deluded himself when he thought he was a novelist. All sentiment is absent from *Immaturity*, and he finally gave up fiction. Like Dickens he destroyed all letters sent to him. [Briefly traces Shaw's adventures among the ladies with reference to politics and literature. [Illustrated.] [In French.]

888 Minney, R[ubeigh]. J[ames]. THE EDWARDIAN AGE (Bost: Little, Brown, 1964), pp. 2, 20, 112, 169.
King Edward, who liked the theater but rarely went to see serious drama, saw *Arms and the Man* and found Shaw "a damned crank." Few of Shaw's plays ran even 50 nights in this period. After the fashion of the time, Shaw, with Bertrand Russell, often went for walks of up to 20 miles a day. Shaw sometimes pushed a bicycle, occasionally mounting it and pedalling furiously ahead of the exasperated Russell. In 1906, Shaw was among those who attended a banquet at London's Savoy Hotel honoring suffragettes who had served prison sentences.

889 Monleón, José. "*Pygmalion* de Bernard Shaw," PRIMER ACTO (Spain), LVII (Oct 1964), 50-51.
[Essay-review of Adolfo Marsillach's production of *Pygmalion*.] Shaw is rarely performed on the Spanish stage because of his lack of respect for traditional values, because producers were too timid or lazy to try new techniques, because of the intellectual dialogue, and finally because Shaw demanded that the audience awaken from its lethargy which the Spanish public was unwilling to do. [In Spanish.]

890 Morgan, Margery M. "Strindberg and the English Theatre," MD, VII (Sept 1964), 161-73.
[Strindberg's earliest reception in England, the connections with Shaw, and some speculations about Strindberg's influence on Shaw.]

891 Nedich, Borivoje. "Beleshke uz prevod komedije *Pigmalion*" (Notes on Translation of the Comedy *Pygmalion*) in B. Sho, PIGMALION (Belgrade: Rad, 1964), 101-5.
[Not seen.] [In Serbian.]

892 Nethercot, Arthur H. "A Plea for *Bernard* Shaw," ShawR, VII (Jan 1964), 2-10.
Although exhibiting some ambivalence toward the name George, Shaw seems to have preferred the name Bernard. Since he is now dead, we ought to respect his desire to be known simply as Bernard Shaw.

893 Nethercot, Arthur H. "Shaw's Feud with Higher Education," JOURNAL OF GENERAL EDUCATION, XVI (1964), 105-19.
Shaw's plays contain at least 25 or 30 examples of individuals who have suffered the negative effects of higher education. Yet Shaw believed in the value of education, if only to the extent that it consisted of the exercise of intellectual curiosity; asking questions is more important than receiving answers.

894 Nolte, William H. "GBS and HLM," SOUTHWEST REVIEW, XLIX (1964), 163-73.
Although comparable in many ways, Shaw and H. L. Menken differed significantly in that Shaw was a revolutionary, committed to the implementation of new ideas for old, while Mencken was essentially skeptical of all ideas. It is not surprising, then, that Mencken's early enthusiasm for Shaw, revealed in his GEORGE BERNARD SHAW: HIS PLAYS (1904) would later cool, as seen in his subsequent remarks on Shaw's plays.

895 Nowell-Smith, Simon (ed). EDWARDIAN ENGLAND, 1901-1914 (NY and Lond: Oxford UP, 1964), pp. 78, 163, 295-96, 297-300, 308, 312, 318, 325, 338-39, 341, 345, 365, 373, 377-78, 379, 380, 395-97, 401, 402, 407, 428, 429.

[Shaw's place, under such headlings as "The Political
Scene," "Thought," "Reading," and "Theatre," in the
English scene, 1901-1914. Factual, not critical.]

896 Odajima, Yushi. "G. B. Shaw - Sono Gendaiteki
Igi" (G. B. Shaw - His Present Significance),
HIGEKI KIGEKI (Tokyo, XVIII (Feb 1964), 14-19.
Although Shaw is now almost ignored in Japan, he has still
a number of positive merits to us: his basic attitude
toward theater, his satirical method, his dramaturgy, his
dramatic language and laughter. [In Japanese.]

897 Okumura, Saburo. "Shingeki Undo to Bernard Shaw
- Shaw no Gikyokushuppan no Haikei to sono Mokuteki-
" (The New Drama Movement and Bernard Shaw - the
Background of Shaw's Publication of His Plays and
Its Purpose), KAGAWA DAIGAKU GAKUGEIGAKUBU KENKYUHO-
KOKU (Takamatsu), Part I, No. 18 (Aug 1964), pp. 46-
78.
There were three reasons or motives behind Shaw's
venturing on publishing his own plays with full use of
"literary expression" (i.e., detailed stage directions,
long prefaces, and so forth): 1) the existence of
censorship; 2) to bring the plays into the homes of middle
class, many of whom were not habitual theater goers; and
3) to secure an authentic representation of his own work.
This "literary expression" was the means for Shaw to
protect himself from theater managers, audiences, critics
and actors against misrepresentation of his plays. In
short Shaw's venture on publishing his plays was a
movement for the renovation of the Victorian theater
world. [In Japanese.]

898 Reinert, Otto. "Comment" and "(George) Bernard
Shaw" DRAMA: AN INTRODUCTORY ANTHOLOGY, ALTERNATE
EDITION, ed by Otto Reinert (Bost and Toronto:
Little, Brown, 1964), pp. 590-96, 880-81; reprinted
as MODERN DRAMA, ALTERNATE EDITION, ed by Otto
Reinert (Bost and Toronto: Little, Brown, 1966),
pp. 222-28, 617-18.
The paradox at the heart of *Caesar and Cleopatra* is that
it is a play that is neither heroic nor romantic. The
pageantry, Shaw makes clear in the Preface, is not an end
in itself. Shaw deemphasizes the historical glamor to
show us the essential contemporaneity of the past. In
this, Shaw's method is the same as Shakespeare's. The
principal conflict in the play is not between Rome and

Egypt but between teacher and pupil, between needful change and resistance to change. A thesis play, *Caesar* includes the earliest reference to the idea of the world's ultimate salvation necessitating the evolution of the Superman. [Appendix includes a brief biographical note on Shaw with a list of suggested reading.]

899 Rodenbeck, John von Behren, Jr. "Alliance and Misalliance: A Critical Study of Bernard Shaw's Novels," DA, XXV (1964), 3583. Unpublished dissertation, University of Virginia, 1963.

900 [Ross, Robert?]. "Two Edwardian Satires on Shaw," Shaw R, VII (Sept 1964), 87–94.
Although probably a better self-parodist, Shaw did not escape being lampooned by others. One such satire was SOME DOCTORED DILEMMA, which appeared anonymously in THE ACADEMY, edited by Lord Alfred Douglas, and probably the work of Robert Ross, Wilde's literary executor. Another satire is BRUCE'S PLAY, which is Chapter XVII of Ada Leverson's LOVE'S SHADOW. [Texts of both reprinted.]

901 Rosset, B. C. "McNulty's HOW I ROBBED THE BANK OF IRELAND," Shaw R, VII (May 1964), 47–53.
[The text, with an introductory note, of a short story by Matthew Edward McNulty, Shaw's friend from boyhood, in which the "Monster" may be "a friendly dig at Shaw."]

902 Rosset, B. C. SHAW OF DUBLIN: THE FORMATIVE YEARS (University Park, Pennsylvania: Pennsylvania State UP, 1964).
[An account of the lives of George Carr Shaw, Lucinda Elizabeth Gurly, George John Lee, and Shaw to the death of George John Lee in 1886. Supports the conclusion that Shaw's mature personality was formed by his hatred of his mother because of her liaison with George John Lee and his consequent uncertainty whether Lee or George Carr Shaw was his actual father. Illustrations.]

903 Roy, R. N. BERNARD SHAW'S PHILOSOPHY OF LIFE (Calcutta, India: Firma K. L. Mukhopadhyay, 1964, 1970). [First submitted as a dissertation to the faculty at the Univ. of Calcutta.]
I. The Making of a Philosopher. [Biographical summary.]
II. The Novels: Shaw Knew It All Along. Shaw's novels

are artistic failures, but although inchoate, their ideas
are substantially those of the more successful dramas.
III.   Sex, Marriage, and Family.   IV.   In Economics All
Roads Lead to Socialism.   V.   Political Philosophy.   VI.
The Philosophy of Creative Evolution.

904 Sainer, Arthur. THE SLEEPWALKER AND THE ASSAS-
SIN, A VIEW OF THE CONTEMPORARY THEATRE (NY:
Bridgehead Books, 1964).
[Theatrical reviews, largely collected from VILLAGE VOICE;
reviews of DEAR LIAR, pp. 44-45, and *Mrs. Warren's
Profession*, p. 78.]

905 SHAW-SCRIPT: A QUARTERLY IN THE SHAVIAN ALPHA-
BET (Worcester, England [nos. 1-8 (1964?-1965)].
[A publication containing short pieces, mostly not about
Shaw, printed in 'Shavian' for the purpose of keeping
readers "informed, entertained and practiced in reading."]

906 "Shou" (Shaw), UKRAINS'KA RADIANS'KA ENTSIKLO-
PEDIIA (Ukrainian Workers' Encyclopedia) XVI, (Kiev:
Akademiîa nauk URSR, 1964), 373-74.
Disillusioned by Fabianism, Shaw turned to the
revolutionary ideas of Marx.   In the *Plays Unpleasant*,
Shaw exposed the hypocrisy of the bourgeois-gentry upper
class; in the *Plays Pleasant*, he derided the false heroics
and lies of bourgeois morality.   The Russian Revolution of
1905-7 strengthened his tendency towards democratism.
Shaw welcomed the October Revolution (1917) and turned
from reformism to an idealistic philosophy, regarding the
"people" as a decisive historical force.   He began to
believe that only the proletariat could bring England out
of the impasse of capitalism; he approached the English
Communist Party and contributed to its publications.   His
last works were devoted to the struggle for peace against
aggressive American imperialism.   [In Ukrainian.]

907 Solomon, Stanley J.   "The Ending of *Pygmalion*:
A Structural View," ETJ, XVI (March 1964), 59-63.
In demonstrating that the dramatic structure of *Pygmalion*
prepares for its "unromantic" ending, it is best to
overlook both Shaw's postscript to the printed version of
the play and his rewritten ending for the movie version.
The structure of the play makes it clear that the original
ending is the only logical one.

908 Solomon, Stanley J. "*Saint Joan* as Epic Tragedy," MD, VI (Feb 1964), 437-49; trans by Jürgen Enkemann and rptd as "Shaws *Saint Joan* als epische Tragödie," in ENGLISCHE LITERATUR VON OSCAR WILDE BIS SAMUEL BECKETT, ed by Willi Erzgräber (Frankfurt/Main: Fischer [Interpretationen], 1970), pp. 48-62.
Saint Joan is best understood as epic drama in which the personal tragedy of Joan herself is an element in the larger story, perhaps equally tragic, of her opposition. Joan is the tragically flawed heroine of her drama, but her opposition's position cannot be slighted, and the play's epilogue, necessary to complete both the story and the meaning, is demanded by the play's structure.

909 Speckhard, Robert R. "Shaw's Therapeutic Satire," MARABAR REVIEW, I (Summer 1964), 94-99.
Shaw was a reluctant satirist who wished to criticize without inflicting pain. In *You Never Can Tell*, the pretensions of the bitter, unhappy Victorian father, Crampton, are ridiculed by his children until he is transformed.

910 Stevenson, Lionel (ed). VICTORIAN FICTION. A GUIDE TO RESEARCH (Cambridge: Harvard UP, 1964), pp. 44, 54, 75-76, 80-81, 101, 106, 113, 114, 115.
[Shaw's role in the critical and scholarly attention to Dickens.]

911 Stockholder, Fred Edward. "G. B. Shaw's German Philosophy of History and the Significant Form of His Plays," DA, XXV (1964), 1221. Unpublished dissertation, University of Washington, 1964.

912 Stokes, E. E., Jr. "Jonson's 'Humour' Plays and Some Later Plays of Bernard Shaw," SHAVIAN, II (Oct 1964), 13-18.
The symbolic and allegorical tendencies of Shaw's later plays cause them to resemble the Jonsonian "humour" plays. Examples of the similarities in technique can even be noted in such early plays as *Major Barbara* and *Arms and the Man*.

913 Suzuki, Hidechika. "Shaw no Sakugekirinen to sono Jissai" (Shaw's Dramaturgy and Practice),

JINBUN RONKYU (Kwansei Gakuin University, Nishino-
miya), XV (Oct 1964), 17-31.
As a discussion play *Mrs. Warren's Profession* is a
brilliant realization of the ideas set forth in *The
Quintessence of Ibsenism*, particularly in the chapter "The
Technical Novelty in Ibsen's Plays." [In Japanese.]

914 Talley, Jerry B. "Religious Themes in the
Dramatic Works of George Bernard Shaw, T. S. Eliot,
and Paul Claudel," DA, XXV (1964), 3750. Unpublished dissertation, University of Denver, 1964.

915 Taubman, Howard. "As Ever, Shaw," NYT, 7 Dec
1964, p. 45.
Man and Superman has not lost its headiness. The "Don
Juan in Hell" dream scene is Shaw at his most dazzling.

916 Ward, A. C. TWENTIETH-CENTURY ENGLISH LITERA-
TURE 1901-1960 (NY: Barnes & Noble enlgd ed; Lond:
Methuen, 1964; first publ. 1928), pp. 94-105.
Shaw led the proponents of change in the early twentieth
century, yet by the thirties, much of his protest seemed
timid. [Brief sketch of life and works.]

917 Watson, Barbara Bellow. A SHAVIAN GUIDE TO THE
INTELLIGENT WOMAN (NY: Norton; Lond: Chatto &
Windus, 1964; rptd with an introduction, NY:
Norton, 1972).
After 80 years, much of what Shaw had to say about women
through his women characters, although still viable where
not already commonplace, is ignored. His women characters
have been scorned, however, by two types of critics, the
lady-like and the sensualist. Shaw was not a feminist,
which implies a male-female conflict; he went beyond. It
was to the intelligent woman who realized the things wrong
with the idealized notion of woman that Shaw addressed
himself. In his first literary work, *My Dear Dorothea*,
Shaw attacked the womanly ideal. His Dorothea is urged to
be selfish, to put independence before any other concern.
This was not for women only, as *Major Barbara*'s Undershaft
shows.

In the sense that she does what women would like to do,
Ann Whitefield is Everywoman. Candida lives in an
ironical doll's house where she protects Morell but
resents rather than joys in her self-sacrifice. Cicely

Waynflete is Ann Whitefield without the sexual element. *Heartbreak House* is so bleak because its women, superficially Shavian, conform to the genteel literary tradition of the womanly ideal.

For Shaw, Socialism would allow for the free operation of the Life Force. Thus the woman's role is of major importance, but it is the selectiveness rather than the strength of the sexual impulse operating through the woman that is of most value in Creative Evolution. Shaw gives us no picture of the new woman as mother, because the old rules make it impossible for the new woman to do anything but renounce motherhood and marriage.

If Shaw chose to depict marriage as the unconscious working of the Life Force, he also recognized that in a capitalist society it was the only career for women.

The Shavian career woman is an image of the potential in women. His working woman is never less than absolutely feminine. Shaw's attitude toward the Suffrage movement at its height seemed inexplicable. Time has confirmed Shaw's conviction that giving women the vote was no more than an act of simple justice, but that the vote can, of itself, solve no really difficult problems for women.

Shaw's complete woman is as absolute an idea as the complete man. In his treatment of women, Shaw inspires us to the celebration of our common humanity.

918 Webb, Clifford. "Shaw and the Twentieth Century Theatre," SHAVIAN, II (June 1964), 13-17.
With respect to the contemporary theater, Shaw cannot be said to have founded a school or to have had any significant followers. His chief influence lies in his reformation of nineteenth-century drama.

919 Weintraub, Stanley. "Bernard Shaw's Other Saint Joan," SHAVIAN, II (Oct 1964), 7-13; rptd SOUTH ATLANTIC QUARTERLY, LXIV (Spring 1965), 194-205; rptd StJFYA, pp. 230-41.
Although it is unlikely that Shaw or T. E. Lawrence "ever saw Lawrence of Arabia in the Joan of Arc" that Shaw created in *Saint Joan*, there are several remarkable parallels between the two. Shaw was reading Lawrence's SEVEN PILLARS OF WISDOM in 1923 while he was writing *Joan*. Both Joan and Lawrence were "adventurous, imaginative, ascetic, contemplative," and both were destroyed by a

world unready for spiritual idealism. The description of Joan by her contemporaries fits Lawrence as well. Had Joan lived, Shaw conjectured that she would have tried to retire to obscurity--as Lawrence did after World War I. Shaw seems to have mentally associated Joan, Napoleon, Lawrence, and Trotsky as charismatic military leaders. Joan and Lawrence lived and ate with the common soldiers; their military skill consisted of a "pick-up" knowledge of weaponry, common sense, courage, and charisma. In Shaw's view, Joan and Lawrence were also possessed of intellectual and moral passions that were more powerful than sexual passion. Joan does not, however, have a taste for self-conscious, "living martyrdom," a trait that Shaw disapproved of in Lawrence.

920 Weintraub, Stanley. "The Two Sides of 'Lawrence of Arabia': Aubrey and Meek," Shaw R, VII (May 1964), 54-57; rptd in BERNARD SHAW'S PLAYS, ed by Warren Sylvester Smith (1970).
Although T. E. Lawrence made nearly two dozen suggestions, which were accepted by Shaw, for improving the characterization of Private Meek (Lawrence in his post-Arabian phase) in *Too True to Be Good*, neither he nor Shaw seemed inclined to tamper with the not easily understood character Aubrey Bagot.

921 Weisert, John J. "One amongst So Many: A Minority Report from Germany," Shaw R, VII (May 1964), 64-65.
Beginning in late 1925, just as Germany was about "to mark Shaw's seventieth anniversary with nearly universal adulation," there appeared in various German publications a number of rather heavy-handed attempts by Herbert Eulenberg, "arch Teutonic anti-Shavian," to discredit Shaw. The effort was unsuccessful.

922 Wellwarth, George E. THE THEATRE OF PROTEST AND PARADOX (NY: New York UP, 1964, 1965, 1971), pp. 2, 15, 37, 110, 121n, 134, 142, 157, 158, 179, 196, 197, 203n, 231, 241, 262, 267, 284.
Modern avant-garde drama is only the successor to the Ibsen-Shaw social drama.

923 Worth, Katharine J. "Shaw and John Osborne," SHAVIAN, II (Oct 1964), 29-35.

In its Socialist realism, Osborne's drama is most reminiscent of Shaw, and there are many striking similarities between the works of the two playwrights.

1965

---

924 Abbott, Anthony S. SHAW AND CHRISTIANITY (NY: Seabury P, 1965); part rptd in TCIMB (1970).
Shaw was both a playwright and a prophet, a revealer of truth about the *present*, who used exaggeration, distortion, and caricature. His Creative Evolution was "a kind of compromise between the naturalism of the Darwinians and the orthodox theology of the defenders of Christianity." Shaw's upbringing amid the Protestant-Catholic conflicts in Ireland made him a rebel not against Christianity or any particular denomination, but "against the common practice of the Christian religion in a supposedly Christian land." *The Devil's Disciple* and *The Shewing-up of Blanco Posnet* contrast true religion with the false religion of the Philistines. *Major Barbara* and *Androcles and the Lion* dramatize the union of spiritual and material forces, idealism and realism. In *Saint Joan*, on the other hand, there is no union of the real and the ideal, because Joan, the lonely prophet, is too idealistic. *The Simpleton of the Unexpected Isles* is an "urgent message" from an aging Shaw in which he restates his views on "sex, eugenics, politics, patriotism, faith, love, and the end of the world." The play's main theme is that failure to find a solution to society's problems is not important so long as one does not despair. For a while it appeared that Shaw, like the liberal Christians of the late nineteenth and early twentieth centuries, was outdated, but now we can see Shaw's continuing importance, in his plays at least, because his ideas are similar to those of Bultmann, Tillich, and Bonhoeffer. [Superficial. As Abbott says in the Preface, "this book is addressed primarily to neither the Shavian specialist nor the professional theologian, but to . . . the public."]

925 Alvaro, Francisco. "*Pigmalión*," EL ESPECTADOR Y LA CRITICA (The Spectator and the Critic) (Valladolid: Talleres Graficos Ceres, 1965), pp. 268-73.
Pygmalion's presentation by the Company of Adolfo Marsillach in Madrid in 1964 followed the original text. Though it was performed with gravity balanced with humor, *ABC* objected to what it considered its exaggerated

farcical rhythm. Some viewed it as nothing but a simple study of types and situations. [In Spanish.]

926 Amalric, Jean-Claude. "Satire et comique plaisants et déplaisants: *Mrs. Warren's Profession* et *Arms and the Man* (Satire and Plays Pleasant and Unpleasant), ASPECTS DU COMIQUE DANS LA LITTÉRATURE ANGLAISE (Aspects of Comedy in English Literature), Société des Anglicistes de l'Enseignement Supérieur, Actes du Congrès de Lille (Paris: Didier, 1965), pp. 28-47.
Violent social satire based on political conviction and expressed with bitter sarcasm and intensely ironic comedy in *Mrs. Warren's Profession* gives way in *Arms and the Man* to more general and playful commentary on human behavior. [In French.]

927 Archer, Peter. "Shaw and Human Rights," SHAVIAN, III (Winter 1965), 6-8.
Some of the economic, social, and cultural rights set forth in the Universal Declaration of Human Rights adopted by the United Nations in 1948 were "very close to Shaw's heart." He too advocated freedom of opinion and speech and toleration for those we believe to be wrong. He was also able to portray abstractions to make his audiences feel the personal tragedies of people who are deprived of their rights.

928 Arnold, Armin. G. B. SHAW (Berlin: Colloquium Verlag [Köpfe des XX. Jahrhunderts, Band 39], 1965).
[A short introduction to Shaw, consisting mainly of biographical data and plot summaries. Arnold's conclusion: "Shaw was perhaps no great thinker but he was cleverer than most. A dozen of his comedies belong to the best world theater has to offer."] [In German.]

929 Auden, W. H. "One of the Family," NY, XLI (23 Oct 1965), pp. 227-44; rptd in J. G. Riewald (ed), THE SURPRISE OF EXCELLENCE (1974).
[Anecdote about Max Beerbohm altering photographs of Shaw and bewildering him.]

930 Austin, Don. "Comedy through Tragedy: Dramatic Structure in *Saint Joan*, Shaw R, VIII (May 1965), 52-62.
The happy ending of Shaw's version of the Joan of Arc story "is accomplished, not in spite of death, but by way of death." The main comic technique is the institutionalized *senex* (in this play, representatives of church and State) to oppose the young individual. Time reconciles age and youth on youth's terms, but only after Joan's sacrifice. Joan gradually passes from romantic illusions about war to practical strategy, from self-ignorance to self-understanding, and from despair to true hope. In the timeless Epilogue, the mocking levity returns to produce an expanded, Dantean comedy.

931 Bainbridge, John. "Satisfying the Ghost of G.B.S.," NY, XLI (6 Nov 1965), 137-72.
During his lifetime, Shaw bequeathed his house to the National Trust, but since Shaw's death the maintenance of Shaw's Corner has cost the Trust money because the Shaw Memorial Fund failed, the entrance fee produced only modest revenues, and no permanent tenant can be found. Shaw's Will caused even more difficulties.

932 Bateson, F. W. A GUIDE TO ENGLISH LITERATURE (NY: Doubleday [Doubleday Anchor Original]; Chicago: Aldine, 1965, 1968; NY: Gordian P, 1976), p. 185.
[Very brief reading list.]

933 Batson, Eric J. "From Our London Correspondent," ISh, III (Spring 1965), 43.
The kernel of *Major Barbara*'s meaning is especially clear in the oratorio sung in the Labor Church in the film version: The world must tame the Undershafts so that "Creation not destruction,/Henceforce shall make us great."

934 Behrman, S. N. "'Let Her Bring Me Yes!': Gabriel Pascal and Bernard Shaw," and "'We Go See Old Man': Bernard Shaw and Gabriel Pascal," THE SUSPENDED DRAWING ROOM (NY: Stein & Day, 1965; Lond: H. Hamilton, 1966), pp. 13-14, 17-19, 65-94.
Shaw met Pascal on the Riviera where he told Pascal to come see him in England when he was broke. Pascal did visit Shaw several years--and failures--later, told him a

few "lovely episodes" of his life, and won Shaw's permission to film one of his plays. With the help of Leslie Howard, Pascal made a successful *Pygmalion*, but *Major Barbara*, which he directed himself, was unsuccessful. The superb "short" that Shaw made to precede *Barbara* captures the essence of his credo and style. Pascal planned films of *Candida* and *Saint Joan* (even had Garbo under contract). He ended up making a fabulously expensive *Caesar and Cleopatra*. This too failed. [Behrman reminisces about his relationship with Pascal and his (Behrman's) meeting with Shaw. Excerpts from a few of Shaw's letters to Pascal are included.

935 Berst, Charles A. "Bernard Shaw's Comic Perspective: A View of Self and Reality," D A, X X VI (1965), 2743-44. Unpublished dissertation, University of Washington, 1965.

936 Bosworth, R. F. "What's in the Name Szczepanowska?" Shaw R, VIII (Sept 1965), 112.
Shaw probably named this character in *Misalliance* after a real-life friend of John Ruskin.

937 Brown, Ivor. SHAW IN HIS TIME (Lond: Thomas Nelson & Sons, 1965).
[Life and works, which relies heavily on Shaw's own writings and previuosly published studies.]

938 Brown, Ivor. "Those Angry Authors—Why Their Protests Fail," SRL, XLVIII (28 Aug 1965), 18-19, 65.
Shaw used drama to protest stage censorship, the abuse of the English language (in *Pygmalion*), and rack-renting (in *Widowers' Houses*). His protests are eminently readable but ineffective because they do not take into account the personalities of the statesmen.

939 Brustein, Robert. SEASONS OF DISCONTENT: DRAMATIC OPINIONS 1959-1965 (NY: Simon & Schuster, 1965), pp. 91, 143-44, 233, 333.
Jack Tanner in *Man and Superman*, unlike Robin Flood in Inge's DARK AT THE TOP OF THE STAIRS, does not give up his genius when he consents to marriage. Shaw's play thus opens up onto moral and political horizons. *Too True to Be Good* lacks form because Shaw could not decide whether

to write a comedy or to express his post-war nihilism. Albert Marre's 1963 production updates the play and deletes all the depressing ideas but fails to solve this structural weakness. The only good scene in the 1962 Old Vic revival of *Saint Joan* is the colloquy between Cauchon and Warwick, "an amusing, elementary history course in the rise of Protestantism and Nationalism."

940 Bryden, Ronald. "G.B.S. at 109," NStat, LXX (3 Dec 1965), 898.
Shaw is undergoing a revival, but it is doubtful that the audiences really accept his intellectuality and Socialism. Shaw created two types of non-realistic dramatic characters: 1) music hall caricatures that anticipate Brecht's characters, and 2) star roles--like Lady Cicely in *Captain Brassbound's Conversion* and Ann Whitefield and Jack Tanner in *Man and Superman*--that emblematize abstractions. [Review-article on 1965 productions of *Captain Brassbound* and *Superman*.]

941 Bryden, Ronald. "Shaw's Shyness," NStat, LXX (1 Oct 1965), 492-93.
The key to Shaw is that his mask, which he made in the 1874-1894 period, hid a shy, tragically insecure man. He never expected to persuade anyone and thereby relieve his loneliness. Shaw's letters to Alice Lockett reveal a battle of the sexes that appeared later in the dueling between the New Women and the Supermen in Shaw's plays. A great Shaw play is one in which Shaw reveals his loneliness. *Heartbreak House* is great; *Too True to Be Good* is nearly great. [A review - article of COLLECTED LETTERS, 1874-1897 (1965), and a production of *Too True*.

942 Budach, Hildegard. "*Heiraten* von George Bernard Shaw" (*Getting Married* by George Bernard Shaw), DIE VOLKSBÜHNE, XVI(1965-66), 76-77.
Shaw's criticism of his country's marriage laws resulted from his high opinion of the rights of the individual. Marriage remained one of his favorite topics throughout his life. *Getting Married* is not one of his better works, but it is more amusing than the plays of most of his contemporaries. [In German.]

943 Burgess, Anthony. "The Two Shaws," Spec, 14 May 1965, pp. 635-36.

In the Prefaces, Shaw appeared as a rationalist, but in the plays he revealed a sense of the prophetic, the numinous. The rationalist side appeals to adolescents, and Shaw himself was an adolescent because he lived in a time that required the erection of something new to replace religion. Shavianism, however, is only a collection of hand-me-down manifestoes unified by a personality. Yet "the comic assertion of self often looks like an attempt to convince himself that he exists." Like Shakespeare, he had no personality. Shaw's greatness lies in irrepressible sense of mystery that appears in plays like *Back to Methuselah*. Nevertheless, the two sides of Shaw meet "in a tradition of dissent whose prose is inspired by the Bible." [Review-article on THE COMPLETE PLAYS OF BERNARD SHAW & THE COMPLETE PREFACES OF BERNARD SHAW (1965).]

944 Carpenter, Charles A., Jr. "The Controversial Ending of *Pygmalion*," ShawR, VIII (Sept 1965), 114. As a remark he made to Flora Robson shows, Shaw did not approve of the Romeo ending some interpreters insist on giving to *Pygmalion*.

945 Corrigan, Robert W. "The British Drama in the Twentieth Century," LAUREL BRITISH DRAMA: THE TWENTIETH CENTURY, ed by Robert W. Corrigan (NY: Dell, 1965), pp. 9-10, 12-16; rwkd in Corrigan, Robert W. "The Collapse of the Shavian Cosmos," THE THEATRE IN SEARCH OF A FIX (NY: Delacorte P, 1973), pp. 161-74. With *Heartbreak House*, Shaw brought British drama into the mainstream of modern continental drama, for in this play he showed that there is nothing to hope for. Man lives in an irrational world dominated by unconscious forces and irreconcilable conflicts. In *Major Barbara* Shaw suggested that salvation was possible if only people were bold and strong, but by the end of *Heartbreak* even Captain Shotover and Ellie Dunn have lost their faith. In Heartbreak House, that is, in Europe before the war, "nothing is real or true."

946 Costello, Donald P. THE SERPENT'S EYE: SHAW AND THE CINEMA (Notre Dame, Indiana, & Lond: U of Notre Dame P, 1965). Chapter on *Pygmalion* rptd in FILM AND LITERATURE: CONTRASTS IN MEDIA, ed by Fred H[arold] Marcus (Scranton/Lond/Toronto: Chandler,

1971), pp. 228-42; on *Major Barbara* rptd TCIMB ed by Rose Zimbardo (1970).
A devotee of photography, Shaw took a special interest in the cinema because he saw in it a "serpent's eye" that could fascinate a mass audience. Shaw wanted to have his plays filmed, but only according to his drama-oriented theory. Shaw began to have his way with the filming of the cathedral scene from *Saint Joan* (1927) and *How He Lied to Her Husband* (1931). He required the same approach in the 1932 *Arms and the Man*, with the result that the film lost even more money than *How He Lied*. Shaw was unable to exert such tight control over foreign productions of *Pygmalion* (German, 1935; Dutch, 1937). [Costello describes, scene by scene, the film *Pygmalion's* deviations both from the play text and from the 1941 Penguin "screen version."] Alan Jay Lerner used much of Pascal's new material in MY FAIR LADY. [A scene by scene analysis of the deviations of the film *Major Barbara* from the play and 1951 Penguin "screen version."] He soon after wrote a screen-play--which was never filmed or published--of *Arms and the Man*. [A scene by scene analysis of the deviations of the film *Caesar and Cleopatra* from both the play and the unpublished shooting script.]

He produced only one more film--an RKO travesty of *Androcles and the Lion*. Most of the later Shaw film adaptations were failures: Preminger's *Saint Joan* (1957), the Burt Lancaster *Devil's Disciple* (1959), and the German versions of *Arms* (1958) and *Mrs. Warren's Profession* (1959). However, *The Doctor's Dilemma* (1958) and *The Millionairess* (1961), were successful. [Appendices include a list of film adaptations of Shaw plays; the opening two scenes from Shaw's unpublished film version of *Disciple*; a textual comparison of play, screen-play, and sound track versions of Act V of *Pygmalion*; Shaw's unpublished screen scenario for *Arms* and an extensive bibliography on film adaptations of Shaw's plays. The book is heavily illustrated throughout.]

947 Crompton, Louis. "[A Dull Don Juan in Shaw?]," PRAIRIE SCHOONER, XXXIX (Summer 1965), 183-85.
Shaw's Don Juan in *Man and Superman*--based on a real-life Don Juan, Shaw himself--is not fatigued by love of women but eager to conquer new and "more challenging mountains."

948 Crompton, Louis. "Shaw's *Heartbreak House*," PRAIRIE SCHOONER, XXXIX (Spring 1965), 17-32.

Heartbreak House is experimental and reactionary, imbued
with the spirit of both Chekhov and Carlyle. Shaw used
Chekhovism to gain the attention of the intelligentsia
while he prophesied their impending doom. Ellie Dunn, the
center of the action of the play, experiences two changes
of heart. She begins as a protegé of Hesione, who wants
to lead men, like her otherwise courageous husband Hector,
into the trap of marriage and happiness. But Ellie soon
turns from romantic illusion to cynicism. By the end of
the play, however, she has become a disciple of Captain
Shotover. Shotover has always had a sense of purpose in
his life. Now, pondering the problem of "social power,"
he has concluded that the selfish holders of private
power--the frivolous romantics as well as the Mangans--
must be destroyed. His message to Ellie is that she must
not sell her soul but must accept social responsibility.
Love is not enough.

949 Dalmasso, Osvaldo de. "Molière, George Bernard
Shaw y los médicos" (Molière, George Bernard Shaw
and the Doctors), LYRA (Argentina), II (Sept-Dec
1965), n.p.
Both Molière in THE IMAGINARY INVALID and Shaw in *The
Doctor's Dilemma* strongly criticize the ignorance and
arrogance of doctors. [In Spanish.]

950 Davis, Robert B. "A Study Guide to Shaw's *Saint
Joan*," EXERCISE EXCHANGE, XIII (Nov 1965), 26-27.
[Study questions.]

951 Dietrich, Richard Farr. "The Emerging Superman:
A Study of Shaw's Novels," DA, XXVI (1965), 1644.
Unpublished dissertation, Florida State University,
1965.

952 Dunlap, Joseph R. "Richards, Scott, Ibsen and
Shaw, or Leaves from a Typographical Family Tree,"
ISh, III (Spring 1965), 44-46.
"In the light . . . of Shaw's remarks . . . we may place
one if not both of Walter Scott's publications of Ibsen's
dramas on the typographical family tree of *Plays Pleasant
and Unpleasant*."

953 Fredeman, William E. PRE-RAPHAELITISM: A BIBLIOCRITICAL STUDY (Cambridge: Harvard UP, 1965), pp. 5, 166, 273.
[An annotated bibliography of materials by and about the Pre-Raphaelites, including a few Shaw items.]

954 Frederick, Moritia-Leah. "Notes Toward the Establishment of a Shaw Discography," ISh, IV (Winter 1965-66), 27-28.
[A brief annotated list of recent LP recordings of readings and play performances.]

955 Garis, Robert. THE DICKENS THEATRE: A REASSESSMENT OF THE NOVELS (Oxford: Clarendon P, 1965), pp. 21-28.
Shaw ably distinguished between the "illusion of naturalness" (which is *not* to say the illusion of reality) that Duse created on stage and the "theatrical" style of Bernhardt. He truly understood both actresses; though he considered Duse's dignified, smooth artistry superior, he could not resist Bernhardt's intensity. Dickens's art is proud and self-conscious, "theatrical," like Bernhardt's.

956 Gertler, Mark. MARK GERTLER, SELECTED LETTERS, ed by Noel Carrington (Lond: Rupert Hart-Davis, 1965), pp. 59-61; rptd "Scraps and Shavings," SHAVIAN, III (Spring-Summer 1967), 32.
[Gertler's unhappy reaction to a performance of *The Doctor's Dilemma*, because he was horrified by the performance and the characterization of the artist.]

957 Gilliatt, Penelope. "Shaw" [First printed 2 May 1965, London, place unknown]; rptd in UNHOLY FOOLS, WITS, COMICS, DISTURBERS OF THE PEACE: FILM & THEATER (NY: Viking P, 1973), pp. 58-59.
Mrs. Warren's Profession works because of the topicality it had in 1894, not in spite of it.

958 Gilliatt, Penelope. "Shaw" [First printed 3 Oct 1965, London, place unknown; rptd in UNHOLY FOOLS, WITS, COMICS, DISTURBERS OF THE PEACE: FILM & THEATER (NY: Viking P, 1973), p. 60.
Fanny's First Play gives Shaw the pleasure of modesty, trumpet-blowing, and critic-proofness all at once.

959 Gilmartin, Andrina.   "Mr. Shaw's Many Mothers,"
ShawR, VIII (Sept 1965), 93-103.
Shaw posited three classes of mothers: 1) instinctive,
loving mothers, 2) women who could make satisfactory
mothers with some guidance, and 3) bad mothers who beat
their children.   Kitty Warren starts out as adequate, but
ends as an "impossible creature" who would raise her
daughter to be a prostitute.   Catherine Petkoff *in Arms
and the Man* is only adequate because she vacillates
between realism and romanticism.   Candida, mother to a
grown man, is an unfit, obtuse, "tiger mother."   Mrs.
Clandon in *You Never Can Tell* is incapable of maternal
kindness.   Mrs. Whitefield in *Man and Superman* is a conventional but admirable mother of a child who needs *no*
mother.   Lady Britomart in *Major Barbara* is unscrupulous,
greedy, and inconsistent, but her money makes a difference.   Mrs. Tarleton in *Misalliance* is sensible, Mrs.
Higgins is an independent mother of an independent son in
Pygmalion, and Mrs. O'Flaherty is a son-beater whose son
"was more afraid of running than of fighting."

960 Goodman, Phyllis M.   "Beethoven as the Prototype
of Owen Jack," ShawR, VII (Jan 1965), 12-24.
The parallels between Owen Jack in *Love among the Artists*
and Ludwig van Beethoven, about whom Shaw could have read
widely in the British Museum, are in fact numerous and
concrete.   Jack is similar to Beethoven in appearance,
"foreign" background, and resonant voice.   Both used
simple calling cards at first, needed recognition, but
were arrogantly confident of their genius.   Jack's setting
of PROMETHEUS UNBOUND parallels Beethoven's Ninth
Symphony.   Both men were imperious with servants, returned
to music after being rejected, for once, in a serious love
affair, and both despised dilletantes.

961 Gordon, John D.   "An Anniversary Exhibition:
The Henry W. and Albert A. Berg Collection 1940-
1965," BNYPL, LXIX (Oct-Nov 1965), 537, 602.
[A brief account of Shaw's early years in London and the
writing of *Widowers' Houses*, a holograph copy of which is
in the Berg collection along with a considerable number of
other Shaw materials.]   [Also published as a separate
pamphlet.]

962 Gordon, John D.   "Novels in Manuscript: An
Exhibition from the Berg Collection," BNYPL, LXIX
(May-June 1965), 317, 396.

[Brief account of Shaw's novel-writing years and a description of the six "well corrected" manuscript pages of *Love among the Artists* that are in the Berg Collection.] [Also published as separate pamphlet.]

963 Grazhdanskaĭa, Zoĭa Tikhonovna. BERNARD SHOU (Bernard Shaw) (Moscow: Prosveshcheniĭe, 1965). *The Quintessence of Ibsenism* provides not only one of the most interesting essays on Ibsen's plays but also a blueprint for Shaw's social-ethical insights and the themes that Shaw developed in his plays. In his personal philosophy and his art, Shaw gradually grew away from his early, naive Fabianism. *Candida*'s Marchbanks represents Shaw's first positive, non-Fabian hero. The deromanticized, ambiguous Napoleon of *Man of Destiny* and the rebellious, undirected Richard Dudgeon of *The Devil's Disciple* follow in the same direction. The naive, utopian *Captain Brassbound's Conversion* and *Caesar and Cleopatra*, which idealizes, with historical inaccuracy, "the wise and strong hero," represent two backward steps. The Boer War, however, brought Shaw to a recognition of the impossibility of the perfectibility of the ordinary man. In *Man and Superman*, Shaw developed the concept of the non-Nietzschean Superman. Broadbent in *John Bull's Other Island* is the first in a series of "false supermen" that leads eventually to the complete rejection of the Fabian hero and the creation of Joan in *Saint Joan*, a heroine of the people. *The Apple Cart* is one of Shaw's masterpieces. Shaw's visit to the Soviet Union in July 1931 had a profound influence on him and motivated him to promote Soviet achievements and disparage capitalist bosses, the confused bourgeois intelligentsia, and the short-sighted bourgeois democracy. In Shaw's last years, characterization declined to caricature in keeping with the fantastic nature of his plays. [In Russian.]

964 Gribben, John L. "Shaw's Saint Joan: A Tragic Heroine," THOUGHT, XL (1965), 549-66. Shaw's *Saint Joan* is in fact an Aristotelian tragedy. Contrary to what S. H. Butcher says, saints--when they are visualized as real flesh and blood people--do suffer and do adapt to the will of God with much cost to themselves. The compensation of Heaven does not lessen the impact of this struggle. The tragic flaw of martyrs and saints is their persistent inability to comprehend why the world rejects them. The unchanging essence of Aristotle's definition of tragedy is the teleological argument: tragedy is designed to "excite pity and fear in such a way that these emotions are properly purged." T. S. Eliot's MURDER IN THE CATHEDRAL, through mystic symbolism, arouses and purges pity and fear. *Saint Joan*, as Shaw finally wrote it, is also a tragedy. Joan's flaw was "her genius and her ingenuity that leads her to expose dullards and to destroy herself." The three agons of her tragedy are 1) the "pious murder" of the court's judgment, 2) Joan's inability to persuade the judges that her inspiration was real, and 3) the final rejection of Joan in the Epilogue.

965 Guseva, E. "Šou-Kritik" (Shaw the Critic), VOPROSY LITERATURY, IX (1965), 220-24.
Shaw's early Socialist activities permanently influenced his life and writings--including his plays. He championed Ibsen, Wagner, Whistler, and the Impressionists while reshaping their revolutionary ideas in his dramas. Although Shaw attacked Shakespeare, he did so primarily to advance Ibsenism. He admired Tolstoy's iconoclasm. Shaw's criticism of nineteenth-century theater is still interesting because his comments on acting, actors, and producers so brilliantly reveal his own aesthetic. [Review-article on BERNARD SOU O DRAME I TEATRE (Bernard Shaw on Drama and Theatre), ed by A. Anikst & E. Kornilovaia (Moscow: Izdatel'stvo Inostrannoi Literatury, 1963) [Not seen.] [In Russian.]

966 Györe, Imre, "Az eretnek öröksege. Shaw halálának 15. Évfórdulojára," (On the Fifteenth Anniversary of Shaw's Death), MAGYAR NEMZET, XXI: 257 (1965), 9.
[Not seen.] [In Hungarian.]

967 Harnsberger, Caroline Thomas (comp). BERNARD SHAW: SELECTIONS OF HIS WIT AND WISDOM (Chicago & NY: Follett, 1965).
[Short excerpts from Shaw's published works and conversations. The selections are grouped under topic headings proceeding alphabetically from Absolution to Youth. Also included are a bibliography of primary and secondary works, chronologies of Shaw's life and works, and indexes.]

968 H[epple?], P[eter]. "*Fanny's First Play*," THEATRE WORLD, LXI (Nov 1965), 7, 20-21.

A potboiler like Shaw's *Fanny's First Play* at the Mermaid is worth twelve of the works of any average playwright. [Photographs.]

969 Hogan Robert. "The Novels of Bernard Shaw," ENGLISH LITERATURE IN TRANSITION, VIII (1965), 63-114.
Shaw's diffidence about his novels has misled critics into underrating them. *Immaturity* is not a chaotically structured *Bildungsroman* about Robert Smith but a gallery of immature characters who represent society. This theme is significant, though Shaw's plotting and characterization are weak. The style of this novel is fluent, even witty. *The Irrational Knot*, perhaps Shaw's most "artistically finished" novel, is neither a comedy nor a tragedy but a "triumph" of the infallible man. Shaw's exposure of marriage is based on his belief that in a successful marriage, one partner had to be ordinary, the other "remarkable." This novel also criticizes social structures based on absurd economic and social distinctions. The fragmentary *Love among the Artists* is saved by its portrayal of Owen Jack, another self-sufficient person. Shaw uses Jack to develop his distinction between the true artist, who "is obsessed by his work," and the false artist, who "is obsessed by himself." Byron, in Shaw's most conventional, most popular novel *Cashel Byron's Profession*, is also a diligent master of technique, but he is no superman. In the portrayal of parent-child relationships, Shaw again emphasizes reason over sentimental emotion. Shaw became increasingly dissatisfied with the novel form. *The Unsocial Socialist* appears to have been finished hurriedly in frustration. Yet the first half is a "triumph over the limitations of the novel," because it uses farce to criticize the love and violence of conventional fiction. The second part of the novel fails because it arbitrarily combines a Socialistic theme with a traditional love-story plot. It is an inestimable loss to art that after *Socialist* Shaw turned for 10 years to criticism, lecturing, and politics. His concern for content has not exerted a force on the development of the novel.

970 Hortmann, Wilhelm. ENGLISCHE LITERATUR IM 20. JAHRHUNDERT (English Literature in the Twentieth Century) (Bern and Munich: Francke, 1965), pp. 10-13, 18, 29, 57, 66, 96-98.
[The usual introduction to Shaw's life and works.] As a member of the Fabian Society and as a spokesman on behalf

246

of the Ibsen Movement in England Shaw revolutionized the English theater. His best play is *Saint Joan*. [In German.]

971 Howard de Walden, Margherita. PAGES FROM MY LIFE (Lond: Sidgwick & Jackson, 1965), pp. 96-98, 185.
[Lady Howard de Walden's reminiscences include three episodes about Shaw. In a cowboy "extravaganza" film being made by James Barrie and Harley Granville-Barker, Shaw seized the opportunity to "orate"--even though it was a silent film. At a luncheon that the Shaws attended at the Howard de Waldens, Shaw was mistakenly served fish cutlets instead of nut cutlets. Mrs. Shaw was delighted to have Shaw's pompousness about vegetarianism undercut for once. Lady Howard de Walden was incensed when Shaw refused to appear at a benefit debate for the rebuilding of Queen Charlotte's hospital because he told her that there were already too many babies anyway.]

972 "Idiophone Book," TLS, 11 Feb 1965, p. 112.
Shaw as a dramatist, a recorder of speech sounds, took phonetics seriously. Unfortunately, he did not go far enough in his study of language, and few other artists have shared his interest. [Review of David Crystal and Randolph Quirk, SYSTEMS OF PROSODIC AND PARALINGUISTIC FEATURES IN ENGLISH (The Hague: Mouton, 1964).]

973 Jago, D. M. "Tradition and Progress in Shaw and Wells, Belloc and Chesterton." Unpublished dissertation, University of Leicester, 1965.
[Listed in McNamee, SUPP I.]

974 Kantorovich, I. B. "Kompozitsiia i styl' pozdnei intellektual'noi dramy Shou: k voprosu o svoeobraznii zhanra i khudozestvennoi literatury" (Composition and Style of the Late Intellectual Drama of Shaw: On the Question of originality of Genre and Artistic Literature), UCHENYE ZAPISKI SVERDLOVSKOGO PED. INST. (Sverdlovsk), XXVII (1965), 62-97.
[Not seen.] [In Russian.]

975 Kaufmann, R. J. (ed). G. B. SHAW: A COLLECTION OF CRITICAL ESSAYS (Englewood Cliffs, NJ: Prentice-

Hall [Twentieth Century Views], 1965).
Contents, abstracted separately under date of first
publication: R. J. Kaufmann, "Introduction" (1965);
Bertolt Brecht, "Ovation for Shaw," MD (1959); Erik H.
Erikson, "The Problem of Ego Identity," JOURNAL OF THE
AMERICAN PSYCHOANALYTIC ASSOCIATION (1956); Richard M.
Ohmann, "Born to Set It Right: The Roots of Shaw's
Style," SHAW: THE STYLE AND THE MAN (1962); Bruce R.
Park, "A Mote in the Critic's Eye: Bernard Shaw and
Comedy," TEXAS STUDIES (1958); Eric Bentley, "The Making
of a Dramatist (1892-1903)," TULANE DRAMA REVIEW (1960);
Norbert F. O'Donnell, "The Conflict of Wills in Shaw's
Tragicomedy," MD, (1962); Louis Crompton, "Shaw's
Challenge to Liberalism," PRAIRIE SCHOONER, (1963); Robert
Brustein, "Bernard Shaw: The Face Behind the Mask," THE
THEATRE OF REVOLT (1964); G. Wilson Knight, "Shaw's
Integral Theatre" [original title, "Shaw"], from THE
GOLDEN LABYRINTH (1962); Margery M. Morgan, "*Back to
Methuselah*: The Poet and the City," ESSAYS AND STUDIES
1960 (1960; Louis L. Martz, "The Saint as Tragic Hero"
[original title, "The Saint as Tragic Hero: *Saint Joan*
and *Murder in the Cathedral*"], TRAGIC THEMES IN WESTERN
LITERATURE, (1955); T. R. Henn, "The Shavian Machine," THE
HARVEST OF TRAGEDY (1956); Irving Fiske, "Bernard Shaw and
William Blake" [original title, "Bernard Shaw's Debt to
William Blake"], from SHAVIAN, Tract No. 2 (1951); also
included by not abstracted: "Chronology of Important
Dates," pp. 179-80; "Notes on the Editor and Authors," p.
181; "Selected Bibliography," p. 182, specific items
mentioned being abstracted under the dates of first
publication.

976 Kaufmann, R. J. "Introduction," G. B. SHAW: A
COLLECTION OF CRITICAL ESSAYS (Englewood Cliffs, NJ:
Prentice-Hall, [Twentieth Century Views], 1965), pp.
1-13.
Shaw invented the GBS *persona* to provoke strong reactions
from skeptical critics. Like Socrates, he devised
"instruments of moral vexation" to "force the pace of
thought." But society gave little heed to Shaw, and after
the social order "committed suicide" in World War I, Shaw
was never quite the same. Shaw's splendid activity as an
artist was, in a sense, a tragic failure. The critics in
this collection [their points of view are summarized here]
try to free Shaw from the accumulated misunderstandings.

977 Keo[u]gh, Lawrence C. "Horror and Humor in
Shaw," SHAVIAN, III (Winter 1965), 9-15.

Shaw was an extremely sensitive person who used the mask
of a buffoon to protect himself from and, paradoxically,
to express the horrors of his childhood and life itself.
[Includes extensive quotations from Shaw's letters and
conversations with his biographers.]

978 Kirov, T. "Bernard Sou" (Bernard Shaw),
SUVREMENNI ANGLIISKI PISATELI (Contemporary English
Writers) (Sofia: Nauka i izkustvo, 1965), pp. 245-
65.

In the *Plays Unpleasant*, Shaw conducts a battle on a wide
front against social and moral problems, exposing the
decay underlying the pretended honesty of contemporary
society. Likewise, the *Plays Pleasant*, despite their
title, do not put an end to the battle but transfer it to
social questions. In the *Three Plays for Puritans*, Shaw
does not so much attack Puritanism and Christianity as the
effects they have on human character. Shaw's plays
contain serious and unserious passages, and he was
interested in reality and truth. The most serious
conclusions could be formulated in witty paradox. [In
Bulgarian.]

979 Kocztur, Gizella. "A Hungarian View of George
Bernard Shaw's Works," CShav, VI (Jan-Feb 1965), 4-
18.

Shaw is better known in Hungary than most Hungarian
playwrights. [Survey of the development of the image of
Shaw in Hungary. Bibliography of translations and
publication of Shaw's works in Hungary; Shaw's plays on
the Hungarian stage, works written about Shaw.]

980 Komatsu, Motoya. "Shaw Metosera ni Kaere
Kosatsu (1) -Kareno Chojin o megutte-" (On Shaw's
Back to Methuselah [1] -His Superman-), AKITA DAIGA-
KU GAKUGEIGAKUBU KENKYUKIYO (Akita), (Jinbunkagaku)
No. 15 (March 1965), pp. 21-28. "Shaw Metosera ni
Kaere Kosatsu (2) -Kareno Yume to Kibo-" (On Shaw's
Back to Methuselah [2] -His Dream and Hope-), AKITA
DAIGAKU KYOIKUGAKUBU KENKYUKIYO (Akita), (Jinbunk-
agaku, Shakaikagaku) No 22 (Feb 1972), pp. 14-26.

Though it is full of disappointments as a dramatic piece,
Back to Methuselah is unrivaled as science fiction. We
must not forget in reading it that Shaw is an optimist as
well as a rigorous individualist, who opposes any kind of
idea or system that will be a burden on human beings. [In
Japanese.]

981 Kozelka, Paul. "Foreward," "Introductory Note to *The Devil's Disciple*," "Introductory Note to *Candida*," "Introductory Note to *Man and Superman*," FOUR PLAYS BY BERNARD SHAW, ed by Paul Kozelka (NY: Washington Square Press, 1965), pp. ix-xii, 3-4, 81, 149, 259-60.
Outwardly prepossessing, inwardly shy, Shaw was spiritually and morally strong. *The Devil's Disciple* inverts melodramatic techniques and values to attack the uselessness of war. *Candida* introduced Shaw's versions of the New Woman and Christian Socialism into English theater. In *Caesar and Cleopatra*, Shaw gave Caesar all the qualities in a leader that he most admired—ruthlessness, lack of sentimentality, wit, fairness, and egotism—and he has Cleopatra develop into a woman who can rule. Shaw wrote *Man and Superman* to show that if man did not use his brains to achieve his full potential, the Life Force (God) would replace him with another breed. [Also includes "Suggested Readings," items listed abstracted under date of first publication.]

982 Lambert, J. W. "Plays in Performance," DRAMA ns LXXIX (Winter 1965), 17-24.
Fanny's First Play and *Too True to Be Good* still have much to tell us about society. [Photograph of *Too True*.]

983 Laurence, Dan H. (ed), BERNARD SHAW, COLLECTED LETTERS, 1874-1897, ed with intro and notes by Dan H. Laurence (Lond: Max Reinhardt, 1965; NY: Dodd, Mead, 1965).
[Laurence supplies a general introduction, lucid sketches of Shaw's life up to 1897, and explanatory headnotes. Also included are illustrations, an Index of Recipients, and a General Index compiled by Eric J. Batson.]

984 Laurence, Dan H. "A Note on the Texts" and [headnotes], SELECTED NON-DRAMATIC WRITINGS OF BERNARD SHAW, ed by Dan H. Laurence (Bost: Houghton Mifflin, 1965), pp. [xiii]-xiv, 2, 206, 347, 378, 391, 406, 427, 433, 446.
[A brief note on Shaw's spelling and other typographical idiosyncrasies and notes on the textual history of *An Unsocial Socialist, The Quintessence of Ibsenism,* "A Degenerate's View of Nordau," "On Going to Church," "Socialism for Millionaires," "The Illusion of Socialism," "Tolstoy on Art," "In the Days of Youth," and "Who I Am, and What I Think."]

985 Leary, Daniel J. MAJOR BARBARA: A CRITICAL COMMENTARY (NY: American R. D. M. [Study-Master Series], 1965).
Major Barbara is Shaw's DIVINE COMEDY. Act I presents with some nostalgia the surface of the old order. The Act II descent into hell brings into clear focus, through action and symbolism, the conflict between Undershaft's capitalism and Barbara's institutionalized Christianity. The conflict is resolved in Act III, however, when Cusins is reborn as the Superman and Barbara becomes a Shavian realist filled with the Life Force. [Also includes a cursory biography, summary of the Preface to *Barbara*, glossary, character analysis, critical appraisal, two reviews by Desmond MacCarthy, study topics, and a brief bibliography.]

986 Leary, Daniel J. "The Rest Could Not Be Silence," ISh, III (Spring 1965), 40-42.
In the Epilogue to *Saint Joan*, Shaw presents us with a world that continues to reject greatness. It also suggests Joan's continuity.

987 Leigh-Taylor, N. H. (ed). "Introduction," BERNARD SHAW'S READY-RECKONER: A GUIDE TO CIVILIZA-TION, ed with intro by N. H. Leigh-Taylor (NY: Random House, 1965), pp. xv-xxxiv.
Shaw was a prophet of sociological truths. He consistently advocated Socialism and equalitarian communism. He will either go down in history "as the clearest head of the twentieth century," or "he will earn some such title as Great Confessor to the Age of the Communist-Capitalist showdown." [The book is composed of selections from Shaw's writings arranged under the following headings: Poverty, Christianity, Crime and Punishment, Democracy, Capitalism, Socialism, Human Relations, and Education.]

988 Lewis, Cecil. "Foreword: George Bernard Shaw: A Biographical Note," THE SERPENT'S EYE: SHAW AND THE CINEMA, by Donald P. Costello (Notre Dame, Indiana and Lond: U of Notre Dame P, 1965), pp. vii-xiii.
[Lewis recounts his relationship with Shaw, who launched him on his film career by letting him make movies of *How He Lied to Her Husband* and *Arms and the Man*.] Both failed because they were uncinematic. One cannot blame Shaw for

his resistance to adaptation, however, because he did not want anyone to "castrate his plays" of their paradox.

989 Luck, Georg. "Didaktische Poesie" (Didactic Literature) in DAS FISCHER LEXIKON. LITERATUR II/1 (The Fischer Encyclopedia. Litearture II/1), ed by Wolf-Hartmut Friedrich and Walther Killy (Frankfurt/M.: Fischer, 1965), pp. 151-62.
The English drama has always been mainly didactic. Therefore Shaw is a typical English playwright. His didactic tendencies recall both Thomas Mann and Bertolt Brecht. [In German.]

990 M., H. G. "*Widowers' Houses*," THEATRE WORLD, LXI (April 1965), 5.
Shaw's humor and wit can make even the human absurdity and hopelessness of *Widowers' Houses* tolerable. [Review of Theatre Royal production.]

991 McDowell, Frederick P. W. "Shaw's Eminent Contemporaries," ISh, IV (Winter 1965-1966), 20-24.
Sydney Carlyle Cockerell, Max Beerbohm, and Shaw were "heirs in Edwardian times to the Victorian age." Shaw is as much the idealist as the iconoclast. To understand Cockerell, who was Shaw's friend, and Beerbohm, who shared Shaw's sense of humor, fun, and beauty, is to better understand Shaw himself. [Review-article on Wilfrid Blunt, COCKERELL (1965) and David Cecil, MAX: A BIOGRAPHY (1965).]

992 Mander, Gertrud. GEORGE BERNARD SHAW (Velber bei Hannover: Friedrich Verlag, 1965).
Shaw is an excellent propagandist and dramatist, not so much an original thinker. Characteristic for him are his phoenix-like ability to change, his dialectical way of thinking (which makes it difficult to grasp him), his gift to entertain, his optimistic belief in social progress, and his belief in the changeability of the world. There are several reasons why today (1965) interest in Shaw has diminished. It is a reaction to too much Shaw. Moreover, a more tragic view of the world has eclipsed Shaw's optimism. His dramatic innovations were surpassed by others. Shaw's dramatic concept consisted mainly in attacking the well-made play and Victorian society from within by inversion of accepted models. In the center of

his plays are his characters. Because they are full of
contradictions, they are real and natural rather than
mechanical. As a rule his male characters are more
realistic than his female characters. Mostly his
characters are active and full of life and energy rather
than introspective and melancholic. They are shown in
their societal context. Shaw's "religion" is not
transcendental but directed towards the creation of more
perfect individuals and a more perfect society here on
earth. Despite many differences there are many
similarities between Shaw and Bertolt Brecht. Both
playwrights use their anti-illusionary theater for both
entertainment and instruction. The core of Shaw's plays
is the speeches; it is mainly because of them that his
plays are the most brilliant comedies since Shakespeare.
[Mander's book is intended as an introduction to Shaw. It
consists of a chronology, a chapter providing general
comments on Shaw's time and his work, several chapters
discussing selected plays, and a concluding chapter
dealing with the stage reception of Shaw's plays.] [In
German.]

993 Mason, M. A. "The Early Plays of Bernard Shaw,
up to 1910, in Relation to the Social Background and
Ideas of the time." Unpublished dissertation,
University of London, Kings College, 1965.
[Listed in McNamee, SUPP I.]

994 Masumoto, Masahiko. "Nihon niokeru Bernard Shaw
(1) -Hoyaku Bunkenmokuroku-" (Bernard Shaw in Japan
(1) -a List of Japanese Translations), NANZAN REVIEW
(Nanzan University, Nagoya), No. 3 (Dec 1965), 67-
111.
[Lists 260 items published between 1909 and 1965, with a
survey of Shaw's reception in Japan up to 1910.] [In
Japanese.]

995 Masumoto, Masahiko. "*Pygmalion* no Ketsumatsu"
(The Denouement of *Pygmalion*), AKADEMIA (Nanzan
University, Nagoya), No. 45/46 (Jan 1965), 77-94.
There are at least three different endings in *Pygmalion*;
one is to be found, for example, in *The Complete Plays of
Bernard Shaw* (1931); another is in the alleged 'film
version' of the play published in 1941 by Penguin Books;
the third is in the film made in 1938. Although the
majority opinion holds that Shaw changed his attitude
on the relationship between Higgins and Eliza--hence the

different versions--these versions do not contradict themselves, but are variations on the same consistent and coherent ideas that Shaw has never abandoned. *Pygmalion* is not a mere Cinderella-like romantic play like MY FAIR LADY. An analysis of the play, focusing its theme on the development of Eliza, together with the examination of text variants and Shaw's basic attitude, will support this conclusion. [In Japanese.]

996 Masumoto, Masahiko. "Shaw in Japan--the First Period," ISh, IV (Winter 1965-1966), 30-31.
Socialist writers and innovative theater directors were among the first in Japan to show an interest in Shaw. By 1910 several translations of Shaw plays had been published and the first Japanese performance of a Shaw play (*The Shewing-up of Blanco Posnet*) had been given.

997 Matlaw, Laura T. "Shawloha!" ISh, III (Spring 1965), 38-39.
[A recounting, by a seventh-grader, of Shaw's 1933 and 1936 visits to Hawaii. Based on newspaper reports. Photograph.]

998 Mikhailovskiĭ, Boris Vasil'evich. TVORCHESTVO M. GOR'KOGO I MIROVAIA LITERATURA (Gorky's Works and World Literature), (Moscow: "Nauka," 1965), 568-70.
Shaw's social and psychological paradoxes have something in common with the dialectical dramaturgy of Gorky. In Shaw's paradoxical development of conflicts in *Major Barbara, Candida* and elsewhere, he criticized attempts to establish Christian ethics in contemporary bourgeois society. Both playwrights sought to expose not only the contradictions in capitalist society but also to strip away the illusions cultivated by bourgeois society. Shaw criticized the pretensions and illusions of bourgeois heroes who feel morally superior, though these feelings are illusory, as in Gorky's free-thinking, or progressive, or humanistic characters whom he shows to be the product of ideological aberrations. The plays of both often have a sub-text which argues against familiar aesthetic, moral or philosophical concepts. [In Russian.]

999 Mills, Carl Henry. "The Intellectual and Literary Background of George Bernard Shaw's *Man and Superman*," DA, XXVI (1965), 2727-28. Unpublished dissertation, University of Nebraska, 1965.

1000 Mills, John A. "Language and Laughter in Shavian Comedy," QUARTERLY JOURNAL OF SPEECH, LI (Dec 1965), 433-41.
In his plays, Shaw relies primarily on a neutral, plain style composed of "vernacular and idiomatic elements, of antithetical constructions, and of repetition." This style is in no way funny in itself, but it is a perfect means of teaching revolution to the masses by ridiculing outmoded ideas. It is also highly dramatic. [Examples are taken mainly from *The Devil's Disciple, Man and Superman, Caesar and Cleopatra,* and *Major Barbara.*]

1001 Mills, John A. "Shaw's Linguistic Satire," ShawR, VIII (Jan 1965), 2-11.
Shaw used linguistic satire--the mocking of special vocabularies and coterie syntaxes--to support his main themes. In *Arms and the Man*, Sergius's grand romantic-novel vocabulary, artificial syntax, metaphor, and alliteration are comically juxtaposed to the efficient language of Bluntschli. *Candida*'s Morell, even when passion is called for, speaks with "flaccid tumidity"; and Marchbanks uses a post-romantic jargon. Morell and Marchbanks are less comic, however, because they experience genuine anguish, and they change. *Captain Brassbound's Conversion* inverts melodrama by exposing the folly of vengeance. Shaw wants Brassbound to be a sympathetic character, so only occasionally does he have Brassbound use the self-conscious laconicism and bombast of an avenger.

1002 Niàfïed, Uladzimir. STAVLENIE BELORUSSKOGO SOVETSKOGO TEATRA 1917-1941 (Evolution of the Belorussian Soviet Theater 1917-1941) (Minsk: "Nauka i tekhnika," 1965).
Between 1921 and Autumn 1923, the Belorussian State Theater (Minsk/Vitebsk) produced *The Devil's Disciple* because it was appropriate, since it dealt with a war against English colonialists, to the revolutionary period. In 1922 *Arms and the Man* was planned for production at the "Youth Theater" in Vitebsk but was cancelled. [In Russian.]

1003 Nickson, Richard. 'GBS: Words to the Unwise," ISh, III (Spring 1965), 49.
[Parody of YOU ARE OLD, FATHER WILLIAM with Shaw as the hero, condemning the use of atomic weaponry.]

1004 Obraztsova, Anna Georgievna. DRAMATURGICHESKII METOD BERNARDA SHOU (Dramaturgical Method of Bernard Shaw) (Moscow: "Nauka," 1965).
One aspect of Shaw's work that remains obscure despite extensive, insightful criticism of all the plays is the Shavian paradox. Paradox is the essence of Shaw's dramatic conflict, character, and dramatic form. The elaborate stage directions and long prefaces are integral to the intellectual disputes of Shaw's drama. His heroes are uncommon, strong, and unscrupulous out of necessity. Shaw's structures are paradoxical, and his action is intellectual because bourgeois society is irrational and chaotic. Undershaft in *Major Barbara* is an expression of the absolute power of capitalism. *Saint Joan*, which both "Shakespearizes" and Schillerizes" history, shows that there has been *no* progress in history. As Shaw's dramaturgy progresses, his plays take place on a broader and broader setting, theme is piled upon theme, and genre becomes indefinable. Characters proliferate, paradoxes become tragic and grotesque, and fantasy becomes the only vehicle by which Shaw can adequately express his horror of the monstrous socio-economic evil he observes. [In Russian.]

1005 "Ocho oscares para MY FAIR LADY" (Eight Oscars for MY FAIR LADY), CUADERNOS DE SUR (Argentina), II (11 June 1965), 538.
The film version of *Pygmalion*, MY FAIR LADY, marks an epoch for its impact, influence, and publicity. [In Spanish.]

1006 O'Donovan, John. SHAW AND THE CHARLATAN GENIUS: A MEMOIR (Dublin: Dolmen P; Lond: Oxford UP 1965; Chester Springs, PA: Dufour Editions, 1966).
Shaw's "authentic account" in *Sixteen Self-Sketches* of George John Vandeleur Lee was by no means complete or forthright. Shaw blamed the demise of his parents' marriage on the 16-year gap in their ages and on his father's drunkenness and impecuniosity; nevertheless, the main cause was George John Lee. Bessie Shaw and Lee very likely had an affair in Dublin and London, though there is no reason to believe that Lee was Shaw's father. Shaw concealed Lee's religion. That he was Roman Catholic explains why Shaw was sent on Lee's advice to the Central Model Boys' School and why Sir Frederick Shaw stopped inviting the George Carr Shaw family to his home. Shaw seems to have at least considered the possibility that the

attractive, genial Lee was his father. An "illegitimacy
theme" runs through his plays (Higgins in *Pygmalion* may be
based upon Lee):   Shaw's character and tastes resembled
Lee's more than George Carr Shaw's.   Lee failed in London,
but he did help Shaw by having him ghost write some music
criticism for the HORNET.   Lee meanwhile may have become
involved with Shaw's sister Lucy.   [The book concludes
with brief appendices on George Carr Shaw's drunkenness,
Catholic-Prostestant hate in 19h century Ireland, a poem
to one of Lee's singers, Lee's Dublin musical contemporaries, a description of the programmes from Lee's Dublin
concerts, typical reviews of Lee's concerts, the attribution of the authorship of Lee's THE VOICE to Malachi J.
Kilgarriff, and brief accounts of H. Julian Marshall,
publisher of the VOICE, Charles Cummins, and Mrs. George
Ferdinand Shaw. [Illustrated.]

1007 Oldsey, Bernard S., and Stanley Weintraub.
"Ambassadors at Large: Other Writings," THE ART OF
WILLIAM GOLDING (NY: Harcourt, Brace & World,
1965), pp. 147-58.
William Golding's THE BRASS BUTTERFLY demonstrates Shavian
paradoxes, wit, and technique.

1008 Ozu, Jiro.   "Igirisukindaigeki to Bernard Shaw"
(English Modern Drama and Bernard Shaw), KINDAI
GEKISHU (Modern Dramas) (Tokyo: Chikuma Shobo
[Sekai Bungaku Taikei (Collections of World Litera-
ture) vol. 90], 1965), pp. 381-84.
Shaw's dramas are written from the viewpoint of the comic
vision, whereas Ibsen, whom he admired greatly, tried to
grasp reality with the tragic vision. [In Japanese.]

1009 Pálfy, István.   "George Bernard Shaw's Reception in Hungary, 1914-1939," HUNGARIAN STUDIES IN
ENGLISH, II (Dec 1965), 93-104.
At the beginning of World War I, when productions of
"entente" dramatists were forbidden, attention shifted to
Shaw's non-theatrical works.   *Common Sense about the War*
was especially popular because the progressives approved
of Shaw's contention that Entente and Central Powers were
mutually responsible for the war, while conservatives took
Shaw's statements to apply only to England and Russia.
Thus, by 1916, *Candida* was on the stage and Sandor Hevesi
was publishing more translations of Shaw plays and
articles on Shaw.   During the Hungarian Soviet Republic
(1919), the nationalized theaters presented Shaw plays to

appreciative audiences of industrial workers. During the early 1920's, fine productions of *Man and Superman* and *Saint Joan* were given, and more translations and articles were published. In 1926, however, the "right-wing elements and army officers" closed a production of *Arms and the Man*, and Shaw's anti-Horthy comments in 1928 so angered the chauvinistic ruling class and liberal press that his plays were practically banished for two years, though Ferenc Hont did give an innovative performance of *Joan* in 1928. In 1929, interest again turned to Shaw's Fabianism and non-theatrical works. Shaw's apparent admiration for dictators in *The Apple Cart* caused considerable controversy, but revivals of *Joan* and *The Devil's Disciple* proved that the Shavian superman had "very little in common with the 'ideal superman-dictator' of the fascist ideology." The Shaw cult was extinguished in 1939 because of the spread of Hungarian fascism and the death of Hevesi.

1010 Pearson, Hesketh. "The Flawless Hamlet" and "Superman of the Theatre," EXTRAORDINARY PEOPLE (Lond: Heinemann; NY & Evanston: Harper & Row, 1965), pp. 165-74, *passim*, 237-60.
Shaw thought Forbes-Robertson's Hamlet was incomparable. He wrote *Caesar and Cleopatra* with Forbes-Robertson in mind for Caesar, but it was several years before the actor had the intelligence to produce the play--and add another great performance to his career. Shaw was a master of every aspect of the theater. He wrote hard-hitting, informed music and drama criticism. He wrote great plays in the tradition of Euripides, Shakespeare, and Molière. His shrewd business sense was useful to Vedrenne and Barker at the Court Theatre. When producing [directing] one of his plays, he would show the actors how to deliver his modern plays in a classical, operatic style. He exaggerated his demonstrations to the actors so that they would not merely imitate him. Since he did not care for Gilbert and Sullivan or for THE CHOCOLATE SOLDIER, "we can conclude that MY FAIR LADY would have exasperated him. But if it has increased the circulation of his works, he might have excused it."

1011 Pearson, Hesketh. HESKETH PEARSON BY HIMSELF (Lond: Heinemann, 1965; NY: Harper & Row, 1966, © 1965), pp. 48, 110, 126, 146, 158-59, 188-89, 261-78.
Shaw, consistently friendly and helpful, offered good advice on financial matters, supplied much needed

information, and even wrote portions of the *G.B.S.* biography--in the biographer's style. In spite of his criticism of police-state tactics, Shaw still approved of the Soviet regime. Perhaps the greatest disappointment in Shaw's life was his estrangement from Granville Barker. [Pearson reminisces about his relationship with Shaw, especially during the writing of *G.B.S.*: A FULL LENGTH PORTRAIT (1942).]

1012 Petrie, Sir Charles. THE EDWARDIANS (NY: W. W. Norton, 1965), pp. 28, 34, 35.
[Discusses Shaw and the Theater and the Fabian Society.]

1013 Pilecki, Gerard Anthony. SHAW'S *GENEVA*: A CRITICAL STUDY OF THE EVOLUTION OF THE TEXT IN RELATION TO SHAW'S POLITICAL THOUGHT AND DRAMATIC PRACTICE (The Hague: Mouton; N Y: Humanities Press [Studies in English Literature, vol VIII], 1965).
[A study of the revisions of *Geneva* in the light of Shaw's political reviews and of his interest in expressing his ideas and his concern for dramatic values.] The importance of *Geneva* to Shaw lies in his desire to arouse men's conscience over peace. He revised in order to polish the dialogue, to update the play, and to reflect changes in his own attitude. The play fails because it "closely reflects the pre-war world, but in a completely distorted way."

1014 Pritchett, V. S. "Encounters with Yeats," NStat, LXIX (4 June 1965), 879-80; rptd in W. B. YEATS: INTERVIEWS AND RECOLLECTIONS (Lond and Bassingstoke: Macmillan; N Y: Harper and Row, 1976), p. 347.
W. B. Yeats felt Shaw had no principles.

1015 Pul'khritudova, E. "Neizvestnyĭ Shou: p'esa B. Shou *Millionersha* v teatre im. Vakhtangova, Moskva" (Unknown Shaw: Shaw's *Millionairess* at the Vakhtangov Theater, Moscow), TEATR (Moscow) no. 4 (1965), 13-16.
The plays of Shaw are not often seen on our stages. His little known *The Millionairess* is a novelty. Gradually, the audience realizes that this eccentric comedy of manners is turning into a social drama of an individual

born "outside his class" and is a judgment upon Epiphania. [In Russian.]

1016 Radin, Nikolai Mariiusovich. AVTOBIOGRAFIIA (Autobiography), (Moscow: Vserossiiskoe teatral'noe obshchestve, 1965.
[Radin created roles in *Mrs. Warren's Profession, Caesar and Cleopatra, The Devil's Disciple, Arms and the Man, Pygmalion,* and *The Doctor's Dilemma.*]

1017 Ray, Gordon N. "Introductory Note," SELECTED NON-DRAMATIC WRITINGS OF BERNARD SHAW, ed by Dan H. Laurence (Bost: Houghton Mifflin, 1965), pp. vii-xi.
Shaw's early writing possessed an irresistible vitality that is missing from his strident late works. *An Unsocial Socialist* and *The Quintessence of Ibsenism*, though flawed, present Shaw's attempts to reject the Victorian social order. The characters, situations, and dialogue of the early non-dramatic writings also anticipate Shaw's drama, an artistic form whose exigencies he did master.

1018 "Rediscovery of Bernard Shaw," TIMES (Lond), 8 Dec 1965, p. 5; rptd in THE CURTAIN RISES: AN ANTHOLOGY OF THE INTERNATIONAL THEATRE, comp by Dick Richards (Lond: Leslie Frewin, 1966), pp. 130-32.
We can now see that Shaw's best plays are not those on trivial, current debating topics, but rather those like *Heartbreak House* in which enduring themes rise out of revolutionary, non-narrative dramatic structures.

1019 Regan, Arthur E. "Farce and Fantasy in Bernard Shaw." Unpublished dissertation, Harvard University, 1965.
[Listed in McNamee, SUPP I.]

1020 Romm, Anna Sergeevna. DZHORDZH BERNARD SHOU (George Bernard Shaw) (Moscow & Leningrad: Iskusstvo, 1965).
Shaw's basic philosophical, social, and aesthetic ideas reflect his intense hatred for the existing, bourgeois social order. In *Saint Joan*, the theme of the conflict between the vital individual and the stultifying, capitalist society reaches maturity. Joan's monologues sound like Shaw's personal testament, and the play assumes a

lyrical pathos undiluted by irony or scepticism.   In
Shaw's later works, melancholy gives way to bitterness,
and a series of apocalyptic plays indicates capitalism's
inevitable doom and the impossibility of a successful
bridge to the rational paradise of Beotia--the symbol of
the Soviet Union in *Too True to Be Good*. [An introductory
work for the non-scholar.   Adheres to Communist Party
line.]   [In Russian.]

1021 Rothenstein, John.   SUMMER'S LEASE: BEING
VOLUME ONE OF AN AUTOBIOGRAPHY (Lond: H. Hamilton,
1965; NY: Holt, Rinehart and Winston, 1966), pp.
71-72, 110, 214-15.
[Shaw once told Rothenstein that T. E. Lawrence, though
brilliant, was "not fitted to exercise supreme power"
because he could not make up his mind about the two
crucial questions: government and religion.   Like other
intellectuals, Shaw was not treated with respect in
England.   Rothenstein felt that Shaw's defense of Italy's
invasion of Abyssinia was not based on an understanding of
the complexities of the issue.]

1022 Roy, Emil.   "World-View in Shaw," DramS, IV
(Winter 1965), 209-19.
A substitute for the medieval Catholic Church, Shaw's
theater consists of "a series of interlocking metaphorical
operations: an identification by analogy of the religious
essence of all reforming institutions; the dialectic
progression which results from the conflict of unsettled
ideals in Shaw's mind, to which all his dramatic
presentations refer."   "The embodiment of this
institutional *elan vital* in a single character in each
play" is achieved through a process of symbolic
transcendentalism.   The settings in Shaw's plays are
usually polarized to represent value alternatives in the
dialectic progression of the action.   The devil's advocate
appears as early as *The Philanderer, Mrs. Warren's
Profession,* and *Arms and the Man.* Shaw also varies this
pattern.   In *Captain Brassbound's Conversion, Man and
Superman,* and *The Doctor's Dilemma,* the "mock-diabolic"
Ironist exposes imposters through ridicule; in *Candida,
Don Juan in Hell, Saint Joan* and *Heartbreak House,* the
Shavian hero, after attacking society, perhaps acquiring a
convert, and gaining enlightenment himself, withdraws to a
void filled with potentiality.   The purpose of Shaw's
drama is purgative and redemptive.   In *Getting Married,*
Mrs. George's vision of love is a metaphor for the

"quintessential quality of all religions" toward which the play's dialectic strives.

1023 Schor, Edith. ARMS AND THE MAN: A CRITICAL COMMENTARY (NY: American R. D. M. Study-Master Series, 1965).
[Includes biography, general introduction to the play, plot summary, notes, critical appraisal, character analysis, study topics, and bibliography.]

1024 Scott, William. "'Geordie' Bernard Shaw," SHAVIAN, III (Spring 1965), 10-16.
Almost from the beginning, the People's Theatre of Newcastle-upon-Tyne performed Shaw plays. They gave the first and second amateur performances of *Back to Methuselah*, and produced *Saint Joan* six times between 1927 and 1937. Shaw made two visits to the People's Theatre. In 1921, when he came to see *Man and Superman*, he was restrained. He gave no curtain speech and called the performance "infamous." More genial in 1936, however, he praised the devotion of the actors, especially Greta Burke, for their performance of *Candida*.

1025 Shedd, Robert G. "Modern Drama: A Selective Bibliography of Works Published in English in 1963-64," MD, VIII (Sept 1965), 204, 219-21.
[Very selective bibliography that focuses on books and scholarly articles. With a break for the years 1969-1973, this bibliography is published annually. The editors responsible, in addition to Shedd, are Elizabeth Towne Norton, John D. Haskell, Jr., and Charles A. Carpenter.]

1026 Smith, J. Percy. THE UNREPENTANT PILGRIM: A STUDY OF THE DEVELOPMENT OF BERNARD SHAW (Bost: Houghton Mifflin, 1965; Lond: Gollancz, 1966).
[History of Shaw's beliefs, emphasizing Creative Evolution and Socialism, as they appear in his criticism, novels and plays. Many good insights, but weakened by factual and documentation errors.]

1027 Smoker, Barbara. "Speech and Spelling," SHAVIAN, III (Summer 1965), 20-24.
Shaw wanted a new alphabet primarily for aesthetic reasons, but at the end of his life he appealed to the public on economical grounds. Sir James Pitman did not,

in fact, fight very hard in the courts for the alphabet trust specified in Shaw's Will. If a new alphabet is ever to be established, it must be introduced first to children who have not been exposed to another alphabet. [Review-article on GEORGE BERNARD SHAW ON LANGUAGE ed by Abraham Tauber (1963)].

1028 Speckhard, Robert R. "Shaw and Aristophanes: How the Comedy of Ideas Works," ShawR, VIII (Sept 1965), 82-92.
To help the audience identify the vital protagonist in the Shavian play of ideas, Shaw used a technique similar to the *Eiron-Alazon* conflict in Aristophanes' comedies: The audience sympathizes with the underdog *Eiron*-Buffoon, who is smarter than he appears to be, and rejects the pretentious *Alazon*. In *Captain Brassbound's Conversion* Lady Cicely is the *Eiron*; Hallam and Brassbound are *Alazons*. The progress of the play is the reversal of the positions of protagonist and antagonist until the apparent fool triumphs. Other Shaw *Eiron*-Buffoons include Bluntschli, Marchbanks, William the Waiter (*You Never Can Tell*), Ann Whitefield, and Androcles. Shaw's device is less theatrical than Aristophanes's because he used realistic social types. He also used the Socratic polite *Eiron* and originated the Ironical Rogue protagonist (e.g., Jack Tanner) to oppose the "complacently conceited" type of *Alazon*. Finally, Shaw made the *Eiron-Alazon* confrontation more complex. Tanner is an *Eiron* who becomes an *Alazon*, and Keegan, the *Eiron* in *John Bull's Other Island*, does not disconcert the *Alazon*, Broadbent. "Shavian comedy of ideas is not a debate or discussion, but a confrontation of two different types of personalities in which ideas are weapons."

1029 Stamm, Julian L. "Shaw's *Man and Superman*: His Struggle for Sublimation," AMERICAN IMAGO, XXII (Winter 1965), 250-54.
The Don Juan theme of *Man and Superman* is a thinly veiled sublimation of Shaw's relationship with his mother and his ambivalent attitudes toward sex. The philosophical, desexualized Don Juan is a reflection of Shaw's unconsummated marriage to Charlotte Payne-Townshend. "In Charlotte, Shaw sought a mother substitute. His unconscious incestuous wishes had [previously] prevented him from considering marriage at all." The dream scene of Act III presents the unconscious conflicts of Jack Tanner, who is Shaw's central voice in the play. Tanner fears the father role; Don Juan, the model of the Superman, wants to

avoid Ana and seek solitude in heaven. On the other hand, Shaw urges "the union of the super-being with mother, to create the Superman." Shaw's devotion to classical music was also a sublimation of and substitute for his desire for his mother. Through witty, satirical plays, Shaw expressed his conflicts on an oral level. "With his speech he devoured and created." Because of his closer relationship with his father, Shaw developed a homosexual aspect to his nature. [Facile.]

1030 Stavrou, C. N. "The Love Songs of J. Swift, G. Bernard Shaw and J. A. A. Joyce," MIDWEST QUARTERLY, VI (Winter 1965), 135-62.
Because of the Traditional Rationalism, Humanism, and Christianity in their intellectual heritage and sensibility, Swift, Shaw, and Joyce could not espouse paganism or hedonism. Shaw advocated social reform, but he really loved his art--including his persona--more than humanity. Shaw praised his New Women for virtues usually considered masculine. His abnegation of the flesh was thorough. His heroines claim to be in the grips of the Life Force, but they act like ordinary women trying to get and hold a husband. Shaw forces the audience to "dwell on licentiousness" precisely because he pretends there is none in the plays. In real life Candida would have seduced Marchbanks. Shaw's women are more like mothers than lovers. "*Back to Methuselah* prefigures a newfoundland more bleak and dreary than any number of Houyhnhnmlands." Shaw wished for an alternative to marriage; he was not, however, a true ascetic but only an inverted romantic. Swift, Shaw, and Joyce fail to understand that love, because it safeguards life, "is the index to man's acceptance of his limitations and of his willingness to establish a bond with another of his kind."

1031 Stokes, E. E., Jr. "Bernard Shaw's Debt to John Bunyan," Shaw R, VIII (May 1965), 42-51.
Bunyan exerted a life-long influence on Shaw, though Shaw was careful to distinguish between Bunyan's moralism and optimism, which he approved of, and his orthodox Puritan theology, which he did not. Shaw admired the realism and vigor of Bunyan's style; Bunyan was an artist-philosopher. This influence is not surprising since Shaw himself was a Puritan of a "higher" sort, one who believed in seriousness, work, purposiveness in life, exalted the intellectual side over the physical, and felt a sense of duty to "human society and its improvement." From Bunyan, Shaw learned that art must have a philosophy and a social

message. He was also influenced by Bunyan's method of moral allegory. *Too True to Be Good* explicitly borrows an insight about war from PILGRIM'S PROGRESS and applies it to the twentieth century. Shaw did not "Shavianize" Bunyan.

1032 Strozier, Robert. "The Undramatic Dramatist: Mrs. Warren's Shaw," SHAVIAN, III (Summer 1965), 11-14.

"In *Mrs. Warren's Profession* the drama is weakened by the propaganda which ironically would be more effective if artistically presented." The incest theme is weak dramatically and serves no purpose in the drama. Furthermore, Shaw's method of restraining the reader's emotion and forcing him to think about the play's themes lacks subtlety.

1033 Styan, J. L. THE DRAMATIC EXPERIENCE (Cambridge: Cambridge UP, 1965), pp. 10-12, 37, 42, 74-77, 78-80, 96, 124, and *passim*.

In *Saint Joan*, Shaw creates a by-play with the audience without the use of asides or prologue. He draws the audience's attention through the proscenium and into the play by giving us, in contrast to what we expect and in contrast to the meek Steward of the first scene, a brisk, business-like Joan who speaks with a musical breathlessness. In a modern play like *Pygmalion*, the audience may remain aloof and critical of all the characters. This is a hazard for some playwrights, but an advantage for Shaw, who wants us to *think* about the play. He made good use of actors' voices in communicating meaning in the theater. Plot was relatively unimportant except as a means for creating dramatic dialectic. At the end of Act II of *Major Barbara*, for example, Shaw uses verbal, visual, musical, and mood contrasts to highlight the differing reactions of the characters to Bodger's offer. These contrasts, again, force the audience to think.

1034 Suga, Yasuo. "Shaw to Sono Jidai" (Shaw and His Age), in SEKAI NO ENGEKI YOROPPAHEN (The World Theater: Europe), ed by Tsuneari Fukuda and Takashi Iwaso (Tokyo: Mikasa Shobo [Gendai No Egeki, IV], 1965), pp. 16-27.

Shaw's greatness as a dramatist lies in the fact that he possessed objectivity which is the privilege allowed to a dramatist. He created a unique comedy of extravaganza, which is different from Shakespeare's, Moliere's, Congreve's, Sheridan's or Wilde's. [In Japanese.]

1035 Tauber, Abraham. "'Thruway'--According to Webster, Dewey, and George Bernard Shaw," QUARTERLY JOURNAL OF SPEECH, LI (April 1965), 229-31.
"Thruway," a spelling simplification originally proposed in America by Melvil Dewey, has been officially accepted-- for highways in the state of New York. Down through the centuries many, including Noah Webster, have proposed spelling reforms; Shaw, however, advocated an entirely new alphabet. Partly on the basis of the momentum gained by Shaw's proposals, some progress has been made in England and America in using a phonetic alphabet to teach reading.

1036 Thomas, J. D. "'The Soul of Man under Socialism': An Essay in Context," RICE UNIVERSITY STUDIES, LI (Winter 1965), 83-95.
Like most of his contemporaries, Oscar Wilde considered Socialism, including Fabian Socialism, the opposite of Individualism and artistic freedom. The ideas in "The Soul of Man under Socialism" closely resemble the communist anarchism of William Morris as well as the evolutionary Socialism of Sydney Olivier, a Fabianist who nevertheless emphasized individual freedom. It is very likely, however, that the specific inspiration for Wilde's essay was Shaw's 1890 Fabian Society lecture that later became *The Quintessence of Ibsenism*, for Shaw's analysis of Ibsen also emphasized individualism, artistic freedom, and the repudiation of duty.

1037 Timko, Michael. "*Entente Cordiale*: The Dramatic Criticism of Shaw and Wells," MD, VIII (May 1965), 39-46.
As drama critics and friends, Shaw and H. G. Wells fought "side by side to combat mediocrity and humbug in literature as well as in life." From January to May 1895, there were 21 plays that both Shaw and Wells reviewed for their respective papers. A comparison of their reviews of AN IDEAL HUSBAND, THYRZA FLEMING, GUY DOMVILLE, KING ARTHUR, THE IMPORTANCE OF BEING EARNEST, AN M.P.'S WIFE, GENTLEMAN JOE, and THE NOTORIOUS MRS. EBBSMITH shows that though Shaw was the more confident, brilliant reviewer, the two critics did agree on their evaluations--except of THE IMPORTANCE OF BEING EARNEST, which Shaw took much too seriously. They frequently agreed even on the particular strengths and weaknesses of a play. They also disagreed:

266

Shaw preferred Jones, Wells preferred Pinero; Wells was dissatisfied with Ibsen and narrow, joyless Ibsenism, while Shaw interpreted Ibsen as an "ethical philosopher and social polemist." Wells deserves his due as a lesser, but important reviver of British drama.

1038 "*Too True to Be Good*," THEATRE WORLD, LXI (Oct 1965), 8-9.
[Photographs of the "delightful revival" of *Too True to Be Good* at the Edinburgh Festival and then at the Lyceum Theatre, London.]

1039 Trewin, J. C. "Plays in Performance," DRAMA, ns LXXVII (Summer 1965), 16-23.
Widowers' Houses, *Mrs. Warren's Profession*, *Candida*, and *Heartbreak House* are all exciting. [Photograph of *Widowers'*.]

1040 Turner, Justin G. "George Bernard Shaw: Composer," CORANTO: JOURNAL OF THE FRIENDS OF THE LIBRARIES, II (Spring 1965), 3-6.
From a letter dated 31 March 1884 to Mrs. (Caroline) Radford and two sheets of music in Shaw's handwriting, it would appear that Shaw did compose as well as perform and review music. In 1950 Shaw nevertheless persistently denied that that qualified him to be called a "composer." [The 1884 letter and Shaw's 1950 reaction to it are printed here.]

1041 Veth, Kurt, Jutta Peters, Peter Sindermann, and Ingrid Seyfarth. "Aufstieg und Fall des Mädchens Johanna. *Die Heilige Johanna* von Shaw am Landestheater Halle" (Rise and Fall of the Maiden Joan. Shaw's *Saint Joan* in Halle), THEATER DER ZEIT, XX (16 March 1965), 12-16.
Director Kurt Veth took a Brechtian approach to *Saint Joan*. He stressed the basic social gestus (*Grundgestus*) of each scene, he presented the characters in specific historic situations, and he did not attempt to smooth over contradictions. [In German.]

1042 Wagenknecht, Edward. DICKENS AND THE SCANDAL-MONGERS (Norman: U of Oklahoma P, 1965), pp. 21-22, 23, 43, 133, 151.

Shaw contradicted himself in his testimony about Dickens's relationship with Ellen Ternan, so his word is worthless in any attempt to settle this controversy. Shaw found GREAT EXPECTATIONS a profoundly sad book, but he, typically, looked at only one side of the question.

1043 Weales, Gerald. "Tennessee Williams Borrows a Little Shaw," ShawR, VIII (May 1965), 63-64.
Tennessee Williams and Donald Windham's YOU TOUCHED ME! borrows Captain Rockley's sea-faring past and Hadrian's flute from *Heartbreak House*.

1044 Weintraub, Stanley. REGGIE: A PORTRAIT OF REGINALD TURNER (NY: Braziller, 1965), pp. 154, 156, and *passim*.
In a letter to Robbie Ross, Shaw described Oscar Wilde's DE PROFUNDIS as a gigantic *blague* for the benefit of the British public. Reggie Turner did not believe that Shaw made good use of dialogue to let his characters reveal their inner lives.

1045 Weisert, John J. "More on Shavian Oratory," ShawR, VIII (Sept 1965), 112-13.
[Weisert introduces and translates an account from the 4 March 1909 *Louisville Anzeiger* of a speech Shaw gave calling for the "communication of bread" and city ownership of land.]

1046 Weissman, Philip. CREATIVITY IN THE THEATER: A PSYCHOANALYTIC STUDY (NY & Lond: Basic Books, 1965), 6, 22, 26, 54, 56, 146-72.
Shaw, like playwrights in general, used his dissociative capacity to transform "personal enactments" into "creative enactments," plays. In *Pygmalion* Shaw unconsciously re-created the forgotten oedipal scene: Eliza represents Shaw's mother; Higgins is both Vandaleur Lee, the interloping father figure in the Shaw household, and Shaw himself. Col. Pickering is a realistic version of the father figure, Mr. Doolittle derives from Shaw's maternal grandfather, and Mrs. Higgins is a realistic portrayal of Shaw's mother. The play also transformed Shaw's current relationships with women. He conceived of *Pygmalion* in 1897 with Mrs. Patrick Campbell in mind to play Eliza. In 1912, when his mother was dying, he returned to the play and to Mrs. Campbell personally. His attitude toward Mrs. Campbell and other actresses was an

enactment of the oedipal scene, since he could possess these women by writing roles for them just as Lee, the voice teacher, had possessed Mrs. Shaw. Because Mrs. Shaw neglected her son, he viewed her from a distance; he idolized her. On his honeymoon with Charlotte, another mother figure, Shaw was physically incapacitated, a sublimation of castration anxiety. *Caesar and Cleopatra, The Devil's Disciple, Captain Brassbound's Conversion,* and *Back to Methuselah* all deal with the same oedipal scene. Shaw's resistance to the idea that Higgins and Eliza should marry is further proof that the characters embody an unresolved mother-child relationship. Shaw alternated between sexualized feelings directed toward a real person and desexualized feelings enacted in plays. Through art Shaw could be omnipotent. If he had had no dramatic talent, "he would still have had to cope with an unresolved problem of childhood omnipotence."

1047 Wellek, René. A HISTORY OF MODERN CRITICISM: 1750-1950, Vol. IV (New Haven & Lond: Yale U P, 1965), 223, 336, 428-32.
Shaw was neither a Marxist nor a sociological critic, but an "ideologist and didacticist" in the Victorian realistic tradition. *The Quintessence of Ibsenism* concentrates on Ibsen's--and Shaw's--content. Shaw applied the same standards of realism, commonsense, and progressivism to his nineteenth-century contemporaries and to Shakespeare-- and found them all deficient. Because he was "deeply insensitive to the inner life of man," Shaw could not understand poetry, the problems of the novel, or art in general.

1048 White, William. "Shaw on Dante: Unpublished?" ShawR, VIII (Sept 1965), 111.
[A query as to whether a marginal note by Shaw, printed here in full, had been previously published.]

1049 Zadrima, Anton. "Bernard Šo na Cetinju" (Bernard Shaw in Setinja), POBJEDA, XII (1965), 2474.
[Shaw visits in 1929. Not seen.] [In Croatian?]

1050 Zimmerman, Wolfgang. "G. B. Shaw: *Der Arzt am Scheideweg*" (G. B. Shaw: *The Doctor's Dilemma*), DIE VOLKSBÜHNE, XVI (1965-66), 93-95.

Neither Dubedat nor Ridgeon is the object of Shaw's scorn but society at large. Shaw's criticism of society should not be seen so much from a Socialist perspective but through the mirror of German classicism. [In German.]

1966

1051 Adam, Ruth. WHAT SHAW *REALLY* SAID (Lond: Macdonald, 1966; NY: Schocken, 1967, © 1966). [Includes an introductory biographical chapter, 12 chapters on Shaw's ideas, and summaries of the best-known plays and essays. The topical chapters, which consist of a running commentary liberally illustrated with quotations, are: About God, About Sex and Marriage, About Socialism, About Democracy, About Crime and Punishment, About War, About Doctors, About Bringing up Children, About the English, About the Theater, About the Future, About a New Alphabet. Superficial.]

1052 Adams, Elsie Bonita. "Bernard Shaw and the Aesthetes," DA, XXVI (1966), 6692. Dissertation, Michigan State University, 1966, published as BERNARD SHAW AND THE AESTHETES (Columbus: Ohio State UP, 1971).

1053 Adams, Elsie B[onita]. "Bernard Shaw's Pre-Raphaelite Drama," PMLA, LXXXI (Oct 1966), 428-38. In the Preface to *Plays Pleasant*, Shaw called himself a Pre-Raphaelite dramatist and *Candida* a Pre-Raphaelite play. F. G. Stephens's description of the Pre-Raphaelite artists applies equally to Shaw: His characters are "pure transcripts . . . from nature instead of conventionalities . . . from the Old Masters." Shaw too wanted minute detail and moral purpose. *Candida* is Pre-Raphaelite because it is a "modern analogue to medieval religious art" and because it "demands a re-evaluation of the nature and function of the artist." It also revolts against Pre-Raphaelitism at its best to assert something higher--the Shavian woman, freedom for the artist, and Creative Evolution.

1054 "After the Revolution," ISh, V (Winter 1966-1967), 17, 20, 24.

In an 1888 April Fool's parody, Shaw projected the
personalities of his Socialist friends and colleagues into
a post-revolutionary future where they seem ready to start
a revisionist, counter-revolution. [Introduction to
"Curious Extract from the TIMES of the 1st April, 1900,"
presumably by Shaw, reprinted from TODAY: A MAGAZINE OF
SCIENTIFIC SOCIALISM, IX, No. 53, April 1888.]

1055 Anikst, A. "Vstrecha dvukh zvedz: ob
ispolnenii glavnikh rolei R. Pliattom i M.
Dzhaparidze v spektakle moskovskogo dramaticheskogo
teatra im. Mossoveta *Tsezar' i Kleopatra* po p'ese
B.Shou," (Meeting of Two Stars: On the Performance
of the Leading roles by R. Pliatt and M. Dzhaparidze
in the Spectacle of the Moscow "Mossovet" Dramatic
Theater after *Caesar and Cleopatra* by B. Shaw),
TEATR (Moscow), (1968), 74-77.
Caesar and Cleopatra is already in its second successful
season at the "Mossovet" Theater. Recently, the Georgian
actress Medeia Dzhaparidze took over the role of
Cleopatra. Previously, the play should have been entitled
"Caesar and Others," when R. Pliatt starred. But the star
system is foreign to our theater, thanks to Stanislavsky
50 years ago, though the individuality of players is
always respected. Shaw wrote the play with Imperialist
England of the late nineteenth century in mind, and the
stage designer emphasizes this by using cuttings from
English newspapers from the Boer War period (including the
TIMES) instead of hieroglyphics on the walls of Ancient
Egypt. [In Russian.]

1056 Anisimov, I. "Shou na storone novogo mira"
(Shaw on the Side of a New World), NOVAIA EPOKHA
VSEMIRNOI LITERATURY (A New Epoch in World Literature) (Moscow: "Sovetskii pisatel'," 1966) pp. 204-
29.
Shaw began writing plays accusing the deformities, lying,
cynicism and inhumanity of bourgeois reality. His
ruthless frankness at once became a generally admitted
trait of his output. Paradox became Shaw's vital power,
not merely an intellectual game; it was marked by the
paradox of capitalism, in which people without honor wear
masks of respectability and utter shameful thoughts in
high phrases. Capitalism, a world in which everything is
upside-down, is a key to the interpretation of all Shaw's
paradoxes. The Socialist Revolution had a profound effect
upon Shaw, and he welcomed it. He sent *Back to Methuselah*
to Lenin, who read the Preface attentively as criticism of

bourgeois democracy (though the notion of Creative Evolution in the play is futile). Shaw's visit to the Soviet Union in 1931 made him still more perspicacious towards capitalism. [In Russian.]

1057 Arkadin. "Film Clips," SIGHT AND SOUND, XXXV (Spring 1966), 98.
While it is true that all of the Shaw films except *Pygmalion* are failures, the fault is not entirely due to Shaw's theater-oriented theory of film and film adaptation. Cecil Lewis and Gabriel Pascal were not first-rate film artists, for one thing. Secondly, the weaknesses that appear in the films are in fact only exaggerations of the weaknesses in the original plays. [Review-note on Donald Costello, THE SERPENT'S EYE: SHAW AND THE CINEMA (1965).]

1058 Armstrong, William A. "George Bernard Shaw: The Playwright as Producer," MD, VIII (Feb 1966), 347-61.
Shaw did not get along well with the actor-managers, since they "harked back" to nineteenth-century romanticism and since he deplored their Shakespeare productions. Shaw's own training as a producer was primarily musical. He rehearsed and criticized his actors with perspicacity and wit. He wrote his plays for the picture-frame stage, but he believed a superior stage would evolve in the future.

1059 Arnold, Armin. "Der neue Mensch als Methusalem: G. B. Shaws Langleber" (The New Man as Methuselah: G. B. Shaw's Longliver), DIE LITERATUR DES EXPRESSIONISMUS: SPRACHLICHE UND THEMATISCHE QUELLEN (The Literature of Expressionism: Verbal and Thematic Sources) (Stuttgart: Kohlhammer, 1966), pp. 107-13.
[Not seen.] [In German.]

1060 Baquero, Acadio. DON JUAN Y SU EVOLUCION DRAMATICA (Don Juan and His Dramatic Development), (Madrid: np, 1966).
[Not seen.] [In Spanish.]

1061 Bastable, Adolphus (pseud). "Our Theatres in the Sixties," SHAVIAN, III (Summer 1966), 25-26.

The effect of *The Simpleton of the Unexpected Isles* "is much the same as that created by a charade played by intelligent people." The result is good fun but not good art. [Review of 1966 Birmingham Repertory Theatre production of *Simpleton*.]

1062 Baylen, Joseph O. "G.B.S. on the 'Art of Living,' 1908," UNIVERSITY OF MISSISSIPPI STUDIES IN ENGLISH, VII (1966), 89-92.
In December 1907, the REVIEW OF REVIEWS asked prominent British men of science, letters, art, politics, and religion to recommend the "best regimen as to food and drink and tobacco." The replies were published in the March 1908 issue. Shaw used the opportunity not only to advance his ideas about vegetarianism and abstinence from tobacco, but also to criticize the habits of Edwardian England and foster his G.B.S. image. [Shaw's letter is reprinted.]

1063 Beard, Harry R. "Das Englische Theater" (English Theater) DAS ATLANTISBUCH DES THEATERS (The Atlantis-Book of the Theater) (Zürich and Freiburg: Atlantis, 1966), pp. 621-72.
[On Shaw's difficulties with stage directors (especially Henry Irving's refusal to perform Shaw's *Man of Destiny*) and on his successes at the Royal Court Theatre, the Avenue Theatre and the Gaiety Theatre (Manchester).] [In German.]

1064 Bentley, Roy (comp). STUDENTS' SOURCES FOR SHAKESPEARE'S *HAMLET*, SHAW'S *SAINT JOAN*, CONRAD'S *HEART OF DARKNESS* (Agincourt, Ontario: Book Society of Canada, 1966), pp. 39-74.
Contents, abstracted separately under date of first publication: Thomas E. Connolly, "Shaw's *Saint Joan*, EXPLICATOR (1955); Hans Stoppel, "Shaw and Sainthood," ENGLISH STUDIES (April 1955); Dorothy Dupler, "An Analytical Study of the Use of Rhetorical Devices in Three Selected Plays of George Bernard Shaw: *Saint Joan, Androcles and the Lion,* and *Candida*," DA, XXII (1963); John Fielden, "Shaw's *Saint Joan* as Tragedy," TWENTIETH CENTURY LITERATURE, III (July 1957). Also included but not abstracted: Jeanne d'Arc, "Joan of Arc: 'I Have Nothing More to Say'," from JOAN OF ARC, A SELF PORTAIT, trans by Willard Trask (NY: Stackpole, 1936).

1065 "Bernard Shaw and Hollywood," CShav, VII (Jan-Dec 1966), n.p. [Reprints of articles from the Los Angeles *Examiner* about Shaw and the Movies.]

1066 BERST, C[harles] A. "Propaganda and Art in *Mrs. Warren's Profession*," ELH: JOURNAL OF ENGLISH LITERARY HISTORY, XXXIII (Sept 1966), 390-404; rptd in slightly revised form as Chapter One in BERNARD SHAW AND THE ART OF DRAMA by Charles A. Berst (1973).
Mrs. Warren's Profession is didactic, but Shaw's art "qualifies, modifies and even contradicts at times simple, over-arching propagandistic conclusions" such as those Shaw advaces in the Preface. The play does not entirely support the claim that poverty is the sole cause of prostitution, nor is the play really moral. The play is developed on three levels: 1) a moral allegory in which Vivie resists the temptations of religion, aesthetics, love, and luxury; 2) a realistic tragedy in which Vivie's moral victory is seen to be an illusion by comparison with her mother's clear-sighted, unconventional vitality; and 3) a pervasive comic element which lightens the allegory and the tragedy. Vivie is possessed of a machine-like inflexibility that makes her comic in a Bergsonian way.

1067 Berst, Charles A. "Romance and Reality in *Arms and the Man*," MODERN LANGUAGE QUARTERLY, XXVII (June 1966), 197-211; rptd in slightly revised form as Chapter Two in BERNARD SHAW AND THE ART OF DRAMA, by Charles A. Berst (1973).
Arms and the Man dramatizes, not the simple confrontation between romantic illusion and prosaic reality, but the complex, interlocking relationship between romanticism and realism. Raina evolves from romance to reality, ultimately affirming the "'prosaic' romance of compassion and maternal affection." By Act III, Bluntschli's apparent common sense has acquired a romantic aura, making him more truly romantic than Sergius. Sergius himself is a "comedic Hamlet," a self-conscious man caught between noble impulses toward an unachievable "higher love," and natural physical desires. Louka is a realist with romantic ambition. Only Nicola is a complete, mundane realist. The ending of the play resolves these disparate elements through the marriages. Unfortunately for Shaw, the humor that he used as "a vehicle for thought" in this play has tended to obscure his subtle satire on war and the genteel classes and his exploration of the romantic-realist spectrum in human disposition.

1068 Brashear, William R. "O'Neill and Shaw: The Play as Will and Idea," CRITICISM, VIII (Spring 1966), 155-69.

O'Neill is the voice of the will, Shaw the voice of the intellect. Both read Schopenhauer and Nietzsche, but Shaw did not really understand that Schopenhauer's Will to Live is the same as Kant's *noumena*, an unknowable substratum world of flux. Shaw used his intellect to abstract a concept of the will and identified the will with the spirit. What Shaw means by "thought" in *Back to Methuselah* is not Schopenhauer's and Bergson's "vital process of consciousness," but the Socratic intellect. This does make Shaw a master of Bergsonian comedy, however, for to Bergson the comic mode is the intellectual mode. O'Neill, on the other hand, is close to Schopenhauer and Nietzsche because he delights in the reality behind the phenomena. His dynamic tragedies show the struggle of the individual for identity in the chaotic realm of cosmic consciousness. Shaw's vision has no contact with the vital flux of life and therefore is ultimately more pessimistic than O'Neill's.

1069 Budziński, Franciszek. "Niektóre Problemy Przejścia od Kapitalizmu do Socjalizmu w Pogladach George-Bernarda Shawa" (Some Problems in Shaw's Conversion from Capitalism to Socialism), STUDIA Z HISTORII MYŚLI SPOLECZNO-EKONOMICZNEJ (Warsaw), XII (1966), 77-96.

Although Marx had a great influence on Shaw's thought, Shaw is in debt to Marx for opening his eyes to the abuses of the Bourgeoisie, but in denying Marxist solutions to the problems, he proves he completely misunderstood Marx's theories. Shaw felt that the individual was responsible for the situation, and he turned to Darwin, Spencer, Nietzsche, Butler, and Bergson. [Traces the history of Shaw's dilemma about Socialism, democracy, capitalism, and freedom.] He reduces all economic problems to equality of income. He lacked a clear vision of Socialism and the means leading to it. He wanted to love justice, but he turned from reality and created abstractions. [In Polish.]

1070 Bühler, Renate. "Drei Lustspiele im Unterricht: Aristopphanes, DIE FRÖSCHE, Plautus, AMPHYTRION, Shaw, *Pygmalion*" (Teaching 3 Comedies: Aristophanes, THE FROGS; Plautus, AMPHYTRION; Shaw, *Pygmalion*), DER DEUTSCHUNTERRRICHT, XVIII (June 1966), 88-106.

The three comedies represent three different types of comedies. Shaw's *Pygmalion* as well suited for schools because of its topic: education. The main question is what constitutes a well-educated person. [In German.]

1071 Burgaft, E. "Ironiia i avtoironiia Bernarda Shou" (Irony and Auto-irony in Bernard Shaw), VOPROSY RUSSKOI I ZARUBEZHNOI LITERATURY (Kuibishev), II (1966), 461-82.
Inner doubts in his own ideas, influenced partly by Fabian doctrines of gradual reform, caused auto-irony in Shaw's works evident in the ironic sub-text or "stifled voice" of the author. The voice is audible as early as the *Unpleasant Plays*, and it is still clearer in the plays of the early 1900's. Later, Shaw began to mask social themes under the cover of history, or comedies of manners, or apparently innocent moral and ethical problems, e.g. the conflict between illusion and reality, false heroism, etc. During the economic crisis of the 1930's, Shaw depicts bourgeois England in Swiftian colors and uses auto-parody as in *Farfetched Fables*. [In Russian.]

1072 Bush, Alfred L. "The Exhibition: A Retrospective View," WILDE AND THE NINETIES: AN ESSAY AND AN EXHIBITION, ed by Charles Ryskamp (Princeton: Princeton UP, 1966), pp. 32-33, 47, 50. [A description of the 1966 exhibition of Oscar Wilde materials at Princeton University, including some Shaw plays, criticism, and Socialist tracts.]

1073 Caputi, Anthony (ed). MODERN DRAMA: AUTHORITATIVE TEXTS OF THE WILD DUCK, THREE SISTERS, THE DEVIL'S DISCIPLE, A DREAM PLAY, DESIRE UNDER THE ELMS, HENRY IV, BACKGROUNDS AND CRITICISM (NY: Norton [Norton Critical Editions]), pp. 392-419.
Contents relevant to Shaw, abstracted separately under date of first publication: Anthony Caputi, "On Reading Modern Plays" (1966); Charles A. Carpenter, "The Quintessence of Shaw's Ethical Position" (1966); Eric Bentley, "Melodrama and Education," from BERNARD SHAW (1947); Martin Meisel, "Rebels and Redcoats," from SHAW AND THE NINETEENTH CENTURY THEATER (1963); "Selected Bibliography," items here being abstracted under date of first publication. By Shaw and not abstracted: "Ideals and Idealists," from *The Quintessence of Ibsenism*; and "On Diabolonian Ethics," from "Preface" to *Three Plays for Puritans*.

1074 [Caputi, Anthony]. "On Reading Modern Plays,"
MODERN DRAMA: AUTHORITATIVE TEXTS OF THE WILD DUCK,
THREE SISTERS, THE DEVIL'S DISCIPLE, A DREAM PLAY,
DESIRE UNDER THE ELMS, HENRY IV, BACKGROUNDS AND
CRITICISM, ed by Anthony Caputi (NY: Norton [Norton
Critical Editions]), 1966, pp. xi-xxvii.
[Briefly introduces Shaw as a modernist who adapted
realistic dramatic forms.]

1075 Carpenter, Charles A. "The Quintessence of
Shaw's Ethical Position," MODERN DRAMA: AUTHORITA-
TIVE TEXTS OF THE WILD DUCK, THREE SISTERS, THE
DEVIL'S DISCIPLE, A DREAM PLAY, DESIRE UNDER THE
ELMS, HENRY IV, BACKGROUNDS AND CRITICISM, ed by
Anthony Caputi (NY: Norton [Norton Critical Edi-
tions], 1966), pp. 402-08.
At one extreme Shaw was a semi-mystic possessed by a
"world betterment craze"; at the other he was a "cerebral
philosopher." But at the center, Shaw was an ethical
meliorist. In *The Quintessence of Ibsenism*, as in all of
his work, Shaw's emphasis is on "destroying ideals,
cultivating the intellect, and implanting ideas as the
principal means to the 'supreme end' of evolution." Man
must both follow and direct his inner "living will."

1076 Carpenter, Charles A. "Shaw's Collected
Letters," MD, IX (Sept 1966), 190-94.
One of the forms of Shaw's "self-permeation" from 1874 to
1897 was his letters. He used them in "his overall
campaign to de-sentimentalize, humanize, and socialize the
human race." [Review-article on BERNARD SHAW: COLLECTED
LETTERS, 1874-1897, ed by Dan H. Laurence (1965).]

1077 Carrington, Norman Thomas. NOTES ON G. BERNARD
SHAW: ANDROCLES AND THE LION (Bath: Brodie [Notes
on Chosen English Texts], [1966]).
[Includes a cursory biography, Florio's translation of
Montaigne's version of the Androcles story, a superficial
analysis of Shaw's characters, explanatory notes, and
study questions.]

1078 Coburn, Alvin Langdon. ALVIN LANGDON COBURN,
PHOTOGRAPHER: AN AUTOBIOGRAPHY, ed by Helmut &
Alison Gernsheim (NY & Washington: Frederick A.
Praeger, 1966), pp. 5, 13, 24-28, 32, 36-42, 53, 74,
76, 80, 96, 98, 104.

An enthusiastic photographer himself, Shaw readily consented to sit for Coburn and to provide him with introductions to other famous people. Shaw wrote a preface to the catalogue of Coburn's 1906 show and a foreword to his book LONDON. [Includes a limerick Shaw wrote to Coburn, a Shaw letter, the previously unpublished foreword to LONDON, and several of Coburn's photographs of Shaw.]

1079 Cohn, Ruby, and Bernard F. Dukore (eds). "George Bernard Shaw [1856-1950]," TWENTIETH-CENTURY DRAMA: ENGLAND, IRELAND, THE UNITED STATES (NY: Random House, 1966), pp. 3-8.
Shaw was concerned with the major social issues of nearly a century--from Darwinism and Socialism to motion pictures. An eager reader and playgoer, Shaw utilized and vitalized with wit and paradox the nineteenth-century traditions; his intellectual theater was set in a framework of "hi-jinks and hokum." In *Major Barbara*, Undershaft, Cusins, and Barbara form a "mystic trinity" of body, mind, and soul. Cusins and Barbara experience true conversion, yet they will try to use Undershaft's "realism and power" for their own ends, making their own converts. The play is filled with Greek motifs and the archetypal patterns of death, resurrection, and apotheosis. [Includes a chronology and a bibliography of major works about Shaw.]

1080 Coleman, D. C. "Fun and Games: Two Pictures of Heartbreak House," DramS, V (Winter 1966-1967), 223-36.
Albee's WHO'S AFRAID OF VIRGINIA WOOLF? echoes Shaw's *Heartbreak House* in structure and theme. In both plays the setting is an "emancipated parlor" that represents a whole culture, a culture in which the "success" of the dominant older generation has had "a dispiriting influence" on the younger generation. Dialogue, the center of action of both plays, is used to strip the characters of their illusions, and games are used to advance this action. *Heartbreak* includes two games of "Humiliate the Host"; in one Hector is exposed, in the other Ellie discovers that Captain Shotover is now only playing a role that he once lived. The seductive but frustrating game of "Hump the Hostess" is played by Hesione and Ariadne, but more genteelly than Martha plays it in VIRGINIA WOOLF. And Shaw too attacks the "mother-women" who treat men like children. Just as "Get the Guests" in VIRGINIA WOOLF is used to open the eyes of the

younger generation, Shaw uses domestic sport to remove the scales from the eyes of Ellie and Mazzini. Ellie, like Nick and Honey, learns from her experiences. However, *Heartbreak* is less complex and more pessimistic than VIRGINIA WOOLF. Albee's characters, unable to clearly distinguish between truth and illusion, deceive even themselves; Shaw's shed their masks easily, but Ellie, finally, learns nothing constructive from her experiences.

1081 Coleman, D. C. "Shaw, Hitler, and the Satiric Fiction," DALHOUSIE REVIEW, XLVI (Winter 1966-1967), [443]-56.
As a satire, Shaw's *Geneva* is a failure. Satire uses a "deliberate fiction" as an indirect means to attack real victims. The fiction is not an end in itself. The satirist exaggerates human errors, but he must know the truth. Shaw wanted to be didactic and prophetic. His failure as a satirist is clearest in his handling of Battler. He avoided the absolute confrontation of social good and social evil, perhaps because he lacked the moralist's sense of humor. He also lacked foresight and even hindsight. He never understood Hitler's treatment of the Jews. Because he preferred the Superman over Parliamentary democracy, and because he wished to argue for toleration among nations, Shaw did not distinguish between Battler and the other politicians in the play, even in his post-war revision. Thus *Geneva* is a "satire manque."

1082 Cordell, Richard A. ["Comments on Shaw on del Sartism"], ISh, V (Fall 1966), 3-4.
Shaw's 1 September 1886 "Art Corner" column [reprinted here] shows that he was a great personal essayist. He reveals himself, and his comments on acting are memorable and relevant.

1083 Cvetković, Sava. REPERTOAR NARODNOG POZORIŠTA U BEOGRADU 1868-1965 (Repertoire of the National Theater in Belgrade 1868-1965) (Belgrade: Muzej pozorištne umetnosti, 1966).
In 1921, *Mrs. Warren's Profession* was produced at the Belgrade National Theatre: *Pygmalion* (1922), *The Doctor's Dilemma* (1923), *The Devil's Disciple* (1924), *Saint Joan* (1926), *Caesar and Cleopatra* (1933), *Pygmalion* (1938), *Androcles and the Lion* (1952), *Joan* (1960), and *The Millionairess* (1964). [In Serbian.]

1084 Donaghy, Henry. "A Comparison of the Thought of George Bernard Shaw and G. K. Chesterton," DA, XXVII (1966), 3868A. Unpublished dissertation, New York University, 1966.

1085 Dukore, Bernard F. "The Undershaft Maxims," MD, IX (May 1966), 90-100; rptd TCIMB, ed by Rose Zimbardo (1970).
The Undershaft Maxims in *Major Barbara* state that power is a part of a divine plan, amoral in itself, wielded but not owned, pragmatic, and necessary. These principles are implicit throughout the play, but Undershaft uses the Maxims in Act III to convert Cusins, and Cusins uses all but the second ("All have the right to fight: none have the right to judge") to persuade Barbara that he is right to take on the munitions factory. The maxim that Cusins will write up may very well be similar to his statement that he wants "a power simple enough for common men to use, yet strong enough to force the intellectual oligarchy to'.use its genius for the general good."

1086 Egrí, Péter. "Ibsen, Joyce, Shaw," FILOLÓGIAI KÖZLÖNY, XII (1966), 109-33.
Ibsen's tragicomedy, from his second period, is a seminal influence on Shaw and Joyce. Joyce's mysticism and decadence, however, are very different from Shaw's realism. [Mostly analysis of Ibsen and Ibsen's influence on Joyce.] [In Hungarian.]

1087 Esslin, Martin. "Martin Esslin at *You Never Can Tell*/Haymarket," P&P, XIII (March 1966), 12-15.
Shaw wrote *You Never Can Tell* to break into the fashionable West End theaters; thus it, like other Shaw plays, uses the forms of the conventional theater of the 1890's. The problem is that even Shaw's revolutionary *ideas* are now "commonplace and irrelevant." Shaw plays are being revived because West End managers have discovered that "much of Shaw is perfectly good musical comedy without an expensive score, chorus girls and dances." [For a contrasting view of the "Shaw revival," see Simon Trussler, "Why Shaw?" (1966).]

1088 Evans, T. F. "Notes from London--February 1966," ISh, IV (Spring 1966), 45.

Fifteen years after Shaw's death, four of his plays are being produced, and the B. B. C. has broadcast several other Shaw offerings.

1089 Gilliatt, Penelope.   "Shaw" [First printed 9 Jan 1966, London, place unknown.], UNHOLY FOOLS, WITS, COMICS, DISTURBERS OF THE PEACE: FILM & THEATER (NY: Viking Press, 1973), p. 61.

Shaw's plays are exegetical, but his shrewdness is totally successful.

1090 Gordon, David J.   "Two Anti-Puritan Puritans: Bernard Shaw and D. H. Lawrence," YALE REVIEW, LVI (Autumn 1966), 76-90; rptd in LITERARY ART AND THE UNCONSCIOUS (Baton Rouge: Louisiana State UP, 1977), pp. 153-70.

Shaw and Lawrence opposed Puritanism, in the usual sense of the word, because they did not classify instincts as "vice" and suppression of instinct through fear as "virtue." Nevertheless, Shaw and Lawrence were Puritans in a deeper sense. They zealously advocated vital energy as "a new moral center beyond good and evil." This transcendance was to be achieved through a renunciation combined with compensation at a higher level. Their drive toward renunciation points to "some unadmitted guilt connected with the normal social roles of the male adult." If energetic men like Lawrence and Shaw cannot reduce this obstructing guilt by modifying their wishes and moral will, they may turn to "more extreme modes of resolution, such as apotheosis and martyrdom." Shaw's reluctant attraction to martyrdom is seen in his tendency to have martyrs and conquerors as twin heroes (e.g., Dudgeon and Anderson in *The Devil's Disciple*) or to combine the martyr and conqueror (e.g., Caesar and Joan). Shaw and Lawrence believed every evil except "mere" mortality could be overcome by will, courage. But their liberating system of sacrificing the self to a higher will is actually oppressive when forced on others in order to create a new social order. Their need to overcome their sense of exclusion was so strong that they attempted to "adapt the whole world to themselves." Nevertheless, some areas of their work are not touched by this conflict. Shaw compromised his moral absolution by presenting his ideas in comedies. Both Lawrence and Shaw moved back and forth between direct assertion in discourse and hypothetical creations in literary fictions.

1091 Guthke, Karl S. MODERN TRAGICOMEDY: AN INVESTIGATION INTO THE NATURE OF THE GENRE (NY: Random House, 1966), pp. 71, 107-9, 140, 147, 182. Tragicomedy knows no answers to the complexities and ambiguities of life. Satire, on the other hand, assumes the existence of a norm. Thus Shaw, in spite of his tendency to label his plays as tragicomedies, actually wrote satires. Shaw's association of tragicomedy with a particular historical moment implies that when that moment is surpassed, tragicomedy will be surpassed also. Nevertheless, Shaw was correct in labeling Ibsen's THE WILD DUCK as a tragicomedy.

1092 Hagnell, Viveka. "Bernard Shaws scenanvisningar" (Bernard Shaw's Stage Directions), DRAMA-FORSKNING, II (1966), 132-36. Although Shaw blamed his extensive use of stage directions on the theater censorship which forced him to prepare his plays for a reading public, he obviously used the stage directions for many purposes. Shaw was an originator in the length and the wit of his stage directions. In making his plays readable, Shaw was furthering his main purpose in writing plays, that of changing the prevailing social situation and freeing the public from romantic illusions. The reader of the directions can gain a much deeper understanding of a play than a viewer can. The stage directions found at the beginning of scenes can be divided into five categories. 1) The directions which give direct factual description constitute the most frequent but the least original type. 2) Often the descriptions of characters become principally explanations, in which Shaw functions as omniscient author. 3) Some stage directions narrate what has happened to the characters between acts, before the play began, after the play ends, or even if their circumstances had been different. 4) The stage directions bearing general commentary have perhaps the loosest of relationships to the action of their plays; Shaw uses such commentary to indicate where his sympathies lie and why. 5) This category includes suggestions about technique, usually involving some element of style and couched in language that avoids the use of technical terminology. Reading the dialogue of a play alone, without the stage directions, leads to an imperfect understanding of Shaw's intentions with regard to characters. [This spare article has the appearance of being an abstract.] [In Swedish.]

1093 Hamer, Douglas. "Some of Shaw's 1889 Political Opinions," N & Q, XIII (Sept 1966), 343-44.
Shaw was a propagandist of Fabian Socialism even to Cambridge conversation groups. He never believed, however, that women could understand Socialism. [Includes a transcript from G. C. Moore Smith's commonplace book of a conversation he had with Shaw.]

1094 Heergešić, Branko. "Konačno ipak--Shawovi predgovori: *Lica i nalicja* (At All Events--Shaw's Prefaces: *Man and Superman*), REPUBLIKA (Belgrade), XXII (1966), 114.
Shaw is known in our country by works about him rather than his plays. Now that Shaw is dead, he can no longer correct such works. S. Nedic's introduction to this translation of *Man and Superman* describes Shaw's various theories--political, moral, scientific, religious, and artistic. [In Serbian.]

1095 Holt, Charles Loyd. "*Candida*: The Music of Ideas," Shaw R, IX (Jan 1966), 2-14.
Since the main element of musical structure is systematic repetition, the basic element of the music metaphor in drama is "controlled repetition of language, idea, or symbol." *Candida* is a "musical" version of the Faust drama, at least partly based on Gounod's opera. Both works are about people of action and decision in a world dominated by tradition and talk. The first act of *Candida* is "a madrigal-like opening movement in a three-movement chamber symphony whose final development is something comparable to a climactic operatic trio." The thematic motifs, developed by statement, variation, and counterpoint, are 1) understanding or affirmation, 2) love, or understanding between two people, 3) decision, and 4) action. Whereas in FAUST, in Shaw's terminology, Marguerite is a Philistine, Faust an Idealist, and Mephistopheles a Realist, in *Candida* each of the main characters is Philistine, Idealist, and Realist. Act II uses a rondo form to expose but not mock Marchbanks' ideas. The ending of Act III most closely resembles FAUST. Candida, like Marguerite, leads the melodic development upward toward transcendence; Morell, like Faust, finally "understands" through acceptance rather than awareness. Perhaps Marchbanks does too?

1096 Holt, Charles Loyd. "Mozart, Shaw and *Man and Superman*," Shaw R, IX (Sept 1966), 102-16.
Shaw admired Mozart above all other composers and DON GIOVANNI above all other operas. *Man and Superman* "is an opera entire: libretto, 'symmetrical lyric with rhymes,' and . . . a complete music that stalks loftily towards new horizons in modern drama." Shaw musically inverts Mozart's characters and uses coincidences as a structural frame against which motifs are played to vary and expand the theme. The Act III dream sequence is a quartet on the themes of women, love, sex, marriage, among others.

1097 Holt, Charles Loyd. "Music and the Young Shaw," SHAVIAN, III (Spring 1966), 9-13.
As a youth, Shaw looked at music and literature as the same thing, and he later insisted that his drama was founded on music. G. J. V. Lee, the music teacher, influenced Shaw's dramaturgy. Not only is opera, with its direct, full-blown emotions, part of the Shavian aesthetic, but Shaw's plays are the logical "close" to the English opera tradition of Purcell and Gilbert and Sullivan.

1098 Hornby, Richard. "Bernard Shaw's Dark Comedies," DA, XXVII (1966), 477A. Unpublished dissertation, Tulane University, 1966.

1099 Hornby, Richard (comp). "Books and Theatre: A Bibliography," TULANE DRAMA REVIEW, X (Summer 1966), 239-64.
[Includes editions of Shaw plays and books about Shaw published in the U.S. between 1 February 1965 and 31 January 1966.]

1100 Hubenka, Lloyd John. "The Religious Philosophy of Bernard Shaw," DA, XXVII (1966), 477A. Unpublished dissertation, University of Nebraska, 1966.

1101 Hughes, Emrys. BERNARD SHOU (Moscow: Molodaia gvardiia, 1966; rptd 1968).
[This biography of Shaw, written in English and trans by B. Nosika, apparently was never published in English. It has also been translated into Lithuanian as BERNARDOS ŠO (Vilnius: "Vaga," 1973). Unseen.] [In Russian.]

1102 Hugo, Leon. "Shaw in Durban," SHAVIAN, III (Spring 1966), 5-8.
[Hugo introduces and reprints an interview with Shaw (published in 1935 in THE NATAL ADVERTISER) about the death of T. E. Lawrence.]

1103 Irving, Laurence. "Bernard Shaw," TLS, 7 July 1966, p. 595.
Shaw was hostile to Henry Irving until 1937, after which he relented and even admitted that he had been unfair.

1104 Johnson, E. D. H. "The Eighteen Nineties: Perspectives," WILDE AND THE NINETIES: AN ESSAY AND AN EXHIBITION, ed by Charles Ryskamp (Princeton: Princeton UP, 1966), p. 27.
Shaw and his contemporaries in the 1890's possessed a passionate, vital need to discard the old and taste the new. They were not simply "decadents" or "precursors" of the twentieth century.

1105 Kantorovich, Iosif B. "Bernard Shou v bor'be za novuiû dramy (Problema tvorcheskogo metoda i zhanr)" (Bernard Shaw and the Struggle for a New Drama [Problems of Creative Method and Genre]), Dissertation, Moscow University, 1966. [In Russian.]

1106 Kantorovich, I[osif]. B. "Transformatŝiia traditŝionikh zhanrov v intellektual'noĭ drame Bernarda Shou: Rozhdestvenskaiâ pantomima i 'drama-basniâ' *Androkle i lev*" (Transformation of Traditional Genres in Bernard Shaw's Intellectual Drama: Christmas Pantomime and "Drama-Fairy Tale" *Androcles and the Lion*), UCHENYE ZAPISKI URAL'SKOGO UNIVER-SITA, XLIV (SERIIÂ FILOLOGIIÂ), Vyp 1 (1966), 5-16.
[Not seen.] [In Russian.]

1107 Keough, Lawrence C. "The Theme of Violence in Shaw," SHAVIAN, III (Winter 1966-1967), 12-17.
Shaw consistently advocated direct action and violence, so it is logical that he admired Gene Tunney and praised the dictators. Bluntschli, the man of action in *Arms and the Man*, avoids violence only because of his "child-like, clear-minded approach to reality." As Shaw grew more pessimistic, he showed violence taking over in his plays.

Ellie, at the end of *Heartbreak House*, looks forward to the impending destruction of her society, and Joan is doomed from the beginning of *Saint Joan*.

1108 Ketels, Violet B. "Shaw, Snow, andn the New Men," PERSONALIST, XLVII (1966), 520-31.
Shaw's *Major Barbara*, like C. P. Snow's Strangers and Brothers novel-sequence, presents the overthrow of the traditional religious ethic in favor of an evolving humanist ethic; Cusins is one of Snow's "new men." The new men are educated, morally responsible seekers after truth and reality. They are willing to make decisions in the present, but they also have foresight and the willingness to attempt a reconstruction of value to keep society from dooming itself "in meaningless existential drift." A fundamental ethical proposition for both Shaw and Snow is that poverty--national or global--cannot be tolerated.

1109 Kocztur, G. "Bibliography of Works about Shaw," ACTA LITTERARIA (Academy of Sciences, Budapest), Nos. 3/4 (1966), 463-76.
[A Shavian bibliography.]

1110 Kranidas, Thomas. "Sir Francis Bacon and Shaw's Pygmalion," ShawR, IX (May 1966), 77.
Shaw's Higgins is remarkably similar to Bacon's Pygmalion (in THE ADVANCEMENT OF LEARNING), who is an emblem of the vanity of falling in love with words instead of matter.

1111 Krättli, Anton. "Theaterkritik" (Theater Criticism) in DAS ATLANTISBUCH DES THEATERS (The Atlantis-Book of the Theater), ed by Martin Hürlimann (Zürich and Freiburg: Atlantis, 1966), pp. 371-86.
[Briefly portrays Shaw as a drama critic and as an opera critic.] As a critic Shaw was sarcastic and cunning. [In German.]

1112 Lambert, J. W. "Plays in Performance," DRAMA, ns LXXX (Spring 1966), 16-27.
The Philanderer barely outlives its topicality. Shaw never again let so much pain show. Alan Badel plays Tanner in *Man and Superman* as though he were a charlatan, which is enjoyable but not right. The production of *You*

Never Can Tell is not so delightful; Ralph Richardson
gives only a glimpse of what he might do. [Photograph of
Never Can.]

1113 Lambert, J. W. "Plays in Performance," DRAMA,
ns LXXXII (Autumn 1966), 20-28.
Shaw borrowed freely from the popular theater, and the
theatrical effects enliven plays like *The Doctor's
Dilemma*.

1114 Lambert, J. W. "Plays in Performance," DRAMA,
ns LXXXIII (Winter 1966), 20-28.
Max Adrian portrayed all the gusto, wit, and sadness of
Shaw as he spouted extracts from Shaw's writings. [Review
also of the *The Man of Destiny* and *O'Flaherty, V.C.*
Photograph of *O'Flaherty.*]

1115 Leary, Daniel J. "The Evolutionary Dialectic
of Shaw and Teilhard: A Perennial Philosophy,"
ShawR, IX (Jan 1966), 15-34.
Shaw's ideology is founded on a firm dialectic structure
which systematically incorporates the insights of many
nineteenth-century thinkers. This ideology, the
significance of which is underscored by its parallels to
the ideas of Pierre Teilhard de Chardin, is expressed in
the emotional experiences of Shaw's plays. In Shaw's
dialectic, Creative Evolution is thesis, ontology (Nature
of Pantheism) is antithesis, and the open morality of the
Superman is synthesis. Teilhard and Shaw were trying to
reconcile the Cartesian dichotomy between science and
religion, matter and spirit. Rejecting Schopenhauer's
purposeless Will, Shaw optimistically believed that
evolution proceeded toward a higher degree of self-
consciousness. Teilhard also emphasized increasing self-
consciousness, evolutionary purpose, and optimism. Both
Shaw and Teilhard were influenced by Bergson and Lamarck.
Shaw's Superman and Teilhard's Seer are creative,
energetic, responsible beings "headed toward the same non-
material and ultimate biological leap." Shaw's and
Teilhard's dialectic progression is "from a simpler form
of energy, through the illusions of matter, to a more
complex, yet unencumbered form of energy." Shaw's
perennial religion, which puts him at the center of his
culture, is at the heart of such great plays as *Back to
Methuselah, Caesar and Cleopatra,* and *Saint Joan.* Late in
life, Shaw lost his optimism, however, and his last plays
resemble the theater of the absurd.

1116 Leary, Daniel J. "Is *The Simpleton* Silly?" ISh, V (Winter 1966/67), 25.
Edmund Wilson is incorrect to consider *The Simpleton of the Unexpected Isles* "silly." It is *Back to Methuselah* in miniature. Both present "self-willed death, desire for life, and the power of Will"; both show that man must outlive his passions.

1117 Leonard, Hugh. "Shaw's Hatpeg," P&P, XIII (Jan 1966), 12-13.
Without the hell scene, *Man and Superman* is an empty hatpeg. [Review of *Superman* at the New Arts, London. Photographs.]

1118 "Life and Letters," TLS, 16 June 1966, pp. 525-27, 580.
Beginning with his first recorded letter, Shaw affected, apparently for the sake of originality, a flippancy, an abnegation of feeling toward every subject, even death. He is aphoristic, but well-wrought aphorisms are not real wisdom. "After the heroics have been thrown away one is forced, both in the 'positive' plays and in the letters, to doubt whether he really knew anything of what people are like." Shaw's narrowness of feelings produced "insufferable" solutions, "clever but extremely empty" plays, and a "charade" of a philosophy. Shaw seems to have felt and expressed some genuine feelings for Charlotte Payne-Townshend and Janet Achurch, who was an uncomplicated sort of person whom he could understand. But his letters to Ellen Terry are filled with "nauseating" language unsupported by any feeling of love. Nevertheless, Shaw was generous and thoughtful. He believed in himself and some vague religion. His comments on music are superb, but on too many other subjects, including Shakespeare, he is ignorant. [Review-article on Bernard Shaw, COLLECTED LETTERS, 1874-1897 (1965).]

1119 McDowell, Frederick P. W. "Shaw's 'Real, Creative, Material World': The Correspondence," DramS, V (Spring 1966), 78-86.
Shaw's letters from 1874 to 1897 reveal him "incisively as a personality." The correspondence clarifies his relationships with women, his Socialist activities, his music and drama criticism, and his dominating passion--to be a great writer. The Shavian approach to drama is evident as early as 1880 in his anti-conventional novels. He reveals himself as both pure artist, concerned with

aesthetics and as "a moralist in literature." He applied
his shrewd intellect to himself and others. Courageous,
well-informed and open-minded, he illuminates one side of
an interesting era in history. His letters, themselves
fine examples of the informal essay, reveal his belief in
the need for a pragmatic sense of "the real, creative,
material world" to counteract inflated moral idealism. [A
review-essay of George Bernard Shaw, COLLECTED LETTERS,
1874-1897 (1965).]

1120 MacGreevy, Thomas. "W. B. Yeats--A Generation
Later," UNIVERSITY REVIEW (Dublin), III (1966), 3-4;
rptd in W. B. YEATS: INTERVIEWS AND RECOLLECTIONS,
ed by E. H. Mikhail (Lond and Bassingstoke:
Macmillan; NY: Harper & Row, 1977), pp. 413-14.
Although Yeats laughed at Shaw's comedy, he detested
Shaw's tendency to deal with the inexplicable with a smart
phrase. He wished Shaw's actors spoke like poets rather
than lawyers. Shaw's Preface to *Androcles and the Lion* is
responsible for much of the disturbed attitude of today's
youth.

1121 Mackerness, E. D. "Corno Inglese: Notes on
the Texture of George Bernard Shaw's Musical Criti-
cism," RENAISSANCE AND MODERN ESSAYS, PRESENTED TO
VIVIAN DE SOLA PINTO IN CELEBRATION OF HIS SEVEN-
TIETH BIRTHDAY, ed by G. R. Hibbard with George A.
Panichas and Allan Rodway (NY: Barnes & Noble;
Lond: Routledge & Kegan Paul, 1966), pp. 147-57.
The raciness and readability of Shaw's best reviews
conceal ulterior motives. He satirized the academic
critics for their reduction of art to dogma and system.
He attacked choral festivals because they substituted
fatuous, specially-commissioned sacred oratorios for
devotional exercise. Shaw's apt Dickensian analogies are
aimed at the non-musical sensibilities of his audience.
He wrote in the "radical" journalism tradition: he wanted
music to be available to the masses.

1122 McKinley, R. D. "George Bernard Shaw and the
Atonement," DALHOUSIE REVIEW, XLVI (Autumn 1966),
[356]-65.
The Cross, the focus of Christianity, is a paradox of
exaltation and humiliation, love and hate; it was also a
"stumbling block" for Shaw's aesthetic sense, morality,
and intellect. He rejected the doctrine of Atonement
through blood sacrifice, blaming it, wrongly, on St.

Paul. Shaw was not alone in rejecting nineteenth-century concepts of Atonement, however. Shaw too believed that moral responsibility was the means to salvation. Atonement through vicarious sacrifice, he said in the Preface to *Androcles and the Lion*, was an attempt to bribe God, just as men attempted to bribe judges in a capitalistic society. Shaw was wrong to imply in *Major Barbara*, however, that Bodger and Undershaft could buy salvation. At most they could buy only salve for their consciences. Shaw did not really understand the Christian concept of sin--which is alienation from God, not merely a violation of a moral law. He did not look for the kernel of truth in the doctrine of Atonement.

1123 McMillin, Scott. "G.B.S. and Bunyan's Badman," ShawR, IX (Sept 1966), 90-99.
Judging from the annotations Shaw made, probably in 1949, to LIFE AND DEATH OF MR. BADMAN, Shaw was not deeply influenced by any of Bunyan's works except PILGRIM'S PROGRESS. [McMillin's note is followed by a complete transcription of Shaw's annotations to BADMAN.]

1124 Manson, Donald Duane. "Bernard Shaw's Use of Wit in Selected Speeches," DA, XXVII (1966), 3973A. Unpublished dissertation, Pennsylvania State University, 1967.

1125 Martin, Kingsley. FATHER FIGURES: A FIRST VOLUME OF AUTOBIOGRAPHY, 1897-1931 (Lond: Hutchinson, 1966), pp. 33, 36, 52, 74, 77, 91-93, 96, 98, 139, 153, 155, 159, 185, 188, 192, 210-11.
[Passing references to Shaw, including Shaw as a "father figure," and his relationship with the NEW STATESMAN.]

1126 Masumoto, Masahiko. "Shaw in Japan--the Second Period," ISh, V (Winter 1966-1967), 22-23.
The two decades from 1911 to 1929 witnessed Shaw's greatest popularity in Japan, but his true dimensions have never been fully exhibited since his major plays, except for *Saint Joan*, have never been performed.

1127 Mills, John A. "The Comic in Words: Shaw's Cockneys," DramS, V (Summer 1966), 137-50.
Cockney dialect itself has comic potential, but Shaw manipulates the language to increase the comic effect and

to support characterization and theme. Burgess in *Candida* mixes elegant phrasing with cockney solecisms and pronunciation. Felix Drinkwater in *Captain Brassbound's Conversion* adds idiosyncratic, repetitive syntax to his extreme vulgarization of vowel sounds. Moreover, the "antic disparity" between the nicety of his vocabulary and sentiments (borrowed from pulp fiction at that) and the vulgarity of his sounds is used to reveal his basic insincerity. Cockney dialect is used in *Major Barbara* primarily for realism, but in *Pygmalion* Shaw returned to the comic cockney. Alfred Doolittle, like his predecessors, links semi-refined vocabulary and syntax to vulgar sounds. This is integral to his character, for he truly is a cockney "thinking man." Eliza presents two new possibilities. As Higgins' fledgling pupil, she sometimes produces a comic effect by combining elegant sounds with cockney vocabulary, and her cockney language is essential to the action and theme of the play.

1128 Morison, Stanley. "Foreword," MORRIS AS I KNEW HIM, by Bernard Shaw, with Introduction by Basil Blackwell (Lond: William Morris Society, 1966), pp. [5-6].
Shaw wrote "Account of William Morris as I Knew Him" in 1936 as an introduction to the second volume of WILLIAM MORRIS: ARTIST, WRITER, SOCIALIST, a collection of Morris's doctrinal and expository lectures on Socialism. Although the "Account" naturally emphasizes Morris's relationship to Socialist history, it is also an intimate biography. Shaw even managed to be, for him, quite modest, producing a "sober essay in Morrisian hagiography."

1129 Neel, Boyd. "Shaw and Music," SHAW SEMINAR PAPERS-65 (Toronto, Winnipeg, Vancouver: Copp Clark, 1966), pp. 53-61.
Shaw as a music critic was an agitator at the moment that English music badly needed a good shaking-up.

1130 Nethercot, Arthur H. "Zeppelins over Heartbreak House," ShawR, IX (May 1966), 46-51; rptd in BERNARD SHAW'S PLAYS, ed by Warren Sylvester Smith (1970).
For the conlcusion of *Heartbreak House*, Shaw used details from an actual bombing raid that he witnessed. However, his treatment is generalized (he does not identify the attackers, the type of flying machine, or even use the

words "bomb" and "war") in order to make the play highly symbolic. From the sky will come either of the two alternatives for mankind: replacement by the Superman or total destruction. The ending of the play is too nicely selective in its destruction of the two kinds of "burglars" and the rectory.

1131 Nickson, Richard. GEORGE BERNARD SHAW'S MAN AND SUPERMAN (NY: Monarch Press [Monarch Notes and Study Guides], 1966).
[Not seen.]

1132 Nicolson, Harold. DIARIES AND LETTERS 1930-1939, ed by Nigel Nicolson (Lond: Collins; NY: Athenem, 1966), pp. 52, 75.
In conversation, Shaw said that boanerges in *The Apple Cart* was modeled on Bradlaugh but agreed nevertheless that the role was John Burns "to the life." The politician in *John Bull's Other Island* was not a portrayal of Haldane, but the waiter in *You Never Can Tell* was. Shaw claimed that he wrote plays on the spur of inspiration and worked out the details of dramatic form later.

1133 O'Donovan, John. THE SHAWS OF SYNGE STREET (Dixon, California: Proscenium PC ["Lost Play" Series, No. 2], 1966).
[A love-triangle tragi-comedy based, loosely, on the real-life relationship between George John Vandaleur Lee, Mrs. George Carr Shaw (Shaw's mother), and Mrs. George Ferdinand Shaw. Lucy Shaw, Shaw's sister, is also toyed with by the insatiable Lee. George Carr Shaw is portrayed as a comic drunk who is as ineffectual in business as he is in keeping his wife at home. Shaw himself appears only briefly, at the end of the last act after his mother has left for London.]

1134 Okumura, Saburo. "Bernard Shaw no Shakespeare Hihyo" (Bernard Shaw's Shakespeare Criticism), SHIKAI (Kyoto), No. 7 (June 1966), 31-42.
If read as a whole, Shaw's Shakespeare criticism is not irresponsible disparagements. We must not forget the dramatic circumstances and the general attitude to Shakespeare at the turn of the century. Shaw attacked the philosophical side of Shakespeare, while he praised his craft and power of expression without reserve. Most

important in Shaw's Shakespeare criticism is his call for a return to Elizabethan-type production. [In Japanese.]

1135 Okumura, Saburo. "Bernard Shaw to Fasizumu" (Bernard Shaw and Fascism), JINBUN KENKYU (Osaka Municipal University, Osaka), XVII (Dec 1966), 1001-1016.
The preface to *The Millionairess* has often furnished Shaw critics with the authority to label him an admirer of Hitler and Mussolini. However, Shaw really discusses the subject of the born boss, criticizing the defects of parliamentary democracy and advocating the necessity of communism. Shaw never admires born bosses uncritically; rather he discusses the means to defend ourselves from the atrocities of such bosses. His method of argument is that of a satirist who habitually simplifies and exaggerates. That may be a cause of unfortunate misunderstanding. [In Japanese.]

1136 Okumura, Saburo. "Bernard Shaw to Kiristokyo" (Bernard Shaw and Christianity), KAGAWA DAIGAKU GAKUGEIGAKUBU KENKYUHOKOKU (Takamatsu), Part I, No. 19, (Feb 1966), pp. 1-39.
It is wrong to think that Shaw was an atheist in his youth, then turned a Creative Evolutionist in the middle age, and finally returned to Christianity in his old age. In reality he was all of them throughout his long life, and they coexisted harmoniously in him. [A detailed examination of Shaw's view of Christianity as expressed in the preface to *Androcles and the Lion*.] [In Japanese.]

1137 Omerov, I. M. "Tema borby protiv imperializma, zakhvatnicheskikh voin i kolonializma v tvorchestva B. Shou" (Theme of Struggle against Imperialism, Wars and Colonialism in the Works of B. Shaw). Unpublished dissertation (Baku), 1966. [Listed in NAUCHNYE TRUDY SVERDLOVSKOGO PED. INSTITUTA, 218 (1974), 65.]
[In Russian.]

1138 Parker, Francine. "Some Thoughts on Directing and on Directing a Shaw Disquisitory Play," CShav, VII (Jan-Dec 1966), n.p.
[The author's experiences staging *Press Cuttings* and her discovery that the "author knows best" and the director should serve the author, and that Shaw's play is

constructed like music, with the characters like instruments presenting variations on themes.]

1139 Parker, R. B. "Bernard Shaw and Sean O'Casey," QQ, LXXIII (Spring 1966), 13-34; rptd SHAW SEMMINAR PAPERS--65 (Toronto, Winnipeg, Vancouver: Copp Clark, 1966), pp. 1-29.

O'Casey loved and admired Shaw. Even before they met, O'Casey had been influenced by Shaw's drama, especially *John Bull's Other Island*. Shaw's support for O'Casey in THE SILVER TASSIE battle with the Abbey Theatre helped O'Casey be independent (though it should be added that O'Casey's intransigence was quite un-Shavian). O'Casey shared Shaw's Christian, pacifist brand of Socialism and was strongly influenced by Shaw's evolutionary vitalism, "aristocratism," and mocking laughter. Both men were feminists, perhaps because their mothers were such strong people. Both playwrights attacked Irish Catholicism and romanticism, but Shaw did so with more reasonableness and consistency. Shaw's use of farce, dialogue, and melodrama is also more sophisticated: Shaw built dramas into complex musical structures while O'Casey used music in a naive, melodramatic way.

1140 Pathak, N. C. "The Human Appeal of Shaw's Characters," CALCUTTA REVIEW, CLXXIX (1966), 35-42. [Not seen.]

1141 Perovic, Sreten. "George Bernard Shaw: *Pigmalion*," POBJEDA, XXIII (1966), 2487. [Not seen.] [In Croatian?]

1142 Reitemeier, Rüdiger. "Sündenfall und Übermensch in G. B. Shaws *Back to Methuselah*" (The Fall of Man and Superman in G. B. Shaw's *Back to Methuselah*), GERMANISCH-ROMANISCHE MONATSSCHRIFT, Neue Folge, XVI (Jan 1966), 65-76.

The history of mankind which begins with the creation of Adam and Eve is characterized by the struggle between matter and mind. Through the process of creative evolution this history will end with the victory of mind over matter. All the fragmented parts of life will return to the all embracing and unifying Life Force, from which they once emanated. [In German.]

1143 Rockman, R. REVIEW NOTES AND STUDY GUIDE TO THE MAJOR PLAYS OF SHAW (NY: Monarch Press, 1966). [Not seen.]

1144 Rodale, J. I. RODALE'S SYSTEM FOR MENTAL POWER AND NATURAL HEALTH (Englewood Cliffs, NJ: Prentice-Hall, 1966), pp. 3-6.
Had Shaw eaten meat, his writing might have been less vicious. Eating eggs kept him mentally alert.

1145 Romm, A. S. "O dramaticheskoĭ strukture *Nepriiătnykh p'es* B. Shou" (On the Dramatic Structure of Shaw's *Unpleasant Plays*), UCHENYE ZAPISKI LENINGRADSKOGO PEDAGOGICHESKOGO INSTITUTA (Leningrad) CCLXXV (1966), 359-72.
The dramatic secret of the *Unpleasant Plays* (we omit *The Philanderer*) is the existence of invisible characters: the tenants in *Widowers' Houses* and the brothels of Mrs. Warren. Both are constructed on an analytical principle in which the role of classical Destiny is taken by the economic laws of bourgeois society. They are the invisible directors of the tragicomedy of contemporary life. The *Unpleasant Plays* refer not only to all-powerful Destiny, but also to the possibilities of mastering it. Shaw was by no means a fatalist. They provide a key to the labyrinth of the works of the most paradoxical of European playwrights and allow us to reach conclusions regarding twentieth-century realism and its relationship to the art of the past. [In Russian.]

1146 Romm, A. S. "Sotsaial'no-filosoficheskaiă problematika p'esy Shou *Pigmalion*" (Social and Philosophical Problems in Shaw's *Pygmalion*), UCHENYE ZAPISKI LENINGRADSKOGO GOSUDARSTVENNOGO PEDAGOGICHE-SKOGO INSTITUTA (Leningrad), CCCVI (1966), 223-39.
To Shaw, Capitalism was a stagnant world of spiritual blindness, preventing the development of mankind. But to awaken the individual was not enough for Shaw: some real occupation had to be found, though under conditions of the collapsing bourgeois system this became increasingly difficult. The Fabians could not help, and Shaw now enters upon a new phase of creativity with *Pygmalion*. [In Russian.]

1147 Rosenblood, Norman (ed). *SHAW SEMINAR PAPERS-65* (Toronto, Winnipeg, Vancouver: Copp Clark, 1966).
Table of Contents, abstracted separately under the name of the author; Norman Rosenblood, "Introduction"; R. B. Parker, "Bernard Shaw and Sean O'Casey," QQ (1966); Stanley Weintraub, "The Avant-Garde Shaw"; Boyd Neel, "Shaw and Music"; Robert F. Whitman, "The Dialectic Structure in Shaw's Plays."

1148 Rosenblood, Norman. "Introduction," SHAW SEMINAR PAPERS-65 (Toronto, Winnipeg, Vancouver: Copp Clark, 1966), pp. vii-ix.
[Survey of contents and explanation of Shaw Seminar at Niagara-on-the-Lake.]

1149 Schwartz, Grace H. SHAW'S PYGMALION (NY: Monarch Press [Monarch Notes and Study Guides], 1966).
[Not Seen.]

1150 Sekulic, I. "Oko Shoove *Kandide* u Beogradu" (On Shaw's *Candida* in Belgrade), ESEJI O UMETNOST (Essays on Art) (Novi Sad/Belgrade: 1966), pp. 41-63.
[Not seen.] [In Serbian.]

1151 Selenič, Slobodan. "Bernard Shaw, *Sveta Jovanka*" (Bernard Shaw, *Saint Joan*), BORBA (Belgrade), XXV (1966), 30.
[Not seen.] [In Serbian.]

1152 Seyfarth, Heinz. "George Bernard Shaw: *Der Kaiser von Amerika*" (*The Apple Cart*), DIE VOLKSBÜHNE, XVII (1966-67), 93-94.
Shaw will achieve immortality as a poet. His philosophical and social ideas are second hand; they died with him. *The Apple Cart* is structured like an opera. Its wit rests on paradox. [In German.]

1153 "Shaw in New York," ISh, IV (Spring 1966), 33.
[Brief account of Shaw's arrival in New York for his one-day visit and speech on 11 April 1933.]

1154 Sherin, Edwin. "A Director's Notes on *Saint Joan*," Shaw R, IX (May 1966), 75-76.
Saint Joan's complex characters are our contemporaries, "revealed in the ironic light of history." [Program notes from 1965 Washington, D.C., Arena Stage production.]

1155 Silverman, Albert H. "Bernard Shaw's Political Extravaganzas," DramS, V (Winter 1966-1967), 213-22.
In the late political extravaganzas--*The Apple Cart, Two True to Be Good, On the Rocks, The Simpleton of the Unexpected Isles,* and *Geneva*--Shaw paradoxically unites humor and tragedy, optimism and pessimism. The pessimism lies in his disillusionment with democracy, realiity, human institutions; the optimism in the Life Force mystique. Beginning with *Heartbreak House,* Shaw had turned from gay laughter to derisive, Olympian laughter, the modern cosmic kind of comedy that he had found in Ibsen's WILD DUCK. For Shaw, pure tragedy probably was "a romantic illusion," to be uncovered like other illusions. In *Cart* Shaw returned to the attack on illusions that he had waged in *Plays Unpleasant* but abandoned in *Plays Pleasant*. *Cart* is an intellectual problem play and a "music of ideas"--a discussion play that uses a musical structure to develop its themes. The political extravaganzas are also Shavian fantasies in which reality is no longer distinguishable from fantasy. Although humans are irrational, and post-war events too unrealistic to be believed in, the blind actions of political leaders are real. Shaw's political extravanganzas grow out of his "disquisitory play" form, but in the late plays there is even more use of monologue and soliloquy. At the end of *Too True,* nevertheless, Shaw seems to confess the futility of his talking.

1156 Skriletz, Dorothy J. "Bernard Shaw: Public Speaker," DA, XXVII (1966), 1466A-67A. Unpublished dissertation, Michigan State University, 1966.

1157 Sokolíanskiĭ, M. G. "Maksim Gor'kiĭ i Dzhordzh Bernard Shou" (Maxim Gorky and George Bernard Shaw), VOPROSY RUSSKOĬ LITERATURY (Chernovits), I (1966), 106-112.
[Not seen.] [In Russian.]

1158 Speckhard, Robert R. "Shaw and Aristophanes: Symbolic Marriage and the Magical Doctor/Cook in Shavian Comedy," Shaw R, IX (May 1966), 56-65.
Shaw uses symbolic marriages and magical Doctor/Cooks, Archetypes also found in Aristophanes' plays, to create icons for modern man. [A superficial analysis of the symbolic "marriages" in *Man and Superman, Major Barbara, Androcles and the Lion,* and *Heartbreak House.*]

1159 Sudo, Nobuo. "G. B. Shaw: *Saint Joan* Ko" (On G. B. Shaw's *Saint Joan*), MEIJIGAKUIN RONSO (Tokyo), No. 116 (Aug 1966), pp. 1-17.
Saint Joan is a chronicle play which depicts man's senseless acts against Joan. This is Shaw's appeal to man to have a nobler religion and more abundant life. [In Japanese.]

1160 Torchiana, Donald. W. B. YEATS AND GEORGIAN IRELAND (Evanston, Illinois: Northwestern UP, 1966), pp. 216, 358-59.
Yeats considered Shaw to be one of the four greatest Irishmen (Berkeley, Swift, and Burke being the others). Yeats shared Shaw's aversion to the "spoilt priest" of Ireland, but he could not agree with Shaw's optimistic view of the future Socialist state.

1161 Trussler, Simon. "Why Shaw?" P&P, XIII (March 1966), 48-51, 73.
The "Shaw revival" in England began by coincidence when several of Shaw's plays were performed by different companies within a twelve-month timespan in 1965-1966. The Brechtian revolution had prepared the way for a revival of interest in Shaw since Brecht too used the theater for didactic, intellectual purposes. Only recently have audiences begun to realize that even in his comedies Shaw is a serious artist and a superb craftsman. The substance of his plays is not dated because it is complex and not really topical. The key to directing and acting a Shaw play is to find in the text the "Shavian style": musical form, thought, and emphasis on language. "You've got to give a performance every bit as precise as in opera." [Based on interviews with Ralph Richardson, Alan Badel, Frank Dunlop, Don Taylor, and Ronald Eyre.] [For a contrasting view of the "Shaw revival," see Esslin, Martin. "Martin Esslin at *You Never Can Tell*/Haymarket" (1966).]

1162 Tsonkov, A. "Bernard Shou 110 g. ot rozhdeneto mu" (Bernard Shaw's 110th Anniversary), UCHIT. DELO (Sofia), No. 58 (26 July 1966).
[Not seen.] [In Bulgarian.]

1163 Tul'chinska, B. N. "Pro zhanrovu spetsifiku rannikh p'es Bernarda Shou" (On Generic Specifications of Shaw's Early Plays), VISTNIK KHARKOVSKOGO UNIVERSITETU (Kharkov), Seriiâ fil. No. 3 (1966), 89-95.
[Not seen.] [In Ukrainian.]

1164 Ussher, Arland. "Irish Literature," ZEITSCHRIFT FÜR ANGLISTIK UND AMERIKANISTIK, XIV (1966), 30-55.
Shaw is the spiritual father of my generation. He taught us to open our eyes and look at facts.

1165 Valency, Maurice. THE BREAKING STRING: THE PLAYS OF ANTON CHEKHOV (NY: Oxford UP, 1966), pp. 22, 44.
Shaw's satanic heroes turn nineteenth-century diabolism into useful channels. Jack Tanner of *Man and Superman* is the logical conclusion to the romantic rebel hero. Shaw used the traditional characterization technique of giving each character a dominant trait--with the variation that the trait could be revealed at any moment as merely a mask hiding a contradictory trait.

1166 Vincent, Clare. "In Search of a Likeness: Some European Portrait Sculpture," METROPOLITAN MUSEUM OF ART BULLETIN, ns XXIV (April 1966), 249-[51].
Auguste Rodin did not capture the comic essence of Shaw in his otherwise fine sculpture. Jacob Epstein's rough, experimental bust portrays, in Shaw's words, "a barbarous joker, not a high comedian." Shaw was perhaps best captured in a photograph by Edward Steichen. [Illustrated.]

1167 Wardle, Irving. "Back to Shaw," List, LXXV (13 Jan 1966), 56-58.
It is yet to be seen whether the current [1965-66] Shaw revival will bring audiences closer to Shaw's message. He was "obsessively" concerned with one idea, Creative

Evolution, and *Back to Methuselah* gives complete expression to this idea. In form, *Methuselah* is a summary of Shaw's methods: *In the Beginning* is an ironic history play, *The Gospel of the Brothers Barnabas* is a disquisitory play, and *The Thing Happens* is an extravaganza. Creative Evolution is not science but a faith. In *Methuselah*, Shaw gave free rein to his philosophical side. [Introduction to the BBC Third Programme production of *Back to Methuselah*.]

1168 Watanabe, Michio. "Kikuchi Kan to Bernard Shaw" (Kan Kikuchi and Bernard Shaw), HIKAKUBUNKA (Tokyo Woman's Christian College, Tokyo), No. 12 (Feb 1966), 125-32.
Kan Kikuchi [Japanese writer and editor, 1888-1948] is reputed to have been deeply influenced, particularly in his youth, by Shaw. However, there is no independent essay on Shaw to be found in his Collected Works (10 vols). He was dissatisfied with Shaw's destructive tendency and the artistic deficiency of the problem play in general. [In Japanese.]

1169 Weightman, John. "Ideas and the Drama," ENCOUN-TER, XXVII (Sept 1966), 46-48; (Oct 1966), 57-59.
Shaw attempted to "inject" ideas into the theater, but in *The Doctor's Dilemma, You Never Can Tell,* and *Man and Superman*, his ideas operate on one level while characterization and action operate on a very different level. *Dilemma* is dated because the action is out of focus. Dubedat, the Superman figure, is murdered. Evolutionary theory and Deism are fused with such optimism in *Never Can* and *Superman* that there are no truly evil characters and no conflict. As a result, the plays are "eunuch-like." The conservative structures and "structural messages" of these plays are stronger than their revolutionary ideas. [Review of the 1966 London productions.]

1170 Weintraub, Stanley. "The Avant-Garde Shaw," SHAW SEMINAR PAPERS-65 (Toronto, Winnipeg, Vancouver: Copp Clark, 1966), pp. 31-52; rptd in BERNARD SHAW'S PLAYS, ed by Warren Sylvester Smith (1970).
Much that has been associated with the most advanced theater in our generation can be found in Shaw's plays: theater-in-the-round, cinematic technique, universal (contemporary) themes, anti-realist devices, the actor-

character.   He rejects illusion in favor of a theater that might remedy the ills of civilization. Philosophically he is still current; theologically he is still heretical.

1171 Weintraub, Stanley.   "'The Beardsley': An Introduction," THE SAVOY: NINETIES EXPERIMENT (University Park & Lond: Pennsylvania State UP, 1966), pp. xx, xxi.
Aubrey Beardsley was largely responsible for determining the character of the SAVOY. Beardsley admired Shaw, and it was probably he who secured Shaw's contribution ("On Going to Church") for the first issue. Nevertheless, Shaw was among those who objected to the eroticism in a Beardsley drawing also intended for the first issue. "On Going to Church" is a clear, finely written statement of Shaw's life-long belief in mysticism and the need for religion.

1172 Weintraub, Stanley.   "Editor's Introduction: The Court and the Shavian Revolution," DESMOND MAC CARTHY'S THE COURT THEATRE 1904-1907: A COMMENTARY AND CRITICISM, ed by Stanley Weintraub (Coral Gables, Florida: U of Miami P [Books of the Theatre Series, No. 6], 1966), pp. xi-xxvi.
Harley Granville-Barker, John E. Vedrenne, and Shaw, actor-manager, business manager, and playwright respectively, were responsible for bringing English drama into the twentieth century. Of the 988 performances in the Court Theatre's four seasons, 701 were of Shaw plays. King Edward VII's command performance of *John Bull's Other Island* put the seal of approval on Shaw's plays. Shaw directed most of the productions of his plays and got along well with the actors and Barker, even though Barker's realistic acting style was very different from his own preference for operatic, larger-than-life acting. Shaw even criticized his own plays--once when *How He Lied to Her Husband* did not make a profit, and once when Ellen Terry gave an inadequate performance in *Captain Brassbound's Conversion*. Shaw encouraged others to write new dramas for the Court Theatre. When the Court closed, Shaw blasted the critics, but at least one of them, Max Beerbohm, had already recognized the importance of the new movement.

1173 White, Jean Westrum. "Shaw on the New York Stage," DA, XXVII (1966), 1144A. Unpublished dissertation, New York University, 1965.

1174 Whitman, Robert F. "The Dialectic Structure in Shaw's Plays," S H A W S E M I N A R P A P E R S-65 (Toronto, Winnipeg, Vancouver: Copp Clark, 1966), pp. 63-84.
Although Shaw believed that the importance of his plays lay in the ideas they contained, he was under no illusion about the absolute truth of his message. The Hegelian thesis-antithesis-synthesis underlies the form of Shaw's plays, such as *Arms and Man, Major Barbara* and *Man and Superman*.

1175 Whitman, Wanda. "Shaw and the Press Gang in New York - 1933," ISh, IV (Spring 1966), 34-36.
[A précis of articles by Lewis Gannett, Morris Watson, Lawrence Langner, and Edmund Wilson on Shaw's stop in New York on 11 April 1933. Illustrated.]

1176 Zavadskiĭ, Ĩu. A. "O filosofskikh dramakh Shou i sovremennoĭ teatral'noĭ estetike (Zametki rezhissera)" (On Shaw's Philosophical Dramas and Contemporary Theatrical Aesthetics), V O P R O S Y F I L O S O F I I (Moscow) X X (1966), 11, 93-8; trans by F. Koblischke, "Die Philosophischen Dramen Shaws und die moderne Theaterasthetik," K U N S T U N D L I T E R A T U R, X V (1967), 482-88.
Nowadays, Shaw's plays are produced more frequently in the Soviet Union than in the twenties and thirties, and even ten years ago. His success coincides with the deep interest of producers and players in Brecht's plays. Shaw blended politics, sociology, and economics into drama. My first encounter with Shaw's work was *The Devil's Disciple*, produced at the "Zavadskii Studio" in Moscow, in 1933, and *Caesar and Cleopatra* some years later at the "Mossovet Theater," with Pliatt. We decided to introduce Shaw himself to comment at the start and end of performances. Legends that Shaw's plays are "unplayable" have harmed his reputation. In her book, A. Obraztsova (*Dramatic Method of Shaw*, Moscow, "Nauka," 1965) provides a guide to questions of Shaw's theatrical aesthetics, which I do not attempt to answer. Shaw's main aim was to teach readers and audiences to think, and having thought, to act. Shaw's method is reflected in contemporary Soviet dramaturgy e.g. D. Pavlovaĩa's "Conscience," which depicts Party meetings and the like. Shaw's method of dramatizing ideas has raised the intellectual standard of contemporary theatrical art, based on the development of the audiences' awareness. Audiences now want to think, and to evaluate and analyze events. [In Russian.]

302

1177 Zograd, N. G. MALYI TEATR V KONTSE XIX-NACHALE XX WW (The Malyi Theater at the End of the Nineteenth to the Beginning of the Twentieth Centuries) (Moscow: Nauka, 1966), pp. 337, 427, 492.
Permission to produce *Candida* was obtained for the Malyi Theater (Moscow) in 1908, but the Committee preferred Pinero's HIS HOUSE IN ORDER. In 1909 *Ceasar and Cleopatra* caused wide differences in critical reaction. APOLLO said it was a satire on the English ruling class, whereas RUSSKAYA MYSL (Russian Thought) saw it as having analogies with Russia, collapsing from inner weakness, with the revolutionary philosopher Caesar establishing a new order. In 1915 *Misalliance* was postponed until 1916/1917 because Shaw was accused of Germanophilia. [In Russian.]

1967

1178 Adams, Elsie B. "The Portrait of the Artist in Bernard Shaw's Novels," ELT, X (1967), 130-49.
In each of his first three novels Shaw contrasts a true artist with an aesthete (here defined as a dilettante or a sham artist) and often also with a Philistine and a practical man of affairs. Through these contrasts in the novels the following Shavian attitudes toward art become clear: the true artist cares nothing for the expectations of society; great art has the beauty of truth; art is created to express truth, not to make money, but the true artist is nevertheless practical enough to accept money for his work; the true artist cannot dilute his devotion to art by marrying. The sham artists in these novels are anticipations of such characters a Praed, Octavius, and Apollodorus in the plays, and the real artists are anticipations of Dubedat, Shaw's conception of Shakespeare in *The Dark Lady of the Sonnets*, Henry Higgins, and the Marchbanks of the end of *Candida*. The "true artists" of Shaw's novels and plays share many of the qualities of the genuine artists of the late nineteenth century aesthetic movement, whereas the "aesthetes," or sham artists, in Shaw's works are reminiscent of the late nineteenth century parodies of the artists of the aesthetic movement.

1179 Adler, Jacob H. "A Source for Eliot in Shaw," N&Q, XIV (1967), 256-57.
T. S. Eliot admitted some indebtedness of MURDER IN THE CATHEDRAL to *Saint Joan*. Probably the questions of

martyrdom debated in MURDER IN THE CATHEDRAL were influenced by the discussions of martyrdom both in the Epilogue to *Joan* and in *Androcles and the Lion.* In addition, the description of the death of Celia Copplestone in THE COCKTAIL PARTY was probably influenced by the false description of Bluntschli's death [sic] given by Bluntschli himself in *Arms and the Man.*

1180 Albert, Sidney P. "To the Editor," SHAVIAN, III (Spring-Summer 1967), 31.
The source for the name "Miss Vavasour" by which the Reverend Samuel Gardner addresses Mrs. Warren in the first act of *Mrs. Warren's Profession* is very likely the character Lilian Vavasour of Tom Taylor's NEW MEN AND OLD ACRES, a character with whom Shaw professed himself smitten when he saw the role played by Ellen Terry.

1181 Altshuler, Thelma, and Richard Paul Janaro. RESPONSES TO DRAMA: AN INTRODUCTION TO PLAYS AND MOVIES (Bost: Houghton Mifflin, 1967), pp. 65-66, 88, 121, 127, 129-32, 221, 241-43, 332, 333, 334, 337.
MY FAIR LADY, which embodies the Joseph plot of the success of the underdog, sentimentalizes and romanticizes Henry Higgins in order to provide a popular romantic ending instead of the credible, no-nonsense ending which Shaw gives *Pygmalion.* In *Saint Joan* Shaw "identifies himself" with Joan and with Christ "to form a modern-day trinity" which is persecuted by the unperceptive. The number and range of themes included in the best of Shaw's plays are such that they achieve universality. Each of Shaw's best plays presents a character who is clearly a spokesman for Shaw. This character--often a rogue hero of superman proportions, such as Andrew Undershaft of *Major Barbara*--fulfills the philosophical role carried by the chorus in the Greek tragedies. The influence of Nietzsche on this superman character is so great that a familiarity with the ideas of Nietzsche adds much to the understanding of the plays. Shaw's realism was tempered by his use of fantasy, as in the Hell scene of *Man and Superman,* by the impossibly heightened and sustained wit of his supermen, and by his disregard for historical fact in his interpretation of heroic characters of the past.

1182 Amalric, Jean-Claude. "Reliefs du festin Shavien: Recueils et lettres publiés depuis la mort de Bernard Shaw" (Leftovers from the Shavian Feast:

Selections and Letters Published since the Death of
Bernard Shaw), ÉTUDES ANGLAISES, XX (1967), 165-68.
Since the death of Shaw numerous collections of his
articles, speeches, and letters, some previously
unpublished and some published but not easily accessible,
have appeared in print.   All these collections are
valuable in several ways: biographically, particularly in
that they make it clear that "le visage de Bernard Shaw et
le masque de G.B.S." coincide very little; historically,
in that they present a history of the theater of Shaw's
time through his words as critic, as dramatist, and as
director; and philosophically, in that they contribute to
the study of the development of the ideas of Shaw. [In
French.]

1183 Andrews, Alan. "Mendoza and Sir Arthur Conan
Doyle," ShawR, X (Jan 1967), 2-5.
As Shaw himself acknowledged, *Man and Superman's* Mendoza
was inspired by the bourgeois poet-brigand El Cuchillo and
some of the other characters of Arthur Conan Doyle's THE
EXPLOITS OF BRIGADIER GERARD who are involved in the
capture of Gerard in the mountains of Spain.

1184 *"Arms and the Man,"* SHAW FESTIVAL 1967
[Souvenir Program], (Ottawa: Rothmans, 1967), pp.
[11-12].
Arms and the Man was the first of Shaw's plays to have a
commercial success and therefore could be considered to
represent a "turning point . . . in the development of the
modern theatre." Among those he worked with in the
theater Shaw was considered a genius at directing and
acting as well as at writing plays.   The personal and
persistent attention he gave to the proper acting of his
plays is demonstrated by his correspondence with Alma
Murray, who originally played Raina.

1185 Armytage, W. H. G. "Superman and the System
(Conclusion)," RIVERSIDE QUARTERLY, III (1967), 44-
51; rptd in W. H. G. Armytage, YESTERDAY'S TOMOR-
ROWS: A HISTORICAL SURVEY OF FUTURE SOCIETIES
(Lond: Routledge and Kegan Paul; Toronto: U of
Toronto P, 1968).   [Part I of this study, which
dealt with the ideas of H. G. Wells and of Nietzsche
about the Superman, appeared in RIVERSIDE QUARTERLY,
II (1966), 232-42.
In this concluding section Armytage discusses the ideas of
Shaw, of "later German apostles," of D. H. Lawrence, and

of Yeats on the subject of the superman. The section devoted to Shaw, subtitled "The Shavian Apocalypse," mentions briefly the Superman concept in *Man and Superman* and then summarizes, virtually without comment, the development of the concept in *Back to Methuselah*.]

1186 Ayling, Ronald. "Preface," BLASTS AND BENEDICTIONS: ARTICLES AND STORIES, by Sean O'Casey (Lond, Melbourne, Toronto: Macmillan; NY: St. Martin's, 1967), pp. ix, xviii.
The title of the book comes from a remark of O'Casey's about Shaw's "sending his blasts and benedictions everywhere." Though a communist sympathizer himself, O'Casey defended Shaw against criticisms of English communists.

1187 B., T. Y. "Shaws on the Stage," SHAVIAN, III (Spring-Summer 1967), 17.
THE SHAWS OF SYNGE STREET by John O'Donovan (1966) is a lively, intelligent play which, in spite of its humor, has a pervasive note of sadness. Its view of the relationship between Shaw's mother and George Vandeleur Lee is not that given by Shaw himself.

1188 Barnes, Clive. "Theater: Max Adrian Pretending to Be G. B. Shaw," NYT, 13 Oct 1967.
BY GEORGE presents an autobiography of Shaw in excerpts from his writings selected by Michael Voysey and performed by Max Adrian. Although the performance does not seem to get across the real Shaw and although a two-hour lecture, even by a witty lecturer, is not really a dramatic experience, the very use of Shaw's prose insures that this production has more of interest to offer than is likely to be found in other plays of the season.

1189 Barnet, Sylvan, Morton Berman and William Burto (eds). TRAGEDY AND COMEDY: AN ANTHOLOGY OF DRAMA (Bost: Little, Brown, 1967), pp. 577, 658-61.
As a writer of comedy Shaw accepts the conventional theory that the purpose of comedy is to "chasten morals," and he uses stock characters. However, his comedies are unconventional in that they do not persuade their errant characters to return to the accepted morality of their society but instead, as in *Major Barbara*, attempt through discussion to establish a new morality and a new kind of society.

1190 Bastable, Adolphus [pseud]. "Our Theatres in the Sixties," SHAVIAN, III (Spring-Summer 1967), 13-16.

The Mermaid Theatre recently staged three of Shaw's short plays: *Augustus Does His Bit, Press Cuttings,* and *Passion, Poison and Petrifaction.* The first and last of these are merely light and pleasant entertainments, but *Press Cuttings,* though full of satire which was topical in its own time, still has great pertinence today. *Getting Married,* which is currently being produced in London, has only the intellect, not the life, except in brief passages. *On the Rocks,* which will be produced in Scotland at the Pitlochry Festival, has both "shrewd sense" and humor and probably will have a surprising contemporary relevance.

1191 Bastable, Adolphus [pseud]. "Our Theatres in the Sixties," SHAVIAN, III (Autumn 1967), 17-22.

Of the two Shakespearean plays presented this year at Stratford-on-Avon, Shaw had commented only incidentally on the first, CORIOLANUS, but had written extensively in analysis and praise of ALL'S WELL THAT ENDS WELL, seeing the direct and purposeful Helena as an anticipation of some of the heroines of his own and Ibsen's plays. An interesting parallel might be drawn between Helena and Ann Whitefield. *Heartbreak House,* in its revival at the Festival Theatre at Chichester, has been praised very highly by the critics. The ending still seems unsatisfactory to this reviewer, however, and it seems possible that Shaw's own uncertainty is reflected in this ending. Desmond MacCarthy's assertion that Hushabye, Lady Utterword, Mazzini Dunn, and Ellie would all be more likely to react through positive actions than through negative despair to the situation at the end of the play seems valid. Nevertheless, the play is "a deeply penetrating and shrewdly observed, richly comic and ultimately poetic interpretation of English society," which certainly refutes the notion that Shaw could not deal dramatically with emotions, but only with ideas.

1192 Bastable, Adolphus [pseud]. "Our Theatres in the Sixties," SHAVIAN, III (Winter 1966-67), 18-22.

Max Adrian's impersonation of Shaw in AN EVENING WITH GBS is very good. However, the Shavian material used, selected by Michael Voysey, was almost all very light and thus did not truly represent Shaw since it conveyed none of his reforming zeal and expressed few of his serious social and economic ideas. The recent production of *The*

Doctor's Dilemma, as usual, gave top billing to the actress who played Jennifer although Shaw said, and the performances prove him right, that her part was not the most important one. *O'Flaherty, V.C.* and *The Man of Destiny* were recently played together, with Ian McKellen playing both O'Flaherty, in the very thought-provoking and yet highly entertaining "recruiting pamphlet," and the less effective role of Napoleon in *Destiny.*

1193 Bhalla, Alok. "An Obstinate Margin in Tragedy (Shaw's *Saint Joan*)," QUEST, LIV (Summer 1967), 45-51.
Tragedy arises sout of the inability of man to achieve "communion with the vast design" of life and of the universe. Shaw's *Saint Joan* is not a tragedy, but a religious play, because Joan never doubts that she has such communion with God. Joan has no real suffering because she is not very human, but instead she is like one already beyond the passions and limitations of humanity. Because of this lack of real suffering and of humanity, Joan is almost a sentimental figure, and because of the lack of evil in the universe of the play, the play becomes a melodrama. The Epilogue is unnecessary and adds to the sentimentality of the play.

1194 Bindley, P. J. "Shaw and Religion," SHAVIAN, III (Winter 1966-67), 28-30.
SHAW AND CHRISTIANITY by Anthony S. Abbott (1965) is superficial and simplistic in its attempts to set forth Shaw's religious position. Shaw was too full of life and too much a questioner to find a religious home in the churches of his time, but his own "religion of the Life Force" was never consistently worked out, as Abbott tries to prove that it was.

1195 Blanch, Robert J. "The Myth of Don Juan in *Man and Superman*," REVUE DES LANGUES VIVANTES, XXXIII (1967), 158-63.
From the original Don Juan of Tirso de Molina in the seventeenth century, the figure of Don Juan went through a number of changes in his various depictions before finally arriving at Shaw's Don Juan, a complete reversal of the original sexual libertine. Shaw's Don Juan attempts to escape the determined advances of woman, who wishes to use him for purposes of procreation in order to bring about the eventual production of the superman. He is an anti-establishment rebel interested in the improvement of

society and a long-winded philosopher who desires to live the contemplative life. He has no interest in personal goals but desires merely to be used by the Life Force in its continuing struggle to produce an improved human being.

1196 Bodelsen, C. A. "Bernard Shaw," FREMMEDE DIGTERE I DET 20 ÅRHUNDREDE (Foreign Authors in the Twentieth Century), ed by Sven Møller Kristensen (Copenhagen: G.E.C. Gads Forlag, 1967), I, 9-28. Shaw's upbringing in the decaying Anglo-Irish middle class which was losing its economic and political power but still desperately clinging to the external symbols of its past status was the ideal preparation for a future critic of the late Victorian English society. When he began writing plays Shaw had to create not only his plays but also the public for them. Therefore he used the dramatic forms the public was accustomed to but infused his own ideas into them. In *The Devil's Disciple, Caesar and Cleopatra* and *Saint Joan* Shaw used an even older form, the Shakespearean chronicle play, with the purpose of showing his own interpretations of the leading characters. Shaw's dramatic style gradually left conventional plot structure behind and moved in the direction of philosophical discussions with little plot, as in *Heartbreak House* and *Back to Methuselah*. Shaw's own morality was basically rationalistic. Some of his opinions--those favoring capital punishment and the annexation of the Boer Republic, for example--seem to run counter to his basic beliefs but actually reflect his valuation of order and organization over freedom. He insisted that his Socialism was not based on any sentimental love for the underprivileged but on his belief that poverty was immoral and that money was the greatest power in the world, beliefs which he set forth in his Preface to *Major Barbara*. *The Apple Cart* and *On the Rocks* reflect his uneasiness about the combination of English Socialism with the Labour Party. The basis of Shaw's moral philosophy is not much different from that of the Sermon on the Mount, as is made clear in his foreword to *Androcles and the Lion*. In Shaw's theory, what the Life Force wants of men is that they work steadily to improve the world, without concerning themselves over whether they individually are having good or bad luck in life. Though he considered himself a philosopher who was writing plays mainly to advance his own ideas, Shaw converted few to his beliefs, and "it was less as original thinker than as artist--as stylist, depicter of characters, and polemicist--that he was a genius." [In Danish.]

309

1197 Brophy, Brigid. "I Never Eat Dead," SHAVIAN, III (Winter 1966-67), 7-11.
Shavians (and others) should be vegetarians, not in slavish imitation of Shaw, but by using their minds as Shaw did to question the reasoning and morality underlying the custom of eating meat and by following the reasoning set forth by Shaw in the Preface to *Androcles and the Lion*.

1198 Browne, E. Martin. "Religious Drama in Great Britain and America," THE OXFORD COMPANION TO THE THEATRE, ed by Phyllis Hartnoll, (Lond, NY, Toronto: Oxford UP, 3rd ed. 1967), pp. 793-94.
[This article appears for the first time in the third edition.] After the subject of religion had been virtually absent from the British stage for more than 200 years, it was first reintroduced by playwrights such as Henry Arthur Jones, who presented plays having religious settings and playing upon religious emotions. Religious ideas were reintroduced to the stage principally by Shaw, in such plays as *The Devil's Disciple, Saint Joan,* and *Androcles and the Lion*.

1199 Butler, Anthony. "The Guardians," THE STORY OF THE ABBEY THEATRE, ed by Sean McCann (Lond: Four Square Books [New English Library], 1967), pp. 18-52.
Yeats and Shaw were for a time rivals for the affection of Annie Elizabeth Fredericka Horniman; Shaw referred to her as his "octopus," and she used the German word for octopus, "tintenfisch," as her telegraph code name. Yeats and Lady Gregory supported Shaw's *The Shewing-up of Blanco Posnet* at the Abbey when the British officials opposed its presentation, but in 1914 they postponed a presentation of *O'Flaherty V.C.* to avoid offending the British garrison.

1200 Canaris, Volker. "Kritische Chronik: Köln" (Critical Chronicle: Cologne), TH, VIII (Dec 1967), 57.
[Reviews *Man and Superman.*] It is impossible to perform Shaw's comedy because its wit is out of date. [In German.]

1201 Carrington, Norman T. G. BERNARD SHAW: ARMS AND THE MAN, ed by Norman T. Carrington (Bath: Brodie [Notes on Chosen English Texts] [1967]).

[This 43-page pamphlet is designed for the use of students. It is divided into four major sections, the first giving both biographical information about Shaw and a brief critical survey of his works; the second discussing the title, plot, theme, characters, and style of *Arms and the Man*; the third containing an act-by-act summary of the play and explanatory notes for terms, chiefly names of persons and places, which students might find difficult; and the fourth containing fifteen questions for use in analyzing the principal features of the play.]

1202 Cassell, Richard A., and Henry Knepler (eds). WHAT IS THE PLAY? (Glenview, Illinois: Scott, Foresman, 1967), pp. 3, 4, 31-32, 86-87, 171.
Though Shaw was a supporter of Ibsen's plays and themes, in his own plays he used comedy instead of the "earnest, dogged, direct" method of Ibsen to advance those themes. In *Arms and the Man* Shaw used wit to attack romantic conceptions of "war, soldier-heroes, and love" and to ridicule the typical melodrama of the Victorian stage. Though the play was not successful at first, there is no question that the wit is still enjoyable. Shaw develops the four main characters in such a way that the viewer will not have one unchanging reaction to each but a series of reactions as the characters changes and as he is seen in different lights.

1203 Chapman, John. "Max Adrian as G. B. Shaw," DAILY NEWS (NY), 13 Oct 1967.
BY GEORGE, Max Adrian's one-man presentation of material from the writings of Shaw selected and arranged by Michael Voysey, is entertaining but superficial in the picture of Shaw which it reflects.

1204 Cheshire, David. THEATRE: HISTORY, CRITICISM AND REFERENCE, ed by K. C. Harrison (Lond: Bingley [Readers Guide], Hamden, Conn.: Archon, 1967), pp. 64-66, 83-84, 85, 87.
The variety and quantity of Shaw's work in many fields is remarkable.

1205 Chew, Samuel C., and Richrd D. Altick. THE NINETEENTH CENTURY AND AFTER (1789-1939), Book IV of A LITERARY HISTORY OF ENGLAND, Albert C. Baugh (ed), (New York: Appleton-Century-Crofts, 2nd ed., 1967), pp. 1483, 1488, 1518-19, 1520-25, S1520. [Reprints without any change the pages of the 1948 edition dealing with Shaw, but in the "Bibliographical Supplement" lists 55 works published since 1948.]

1206 Churchill, Randolph S. WINSTON S. CHURCHILL, Vol. II: *1901-1914: YOUNG STATESMAN* (Bost: Houghton Mifflin, 1967), pp. 1, 247.
Referring to his and Churchill's deficiencies in formal education, Shaw noted that they were both "officially classed as ignoramuses." By the 1906 election H. G. Wells, though still Socialistic in his thinking, was no longer an advocate of the position of Shaw and the Fabians.

1207 Clay, James H[ubert], and Daniel Krempel. THE THEATRICAL IMAGE (NY: McGraw-Hill, 1967), pp. 40-41, 98, 100, 130.
Though many critics feel that the Epilogue to *Saint Joan* is unnecessary and inappropriate, it is a necessary part of the "commanding image" of the play. The role of Eliza in *Pygmalion* provides the actress an opportunity to display her ability to produce a wide range of voice tones as well as sounds.

1208 Clayes, Stanley A., and Martin S. Stanford. SUGGESTIONS FOR INSTRUCTORS TO ACCOMPANY STANLEY A. CLAYES' DRAMA & DISCUSSION (NY: Appleton-Century-Crofts, 1967), pp. 38-46.
[This instructors' manual includes for each play in DRAMA & DISCUSSION "A Perspective" and "Questions," both composed by the authors of the manual, and "Commentaries," which are brief excerpts from a variety of critical articles about the play. "A Perspective" and "Questions" pertaining to *Saint Joan* attempt to point out Shaw's purposes in the play and the ways in which he accomplishes those purposes. "Commentaries" concerning *Saint Joan* are excerpts from W. P. Barrett, THE TRIAL OF JEANNE D'ARC (1931); rptd in St. John Ervine, BERNARD SHAW (1956); Bernard Shaw, "Sullivan, Shakespeare, and Shaw," ATLANTIC MONTHLY (March 1948); Eric Bentley, BERNARD SHAW (1947); Arthur Nethercot, MEN AND SUPERMEN: THE SHAVIAN PORTRAIT GALLERY (1954); John Gassner, "Bernard Shaw and the Making of the Modern Mind," COLLEGE ENGLISH (April 1962); Homer E. Woodbridge, GEORGE BERNARD SHAW: CREATIVE ARTIST (1963); William Irvine, THE UNIVERSE OF G.B.S. (1949);

William Heilig, (Unpublished work); Richard M. Ohmann, SHAW: THE STYLE AND THE MAN (1962).]

1209 Cleaver, James. THEATRE THROUGH THE AGES (NY: Hart Publishing Co., 1967), pp. 200, 214, 259, 267, 297, 301-9, 310, 317, 346, 381, 384, 402, 417, 418. Though Shaw's plays are vehicles for his reformist ideas and beliefs, they are also great drama by virtue of their "individual characters," their stimulating and thought-provoking dialogue, and their structure. [Contains a history of Shaw as dramatist with individual comments on 35 of his plays.]

1210 Cole, Marion (ed). FOGIE: THE LIFE OF ELSIE FOGERTY, C.B.E. (Lond: Peter Davies, 1967), pp. 21, 29, 38, 45, 78-79, 114-15, 117, 130-33, 135, 179, 184, 190, 200, 210.
Shaw and Elsie Fogerty appreciated one another's qualities. In their "lively " conversations she concentrated both sincere attention and "calculated flattery" on him. He praised her persistence and forcefulness. Lewis Casson feels that Shaw's Saint Joan embodies qualities which he had seen in Fogie. Fogie saw some incongruity in the notion of Shaw's writing *Saint Joan*, but felt that the Sybil Thorndike-Lewis Casson production revealed it as of a different quality from all the other Shaw plays. Shaw always attended the Malvern Festival, where *The Apple Cart* was the first play performed and where many of his other plays, including his "tremendous" *Back to Methuselah*, were produced. Shaw and George Whitworth did more than anyone else to bring about a National Theatre. Edith Evans recalls the help Fogie gave her when she was playing Lady Utterword in *Heartbreak House*, and Gwynneth Galton recalls a postcard Shaw sent her when she was playing Fanny in *Fanny's First Play*.

1211 Coleman, D. C. "Bernard Shaw and BRAVE NEW WORLD," ShawR, X (Jan 1967), 6-8.
Aldous Huxley's BRAVE NEW WORLD deliberately attacks some of Shaw's Utopian ideas, particularly those associated with *Back to Methuselah*. On the other hand, the utopia held up to ridicule in BRAVE NEW WORLD is in many respects very much like the Hell which Shaw depicted as a hell in *Man and Superman*.

1212 Cooke, Richard P. "The Theater: Shaw Reactivated," WALL STREET JOURNAL, 17 Oct 1967.
In preparing BY GEORGE, Michael Voysey has made "excellent" selections from Shaw's writings, and Max Adrian's representation is "entertaining" and "stimulating," though perhaps it shows more of Shaw's jesting than of his serious side.

1213 Cordell, Richard A. "Letters to the Editors," ISh, V (Spring 1967), 42.
The "Curious Extract from the TIMES" published in your Winter issue is certainly by Shaw though not "Shaw at his best."

1214 Cordell, Richard A. "Shavian Notes," ISh, VI (Fall 1967), 11.
When a play by Shaw is presented it is still likely to be labeled "the funniest and wittiest comedy in town," as witness the recent production of *Arms and the Man* and the current production of *Getting Married*. Shaw, like Aeschylus, Euripides, and Aristophanes, is a "subversive" because his plays make people think.

1215 Cordell, Richard A. "Shavian Notes," ISh, VI (Winter 1967-68), 10.
[Gives brief notes of information about performances of *Heartbreak House*, *The Man of Destiny*, *Caesar and Cleopatra*, and *Great Catherine* and recommends Robert Hogan's analysis, in ENGLISH LITERATURE IN TRANSITION (1965), of the novels of Shaw.]

1216 Corrigan, Robert W[illoughby]. "George Bernard Shaw: 1856-1950," MASTERPIECES OF THE MODERN ENGLISH THEATRE, ed by Robert W. Corrigan (NY: Collier Books, Macmillan, 1967), p. 110.
Shaw was the creator of "the modern comedy of ideas." Though his plays fall within the realistic tradition, he used his brilliant intellect and wit, his "love of fun," his gift for paradox, and his mastery of theatrical technique to shock people into thinking, particularly into thinking about social problems, with the ultimate goal that they should improve the society in which they live.

1217 Corrigan, Robert W[illoughby]. "Melodrama and the Popular Tradition in Nineteenth-Century British

Theatre," THE NINETEENTH CENTURY, ed by Robert W. Corrigan, Laurel British Drama Series (NY: Dell, 1967), pp. 7-22; rwkd in Corrigan, Robert W. "The Collapse of the Shavian Cosmos," THE THEATRE IN SEARCH OF A FIX (NY: Delacorte Press, 1973), pp. 161-74.

Although Shaw criticized Victorian melodrama very severely, he nevertheless used many of the techniques and stock characters of that melodrama in his own plays. It was really the morality expressed in this melodrama that he repudiated, and yet he relied upon the Victorian framework of morals and manners as the context within which he could mount his attack. *Heartbreak House* illustrates what happened to Shaw when that Victorian framework crumbled: his sense of an ordered world vanished, and with it his ability to give an ordered structure to his plays.

1218 Corrigan, Robert W[illoughby]. "The Modern British Theatre and the Wide Embrace," MASTERPIECES OF THE MODERN ENGLISH THEATRE, ed by Robert W. Corrigan (NY: Collier Books, Macmillan, 1967), pp. 7-10.

The history of the modern British theater can be divided into three periods, with Shaw as the outstanding playwright of the first of these, from the turn of the century to the thirties. Furthermore, no playwright since Shaw has been able to approach his stature as a dramatist.

1219 Coward, Noël, with Michael MacOwan. "Noël Coward: A Postscript," GREAT ACTING, ed by Hal Burton (NY: Bonanza Books, Crown, 1967), pp. 154-60, 164-77.

[Based on one of a series of interviews of great actors conducted on BBC-2 television in 1965 and 1966.] In playing *The Apple Cart* I took the director's advice and played King Magnus as "basically a sad man." Shaw probably did not see him that way, and the original production did not play the last act "with sentiment" as did our 1952 production. Personally, Shaw was a very kind man and gave me much help and good advice when I was starting out as a playwright.

1220 Cowell, Raymond. TWELVE MODERN DRAMATISTS (Lond, NY: Pergamon, 1967), pp. 5, 15, 49-50, 56, 66.

Though heavily influenced by Ibsen, in his own day Shaw seemed highly original because he was overthrowing the conventions of the English Victorian stage. However, his plays, which do not have "the organizing principle of a central vision," are too much concerned with the discussion and debate of abstract ideas, and their value today lies mainly in their wit. *Saint Joan*, Shaw's "finest achievement," lacks the "didacticism and opinion-mongering" which have marred his other plays. The play, whose best qualities stem from the fact that it relies heavily on the transcripts of the original trial, shows both the political leaders of England and the religious leaders of the Church as determined to remove the danger to their institutions which Joan represents. In Scene Six Joan rises to tragic heights in her recognition "of her own nature and of that of the world which has rejected her, and which she now rejects."

1221 Crompton, Louis. "Improving *Pygmalion*," PRAIRIE SCHOONER, XLI (Spring 1967), 73-83.
Despite the romantic interpretations given the conclusion of *Pygmalion* by stage, movie, and musical productions and by some literary critics, the evidence of the play itself is that Higgins and Eliza will not marry and would not be happy together if they did. The comedy of manners in the play is also often misinterpreted. Though Shaw used Doolittle as a means to poke fun at middle-class morality, he nevertheless makes it clear that society is better off when Doolittle has been forced into the middle class; his loss in personal freedom is compensated by society's gain when a blackmailer and pimp is turned into a responsible, law-abiding citizen.

Although Eliza has become an independent person by the conclusion of the play, she still demands from the world a loving response to herself, a response which she cannot get from Higgins but can get from Freddy. Higgins, on the other hand, is a "world-betterer" and as such is not concerned with the response of the world to himself.

1222 Dannenberg, Peter. "Kritische Chronik: Kiel" (Critical Chronicle: Kiel), TH, VIII (March 1967), 44-45.
Helmut Geng's production of *Saint Joan* is performed like a historical picture-sheet; it recalls the plays of Schiller. [In German.]

1223 Del Amo, Alvaro. *"Androcles y el león* de Bernard Shaw (Bernard Shaw's *Androcles and the Lion*), PRIMER ACTO (Spain), LXXXVI (July 1967), 62. [Essay-review of production of *Androcles and the Lion* by the Escuela de Arte Dramatico.] Shaw should not be considered only as a witty and clever author because this obscures the real and complex writer who is mainly concerned with clashes of ideologies, the use of classical myths in order to understand the present, and the treatment of the "happy ending." [In Spanish.]

1224 Dent, Alan. *"Heartbreak House,"* CHICHESTER 67 [Chichester Festival Theatre Souvenir Program], ed by David Fairweather (Birmingham, England; Lond: Weather Oak P, 1967), pp. 34-35. Captain Shotover of *Heartbreak House* is fundamentally a portrait of Shaw himself in his maturity. With a few notable exceptions, the English critics at its first production did not appreciate the greatness of the play, and for the most part they concentrated on its defects in their criticisms. Though Shaw admitted modeling Hesione Hushabye on Mrs. Patrick Campbell, he steadfastly refused to allow Mrs. Campbell to play that or any other role in the play, because of her lack of a professional attitude toward acting. [Includes lists of cast and producers for the first London production and for four London revivals.]

1225 DiClaudio, Giuseppe. NOTE SUL TEATRO DI G. B. SHAW (Notes on the Theater of G. B. Shaw) (Bologna: Cooperative Libraria Universitaria Editoriale, 1967). [Lecture notes for the Faculty for teachers: 1) General Introduction, 2) Biographical Survey, 3) Intellectual Development, 4) Shaw's Criticism, 5) History of Shaw's Theatrical Career, 6) Critical Reception, 7) Shaw's Dramatic Technique, 8) Commentary on Selected Plays, and 9) Bibliography. For preparation for the examination in the History of the Theater.] [In Italian.]

1226 Dieckmann, Jörg. "Kritische Chronik: Karlsruhe" (Critical Chronicle: Karlsruhe), TH, VIII (Feb 1967), 45-47. The cast of Willi Rohde's production of *Saint Joan* at the Badisches Staatstheater was not satisfactory. [In German.]

1227 Doherty, Brian. "Archer's Review of *Arms and the Man*: Playwright Answers Critic," SHAW FESTIVAL 1967 [Souvenir Program], (Ottawa: Rothmans, 1967), p. 17.

From the time of their meeting when both were 27 years old Shaw and William Archer developed a mutual respect and a deep and lasting friendship. Nevertheless, they often had, and expressed frankly, important differences of opinion about their strong mutual interest, drama. When Archer criticized *Arms and the Man* for its "Gilbertian irony," Shaw denied that its irony was Gilbertian, asserting that Gilbert was cynical and pessimistic, whereas his own irony was "positive." To Archer's criticism that Shaw saw only the "seamy side" of people and that Raina is "bloodless" and fickle, Shaw replied that these criticisms stemmed from Archer's hopeless idealism and lack of awareness of the realities of human nature.

1228 Donaghy, Henry J[ames]. "Chesterton on Shaw's Views of Catholicism," ShawR, X (Sept 1967), 108-16.

One reason why Shaw and Chesterton could not agree about Catholicism was that each had a different conception of the Catholic Church. Chesterton pointed out that Shaw did not understand true paradox, an inherent element in Christianity and Catholicism, and that Shaw's apparent paradoxes really resulted from his being so consistent as to carry concepts through to their ultimate conclusions. Because Shaw could not understand paradox, he could not realize that Christianity allows a man to experience pessimism without being a pessimist. On the other hand, Shaw's apparent optimism about man was really at basis pessimism since he felt that man is hopeless and will have to be scrapped in favor of a Superman who is yet to come. Though Shaw could not see Christian asceticism for what it really is, a way to release one's true nature, in the Preface to *Man and Superman* he does advocate man's putting aside his own desires and devoting his whole life to the advancement of the Life Force. Shaw's correspondence with Chesterton makes it clear that Shaw's concept of Catholicism was that embodied in Father Dempsey of *John Bull's Other Island*, not that of Father Keegan, who, like Chesterton, was an exceptional Catholic in Shaw's view.

1229 Dooley, Roger B. "Theater Review: BY GEORGE," ISh, VI (Winter 1967-68), 14.

Composed entirely of the words of Shaw selected and arranged by Michael Voysey, BY GEORGE, in which Max Adrian

plays Shaw, presents the personal as well as the public
voice of Shaw on many topics in a production on an
"intellectual level . . . far above most current theater."

1230 Dorcey, Donal. "The Big Occasions," THE STORY
OF THE ABBEY THEATRE, ed Sean McCann (Lond: Four
Square Books [New English Library], 1967), pp. 126-
57.
When, in 1909, *The Shewing-up of Blanco Posnet* was refused
a license by the British censor, Shaw offered the play to
the Abbey.   Though public protest and official pressure
before the opening night made it appear that by presenting
the play the Abbey would be endangering its own existence,
Yeats and Lady Gregory insisted on its presentation.   The
actual performance was something of an anti-climax
because, though many reviewers found the play artistically
disappointing, few critics or other theater-goers could
find any offense to morality or religion in it.

1231 Downer, Alan S.   "Introduction," PYGMALION AND
OTHER PLAYS, by Bernard Shaw (NY: Dodd, Mead,
1967), pp. ix-xv.
Shaw's great gift was the ability to give serious and
revolutionary ideas comic form, so that his reforming
dramas were highly entertaining. *Caesar and Cleopatra* is
the story of Caesar's creating a queen out of a spoiled
and undisciplined child.   Caesar is just one in a long
line of Shavian heroes, beginning with Bluntschli of *Arms
and the Man*, who themselves do not do what they like but
what must be done and who exalt the power of reason over
the appeals of emotion.   Many of these heroes are
iconoclasts, as are both the minister and the ne'er-do-
well of *The Devil's Disciple*.   They are leaders in the
march of Creative Evolution, being spurred on by the Life
Force to move ahead of the rest of mankind so that mankind
may follow. *Pygmalion*, like *Caesar*, is about a man's
drive to educate a girl in order to cut her loose from the
role into which society would freeze her.   The success
achieved by the agents of the Life Force in the three
plays published here demonstrates that in this early
period Shaw was a "convinced optimist."

1232 Doyle, P.A.   "Shaw on Immortality and on
Illustrating His Dramatis Personae: Two Unpublished
Letters," BNYPL, LXXI (1967), 59-60.
Two recently discovered Shaw letters add to our store of
knowledge about his opinions.   One, written to Frederick

H. Evans, a bookseller and friend, is relevant to the views about the immortality of man which Shaw dramatizes in *Man and Superman* and *Back to Methuselah*. Shaw points out that most people think that a man becomes an angel after death; Shaw himself thinks that man will continue to evolve until he becomes a superman. The other letter, a reply to a request by a journalist, Ralph Watson Hallows, for help from Shaw in illustrating the characters of his plays, asserts that Shaw did not visualize the physical qualities of his *dramatis personae*, but only their characters, and therefore could not help Hallows in this respect.

1233 Dukore, Bernard F. "Introduction, to *Macbeth Skit*, by George Bernard Shaw," ETJ, XIX (Oct 1967), 343-44.

Shaw showed an interest in MACBETH throughout his life, from his teenage days when he and some fellow students organized an acting club whose first production was MACBETH. His concern with MACBETH is evident in his many discussions of it in columns of dramatic criticism, in prefaces to his plays, and in personal letters, and in a number of short parodies: *The Dark Lady of the Sonnets, A Dressing Room Secret*, the conversion of MACBETH V.viii into the form of a chapter of a novel, and the *Macbeth Skit* printed here for the first time, a parody of portions of MACBETH I.v and I.vii.

1234 Dukore, Bernard F. "Shaw's Doomsday," ETJ, XIX (March 1967), 61-71.

The Simpleton of the Unexpected Isles has the simplistic form of a child's fable and like such a fable carries a clear moral, that "one should live one's life as though every day were Judgment Day." This moral is related to the belief expressed in *Man and Superman* that the "true joy of life" consists in wearing oneself out in the service of the Life Force rather than in devoting one's life to the pursuit of one's own happiness. This is a return to the Socialistic doctrines of *Mrs. Warren's Profession* and *Widowers' Houses*. The most important unifying element is the judgment motif. The four children symbolize the four romantic illusions which mislead the world--"Love, Pride, Heroism, and Empire," just as in *Heartbreak House* four of the characters represent these same four illusions. Pra and Prola survive the Day of Judgment because they are ready to accept failure and defeat as mere stages in the progress toward the goal of an improved world, and they are ready to continue to wrestle with life as it comes to achieve this improvement.

1235 Dunlap, Joseph R. "A Further Note on the 'Curious Extract from the TIMES,'" ISh, VI (Winter 1967-68), 7.
Investigation has revealed that in deciphering Shaw's diary entry of 12 March 1888, Blanche Patch misread Shaw's shorthand for "April" as "Ag" and therefore put the mystifying date of 1 August 1900 in place of the significant date of April 1 in Shaw's reference to the topic of his article.

1236 Dunlap, Joseph R. "Future Times," ISh, V (Spring 1967), 44.
Just as Shaw in 1888 published an excerpt from the 1 April 1900 issue of the TIMES, Mark Twain in 1898 published excerpts from the 1 April, 5 April, and 23 April 1904 issues of the TIMES. Both writers gave satirical glimpses of the future in their excerpts, and some of their satiric predictions came surprisingly close to later developments.

1237 Dunlap, Joseph R. "Letters to the Editors," ISh, V (Spring 1967), 43.
In his "Curious Extract from the TIMES" Shaw takes a realistic view of the results of any possible revolution: first, the unsuccessful revolutionists are not killed, but the possibility of their taking any effective action is negated by their being relegated to the House of Lords; and second, the results achieved by the revolution are far different from those anticipated by the revolutionists.

1238 "Editorial," SHAVIAN, III (Autumn 1967), 1-5.
Shaw's *On the Rocks* dealt with his doubts about the ability of parliamentary governments to solve the economic and military problems of modern society and expressed the view that a strong dictator is needed to force people to cope sensibly with these problems. Almost 60 years ago the Joint Committee of both Houses of Parliament, after considering the views of Shaw on the subject, made recommendations which would have diminished the Lord Chamberlain's power to censor stage plays, but these recommendations were never put into effect. A 1966 joint committee has now made recommendations which, if put into effect, would virtually restore freedom of speech to the stage. Shaw's initials, carved on a beech tree at Coole

Park, the former estate of Lady Gregory, among the initials of other founders of the Abbey Theatre, and a statue of Troubetskoy in the National Gallery in Dublin are both indications of Shaw's Irish background.

1239 "Editor's Note" to "The Abolition of Christmas," SHAVIAN, III (Autumn 1967), 7.
A note in Shaw's diary dated Christmas Day 1888 indicates that on that day he wrote a letter to the STAR advocating the abolition of Christmas. Though signed "William Watkins Smyth" of the "Christmas Day Abolition Society," the following letter, which appeared in the STAR two days later, is probably that written by Shaw.

1240 "Editor's Note to (P) Shaw! A Page from an Interviewer's Log-book,'" ISh, VI (Fall 1967), 9.
A reference to the equator in "(P) Shaw! A Page from an Interviewer's Logbook," first published in PUNCH, OR THE LONDON CHARIVARI on 10 October 1896, may not have been intended as a reference to the geographical equator but rather as a name for the TIMES, as is suggested by a passage in Laurence Thompson's life of Robert Blatchford in which the term "the equator" is clearly used as a name for the TIMES.

1241 Evans, Edith, with Michael Elliott. "Edith Evans," GREAT ACTING, ed by Hal Burton (NY: Bonanza Books, Crown, 1967), pp. 111-12, 121-35.
[Based on one of a series of interviews of great actors conducted on BBC-2 television in 1965 and 1966.] I gave up 35 pounds a week in a London theater for the chance to play the She-Ancient in *Back to Methuselah*, "a great play," for 8 pounds a week in Birmingham. Shaw was right in his statement that Rosalind of AS YOU LIKE IT was at the best time of a woman's life.

1242 Evans, T. F. "At His Beddes Heed," SHAVIAN, III (Winter 1966-67), 26-27.
THE DRAMA BEDSIDE BOOK [ed H. F. Rubinstein and J. C. Trewin (Lond: Gollancz, 1966)] includes four passages from Shaw, using two of them to "frame" the collection: a passage from *In the Beginning*, the first play of *Back to Methuselah*, opens the anthology and a passage from *As Far as Thought Can Reach*, the last play of *Methuselah*, closes it. The two other Shavian excerpts are from *John Bull's Other Island* and *Androcles and the Lion*.

1243 Evans, T. F. "Editorial," SHAVIAN, III
(Spring-Summer 1967), 1-4.
In connection with the current controversy over the
proposed staging of Rolf Hochhuth's THE SOLDIERS at the
National Theatre, a recent letter published in the
GUARDIAN states that if the staging is allowed that action
will support Shaw's statement that the English do not
deserve great men. It would be more appropriate, however,
to cite on the other side of the controversy Shaw's long
and well-known opposition to censorship of the stage. In
connection with the current controversy over the possible
banning of the film based on Joyce's ULYSSES, it might be
appropriate to recall Shaw's praise of the book as a
"literary masterpiece" which contained both "realism" and
"poetry."

1244 Evans, T. F. "Editorial," SHAVIAN, III (Winter
1966-67), 1-5.
A passage from *An Unsocial Socialist*, which predicts that
the time will come when either Socialism or ruin must
engulf England, is one that few would disagree with today.
William Gaskill's desire to ban critics from performances
at the Royal Court Theater calls to mind Henry Irving's
similar attempt to ban Shaw from the Lyceum because he had
never written a sympathetic review of any of Irving's
productions.

1245 Evans, T. F. "Notes from London: June 1967,"
ISh, VI (Fall 1967), 5.
The current revival of *Getting Married* points up its
relevance to the contemporary efforts to reform the
divorce laws; the play, though providing much sensible
discussion of the problems surrounding marriage, is not
really good theater.

1246 Evans, T. F. "The 'Shaw Revival,'" SHAW
FESTIVAL 1967 [Souvenir Program], (Ottawa:
Rothmans, 1967), p. 2.
Though Shaw's plays have never lost their popularity in
England outside London, they are only now being revived at
the London West End theaters, frequently in productions
which have first appeared in other cities. *Too True to Be
Good*, recently produced with unexpected success in
Edinburgh and London, was praised by one critic as having
been 30 years ahead of the "unshavian *avant garde*," and
Press Cuttings, produced together with two other short

plays, was praised by another as having foreshadowed
certain elements of Bertolt Brecht's style.

1247 Ewen, Frederic. BERTOLT BRECHT: HIS LIFE, HIS
ART AND HIS TIMES (NY: Citadel, 1967), pp. 30, 45,
120, 124, 163-64, 200, 232, 261, 264, 268, 279.
[Most of these pages merely mention Shaw or one of his
plays in passing.] Brecht praised Shaw's humor, his
reasoning, and the importance of "opinions" in Shaw's
plays. There are some interesting similarities between
SAINT JOAN OF THE STOCKYARDS and Shaw's *Saint Joan* and
Major Barbara.

1248 Fatur, Bogomil. "Shaw kot družbeni fenomenon"
(Shaw as a Social Phenomenon), OSEBNOSTI--DELA--
IDEJE (Characteristics--Deeds--Ideas) (Maribor:
"Založba obzorja," 1967), pp. 129-40. [Dated 1951.]
Ideologically, Shaw was a bourgeois Socialist who never
overcame his Fabianism. As a young man he studied Marx
but never became a revolutionary and remained a fervent
spokesman of Fabian Socialism and ideas. [In Slovene.]

1249 Findlater, Richard [pseud of Kenneth Bruce
Findlater Bain]. BANNED! A REVIEW OF THEATRICAL
CENSORSHIP IN BRITAIN (Lond: MacGibbon & Kee,
1967), pp. 45, 75-76, 77, 79, 80, 81, 82, 85, 86,
87, 89, 91, 92, 99, 101-3, 104, 105, 112, 114, 115,
120, 125, 126, 127, 136, 150, 170-71, 204, 207.
Both as drama critic and as playwright Shaw fought
censorship. Each of the three Shaw plays refused a
license by the censor--*Mrs. Warren's Profession, The
Shewing-up of Blanco Posnet,* and *Press Cuttings*--had a
significant effect in weakening the censorship. In
addition Shaw publicly supported plays by Ibsen, Brieux,
Granville-Barker and others to which the censor refused a
license.

1250 Fletcher, Ifan Kyrle. "Charles Ricketts and
the Theatre," THEATRE NOTEBOOK, XXII (Autumn 1967),
6-23.
Charles Ricketts, the versatile artist, found his "finest
possibilities" as a stage designer in his work for
productions of Shaw plays. Those for which he was either
partially or wholly responsible for the designing of stage
settings and costumes were the "Don Juan in Hell" portion
of *Man and Superman, The Man of Destiny, Arms and the Man,*

*The Dark Lady of the Sonnets, Fanny's First Play,
Annajanska,* and *Saint Joan.*

1251 Fordyce, William DeLorme Trow. "Bernard Shaw
and the Comedy of Medicine: A Study of *The Doctor's
Dilemma.*" Unpublished Dissertation, Harvard University, 1967.
[Listed in McNamee.]

1252 Freedman, Morris. THE MORAL IMPULSE: MODERN
DRAMA FROM IBSEN TO THE PRESENT (Carbondale,
Edwardsville: Southern Illinois UP; Lond, Amsterdam: Feffer & Simons, 1967), pp. 45-62, et passim.
[This book sees the drama produced by the most important
of modern playwrights—Ibsen, Strindberg, Chekhov, Shaw,
Wilde, O'Casey, Pirandello, Lorca, Brecht, and the "angry"
and "Absurdist" writers—as having for its basis and
motivating force the "moral impulse"—the impulse to
examine honestly both the social and the personal
realities of man's life. Chapter 4, dealing with Shaw, is
entitled "Shaw's Moral Seriousness."]

The fundamental theme of all Shaw's drama is "that only
the hardest truth, the barest reality, can 'make us
free,'" The conflict in Shaw's plays is a struggle
between and among complex human beings, none of whom sees
the truth completely and freely. In *Saint Joan* the
members of the Catholic clergy are not evil but are
earnestly attempting to do what is right; Joan has no
understanding of the threat she poses to the Church and to
feudalism and is important because she is "a heroine of
life itself." *Major Barbara* points out that one of the
great evils of poverty is that it "destroys the human
possibility" to such an extent that even munitions making
seems good by comparison with it. *Pygmalion* is the story
of a man who is incomplete as a human being because of his
inability to respond to a woman emotionally. *The Doctor's
Dilemma* is basically about the moral evil of one
particular, individual doctor. *Androcles and the Lion,*
though a farce, has a fundamentally serious and moral
concern made evident through the responses of Lavinia and
Androcles to their world. Don Juan-Jack Tanner,
Marchbanks, and Caesar approach greatness because of their
ability to see through the easy sentimentality which
society passes out as truth to the much harder truth which
can be discerned only through disciplined insistence on
seeing the reality of each individual human relation and
situation.

1253 Fridberg, L. M. "Struktorno-sintakticheskie elementy avtorskoĭ obrabotki ĭazyka v voproso-otvetnykh stikakh dialoga dramaticheskogo proizved-eniĭa (Na materiale p'esy B. Shou *Major Barbara*)" (Structural and Syntactic Elements of Authorial Adaptation of Language in Question-Answer Lines of Dialogue in a Dramatic Work [On Material from Shaw's *Major Barbara*]), VOPROSY ROMANO-GERMANSKOĭ FILOLOGIĭ (Tashkent), vyp. XV (1967), 97-114. [Not seen.] [In Russian.]

1254 Fromm, Harold. BERNARD SHAW AND THE THEATER IN THE NINETIES: A STUDY OF SHAW'S DRAMATIC CRITICISM (Lawrence: U of Kansas P, 1967); part rptd TCIMB, ed by Rose Zimbardo (1970).
In his role as drama critic in the nineties, Shaw set forth the major beliefs about drama which guided him later. Shaw felt that for characters to be psychologically realistic they must exhibit the qualities of the Irrational Will. The one departure from realistic psychology for which Shaw did find justification in the drama was an unrealistic self-awareness and ability to explain themselves on the part of the characters. Though the ultimate goal of the Life Force is to produce human beings who are, like the Ancients of *Back to Methuselah*, capable of living in a world devoid of human sexuality or other material attachments, a world of pure thought akin to Christian immortality or the Platonic realm of pure ideas, the Life Force uses both sex and esthetic appreciation as the means. *Man and Superman* shows that for men sex has to be that means, but for some the means is art. The three major influences on the nineteenth-century drama which Shaw attacked in his reviews (and in his own plays) were, first, the need for spectacle; second, the Robertsonian drama, which emphasized realism; and third, the well-made play. Shaw believed that the stage should present to the audience real problems, real circumstances, and real characters from their own lives for their edification, not primarily for entertainment. Shaw's pronouncements on Ibsen's plays fall into three separate categories: those written in his early days of activity with the Fabian Society, when he looked to Ibsen's plays mainly for the Socialistic theories he could find there--the period in which he wrote *The Quintessence of Ibsenism*; those written as reviews of plays when he was a drama critic for the SATURDAY REVIEW, a period when he was considering the plays for all their qualities as plays, not just for their themes; and those written as parts of prefaces to his own plays, a period when he was

writing not only as a critic but also as a historian of
drama. Though the audiences of the nineties were not
ready for the serioius drama of such writers as Ibsen and
Shaw himself, Shaw did not give them up in despair;
instead he felt that it was the duty of the theater to
educate its audiences to such a readiness.

1255 Fulton, Renée J.   "Letters to the Editors, ISh,
   V (Spring 1967), 42.
[The writer asks what evidence there is to support the
belief that the "Curious Extract from the TIMES" published
in the Winter issue is by Shaw. See Richard A. Cordell.]

1256 Furlong, William B.   "Shaw and Chesterton: The
   Link Was Magic," ShawR, X (Sept 1967), 100-7.
From his earliest association with Chesterton Shaw took
the position of his mentor in both financial and literary
affairs. As is evident from his "Chesterbelloc" essay and
from many of his letters to Chesterton and Mrs.
Chesterton, Shaw was particularly and continually strong
in his insistence that Chesterton's talent was primarily
dramatic. Only after much effort did he prod Chesterton
into writing MAGIC, a play in which Chesterton "pummeled
Shaw's position on everything from vegetarianism to
religion," as Shaw had known he would. However,
Chesterton used techniques of intellectual conflict,
including paradox, epigram, and dialects, strikingly
similar to Shaw's. Shaw was unreserved in his praise of
MAGIC, as were other critics and the popular audiences,
but except for an "interesting stage essay THE JUDGMENT OF
DR. JOHNSON" Chesterton never wrote for the stage again.

1257 "G.B.S. and the Leading Ladies," SHAW FESTIVAL
   1967 [Souvenir Program], (Ottawa: Rothmans, 1967),
   p. 18.
As a drama critic Shaw wrote a famous comparison of Sarah
Bernhardt and Eleanora Duse, and he often wrote long,
extravagant, and persuasive letters to prospective leading
ladies for his plays. [Here are reprinted Shaw's 1895
review comparing Bernhardt and Duse and a 1913 letter to
Mrs. Patrick Campbell.]

1258 Gentle, Leonard I.   "Letters to the Editor:
   G.B.S.--Composer?" MUSICAL OPINION, XCI (Dec 1967),
   138-39.

The music from *Saint Joan* about which Jack Werner inquires is probably based on "Sound the Battle-cry," which is in both the Baptist and the Salvation Army hymnbooks.

1259 Gerould, Daniel C. "Soviet Shaw, Slavic Shaw: Moscow, 1967," ShawR, X (Sept 1967), 84-92.
The Russians go to Shaw's works for truth, not wit, because they find his underlying economic and social theories consisten⌐ with their own. The productions of *Heartbreak House, The Millionairess, Arms and the Man,* and *Caesar and Cleopatra* now playing in Russia are extremely popular. The Russians compare *Heartbreak* to Chekhov's THE THREE SISTERS, "the most tragic and emotional" of Chekhov's plays, instead of THE CHERRY ORCHARD, "the most comic." On the other hand, *The Millionairess* is played, with its alternate ending, as lively farce rather than intellectual wit, since the satire on capitalism is rather irrelevant in a non-capitalist society like Russia. The production of *Arms* (called THE CHOCOLATE SOLDIER) also slights the intellectual aspects of the play in favor of a highly physical "virile and earthy" presentation. Rostislav Pliatt, who appeaers as Shaw in the current Russian production of DEAR LIAR, appears not only as Caesar in *Caesar* but also as Shaw before and after the play to comment on its relevance to the modern world. These Russian productions of Shaw's plays not only reveal the Russian love of Shaw but also do much to refute the common Western criticism that Shaw's characters are bloodless intellectual abstractions rather than real live people.

1260 Goslin, Vernon. "To the Editor: Andrew Undershaft," SHAVIAN, III (Autumn 1967), 34.
Research in the registers of a number of churches in London shows an interesting range of names that Undershaft was fortunate enough to miss when his creator saw fit to have him discovered in the parish of St. Andrew Undershaft.

1261 Gottfried, Martin. "Theatre: BY GEORGE," WOMEN'S WEAR DAILY, 13 Oct 1967.
In this presentation of Shaw from his own writings there is too much self-indulgent self-contemplation of Shaw the person and little or nothing about his really important achievement, his plays, which are currently not recognized as the "classics" they are. The production is not interesting, nor does it give any true insight into Shaw.

1262 Gould, Jack.   "TV: Earnest *Saint Joan*," NYT, 5 Dec 1967, p. 95.
Much of Shaw's wit in *Saint Joan* was lost, and the pace of the play was weakened by the cuts made to fit the play into the two-hour Hall of Fame time slot.   Only in the trial scene did Geneviève Bujold manage to achieve the difficult combination of naive innocence and emotional depth which the role demands.   The view of Joan seen through the flames is an example of just the kind of sensationalism that Shaw criticized in his preface to the play.

1263 Grecco, Stephen.   "Vivie Warren's Profession: A New Look at *Mrs. Warren's Profession*," ShawR, X (Sept 1967), 93-99.
Mrs. Warren's Profession is a highly autobiographical play, with Mrs. Warren modeled on Shaw's mother, Vivie on his sister Lucy, Crofts on George Vandeleur Lee, Frank on Shaw himself, the Reverend Samuel Gardner on Shaw's father, and Praed possibly on Shaw's uncle, Walter John Gurly.   These possibly unconscious portrayals from life reveal Shaw's repressed Oedipal feelings for his dominating mother and his very masculine sister, the feminine quality of his own nature, and his dislike for and envy of Lee.

1264 "Green Crow Cawing," TLS, LXVI (26 Jan 1967), 65.
In BLASTS AND BENEDICTIONS Sean O'Casey approved Shaw's relation with Mrs. Patrick Campbell, asserting that it was natural for Shaw to want the companionship of someone more glamorous than Mrs. Shaw and her friends.

1265 Grossman, Manuel L.   "Propaganda Techniques in Selected Essays of George Bernard Shaw," SOUTHERN SPEECH JOURNAL, XXXII (Spring 1967), 225-236.
In the preface to *On the Rocks* and in *Everybody's Political What's What* Shaw asserted positively that he was a propagandist.   In "Socialism and Superior Brains" the literary allusions and Latin terms indicate that he is aiming this essay at a well-educated audience.   There he uses irony, ridicule, and exaggerated comparisons and analogies as his principal propaganda techniques.   In "Vivisection" Shaw first makes an emotional appeal to his audience and then develops within the framework of that emotional appeal all the propaganda techniques used in "Socialism," along with a number of others with greater

emotional impact, such as invective. In "The Censorship of the Stage in England," directed at an American audience, Shaw also begins with emotional appeals to American prejudices against the English and to American fears of anything smacking of tyranny, and then within this emotional framework he uses the more intellectual appeals which he has also used in the other two essays.

1266 Guernsey, Otis L., Jr. (ed.) THE BEST PLAYS OF 1966-1967: THE BURNS MANTLE YEARBOOK (NY, Toronto: Dodd, Mead, 1967), pp. 63, 65, 70, 87, 90, 92, 93, 95, 96, 97, 98, 99, 122, 126, 127, 422.
[Contains passing references to performances of *Captain Brassbound's Conversion, The Devil's Disciple, The Doctor's Dilemma, Getting Married, Major Barbara, Man and Superman, Man of Destiny, Misalliance, The Music Cure, O'Flaherty V.C., Saint Joan, You Never Can Tell,* and Margaret Webster's SEVEN AGES OF BERNARD SHAW.]

1267 Guerrero Zamora, Juan. HISTORIA DEL TEATRO CONTEMPORANEO, (History of the Contemporary Theater), IV (Barcelona: Flors, 1967), 141-67.
[Not seen.] [In Spanish.]

1268 Hatlen, Theodore W. "Principles," "Bernard Shaw (1856-1890)," and "Review Questions" for *Major Barbara,* DRAMA: PRINCIPLES AND PLAYS, ed by Theodore W. Hatlen (NY: Appleton-Century-Crofts, 1967), pp. 21, 23, 39, 40, 43, 44, 47, 49, 50, 319, 370.
After a varied career including the writing of novels, music criticism, and drama criticism, and active support of Socialism, Shaw began writing plays, first in the realistic style attacking social problems and later leaving behind the purely realistic style but still aiming his comic thrust at the problems of modern life, as he did in *Major Barbara.* He has gradually won recognition "as the creator of the most significant collection of dramatic literature in the twentieth century." [Nineteen review questions following the text of *Major Barbara* deal primarily with theme and structure.]

1269 Henderson, Philip. WILLIAM MORRIS: HIS LIFE, WORK AND FRIENDS (NY, Toronto, Lond, Sydney: McGraw-Hill, 1967), pp. 166, 170, 223, 230, 246-47, 261, 264, 265, 273, 277, 283, 290, 298-300, 303,

306, 309, 312-13, 319-21, 330, 339, 340, 342, 344, 367, 370, 374, 376, 377, 378.
Shaw and May Morris were apparently in love, but Shaw was prevented by his poverty from marrying her. Along with Morris, Shaw was a frequent and effective speaker for Socialism at street corner and other gatherings. Shaw found in the Social Democratic Federation too much theorizing and not enough of the hard facts about capitalism on which the Fabian Society, particularly through the work of Sidney Webb, concentrated. On at least two occasions Shaw paid eloquent tribute to Morris' greatness.

1270 Hogan, Robert. AFTER THE IRISH RENAISSANCE: A CRITICAL HISTORY OF THE IRISH DRAMA SINCE THE PLOUGH AND THE STARS (Minneapolis: U of Minnesota P, 1967), 49, 78-79, 144, passim.
Louis D'Alton's THIS OTHER EDEN is similar to *John Bull's Other Island* both in theme and in technique, but if it is Shavian it is "minor Shaw." THE LESS WE ARE TOGETHER by John O'Donovan, who is "about the closest approach to an Irish Shavian," has some similarities to *The Apple Cart*. O'Donovan's THE SHAWS OF SYNGE STREET, though a good play, is not reliable biography. Denis Johnston's THE GOLDEN CUCKOO shows some influence of *Saint Joan.*

1271 Hogan, Robert, and Herbert Bogart (eds).   THE PLAIN STYLE: A RHETORIC AND READER (NY: American Book Co., 1967), pp. 77-80.
Though Shaw is a master of all the literary and rhetorical devices of style, his basic style is plain and fluent, and when necessary he incorporates such devices into his style without disrupting its characteristic plainness. In the selection printed here--"How Frank Ought to Have Done It"--he first establishes a "mock pomposity" that he subsequently punctures. [This anthology also reprints on pages 303-07 Sean O'Casey's "A Whisper about Bernard Shaw," from O'Casey's THE GREEN CROW (1956), and on pages 308-19 O'Casey's "The Bald Primaqueera," which first appeared in the ATLANTIC MONTHLY (1965) and was subsequently reprinted in O'Casey's BLASTS AND BENEDICTIONS: ARTICLES AND STORIES, ed by Ronald Ayling (1967).]

1272 Hogan, Robert, and Michael J. O'Neill. "Introduction," JOSEPH HOLLOWAY'S ABBEY THEATRE: A SELECTION FROM HIS UNPUBLISHED JOURNAL "IMPRESSIONS

OF A DUBLIN PLAYGOER," ed by Robert Hogan and Michael J. O'Neill (Carbondale and Edwardsville: Southern Illinois UP; Lond and Amsterdam: Feffer & Simons, 1967), pp. xvi-xvii, xx-xxi, xxiii.
[Brief references to Shaw.]

1273 Holloway, Joseph. JOSEPH HOLLOWAY'S ABBEY THEATRE: A SELECTION FROM HIS UNPUBLISHED JOURNAL "IMPRESSIONS OF A DUBLIN PLAYGOER," ed by Robert Hogan and Michael J. O'Neill (Carbondale and Edwardsville: Southern Illinois UP; Lond and Amsterdam: Feffer & Simons, Inc., 1967), pp. 97, 99, 101, 109, 116, 129, 132, 142, 151, 171, 188, 191, 197-98, 203, 229-30, 232, 234, 246, 247, 250, 258-59, 279, 280-81, 282, 283, 285.
[Full-paragraph accounts of two speeches by Shaw, one on "Literature in Ireland" and one on "The Poor Law and Destitution in Ireland"; all the other cited pages contain mere passing references to Shaw.]

1274 Hornby, Richard. "Bernard Shaw's Dark Comedies," DA, XXVII (1967), 3539A-40A. Unpublished dissertation, Tulane University, 1966.

1275 Huggett, Richard. "Inhospitable Shaws" [Letter to Editor], Spec, CCXVIII (17 March 1967), 320.
Despite Spurling's opinion to the contrary (1967), Shaw's greatness is attested both by his critical reputation and by the popularity of his plays.

1276 Hugo, L. H. "Some Aspects of Bernard Shaw's Philosophy," UNISA ENGLISH STUDIES, IV (1967), 1-15.
[The text of this article was part of a program presented on 17 March 1967, in which each of the four sections of Hugo's speech served as an introduction to a reading from a Shaw play by the Pretoria Theatre Study Group.]

Shaw's Socialism affected all of his plays to some extent or other. Some, such as *Widowers' Houses* and *Major Barbara*, have specific theories from "scientific economics" as their bases. Others are affected by the ethics of Socialism. More specifically, "the prime ethic in Shavian drama is simple humanitarianism." One of Liza's stories in Act III of *Pygmalion* does more than make the audience laugh. It also affords a vivid "exposure of the abyss between money and no-money." In *The Doctor's*

Dilemma Dubedat is given up to death by Dr. Ridgeon for
the same reason that Joan is put to death in *Saint Joan*--
because he is so far ahead of his time as to make society
uncomfortable by his unorthodox behavior.

Shaw's musical background had a strong influence on his
dramatic technique, as is evident not only in the Don Juan
in Hell scene in *Man and Superman* but also in the "verbal
music" of his "fantasia" *Heartbreak House.*

Though Shaw subscribed to no organized religion, he was a
very religious person, and "it is as a religious dramatist
that we should finally see Shaw."

   1277 Hurd, Michael. "A Shavian Dilemma" [Letter to
      Editor], MUSICAL TIMES, CVIII (Sept 1967), 812.
In a 1916 note Shaw indicated that the only tune he remem-
bered "composing or appropriating" was a variation of
"Yankee Doodle." The tune from *Saint Joan* about which
Jack Werner inquires seems to have come from the same
source.

   1278 Jemnitz, János. FRIEDRICH ADLER ÉS GEORGE
   BERNARD SHAW VITÁJA AS OLASZ FASIZMUSRÓL (The Debate
   on Italian Fascism between Friedrich Adler and
   George Bernard Shaw) (Budapest: Akadémiai Kiadó,
   1967).
[Not seen.] [In Hungarian.]

   1279 Jones, D. A. N. "Politics in the Theatre,"
      TLS, LXVI (27 July 1967), 681-82.
The theater can be used effectively for political
didacticism, as Shaw has shown. Shaw has said that the
viewer should feel so involved in the problems being
presented on the stage that he leaves the theater with a
feeling that he must be actively engaged in finding a
solution to the problems for himself and for civilization.

   1280 Jones, Raymond. "Christian or Religious?"
      SHAVIAN, III (Spring-Summer 1967), 20-22.
SHAW ON RELIGION, by Warren Sylvester Smith (1967), is an
anthology which shows many similarities between Shaw's
thinking and the thinking of the modern theologians who
find the ancient forms and liturgies of the Christian
churches empty of meaning and who seek to break down the
barriers between Christianity and the other faiths of the

333

world. Yet there are many differences between Shaw's concept of the impersonal Life Force and the more personal concept of God held by even the most revolutionary modern Christian theologians.

1281 Kantorovich, I. B. "Bernard Shou i sovremennaîa zarubezhnaîa drama" (Bernard Shaw and Contemporary Foreign Drama), FILOLOGICHESKII NAUKI (Moscow), X (1967), 76-88.

As Engels forecast, the end of the 80's and the 90's in England saw the formation of Socialist teachings and organizations. It fell to Shaw to found an entire new generation of playwrights and establish new realistic social drama, which he thought of as drama of great ideas, intellectual drama. The central place was occupied by rationalism, Ibsenite humanistic ideals, and the displacement of bourgeois morals and bourgeois society as a whole. At first Shaw founded his work on the progressive traditions of English literature. The writers of critical realism uncovered the secrets of bourgeois family life. Ibsen took the next step, and Shaw developed Ibsen's ideological and aesthetic struggles. But Shaw clearly saw the inadequacy of the Ibsen tradition and conceived a mixed genre of narrative, statement, description, dialogue and drama. Prefaces, stage-directions, and afterwords increased, and Shaw turned to the traditions of Russian "classical" realism, as he wrote to L. N. Tolstoi on 14 February 1910. The October Socialist Revolution was a turning-point in Shaw's evolution; *Heartbreak House, a Fantasia in the Russian Manner on English Themes* marks the transition to his later work. But *Heartbreak* is not as much like Chekhov's THE CHERRY ORCHARD as some critics claim. The similarity is more didactic than aesthetic. Shaw transferred the lyricism of Chekhov's style and composition to Clifford Odets. Strindberg also drew some symbolic motifs from Shaw in THE GHOST SONATA (1907). *Man and Superman* is also a fantasia in the Russian manner and is close to the Chekhov tradition though in a new dramatic method of a rationalist fantasia, as are *Back to Methuselah* and *The Apple Cart*. But the concentrated thought in the later plays is not merely metaphysical or detached from reality. Pirandello cannot be imagined without Shaw's and Ibsen's contributions to new contemporary dramaturgy. Sean O'Casey continued Shaw's dramaturgy, with his interest in private lives and use of satire, though O'Casey never shared Shaw's Fabian illusions. Likewise the expressionist theater of Georg Kaiser and Ernst Toller derives from Shaw. [In Russian.]

1282 Kantorovich, I. B.   "A Russian Study of Shaw's Dramatic Method," SHAVIAN, III (Spring-Summer 19697), 18-19.

THE DRAMATIC METHOD OF BERNARD SHAW by A. G. Obrraztzova (1965) considers Shaw's dramatic method in relation to four problems, discussed under the chapter headings "Dramatic Conflict," "Characters," "Paradox," and "The Nature of Genre." The author sees the dramatic conflict as consisting in a clash of ideas, this conflict overwhelming all other elements of the play. The characters exist mainly to carry out this conflict. This examination is very thorough and considers the problems from many sides, but it does fail to give complete analyses of any of the plays or to consider the dramatic methods of Shaw's contemporaries.

1283 Kaufmann, R. J.   "Shaw's Elitist Vision: A Serial Criticism of the Plays of the First Decade," KOMOS, I (1967), 97-104.

The plays which Shaw wrote in the 1890's are in some respects better than his later plays because in these first ten plays he was still searching for answers to questions about society and the individual rather than simply using the plays to dramatize increasingly firm convictions. *Widowers' Houses* shows the conflict between tact, the individual's sensing and producing the socially expected responses, and the desire of the individual person to be himself. In both *The Philanderer* and *Mrs. Warren's Profession* all the major characters are posing, some accepting the roles which society decrees for them and others posing as rebels. In *Arms and the Man* Bluntschli is the "dehypocritizer" who exposes the romantic roles which people play, but in *Candida* all the men are poseurs until Candida shatters their romantic illusions about themselves. The plays following *Candida* explore the "feminine component in genius," whether it is found in men or in women. *The Man of Destiny* finds Napoleon's genius to reside in his emotional balance, which prevents his reacting in the socially expected manner to temptations to jealousy and pride. In *You Never Can Tell* the younger generation reject entirely the social expectations of their elders, and in *The Devil's Disciple* Shaw discovered the "true enemy," the sterile and hypocritical puritanism which Mrs. Dudgeon represents. The Egyptian society in *Caesar and Cleopatra* is as sterile and bankrupt as the puritan one represented by Mrs. Dudgeon, and Caesar stands out in contrast to it because his actions spring from his broad and spontaneous perceptions of the world around him. Lady Cicely, of *Captain*

Brassbound's Conversion, has qualities of both Caesar and Candida.

1284 Keough, Lawrence, C. "The Theme of Violence in Shaw," SHAVIAN, III (Winter 1966-67), 12-17.
The violence which erupted in *Heartbreak House* and *Saint Joan* was actually latent in all of Shaw's plays. From the very beginning his plays tended to portray situations in which a strong and effective person controls and suppresses the violence and disorder around him, as is the case with Bluntschli in *Arms and the Man*. The violence was unleashed in the later plays when Shaw's growing pessimism made him less certain that strong leaders could indeed control the violence and disorder of the world. Ellie and Joan are alike in several respects, especially in their attempts to oppose "the Establishment," but neither succeeds, and both are in one sense or another defeated by violence.

1285 Kernan, Alvin B. "George Bernard Shaw," MAJOR BRITISH WRITERS, SHORTER EDITION, ed by G. B. Harrison (NY: Harcourt, Brace & World, 1967), pp. 883-88.
Shaw believed in the power of human reason in the service of the Life Force to cut through human idiocy. In *Saint Joan* Shaw sets a clever trap; he exposes Joan's new ideas as our old ideas, that have created World War I. Her supernatural guides are only the projections of the clear mind and creative imagination of a genius.

1286 Kerr, Walter. "London: One Shaw after Another," NYT, 27 Aug 1967, II, pp. 1, 5, 9.
The clarity of Shaw's *Heartbreak House*, now at the Chichester Festival Theater, at first seems disturbing. One has a tendency to look for obscure meanings and miss the one clear, straightforward theme which overrides all the other meanings of the play--that England must learn to navigate or it will drift into doom. As is usual Shaw loves all the characters of *Heartbreak* in spite of their foolishness, but he does not hesitate to expose their foolishness mercilessly. This is Shaw's best play and "one of the great plays of the century."

1287 Knappert, Jan. "Review of Shaw, *On Language*," LINGUISTICS (The Hague), Aug 1967, pp. 125-26.

Though Shaw's comments on language are often original and perceptive, his "naivete" is shown by his irrational bias against Esperanto and his belief that English could be reformed by making the spelling consistent and doing away with illogical or unnecessary grammatical features. Equally unrealistic is his advocacy of the substitution of a new 42-letter alphabet for the Roman alphabet. Such a substitution could make possible a clearer relationship between letter and sound, but it would deprive English of the advantages of having an alphabet which is almost universally used.

1288 Knepper, Bill Garton. *"Back to Methuselah* and the Utopian Tradition," DA, XXVIII (1967), 681A. Unpublished dissertation, University of Nebraska, 1967.

1289 Kumar, V. GEORGE BERNARD SHAW: A CRITICAL STUDY (Meerut: Sarita Prakashan, 1967).
[This pamphlet devotes less than one-third of its 76 pages to general discussion of Shaw--a brief biography; very brief considerations of *Arms and the Man, Candida,* and *The Apple Cart;* brief comments about *Androcles and the Lion, Back to Methuselah, Caesar and Cleopatra, The Doctor's Dilemma, Getting Married, Heartbreak House, Major Barbara, The Philanderer, Pygmalion, Widowers' Houses,* and *You Never Can Tell;* and brief discussions of Shaw's social, philosophic, and aesthetic beliefs--and then gives the rest of its attention to a rather lengthy consideration of *Saint Joan.*]

Because Shaw is more concerned about expressing his philosophy than about art in his plays, because he does not discipline his wit, and because he lacks understanding of deep emotions, his plays are in some respects inartistic. Shaw's dialogue, like that of other naturalistic playwrights, does not convey emotion well, but in Shaw's case this quality may not be an important defect since his purpose in the plays is intellectual and comedic, not emotional. Shaw's dramatic technique consists in making concrete the political, dramatic technique consists in making concrete the political, economic, and social environment of the individuals in his plays and showing the conflict between one individual and that environment.

Though *Saint Joan* is not factually accurate, it does convey the true flavor of medieval times, and it avoids most of the romanticizing and melodrama in which other versions of the story have tended to indulge. As he portrays Joan, her chief qualities are an instinctive common sense or practical judgment which is an indication that she is one of the Life Force's attempts at a Superman, though still in the unselfconscious stage; a firm confidence in this judgment, which her strong imagination makes her conceive as coming in the form of voices sent by God; a selfless devotion to a cause; and sexlessness. The Epilogue is important to the play because it shows that the burning of Joan was not the end of her story.

1290 Lambert, J. W. "Plays in Performance," DRAMA, nx LXXXIV (Spring 1967), 16-24.
Aleksei Arbuzov's THE PROMISE echoes *Candida*.

1291 Laurence, Dan H. "George Bernard Shaw," FOUR OAKS LIBRARY, ed by Gabriel Austin (Somerville, NJ: privately printed, 1967), pp. 93-97.
In 1903 Shaw, desiring to find a new publisher since his old one had not been very successful in selling his books, reached an agreement to have his forthcoming play, *Man and Superman*, printed himself and published on commission through Constable and Co., which was at that time under the management of two relative newcomers to the publishing business--Otto Kyllmann and W. M. Meredith--whom Shaw could influence to follow the publishing practices he suggested. The bulk of the 47-year-long correspondence which was thus initiated between Shaw and Constable's is in the Hyde collection at the Four Oaks Library, along with many other documents relating to Shaw and his plays.

1292 Laurence, Dan H. "Letters to the Editors," ISh, V (Spring 1967), 43.
Shaw's diary entry for 12 March 1888 supports the belief that the "Curious Extract from the TIMES" is by Shaw.

1293 Leonard, Hugh. "Shaw in Limbo," P&P, XIV (April 1967), 46-47.
The program of Shaw one-acters at the Mermaid, *Augustus Does His Bit, Press Cuttings,* and *Passion Poison, and Petrifaction* "might be compared with a meal designed for an invalid who is forbidden to eat solids." They are worth a visit. [Photographs.]

1294 Leonard, Hugh. "Stars Galore," P&P, XIV (June 1967), 20-21.
Getting Married at the Strand is Shaw at not far from his worst. It displays a puritanical distaste for sex. [Photographs.]

1295 Levine, Carl. "Social Criticism in Shaw and Nietzsche," ShawR, X (Jan 1967), 9-17.
Though Shaw, in the Preface to *Major Barbara*, vigorously denied that his concept of the Superman and related social and religious concepts had been derived from Nietzsche, Shaw's beliefs were certainly similar to those of Nietzsche in a number of important respects. Shaw, like Nietzsche, had a contempt for the hypocrisy of the average man, as is evident in *The Man of Destiny, Pygmalion,* and *Candida*; a belief, set forth in *Barbara*, that before man can improve himself and his society, he must discard the outmoded beliefs and practices of the past and present; a belief, expressed in *The Perfect Wagnerite*, in the Superman; a belief, demonstrated in *Getting Married* and *Man and Superman*, that the institution of marriage should be discarded; a belief in the necessity of breeding human beings in accordance with sound eugenic principles; and a belief that man's goal should be, not power over others, but power over self. There are, however, important differences between Shaw's and Nietzsche's beliefs. Nietzsche attacked fundamental Christian dogma, whereas Shaw, as he made clear in *Barbara* and *Androcles and the Lion*, attacked only the Christian religion as it has been practiced, asserting that the basic teachings of Christ are sound and should be followed. Though Shaw criticized the weaknesses of the average man, he did not, as Nietzsche did, reject democracy and Socialism; as is evident from *The Revolutionist's Handbook* appended to *Superman*, Shaw merely insisted that democracy and Socialism should be used as means to raise the average man to a superior level rather than as a means to bring the superior man down to the level of the average man. Shaw envisioned in *Superman* and *Back to Methuselah* the possibility that all of mankind will eventually evolve into a race of Supermen.

1296 Lewis, Theophilus. "Theatre," AMERICA, CXVI (24 June 1967), 879-80.
The Syracuse Repertory Theatre's production of *The Devil's Disciple* is an "impudent melodrama" peopled by "robust characters" easy to understand and represent.

1297 Lewis, Theophilus. "Theatre," AMERICA, CXVII
(15 July 1967), 63-64.
The Sheridan Square has a very effective production of
Arms and the Man, a play which has as much pertinence
today in its criticism of war as it had when it was
written. The play offers social criticism on a wide range
of subjects, especially on social pretensions.

1298 Ley-Piscator, Maria [von Czada]. THE PISCATOR
EXPERIMENT: THE POLITICAL THEATRE (NY: James H.
Heineman, 1967), pp. 34, 37, 111, 162, 177, 225,
231, 270, 271, 295, 296.
Shaw was an Epic playwright by virtue of the fact that he
was a thinker. *Saint Joan, Arms and the Man, Back to
Methuselah,* and *Androcles and the Lion* are on Epic
subjects, and in producing the latter play Piscator gave
it Epic treatment.

1299 Lid, R[ichard] W., and Daniel Bernd (eds).
PLAYS: CLASSIC & CONTEMPORARY (Phila & NY: J. B.
Lippincott [Lippincott College English Series],
1967), pp. 352-53.
In *The Doctor's Dilemma* Shaw explores the ethical problems
which are inevitably bound up with the responsibilities
assumed by members of the medical profession, and by
extension all professions. The play offers no solutions,
but makes the audience aware of the problems as real
problems with which they themselves must deal.

1300 "The Life Force and the Crosstians," TLS, 23
March 1967, p. 247.
[Review of SHAW ON RELIGION, ed by Warren Sylvester Smith
(1967).] Though Shaw criticized Christianity, he did not
reject it entirely. His criticisms of it, though worded
in an original way, were not original but were the
criticisms being made by the Theological Modernists,
including his friend R. J. Campbell. Shaw's theories
about the Life Force were not a substitute for
Christianity but his way of explaining Christianity.

1301 Loney, Glenn. "Theatre Abroad: Oh to Be in
England--A London Theatre Album," ETJ, XIX (March
1967), 87-95.
This season's revivals of Shaw's *The Doctor's Dilemma, You
Never Can Tell,* and *Man and Superman* have been very
successful commercially even though the productions of

Dilemma and *Superman* were not as good as some previous ones have been.

1302 McBride, Joseph. "Shaw Impersonated," SHAVIAN, III (Spring-Summer 1967), 9-12.
Bramwell Fletcher, playing Shaw in THE BERNARD SHAW STORY on the college circuit in the United States, explains that he has not tried to give a slavish imitation of all Shaw's physical qualities but rather to concentrate on what Shaw said. Except for the necessary *and*'s, *but*'s, and other transitional words, all the words are from Shaw.

1303 McDonald, David J., Jr. "A TV Study Guide: George Bernard Shaw's *Saint Joan*," CLEARING HOUSE, XLII (Nov 1967), 188-90.
[After a brief introduction, the main body of this article is a study guide in outline form.] Though Shaw considered himself a realist and considered *Saint Joan* "classical" in structure, actually the play is "a romantic melodrama and comedy."

1304 McKee, Irving. "To the Editor: Mrs. Warren and Miss Vavasour," SHAVIAN, III (Winter 1966-67), 33.
Conyers Read's LORD BURGHLEY AND QUEEN ELIZABETH has an account of the Earl of Oxford's love affair with Ann Vavasour, whom Oxford's father-in-law called "a drab, that is to say, a whore." This account sheds new light on Shaw's reason for having the Reverend Samuel Gardner call Mrs. Warren Miss Vavasour at the end of Act I of *Mrs. Warren's Profession*.

1305 Maiskiĭ, Ivan Mikhailovich. "Bernard Shou" (Bernard Shaw), B. SHOU I DRUGIE: VOSPOMINANIIA (B. Shaw and Others: Memoirs) (Moscow: Iskusstvo, 1966), 13-53.
In 1935, Shaw told Maisky the point of departure for *The Doctor's Dilemma* was the marriage of Engels and Eveling [Eleanor Marx and Edward Aveling?], and to show that the medical profession should be "municipalized." Shaw's plays after World War I have less artistic value than those before it, but were more effective as weapons of open political struggle and as political pamphlets. Shaw was an individual rebel with no followers, in the English style, despite his Irish origins. [In Russian.]

1306 Maisky, Ivan. "Meetings with George Bernard Shaw," SPUTNIK (Nov 1967), pp. 163-75.
[A translation by the author of an article which first appeared in Russian in NOVY MIR]. During my eleven-year acquaintanceship with Shaw while I was Soviet ambassador to England (1932-43), Shaw and his wife extended many courtesies to my wife and me. The outstanding quality of Shaw's personality was "his enormous, bubbling vitality" (this despite the fact that at the beginning of this acquaintanceship Shaw was already 76 years old). He was always a great defender of Soviet Russia. Paradoxically, he once insisted that Russian communism was a great example of Fabianism. Though he proposed some criticisms of and amendments to the Soviet constitution, he nevertheless found it acceptable as it was.

1307 Manson, Donald Duane. "Bernard Shaw's Use of Wit in Selected Speeches," DA, XXVII (1967), 3973A. Unpublished dissertation, Pennsylvania State University, 1966.

1308 Marek, Jiří. "George Bernard Shaw," CIZÍ JAZYKY VE ŠKOLE, X (1967), 8-13.
[Summaries of Shaw's major plays with brief, Socialistically tendentious interpretation. Short biography.] [In Czechoslovak.]

1309 Martin, Wallace. *THE NEW AGE* UNDER ORAGE: CHAPTERS IN ENGLISH CULTURAL HISTORY (Manchester: Manchester UP; NY: Barnes & Noble, 1967), pp. 1, 4, 20, 21, 22, 24, 26, 35, 40, 42, 55, 62, 65, 66, 68, 70-78, 83, 108-9, 122, 125, 128-29, 161, 194, 197.
Shaw and one other person each contributed 500 pounds in 1907 to establish the NEW AGE, Shaw's contribution coming from his profits from *The Doctor's Dilemma*. In its early years Shaw contributed articles frequently to the NEW AGE, offering them without receiving payment. One of his contributions was the now-famous article on the "Chesterbelloc" which was part of a continuing debate between Shaw, Wells, Chesterton, and Belloc on "the cultural and spiritual meaning of Socialism." In analyzing the plays of Ibsen, Shaw and William Archer concentrated on the search for a "message" in them, as Shaw demonstrated in *The Quintessence of Ibsenism*, and according to Ashley Dukes both Shaw and Archer were unable to see Chekhov's THE CHERRY ORCHARD as a "work of art." In addition to his contribution to the founding of the NEW

A G E, Shaw was also active in the movement to organize the Fabian Arts Group, with "the object of interpreting the relationship of art and philosophy to Socialism," and his criticism of the actor-manager system in the theater helped to create the demand for a type of theater organization which was more suitable for the presentation of the drama of ideas, a demand which resulted in the founding of the Court Theatre under the management of J. E. Vedrenne and Harley Granville-Barker.

1310 Masumoto, Masahiko. "Bernard Shaw in Japan (II)--List of Plays Performed," RESEARCH BULLETIN (Nagoya, Japan), XI (1967), 152-78.

1311 Masumoto, Masahiko. "THE BILLIONAIRESS and Max Adrian in Japan," ISh, VI (Fall 1967), 6-7.
THE BILLIONAIRESS, Tsuneari Fukuda's very free adaptation of *The Millionairess*, is a satire in "Shavian style" on the contemporary culture of Japan which was presented in Tokyo during March. Max Adrian plays the part of Shaw in MAX ADRIAN AND GEORGE BERNARD SHAW, written by Michael Voysey and presented in Tokyo and Osaka in June of this year after last year's successful run at the Edinburgh Festival under the title A NIGHT WITH G.B.S. The success of these two productions in Japan augurs well for the forthcoming production there of *Caesar and Cleopatra*.

1312 Masumoto, Masahiko. "Nihon niokeru Bernard Shaw (2) -Joen Mokuroku-" (Shaw in Japan (2) -List of Plays Performed), KIYO (Dept. of General Education, Nagoya University, Nagoya), (Gaikokugo, Gaiko-kubungaku) No. 11 (March 1967), pp. 152-78.
[A list of all Shaw productions in Japan from 1910 through 1965, with a brief survey of Shaw on the Japanese stage in the 1910's through 1920's.] [In Japanese.]

1313 Mayne, Fred. THE WIT AND SATIRE OF BERNARD SHAW (Lond: Edward Arnold; NY: St. Martin's Press, 1967); part rptd TCIMB.
Shaw used wit as a means to further his didactic purposes. His wit combines the qualities of "inevitableness and surprise." The speech of those characters who are setting forth Shaw's point of view is always more full of these qualities than is the speech of those giving the opposing views. The element of surprise is produced by anticlimax, by a looseness of structure which contributes to the

effectiveness of both anticlimax and paradoxical witticisms, by a condensation produced by omission, and by the use of the concrete. In the construction of whole plays Shaw uses the inversion of paradox to carry out his themes. Many of his plays have a structure similar to that of the Socratic dialogue. *Major Barbara, John Bull's Other Island, Arms and the Man, Man and Superman, The Devil's Disciple, Candida, The Apple Cart, How He Lied to Her Husband, Widowers' Houses,* and *Mrs. Warren's Profession* all have this structure. Shaw's characters fall into two categories: those being satirized for having become types (the romantic idealists) and those who have for the most part retained individuality and humanity (the realists), and Shaw's wit arises out of the conflict between the two. Since subtle irony is apt to be missed in oral presentation, Shaw underscores it heavily.

For the most part in Shaw wit is used in the service of truth; even where a witticism tells only a half truth, it eventually leads to the discovery of the truth. Nevertheless, as a "polemical writer" Shaw "says what he thinks"; as a playwright Shaw "says what he feels." The effects of the changes in Shaw's life and opinions can be traced from the early Socialistic plays, *Widowers' Houses* and *Mrs. Warren;* through the period in which the comedy springs from the contrast between the realistic man of action and the romantic idealist, culminating in his making heroes of "an extroverted idiot like Broadbent" and "an 'unashamed,' rapacious, and essentially amoral armaments manufacturer like Undershaft"; then through the period of despair in which *Heartbreak House* was written; then through the attempt at throwing off this despair by fashioning a religio-philosophical system in *Back to Methuselah;* then the return to reality, though a darker one, in *Saint Joan;* and then through the final period, in which the frivolous and farcical nature of the plays masks a despairing pessimism. It is in the plays produced between *Barbara* and *Heartbreak* and those produced after *Joan,* when Shaw no longer had any faith in his earlier beliefs or in the educability of man, that his wit becomes a device for evading reality rather than a means of discovering truth.

1314 Meier, Erika. REALISM AND REALITY: THE FUNCTION OF THE STAGE DIRECTIONS IN THE NEW DRAMA FROM THOMAS WILLIAM ROBERTSON TO GEORGE BERNARD SHAW, published dissertation, University of Basel (Bern: Francke Verlag [The Cooper Monographs on English and American Language and Literature],

1967), pp. 5, 6, 19, 30, 38, 55, 58, 65, 68, 71-72,
77, 86, 105, 107-8, 112, 115, 124, 148, 167, 169-70,
184, 186, 193, 195, 196-293.
A study of the stage directions and the relationship
between the stage directions and the dialogue in selected
plays of six nineteenth-century playwrights reveals that
one of them, Shaw, in his first ten plays, the last of
which was written in 1900, succeeded in achieving a
successful amalgamation of theatricality and realism. In
spite of his criticism of the farcical and melodramatic
theatricality of the Victorian drama and the unrealistic
structure of its well-made plays, Shaw himself often used
techniques and scenes clearly derived from farce and melodrama and a tight plot structure derived from the well-
made play; however, the originality of thought in his
plays transformed these techniques and qualities and made
their use original. This originality of thought is
apparent in his revolutionary depictions of women and of
heroes. A study of these plays reveals that the lengthy
stage directions are not used to fill a need created by a
lack of skill in creating dialogue which will convey the
needed information dramatically.

1315 Mensching, Gerhard. "Die Kirche auf dem
Theater: Shaw--Schnitzler--Brecht--Hochhuth" (The
Church on Stage: Shaw--Schnitzler--Brecht--
Hochhuth), RELIGION UND RELIGIONEN. FESTSCHRIFT FÜR
GUSTAV MENSCHING ZU SEINEM 65. GEBURTSTAG (Religion
and Religions. Festschrift for Gustav Mensching on
His 65th Birthday) (Bonn: Roehrscheid, 1967), pp.
332-45.
A closer examination of Shaw's *Saint Joan*, Brecht's
GALILEO, Schnitzler's PROFESSOR BERNHARDI and Hochhuth's
THE DEPUTY shows that in all four plays the individual
characters representing the church reveal the incongruity
between ideology and morality. Saint Joan, Galileo,
Professor Bernhardi and Riccardo Fontana fail because they
as individuals do not recognize the true interests of the
church as an institution of power. [In German.]

1316 Meyer, Michael. IBSEN: A BIOGRAPHY (Garden
City, NY: Doubleday, 1967).
[This book has numerous brief references to Shaw, mostly
to his opinions of Ibsen's plays, as expressed in reviews
of their performances and in *The Quintessence of Ibsenism*,
and to the influence of his criticism on Ibsen's reputation.]

1317 Miller, James E., Jr., and Bernice Slote (eds).
THE DIMENSIONS OF LITERATURE: A CRITICAL ANTHOLOGY
(NY, Toronto: Dodd, Mead, 1967), pp. 446-47, 625.
Arms and the Man was not at first successful in England,
but after a success in America it gradually achieved
general popularity. Shaw's Preface indicates that his
purpose is to attack romantic ideals, especially those
about war, and substitute for them realistic thinking.
Yeats said that the play represented "inorganic, logical
straightness" instead of the "crooked road of life" and
that it gave him a nightmare about an efficient,
energetic, and ruthlessly smiling sewing machine.

1318 Mills, Carl Henry. "*Man and Superman* and the
Don Juan Legend," COMPARATIVE LITERATURE XIX (Summer
1967), 216-25.
In *Man and Superman* Shaw did not ignore or reverse the Don
Juan legend created and preserved by literary tradition
but instead adopted the major outlines of that legend,
borrowing something from all the major works which had
previously dealt with it and continuing the development of
that legend in the direction in which it had already been
led by earlier authors. From Tirso de Molina's EL
BURLADOR DE SEVILLA he adopted the moral attitude which
condemned the wastefulness of romantic libertinism, from
Molière's DOM JUAN, OU LE FESTIN DE PIERRE Shaw adopted
the satiric technique, adapting it to his own purposes,
from Mozart's DON GIOVANNI he adopted the musical form,
creating the "operatic ideological play," and from
Goethe's FAUST (Faust being a Don Juan figure because he
devotes his life to and sells his soul for the satisfaction of his appetites and desires) he adopted a philosophy
of life which sets up as the goal of life not the satisfaction of personal desires but the service of humanity
through the service of the creative Life Force. Shaw's
treatment of the Don Juan legend in *Superman* had been
foreshadowed by his treatment of that legend in his 1887
short story "Don Giovanni Explains."

1319 Moore, Doris Langley. E. NESBIT: A BIOGRAPHY.
(Lond: Ernest Benn, 1st revd. ed. 1967), pp. 13, 15-
16, 18, 20-24, 103, 112, 113, 115, 118, 132-36, 151-
53, 189, 208, 230, 241, 247, 252, 287, 295, 296.
Though Shaw was at first unwilling to give any information
for use in this biography since he feared that it might
become "a mere whitewashing operation," once his curiosity
was piqued he agreed to help, gave a large amount of

information about Nesbit and about many of the other people associated with the Fabian Society in its early days, and subsequently read proof copies of the biography, making improvements in the language but never censoring. [Material on pp. 13-24 not in eds of 1933 or 1951.]

1320 Morgan, Margery M.   "Introduction," *You Never Can Tell*, by George Bernard Shaw (Syndey, Melbourne, Brisbane: Hicks Smith & Sons [Gateway Library], 1967), pp. 7-32; rptd in Margery M. Morgan, THE SHAVIAN PLAYGROUND, Chapter 5 (1972).
Shaw was "chiefly responsible" for the revitalization of the English drama in the late nineteenth century after its two-century downhill slide.   Stock characters from the Christmas Pantomimes influenced *Androcles and the Lion, Major Barbara,* and *Saint Joan,* and stock characters from the Commedia dell'Arte tradition influenced *You Never Can Tell.*   The Family situation in the play is in many respects autobiographical, with the father, the mother, and the sisters modeled in part on Shaw's parental family and with both Philip and Valentine reflecting different aspects of Shaw's own characters and situation.   But the play goes beyond the autobiographical, both in dramatizing some of the major concerns of the late Victorian period-- the reaction against the repressive Victorian family unit and the advancement of the feminist movement, for example--and in achieving the true comic view, in which detachment from personal griefs and desires enables one to transcend them and realize a proper balance between feeling and thinking.

1321 Morgan, Margery M.   "Shaw, Yeats, Nietzsche, and the Religion of Art," KOMOS, I (1967), 24-34.
There is a close relationship between "Shaw's *Major Barbara* and Yeats's THE RESURRECTION, partly through the independent influence on each one of Nietzsche's BIRTH OF TRAGEDY FROM THE SPIRIT OF MUSIC and partly through the direct influence of *Barbara* on THE RESURRECTION.   Both plays are reactions to the "death of God" theory of Nietzsche, both are "plays of conversion," and both end with a "resurrection of religion in the illuminated mind." Both were influenced by Gilbert Murray.   Both have some elements in common with Ibsen's EMPEROR AND GALILEAN.

1322 Morriss, A. H.   "Letters to the Editor: G.B.S.--Composer?" MUSICAL OPINION, XCI (Dec 1967), 138.

With regard to the music in *Saint Joan* which is discussed by Jack Werner in a letter which appeared in both the MUSICAL TIMES and the November issue of MUSIC OPINION, in the 1924 Constable edition the penultimate note is an F, but in the 1934 Odhams edition this note is a D-flat.

1323 Müllenbrock, Heinz J. "Shaws Behandlung der irischen Frage in *John Bull's Other Island*" (Shaw's Treatment of the Irish Question in John *Bull's Other Island*), LITERATUR UND ZEITGESCHICHTE IN ENGLAND ZWISCHEN DEM ENDE DES 19. JAHRHUNDERTS AND DEM AUSBRUCH DES ERSTEN WELTKRIEGS (Literature and Contemporary History in England Between the End of the Nineteenth Century and the Outbreak of the First World War) (Hamburg: De Gruyter, 1967), pp. 66-73; see also 10-12, 199-203.

1324 Muggeridge, Kitty, and Ruth Adam. BEATRICE WEBB: A LIFE, 1858-1943 (Lond: Secker & Warburg, 1967; NY: Knopf, 1968), pp. 107, 113, 116, 118, 119, 121-22, 130-31, 133-40, 142. 146-47, 150-55, 159-61, 163, 166, 169, 171-72, 174, 176-78, 196-201, 203-4, 208, 210, 216, 223-24, 226, 229-31, 233-35, 237, 240, 244, 247-48, 251, 254, 257.
Sidney Webb, Graham Wallas, and Shaw, the "three musketeers" of the early days of the Fabian Society, remained close even after Webb's marriage, sharing their time, energy, knowledge, and money in a true communist fashion. Shaw invented the "Sunday husband" concept as a method of improving marriages by allowing the wife the experience of intellectual and romantic refreshment with a man other than her husband, and he was the Sunday husband of Kate Salt for a time. Beatrice Webb and Shaw both wanted the same thing from Sidney Webb--the stability which his sound factual and analytical mind gave to their imaginations--and thus they were in a sense competitiors for Webb's time and attention. Shaw felt that he and Beatrice could have a much closer intellectual intimacy than she and Sidney Webb ever would and that this knowledge created an awkwardness between Shaw and Beatrice. She was the model for all the independent, aggressive, man-taming, yet charming women in his plays, such as Ann of *Man and Superman*, Lavinia of *Androcles and the Lion*, and Vivie of *Mrs. Warren's Profession*. As Shaw's plays became increasingly successful, Beatrice Webb felt that his growing wealth and the adulation he received were causing him to lose sight of his old Socialist beliefs and were making him so full of his own opinion

that he could not listen to others.   She was particularly distressed by the theme of *Major Barbara* that poverty was not an indication of the need for reform of the poor but an indication of the need for reform of society, by his anti-democratic ideas and his admiration of Mussolini, and by his portraying of a king as an admirable ruler in *The Apple Cart.*

1325 Muir, Kenneth.   "Shaw, George Bernard," ENCY-CLOPEDIA OF WORLD LITERATURE IN THE TWENTIETH CENTURY, ed by Wolfgang Bernard Fleischmann (NY: Frederick Ungar, 1967), III 260-66.
[This encyclopedia is an "enlarged and updated" edition of LEXIKON DER WELTLITERATUR IM 20. JAHRHUNDERT (Freiburg: Verlag Herder).]   [This article opens with a barebones biography of Shaw, followed by brief descriptions of and commentaries on 17 of the major plays and reprints of brief excerpts from commentaries by Max Beerbohm, Havelock Ellis, James Huneker, Ernest A. Boyd, St. John G. Ervine, Frank Harris, Hesketh Pearson, Laurence Housman, Eric Bentley, C.E.M. Joad, Joseph Wood Krutch, and J. B. Priestley.]   Despite his own claims and those of many critics to the contrary, Shaw's plays are not merely propaganda pieces,   nor   are   his   characters   solely abstractions mouthing his ideas.   His best plays have a conflict of ideas and are "the finest examples in English of the comedy of ideas."   He was a "superb prose stylist--eloquent, witty, and lucid."

1326 Murray, D. Stark.   "New Ethical Problems in Medicine," ETHICAL RECORD, LXXII (July-Aug 1967), 10-12.
[Summary of a lecture given on 16 April 1967.]   Britain has to some extent achieved a reform which Shaw called for in his "Preface" to *The Doctor's Dilemma*--the removal of the profit motive from the practice of medicine--but in some circumstances the profit motive still lingers.

1327 Nickson, Richard.   "Shaw on the Dictators: Labels and Libels," CEA CRITIC, XXIX (May 1967), 3, 8-9.
Shaw condemned the use of political labels because they are so often misleading and misconstrued, and with regard to himself he objected seriously to the labels "fascist" or "dictator-worshipper," which were often applied to him, particularly by journalists.   He admired those governments, whatever their labels, which he felt were

overthrowing capitalism in favor of some form of Socialism, governments not necessarily "by everybody," but "for the benefit of everybody." In spite of his praise of both Soviet and fascist leaders, he was opposed to totalitarianism.

1328 Nikitina, A. I., and A. S. Romm, "Bernard Shou--korespondent P. A. Kropotkina" (Bernard Shaw--Correspondent of P. A. Kropotkin), RUSSKAĬA LITERATURA (Leningrad), II (1967), 137-40.
Russia attracted Shaw's attention long before 1917. For many years Shaw and P. A. Kropotkin were friends with deep mutual respect. Kropotkin had been exiled from Russia in the 1870's for Socialist activities and became influential in Socialist circles in Western Europe. His archives, now in the Central State Archives, Moscow, contain three letters from Shaw. In the first two (1902, 1905), Shaw offers Kropotkin financial assistance. In the third (1908), Shaw criticizes the West European press for its sensational treatment of the repressions proceeding in Russia against the Socialist and revolutionary movement. [In Russian.]

1329 NOTES ON GEORGE BERNARD SHAW'S *SAINT JOAN* (Lond: Methuen [Study-Aid Series], 1967).
[This 64-page study guide contains brief summaries of the history of drama; of Shaw's life and career; of the histories of France, the Church, and feudalism during Joan of Arc's lifetime; of Shaw's Preface to *Saint Joan*; and of the play itself. In addition it provides a glossary of terms used and persons referred to in the Preface; sample discussion and objective questions, some with suggested answers; character sketches of the principal persons in the play; very brief discussions of the good and poor qualities of the play; and a brief bibliographical note.]

1330 Nowell-Smith, Simon (ed.) LETTERS TO MACMILLAN (Lond, Melbourne, Toronto: Macmillan; NY: St. Martin's P, 1967), pp. 15, 190, 194, 366.
Macmillan rejected all five of Shaw's novels, indicating, however, that they showed promise. In a letter to Harold Macmillan, Sean O'Casey comments that Shaw recognized at once the wording and judgment from the Bible in O'Casey's THE STAR TURNS RED.

1331 Nyssen, Leo. "Kritische Chronik: Bochum" (Critical Chronicle: Bochum), VIII (Nov 1967), 47. The setting of Schalla's production (or *Caesar and Cleopatra*) is imaginary and not historical. The actor Hans Häckermann interprets Caesar's resignation very well. Heinrich Böll's translation of *Caesar and Cleopatra* is an excellent transposition of Shaw's imagery. [In German.]

1332 O'Casey, Sean. "The Bald Primaqueera," BLASTS AND BENEDICTIONS: ARTICLES AND STORIES, by Sean O'Casey, ed by Ronald Ayling (Lond, Melbourne, Toronto: Macmillan; NY: St. Martin's, 1967), p. 66.
The playwrights of the Theatre of the Absurd and the Theatre of Cruelty have an ugly vision of the world; their vision is opposite to that of Peter Keegan, of *John Bull's Other Island*, but is equally "the vision of a madman."

1333 O'Casey, Sean. BLASTS AND BENEDICTIONS: ARTICLES AND STORIES, ed Ronald Ayling (Lond, Melbourne, Toronto: Macmillan; NY: St. Martin's, 1967), pp. ix, xviii, 24-25, 27, 28, 48-49, 66, 90, 106, 143, 179, 195-204, 221, 256, 258.
In this collection of articles and stories by Sean O'Casey the following selections mention Shaw, some merely in passim references but two, readily identifiable by their titles, in lengthy discussions: Ronald Ayling, "Preface," pp. ix-xix; "The Play of Ideas," NS&Nation (1950); "Melpomene an' Thalia Beggin' for Bread," NYTMag (9 Nov 1958); "Dramatis Personae Ibsenisensis," AMERICAN SPECTATOR (NY) (July 1933); "The Bald Primaqueera," not previously published; "THE PLOUGH AND THE STARS: A Reply to the Critics," IRISH TIMES (19 Feb 1926), IRISH INDEPENDENT (20 Feb 1926); "THE SILVER TASSIE" [originally entitled "The Plays of Sean O'Casey: A Reply"], NINETEENTH CENTURY (Sept 1928); "COCKADOODLE DOO" [part of which appeared under the title "O'Casey's Credo" in NYT (9 Nov 1958)]; "Literature in Ireland," INTERNATIONAL LITERATURE (Dec 1939); "G.B.S. Speaks out of the Whirlwind" [Book review of *Three Plays: Too True to Be Good, A Village Wooing,* and *On the Rocks*, by Shaw (Constable, 1934)], List (7 Mar 1934); "Shaw's Primrose Path" [originally entitled "With Love and Kisses from Mr. Shaw," this article reviews BERNARD SHAW AND MRS. PATRICK CAMPBELL: THEIR CORRESPONDENCE, ed Alan Dent (NY: Alfred A. Knopf, 1952)], NYT (9 Nov 1952); "A Prophet in the Theatre" [Review of ROBERT LORAINE, by Winifred Loraine (Collins, 1938)], SUNDAY TIMES (18 Sept 1938);

"There Go the Irish," from THEY GO, THE IRISH: A MISCELLANY OF WAR-TIME WRITING (1944).

1334 Okumura, Saburo. "Gendai Yutopia toshiteno *Metosera ni Kaere*" (*Back to Methuselah*: A Modern Utopia), ALBION (Kyoto University, Kyoto), ns No. 13 (Oct 1967) 66-79.
In *Back to Methuselah* Shaw took up the biblical subjects, (the fall of Adam and Eve and salvation of mankind, and propounded it in the context of evolution, not of eschatology. The fall in the play began when Adam and Eve invented natural birth. Salvation, on the other hand, is to be realized in the shape of the evolution of man into superman: the Ancient. It is important to know that longevity will not be given to everybody who wills it hard enough, but it is possible only by the tremendous miracle-working force of will. The vital portions of this play are Parts III, IV and V, where Long-livers and Ancients make their appearances. They show satirically man's shortcomings. *Methuselah* is a sort of negative utopia: reversal of an easy idealization of the superman and his society. [In Japanese.]

1335 Olivier, Laurence, with Kenneth Tynan. "Laurence Olivier," GREAT ACTING, ed by Hal Burton (NY: Bonanza Books, Crown, 1967), pp. 11-40.
[Based on one of a series of interviews of great actors conducted on BBC-2 TV in 1965 and 1966.] To my comment that Sergius, the role I was playing in *Arms and the Man*, was a "stupid, idiot part," Tyrone Guthrie replied that I would never play it well unless I loved the character. "*Arms* was a success on its own" at the Old Vic.

1336 Osborn, Margaret Elizabeth. "The Concept of Imagination in Edwardian Drama," DA, XXVIII (1967), 1443A. Unpublished dissertation, University of Pennsylvania, 1967.

1337 Parkinson, C. Northcote. LEFT LUGGAGE: A CAUSTIC HISTORY OF BRITISH SOCIALISM FROM MARX TO WILSON (Bost: Houghton Mifflin, 1967), 3, 56-59, 64-69, 99-101, 105, 136, 149-51, 166, 184.
Shaw and the Webbs were the creators of the British Labour Party. The great influence of Shaw was responsible for

destroying the effectiveness in Britain of Marxism, "liberalism as an intellectual force" and "middle-class humanitarianism as applied to the poor," and substituting for all of these a Socialism which was "little more than the application of democratic principles to an industrial society." Shaw's Socialistic views were set forth not only in such tracts as *Fabian Essays in Socialism* and *The Intelligent Woman's Guide to Socialism and Capitalism*, but also in most of his plays, especially in *Major Barbara*. As Chesterton pointed out, Shaw made a considerable sacrifice of his potential in art in order to serve the cause of Socialism. None of the left-wing or reformist dramatists who have followed Shaw in the theater have either his knowledge or his genius.

1338 Pietzsch, Ingeborg. "Berlin, Volksbühne: *Caesar und Cleopatra* von G. B. Shaw" (Berlin, Volksbühne: *Caesar and Cleopatra* by G. B. Shaw), THEATER DER ZEIT, XXII (1967), 28-29.
The emphasis in the Volksbühne production of *Caesar and Cleopatra* is on the political power play. [In German.]

1339 Popkin, Henry. "Introduction," ARMS AND THE MAN, ed by Henry Popkin (NY: Avon Books, 1967), pp. 9-18.
The outstanding quality of Shaw's style is "bald assertiveness applied to defeating expectation," a technique used both in his dramatic criticism and in his own plays. Often the "bald assertions" are very sound, but at other times, as in the ideas about Bulgarians and their way of life expressed in *Arms and the Man*, they lack any factual or logical basis. The reversal of expectations usually involves the upsetting of some conventional idea in favor of a more realistic idea about which Shaw felt very strongly. In *Arms* the reversal of the stereotypes of the professional soldier and of the ideal lover reflects Shaw's pacifism and his anti-romantic views of life. Similar reversals occur in other plays. Though his plays are primarily vehicles for the expression of his ideas and though his surprising supermen are unheroic and usually have no interest in romantic passion, plays do not lack passion because Shaw's passionate involvement with ideas made his plays passionate and "even poetic."

1340 Rahill, Frank. THE WORLD OF MELODRAMA (University Park, Lond: Pennsylvania State UP, 1967), pp. 78, 185.
Bluntschli's entrance through a balcony window in *Arms and the Man* was probably suggested to Shaw by a similar entrance in DON CÉSAR DE BAZAN by Adolphe Dennery and Dumanoir. Perhaps Chaplain Brudenell of *The Devil's Disciple* was suggested to Shaw by Blount, the fighting parson in Dion Boucicault's JESSIE BROWN; OR, THE RELIEF OF LUCKNOW. [Though Rahill names Brudenell, his description of Blount suggests that he may have had Anderson in mind instead.]

1341 Rama Rao, Sarvepalli. THE VALUES OF SHAVIAN DRAMA AND THEIR VALIDITY (Tirupati: Sri Venkateswara University [1967?]). [Dissertation, Nagpur University (1957?).]
Though in his plays Shaw often sacrificed both artistic values and realism to accomplish his teaching purpose, he did succeed in ridding the stage of the notion that its purpose is to provide an evening of "escape" for its audience and also in combatting the theory of totalitarian societies that the drama should be used as a tool of indoctrination. Shaw viewed the stage as a pulpit for his preaching, not in order to gain blind acceptance of his views but in order to break down his audience's credulity and its tendency to make emotional choices and to inculcate in his audiences instead the habits of questioning, of scepticism, and of using intelligence instead of emotions in making choices. In opposition to the melodrama of the nineteenth century Shaw populated his plays with characters who are ordinary, everyday people whose good and evil actions are reflections of their degree of intelligence and perceptiveness rather than indications of basically good or evil natures. These characters can be classified as Positive and Negative Characters--the Positive Characters being those who see reality clearly, accept it, and deal with it intelligently, and the Negative ones being those who are blind to reality, who accept unquestioningly the illusions which society disseminates about itself, and who make their decisions emotionally on the basis of such illusions. The characters are, of course, not extremes of either kind, but rather mixtures of Positive and Negative characteristics. In the plays the traditional dramatic conflict has given place to a debate between the Positive and the Negative Characters, sometimes with a conversion or at least a partial conversion of a Negative Character to a Positive Character.

The plays can be grouped into six categories in order to demonstrate the interaction of the Positive and Negative Characters in them: the economic plays, the political plays, the historical plays, the social plays, the plays dealing with personal relations, and the religious and philosophical plays.

1342 Redgrave, Michael. THE ACTOR'S WAYS AND MEANS (Lond, Melbourne, Toronto: Heinemann, 1953), pp. 20-21, 25, 87, 88.
Shaw's dramatic criticism was sometimes "savage," but it arose from a love of the theater. He inveighed against the star system and was one of the most influential of those who helped to make the author's play rather than the starring actor the most important element in the theater.

1343 Redgrave, Michael, with Richard Findlater. "Michael Redgrave," GREAT ACTING, ed by Hal Burton (NY: Bonanza Books, Crown, 1967), pp. 99-110.
[Based on one of a series of interviews of great actors conducted on BBC-2 television in 1965 and 1966.] Shaw was correct in his statement that one-half hour of singing every day would improve anyone's health.

1344 Richardson, Ralph, with Derek Hart. "Ralph Richardson," GREAT ACTING, ed by Hal Burton (NY: Bonanza Books, Crown, 1967), pp. 62-80.
[Based on one of a series of interviews of great actors conducted on BBC-2 television in 1965 and 1966.] Shaw often showed up at rehearsals of *Arms and the Man*. His advice on playing the role of Bluntschli was always given in a very polite and encouraging way. He pointed out that "acting" should never be allowed to interfere with the rapid flow of wit in the lines and characterized the play as "a musical play, a knockabout musical comedy."

1345 Rischbieter, Henning. "Eine Bühne für Protagonisten. Report über ein Theater: Thalia Theater Hamburg" (A Stage for Protagonists. Report on a Theater: Thalia Theater Hamburg), TH, VIII (May 1967), 18-23.
Willi Schmidt's production of *The Apple Cart* was not reduced to a few gags but was presented in an excellent progression of effects. Shaw's attack against democratic illusions is malicious. [In German.]

1346 Roberts, Peter. "Not So Chekovian," P&P, XIV (Sept 1967), 14-15, 27.
Heartbreak House, once considered shocking, is now a peg on which to hang star performers. The production at Chichester reveals Shaw as a clumsy craftsman. [Photographs.]

1347 Robson, William A. "Bernard Shaw and THE POLITICAL QUARTERLY," POLITICS AND GOVERNMENT AT HOME AND ABROAD, by William A. Robson (Lond: George Allen & Unwin, 1967), pp. 48-67.
When Shaw was first approached, through a personal interview, about a contribution to the founding of the POLITICAL QUARTERLY, he offered advice on the operation of the quarterly and said he would consider making a contribution. Since no one else connected with the project was able to supply or persuade others to supply even one-tenth of the amount furnished by Shaw, it was really Shaw's contribution which made the quarterly possible at all. In addition, he made three literary contributions to the quarterly--in 1931, 1933, and 1935. In 1933 a request for additional funds from Shaw--a request which was denied because Shaw felt he could not subsidize what he regarded as a failing venture-- stimulated an exchange of letters with Shaw on the merits of democracy and parliamentary government versus those of dictatorships. A review in the POLITICAL QUARTERLY of a volume of Shaw's collected Prefaces noted, among other things, that in spite of all his criticisms of democracy Shaw really favored it but was led away from it by his attempts to make the "democratic process foolproof." *Everybody's Political What's What* (1944) revealed that Shaw's respect for dictatorships had diminished considerably; in that work he viewed rule by dictators as unworkable and asserted that government should be by groups of qualified professionals who were replaced periodically and who were constantly subject to severe criticism by the people.

1348 Roll-Hansen, Diderik. "Shaw's *Pygmalion*: The Two Versions of 1916 and 1941," REVIEW OF ENGLISH LITERATURE, VIII (July 1967), 81-90.
The 1941 edition of *Pygmalion*, which purports to be a script of the film version, is actually closer to the earlier 1916 play version than to the film version but is not in a form which could satisfactorily be produced either on stage or on film. The 1916 version is full of "stage tricks" which do not transfer well to film, but the

revisions which Shaw incorporated into the 1941 published
version do not satisfactorily bridge the gap between the
requirements of the stage and those of the screen and are
in some cases obviously more intent upon conveying to the
reader a social message than upon adapting the play to the
needs of the screen. The result is that this 1941 version
is in some passages an incongruous blend of satiric comedy
and solemn social criticism, reminiscent of *Widowers'
Houses*. In the original theatrical version of *Pygmalion*
Shaw achieved a very satisfactory blend of "a romantic
comedy based on the Cinderella theme and a satiric comedy
of ideas." Records of the actual performance of Mrs.
Patrick Campbell, the first stage Eliza, indicate that
Higgins was indeed "trapped" into marriage by a triumphant
Eliza, so that the original stage version of the play
carried out the theme of the "biter bit." It was
apparently only because audiences failed to interpret this
as a satiric theme but instead saw the play as having a
sentimentally romantic ending that Shaw rejected this
interpretation of the ending and subsequently insisted
that Eliza would instead marry Freddy.

1349 Rollins, Ronald G. "Shaw and O'Casey: John
Bull and His Other Island," Shaw R, X (May 1967), 60-
69.
Though Shaw's *John Bull's Other Island* and O'Casey's
PURPLE DUST are alike in basic plot situation and in
theme, both demonstrating the "mental and spiritual
torpidity and economic stagnation that invariably follow
when people develop a paralyzing preoccupation with the
remote and illusory," they are different in technique,
particularly in character portrayal, Shaw's characters
being far more complex than those of O'Casey. In
addition, Shaw's play is more cerebral and O'Casey's more
farcical; O'Casey enriches his play with symbolism and
with mythical motifs, both of which are lacking in Shaw's.

1350 Royall, Walter L. "DeFonblanque and Shaw's
Burgoyne," Shaw R, X (May 1967), 42-49.
E. B. DeFonblanque's POLITICAL AND MILITARY EPISODES
DERIVED FROM THE LIFE AND CORRESPONDENCE OF THE RIGHT HON.
JOHN BURGOYNE, published in London in 1876, is undoubtedly
the source of Shaw's portrayal of Burgoyne in *The Devil's
Disciple*, as suggested by Shaw's two references to
DeFonblanque in the "Notes to *The Devil's Disciple*." Shaw
asserts that in the depiction of Burgoyne he attempted "as
faithful a portrait as it is in the nature of stage por-
traits to be," and this claim is validated by the number

of passages in DeFonblanque's biography which support Shaw's depiction of elements of Burgoyne's character and personality.

1351 Russell, Bertrand. THE AUTOBIOGRAPHY OF BERTRAND RUSSELL, Vol I (Lond: George Allen and Unwin; NY: Little, Brown, 1967), pp. 74, 106-7, 288-89; letter to G. L. Dickinson rptd SHAW, THE CRITICAL HERITAGE (1976).

The essence of Fabianism was the worship of the state, and it led Shaw to an undue tolerance of Mussolini and Hitler and an absurd adulation of the Soviet Government. [In a letter to Goldsworthy Lowes Dickinson:] "I think envy plays a part in [Shaw's] philosophy in this sense, that if he allowed himself to admit the goodness of things which he lacks and others possess . . . he would find life unendurable."

1352 Saffron, John. "Caesar and Bluntschli: Shaw's View of Heroism," SHAVIAN, III (Autumn 1967), 10-14.

Shaw's Caesar and his Captain Bluntschli are alike in several important respects, and both are used by Shaw to dramatize his conception of heroism. Both are "pragmatic" and "flexible" in their attitudes and actions in connection with war and romantic love. Neither is guided by traditions, conventions, or moral preconceptions. Each is presented in conjunction with a foil who does show conventionality, dogmatism, and inflexibility and whose views and actions are made to look ineffective and ridiculous.

1353 Saint-Paulien [pseud of Maurice I. Sicard]. "Le séducteur de Kierkegaard, et le Don Juan misogyne et socialisé de George Bernard Shaw" (The Seducer of Kierkegaard), and the Misogynist and Socialist Don Juan of George Bernard Shaw), DON JUAN: MYTHE ET RÉALITÉ (Don Juan: Myth and Reality) (Paris: Plon, 1967), pp. 241-52.

[Not seen.] [In French.]

1354 Schultheiss, Thomas. "Conrad on Stage Censorship," AMERICAN NOTES & QUERIES, V (April 1967), 117-18.

Conrad, Shaw, and 72 others signed a letter of protest against censorship of the drama which appeared in the TIMES in October 1907. Subsequently Shaw set forth his opposition to such censorship in the Preface to *The Shewing-up of Blanco Posnet.*

1355 Shayon, Robert Lewis. "Shaw at the Stake," SRL, L (30 Dec 1967), 37.
It is doubtful that Shaw would have approved the cutting of *Saint Joan* done by the Hallmark Hall of Fame production on NBC-TV to make the play fit into the two-hour time slot. In his Preface to the play Shaw inveighed against those who wanted to cut out the Epilogue and "all the references to such undramatic and tedious matters as the Church, the feudal system, the Inquisition, the theory of heresy, and so forth," the very materials which were removed from the play for this televised performance and those which gave the play life and significance.

1356 Shiels, Thomas A. "The Relationship between Holmes and Shaw," BAKER STREET JOURNAL, XVII (June 1967), 90-91.
Contrary to popular belief, Shaw and Holmes did not meet at the 1890 concert of violinist Pablo de Sarasate in London, but five years earlier when both Shaw and Holmes were involved, along with the Salvation Army, in the exposure of prostitution which led to reforms in the laws regarding the age of consent.

1357 Silverman, Albert H. "Bernard Shaw's Political Extravaganzas," DramS, V (Winter 1966-67), 213-22.
In the five late plays of Shaw often called "political extravaganzas"--*The Apple Cart, Too True to Be Good, On the Rocks, The Simpleton of the Unexpected Isles,* and *Geneva*--the comic extravaganza form is particularly well suited to the simultaneous expression of Shaw's disillusionment with and pessimism about contemporary man and society, on the one hand, and his "insistent optimism" about the future development of man and society, on the other. All these extravaganzas derive their form and comic attitude from *Heartbreak House,* which reflected the kind of comedy Shaw found in Ibsen's THE WILD DUCK. These extravaganzas represent a return to the purposes of Shaw's early *Plays Unpleasant,* to substitute the discussion of ideas for the exploitation of emotion on the stage and "to force the spectator to face unpleasant facts." The extravaganzas derive their humor and their sting from their exaggerated and fantastic treatment of reality and from their subsequent revelations that the realities of contemporary political life are as fantastic as the

supposed exaggerations, so that it is impossible to distinguish political reality from the fantasy of the plays. The repetition, transformation and variation of themes through the discussions in the plays give the plays a thematic structure similar to that of a musical composition.

1358 Smith, Warren Sylvester. "An Early GBS Love Poem," Shaw R, X (May 1967), 70-72.
A poem Shaw scribbled in a notebook which he used during his first years in Britain is lacking in interest as poetry but may make some valuable biographical suggestions, particularly about Shaw's early love life.

1359 Smith, Warren Sylvester. "Introduction," SHAW ON RELIGION, ed by Warren Sylvester Smith (NY: Dodd, Mead; Lond: Constable, 1967), pp. 7-16.
This collection of discussions of religion by Shaw is not designed primarily for Shaw scholars and devotees, but instead for anyone interested in the current popular religious debate concerning whether or not God is dead and what kind of church is needed in the life of modern man. Shaw's status as an outsider in religion, as in other matters of conventional belief and practice, enabled him to take a detached view of religion and is the source of much of the humor of his style. Though irreverent, Shaw was nevertheless very religious and was opposed to atheism, seeing God as a Divine Immanence or Divine Providence. The selections range in date from Shaw's fortieth year to within a year of his death.

1360 Smith, Warren Sylvester. THE LONDON HERETICS: 1870-1914 (Lond: Constable, 1967; NY: Dodd, Mead & Company, 1968), pp. 4, 10, 17, 18, 19, 20, 22, 24, 57, 59, 71, 73, 74, 75, 78, 82, 83, 114, 117, 127, 130, 131, 134, 135-36, 137, 145, 156, 161, 187, 188, 190, 191, 211, 215, 254, 255, 256-58, 260, 270-79, 283; pp. 279-79 rptd in BERNARD SHAW'S PLAYS, ed by Warren Sylvester Smith (1970).
In the period covered by this study, Shaw's life touched upon the lives of almost all the "London heretics." Some were models for characters in his plays: Edward Aveling for Louis Dubedat; Eleanor Marx for Jennifer Dubedat; Annie Besant for Mrs. Clandon; Stewart Headlam (in addition to Stopford Brooke, Canon Shuttleworth, and Fleming Williams) for James Morell. Some of the works of the "heretics" provide parallels with later works of Shaw.

Shaw's predictions in *Back to Methuselah* about the future
of man are anticipated by Winwood Reade in THE MARTYRDOM
OF MAN. Moncure Conway's CHRISTIANITY provides a parallel
to Shaw's Preface to *Androcles and the Lion*. An early
address by Shaw himself on "Acting by One Who Does Not
Believe in It, or the Place of the Stage in the Fool's
Paradise of Art" anticipated some of his observations on
the use of art in the Preface to *Man and Superman*.

The gatherings and meetings of the various reform groups
constituted a "night school" for Shaw in which he trained
himself as a public speaker and committee worker and
through which he developed his own beliefs about religion
and society. Shaw was the only one of the London heretics
who worked out a "substitute religion" of his own for the
religious views he was shattering. He adopted a
Lamarckian rather than a Darwinian interpretation of
evolution because he could not accept the idea of an
unplanned or mindless universe. Shaw remained a believer
in the religion he had constructed for himself, and
through periods of despair and "existential pain" this
religion "formed a steadying and consistent strain in one
of the most complex minds of the twentieth century."
Though this religion is set forth most thoroughly in the
Preface to *Methuselah*, it is evident in all his plays,
particularly *Superman* and the plays following it.

1361 Smoker, Barbara. *"Getting Married* in London,"
ISh, VI (Fall 1967), 6.
Though *Getting Married* is "minor Shaw," the brilliant
actors in the current production of it at the Strand
Theatre make the play seem great.

1362 Spurling, Hilary. "Inhospitable Shaws," Spec,
CCXVIII (3 March 1967), 255-56.
Brigid Brophy's THE BURGLAR is another example of the bad
influence on beginning dramatists exerted by Shaw's idea
that drama is nothing but discussion.

1363 Staud, Géza. "G. B. Shaw's Letters to Sándor
Hevesi," THEATRE RESEARCH, VIII (1967), 156-64.
Before Sándor Hevesi began his translations of Shaw's
plays in 1910, few of his plays had been performed in
Hungary, and those few had not been well received, at
least partly because of the poor quality of the
translations. Shaw did not like the first Hevesi
translation, of *Captain Brassbound's Conversion*, but liked

the subsequent ones and gave Hevesi exclusive translation rights for Hungary. From 1910 until his death in 1939 Hevesi translated almost all of Shaw's plays. In 1959 the Theatre Museum in Budapest found six Shaw letters and three letters of Blanche Patch among some of the Hevesi effects which it had purchased. The letters are printed here. [The first of the Shaw letters complains that Hevesi's translation of *Brassbound* was too literal and not creative enough, and also contains a long paragraph on vegetarianism. The others have to do primarily with the appointment of a Hungarian agent for Shaw's works after the death of Teleki, Shaw's first Hungarian agent; with various appointments between Shaw and Hevesi in London; and with the publication and translation of certain Shaw plays and of the Shaw-Ellen Terry correspondence.]

1364 Sullivan, Dan. "Theater: Shaw's *Arms and the Man*," NYT, 23 June 1967, p. 44.
Though the romantic view of war which *Arms and the Man* attacks may now have disappeared, the more general theme of the play, its attack on any romantic view of humanity which fails to take into account the weaknesses and limitations under which humanity labors, still has great pertinence. In the current production of the play at the Sheridan Square Playhouse, John Heffernan projects very well the realistic, unglamorous professional soldier in contrast to the "would-be hero," Sergius. The other performers are disappointing, particularly in their delivery of the lines, but the play is nevertheless effective.

1365 Sumner, W. L. "Letters to the Editor: G.B.S.--Composer?" MUSICAL OPINION, XCI (Dec 1967), 138.
The music from *Saint Joan* which Jack Werner inquires about is Shaw's parody of two tunes to the hymn "For All the Saints."

1366 Swartz, David L., Jr. "Bernard Shaw and Henry James," ShawR, X (May 1967), 50-59.
Oscar Cargill has demonstrated the influence of Shaw's *The Quintessence of Ibsenism* on James's THE AMBASSADORS, and Max Beerbohm has demonstrated the influence of James's RODERICK HUDSON on Shaw's *The Doctor's Dilemma*. Shaw attended the opening night performance of GUY DOMVILLE and in his review gave high praise to the language of the play and to its exaltation of intellect over passion, blaming

its failure not on the play itself but on the inadequacies
of the audience. When James's THE SALOON, with an anti-
military theme very much in accord with Shaw's anti-
military stance in *Arms and the Man*, was rejected by the
Incorporated Stage Society, there ensued a correspondence
between James and Shaw in which their contradictory views
on the purpose of art became evident, with James's view
that the purpose of art is to convey a realistic, personal
and "direct impression of life" coming into conflict with
Shaw's view that the purpose of art is utilitarian and
didactic.

1367 Taylor, Alison. THE STORY OF THE ENGLISH STAGE
(Oxford, Lond: Pergamon, 1967), pp. 61, 62, 63, 64,
66, 70, 77, 79, 82.
[This book is intended for a secondary school audience.]
Shaw helped change the direction of the modern theater by
writing plays about ideas and about real people.

1368 Taylor, John Russell. THE RISE AND FALL OF THE
WELL-MADE PLAY (NY: Hill and Wang, 1967), pp. 81-
88, et passim.
[As its title indicates, this book is a history of the
well-made play. There are numerous passing references to
Shaw, most of them critical of his denigration of the
well-made play, and more than half of the fifth chapter,
entitled "Shaw and Wilde: Attack and a Way of Escape,"
deals with Shaw's effect on the well-made play.]

1369 Tennyson, G[eorge] B[ernhard]. AN INTRODUCTION
TO DRAMA (NY; Holt, Rinehart and Winston, 1967),
pp. 24-25, 32-33.
Even though Shaw's interpretation of Ibsen's plays and his
own as discussion plays has some validity, both his and
Ibsen's plays have underlying patterns which are analogous
to traditional plot structures, as can be demonstrated by
analyzing HEDDA GABLER and *Candida*. Shaw used directions,
prefaces, and even--as in the case of *Caesar and Cleopatra*--prologues and notes for many purposes.

1370 Thompson, Paul. THE WORK OF WILLIAM MORRIS
(NY: Viking P, 1967), pp. 46, 48, 132, 145, 160,
186, 208-9, 213-14.
Even when Shaw had a strong influence on the life of
Morris's daughter May, Morris remained "incurious" about
him. The designs of Shaw's books from *Plays: Pleasant*

and Unpleasant onward were strongly influenced by Morris's ideas about book design. The work of Shaw and the other Fabians on behalf of Socialism did not in fact have the success which Shaw attributed to it in his writings, but actually hampered various Socialistic enterprises, in particular delaying the establishment of the Labour Party.

1371 Thorndike, Sybil, with Michael MacOwan. "Sybil Thorndike," GREAT ACTING, ed by Hal Burton (NY: Bonanza Books, Crown, 1967), pp. 41-61.
[Based on one of a series of interviews of great actors conducted on BBC-2 television in 1965 and 1966.] In spite of the sharp wit of his writing, in person Shaw was always kind, because he was "so feeling" for people. He taught and encouraged me at the beginning of my career when I was understudying Candida on tour. Shaw wrote *Saint Joan* for me to play, but "Shaw himself was a perfect Saint Joan; he could have played it far better than any of us." Lewis Casson directed the cast in theatrical technique, but Shaw directed the delivery of the lines. He and Gilbert Murray, though not "professed Christians," were "the biggest Christians I have known."

1372 Toynbee, Arnold J. ACQUAINTANCES (Lond, NY, Toronto: Oxford UP, 1967), pp. 124-26.
Sidney and Beatrice Webb had an indulgent, parental attitude toward Shaw. They felt they had helped to bring about his marriage, and they rejoiced in his subsequent financial and literary success. To illustrate his naiveté in practical politics they often recounted the story of his abysmal showing when he stood for the London County Council and distributed as an election address a pamphlet which nowhere mentioned the election or his candidacy.

1373 Trilling, Lionel. "Commentary," THE EXPERIENCE OF LITERATURE: A READER WITH COMMENTARIES, ed by Lionel Trilling (Garden City, NY: Doubleday, 1967), pp. 317-21.
Though Shaw labeled *The Doctor's Dilemma* a tragedy, it is obviously a comedy instead. In spite of his professed didacticism, however, Shaw in this play does not set forth his criticisms of the medical profession with any great force; instead, this play makes the same commonsense criticisms of life which are standard fare in any good comedy. Dubedat and Ridgeon hold opposing views about life, and both are mocked.

1374 Tsuzuki, Chushichi. THE LIFE OF ELEANOR MARX, 1855-1898: A SOCIALIST TRAGEDY (Lond and NY: Oxford UP, 1967), pp. 116, 117, 127, 130-31, 151-52, 162, 164-65, 171-72, 181, 182, 183, 202n, 231, 308-9, 327, 329.
[Contains brief references to Shaw as participant in the activities of the Fabian Society and as a Socialist speaker, to his repudiation of the Marxist theory of value, to his opinions of Edward Aveling, to his use of Aveling as a model for Dubedat in his "tragedy" *The Doctor's Dilemma*, to his encouragement of Eleanor Marx's acting ambitions, and to his participation with Eleanor Marx and Aveling in a number of theatrical activities, including promoting the works of Ibsen, taking the part of Krogstad in a reading of NORA (A DOLL'S HOUSE), writing sequels to A DOLL'S HOUSE, and writing for the DRAMATIC REVIEW.]

1375 Turner, Justin G. "G.B.S. Edits Himself," CORANTO (JOURNAL OF THE FRIENDS OF LIBRARIES), V (1967), 20-25.
At the solicitation of its author Shaw made extensive revisions in an undated eleven-page manuscript about his early life written by a trade-unionist whose identity cannot now be ascertained. Only eight pages of the manuscript now survive; whether it was ever published is not known. A comparison of Shaw's revisions with the original version throws into sharp relief the enduring qualities of Shaw's own style: "compression, speed, economy and neatness of word and phrase, and accuracy in matters of fact."

1376 Turner, Michael R. BLUFF YOUR WAY IN THE THEATRE (Lond: Wolfe Publishing, 1967), pp. 21, 23.
Shaw was a "disciple" of Ibsen and realism, but did some experimenting with expressionistic techniques.

1377 Tyson, Brian. "One Man and His Dog: A Study of a Deleted Draft of Bernard Shaw's *The Philanderer*," MD, X (May 1967), 69-78.
The original manuscript of *The Philanderer* reveals that in the first draft of this play Shaw included a dog as an important plot element. There were probably three reasons why Shaw removed the dog from the play: first, the inclusion of the dog plot added a melodramatic element to the play, an element which placed more emphasis on plot machinery than on realism of character portrayal; second,

the dog plot seemed to show too great an influence of W. S. Gilbert on the play, particularly of Gilbertian qualities which Shaw had often criticized; and third, the dog plot was too sentimental. Echoes from the lines dealing with the dog can, however, be discerned in Shaw's "Preface" to *The Doctor's Dilemma*, written many years later. This abandoned plot involving the dog reveals Shaw as a "dog lover," though not a "sentimentalist."

1378 Völker, Klaus. "Kolonial-Klamotte" (A Colonial Old Piece of Trash), TH, VIII (Nov 1967), 42-43. [Reviews Ottofritz Gaillard's production of *Caesar and Cleopatra* at the "Volksbühne Berlin" (East).] Unfortunately Gaillard interprets Caesar as a kind of Hitler. Very often the plot is reduced to a trifling vaudeville. [In German.]

1379 Waal, Carla Rae. JOHANNE DYBWAD: NORWEGIAN ACTRESS (Oslo, Lond & Boston: Universitetsforlaget, 1967), 108, 110, 113, 119, 293, 309. *Pygmalion*, presented with very realistic stage effects, was the "most successful production" of the fall 1914 season at the Nationaltheater in Oslo. The "most interesting" productions by the Nationaltheater in the 1915-16 season were of foreign plays, including *Mrs. Warren's Profession*. In March 1919 the Nationaltheater staged *The Doctor's Dilemma* in a production which proved to be "moderately" successful. The fall 1926 Nationaltheater production of *Saint Joan* failed because the director ignored Shaw's "audacious and witty style" and instead staged the play with the conventional "heavy" atmosphere and tone of historical drama. The Nationaltheater presented *The Apple Cart* in 1931.

1380 Waith, Eugene M. (ed). THE DRAMATIC MOMENT (Englewood Cliffs, NJ: Prentice-Hall, 1967), pp. 1-2, 6, 10-11, 60-62. In the careful detail of the directions about stage settings and in the appropriateness of the dialogue to the characters speaking, Shaw's plays belong to the realistic tradition, but in some other respects they abandon realism for the conventions of satire. In *Major Barbara*, a "play of ideas," wit is used to bring to a focus the conflicting points of view of the major characters, none of which is allowed an unqualified triumph over the others. It is a religious play which contrasts Christianity not only with conventional morality and with materialism, but also with a Dionysiac mysticism.

1381 Wall, Vincent. *"Man and Superman:* Revisited and Re-edited," ISh, V (Spring 1967), 40-41.
A 1905 production of *Man and Superman* without the dream sequence and subsequent productions of the dream sequence alone had Shaw's express approval. From that time through the rest of Shaw's lifetime the play was seldom performed in its entirety.

1382 Watson, Barbara Bellow. "A Shavian Guide to the Intelligent Woman," DA, XXVII (1967), 2549A-50A.
Dissertation, Columbia University, 1963; published under the same title (1964).

1383 Watts, Richard Jr. "Two on the Aisle: Evening about Bernard Shaw," NEW YORK POST, 13 Oct 1967.
Though BY GEORGE with Max Adrian at the Lyceum is an interesting and enjoyable performance, it suffers from the difficulty Michael Voysey obviously had in making the selection from the enormous quantity and wide range of interest of Shaw's writings. The depiction of most of his life is shallow and sketchy, but there is depth and "human warmth" in the third-act interview of Shaw after his wife's death. The audience seemed to respond most to Shaw's rather severe criticism of such performers as Adelina Patti and Henry Irving.

1384 Weintraub, Stanley. BEARDSLEY: A BIOGRAPHY (NY: George Braziller, 1967), pp. 36, 75, 87-88, 90-91, 116, 129, 150, 158, 161n, 195, 274.
A Beardsley poster for the Avenue Theatre, showing an exotic woman with broad shoulders, was used for the first time at the first performance of *Arms and the Man*, leading one commentator to refer to the play as *Shoulders and the Woman*. The play had a mixed reception. Beardsley was a model for "the artist side" of Dubedat, of *The Doctor's Dilemma*.

1385 Werner, Jack. "Letters to the Editor: G.B.S.-Composer?" MUSICAL OPINION, Nov 1967, p. 74.
[Werner asks for the identification of a tune from *Saint Joan* and wonders whether Shaw himself might have composed it.]

1386 Werner, Jack. "Letters to the Editor: G.B.S.-Composer?" MUSICAL OPINION, XCI (Dec 1967), 138.
There is an error in the marking of the music in the first of my two Shaw letters in the November MUSICAL OPINION. Shaw did play the piano and composed music for at least two poems.

1387 "William Archer: A Footnote," ISh, VI (Fall 1967), 4.
[Following a reprint of Archer's review of a 1905 *Man and Superman* production, this three-paragraph informational article traces briefly the enduring relationship between Archer and Shaw as friends and as colleagues.]

1388 Willis, John. THEATRE WORLD: 1966-67 SEASON (NY: Crown Publishers, 1967), pp. 148, 149, 150, 186, 188, 189, 197, 199, 201, 203, 210, 211, 213.
[Primarily a collection of photographs, this book includes pictures from performances of *The Doctor's Dilemma, Major Barbara, Misalliance, Saint Joan, You Never Can Tell,* DEAR LIAR, and THE SEVEN AGES OF BERNARD SHAW.]

1389 Worth, Katharine J. "A Horn of Plenty," SHAVIAN, III (Spring-Summer 1967), 25-27.
BLASTS AND BENEDICTIONS, a collection of articles and stories by Sean O'Casey, edited by Ronald Ayling (1967), shows in several respects how much O'Casey is like Shaw, particularly in the respect that his "blasts," though they "scour," do not "chill." The collection includes a very good comic sketch of Ibsen giving birth to Shaw.

1390 Worth, Katharine J. "The Poets in the American Theatre," AMERICAN THEATRE, ed by John Russell Brown and Bernard Harris (Lond: Edward Arnold [Stratford-Upon-Avon Studies], 1967), pp. 87-107.
[In a brief reference on page 89 Worth says that Robert Lowell and William Carlos Williams have a predilection in their plays for a "dialogue of attack and defence between stage author and stage audience or critic" like that used by Shaw in *Fanny's First Play.*]

1391 Zentner, Karl (comp, trans, and ed). BERNARD SHAW IN DER ANEKDOTE (Bernard Shaw in Anecdotes) 2nd ed. (München: Heimeran, 1967). [KLEINE ANEKDOTEN-

SAMMLUNG, Vol. II, Vol. I being devoted to anecdotes
about Mark Twain.]
[This is a collection of anecdotes involving witty sayings
attributed to Shaw, gathered from many sources but mostly
from newspapers and periodicals of many countries from the
years 1932 to 1965. They are organized into eight
sections--one showing Shaw's selfmockery, one in which
Shaw turns his wit against other people of various
backgrounds, one in which the sharpness of wit comes
primarily from Shaw's insistence on truth, one involving
theater people and theater critics, one involving
reporters, one involving Shaw's friends and colleagues,
one involving women, and a final section which does not
present anecdotes, but aphorisms. The editor's Foreword
presents a brief chronology of Shaw's life and stresses
that the anecdotes have been chosen to show the human side
of Shaw, not Shaw the great author.] [In German.]

1392 Zolotow, Sam. "Diana Sands Gets St. Joan Role
Here," NYT, 14 Aug 1967, p. 34.
Diana Sands says that since Saint Joan, who was not an
American, is to be played by an American, it should not
matter what color that American is.

1968

1393 Albert, Sidney P. "'In More Ways Than One':
Major Barbara's Debt to Gilbert Murray," ETJ, XX
(May 1968), 123-40; rptd in BERNARD SHAW'S PLAYS, ed
by Warren Sylvester Smith (1970).
In both the published text of *Major Barbara* and the screen
play Shaw acknowledges his indebtedness to Gilbert Murray.
While it is well known that Shaw used Murray's translation
of THE BACCHAE and modeled one of the play's *dramatis
personae* upon Murray, it is a less well-known fact that
Murray offered constructive criticism of the completed
version of the play, persuading Shaw to rewrite the third
which improved it greatly. [The Shaw/Murray correspondence is reproduced, five letters, also drafts of the
manuscript of *Major Barbara*.]

1394 Albert, Sidney P. "'Letters of Fire against
the Sky': Bodger's Soul and Shaw's Pub," Shaw R, XI
(Sept 1968), 83-97.

Bodger, whisky magnate and philanthropist in *Major Barbara*, was modeled in part upon Dewar of the Scotch whisky firm and probably also upon members of the Guinness and Bass families, famous brewers with records as politicians and philanthropists. Through him (though he never appears on stage) as well as with the voices of his other characters, Shaw expresses some of his own teetotaler views; in particular, that in order to deal effectively with the drink question, "not only must we face up to existing conditions without comforting illusions; we must go on to seek out the root causes of our social ills."

1395 Alexander, Nigel. A CRITICAL COMMENTARY OF BERNARD SHAW'S ARMS AND THE MAN AND PYGMALION. (Lond: Macmillan [Macmillan Critical Commentaries], 1968.)
[One in a series of *Critical Commentaries* "offered in the belief that, faced with a work of exceptional density of texture or complication of structure, the reader may be helped in his appreciation by a 'conducted tour' or point-by-point critical exposition." Also included: an introduction on "The Play of Ideas," discussion questions, and recommendations for further reading.]

1396 Altwein, Erich F. W. "G.B.S.--ein vergessener Sozialist?" (G.B.S.--a Forgotten Socialist?), GEIST UND TAT, XXIII (1968), 232-34.
Shaw's *The Intelligent Woman's Guide to Socialism and Capitalism* is still relevant today. In several aspects it is a counterpart to Karl Marx's *Das Kapital*. [In German.]

1397 Ashmore, Basil. "Shaw and God," P&P, XV (March 1968), 45.
[Ashmore produced *The Adventures of the Black Girl in Her Search for God* at the Mermaid.] The basic form of a stage work lay concealed in *Black Girl*, waiting to be revealed. The final result is not a play, nor is it a flat reading; it will be unique entertainment, "having the spirit of 1968."

1398 Barnes, Clive. "HER FIRST ROMAN, a Musical, Opens Here," NYT, 21 Oct 1968, p. 53.
Ervin Drake made a terrible mistake when he thought he could make a musical from *Caesar and Cleopatra*.

370

1399 Barnes, Clive.   "The Theater: Shaw's *Saint Joan* at Lincoln Center," NYT, 5 Jan 1968, p. 42.
Saint Joan is not Shaw's best play; the initial exposition is tedious.   Diana Sands plays Joan as a peasant.

1400 Barr, Alan P.   "Diabolian Pundit: G. B. S. as Critic," ShawR, XI (Jan 1968), 22-23.
Fundamental to understanding Shaw as a critic is the fact that he saw himself as "a crusading--even religious-- force, consistently and seriously working for the progression of mankind."   He read other authors selectively and in a way convenient for his argument or crusade, then used his criticism to proselytize for his cause.   Examples of authors used in this way by Shaw are Bunyan, Shakespeare, Ibsen, Wagner, and Nietzsche.

1401 Bently, Joseph.   "Tanner's Decision to Marry in *Man and Superman*," ShawR, XI (1968), 26-28.
Tanner's refusal to marry Ann parallels Don Giovanni's refusal to repent (parallel passages from Shaw and Mozart/daPonte reproduced), and the ensuing damnation of the one is equivalent to the ensuing marriage of the other.   Tanner's sudden reversal of feeling comes as a result of the transformed hell imaged in his mind from the Don Juan sequence in Act III.

1402 Berlogea, Ileana.   G. B. SHAW ÎN ROMÂNIA [G. B. Shaw in Romania] (Bucureşti: Editura Meridiane, 1968).
[Three parts of unequal length: A chapter on *Candida*, one on Romanian criticism of Shaw, one on productions of Shaw's plays.   Lavishly illustrated with production photographs; chronological table of Romanian productions; bibliography.]   For the [Marxist] critic in Romania Shaw represents the right kind of optimism, derived from a strong belief in human values.   Shaw sees poetic values in immediate action, and his brilliant paradoxes bring multiple truth to life.   Shaw's qualities blend harmoniously with the Marxist principle that the stage must be a militant art form with a well-established purpose.   Thus in Romania those Shaw plays that are closer to reality and farther from the grotesque and the fantastic are produced: *Candida, Caesar and Cleopatra, Major Barbara, Mrs. Warren's Profession, Man and Superman, Pygmalion, The Devil's Disciple,* and *Saint Joan,* not *Back to Methuselah, Too True to Be Good, On the Rocks, The Simpleton of the Unexpected Isles,* or *In Good King*

Charles's Golden Days. On the centenary anniversary of Shaw's birth Romanian criticism took the position that he is a healthy, optimistic, lucid observer of the capitalist world. He is a playwright concerned with the individual versus society, individual psychology versus class psychology. He is admired for his wit and his lyricism, as a philosopher and a poet. [Includes an analysis of Radu Lupan's G. B. SHAW (1956), especially the linking of Shaw's biography and his novels.] [In Romanian.]

1403 Berst, Charles A. "The Devil and *Major Barbara*," PMLA, LXXXIII (March 1968), 71-79; rptd in BERNARD SHAW AND THE ART OF DRAMA, by Charles A. Berst (1973).
Focusing on Barbara and aligning her views with Shaw's distort the play. Undershaft reveals society's dependence on money and gunpowder, and though he suggests a basis for reform, he is too ensnared in his profession to effect it himself. As Barbara comes to understand Undershaft's realities, she provides some hope for the future.

1404 Bolitho, Hector. "A Note on Bernard Shaw and H. L. Bates," TEXAS QUARTERLY, XI (1968), 100-12.
During the Second World War Shaw wrote a short article for publication in the Royal Air Force Journal entitled, "To Tokyo on Buttermilk," in which he extolled the virtues of a vegetarian diet and proposed that such a diet be adopted by RAF pilots. H. E. Bates answered in "Back to Methuselah on a Beefsteak." [Both articles are reproduced in facsimile.]

1405 Boulton, Marjorie. THE ANATOMY OF DRAMA (Lond: Routledge & Kegan Paul, 1960), pp. 7, 8, 10, 12, 13, 17, 18, 39, 45, 61, 64, 75, 77, 88, 93, 94, 109, 118, 121, 128, 150, 154, 156, 162, 167, 170, 174, 183.
[Passing references to Shaw as illustration of principles of drama.]

1406 Bozduganov, Nikola. "Sŭvremennikŭt Shou" (Contemporary Shaw) TEATŬR (Sofia), No. 7 (1968), 46-47.
In *Pygmalion* at the Ogniaov Theater (Sofia), social satire is indivisible from the problem of the individual. Love logically crowns the experiment of the contemporary Pygmalion, and ironically Shaw instills a bourgeois style

into Eliza. The producer S. Stoianova stresses this duality and has not neglected the grotesque aspect nor the parody of abstract philosophical digressions. Even the picturesque scenes with Doolittle have their philosophical significance (revolt against bourgeois ideals). [Photographs.] [In Bulgarian.]

1407 Bunich-Remizov, B. B. "Bernard Shou i zhovten'" (Bernard Shaw and October 1917), RADIANSKE LITERATUROZNAVSTVO (Kiev), XII (1963), 58-64.
Shaw's ideological and creative evolution before October 1917 was complex. His interest in the Russian revolutionary movement and Russian literature in translation began in the nineties. Before October 1917, progressive Russian critics valued Shaw's deep understanding and properly evaluated his ideological and creative position. Shaw was disillusioned by the "opportunism" of the Fabian Society, and Lenin was very negative towards them also. *Great Catherine*, which celebrates the October Revolution, was translated into Russian in 1922, in celebration of the October Revolution, but Soviet critics did not appreciate it. [In Russian.]

1408 Castagna, Edwin. "G.B.S. at Pratt," MENCKENIANA, XXVI (Summer 1968), 10-11.
In 1968 the Katz family presented to the Enoch Pratt Free Library a bronze cast of the head of George Bernard Shaw by Jacob Epstein. [Reproduced: the letter of Mr. Leslie Katz offering the sculpture and an article from CARNEGIE MAGAZINE, October 1968, describing the art of the sculptor and his Shaw work.]

1409 Chapman, Raymond. THE VICTORIAN DEBATE, ENGLISH LITERATURE AND SOCIETY 1832-1901 (NY: Basic Books; Lond: Weidenfeld & Nicolson, 1968), pp. 9, 32, 37n, 240, 254, 255, 283, 312, 316n., 319, 320, 330, 334, 341, 344.
[References to Shaw for evidence in cultural history.]

1410 Cocco, Maria Rosaria. "'Malodorous Ibsen,'" ANNALI ISTITUTO UNIVERSITARIO ORIENTALE, NAPOLI, SEZIONE GERMANICA, XI (1968), 171-93.
Except for Shaw, who considered Ibsen superior to Shakespeare, GHOSTS received almost totally negative reviews in England. *Plays Unpleasant* was the most immediate tangible result of Shaw's admiration for Ibsen. The points of

contact between the two writers are: 1) the new woman, 2) the attack on bourgeois society, and 3) the desire to explain human behavior scientifically. Shaw's interest in Ibsen dated from the time he wrote an essay on *Socialism in Contemporary Literature* for the Fabian Society, and Shaw was attracted to the social elements in Ibsen, not "the poetic beauties." [In Italian.]

1411 Cohen, Harriet. "Shaw and the Woolworth Exhibition," SHAVIAN, III (Spring-Summer 1968), 8-10.
To aid Gertrude Harvey, an artist in financial straits, Shaw spponsored the Woolworth Exhibition of Pictures featuring Mrs. Harvey's works and offering them for sale at five pounds each. [The invitation and Shaw's note concerning the economics of fine arts are reproduced.]

1412 Coolidge, Olivia. GEORGE BERNARD SHAW (Bost: Houghton Mifflin, 1968).
[Illustrated biography written for junior high and high school students.]

1413 Cordell, Richard A., "Mr. Bernard Shaw's Plays: The Author's Fees for Professional Productions," ISh, VI (Winter 1968), 8-10.
[Facsimilie copy of Shaw's fees for productions, including other details regarding contracts, followed by notes on current Shaw productions and publications.]

1414 Dobrev, Chadar, "Geroika i ironiîa" (Heroics and Irony), TEATŬR (Sofia), No. 7 (1968), 30-34.
In this production of Shaw's *Saint Joan* at the National Army Theatre in Sofia (July 1968), the settings were geometrically abstract, the acting realistic. Brecht developed the ideas of *Joan* by moving from dialectism to realism, and entered into a polemic with Shaw in his version of the Saint Joan episode. [Photograph.] [In Bulgarian.]

1415 Donaghy, Henry J. "*The Apple Cart*: A Chestertonian Play," ShawR, XI (Sept 1968), 104-8.
In what sense is *The Apple Cart* a Chestertonian play (as suggested by Shaw in a letter to Mrs. Chesterton, 1930)? Both men saw how little democracy succeeded in being democratic, though their utopian visions were very different. In *Cart* Shaw felt uncomfortable coming down on

the side of a king and was unhappy not to be able to offer his Socialist panacea.   Such a position would have been much more congenial to Chesterton.

1416 Dukore, Bernard F. (ed).   SAINT JOAN: A SCREENPLAY BY BERNARD SHAW.   (Seattle, Lond: U of Washington P, 1968).   [Introduction pp. xi-xiii; screenplay pp. 3-137; appendixes, primarily of earlier drafts pp. 141-62.]
Shaw believed that the art of spoken drama on screen is not essentially different from the art of spoken drama on stage; language, not the camera, is primary. This point of view led to difficult relations with Hollywood and resulted in two poorly received films, *How He Lied to Her Husband* and *Arms and the Man*, both directed by Cecil Lewis.   In 1938 Shaw permitted some cutting and adaptation in *Pygmalion* which served to strengthen the romantic aspects and weaken the social yet managed to retain a close resemblance to the original drama.   Not so the movie *Major Barbara*, an enormously cut version of the play, which amounted to little more than a story about a religious girl whose fiancé gets a good job in her father's firm.   The text of *Caesar and Cleopatra* was not much tampered with, but the movie was unsuccessfully directed by Gabriel Pascal, who turned it into what Shaw called a "dull, prosaic, illustrated history."   Shaw completed the screenplay for *Saint Joan* in 1936, but it was never filmed.   He encountered difficulties with censorship boards and was forced to make deletions; other cuts were made simplifying complexities and excising subtleties; and new scenes were added to take advantage of the film medium.   The screenplay of *Joan* may serve as a model of how Shaw wanted his plays filmed since it was never altered by a director.

1417 Egri, Péter.   "A Shaw-drámák Intellektuális Szatírájának Kibontakozása, I" (The Development of Intellectual Satire in Shaw's Plays, I), FILOLÓGIAI KÖZLÖNY, XIV (1968), 124-37.
[Discussion and analysis of Shaw's plays from 1885 to 1903, emphasizing his strong social conscience, his forceful and sympathetic portrayal of women, and his increasingly sharp and witty use of paradoxes.   Brief discussion of Ibsen's positive influence and Nietzsche's negative one.]   [In Hungarian.]

1418 Emmel, Felix. RORORO SCHAUSPIELFÜHRER. VON AISCHYLOS BIS PETER WEISS (RORORO Guide to Drama. From Aeschylos to Peter Weiss) (Reinbek, Hamburg: Rowohlt, 1968), pp. 299-309.
[A survey of Shaw's life and works. Plot summaries of *Major Barbara, The Doctor's Dilemma, Pygmalion,* and *Saint Joan.*] Shaw was a Socialist individualist. [In German.]

1419 Grazhdanskaîa Z. T. BERNARD SHOU POSLE OKTÎAB-RÎA (Bernard Shaw after October) (Moscow: "Prosveshchenie," 1968).
The most important effects on Shaw of the 1917 October Russian revolution included an increase in satirical, grotesque tendencies of his depiction of the bourgeois world. Symbolic and allegorical figures appear, also critical realism, in the historical plays and those set in the future. *Back to Methuselah* represents the philosophical aspect of Shaw's works after 1917; *Saint Joan,* the historical, and *The Apple Cart,* the political. Sometimes these aspects are interwoven. In *Too True to Be Good,* Shaw turns his irony upon himself and his own philosophical theories. *On the Rocks* is the least grotesque of his political plays of the thirties. *Misalliance* is closely linked with his earlier manner, though it sometimes breaks out of the realistic framework and is misunderstood by Western criticism. In *The Simpleton of the Unexpected Isles,* Shaw treats colonial and social themes, with mockery of the English bourgeoisie and government, and shows the moral degradation of British colonial officials. The tragic story of *The Six Of Calais* corresponds to Shaw's anti-war attitude which had first developed among progressive intellectuals during World War I. *In Good King Charles's Golden Days* is linked with contemporary condemnation of political fanaticism and with Einstein's theory of relativity in human characters. The Preface to *Farfetched Fables* contains biographical and social matter as well as much else. Shaw's work influenced Pirandello, Brecht, J. B. Priestley and others. [In Russian.]

1420 Hardwick, Michael and Mollie. WRITER'S HOUSES, A LITERARY JOURNEY IN ENGLAND (Lond: Phoenix House, 1968), pp. 91-95.
[Description with photographs of Shaw's Corner and Ayot St. Lawrence.]

1421 Hartnoll, Phyllis. A CONCISE HISTORY OF THE
THEATRE (Lond: Thames and Hudson, 1968), pp. 204,
209, 211, 218-23, 240, 256, 267.
[Various references to Shaw; emphasis on Shaw as a severe
critic of nineteenth century drama. Contains stage
photographs of the first nights of some of Shaw's plays.]
From 1892 to 1949 Shaw dominated the stage not only in
England but on the Continent.

1422 Holland, Norman N. THE DYNAMICS OF LITERARY
RESPONSE (NY: Oxford UP, 1968), pp. 36, 56, 57,
225, 247, 249-51, 253, 260.
[*Man and Superman* used as evidence for conscious knowledge
of the presence of a myth in a literary work for creating
resonance.]

1423 Holloway, Joseph. JOSEPH HOLLOWAY'S IRISH
THEATRE, Vol I: 1926-1931, ed by Robert Hogan and
Michael J. O'Neill (Dixon, California: Proscenium
P, 1968), pp. 20, 25, 28, 32, 43, 44, 45, 50, 52,
53, 55, 56, 67, 68, 69, 78, 81.
[The journal of theater-going in Dublin by Joseph Holloway
with comments on Shaw plays.

1424 Hopwood, Alison L.   *"Too True to Be Good*:
Prologue to Shaw's Later Plays," ShawR, XI (Sept
1968), 109-18.
Too True to Be Good explores a basic problem of
government: how can men organize society so that it does
not make misfits of everybody, and concurrently a basic
human problem: how can man's life have meaning in a
meaningless universe? It is an Extravaganza in both form
and content and demonstrates Shaw's continuing grasp on a
continually changing world. Through use of comic
surrealism he depicts a twentieth century version of man's
dilemma, but the inconceivability of the universe is
balanced by the equally fundamental truth that it is the
nature of man to make his life meaningful.

1425 Hornby, Richard. "The Symbolic Action of
Heartbreak House," DramS, VII (Winter 1968-69), 5-
24.
Heartbreak House is a "strange" play for Shaw to have
written; with passages similar to Ionesco, Pinter, and
Beckett it seems very un-Shavian. It also has elements
relating it to Tolstoy's FRUITS OF ENLIGHTENMENT (note

Shaw's sub-title, "A Fantasia in the Russian Manner on English Themes") and Shakespeare's KING LEAR, but its closest relative is Shaw's earlier play, *Major Barbara*, with which it shares character types and themes. By use of symbolic action the message is communicated: the natural leaders have failed to give the "men of action" proper guidance; the young have been left to shift for themselves with resultant disaster.

1426 Hutchinson, P. William. "A Comparative Study of the Professional Religionist as a Character in the Plays of George Bernard Shaw." Unpublished dissertation, Northwestern University, 1968. [Listed in DAID.]

1427 Isnardi, Enrico. "Il Teatro del Parradosso: G. B. Shaw" (The Theater of Paradox: G. B. Shaw), RIVISTA LETTERARIA PER I LICEI CLASSICO, SCIENTIFICO, ARTISTICO E PER L'ISTITUTO MAGISTRALE, I (1968-69), 58-59.
Shaw is the last in a long line of playwrights who were performed in England as opponents of the bourgeois theater. *Candida* is his masterpiece. *Heartbreak House* shows that his early optimism is defeated by the vision of the utopians who have seen their ideals shipwrecked. *Saint Joan* seems far from the usual Shaw themes, but the feeling for paradox and cleverness and the puritan view are still there. [In Italian.]

1428 Iufit, A. Z. (ed). RUSSKIĬ SOVETSKIĬ TEATR 1917-1921 (Soviet Russian Theater 1917-1921) (Leningrad: "Iskusstvo," 1968).
On 31 October 1921, V. E. Meĭerhold said in a speech to the company of the No. 1 Theater of the R.S.F.S.R. (Soviet Russian Federative Socialist Republic): "The Artistic Council of the Theaters of the R.S.F.S.R. has included *Great Catherine* in next season's repertoire" (cf. *Vestnik teatra* [1920], 19-20). However, the play was not performed. *The Shewing-up of Blanco Posnet* was put into rehearsal by E. B. Vakhtangov in the Theatrical Section of Narkompros (National Commissariat for Education) in 1919/20 season. [In Russian.]

1429 Keough, Lawrence C. "Henderson Versus Shaw," SHAVIAN, III (Spring-Summer, 1968), 10-13.

The work of Archibald Henderson, Shaw's official biographer, is not only indispensable to the student of Shaw but
also inevitable and unavoidable. Nevertheless his lack of
critical penetration, his verbosity, and the intrusion of
his own ego in the narrative lead to an obscuring of Shaw
more than to an illuminating of him.

1430 Knepler, Henry. THE GILDED STAGE, THE YEARS OF
THE GREAT INTERNATIONAL ACTRESSES (NY: William
Morrow, 1968), pp. 213, 217, 228, 229-30, 232, 234,
291.
[Shaw's Critical reaction to Duse and Bernhardt.]

1431 Knepper, B. G. "Shaw and the Unblessed Poor,"
IOWA ENGLISH YEARBOOK, XIII (1968), 12-17.
Shaw hated poverty and the poor. The immediate solution
is for every man to obtain wealth as he can. His
Socialist solution is to provide a basic income. If man
could not eliminate poverty he must face extinction.

1432 Kon, Militsa. "Ne tol'ko vyduma i smekh" (Not
Only Invention and Laughter), TEATR (Moscow), No. 7
(1968), 25-27.
The Millionairess was produced at the Pushkin Theater,
Krasnoiarsk (1968), as a "musical-farce" described as
"after Shaw," with grotesque situations, eccentric
characters, parody, and paradox. Dancing girls and a
street-singer were introduced. The production reveals
more sharply the satirical essence of the play. The four
acts were reduced to two. [In Russian.]

1433 Kostov, Kiril. "Otmŭshtenieto na Shou" (Shaw's
Revenge), TEATŬR (Sofia), No 4 (1968), 36-38.
Shaw treated history freely in *Caesar and Cleopatra*
(produced at the "Laughter and Tears" Theatre, Sofia) in
order to obtain interesting dramatic action. He chose
Caesar to express his own intellectual ideals. The producer P. Pavlov has seized every opportunity given by the
text for parody, e.g. of Egyptian political limitations,
cult of the gods, etc. Whether Pavlov was justified in
this treatment is doubtful. Of course, Shaw is known for
his humor, love of paradox, and irony. This production
has been turned into a spectacle to arouse laughter, which
Shaw certainly did not intend when he wrote the play.
Consequently it is a failure. [Photographs.] [In
Bulgarian.]

1434 Kudrjavcev, A. "Bernard Shaw: *Sveta Ivana*" (Bernard Shaw: *Saint Joan*), SLOBODNA DALMACIJA, XXVI (1968), 7385.
[Not seen.] [In Croatian.]

1435 Laing, Allan M. "Writing to G. B. S.," ISh, VI (Spring 1968), pp. 34-35.
[Two exchanges between Shaw and Laing (initiated by the latter) on grammatical points.]

1436 Lambert, J. W. "Plays in Performance," DRAMA, ns LXXXVIII (Spring 1968), 16-27.
Heartbreak House is Chekhovian only insofar as it concerns a family on the edge of doom. It is an opera with its own verbal music. Irene Worth gave a virtuoso performance as Hesione Hushabye, a character mischievously named by Shaw, because she does not resemble the passive Trojan lady and she embodies nothing lulling whatever.

1437 Leonard, Hugh. *"The Black Girl in Search of God*," P&P, XV (April 1968), 58.
The adaptation of *The Black Girl in Search of God* by Basil Ashmore is neither prose narrative nor play.

1438 Leonard, Hugh. *"Heartbreak House*," P&P, XV (Jan 1968), 45, 47.
Shaw's plays must be a joy to speak and the devil to act. The characters are shallow disguises of Shaw. [Review of *Heartbreak House* with Irene Worth at the Lyric, London.]

1439 Lester, John A., Jr. JOURNEY THROUGH DESPAIR (Princeton: Princeton UP, 1968), pp. 5, 43, 64, 69-70, 77, 79, 80, 82, 83, 84, 85, 93, 95, 96, 97, 98, 184-85.
[References to Shaw for evidence in cultural history.]

1440 McElderry, B[ruce] R., Jr. "Max Beerbohm: Essayist, Caricaturist, Novelist," ON STAGE AND OFF: EIGHT ESSAYS IN ENGLISH LITERATURE, ed by John W. Ehrstein, John R. Elwood and Robert C. McClean (Pullman: Washington State UP, 1968), pp. 76-86; rptd in THE SURPRISE OF EXCELLENCE: MODERN ESSAYS ON MAX BEERBOHM (1974).

Beerbohm considered himself a poor substitute for Shaw as
a drama critic, but he was independent in judging Shaw's
plays. They were both not bardolators.

1441 Manvell, Roger.   ELLEN TERRY (NY: G. P.
Putnam's Sons, 1968), pp. 9, 46-47, 74, 84, 93, 119,
139, 140, 207, 213-14, 258-87, 290-92, 302, 305,
307, 320, 329, 349, 352-53.
[Traces the relationship between Shaw and Ellen Terry and
Henry Irving.]

1442 Martin, Kingsley.   EDITOR: A SECOND VOLUME OF
AUTOBIOGRAPHY, 1931-45 (Lond: Hutchinson, 1968) and
EDITOR: "NEW STATESMAN" YEARS, 1931-1945 (Chicago:
Henry Regnery, 1968), pp. 47, 69, 70, 71, 72, 81-82,
84, 85-89, 94, 96-107, 108-10, 135, 140, 141, 142,
197, 209, 267-70, 324.
[Discusses Shaw and Beatrice Webb, H. G. Wells, Jung,
Desmond McCarthy, W. H. Rivers, Lady Astor and Maynard
Keynes.]

1443 Masumoto, Masahiko.   "A Note on *Saint Joan* in
Japan," ISh, VII (Fall 1968), 4-5.
Saint Joan is the one exception to the general neglect of
Shaw's plays on the Japanese stage.   There are seven
Japanese translations.   [Brief survey of Japanese produc-
tions of *Joan*.]

1444 Masumoto, Masahiko.   "*Pygmalion* no Ketsumatsu-
Sairon-" (The Denouement of *Pygmalion* -a Second
Thought), IVY (Nagoya University, Nagoya), VII (Jan
1968), 109-19.
The ending of the film of *Pygmalion*, made by Gabriel
Pascal in 1938, is a realization of what is suggested in
the 'Sequel.'   The Higgins-Eliza relationship is one of
the typical patterns in Shaw's dramas.   [In Japanese.]

1445 Mayer, Hans.   "Johanna oder die Vernunft des
Herzens. Über die Jeanne-d'Arc-Stücke von Schiller,
Shaw und Brecht" (Joan or the Rationalism of the
Heart.   About the Jeanne-d'Arc-Plays of Schiller,
Shaw and Brecht), TH, IX (June 1968), 22-27.
Schiller saw in Saint Joan the conflict of modern man, the
conflict between reality and utopia.   Shaw showed the
brutalities of the English ruling class, the superiority

of female logic, and Joan's individualism and spirit of protest (her "protestantism"). Brecht wrote SAINT JOAN OF THE STOCKYARDS against Joan. Later, in THE VISIONS OF SIMONE MACHARD, Brecht presented more of Joan's original "protestantism," and, like Shaw, the conspiracy of the ruling class against her, the representative of the people. [In German.]

1446 Meller, Horst. "*Saint Joan*," ZEITGENÖSSISCHE ENGLISHCHE DICHTUNG, III, DRAMA (Contemporary English Writing, III, Drama) (Frankfurt: Hirschgraben, 1968), pp. 75-98. [Not seen.] [In German?]

1447 Michailowski, Boris. "Gorki und Shaw" (Gorky and Shaw), in MAXIM GORKI: DRAMA UND THEATER (Maxim Gorky: Drama and Theater), ed by Ilse Stauche (Berlin: Henschel, 1968), pp. 34-47. [Not seen.] [In German.]

1448 Miller, J. William. MODERN PLAYWRIGHTS AT WORK, Vol I (NY: Samuel French, 1968), pp. 160-203. [Not seen.]

1449 Moore, Harry T. "Preface," CASHEL BYRON'S PROFESSION by George Bernard Shaw, ed by Stanley Weintraub (Carbondale and Edwardsville: Southern Illinois UP [Crosscurrents/Modern Fiction]; Lond and Amsterdam: Feffer & Simons, 1968), pp. v-vii. *Cashel Byron's Profession* makes the liveliest reading of Shaw's novels. It stands up marvelously. Christopher Morley felt that, if Shaw had continued as a novelist, he would have done something "unlike anything in the course of British fiction."

1450 Murphy, Daniel J. "The Lady Gregory Letters to G. B. Shaw," MD, X (Feb 1968), 331-45. [Fourteen letters from Lady Gregory to Shaw (1909-1925) asking advice on legal, business, and personnel matters of the theater; discussing the production of *The Shewing-up of Blanco Posnet* at the Abbey Theatre, Dublin; expressing hopes of beginning an annual Shaw festival.

1451 Nelson, Raymond Stanley.   "Religion and the Plays of Bernard Shaw," DA, XXIX (1968), 574A. Unpublished dissertation, University of Nebraska, 1968.

1452 Novick, Julius.   "Theatre," NATION, CCVII (9 Sept 1968), 221-22.
Heartbreak House is one of those works that attempt greatly but do not succeed.   An inspired director might make the play seem *in toto* what it is in flashes: "a powerful metaphor for a disintegrating suicidal society," but this production [Shaw Festival, Niagara-on-the-Lake] is not inspired.   The festival also includes a production of Feydeau's LA MAIN PASSE!   In spite of Shaw's disapproval of Feydeau and farce, the two writers seem closer than they did during their lifetimes.

1453 Nurmakhanov, Kalzhan.   SLOVO DRUGA: SBORNIK KRITICHESKIKH STATEĬ (Word of a Friend: Collected Critical Essays) (Alma-Ata: "Zhazushy," 1968), pp. 63-69.
[Not seen.]   [In Russian.]

1454 Okumura, Saburo.   "Isha no Jirenma ni tsuite" (On *The Doctor's Dilemma*), JINBUN KENKYU (Osaka Municipal University, Osaka), XIX (March 1968), 572-86.
The Doctor's Dilemma is an attack, not on the medical profession and doctors, but on people's attitude to them. This is a kind of parody of H. A. Jones' THE PHYSICIAN. Shaw inquired into the subject of a doctor's conscience while criticizing Victorian domestic plays.   [In Japanese.]

1455 Olson, Elder.   THE THEORY OF COMEDY (Bloomington and Lond: U of Indiana P, 1968), pp. 39, 40, 56, 60, 63, 113-24.
In certain respects Shaw resembles Oscar Wilde.   His method is based on the idea that opinion is the most important cause of emotion, and it is related to anticipation.   His dialectic is both constructive and destructive.   He had contempt for the well-made plot.   His discussion is only about the distinctively human issues in human action.   As a thinker, Shaw is a crank, but he is a great playwright.   [Very suggestive, if brief, examination of Shaw.]

1456 Otten, Terry. "Candida and Henry Higgins: Shaw's Mentors to the Human Spirit," DISCOURSE, XI (Summer 1968), 312-16.
Candida and Henry Higgins are kindred spirits; both play the role of spiritual teacher, both assume the task of educating a lost soul. Candida must strip Marchbanks of his self-destroying romantic idealism; Higgins offers Eliza a soul, spiritual freedom from her materialistic values. The success of both Candida and Higgins depends upon their detachment from the object of their concern, and the test of their skill as teachers is whether the disciple obtains self-dependence.

1457 Palester, R. *"Pierwsza sztuka Fanny"* (*Fanny's First Play*), KALENDARZ TEATRU POLSKIEGO (Warsaw), No 20 (1968), 4-10.
[Not seen.] [In Polish.]

1458 Pleasants, Henry. "George Bernard Shaw: Critic of Music," HI-FI STEREO REVIEW, XX (March 1968), 59-63.
Shaw's music criticism was a unique and spectacular performance, and he was rarely wrong. [Photographs.]

1459 Popkin, Henry. "Summer Theater: The Shaw Festival," HUMANIST, XXVIII (Sept-Oct 1968), 27 and *passim*.
[Comment on the pairing of Georges Feydeau's LA MAIN PASSE with Shaw's *Heartbreak House* at the Shaw Festival of Niagara-on-the-Lake (Canada).]

1460 Portîânskaîâ, N. A. "Bernard Shou i irlandskii teatr" (Bernard Shaw and the Irish Theater), UCHENYE ZAPISKI IRKUTSKOGO GOS. PED. INSTITUTA (Irkutsk), XXXIII (1968), 113-22.
Although Shaw did not belong to the Irish Renaissance, his works, due to their general human scope, which avoids narrow nationalism, could not but affect Irish dramaturgy. Shaw's activities on behalf of the theater stimulated the establishment of social dramaturgy and the theater of ideas. His criticial and unmasking attitudes were seized upon in one way or another by his successors in the Irish theater. His influence was felt by all the major writers and dramatists of Ireland. [In Russian.]

1968: 1456-1462

1461 Prang, Helmut. GESCHICHTE DES LUSTSPIELS: VON DER ANTIKE BIS ZUR GEGENWART (A History of Comedy: From Classical Antiquity to the Present Time) (Stuttgart: Alfred Kröner, 1968), pp. viii, 11, 92, 119, 133, 193, 263, 309-14, 315, 321, 331, 335, 344, 354, 360, 366.
Shaw belongs to the very small group of playwrights who have written comedies founded on history. Biting humor and witty satire are the advantages of Shaw's comedies. The lack of dramatic plot is their main weakness. In his social criticism and his 'hero-debunking' he may be compared to many modern German playwights (e.g. Carl Sternheim, Walter Hasenclever, and Ferdinand Bruckner). [In German.]

1462 Pregelj, Zdenko. "Pitanje svobodnog cina u dramama G. B. Shaw" (Question of Free Will in Shaw's Plays), IZRAZ (Sarajevo), XXIII (19968), 450-57.
Shaw successfully combines the basic postulates of the philosophies of Nietzsche and Schopenhauer and adds his own philosophical position. The beginnings of Shaw's philosophy are evident in *Mrs. Warren's Profession, Candida* and more clearly in *Man and Superman* and *Saint Joan*. Mrs. Warren's strength does not lie in her choice of prostitution, but in her deliberate pursuit of that choice, which confirms her individuality. Mrs. Warren is the first in a series of women in Shaw's plays who has not attained the freedom of which Nietzsche writes. Critics saw Mrs. Warren as Shaw's revolutionary engagement in battle for the improvement of women's social position. The situation in which Candida finds herself contrasts with that of Mrs. Warren. It has three possible solutions: the affirmation of freedom as an individual, submission, or the wrecking of a life. She is so imbued with Philistine ideas that she cannot choose Eugene and his absolute freedom. Shaw never consistently accepts Nietzsche's ideas as the only acceptable morality. In creating Ann, Shaw most explicitly shows that morality is an unreal concept. Nietzsche's statement on the "morality" of society and social institutions based on flattery, the belief in property and the social code is reflected in *Man and Superman* where the only moral law is that which places man above the morality of the masses. Joan stands above Mrs. Warren, Candida and Ann and is the most successful of Shaw's women characters. She is the prophet of truth and a social rebel, deeply convinced that the rightness of her actions will lead the to the triumph of the individual over society and its conventions. She must follow her will, and this imperative realizes Schopen-

hauer's philosophical axiom which Shaw has transposed in the play. [In Croatian.]

1463 Punch, A. M. "The Noblest disease," KIPLING JOURNAL, XXXV (Sept 1968), p. 21.
Kipling and Shaw both see work as "the noblest disease" of man.

1464 Racheva, Mariîa. "V direne na geroiko romanti-chniîa Shou" (In Search of the Heroic-Romantic Shaw), NARODNA KULTURA (Sofia), II (1968), 25.
Saint Joan is Shaw's only tragedy, perhaps even a heroic tragedy in the Shakespearian sense. The theme of an individual in revolt against inhuman society is frequent in Shaw's works, but elsewhere the revolt is on a moral and ethical basis, solved by Shaw with irony and scepticism. In *Joan*, the basis of the conflict has political and national significance (feudalism and religion). The production at the National Front Theater (Sofia) demonstrates the intellectual and ideological wealth of *Saint Joan* in all its complexity. [In Bulgarian.]

1465 Regan, Arthur E. "The Fantastic Reality of Bernard Shaw: A Look at *Augustus* and *Too True*," ShawR, XI (Jan 1968), 2-10.
The concept of Playwright as Circus Clown enables one to appreciate much of Shaw's dramatic achievement. *Augustus Does His Bit* is an attack, in the form of a farce, on war and governors who misuse their power to support war; it is an early response by Shaw to the horrors of the First World War. He later reworked the play into *Too True to Be Good*, a fantasy dealing with the absurd violence of the world. Mask and madness, illusion, pretense, and unreality are major elements in this work.

1466 Remizov, B. "Istoriîa odniei druzhbi" (History of a Friendship), VSESVIT (Kiev), V (1968), 92-96.
Maxim Gorky's negative attitude to Shaw before 1911 was unusual in Russian literature, and Gorky knew Tolstoi had accused Shaw (1908) of not being serious. However, Gorky approved Shaw's anti-bourgeois and humanistic attitude. [In Ukrainian.]

1467 Ross, Julian L. "A Piece of Literary Shoplifting," ShawR, XI (Jan 1968), 23-25.

An essay entitled, "The Innocence of Bernard Shaw," by Dixon Scott appeared in 1916. It reappeared in 1949 in "mosaic" plagiarized form under the name of C. E. M. Joad. [Plagiarized passages reproduced.]

1468 Roston, Murray. "Shavian Wit," BIBLICAL DRAMA IN ENGLAND FROM THE MIDDLE AGES TO THE PRESENT DAY (Lond: Faber and Faber, 1968), pp. 257-64.
In *Back to Methuselah*, his rebuttal of neo-Darwinism, Shaw applied to the biblical world his theory of the Will as the inner urging force to create and survive. The play marked a turning point in biblical drama in England, dividing the old school of bibliolaters from the reinterpreters of scriptural themes in the light of modern criteria.

1469 Ruff, William. "Shaw on Wilde and Morris: A Clarification," ShawR, XI (Jan 1968), 32-33.
Shaw can be trusted to tell the truth about a friend; the inaccuracy of a story by Rupert Hart-Davis in THE LETTERS OF OSCAR WILDE can be shown to be Davis's own mistake and the mistake of Hesketh Pearson in OSCAR WILDE HIS LIFE AND WIT.

1470 Russell, Bertrand. THE AUTOBIOGRAPHY OF BERTRAND RUSSELL, Vol II (Lond: George Allen and Unwin; NY: Little, Brown, 1968), pp. 89, 137, 308, 321, 327, 376, 396.
[Passing references to Shaw in letters to Russell; also includes letters from Shaw.]

1471 Salem, James J. "Shaw on Broadway, 1894-1965 (A Checklist)," ShawR, XI (Jan 1968), 29-32.
[List of productions, with opening dates, taken from BEST PLAYS OF THE YEAR AND YEARBOOK OF THE DRAMA IN AMERICA series (NY: Dodd, Mead, beginning 1894.]

1472 Salerno, Henry F. (ed). "George Bernard Shaw (1956-1950)," ENGLISH DRAMA IN TRANSITION, 1880-1920, (NY: Pegasus, 1968), pp. 195-202.
[A brief Shaw biography with data on childhood and career, followed by a brief discussion of selected major works, especially *Major Barbara*, the text of which follows.)

1473 Scriabine, Vera. "Fabian Summer Schools," ISh, VI (Summer 1968), 36-37.
Shaw stayed for weeks at a time at the Fabian Summer Schools lecturing and debating.

1474 Serebriakova, Galina. "Bernard Shou" (Bernard Shaw), O DRUGIKH I O SEBE: NOVELI (On Others and Myself: Short Stories) (Moscow: Sovetskii pisatel' 1968), 203-24.
[Serebriakova met Shaw in 1930. He admired Lenin.] [In Russian.]

1475 "Shaw, George Bernard," DICTIONNAIRE DES LITTERATURES (Encyclopedia of Literature), ed by Philippe van Tieghem, (Paris: Presses Universitaires de France, 1968), vol. III, pp. 3599-600.
[An introduction to Shaw's life and works.] Shaw was a walking paradox. [In French.]

1476 "Shaw w karykaturze" (Shaw in Caricature), KALENDARZ TEATRU POLSKIEGO (Warsaw), No 20 (1968), 32-39.
[Not seen.] [In Polish.]

1477 "Shou, Bernard" (Shaw, Bernard) UKRAINS'KIĬ RADIANS'KIĬ ENTSIKLOPEDICHNIĬ SLOVNIK (Ukrainian Workers' Encyclopedic Dictionary) (Kiïv: Akademiïa nauk Ukrainskoi SRS), III, 811.
Shaw understood that only the proletariat was capable of bringing England out of capitalism. He was close to the Communist Party in England and published in their newspapers. His later works were devoted to the struggle for peace against imperialism. His works published in the Ukraine were: a four-volume edition (1931-2) and *P'esy (Plays)*, (1956). [In Ukrainian.]

1478 Sidnell, M. J. *"John Bull's Other Island:* Yeats and Shaw," MD, XI (Dec 1968), 245-51.
The relationship of Shaw and Yeats has barely been touched upon by biographers, but in the play *John Bull's Other Island*, as well as in the correspondence between the two men regarding its possible staging in Dublin, much is revealed about this relationship. [Yeat's letter to Shaw reproduced in full.]

1479 "'The Stage as a Profession': An 1897
Controversy," ShawR, XI (May 1968), 52-78.
In its 24 November 1897 issue London's MORNING POST
published an article "from a correspondent" on the virtues
of a School of Histrionic Art which would raise the
professional quality and status of theater-related work in
England. This brought forth responses from many actors
and others interested in theater, Shaw among them. [The
original article plus 27 letters, including Shaw's, are
reproduced.]

1480 Stockholder, Fred E. "Shaw's Drawing-Room
Hell: A Reading of *Man and Superman*," ShawR, XI
(May 1968), 42-51.
Jack Tanner, when compared with Sheridan's Charles Surface
in SCHOOL FOR SCANDAL is concerned with the creation of
good on a much larger scale--the ordering of the whole of
human society. As satiric hero, he attempts with wit to
expose the evils within society but thereby threatens
himself with self-exposure and self-destruction. His
comic defeat actually comes when he reveals the
controlling principal of his satire to Ann, his only
potential convert. But when he finally surrenders to her,
he does not surrender his revolutionary principles; he
continues to talk about the Life Force and begins to live
it. He has indeed managed to integrate his world view
with his personal life.

1481 Sturdevant, James R. "Shaw's *Don Juan in Hell*:
A Study in Word Power," ENGLISH JOURNAL, LVII, (Oct
1968), 1002-4.
The dream sequence from *Man and Superman* can serve as a
rich source of words for vocabulary study for high school
students. [Two lists of words from the sequence are
given.]

1482 Szyfman, A. "Shaw w Polsce" (Shaw in Poland),
PRZEGLĄD TEATRALNY HORZYCY (Torun), XLIV (1968), 8-
11.
[Not seen.] [In Polish.]

1483 Tyson, Brian F. "The Evolution of G. B. Shaw's
Plays Unpleasant." Unpublished dissertation, Uni-
versity College London, 1968.
[Listed in DAID.]

1484 Ugarov, V. "Ĕĭnshtein i G.B.S." (Einstein and
G.B.S.), NAUKA I ZHIZN' (Moscow), XII (1968) 66-67.
At the banquet for Einstein held in London, October 1930,
Shaw departed from his custom of speaking impromptu, and
dictated a draft of his speech to Blanche Peet. Shaw
always mocked scientists, except Pythagoras, Aristotle,
Ptolomy, Copernicus, Galileo, Kepler, Newton, and
Einstein, though he differentiates between them: Ptolemy,
Newton and Einstein were creators of a universe; the
others were only concerned with repairing it and contra-
dicted one another. [In Russian.]

1485 Urnov, M. V. "Bernard Shou (1856-1950),"
ISTORIIA ZARUBEZHNOĬ LITERATURY KONTSA XIX-NACHALA
XX VEKA (1871-1917) (Moscow: Izdatel'stvo moskovskogo universiteta, 1968), pp. 239-46.
Shaw, with Romain Rolland, Anatole France and André Bar-
busse, greeted the Socialist Revolution in Russia. But
when asked "Did the October Revolution influence your
work?" Shaw replied, "No. It was my work which influenced the October Revolution." [In Russian.]

1486 Ustanova, R. "Paradoks v dukhe Shoy," (Paradox
in the Spirit of Shaw), TEATR (Moscow), No. 6
(1968), 21-22.
The Devil's Disciple was produced in 1967 at the Tatar
Dramatic Theater in Menzelinsk after being in rehearsal
for three years. It was translated from the Russian into
Tatar, preserving Shaw's style. The company attended
lectures on Shaw's work and on the War of Independence in
North America. The players continue to work on preparing
their roles. The inhabitants of Menzelinsk agree that
Shaw has enriched their national theater. [In Russian.]

1487 Vidmar, Josip. "Drama na raskrščcu" (Drama at
the Crossroads) IZRAZ (Sarajevo), XXIV (1968), 288-
92.
In The Devil's Disciple and other plays, Shaw states that
man is not a uniform uncomplicated being as English
moralists picture him. Shaw pondered the question of
individuality, e.g. Frank in Mrs. Warren's Profession
(though he is not an important character). Comparing The
Doctor's Dilemma with Galsworthy's LOYALTIES, we see that
Shaw believes "Truth is such-and-such," whereas Galsworthy
says "Such is life." In Shaw's plays we see the gesture
of an ideologist; in Galsworthy, that of a wise magician.
[In Serbo-Croatian.]

1488 Wagner, Paul. "Frank Harris and the Maid of Orleans," PRINCETON UNIVERSITY LIBRARY CHRONICLE, XXX (Autumn 1968), 25-38.
In a lettter to Otto Kahn, Frank Harris said he was "appalled by the idea of Bernard Shaw, the skeptic, trying to realize [Joan's] heroic soul. I knew he couldn't do it so I sat down and wrote my play in a month." This play, JOAN LA ROMEE, he sent to Shaw, who responded by saying that there was nothing to do but "drop the thing into the waste paper basket with a good humored laugh, and apologize to posterity for the surviving copies."

1489 Watson, Barbara Bellow. "Sainthood for Millionaires: *Major Barbara*," MD, XI (Dec 1968), 227-44; rptd in BERNARD SHAW'S PLAYS, ed by Warren Sylvester Smith (1970).
In *Major Barbara*, his "Republic of Saints," Shaw shows "that the world must be saved by worldly means, that innocence cannot carry us through, but intellect and will power may." He demonstrated the necessity of true realism, not the "supposed realism of those who accept the *status quo* out of indifference abetted by stupidity . . . or out of moral cowardice of the intellect." Barbara and Undershaft are not saints of God, but saints of this world; and the religion which triumphs over Barbara's Salvation Army Christianity and over Undershaft's religion of capitalism is Shaw's own secular religion of Creative Evolution. This can be seen in the coming together of Barbara and Cusins as well as in the future which is implied at the end of the play.

1490 Weintraub, Stanley. "The Indefatigable Non-Correspondent: G. B. S.," TEXAS QUARTERLY, XI (1968), 113-27.
The most prolific letterwriter in history, Shaw affected a strong dislike for letterwriting. His solution to the problem of an overwhelming inflow of mail was the ready-made reply card. These were color-coded and designed to provide answers to any inquiry or request: for autography or photographs, financial contributions, services as lecturer or author. There was a general-purpose card: "Mr. Bernard Shaw, though he is always glad to receive interesting letters or books, seldom has time to acknowledge them; for his correspondence has increased to such an extent that he must either give up writing private letters or give up writing anything else . . . ." And there were cards detailing his opinions on matters of his special interest: the phonetic alphabet, temperance,

vegetarianism, capital punishment. These correspondence cards of Shaw's expose fascinating aspects of his personality and demonstrate his desire to amuse and inform as many interested persons as he could.

1491 Weintraub, Stanley. "Introduction," CASHEL BYRON'S PROFESSION by George Bernard Shaw, ed by Stanley Weintraub (Carbondale and Edwardsville: Southern Illinois UP [Crosscurrents/Modern Fiction]; Lond and Amsterdam: Feffer & Simons, Inc., 1968), pp. ix-xv.
Shaw thought the form of fiction too unreal. He dramatized, in blank verse, *Cashel Byron's Profession* to secure the copyright before someone else did. Shaw himself toyed with amateur boxing. He parodied absurd Victorian novelistic conventions while going his own way. What was crucially wanting in Shaw was a sense of audience. Writing in a critical vacuum created a sense of unreality.

1492 Weintraub, Stanley. "Mencken to Shaw: 'A Young Man in the Writing Trade' Writes to His Hero," MENCKENIANA, XXVI (Summer 1968), 9-10.
When the still unknown Henry Louis Mencken published his book GEORGE BERNARD SHAW: HIS PLAYS (1905), he sent a copy to Shaw with a very modest accompanying letter. [Letter reproduced in full.]

1493 Weiss, Aureliu. "The Author, the Work, and the Actor: G. B. Shaw and Stage Directions," BRITISH JOURNAL OF AESTHETICS, VIII, (Jan 1968), 49-53).
In his Preface to *Plays: Pleasant and Unpleasant* Shaw raises the problem of the intentions of the playwright being misrepresented by the actors and calls for precise stage directions and character sketches which would show the actor what type of character he was to present. But these analytic descriptions are alien to the movement and function of drama; the preface is better suited to communicating intention. Shaw himself was not really certain as to the purpose of stage directions: whereas he called for dispensing with "emotional directions" in the Preface, he is later of the opinion that these directions should specify "the feeling with which the speech should be delivered."

1494 Wellwarth, George E.   "Gattie's Glass of Water;
or, the Origins of Breakages, Ltd.," Shaw R, XI (Sept
1968), 99-103.
Shaw's admiration for the late Alfred Warwick Gattie,
"that remarkable genius," referred to in his preface to
The Apple Cart, led him to create Breakages, Ltd., the
villain of that play, which was a huge monopolistic
business organization that controlled the nation and stood
for all that Shaw thought was wrong with capitalism. The
real-life equivalent of Breakages, Ltd. took the form of
the Board of Trade and the directors of the railway
companies with whom Gattie was doing constant battle in a
vain attempt to have adopted his brilliant ideas on
transport reform.

1495 White, Terence de Vere. IRELAND (NY: Walker
and Company; Lond: Thames and Hudson, 1968), pp.
10, 11, 12, 100, 101, 110, illus.   No. 34.
[Shaw as an Anglo-Irishman.]

1496 Wilpert,   Gero   von   (ed.).   LEXIKON DER
WELTLITERATUR: HAUPTWERKE DER WELTLITERATUR IN
CHARAKTERISTIKEN UND KURZINTERPRETATIONEN (Diction-
ary of World Literature Presented in Summaries and
Brief Interpretations) (Stuttgart: Alfred Kröner,
1968), pp. 46, 65, 153, 156, 160, 321-22, 420, 432-
33, 438-39, 444-45, 549, 554, 676-77, 681, 682, 714-
15, 720, 850, 1023, 1191.
[Summaries of *Androcles and the Lion, The Doctor's
Dilemma, Caesar and Cleopatra, Candida, Cashel Byron's
Profession, Mrs. Warren's Profession, Widowers' Houses,
Heartbreak House, Saint Joan, Arms and the Man, The Apple
Cart, Captain Brassbound's Conversion, Major Barbara, You
Never Can Tell, The Man of Destiny, Man and Superman, The
Millionairess, Pygmalion, The Devil's Disciple,* and *Back
to Methuselah.*]   [In German.]

1497 Zhaĭchenko,   G.   A.   "Teatry   Moskvy   (po
materialam arkhivov i periodicheskoĭ pechati)" (The
Theaters of Moscow [From Archival Materials and
Periodical Literature]) in RUSSKIĬ SOVETSKIĬ TEATR
1917-1921, ed by A. Z. Ĭufit (Soviet Russian Theater
1917-1921) (Leningrad: "Iskusstvo," 1968) pp. 373-
84.
Arms and the Man was produced 6 November 1918, by the
Rogozhsko-Simonovskiĭ Soviet Theater at the former

"Vulcan" Cinema. *The Doctor's Dilemma* was produced in 1918 at the former Korsh Theater. [In Russian.]

1969

1498 Adams, Elsie B. "A 'Lawrentian' Novel by Bernard Shaw," D. H. LAWRENCE REVIEW, II (1969), 245-53.
Although Shaw and Lawrence had very little in common and did not hold each other in high regard, Shaw wrote a novel, *Cashel Byron's Profession*, which anticipated in its characters and incidents Lawrence's LADY CHATTERLEY'S LOVER. They have unconventional intellectual heroines, strikingly similar settings, lovers of great physical attractiveness and of lower class, and a rejection of the values of the ruling class. Despite these likenesses, one novel is a satire on aristocratic propriety and human frailty and the other a poetic defense of sensual love.

1499 Albert, Sidney P. "Shaw's Advice to the Players of *Major Barbara*," THEATRE SURVEY, X (May 1969), 1-17.
[Material collected to exhibit Shaw's ideas about the production and acting of *Major Barbara*, dealing exclusively with the 1905 Court Theatre production. Material pertaining to subsequent revivals to be published later. Included are rehearsal letters written by Shaw to the two principal players, Louis Calvert (Undershaft) and Annie Russell (Barbara). Also a letter from Shaw to J. E. Vedrenne concerning casting problems, and portions of a talk delivered to a women's club by Annie Russell in 1908, "George Bernard Shaw at Rehearsals of *Major Barbara*." Finally, a summary and critique of the whole rehearsal experience and early *Major Barbara* performances in a letter from Shaw to Eleanor Robson, 24 December 1905.]

1500 Arnold, Armin. "Georg Kaiser und G.B. Shaw: Eine Interpretation der JÜDISCHEN WITWE" (Georg Kaiser and G.B. Shaw: An Interpretation of THE JEWISH WIDOW), GERMAN LIFE AND LETTERS, ns XXIII (Oct 1969), 85-92.
The plot of Georg Kaiser's play THE JEWISH WIDOW (1911) is closely patterned after Shaw's *Man and Superman*. Like

Shaw, Kaiser uses detailed stage directions; his characters, too, talk a lot and act little. Kaiser also uses inversion of traditional concepts, a favorite Shavian device: he inverts the familiar biblical story of Judith. Kaiser's plays THE TEMPTATION (1917) and FLIGHT TO VENICE (1923) also seem to be inspired by Shaw's *Man and Superman*. [In German.]

1501 Barnes, John. "G.B.S. Teaching How and What to Think," SATURDAY REVIEW, (21 June 1969), 35-36. [An essay review of Louis Crompton's SHAW THE DRAMATIST (1969).]

After the *Unpleasant Plays* Shaw was finished with "surgical operations without the benefit of the usual laughing gas," and he took up the melodramatic form which he considered the ideal medium for the moral re-education of the masses. *Arms and the Man* and *The Devil's Disciple* challenged British jingoism and satirized poetic views of love and war. In the much more difficult *Caesar and Cleopatra* Shaw demands that his audience think deeply about the moral and social significance of killing. Only after this did Shaw go on to what Crompton calls "the kingdom peculiarly his own," the period during which he wrote *Major Barbara, Pygmalion, Heartbreak House,* and *Saint Joan,* as always, willing to "hope and think and challenge" his audience.

1502 Barr, Alan P. "'G. B. S.': The Self-Created Persona," UNIVERSITY REVIEW, XXXV (March 1969), 187-96.

Behind Shaw's mask of witty dramatist and court jester is the dedicated serious moralist. The former is a conscious creation, and Shaw wore the mask that the moralist might better convey his message. On the unconscious level this was Shaw's way of solving the problem of ego identity.

1503 Beerbohm, Max. MORE THEATRES, 1898-1903 (Lond: Rupert Hart-Davis, 1969), pp. 11, 12, 13, 17-27, 35, 70, 71, 267, 271, 335-37, 385, 477, 580-82, 596. [Reprints "G.B.S. Oblige (1898), "Mr. Shaw's Profession" (1898), "Mr. Shaw's Profession" (1898), "*Captain Brassbound's Conversion*" (1900), "A Triple Bill" (1902), and other reviews that mention Shaw, all from the SRL.]

1504 Bentley, Eric. "From George Bernard Shaw to G. B. S.," in READER'S ENCYCLOPEDIA OF WORLD DRAMA (NY: Thomas Y. Crowell, 1969), pp. 775-78; rptd ISh, VII (1969), 33-36.
[Biographical facts, development of Shaw's ideas and of his career as critic and writer, his public reception and an evaluation.]

1505 Berst, Charles A. "The Anatomy of Greatness in *Caesar and Cleopatra*," JOURNAL OF ENGLISH AND GERMANIC PHILOLOGY, LXVIII (Jan 1969), 74-91; rptd in BERNARD SHAW AND THE ART OF DRAMA, by Charles A. Berst (1973).
Although it is true that Shaw makes his Caesar effective by making him antiheroic, portraying him from the point of view of his valet, this is not an adequate explanation for the greatness and magic of the role. Just as important as the valet viewpoint is the audience's perspective regarding Caesaar's influence on his "valets." In addition the intimate focus provides insight by contrasting Caesar's public image with the private reality. The number of opposing traits which Shaw has given Caesar probably contributes most strikingly to building the complexity and power of his character; his stature grows as a synthesis of extremes, and it retains all the vital assertion of those extremes while tempering and balancing them with their opposites. Shaw further employs humor, irony, anticlimax, history, fantasy and mystery to create his total dramatic effect.

1506 Boxill, Roger. "Shaw and the Doctors," DAI, XXX (1969), 1553A. Published dissertation, Columbia University, 1966; published as SHAW AND THE DOCTORS (NY and Lond: Basic Books, 1969).

1507 Boxill, Roger. SHAW AND THE DOCTORS. (NY and Lond: Basic Books, 1969).
The views expressed in Shaw's plays and polemics represent the best humanist tradition of medical history. It is the tradition of treating the patient as a human being, of regarding disease as a problem of human welfare, of building mind and body through creating a healthful life. Shaw's non-orthodox views regarding medicine and his love of overstating them have caused him to be labeled a "crank". But he is a crank only in the sense that he "tilts against the windmills of orthodoxy." His

opposition to this orthodoxy was grounded in his Fabian
Socialism and his (anti-Darwinian) Vitalism. Shaw wrote
numerous letters to the *Times* and other journals [several
reproduced here in part] expressing his reservations in
regard to vaccination, vivisection, the germ theory, and
the medical profession as a whole. He discussed the same
issues in longer essays ("What Is to Be Done with the
Doctors?"). As the "twentieth-century Molière" he
presented doctors and medical problems in his dramas (*The
Doctor's Dilemma, Too True to Be Good, The Philanderer*),
as well as in their Prefaces. Whereas Molière wrote
comedies which gave no answers to the problems raised,
Shaw's plays are tragi-comic, with Socialism and Vitalism
given as ready answers.

1508 Boynton, Robert W., and Maynard Mack.
INTRODUCTION TO THE PLAY (NY: Hayden Book Company,
1969; rvsd 1976), pp. 9-10, 30-42, 59-70, 93-96.
[Act by act analysis, with particular discussion of
character, setting and convention, of *The Devil's
Disciple*.]

1509 Brody, Catherine.   "Hallie Flanagan Davis,"
ISh, VIII (1969-70), 29-30.
Hallie Flanagan Davis (1891-1969) was director of the
Federal Theater Project from its inception in 1935 until
Congress ended the Project in 1939. Mrs. Flanagan had
agreed with Shaw that "the function of the theater is to
stir people, to make them think," and Shaw in answer to
her request had granted the Project the right to present
"anything of mine you like." The Shaw cycle eventually
included nine plays.

1510 Brown, Ivor. "The SATURDAY Story," DRAMA, XCV
(Winter 1969), 41-43.
When Max Beerbohm succeeded Shaw as the drama reviewer for
the SATURDAY REVIEW, it became the vehicle of a critical
attitude completely inimical to Shaw and his view of the
theater.

1511 Burgunder, Bernard F.   "Shaw and Ethel
Barrymore?" CORNELL LIBRARY JOURNAL, IX (Autumn
1969), 58-64.
A letter from Shaw to Sally Fairchild, dated 23 March
1897, complains about her having given letters of
introduction to young actresses; he demands that she send

no further "victims" to him. It is probable that the actress in question was Ethel Barrymore. [Complete letter reproduced.]

1512 Carpenter, Charles A. BERNARD SHAW AND THE ART OF DESTROYING IDEALS: THE EARLY PLAYS. (Madison: U of Wisconsin P, 1969).

The great dramatist, thought Shaw, must work for world-betterment; in his early plays he sought to do this by attempting to destroy ideals. His *Unpleasant Plays* is an attack on specific economic and sociological illusions fostered by a capitalist system, and the blame for these evils is squarely placed on the society as a whole. In his *Pleasant Plays* Shaw's method changed, but his aim was the same; instead of attacking ideals by exposing their unpleasant effects, he created characters who appeared ridiculous when acting according to their ideals, thus unsettling these ideals in the mind of the spectator. The *Three Plays for Puritans* approximate the familiar forms of the drama of the nineties, yet they humanize these forms by undermining their "idealistic notions of motivation and supplanting them with Shavian premises reflecting the distinctiveness and primacy of the individual will." Throughout all three of these groups of plays Shaw extolled natural virtue above ideal goodness; his method was not that of amalgamating case and argument, but rather that of "sharpshooting at ideals."

1513 Chappelow, Allan. SHAW--"THE CHUCKER-OUT": A BIOGRAPHICAL EXPOSITION AND CRITIQUE, AND A COMPANION TO AND COMMENTARY ON "SHAW THE VILLAGER." (Lond: Allen & Unwin, 1969; NY: AMS P, 1972).

[A companion volume to SHAW THE VILLAGER (1961) which had been a symposium of the reminiscences of some 60 village people who had known Shaw well, this book brings Shaw back to comment on the topics of fundamental importance raised by the villagers. It is an attempt to assist towards a better understanding of Shaw by clarifying his paradoxical character and attitude to life, but often shared and felt strongly about by the world at large. Shaw's own views, primarily in the form of letters or speeches, are given on such topics as democracy, dictatorship, war, communism, capital punishment, economics, vegetarianism, temperance, morality, love, sex, theater, and reform of the English alphabet. Also included are the texts of his printed postcards, versions of his Will, plus photographs, cartoons, examples of the Shaw alphabet, and lecture cards.]

1514 Cindrić, Pavao *et al.*   HRVATSKO NARODNO KAZALISTE 1894-1969 (The Croatian National Theater 1894-1969) (Zagreb: Naprijed, 1969).
[History of *Mrs. Warren's Profession, Candida, Caesar and Cleopatra, Pygmalion, The Doctor's Dilemma,* and *The Devil's Disciple* in Jugoslavia.]   [In Croatian.]

1515 Cirillo, Nancy Rockmore.   "The Poet Armed: Wagner, D'Annunzio, Shaw," DAI, XXX (1969), 1555A. Unpublished dissertation, New York University, 1968.

1516 Cordell, Richard A., "Bernard Shaw and Common Sense," ISh, VIII (Fall 1969), 17.
[An abstract of Professor Cordell's lecture given to New York Shavians on 24 May 1969, about common sense through the ages and the common sense of Shaw regarding many topics: war, religion, romance, government, economics, medicine, criminology.]

1517 Cordell, Richard A., "Shavian Notes," ISh, VII (1969), 39.
[Notes on significant productions of Shaw plays (*The Devil's Disciple* in Paris in the Cocteau translation); also notes on recently published Shaw-related material.]

1518 Cordell, Richard A., "Shavian Notes," ISh, VIII (1969-70), 20-21.
[A report of noteworthy current Shaw productions with a final word from the author as newly elected president of the New York Shavians, in which he compares the Theater of the Absurd unfavorably with Shavian drama.]

1519 Crane, Gladys Margaret.   "The Characterization of the Comic Women Characters of George Bernard Shaw," DA, XXIX (1969), 3250A-3251A.   Unpublished dissertation, Indiana University, 1968.

1520 Crompton, Louis.   "Introduction," "A Bernard Shaw Chronology," "Selected Bibliography," "Note on the Text and the British Museum Manuscript," and "Notes," ARMS AND THE MAN BY BERNARD SHAW, ed by Louis Crompton (Indianapolis and NY: Bobbs-Merrill [Bobbs-Merrill Shaw Series], 1969), pp. ix-xxi, passim.

Robert Bontine Cunninghame Graham was Shaw's model for
Sergius and Sidney Webb for Bluntschli: The Servo-
Bulgarian war of 1885 served as Shaw's ideal for debunking
war. Ultimately Shaw wanted to raise questions about
human ethics: Naturalism vs. Idealism. Shaw's satire
challenges our critical intellects and our sensibilities.
[Photographs and map.]

1521 Crompton, Louis. SHAW THE DRAMATIST. (Lincoln: U of Nebraska P, 1969); Chap 10 rptd in
BERNARD SHAW'S PLAYS, ed by Warren Sylvester Smith
(1970).
Shaw's major plays may best be understood when considered
in relation to their social, philosophical, and historical
backgrounds. The thinkers and documents which influenced
Shaw, the ideas and values which he held and examined, and
the real-life prototypes who served as models for his
dramatic characters are all a part of that intellectual
ambience out of which the dramas were created. Shaw began
in his *Unpleasant Plays* by attacking the values of the
Victorian bourgeoisie and by exposing their social crimes.
Arms and the Man, when viewed from the point of view of
Shaw's work as a whole, is a narrow play, but it does
provide the reader with a look at a kind of false heroism
before he goes on to discover Shaw's heroic exemplars.
Caesar and Cleopatra is a military melodrama. Here he
asks his audience to think deeply about violence and
justice in a context which dramatizes the conflict between
Old Testament and New Testament morality. Here too Shaw
attempts to define his idea of heroism. With *Major
Barbara*, Shaw created a new genre--the "philosophical
comedy," thus entering a "kingdom peculiarly his own,"
showing his "wit at its most brilliant, his speculations
at their boldest, and his purview broadened to encompass
what he has called 'the destiny of nations.'" In the
tragi-comedy *Heartbreak House*, Shaw is telling us that we
must be prepared, as mortals in a world of men, "to abide
the consequences of our social actions, or negligences;"
whereas in his "world classic," *Back to Methuselah*, he
looks to the future to answer questions as to the root of
social suffering, and the form which an ideal commonwealth
should take. Finally, *Saint Joan* "stands alone as Shaw's
last great tribute to human greatness . . . the final
masterpiece of a man who was willing to hope and think and
challenge his readers to the end."

1522 "Czyżby Renesans Bernarda Shaw?" [Can There Be
a Renaissance of Bernard Shaw?] ORZEŁ BIAŁY
(Brussels), XLIV (1969), 26.
Although it was said that at his death Shaw was obsolete,
the film MY FAIR LADY was a great success, and through it
Shaw found a new audience. Also there has been a torrent
of writing about Shaw. In fact, Shaw is more enduring
than the newer playwrights who seemed to replace him. [In
Polish.]

1523 Dietrich, R. F. PORTRAIT OF THE ARTIST AS A
YOUNG SUPERMAN: A STUDY OF SHAW'S NOVELS (Gaines-
ville: U of Florida P, 1969).
The history of the novels: Shaw's novels arae as true to
life as any fiction, and their language escapes the
"starchy rhetorical patterns" of their time. If plot is a
significant ordering of events to convey a theme, then
Shaw's novels are not plotless. Everything that happens
in *Immaturity* happens because it contributes to the identification of Robert Smith. The characters and incidents
that seem to have no other function than to carry Shaw's
ideas are really integral to the novels' art. *Immaturity*
is Shaw's best novel, and the title does not apply to Shaw
himself.

The novels as autobiography: Smith, the hero of
Immaturity, is a "monster of propriety" because he
overcompensates for his sense of social inferiority by
being extremely correct. The traditional solution of
marriage to the problem of joining society is dismissed,
but professional identity is made available to Smith.

The Irrational Knot focuses on the problems of possessing
an unusual mind. Conolly, the hero, is a "monster of the
mind," of rational control. This inverts the real Shaw.
The pretenses of idealism are exposed by rational realism.
Shaw insisted that the mind, the irrational unconcscious,
was the major source of the irrational in man. Owen Jack,
in *Love among the Artists*, symbolizes Shaw's turn to the
irrational. He is a "monster of the body." The effective
personality finds its energy in brute irrationality. The
problem of *Cashel Byron's Profession* is the synthesis
between the mind and body. Shaw was aware, however, that
moral genius could meet defeat when confronted with brute
savagery.

By the time Shaw wrote *An Unsocial Socialist*, he could see
the humor in the way some people regarded him as a monster
and learned to play the monster role as a joke on those

others as well as on himself. The paradox of the fantastic character G. B. S. is that Shaw was pretending to be something he really was. "The clown was something of a superman."

"Almost all of Shaw's work and life can be understood as an adventure in search of 'god,' the ground of Being, Authority, Motive, and Reality"--a search for a father.

Secular creeds did not provide the Shavian hero with the divine sanction he craved. His adventures in search of god involve him in a kind of romance, "The Romance of the Real." Shaw's call for the Superman is an attempt to restore values to a world where worth was leveled by democracy, and social cohesion was fragmented by capitalism.

1524 England, A[llen]. W[illiam]. MAN AND SUPERMAN (G. BERNARD SHAW) (Oxford: Basil Blackwell [Notes on English Literature], 1968).
Man and Superman was designed to entertain and stimulate thought. An important technical novelty of the play is that discussion is identical with the play itself, but Shaw nevertheless relies on traditional elements of drama. The dramatic action of *Superman* does not fit the philosophical scheme: the deadly struggle between artist-man and mother-woman is not acted out. Shaw's characters are limited, but this is determined by the mode of comedy of manners. Shaw's comedy is genuine and generous. The stage directions may indicate a weakness, but they are useful. Although the Hell scene has no direct affect on the action of the play, there is continuity between the two parts. The action of the scene is the struggle of the characters to establish the purpose of life. Shaw's significance derives more from his imaginative vision than from his philosophical message. [This book was designed primarily for students. Study questions are included.]

1525 Esslin, Martin. *"Back to Methuseslah,"* P&P, XVI (Sept 1969), 24-27.
The National Theatre is testing Shaw in the best possible performance; Shaw was wrong in judging *Back to Methuselah* his masterpiece. It is both dogmatic and dated. There can be no doubt that Shaw's biology is untenable. But it is worth reviving. [Photographs.] [Letter protesting Esslin's views on Shaw's science by Henry Adler, Oct 1969, p. 12, with Esslin's answer.]

1526 Evans, T. F. "Notes from London," ISh, VII (1969), 43.
In surveying the London theater scene one sees very little which would satisfy Shaw's requirement that theater should be among other things "a factory of thought" and "an elucidator of social conduct."

1527 Evans, T. F. "Notes from London," ISh, VII (1969-70), 28.
Two current Shaw productions are *Back to Methuselah* at the National Theatre (evidence of how valuable it is to have a national theater that will choose its productions not solely on commercial grounds) and *You Never Can Tell* in Berlin, excellently performed in spite of a translation which seems not as witty as the original.

1528 Evans, T. F. "Shaw and Education," SHAVIAN, IV (Summer 1969), 16-21.
Education of all kinds always fascinated Shaw; one of his fundamental principles was that children had rights just as parents did, (early discussed in the Preface to *Misalliance*. He denounced all schools as merely places where children can be put out of the way of their parents and where their heads are filled with useless information. He considered that a child should learn certain things to enable it better to carry out tasks beneficial to society (in *Everybody's Political What's What*) but also favored teaching everybody everything, "for we would be savages if we knew nothing beyond the things we can do." In the preface to the YEAR-BOOK OF THE WORKERS' EDUCATIONAL ASSOCIATION (1918), he called for a "civic education" which would include "education in controversy and in liberty, in manners and in courage, in scepticism, in discontent and betterment."

1529 Frazer, Frances. "An Edition of *Three Plays for Puritans*." Unpublished dissertation, Birkbeck, College, Universisty of London, 1969.
[Listed in DAID.]

1530 Furlong, William Benedict. "The Shaw-Chesterton Literary Relationship," DAI, XXIX (1969), 3609A-3610A.
Dissertation, Pennsylvania State University, 1968, published as GBS/GKC: SHAW AND CHESTERTON: THE METAPHYSICAL JESTERS (1970).

1531 Gibbs, A. M. SHAW (Edinburgh: Oliver & Boyd [Writers and Critics], 1969).
The guiding principle of this study is Shaw's own advice, "If you are to get any good out of me you must accept me as a quite straightforward practitioner of the art I make my living by." Thus its central concern is the plays themselves, and Shaw's life is treated only in so far as certain experiences relate directly to his outlook as a dramatist. Though Shaw's intellectual stance is often deeply pessimistic, he wrote "the greater part of his work in the passionate belief or hope that man's lot could be changed for the better." [The plays up through *You Never Can Tell* ("the last and best of the works in *Plays Pleasant*") are handled in the initial chapter; in "Men and Superman" *The Three Plays for Puritans* and *Man and Superman* are analyzed; there follow treatments in chronological order of the major plays up to *Heartbreak House*, which warrants nearly an entire chapter, since it is the "most allusive and poetic" of all Shaw's plays as well as his most powerful attack on contemporary society. *Back to Methuselah, Saint Joan* and the later plays are dealt with briefly, and the final chapter is on "Shaw and the Critics." Selected bibliography included.]

1532 Glicksberg, Charles I. THE IRONIC VISION IN MODERN LITERATURE (The Hague: Martinus Nijhoff, 1969), pp. 36, 178-81, 182, 218.
Because Shaw is a utopian reformer, the Devil in *Man and Superman* is not sufficiently persuasive. His truth of the ironic vision is effectively silenced.

1533 Gottfried, Martin. OPENING NIGHTS: THEATRE CRITICISM OF THE SIXTIES. (NY: G. P. Putnam's Sons, 1969), pp. 184, 272-74.
[Critical survey with remarks about the London production of *You Never Can Tell*.]

1534 Grazhdanskaîa, Z. "Bernard Shou" (Bernard Shaw), in B. SHOU: P'ESY (B. Shaw: Plays) (Moscow: np, 1969), pp. 5-20.
[Not seen.] [In Russian.]

1535 Hatcher, Joe Branch. "G. B. S. on the Minor Dramatists of the Nineties," DAI, XXIX (1969), 2212A-2213A. Unpublished dissertation, University of Kansas, 1968.

1536 Haywood, Charles. "George Bernard Shaw on Incidental Music in the Shakespearian Theater," SHAKESPEARE JAHRBUCH (Weimar), CV (1960), 168-82.
"Shaw, the musically perceptive dramatist, made many discerning comments on the quality and the appropriate use of incidental music in theatrical productions, particularly those of Shakespeare." He was especially critical of noisy, showy, and stylistically unrelated incidental music and favored music which was faithful to the "Age of Shakespeare," that is Tudor music, performed if possible on contemporary instruments.

1537 Haywood, Charles. "George Bernard Shaw on Shakespearian Music and the Actor," SHAKESPEARE QUARTERLY, XX (Autumn 1969), 417-26.
Though Shaw frequently questioned the sense in Shakespeare's plays, he never failed to acknowledge the divine sound they contained. At the same time that he was railing against Shakespeare's "unbearable platitudes, his incredible unsuggestiveness, his intellectual sterility," he was praising the "splendor of sound, the magic of romantic illusion, the majesty of emphasis and every poetic quality that can waken the heart-stir." As music critic and dramatist, Shaw was in a unique position to appreciate Shakespeare's work, and he constantly criticized actors who were deaf to the Shakespearian music, and directors who cut Shakespeare's plays without regard for the music.

1538 "H.G. & G.B.S.: Varied Reflections on Two Edwardian Polymaths," TLS, 27 Nov 1969, pp. 1349-50. [Review of BERNARD SHAW: A REASSESSMENT, by Colin Wilson (1969).]
A place in English letters is still uncertain for both Shaw and Wells. They are best regarded as Edwardian polymaths, as humanists suffering from *Weltverbesserungswahn*. It could be argued that in both men the polemicist eventually dominated the artist (as in *Back to Methuselah*); or alternatively that the limits of art are too narrow and that a new aesthetics of polemics is what is called for.

Response: Hibbs, Christopher. "To the Editor," TLS, 18 Dec 1969, p. 1450. Your reviewer's remarks are hasty and wrong-headed. The review is humorless, vague, unperceptive and pedantic.

[For further response, see Colin Wilson (1969) and James Redmond (1971).]

1539 Holloway, Joseph. JOSEPH HOLLOWAY'S IRISH THEATRE, Vol II: 1932-1937, ed by Robert Hogan and Michael J. O'Neill (Dixon, California: Proscenium P, 1969), pp. 8, 12, 23, 26, 34, 40-41, 48, 49, 68, 80n.
[A journal of theater-going in Dublin by Joseph Holloway with comments on Shaw.]

1540 Huggett, Richard. THE TRUTH ABOUT 'PYGMALION' (Lond: Heinemann; NY: Random House, 1969).
"The utter, grotesque truth" about *Pygmalion*, is a story involving three monstrous egotists: Shaw as author/director of the London production of the play, Mrs. Patrick Campbell in the role of Eliza Doolittle, a role which had been written for her, and Sir Herbert Beerbohm Tree, playing Henry Higgins. This story forms one of the most bizarre chapters in theater history and can be reconstructed from Shaw's director's notes, correspondence between Shaw and Mrs. Pat and his letters and notes to others, photographs, cartoons, newspapers articles. [All of which are reproduced in the volume.]

1541 Hynes, Samuel. "H.G. and G.B.S.," TLS, Nov 1969; rptd in EDWARDIAN OCCASIONS, ESSAYS ON ENGLISH WRITING IN THE EARLY TWENTIETH CENTURY by Samuel Hynes (NY: Oxford UP, 1972), pp. 18-23.
Shaw and Wells have such unstable reputations because of the quality and variety of their public activity. And Shaw and Wells do not pass when measured against the critical commonplaces of the Age of Eliot. Neither played the artist's role in public. They can best be regarded as two Edwardian polymaths. They are both polemicists. They are both "giants who were classics in themselves."

1542 Ivasheva, V. V. "Bernard Shou" (Bernard Shaw), ISTORIIA ZARUBEZHNOĬ LITERATURY POSLE OKTIABR'SKOĬ REVOLUTSKIĬ TOM I [1917-1945]) (History of Foreign Literature after the October Revolution [1917-1945]) (Moscow: Moskovskii universitet, 1969), pp. 207-17.
Heartbreak House was a tragic admission of the crisis of English bourgeois civilization, the lies and inhumanity of capitalist attitudes, and it marks a new stage in Shaw's creative development. Shaw interpreted in his own way

Chekhov's theme of the collapse of traditions and foundations of society. Shaw was one of the first English
writers to recognize the significance of the October
Revolution. However, *Back to Methuselah* reveals the
mistaken direction of Shaw's searchings, Creative Evolution, despite its witty attacks on bourgeois society. In
Saint Joan, Shaw provides a very wide historical
background to Joan's tragic fate. It was a step forward
in comparison with *The Devil's Disciple*, without the
scepticism of the latter. Shaw's realism took the form of
political extravaganzas directed against the political and
economic system of England as in *The Apple Cart*, which is
more profound and more negative towards the economic and
political life of capitalist society than the earlier
Heartbreak. In his journalism of the twenties and
thirties, Shaw sharply attacked the social order,
imperialist wars, colonialism, and up to 1950 he repelled
attacks on communism by critics who called him merely a
joker. [In Russian.]

1543 Jullian, Philippe. OSCAR WILDE, trans from
French (Lond: Constable & Co Ltd, 1969), pp. 35,
133, 184, 200, 255, 275-76, 317-18, 345, 358, 404.
Shaw owed to Wilde the technique of paradox that enabled
him to insult the English without angering them. Only
Shaw supported Wilde in the censorship of SALOMÉ. Shaw
was faithful, but obtuse about Wilde.

1544 Kantorovich, I. B. "Uslovnaîa 'fantastika'
intellektual'noĭ drame Shou (K voprosu o svoeobraz-
nim tvorcheskogo metoda Shou)" (Conventional 'Fantastic' in Shaw's Intellectual Drama [On the
Original Creative Method of Shaw]), UCHENYE ZAPISKI
SVERDLOVSKOGO PED. INST. (Sverdlovsk), VIII (1969),
3-29.
[Not seen.] [In Russian.]

1545 Keough, Lawrence Christopher. "The Critical
Reception of the Major Plays of G. Bernard Shaw
Performed in New York: 1894-1950," DAI, XXIX (1969)
4491A-4492A. Unpublished dissertation, University
of Southern California, 1969.

1546 Keough, Lawrence C[hristopher]. "Shaw's Introduction to New York: The Mansfield Productions
1894-1900," SHAVIAN, IV (Summer 1969), 6-10.

In 1894 and again in 1900 Richard Mansfield produced *Arms and the Man* on the New York stage; in 1897, *The Devil's Disciple*. The plays were received with a mixture of "amusement, delight, scepticism, and impatience." Though the critics were sure that Shaw was a clever entertainer, "they were uncertain of his rank as a dramatist because they did not understand him." [Reviews from NYT, NEW YORK TRIBUNE, and NEW YORK WORLD reproduced.]

1547 Knepper, B. G. "Shaw Rewriting Shaw: A Fragment," Shaw R, XII (Sept 1969), 104-10.
[Reproduction of first and second holograph versions with revisions of *Mrs. Warren's Profession*, Act III.] These when compared with the final version of the play demonstrate that Shaw had developed a sound sense of drama already early in his career.

1548 Knightley, Phillip, and Colin Simpson. THE SECRET LIVES OF LAWRENCE OF ARABIA (Lond: Thomas Nelson and Sons, 1969; NY: McGraw-Hill, 1970), pp. 178, 222, 225, 260, 287, 290-4, 298, 300-2.
Shaw persuaded Lawrence to suppress in THE SEVEN PILLARS OF WISDOM the fact that Britain had no intention of allowing the Arabs a government of their own. Shaw's appeal to the government for a command for Lawrence brought no result. Shaw helped edit THE SEVEN PILLARS.

1549 Koltai, Ralph, in conversation with Michael Billington. "The Designer Talks," P&P, XVII (Nov 1969), 50-53.
[Koltai discusses his designs for the National Theatre production of *Back to Methuselah*.] I tried to achieve a sense of mystery. I found the play boring to read; I got my feeling for it before I read it. [Photographs.]

1550 Kuehne, A. de. "El mito de Pigmalión en Shaw, Pirandello y Solana" (The Myth of Pygmalion in Shaw, Pirandello and Solana), LATIN AMERICAN THEATER REVIEW, II (1969), 31-40.
Mexican playwright Rafael Solana's A SU IMAGEN Y SEMEJANZA depicts a Pygmalion who is a conductor and shows the influence of Shaw. [In Spanish.]

1551 Lambert, J. W. "Plays in Performance, London," DRAMA, XCV (Winter 1969), 14-28.

Only *The Gospel of Brothers Barnabas* from *Back to Methuselah* holds up.

1552 Larson, Gale Kjelshus. "Bernard Shaw's *Caesar and Cleopatra* as History," DAI, XXIX (1969), 4495A. Unpublished dissertation, University of Nebraska, 1968.

1553 Lawrence, Kenneth. "Dialectic and Drama: The Twentieth Century Theater of Ideas," DAI, XXIX (1969), 4496A. Unpublished dissertation, University of Wisconsin, 1968.

1554 Leary, Daniel J. "Dialectical Action in *Major Barbara*," ShawR, XII (May 1969), 46-58.
Shaw constructed *Major Barbara* on a dialectical basis: spiritual/physical, poetic/practical, emotional/intellectual. The overall movement of the play is from Sin (Act I) to Suffering (Act II) and on to Atonement (Act III), and Barbara's own development comes of a synthesis of the qualities she has from her parents with the intellectual balance of Cusins. Further examples of the dialectic action: the ironic caricature offered by Snobby Price and Rummy Mitchens who cannot evolve; the confrontation of the blood and fire message of the Salvation Army with Undershaft's sort of blood and fire; Barbara's final flight toward "the unveiling of an eternal light in the Valley of the Shadow," and her assertion that "There is no wicked side: life is all one . . . ."

1555 Leary, Daniel J. "The Heralds of Convergence: Teilhard and Shaw," VOICES OF CONVERGENCE (Milwaukee: Bruce Publishing Company, 1969), pp. 1-32.
Both Shaw and Pierre Teilhard de Chardin had a theory of the world that was supported by a religion that predates Christianity and has its roots in the archetypal imagination, although they were diametrically opposed on the surface. Shaw as a religious thinker is far from dead, and there is also a religious sensitivity in Shaw the person. In *Back to Methuselah* Shaw puts his Life-Force theory to the test. Both Shaw and Teilhard were evolutionists and had tendencies to pantheism, a Manichean view of matter, and a semi-Pelagian view of man.

1556 Mattews, John F. GEORGE BERNARD SHAW. (NY: Columbia U P [Columbia Essays on Modern Writers Series], 1969).
Next to Shakespeare, Shaw is the most popular dramatist since classical antiquity, and his theater criticism is the most influential since Lessing's HAMBURG DRAMATURGY. Both as critic and playwright he championed what he thought of as realism: "the performance should be true to the play; the play should be true to life." Shaw's eagerness to make the theater a vehicle for truth guided him in his choices for drama topics and in the manner in which he presented them. Though his playwriting lies in the great historic tradition of producing action through conflict of purposes; what makes his plays seem unconventional is that the characters are enormously opinionated and articulate. A favorite Shavian method of characterization, which often constituted the substance of the plots as well, was the process of "discovery of unexpected positive possibilities"; thus whatever the outcome of a Shaw play, its plot was devised on the basis of what would happen if "real people" were involved, and it worked itself out so as to reveal the unexpected truth about such people. In this way Shaw demonstrated his abiding faith in men, even though he had very little faith in institutions--economic, political, or religious.

1557 Mattson, Mary Catherine. "Censorship and the Victorian Drama," DA, XXIX (1969), 4498A. Unpublished dissertation, University of Southern California, 1969.

1558 Maurino, Ferdinando. "And the Ides Failed," ARLINGTON QUARTERLY, II (1969), 50-56.
Shaw's characterization of Caesar has some flaws, but when he "stands before the Sphinx, we have a premonition of what is to come in the final years of Caesar's life."

1559 Mills, John A. LANGUAGE AND LAUGHTER; COMIC DICTION IN THE PLAYS OF BERNARD SHAW. (Tucson: U of Arizona P, 1969).
Shaw often achieves a comic effect through juxtapositions of characters' ideas, their actions, and their use of language. To analyze Shaw's linguistic techniques is to understand better his comedy. Shaw creates a comic clash with dialect by juxtaposing enunciation with vocabulary (Drinkwater in *Captain Brassbound's Conversion* and Eliza in *Pygmalion*). He uses many varieties of linguistic

sapytire to evoke laughter (special style: Sergius; empty verbiage: both Morell and Marchbanks; forensic circumlocution: Broadbent in *John Bull's Other Island*). Shaw on occasion creates characters who speak as automata, for whom language becomes a reflex action; he employs various sorts of word-play and punning; and he even causes the neutral voice in certain situations to contribute to the comic effect.

1560 Minney, R. J. THE BOGUS IMAGE OF GEORGE BERNARD SHAW. (Lond: Frewin; 1969); RECOLLECTIONS OF GEORGE BERNARD SHAW (Englewood Cliffs, New Jersey: Prentice-Hall, 1969).
[This book, which is a mosaic of impressions of Shaw rather than a biography, contains material gathered from occasional conversations with people who knew Shaw together with a good deal taken from his own writings. It gives particular attention to the private in contrast to the public G. B. S. and takes up such matters as his sex life, his tastes in music, his courtship and marriage, his financial affairs, his travels, his daily routine, his visitors, plus numerous anecdotes, such as a Shaw/Bertrand Russell bicycle ride or lunches with Charlotte and famous guests. No footnotes or bibliography.]

1561 Montagu, Ivor. WITH EISENSTEIN IN HOLLYWOOD (NY: International Publishers; Berlin: Seven Seas Books, 1969), pp. 32, 35, 42, 63-65.
[Shaw and Eisenstein. Mary Pickford and Douglas Fairbanks's desire to film *Caesar and Cleopatra*.]

1562 Muir, Kenneth. "Shaw and Shakespeare," FESTSCHRIFT, RUDOLF STAMM, ZU SEINEM SECHZIGSTEN GEBURTSTAG, ed by Edward Kolb and Jörg Hasler, (Bern: Francke, 1969), pp. 13-22.
Shaw's attacks on Shakespeare, whom he had in fact loved from his youth, were motivated by a desire to counteract hypocritical bardolatry and to propagandize for Ibsen and the new drama and thus indirectly for himself as new dramatist as well. Although in many ways Shaw's campaign was justifiable and salutary, he made a great mistake in assuming that the views expressed by Shakespeare's characters were his own. He believed that Shakespeare's philosophy of life was shallow and that he did not have a passion for reforming the world, whereas he himself wrote plays to convert the public to his own views on life and society. Late in life, however, he became anxious to

point out his affinities with Shakespeare. Shaw was ahead of his time in understanding Shakespearian characterization, and he rightly stressed the difference between a dramatic character and a person in real life. Above all he understood and appreciated Shakespeare's mastery of style and the supreme importance of the Shakespearian "musical score," or "word music."

1563 Munitz, Barry. "Joan of Arc and Modern Drama," DAI, XXIX (1969), 2720A. Unpublished dissertation, Princeton University, 1968.

1564 Nadel, Norman. A PICTORIAL HISTORY OF THE THEATRE GUILD, with special material by Lawrence Langner and Armina Marshall and an Introduction by Brooks Atkinson (NY: Crown Publishers, Inc., 1969), pp. 8, 10, 16, 17, 24, 26-28, 34-40, 44-51, 53, 63, 72, 88, 90, 101, 110, 112, 118, 137, 138, 192, 209, 210, 211, 214, 226, 228, 232, 248, 276.
[*Heartbreak House, Back to Methuselah, The Devil's Disciple, Saint Joan, Caesar and Cleopatra, Arms and the Man, The Man of Destiny, Androcles and the Lion, Pygmalion, The Doctor's Dilemma, Major Barbara, Too True to Be Good, The Simpleton of the Unexpected Isles, You Never Can Tell,* and *The Millionairess.* Heavily illustrated with photographs of the productions.]

1565 Naumov, Nićifor. "Junak Šoove Drame" (The Hero of Shavian Drama), ZBORNIK RADOVA POVODOM ČETRDES-ETOGODISNJICE OSNIVANJE KATEDRE ZA ENGLESKI JEZIK I KNJIŽEVNOST (Codex of Works on the Occasion of the Fortieth Anniversary of the Establishment of the Chair of English Language and Literature) (Beograd: Univerzitet u Beogradu, Odsek za Anglistiku, 1969), pp. 245-67.
Every analysis of Shaw's heroes must start with his theory of Creative Evolution. In *Candida, The Devil's Disciple, Major Barbara* and *The Shewing-up of Blanco Posnet* a different aspect of the hero's discovering his purpose is dramatized. Shaw describes the disinterestedness with which his hero pursues his superpersonal aim as well as the atrocious egotism of his disregard for others. The hero possesses a clear sense of reality. He does not fight for Socialism directly because he is not a personified idea but possesses a life of his own. Shaw has contributed to our understanding of a certain type of man. [In Serbian with English summary.]

1566 Nelson, Raymond S. *"Fanny's First Play* and THE
MILL ON THE FLOSS," Shaw R, XII (May 1969), 59-65.
Although Shaw owes much to George Eliot and admired her
spirit of independence, he dismissed her as a "spokesman
of an 'exhausted atmosphere.'" *Fanny's First Play* can be
seen as an ironic adaptation of THE MILL ON THE FLOSS
since both authors develop the same theme (contrasting
live and dead religion through characters who embody the
faiths they live by), though Shaw moves to a drastically
different conclusion.

1567 Nelson, Raymond S. "Shaw and Buchanan,"
ENGLISH LITERATURE IN TRANSITION, 1880-1920, XII
(1969), 99-103.
Robert Buchanan's Devil in his long narrative poem, THE
DEVIL'S CASE (1896) is a relative of sorts of Dick
Dudgeon, Shaw's "Diabolonian" hero of *The Devil's
Disciple*. Buchanan's Devil is the champion of mankind and
an enemy of God, the tyrant, the liar, the great orbidder
and eath-dealer. But whereas this Devil rails against
evils he puts little or nothing in their place. Dick
Dudgeon, on the other hand, is a vitalist and an
evolutionist, a creative and not a destructive force.

1568 Nelson, Raymond S. "Shaw's *Widowers' Houses*,"
RESEARCH STUDIES, XXXVII (March 1969), 27-37.
Shaw is an irrepressible apologist for modern religion.
Widowers' Houses is an attempt to bring the audience to an
awareness of sin and of its responsibility in the
conditions resulting from slum landlordism.

1569 Nelson, Raymond S. "Shaw: Turn-of-the-Century
Prophet," ARLINGTON QUARTERLY, II (Summer 1969),
112-19.
Shaw was a deeply religious man engaged in the salvation
of his contemporaries; he was an artist-philosopher
writing with moral fervor and communicating the ardor of
his vision of God, man, sin, and salvation. By his term
"Life Force," Shaw meant a purposive evolutionary thrust
noticeable in all creation. Evil takes many forms, mostly
social, and the Life Force is bent on the eradication of
them all. For this purpose it enlists individuals, world-
betterers, who are by nature committed to its work and
will. As the general level of life is thus improved, the
entire human race can advance "by various evolutionary
stages through superman on up to godhood itself."

1570 Nelson, Raymond S. "*The Simpleton of the Unexpected Isles*: Shaw's 'Last Judgment'," QQ, LXXVI (Winter 1969), 692-709.
The Simpleton of the Unexpected Isles is an allegorical play, written when Shaw was 78, wherein the Angel of Judgment confronts man with his hypocrisy, self-deception, and lack of understanding; he challenges him to strive toward an upward development of the human race. What ultimately matters is the degree to which individual men cooperate with life's purposes in the development of the coming race. Shaw, the deeply religious, if disconcertingly unorthodox man, is inviting his audience to judge themselves in the mirror of the play.

1571 Nethercot, Arthur H. "Bernard Shaw and Psychoanalysis," MD, XI (Feb 1969), 356-75.
Given Shaw's open-mindedness and his reputation as an "Advanced Thinker" it is surprising that he was so apathetic toward the "New Psychology" or psychoanalysis. One might expect him to have been powerfully attracted to the new doctrines of Freud, since he had always argued for the tearing away of masks which human beings place before their faces to hide the unbearable truth. Yet his early allusions to psychoanalysis revealed doubt and skepticism, and later it was only grudgingly that he admitted that it might have something sensible to say. In *On the Rocks* and *The Millionairess* he made passing humorous reference to psychoanalysis and its practitioners, but it was not until 1948 in his preface to *Farfetched Fables* that he really dealt with the subject at any length. He titled that section "Am I a Pathological Case?" and claimed that the Freudian method, when tried on him, had failed, though he evidenced very little close familiarity with either Freud's works or the writings of others in the field. Shaw's biographers and citics have consistently neglected the subject of his opinions on psychoanalysis, though Archibald Henderson comes closest to coping with it. He calls Shaw a "dramatic psychoanalyst" and relates conversations with his author on psychoanalytic topics. Just before his death Shaw brought together what he called *Sixteen Self Sketches* which show a grudging acceptance of at least some of the principles of psychoanalysis.

1572 Nethercot, Arthur H. "Bernard Shaw, Mathematical Mystic," ShawR, XII (Jan 1969), 2-26.
Looking back on his school days Shaw says in the Preface to *Farfetched Fables*, "I concluded that mathematics are blazing nonsense . . . " but then in the "Sixth and Last

fable" he lists the "mathematical passion" as one of the
mightiest of all passions. Shaw's changing conception of
mathematics can be traced through his writings.

1573 Nickson, Richard. "Barnes Storming," ISh, VIII
     (1969-70), 21.
[An attack on the unfavorable review of the National
Theatre (London) production of *Back to Methuselah* written
by Clive Barnes for the New York Times 31 August 1969.]

1574 Nickson, Richard. "'Methinks It Is like a
     Weasel': Shaw's Pre-Raphaelite Drama," PMLA, LXXXIV
     (May 1969), 597-99.
Correspondence about Elsie Adams, "Bernard Shaw's Pre-
Raphaelite Drama" (1966).   Adams did not faithfully
represent Shaw when she referred to his own claim to be a
Pre-Raphaelite dramatist.

Adams, Elsie B. "A Reply to Mr. Nickson: 'Or like a
Whale' (An Unobtrusive Subtitle)," PMLA, LXXXIV (May
1969), 599-602. Nickson argues pedantically that because
Shaw does not say overtly that he is a Pre-Raphaelite
dramatist, one should not refer to his implicit claim to
be one.

Nickson, Richard.   "'It Is Backed like a Weasel':   A
Rejoinder to Mrs. Adams," PMLA LXXXIV (May 1969), 602-05.
Pre-Raphaelitism scantily figures as topic in Shaw's
published work.

Adams, Elsie B. "A Surrejoinder to Mr. Nickson: Or,
Good, Clean Shavian Fun in Two Volumes," PMLA, LXXIV (May
1969), 605-07. Much of Nickson's rejoinder is true but
beside the point.

1575 NOTES ON GEORGE BERNARD SHAW'S ARMS AND THE MAN
     (Lond: Methuen [Study-aid], 1969).
[Not seen.]

1576 NOTES ON GEORGE BERNARD SHAW'S PYGMALION (Lond:
     Methuen [Study-aid], 1969).
[Not seen.]

1577 Peterson, William S. INTERROGATING THE ORACLE,
A HISTORY OF THE BROWNING SOCIETY (Athens, Ohio:

Ohio UP, 1969), pp. 4, 13, 20, 31, 51, 62, 63, 69, 87, 101, 103, 106, 111-12, 124, 127, 128, 129, 130, 132, 137, 140-41, 144, 145, 149, 150, 152, 189, 202, 217, 223, 230, 234, 237-38.
[Shaw as the voice of devil's advocate in The Browning Society.]

1578 Pettinati, Mario. "A Colazione fra Pirandello e G. B. Shaw" (At Lunch between Pirandello and G. B. Shaw), ELOQUENZA SICILIANA (Rome), IX (1969), 262-66.
[Anecdotes, humorous in tone, told by Pettinati, who served as interpreter for Pirandello during a trip to England. He sat between Pirandello and Shaw at a luncheon given by Lady Lavery for the purpose of Pirandello's meeting Shaw. H. G. Wells was present and toasted Pirandello.] [In Italian.]

1579 Portîanskaîa, N. A. "B. Shou i Shon O'Keisi (Esteticheskie vzglîady)" (Shaw and Sean O'Casey: Aesthetic Views) NEKOTORYE VOPROSY ISTORIÎ MATERII-ALIZMA I ESTETIKI (Some Questions about the History of Materialism and Aesthetics) (Irkutsk: 1969), pp. 71-106.
[Not seen.] [In Russian.]

1580 Rîabov, F. G. "Engel's, Shou, Bebel' i angliîskie vybory 1892 goda," (Engels, Shaw, and Bebel, and the British Elections of 1892), PROMETEÎ (Moscow), VII (1969), 438-39.
On 29 May 1892, Shaw wrote to August Bebel (whom he met in London) remarking on the feeble influence of Socialism among the English working class. Bebel showed the letter to Engels, who had a copy made (the original has not survived). But events of the 1892 elections proved Shaw wrong. [In Russian.]

1581 Rodenbeck, John. "*The Irrational Knot:* Shaw and the Uses of Ibsen," Shaw R, XII (May 1969), 66-76.
The Irrational Knot was first published serially in OUR CORNER (1885-87) and then later in book form (1905). Shaw made more than 300 changes in the text before the book appeared, many of them resulting from his increased knowledge and experience in a variety of areas as well as his heightened awareness of social issues. The fact that

he had become acquainted with Marx and Ibsen between 1885 and 1905 was particularly important.

1582 Rogers, Richard Ernest. "Didacticism, Plot and Comedy: Ways in Which George Bernard Shaw Uses Plot to Keep Comic His Didactic Purpose," DAI, XXX (1969), 5000A. Unpublished dissertation, Indiana University, 1969.

1583 Scheibe, Fred Karl. "In Memoriam II," HARTWICK REVIEW, II (Fall 1966), 47-50.
[A Tribute to Shaw's god-daughter, Edith Livia Cecilia Beatty, who died in 1966. A letter from Shaw to Cecilia Beatty and letters from Miss Beatty and Dan H. Laurence to Professor Scheibe, with reminiscences. Photographs of Shaw and his letter.]

1584 Schöler-Beinhauer, Monica. "George Bernard Shaw und das Wunder" (George Bernard Shaw and the Miracle), LITERATUR IN WISSENSCHAFT UND UNTERRICHT, II (1969), 149-58.
When Shaw discusses miracles in connection with Jesus and Saint Joan, he presents them in such a way that a rational explanation is always possible. However--and that is characteristic for his attitude towards Christianity in general--he does not totally outrule a metaphysical connection. The reasons for this may be that despite his rationalism Shaw is basically a religious man as evidenced by his letters to Dame Laurentia McLachlan, Abbess of Stanbrook. [In German.]

1585 Schonberg, Harold C. "Naturally, Shaw Greatly Disliked Christmas," NYT, 21 Dec 1969, II, p. 19.
Shaw could not abide Handel's MESSIAH as performed in his day. [Surveys Shaw's criticism of music for the English Christmas season.]

1586 Schrickx, W. "Bernard Shaw on Ibsen in a Letter to Henri Logeman" STUDIA GERMANICA GANDENSIA, XI (1969), 167-71.
Professor Henri Logeman, founder of English Studies at the University of Ghent and author of A COMMENTARY, CRITICAL AND EXPLANATORY ON THE NORWEGIAN TEXT OF HENRIK IBSEN'S 'PEER GYNT', wrote Shaw in 1923 inquiring as to the

latter's indebtedness to Ibsen. [Shaw's answer is reproduced in full.]

1587 Scriabine, Vera, "Ben Iben Payne," ISh, VII (1969), 42.
Professor Ben Iben Payne recently received the Award of Merit of the Consular Law Society for his Service to Theater. Mr. Payne both acted in and directed many Shaw plays in England and America.

1588 Searle, William Miner. "The Saint and the Skeptics: Joan of Arc in the Works of Mark Twain, Anatole France, and Bernard Shaw," DAI, XXIX (1969), 4503A. Dissertation, University of California, Berkeley, 1969, published under the same title, 1976.

1589 Seehase, Georg. "Abbild des Klassenkampfes, Aspekte der Wertung demokratischer und sozialistischer Literatur in Grossbritannien" (Image of the Class Struggle, Aspects of the Evaluation of Democratic and Socialist Literature in Great Britain), ZEITSCHRIFT FÜR ANGLISTIK UND AMERIKANISTIK, XVII (1969), 392-405.
Shaw can be considered as a Socialist writer. [In German.]

1590 Seki, Yoshihiko. IGIRISU RODOTOSHI (A History of the Labour Party) (Tokyo: Shakaishisosha, 1969), pp. 17, 26-42, 45, 65, 86, 101, 129, 236.
[Traces Shaw's role as a Fabian in the Labour Party.] [In Japanese.]

1591 Shestakov, D. "Paradoksalisty. O nektorykh osobonnostiakh dramaturgii Ouild i Shou" (Men of Paradox. On Some Features of the Dramaturgy of Wilde and Shaw), TEATR (Moscow), III (1977), 149-62.
[Dated 1969, place of publication unknown.] In *Widowers' Houses* the subject is concealed as is the business of the hero, the question of his conscience. It finally comes to the surface in the form of paradox. Wilde's paradoxes are not functional as are those of Shaw, which derive from the practical common-sense of human experience. For Wilde it was the aim: for Shaw, the means. [In Russian.]

1592 Shimamura, Totaro. "Saint Joan no Epirogu nitsuite" (On the Epilogue in *Saint Joan*), HOKKAIDO EIGO EIBUNGAKU (Sapporo), No 14 (June 1969), 39-47.
Saint Joan is a ritual and, as such, the Epilogue is an indispensable part of the play. The first three scenes should be properly called Prologue, though they were, according to Shaw, "the romance." Thus, the play has the Prologue-Tragedy-Epilogue structure. As a ritual the Prologue depicts the arrival or birth of the Maid, the Tragedy, her departure or death, and the Epilogue, her rebirth as a saint. [In Japanese.]

1593 Shinkuma, Kiyoshi. "A Dramatic Purpose of George Bernard Shaw", NAGOYAGAKUINDAIGAKU RONSHU (Seto), No 19 (Sept 1969), 131-156.
Shaw's purpose in writing *Mrs. Warren's Profession* was to depict symbolically social crimes in dramatic form and to induce guilty conscience among spectators or readers. [In Japanese.]

1594 Silverstein, Paul. "Barns, Booths, and Shaw," Shaw R, XII (Sept 1969), 111-16.
In *Passion, Poison and Petrifaction, or, The Fatal Gazogene: A Brief Tragedy for Barns and Booths*, Shaw wrote a satire on melodramatic structure and content, though indeed, the satire embraces far more than melodrama. The concepts of death, love, honor and jealousy all come in for their respective shares of ridicule as do theatrical techniques (realism) and theatrical questions ("pure" art versus functionality), as well as all manner of character types.

1595 Smith, Warren S[ylvester]. "A Note on the Mathematical Pun .. .," Shaw R, XII (Jan 1969), 26-7.
In the first edition of *The Adventures of the Black Girl in Her Search for God* Shaw had made a mathematical error which he corrrected in the standard edition but at the cost of eliminating a lovely mathematical pun; a later edition restored the passage to its original form.

1596 Sugawara, Takashi. "Eibei Engeki no Inyu" (Introduction of the British and American Drama into Japan), NIPPON NO EIGAKU 100 NEN SHOWAHEN (100 Years of English Studies in Japan, Showa Period) ed by the editorial staff of NIPPON NO EIGAKU 100 NEN (Tokyo: Kenkyusha, 1969), pp. 200-20.

It is deplorable that Shavian drama has failed to bear any fruit on the Japanese stage, which shows up a weakpoint of the Japanese theater. [In Japanese.]

1597 Szladits, Lola L. "New in the Berg Collection, 1962-1964," BNYPL, LXXIII (April 1969), 227-52.
[A descriptive listing of selected acquisitions of the Berg Collection made during the years 1962-1964. Items added to the Bernard Shaw archive include an entire private library; an important item is Shaw's own copy of *The Doctor's Dilemma, Getting Married,* and *The Shewing-up of Blanco Posnet* in the first edition. In the archive of Lady Gregory are included two letters and one note from Bernard Shaw.]

1598 "Taper Forum Offers Adapted Shaw Story," NYT, 22 March 1969, p. 24.
The Adventures of the Black Girl in Her Search for God, adapted by Christopher Isherwood, received lukewarm reviews in Los Angeles.

1599 Trewin, J. C. "Theatre between the Wars, 5-Shaw and the Rest," P&P, XVI (July 1969), 66-71.
Heartbreak House and *Saint Joan* would be on my list of plays from the first seven decades of this century likely to survive. Some of Shaw's later plays have shown that they can hold a theater. [Photographs of productions of *Too True to Be Good, Geneva,* and *The Apple Cart.*]

1600 Tyson, Brian F. "Shaw's First Discussion Play: An Abandoned Act of *The Philanderer,*" ShawR, XII (Sept 1969), 90-103.
In the subsequently abandoned third Act of *The Philanderer,* Shaw had inquired into "the Marriage Question and the problem of Divorce," themes which had been introduced in Act I. Instead of including it in the play, however, he divided the original Act II into two parts, which then became Acts II and III. He wrote a new Act IV and decided to reserve the original Act III for the beginning of a new play. He in fact never used it as such, though parts of it do appear in *Getting Married* and in the *Preface on Doctors.*

1601 Ure, Peter. "Master and Pupil in Bernard Shaw," ESSAYS IN CRITICISM, XIX (April 1969), 118-39; rptd in YEATS AND ANGLO-IRISH LITERATURE: CRITICAL ESSAYS BY PETER URE, ed by C. J. Rawson (Liverpool: Liverpool UP, 1974), pp. 261-280.
Four plays illustrate Shaw's uses of the relationship between master and pupil: *Caesar and Cleopatra, Major Barbara, Pygmalion,* and *Heartbreak House.* Caesar as educator of Cleopatra has as his first task to protect her against herself. As her education continues, she begins to imitate Caesar, but she only learns some of his tricks as ruler and very little of his spirit. Whereas Caesar did not have any specific lesson to teach (it is what he *is* that matters), Undershaft does: Barbara must learn that souls cannot be saved apart from saving society. In *Pygmalion* the master/pupil relationship is developed to the fullest, and an additional aspect in this play is that the educator is also educated by the pupil. Captain Shotover plays the role of educator (of Ellie Dunn) in *Heartbreak*; in fact most of the characters stand in this relationship to her. The first step in her education is to strip away the illusions which close her in. The pattern of master/pupil illustrated in these plays was in modified form an ever-present feature in all of Shaw's life and art.

1602 Ware, James M. "Shaw's 'New' Play: The Black Girl," SHAVIAN, IV (Summer 1969), 11-15.
Christopher Isherwood fashioned a playscript from Shaw's story, *The Adventures of the Black Girl in Her Search for God* which was performed by the Guthrie Theater in the spring of 1969. It was chosen for production "less for its theology than for its pertinence to the American obsession with race relations." Although *The Black Girl* cannot stand up to *Saint Joan*, the two heroines do have much in common. It is a fine example of a morality play in the witty Shavian style.

1603 Weightman, John. "Worshipping the Life Force, Disliking Life," ENCOUNTER, XXXIII (Oct 1969), 31-33.
[Review of the National Theatre production of *Back to Methuselah*, directed by Clifford Williams.] Shaw raises basic philosophic problems: What is man doing here on this earth where he happens to find himself? and Why is life complicated by variouis forms of evil? But by attempting to provide answers to the unanswerable, this play is the least satisfactory of Shaw's major works and

is chiefly interesting as a document about the mind of a man who would not rest in a state of unknowing.

In Part I Shaw demonstrates simultaneously respect for the Life Force and revulsion at the means that the Life Force employs, namely, "all the sexual business." But after Part I it becomes clear that the Life Force itself is a naive and unsatisfactory concept. Shaw claims that man, if he is to survive, must turn himself into a higher species, but he cannot make up his mind as to whether progress depends on God or on the human will. Part V is really very sad, ending with a pie-in-the-sky intonation: "It is enough that there is a Beyond."

1604 Weintraub, Stanley. "Preface" and "Notes," SHAW, AN AUTOBIOGRAPHY, 1856-1898, selected and ed by Stanley Weintraub (NY: Weybright and Talley, 1969; Lond: Reinhardt, 1970), pp. vii-xvi, 297-309. Shaw resisted fashioning a formal autobiography, but he wrote autobiography all his life: his novels and plays, diaries and journals, letters, and his re-writing of the biographies of Frank Harris and Hesketh Pearson, as well as his prefaces, criticism, reviews, essays, and lectures and speeches.

1605 Whalen, Jerome Paul. "Some Structural Similarities in John Bunyan's THE PILGRIM'S PROGRESS and Selected Narrative and Dramatic Works of George Bernard Shaw," DA, XXIX (1969), 3986A. Unpublished dissertation, University of Pittsburgh, 1968.

1606 Williams, Clifford, talks to Vincent Guy. "Director in Interview," P&P, XVI (Aug 1969), 56-57, 63.
I hate Shaw plays when I read them, but when they're on stage, I get more from them. I didn't choose *Back to Methuselah* myself. The allegorical characters are recognizable--like the Bible.

1607 Wilson, Colin. BERNARD SHAW:; A REASSESSMENT. (NY: Atheneum, 1969).
Shaw was possibly the greatest man of his time, but his greatness was primarily that of an original thinker and evolutionist philosopher rather than that of a dramatist. [The connection between Shaw and the author is spelled out in the last chapter, "My Own Part in the Matter" (from the

concluding paragraph: "thinking about him [Shaw] so constantly has given me an odd sense of closeness to him, as if he was the ghost of Hamlet's father, and I carrying out some last request.)   This connection is also implicit throughout the book since all plays are understood as being about the creative workings of the Life Force.] Thus *Man and Superman, John Bull's Other Island, Major Barbara,* and especially *Back to Methuselah* represent the high point of Shaw's dramatic production, whereas *Saint Joan* is "a retrogressive step," and *Heartbreak House,* "Shaw's first failure since *The Philanderer.*"

1608 Wilson, Colin.   "To The Editor," TLS, 18 Dec 1969, p. 1450.
[Rebuttal to review of Wilson's BERNARD SHAW: A REASSESSMENT (1969), "H.G. & G.B.S.:   Varied Reflections on Two Edwardian Polymaths" (1969).]   The book is a reassessment of Shaw, and as such, it is not supposed to be based on new material.   As for the implication that the book is filled with "Wilson Ur-philosophy," I am misrepresented; my philosophical views are reserved for the Appendix. [Reviewer's answer: The book is carelessly documented.   Mr. Wilson writes in the introductory chapter, "My personal attitude to Shaw is explained in the postscript to this bobok, and it is, of course, implicit in the whole book."   Mr. Wilson contradicts this sentence in his letter.]

1970

1609 Albert, Sidney P.   "More Shaw Advice to the Players of *Major Barbara,*" THEATRE SURVEY, XI (1970), 66-85.
William Armstrong had observed that Shaw often wrote private letters or postcards to his actors to supplement the advice he gave them in the theater, and then Armstrong expressed the hope that such documents could be collected to reveal the great mastery of detail and power of persuasion Shaw possessed.   Vast as such an undertaking would be, it is, nevertheless, possible to so proceed in the case of a single play, such as *Major Barbara,* a task already undertaken before Armstrong's proposal.   The letters to Annie Russell, who played Barbara, and to Louis Calvert, who played Undershaft, are extant, and it is

possible to bring together in approximate chronological order the rehearsal letters to both principal players. [Three letters to each are collected here.] A judicious summary and critiques of the whole rehearsal experience with *Barbara* are revealed in a letter Shaw wrote to Eleanor Robson, 24 December 1905. [The letter is reproduced.]

1610 "All about Shaw," ISh, IX (Fall 1970), 5. [Poem, with photographs of Shaw in his famous bathing poses.]

1611 Anzai, Tetsuo. "Chesterton to Shaw" (Chesterton and Shaw), in G. K. CHESTERTON NO SEKAI (The World of G. K. Chesterton), ed by Peter Milward and Kii Nakano (Tokyo: Kenkyusha, 1970), pp. 151-66. Though they stood out in the sharpest contrast in almost all points, Shaw and Chesterton, the most popular controversialists before World War I, cherished a profound respect and friendship for each other. They had common enemies to bombard with laughter, though from diametrically opposite angles. Their targets were 1) Victorian middle class complacency, 2) artistic individualism, 3) shallow cynicism and pessimism, 4) physical science, and 5) sham-atheism and pietism. Their resemblances had a deep common root: mysticism. However, Chesterton's mysticism originated in Catholicism, whereas Shaw's came from Puritanism. GEORGE BERNARD SHAW, one of the best biographical works by Chesterton as well as one of the best books on Shaw generally, revealed their differences clearly. [In Japanese.]

1612 Bader, Earl D. "The Self-Reflexive Language: Uses of paradox in Wilde, Shaw, and Chesterton," DAI, XXX (1970), 4934A. Unpublished dissertation, Indiana University, 1969.

1613 Balashov, P. S. "Oktiâbr' i publitŝistika B. Shou 20-kh godov" (October Revolution and B. Shaw's Journalism of the Twenties), VELIKAIA OKTIABR'SKAIA SOTSIALISTICHESKAIA REVOLUTSIIA I MIROVAIA LITERATURA (The Great October Socialist Revolution and World Literature) (Moscow: Nauka, 1970), pp. 525-37.

Shaw welcomed the October Revolution (1917) and remained
faithful to it, even though sometimes his views were
mistaken.   He considered Lenin a great leader of a new
type.   Shaw's journalism struck a dissonant note in the
anti-Soviet hysteria of 1919-1921, even though his
thoughts were not free from the twists and turns of his
individual viewpoint.   His individualism expressed itself
in paradox, historical reminiscences and analogies which
were not always correct.   He admitted the necessity of
revolution and the dictatorship of the proletariat but, in
his own way, contradictorily.   In his polemics with Henry
Hyndman, Shaw and the latter gradually changed roles.   [In
Russian.]

1614 Bandyopadhyay, Sarit Kumar.   "Trends in Modern
   Bengali Drama," INDIAN WRITING TODAY, IV (July-Sept
   1970), 149-55.
In Bengali drama, Bijan Bhattacharyya and Sambhu Mitra,
like Shaw, concentrated their energy to break the tradition of shallow amusement.   Shaw's naturalism, especially
his form, can be used for contemporary concerns.

1615 Barnett, Gene A.   "Don Juan's Hell," BALL STATE
   UNIVERSITY FORUM, XI (1970), 47-52.
In Bernard Shaw's hell sequence in *Man and Superman*, three
of the characters, Dona Ana, her father the commander, and
Don Juan himself are misplaced, at least according to
their own judgments.   Each of these characters asks
himself, "Why am I here?"   Parallels exist between the
characters in the hell sequence and the characters in the
play proper and offer a resolution to that question posed
by the three.   However, since it is Don Juan/John Tanner's
dream, the question is truly his and the dilemma posed in
that question is what the dream sequence and the play is
all about.   In his dream/nightmare he has come to realize
that he is in the grip of the Life Force, which wills his
fate; his education is complete.

1616 Beerbohm, Max.   LAST THEATRES, 1904-1910 (Lond:
   Rupert Hart-Davis, 1970), pp. 9, 82, 121-24, 135,
   167-69, 178-81, 196, 206, 208, 242-45, 253, 254,
   273, 274, 276, 279, 280, 292-95, 296-99, 324, 399,
   424, 434, 443, 465, 466, 488, 493, 516.
[Reprints: "Dramatic Translation" (1905), "The New
Felicity," (1905), "A 'Yellow Critic'" (1905) "A Great
Dear" (1906)" "G.B.S. Again" (1907), "G.B.S. Republished"

(1907), and other reviews that mention Shaw, all from the SATURDAY REVIEW.]

1617 Bentley, Eric [Russell]. "Ibsen, Shaw, Brecht: Three Stages," THE RARER ACTION: ESSAYS IN HONOR OF FRANCIS FERGUSSON, ed by Alan Cheuse and Richard Koffler (New Brunswick, NJ: Rutgers UP, 1970), pp. 3-23; rptd in THEATRE OF WAR, COMMENTS ON 32 OCCASIONS (NY: Viking P, 1960-1972), pp. 183-211.
Ibsen's plays disturbed Bernard Shaw and led him to modernism and to the theater. If Shaw pushed the idea of the problem drama further than Ibsen, Bertolt Brecht pushed it further than Shaw. No one would argue that Ibsen, Shaw, and Brecht are not social dramatists, but one would have to enlarge the word "social" if it is to fit them in their individual geniuses. Both Shaw and Brecht remained Ibsenites in that they both dealt primarily, if not with neurotic weakness, at least with divided characters. The problem play remained unique in their hands and demonstrated far more art and artifice than has been generally assumed.

1618 Billington, Michael. *"Arms and the Man,"* P&P, XVII (Sept 1970), 32-33.
What is surprising about the Chichester revival of *Arms and the Man* is how well it has stood the test of time; what is disappointing is how John Clements's production failed to make the satire clear. [Photographs.]

1619 Brooke, Sylvia, Lady. QUEEN OF THE HEAD-HUNTERS, THE AUTOBIOGRAPHY OF H. H. THE HON. SYLVIA LADY BROOKE, RANEE OF SARAWAK (Lond: Sidgwick & Jackson, 1970; NY: William Morrow, 1972), pp. 19, 20, 21-23, 30, 42-43, 51, 69-70, 74-75.
[Anecdotes about and letters from Shaw, Sylvia Brooke's "literary godfather." No index.]

1620 Carmody, Terence F. *"Candida,"* ISh, IX (Fall 1970), 13.
Candida at the Longacre Theatre, NY, is a poor production.

1621 Carpenter, Charles A. "Notes on Some Obscurities in the *Revolutionists' Handbook,"* ShawR, XIII (May 1970), 59-64.

426

The Revolutionists' Handbook and Pocket Companion is for
the most part a lucid piece of evolutionary rhetoric,
deserving of full understanding by all its readers, but
many of the references contained in *The Handbook* have been
obscured by the passage of time. [What follows, then, is
an annotated description of the most conspicuous and
elusive obscurities in *The Handbook*.]

1622 Chołodowski, Waldemar. "Lektury i problemy:
George Bernard Shaw. *Żolnierz i bohater*" (Readings
and Problems: George Bernard Shaw. *Arms and the
Man*), TYGODNIK KKULTURALNY (Warsaw), No 15 (1970),
4.
Romanticism is the heritage of all Poles, and we regard
criticism of "banners and hussars" with mixed feelings.
The Polish title, *Soldier and Hero*, of *Arms and the Man*
does not suggest that the words are mutually exclusive.
This "pleasant" play is both sad and contemporary,
reminding us of recent wars in the Third World, commanded
by foreign officers. [In Polish.]

1623 Couchman, Gordon W. "The First Playbill of
Caesar: Shaw's List of Authorities," Shaw R, XIII
(May 1970), 79-82.
The playbill for the copyright performance of *Caesar and
Cleopatra* at the Theatre Royal in Newcastle upon Tyne on
15 March 1899 contains a list of authorities which Shaw
offers to his audiences.   That list is more interesting
for its omissions, works which have a more definite
bearing on Caesar's history, than many of those included;
for example, Dio Cassius, Suetonius, Lucan.   There are
similarities in Shaw's delineation of history at the time
of Caesar with many of the authors he cites, so much so
that the list should possibly be taken more seriously.

1624 Dolch, Martin. *"Pygmalion,"* INSIGHT II:
ANALYSES OF MODERN BRITISH LITERATURE, ed by John V.
Hagopian and Martin Dolch (Frankfurt: Hirschgraben,
1970), pp. 322-30.
[Not seen.]

1625 Downer, Alan S. "The Autobiographer in Spite
of Himself," Shaw R, XIII (Jan 1970), 35-36.
[A review of SHAW: AN AUTOBIOGRAPHY, 1856-1898. Selected
from his Writing by Stanley Weintraub (1969).]   Shaw
himself believed that "all autobiographies are deliberate

lies," and this pastiche account of the first 40 years of his life reveals that Shaw carefully controlled his own public image.

1626 Driver, Tom F. ROMANTIC QUEST AND MODERN QUERY. A HISTORY OF MODERN THEATRE (NY: Delacorte P, 1970), pp. 52, 54, 108, 127-28, 137, 149, 157-58, 170, 190, 191, 216, 247, 249-82, 301, 324, 331, 335, 340, 370, 391.

On the surface Shaw was not a romantic, but only by seeing the romantic beneath the reformer can one discern Shaw's position in the modern theater. Shaw's is the liveliest body of theater criticism in English, but it is not the most fair. Shaw's notion that history tends toward progressive fulfillment belongs to a comic sense. When Shaw went to the popular theater for his inspiration, he was "putting the audience in touch with that force of life which was moving mankind toward its sublime destiny .. . . Underneath the Shavian rhetoric, we may descry the utterly romantic notion of the primitive sublime." In a Shaw play "thinking" is as exciting and as comic as making love. *Candida* is based on the Dionysian idea that the female is superior to the male. The opposition between feminine wit and masculine position is fundamental to all Shaw's best work. *Man and Superman's* motifs are those of *Candida*, but it is in every way a more expansive play. Male surpassed by female, conflict between the generations, and the self deprecator (*eiron*) are the three comic aspects of the play. The bases of Shavian irony are the deception of appearances and the indirect speaking of truth. *Caesar and Cleopatra* is the first of Shaw's extravaganzas. Shaw was so optimistic that in *Heartbreak House* he has not captured the desperation of its time. *Saint Joan* is an extravaganza. Joan's flaw, her genius, is a virtue. Shaw's virtue is that, in spite of his empiricism, he drew his opinions from his intelligence and faith, not experience. His limitation is that he could not learn from experience. His roots in modern drama are in the nineteenth century, but his own flowering was unique, which is why it is almost impossible for other writers to learn from him. He transcends the theater.

1627 Fagan, J. B., and Leon B. Hugo (ed). SHAKESPEAR V. SHAW, ShawR, XIII, (Sept 1970), 105-31.

James Bernard Fagan, the author of "SHAKESPEAR V. SHAW" was born in Belfast, Ireland, in 1873. He went on the

stage in 1895.   In 1918 he took over the management of the
Court Theatre.   He died in Hollywood, California, in 1933.
Shavians will be disappointed in this sketch because Shaw
is "so bereft of words, let alone wit."   [The entire
sketch follows in the next 25 pages.]

    1628 Filipov, Vladimir.   "Ako drugite posledvat
metoda na Lenin . . . "   (If the Others Would Follow
Lenin's Method . . .), LITERATUREN FRONT, 12 Feb
1970, p. 7.
[Not seen.]   [In Bulgarian.]

    1629 Frank, Joseph.   "Take It Off!   Take It Off!"
ShawR, XIII (Jan 1970), 10-12.
One of the techniques which Shaw makes use of in
Heartbreak House is the vaudevillian striptease.   Shaw
uses it to peel off layers of disguises.   Throughout the
play, the characters are stripped of their phoniness.   The
technique is effective, for "most of us would rather hear
a Minsky announcing the end of the world than a Billy
Graham preaching Armageddon."

    1630 Furlong, William B.   GBS/GKC: SHAW AND CHES-
TERTON: THE METAPHYSICAL JESTERS (University Park:
Pennsylvania State UP, 1970).
I.   What about the play?   Shaw's disagreement with GKC in
philosophic principle sparked a series of debates that
eventually resulted in their being hailed as the "Debaters
of the Century."   Shaw importuned Chesterton to write
plays, maintaining they were best suited to Chesterton's
talents.

II.   GKC's GEORGE BERNARD SHAW (1909).   Shaw's reaction to
Chesterton's book provides a clarification of the
intellectual positions of the disputants.   GKC had written
a serious philosophical study of the Shavian mind and
works.   Shaw criticized the factual aspects in order to
put up a smoke screen for his own intellectual privacy.

III.   Genesis of "The Debaters of the Century."   Chesterton provided Shaw with a badly-needed opponent.

IV.   The first public encounter.   Chesterton learned that
Shaw did not waste time nursing rancor over old issues.

V. Debates--formal and informal. Shaw was better at presenting a thesis, at sustaining an argument, and at sheer attacks for the sake of attack. Chesterton demonstrated that his forte was the counterattack.

VI. A new glimpse of Methuselah. In composing his religious testament, Shaw created the character Immenso Champernoon as a thinly disguised GKC.

VII. The last phase, 1928-1936. Shaw's genius was for work; Chesterton's for friendship and enjoyment. Perhaps owing to these differences, their contact was infrequent after 1928 when active controversy ceased.

1631 Govindan, T. C. ESSAYS ON GEORGE BERNARD SHAW (Ottapolam, India: N.S.S. College, 1970).
[The first chapter deals with the theme of "Love and War" and is basically an analysis of *Arms and the Man* and *Saint Joan* in which the writer concludes that the themes of *Arms* found greater significance 30 years later in *Joan*. The second chapter, "A Father for the Superman," presents the idea that Shaw's source for *Man and Superman* was Shakespeare's TWO GENTLEMEN OF VERONA, the difference primarily being that Shakespeare presents *what* happens and Shaw explains *why* it happens. The third chapter, "On the Epilogue of *Saint Joan*," is an argument for the necessity of including the famous epilogue, "The very soul of the play," because it tells the audience that Joan is canonized. Chapter four, "Shaw's *The Devil's Disciple*, shows Dick Dudgeon as a truly religious person, closer to the teaching of Jesus Christ than the supposed Christians. Chapter five, "The Shaping Spirit," argues that Shaw's characters are true to themselves, have the courage of their convictions, and proclaim those convictions to the world. The final chapter, "His Master's Voice," answers the charge that Shaw's characters are simply his mouthpieces.]

1632 Grazhdanskaiâ, Z. T. "Bernard Shaw kak poet" (Bernard Shaw as Poet), FILOLOGICHESKIĬ NAUKI (Moscow), XIII (1970), 20-30.
Western scholars of Shaw repeat one another according to the bourgeois taste of their recipients. Attention has been drawn by Warren Smith ("An Early G.B.S. Love Poem" [1967]) and John O'Donovan (SHAW AND THE CHARLATAN GENIUS [1965]?) to Shaw's use of rhymed and also blank verse in his journal (1873), and in his correspondence with Mrs. Pat Campbell (1912-1913) where he used cockney. Echoes of

Shakespeare also occur, as in *The Admirable Bashville*.
[In Russian.]

1633 Greer, Germaine, "A Whore in Every Home,"
PROGRAM, the National Theatre's production of *Mrs.
Warren's Profession*, 30 Dec 1970; rptd FF, pp. 163-
66.
Shaw as efficiently represses what is bad about Mrs.
Warren's profession as its unspeakable name. The whole
structure of the play relies upon the prurient interest of
the audience. The basic assumption of the play--that a
poor woman can better herself through vice--is the most
effective incentive to prostitution imaginable. the
banishment of the house of ill-fame has merely decon-
trolled the trade not abolished it. If prostitution is
defined by gain, then it is universal; the wife is a
sanctified whore. It is not vice which exploits men and
women, but the profit motive. Shaw could get no closer to
the truth than the feeble Fabian diagnosis that women were
overworked, undervalued and underpaid so that they were
tempted into a life falsely represented as easier. Shaw
does provide an inkling of truth that prostitution is
universal in a capitalist society because of the profit
motive.

1634 Guardia, Alfredo de la. "Inglaterra:
Preeminencia de Bernard Shaw" (England: The Preemi-
nence of Bernard Shaw), VISION DE LA CRITICA
DRAMATICA (View of Dramatic Criticism) (Buenos
Aires: La Pleyade, 1970), pp. 244-48.
Shaw was himself an excellent critic of music and drama,
but was also the subject of other critics like Harris and
Chesterton. [In Spanish.]

1635 Harvey, Robert C. "How Shavian Is the
Pygmalion We Teach?" ENGLISH JOURNAL, LIX (Dec
1970), 1234-38.
The message of *Pygmalion* is clear: speak "good English
and you can be successful." But Shaw's satiric point is
that using surface indicators of human worth can cause us
to be ridiculous. Doolittle makes it to the middle class
on the strength of his ideas. Homage to the theme of
"good English" will not explain the play's conclusion.
Eliza achieves her freedom from social prejudice.

1636 Hegedüs, Géza. G. B. SHAW VILÁGA (The World
of G. B. Shaw) (Budapest: Európa Könyvkiadó, 1970).
[In-depth critical and biographical work. Detailed
bibliography, particularly useful for Hungarian
criticism, and list of Hungarian premieres. Many
photographs, especially of Hungarian productions.]
[In Hungarian.]

1637 Hewitt, Barnard. HISTORY OF THE THEATRE
FROM 1800 TO THE PRESENT (NY: Random House, 1970),
pp. 44, 61, 66, 70, 91.
Shaw understood the artificial nature of his plays, but he
wanted the best realistic production to insure that the
social criticism would not be lost.

1638 Hill, Maureen (ed). NATIONAL PORTRAIT GAL-
LERY: CONCISE CATALOGUE 1856-1969 (Lond: National
Portrait Gallery, 1970), p. 234.
[Describes briefly the three portraits of Shaw in the
National Portrait Gallery--by B. Partridge and J.
Epstein.]

1639 Hollis, Christopher. THE MIND OF CHESTER-
TON (Lond, Sydney and Toronto: Hollis and Carter,
1970), pp. 9, 17, 29, 67, 78-88, 96, 99, 100-1, 116-
17, 118, 145, 161, 215-16, 272, 288.
Shaw was Chesterton's most constant antagonist and his
most constant friend. Both delighted in paradox; both
attacked the Victorians for refusing to acknowledge the
poor. Chesterton's basic criticism of Shaw was that he
respected the traditional taboos of society. Shaw was the
enemy of all "local loyalties"; to Chesterton they were
the stuff that made a man a man. Chesterton believed in
love; Shaw in *élan vital*. Shaw argued that change in
itself was good and therefore did not believe in man as
Chesterton did.

1640 Holloway, Joseph. JOSEPH HOLLOWAY'S IRISH
THEATRE, Vol III: 1938-1944, ed by Robert Hogan and
Michael J. O'Neill (Dixon, California: Proscenium
P, 1970), pp. 6, 8, 9, 35, 47, 55, 59, 68, 79-80,
84, 86, 87-88, 98.
[The journal of theater-going in Dublin by Joseph Holloway
with comments on Shaw.]

1641 Huggett, Richard. THE FIRST NIGHT OF PYGMA-
LION: A COMEDY FOR TWO PEOPLE (Lond: Faber and
Faber, 1970).
[This play was first performed by Richard Huggett and Toni
Block on 30 September 1966 at the National Book League,
London, under the auspices of the Shaw Society. It
combines the dialogue of Bernard Shaw, Mrs. Patrick
Campbell, and Beerbohm Tree, containing factual material
taken from the actual rehearsal of *Pygmalion*, the first
night performance, the subsequent reviews, and the
American tour.]

1642 Hulban, Horia. "Notes on the Style of G. B.
Shaw's Correspondence," ANALELE ŞTIINŢIFICE ALE
UNIVERSITĂŢIL IAŞI, XVI (1970), 129-38.
Metaphorical style is a basic artistic peculiarity of
Shaw's correspondence. "Exquisitely cultivated sense of
beauty" and "great pains and skill of execution" are often
met in the correspondence, as are climax and anticlimax,
paradox, repetition, and balance. [Summary in Romanian.]

1643 Hulse, James W. REVOLUTIONISTS IN LONDON:
A STUDY OF FIVE UNORTHODOX SOCIALISTS (Oxford:
Clarendon P, 1970). [The five Socialists include
Peter Kropotkin, Eduard Bernstein, William Morris,
Sergei Mikhailovich Krovchinskii, alias Stepnick,
and Bernard Shaw; two chapters are devoted to Shaw:
Chapter V: "Shaw: Socialist Maverick," pp. 11-137;
and Chapter VIII: "Shaw: Beyond Socialism," pp.
192-228.]
Shaw supported the Socialist movement to the end of his
life, but he could not avoid pointing out its weaknesses.
Shaw and William Morris had their differences over the
aims and policies of the Socialist League, but after the
"Bloody Sunday" incident in Trafalgar Square, their
differences were less sharp and fell off considerably when
Morris departed from the Socialist League in 1890.

Shaw's early plays, especially *Widowers' Houses* and *Mrs.
Warren's Profession*, are examples of Fabian permeation
into the theater, not directly advocated, but rather as an
"unstated corollary." *Candida*, on the other hand, treats
Socialism directly and is a study in the evolution of
Socialism as well as a revelation of the weaknesses of one
kind of it.

By the end of 1890 Shaw had completed his education in Socialism, and his plays after 1898, *Caesar and Cleopatra* and *Man and Superman* for example, are testimonials to his disenchantment with progress, politics, and Socialism in particular, and point toward his emerging faith in evolutionary biology or metabiology. *Heartbreak House* not only depicts Socialism failing as a healing agent but shows society as a whole incapable of redemption. In *Back to Methuselah* Shaw's image of the future is so fanciful that the play, especially the last two parts of the cycle, reveals little to those studying his Socialism. *Saint Joan* demonstrates Shaw's highest achievement as a playwright and his most impressive statement as a revolutionist. Shaw as rebel could see that Joan's death was a triumph for her cause and the world. The play draws upon the ambiguities and the tensions that were very much a part of Shaw's Socialism. Nothing he wrote after *Joan* adds substantially to his Socialism, a Socialism that was "an amalgamation of his early admiration of Marx's denunciation of capitalism, his preference for the moderate procedures of the Fabians, and his anarchist yearning for the total transformation of society."

1644 Jordan, Robert J. "Theme and Character in *Major Barbara*," TEXAS STUDIES IN LITERATURE AND LANGUAGE, XII (1970), 471-80.
One of the aspects of Shaw's dramatic method is the way in which his plays are often developed as companion pieces. *Major Barbara* and *Man and Superman* are just such companions. The epistle to *Superman* suggests two basic human drives, of every man to be rich at all costs and of every woman to be married at all costs, but the play itself is only concerned with the latter of the two. It remains for *Barbara* to provide the other.

1645 Kantorovich, I. V. "V. I. Lenin i 'vtoraîa epokha' Bernarda Shou" (V. I. Lenin and Bernard Shaw's "Second Epoch"), UCHENYE ZAPISKI SVERDLOVSKOGO GOS. PED. INSTITUTA (Sverdlovsk) CXIX (1970), 123-37.
For Shaw, the central problems of development of a revolution were moral problems, since the morals of the English proletariat were essentially bourgeois. All hopes of revolution thus centered on the intellectual minority. Shaw did not understand the social nature of the Soviet system. His idealistic concept of the historical process restricted his ideological evolution though he understood the current needs of the revolutionary moment. But Shaw's

Fabian illusions prevented him from understanding Lenin's "new method." His extravaganzas of the post-1917 revolutionary period are rationalistic and take place in the kingdom of thought. They are not metaphysical philosophizing but the artistic expression of an ideological generalization of all the concrete disfigurements of bourgeois civilization. Conventional fantasy became a creative godsend which enabled Shaw to expand the ideological content of the extravaganzas, so it became a genre he could use to treat the collossal theme of the crisis of all bourgeois civilization. The result was some loss of his earlier militant realism, but he also gained in critical realism with its dialectical character. [In Russian.]

1646 Kaufman, Michael V. "The Dissonance of Dialectic: Shaw's *Heartbreak House*," Shaw R, XIII (Jan 1970), 2-9.
Shaw's *Heartbreak House* can be viewed from the perspective of musical analogies. His earlier plays, which attempted a creative dialectical synthesis, were analygous musically to a sonata (the essence of which is a struggle between two themes that is resolved). In *Heartbreak* the musical analogy is that of the "fantasia," defined as a monothematic piece of music. *Heartbreak* is not meant to be a dramatic dialectic as are Shaw's earlier plays. By adherence to the monothematic ideal of the baroque fantasia, Shaw gives added strength to his own conception--the failure of dialectical synthesis in the ruling class.

1647 Kaul, A. N. THE ACTION OF ENGLISH COMEDY: STUDIES IN THE ENCOUNTER OF ABSTRACTION AND EX-PERIENCE FROM SHAKESPEARE TO SHAW (New Haven, Connecticut: Yale UP, 1970), pp. 284-327 and passim; pp. 321-26 rptd in StJFYA.
While a full understanding of Shaw is not possible, it is already evident that he is not the simple, one-sided author of popular supposition, but an artist of varied effects and considerable richness and complexity. In *Arms and the Man* seriousness and good sense are the values the play substitutes for the romantic ones which it shatters. However, the final revelation that Bluntschli is an incurable romantic contradicts the picture of him as dramatically presented up to that point. It represents an attempt to distinguish the hero from the servant, not with their common culture but rather beyond it. Needless to

add, the attempt is as intellectually hollow as it is dramatically incoherent, unsuccessful, and unnecessary.

Man and Superman is Shaw's pivotal play, because it looks back to the romantic illusion of *Arms* and forward to *Back to Methuselah*, in its development of the romantic man into the man of experience and the philosophic man. Dramatically, *Methuselah* is a double fantasy, that is, a fantasy about fantasy. Shaw failed to realize that certain ideals are so inseparably a part of the present-day culture that it is not easy to "scrap" them since it would be cutting at the very foundation. Shaw thus wrote not Shavian Comedy but what is increasingly called today tragicomedy.

In *Saint Joan* Shaw was dramatizing the historical origin of the present period. He endorses Joan's triumph without reservation. Shaw's fairness to those who put Joan to death is based on his understanding that in a period of historical crisis there are no easy solutions, and entrenched beliefs are not foolish aberrations. Yet, though he recognized his own time as one of crisis, he made the problems sound all rather easy. This is the basis of his comedy.

1648 Keunen, J. "Napoleon in schaviaanse stijl" (Napoleon in the Style of Shaw), DIETSCHE WARANDE EN BELFORT, CXV (1970), 35-45.
Shaw wrote *The Man of Destiny* as part of his campaign to woo Ellen Terry for Ibsen-style drama. It is essentially comic in tone, with a strong female lead, as is typical of Shaw. The play is operatic in structure, with the many memorable dialogues most effectively interpreted as arias. The comic-opera tone was quite familiar and popular at the time, especially in French works such as Sardou's DORA and MADAME SANS GENE. [In Dutch.]

1649 Lambert, J. W. "Plays in Performance, London," DRAMA, XCVII (Spring 1970), 15-27.
The ever-increasing relevance of Shaw's attack on the soulless corporations emerged from the production of *The Apple Cart*. *Widowers' Houses*, too, "came up fresh as paint." [Photograph of *Widowers'*.]

1650 Lambert, J. W. "Plays in Performance, London," DRAMA, XCIX (Winter 1970), 14-30.

Major Barbara and *Saint Joan* might be companion pieces: in each a young girl challenges authority; she is humbled; in each Shaw strives to give his sympathy to the idealistic girl, though he cannot give her victory.

1651 Leary, Daniel J.   "A Deleted Passage from Shaw's *John Bull's Other Ireland*," BNYPL, VII (1970), 598-606.

Because of the great length of *John Bull's Other Ireland*, Shaw was forced to cut the play for production purposes, deleting, unfortunately, a lengthy passage that has considerable value: 1) it clarifies the character of Tom Broadbent, 2) it anticipates developments of the plot, and 3) it establishes quite early in the play the conflict between dreaming or enthusiasm and efficiency or exploitation.   Shaw allowed no easy synthesis of the dialectic tension in the play: as a result it is one of Shaw's bitterest comedies.   The essence of that bitterness is found in the deleted passage.

1652 Mendelsohn, Michael J.   "Bernard Shaw's Soldiers," ShawR, XIII (Jan 1970), 29-34.

Bernard Shaw was fascinated with the military, war, and the effect it had on people, but he never allowed this fascination to cloud his realistic perception of these military matters.   Shaw uses these matters for dramatic development, and he demonstrates frequently enough that military men are not expected to think, that heroic maneuvers in battle are, as often as not, mistakes that correct themselves by accident, that the romanticism of war is a sham.   Shaw uses the military situation to demonstrate that its leaders are human and more likely to err than to perfect.

1653 Mills, Carl H.   "Shaw's Superman: A Re-examination," ShawR, XIII (May 1970), 48-58.

There are numerous misconceptions of the Shavian Superman. While it is true that Shaw was influenced by such predecessors as Nietzsche, Carlyle, Ibsen, Wagner, and Schopenhauer, it is wrong to think that Shaw assimilated their ideas totally in his conception of the Superman. Shaw's Superman is a synthesis, a refinement of and an improvement of these predecessors, "all brought up to date and conforming to the theory of Creative Evolution formulated by Lamarck, Butler, and Shaw."

1654 Mills, John A. "Acting Is Being: Bernard Shaw on the Art of the Actor," Shaw R, XIII (May 1970), 65-78.

Shaw's attitude toward the art of the actor, as was evinced in his correspondence, his choice of certain players for roles, the fact that he wrote several plays with certain players in mind, and the manner in which he directed productions of his own plays, is not as simple as has often been expressed. The common view is that he was opposed to the acting modes current in his time and preferred the older, more "flamboyant" styles. While he definitely favored technical perfection in an actor, he felt very strongly that an actor could not play a role that was out of the range of his own emotional experience, what Shaw called the "inner truth." Such a view certainly indicates that he was more progressive in his attitudes toward acting than has been commonly recognized.

1655 Monod, Sylvère. "1900-1920: The Age of Chesterton," DICKENSIAN, LXVI (May 1970), 101-20.
[Shaw's criticism of Dickens, especially of HARD TIMES.]

1656 Morgan, Margery M. *"Major Barbara,"* in TCIMB; rptd as Chap 8, THE SHAVIAN PLAYGROUND (1972), pp. 134-57.

The mainspring of *Major Barbara* seems to have been provided by Blake and Nietzsche. The basic conflict of opposites is enacted within a child-parent relationship. Shaw rejects the morbid sentimentality of late Victorian Christianity and the womanly ideal associated with it. "The undercutting of the dramatic resolution in the reduction of Cusins and Barbara in the last moments is functional in referring the problem back to the audience . . . the true resolution of socialist drama belongs not in the work of art but outside it in society."

1657 Mudrick, Marvin. "Shaw," ON CULTURE AND LITERATURE (NY: Horizon P, 1970), 108-16; first published 1964, place unknown.
[Review of Shaw, G. B. *On Language,* ed by Abraham Tauber (1963); THE RELIGIOUS SPEECHES OF BERNARD SHAW, ed by Warren S. Smith (1963); Langner, Lawrence, G.B.S. AND THE LUNATIC; DuCann, C.G.L., THE LOVES OF BERNARD SHAW (1963); Purdom, C. B., A GUIDE TO THE PLAYS OF BERNARD SHAW (1963).] Shaw is no more a dramatist than Voltaire. His plays are so much duller and clumsier than his undramatic works. Shaw writing on the phonetic alphabet

is not even clever.   On religion, he is not much better.
Shaw's Prefaces are better than his plays.

1658 Munteanu, George.   "Liviu Rebreanu şi G. B.
Shaw" (Liviu Rebreanu and G. B. Shaw), TEATRUL
(Bucharest), IV (1970), 62-64.
[Not seen.]   [In Romanian.]

1659 Nelson, Raymond S.   "Blanco Posnet--Adversary
of God," MD, XIII (May 1970), 1-9.
Archibald Henderson characterized Shaw's *The Shewing-up of
Blanco Posnet* as the most sincerely religious of plays and
adds that Shaw is indebted to Tolstoy's POWER OF DARKNESS.
While it might well be asked what the notoriously
unorthodox Shaw has in common with Tolstoy, it is clear
that a similarity exists at three crucial points: both
are concerned with irreligious contempoary life, both have
blackguards as protagonists, and both focus a good deal of
attention on conversion.   Conversion for Shaw is not so
much the reformation of character as it is the redirection
of one's life to purposeful, socially useful ends.   A clue
to what Shaw had in mind in dramatizing Blanco Posnet's
conversion is an interview he wrote which appeared in the
NEW YORK EVENING SUN on 9 December 1911, in which he
states that he has taken the Old Testament prophets to
whom God was a terrible adversary as his models.   Blanco
Posnet, like them, wrestles with God and yields only when
he becomes conscious that the will against which he
struggled was indeed the nobler part of his own will.
Caught in the grip of the "Lord," Shaw's Life Force, he
will spend the rest of his life doing the job for which he
was created.

1660 Nelson, Raymond S.   "The Church, the Stage, and
Shaw," MIDWEST QUARTERLY, XI (1970), 293-308.
Church and stage had been at odds with each other long
before Shaw joined the fray.   Dramatic art for Shaw is a
vehicle for moral instruction, and unlike the earlier
attackers of the stage, Stephen Gosson and Jeremy Collier,
his interest rested not with the welfare of the church,
but with the revitalization of the stage with a living
morality to aid in the understanding and advancement of
man.   Shaw became embroiled in the debate through his
weekly dramatic review for the SATURDAY REVIEW.   He
continually exposed the shallowness and emptiness of those
plays which fell short of true reality.   Shaw took no
sides in the controversary but was a religious man working

in the theater to advance the welfare of men. The dividing line between church and stage becomes in Shaw increasingly hard to find. Convinced of the power of drama in the service of moral purpose, Shaw wrote plays that did more than pander to the public taste. He set out to reform mankind through the art of drama.

1661 Nelson, Raymond S. "Shaw's Keegan," Shaw R, XIII (Sept 1970), 92-95.
The commonly held notion that George Tyrell, a modernist Catholic priest, was the person who served as the inspiration for the character of Keegan in *John Bull's Other Island*, should be challenged, for while some of the characteristics of Keegan are perhaps drawn from other sources, Edward Carpenter was, in fact, the central inspiration for Keegan. Carpenter's character, his ideas, his lifestyle, the circle of friends that surrounded him, and the relationship he bore to Shaw all point to him as the most central source for Keegan.

1662 Nethercot, Arthur H. *"Mrs. Warren's Profession* and THE SECOND MRS. TANQUERAY," Shaw R, XIII (1970), 26-28.
While Shaw stated to Folding Bright that the name "Jarman" never came into his head as the title for *Mrs. Warren's Profession*, his official biographer mentions it, and regardless of Shaw's denial, the title "Mrs. Jarman's Profession" is "a curious illustration of the influence of Paula Tanqueray."

1663 Ogiso, Masafumi. "Bernard Shaw no Joseizo" (Bernard Shaw's Female Characters), JISSEN BUNGAKU (Tokyo), No 41 (Dec 1970), pp. 28-40.
Shaw created four types of female characters: 1) the Womanly Woman (Blanche, Violet, Ann, Julia, Mrs. Warren); 2) the New Woman (Vivie, Grace, Ellie, Raina); 3) the Mother Woman (Candida, Lady Cicely); and 4) the Religious Woman (Barbara, Saint Joan, Lavinia). [In Japanese.]

1664 Pascal, Valerie. THE DISCIPLE AND HIS DEVIL: GABRIEL PASCAL, BERNARD SHAW (NY: McGraw-Hill, 1970).
[Bernard Shaw first appears in this work in chapter five where his initial meeting with Gabriel Pascal in 1935 over the launching of *Pygmalion* for the film adaptation is described in great detail. Subsequent chapters describe

the negotiations for and the actual filming of other Shaw plays. Only the middle chapters of the book have sufficient material on Shaw, but there is at the end of the book two items of interest: a narration of Shaw's death and Pascal's too-late return, and a discussion of developing *Pygmalion* into a musical, the future MY FAIR LADY.]

1665 Ponce, Aníbal. "Bernard Shaw, Meredith y 'La Réclame'" (Bernard Shaw, Meredith and 'Fame'), LOS AUTORES Y LOS LIBROS (The Authors and The Books) (Buenos Aires: Ed. El Viento en el Mundo, 1970), pp. 183-84.
George Meredith failed for having disregarded in his own time the works of writers like Shaw. [In Spanish.]

1666 Priestly, J. B. THE EDWARDIANS (NY and Evanston: Harper & Row, 1970), pp. 89-91, 119, 120, 121, 122, 140-41, 161, 163, 164, 212.
Shaw flourished in the Edwardian atmosphere of hopeful debate. He and some of the other Fabians were sharply anti-democratic. Shaw's plays suffer very little from play reading if it is done intelligently. [Alick P. F. Ritchie caricature of Shaw; the Fabian Window; photographs of *Man and Superman* and *Press Cuttings*.]

1667 Rakitina, L. "Izbrannik Sud'by" (*The Man of Destiny*), TEATR (Moscow), VII (1970), 56-59.
The actor-producer S. Iurskii turned *The Man of Destiny* at the Gorkii Theater into an original genre by using the Preface as a staged prologue, with musical accompaniment by S. Rosentzweig. [In Russian.]

1668 Reuben, Elaine. "The Social Dramatist: A Study of Shaw's English Family Plays," DAI, XXXI (Oct 1970), 1810-11A. Unpublished dissertation, Stanford University,1970.

1669 Richards, Robert F. "Literature and Politics," COLORADO QUARTERLY, XIX (Summer 1970), 97-106.
Shaw makes us think. He used wit to change opinions.

1670 Roby, Kinley. "Arnold Bennett: Shaw's Ten O'Clock Scholar," Shaw R, XIII (Sept 1970), 96, 104.

The relationship between George Bernard Shaw and Arnold Bennett, often acrimonious in public debate, was warm and friendly in their private correspondence. But the public and private relationship between these two men, who were near or at the top of their respective literary professions at the same time, contained intriguing ambivalencies.

1671 Romm, A. S. "Istoricheskaĭa drama Bernarda Shou *Svĭataĭa Ioanna*: problema istorizma Shou" (Bernard Shaw's Historical Drama *Saint Joan*: Problems of Shaw's Historicism), UCHENYE ZAPISKI LENINGRADSKOGO GOS. PED. INST. IM. GERTZENA (Leningrad), CCCLXXVI (1970), 221-47.
Shaw's original philosophy of history enabled him to establish a completely new type of historical drama, which was an innovation not only in ideas but also in dramatic form. He used the principle of mixing different historical periods, making characters of the first century speak the language of the nineteenth, attributing manners and customs of ancient Egypt to his contemporaries, a procedure unacceptable in serious drama before him. The idea of development was at the basis of his philosophy of history. His view of the contempoary world was partly retrospective and enabled him to grasp history as a whole. Certain critics feel *Saint Joan* was a departure from his other plays, though in fact it gives a clearer expression of his philosophy of history. [In Russian.]

1672 Roy, Emil. "Pygmalion Revisited," BALL STATE UNIVERSITY FORUM, XI (1970), 38-46.
The structure of Bernard Shaw's *Pygmalion* is quite conventional. It presents, side by side, the personal comedy of Eliza Doolittle's evolution toward independence and the social comedy of her father's rise into middle-class affluence. These two plot structures, however rewarding in themselves, do not converge upon the traditional expectation of a happy marriage union. Shaw's denial of such an ending underscores his own inner conflicts and is symptomatic of a deep ambivalence pervading the entire play. Higgins comes off as a discarder of all feelings as a human being, a disembodied and passionless observer of events for which he takes no responsibility. Yet he is clearly the hero of the play, whose wit, intelligence, and charm compensate for the negative elements of his character. Eliza will create the ideal man by using Freddy as her biological and Higgins as her intellectual instruments. Ironically, *Pygmalion* is its own sequel.

1673 Ryšánková, Helena. "Bibliografii Sestavila"
(Selective Bibliography), GEORGE BERNARD SHAW,
VZPOMÍNKA PŘI PŘÍLEŽITOSTI 20 VÝROČÍ JENO ÚMRTÍ
(George Bernard Shaw, A Memorial on the 20th Anni-
versary of His Death) (Plzen [Pilsen]:   Knihovna
Města Plzně [City Library of Pilsen], 1970), pp. 15-
38.
[Brief bibliography of works about Shaw. Extensive bib-
liography of Shaw's writings with data of Czechoslovakian
translations and publication.] [In Czechoslovak.]

1674 Sahai, Surendra. ENGLISH DRAMA 1865-1900 (New
Delhi: [W. H. Patwardham] Orient Longman, 1970),
pp. 142-65.
[Chapter VIII presents a commentary on the eight plays
published in *Plays Pleasant and Unpleasant* and *Three Plays
for Puritans*.] *Widowers' Houses* has no conflict in it and
no human interest at all. The characters in *The
Philanderer* are lifeless and at best stagey. The failure
of these plays is due to lack of any interest and an
absence of art. *Mrs. Warren's Profession* is a more mature
play, and it shows Shaw's power as a dramatist.
Especially *Candida* in *Plays Pleasant* shows an even greater
maturity in technique and characterization; it is the
first play in which Shaw successfully combined theme and
technique without overemphasizing either, a fault which
destroyed the artistic effect of his earlier plays.

Three Plays for Puritans is a culmination of Shaw's
developing art. *Caesar and Cleopatra* presents Shaw's
concept of life governed by reason, not impulse, and it
finds its first perfect expression in this play. Shaw is
the only dramatist of the nineteenth century whose ideas
correspond with contemporary philosophy, and as such they
are the best examples of drama in the process of
development.

1675 Schuchter, J. D. "Shaw's *Major Barbara*,"
EXPLICATOR XXVIII (1970), Item 74.
In Roman Catholic hagiology, Barbara is the patron saint
of fusiliers, protector of artillerymen. Hence, in Shaw's
play Barbara's destiny as mistress of the cannon works is
implicit at the outset. Shaw could have hardly chosen a
better name.

1676 Seabrook, Alexander. "G.B.S. and G.K.C.,"
ShawR, XIII (Sept 1970), 132-34. [A Review of SHAW

AND CHESTERTON, THE METAPHYSICAL JESTERS, by William
B. Furlong (1970).]
The most interesting chapters in the book are those
devoted to the great debates between G.B.S. and G.K.C.
The analysis of their debating styles is fine, but the
spontaneous debate between the two reported by Hesketh
Pearson was bogus as Pearson acknowledged in THINKING IT
OVER (1938). Mr. Furlong was hoodwinked along with the
others.

1677 Shinkuma, Kiyoshi. "Shaw a Satirist," NAGOYA
GAKUINDAIGAKU RONSHU (Seto), VII (March 1970), 103-
27.
The Apple Cart is a low burlesque in that a grave subject
is caricatured mockingly. It is also a sardonic picture
in caricature of our cabinet and our democracy. [In
Japanese.]

1678 Smith, Warren Sylvester (ed). BERNARD SHAW'S
PLAYS (NY: W. W. Norton [Norton Critical Edition],
1970).
Contents, abstracted under date of first publication:
Warren Sylvester Smith, "Preface" (1970); "The Plays of
Bernard Shaw," "Notes" and "Selected Bibliography" [not
abstracted]; John Gassner, "Bernard Shaw and the Making of
the Modern Mind," COLLEGE ENGLISH (1962); Martin Meisel,
"Opera and Drama," from SHAW AND THE NINETEENTH-CENTURY
THEATER (1963); Julian B. Kaye, "Shaw and Nineteenth-
Century Political Economists," from SHAW AND THE
NINETEENTH-CENTURY TRADITION (1958); Warren Sylvester
Smith, ["Shaw as Religious Heretic"], from THE LONDON
HERETICS (1967); Stanley Weintraub, "The Avant-Garde
Shaw," from SHAW SEMINAR PAPERS-65; G. K. Chesterton, ["A
1909 View of *Major Barbara*"], from GEORGE BERNARD SHAW
(1909); Barbara Bellow Watson, "Sainthood for
Millionaires," MD (1968); Sydney P. Albert, "'In More Ways
Than One'": *Major Barbara*'s Debt to Gilbert Murray," ETJ
(1968); Michael J. Mendelsohn, "The Heartbreak Houses of
Shaw and Chekhov," ShawR (1963); Harold Clurman, "Notes
for a Production of *Heartbreak House*," TULANE DRAMA REVIEW
(1961); Louis Crompton, "*Heartbreak House*," from SHAW THE
DRAMATIST (1969); Arthur H. Nethercot, "Zepplins over
Heartbreak House," ShawR (1966); from THE TRIAL OF JEANNE
D'ARC [not abstracted]; Luigi Pirandello, "Bernard Shaw's
Saint Joan," NYTMag (1924); Alice Griffin, "The New York
Critics and *Saint Joan*," ShawB (1955); Katherine Haynes
Gatch, "The Last Plays of Bernard Shaw: Dialectic and
Despair," ENGLISH INSTITUTE ESSAYS FOR 1954 (1954);

Stanley Weintraub, "The Two Sides of 'Lawrence of Arabia':
Aubrey and Meek," ShawR (1964); Frederick P. W. McDowell,
["The 'Pentecostal Flame' and the 'Lower Centers'"], ShawR
(1959).

1679 Špot, Josef. "Text Zpracoval," (Introductory
Text), GEORGE BERNARD SHAW, VZPOMÍNKA PŘI PŘÍLEŽI-
TOSTI 20. VÝROČÍ JEHO ÚMRTÍ (George Bernard Shaw, A
Memorial on the 20th Anniversary of His Death)
(Plzeň [Pilsen]: Knihovna Města Plzně [City Library
of Pilsen], 1970), pp. 1-14.
[Biographical Survey of Shaw, the enemy of the
bourgeoisie, from the perspective of the "last twenty
years."] [In Czechoslovak.]

1680 Spurling, Hilary. "*Saint Joan*," P&P, XVIII
(Oct 1970), 30-31.
The curious thing about *Saint Joan*, an irremediably dull
play, is why it should be regarded with such reverent
enthusiasm. [Review of Mermaid production. Photographs.]

1681 Thatcher, David S. "George Bernard Shaw,"
NIETZSCHE IN ENGLAND, 1890-1914 (Toronto: U of
Toronto P, 1970), pp. 175-217.
Shaw was regarded, even by writers more knowledgeable
about Nietzsche's work than himself, as the chief
popularizer of Nietzsche in England. Shaw's point of
contact with Nietzsche emerged indirectly through Ibsen,
Wagner, Schopenhauer, and Nordau. Shaw began to take
Nietzsche seriously around 1901, the beginning of the
composition of *Man and Superman*, but he was never a
systematic, thorough student of Nietzsche. But his
"Nietzscheanism" came under attack from many quarters for
various reasons. Finally, if Nietzsche's attitude towards
Euripides and Carlyle is any guide, Shaw had little
genuine understanding of why Nietzsche proclaimed himself
the first tragic philosopher of modern times.

1682 Tsitnikov, G. I. "Oruzhem Marksistskoĭ Kritiki
(Tvorchestvo Bernarda Shou v otsenke A. V. Luna-
charskogo)" (Armed with Marxist Criticism: Bernard
Shaw's Work as Estimated by A. V. Lunarcharsky),
VOPROSY LITERATURY (Krasnoĭarsk) (1970), 50-66.
[Not seen.] [In Russian.]

1683 Turco, Alfred. "Sir Colenso's White Lie," Shaw R, XIII (Jan 1970), 14-25.

Sir Colenso's dilemma is not whether he should save either Dubedat or Blenkinsop, but whether he should go ahead and "murder" Dubedat in order to get at his wife, Jennifer. This struggle definitely establishes the play as a tragedy as it is subtitled: the tragedy of Sir Colenso's own small, grasping nature given the power of life and death over men. It is a play that manages the ironic mingling of the trite problem play with the technical elements of classical drama.

1684 Vladirmirov, N. "G. B. Shou satitsĭa za mashinku" (G. B. Shaw Sits at His Typewriter), LIT-ERATURNAIĂ GAZETA (Moscow), 3 Dec 1970, p. 15.
[Not seen.] [In Russian.]

1685 Weintraub, Stanley. "The Making of an Irish Patriot: Bernard Shaw 1914-1916," EIRE, IV (1970), 9-27.

In November 1914, smarting under the attacks following publication of his *Common Sense about the War* pamphlet that he was pro-German, Shaw had tried to explain his position by way of Ireland. He tried to turn the Irish extremists who promoted pro-Germanism and Irish insurrection toward moderation. Shaw claimed to reconcile his obligations as a British subject with his objectivity as an Irishman. Shaw visited Lady Gregory during Easter 1915. An outgrowth of this visit was an ironic playlet of war recruiting in Ireland intended to help her hard-pressed Abbey Theatre. *O'Flaherty, V. C.* was also an opportunity to encourage Irish enlistments in the British Army through a play paradoxically calculated to appeal to Irishmen through its satire of Englishmen. Shaw subtitled his playlet "a recruiting pamphlet," and thought of it as "a recruiting poster in disguise."

Shaw went to great lengths to save the life of Sir Roger Casement, one of the Irish revolutionaries. August 1916 saw the beginning in Ireland of a surprising Shavian apotheosis. Shaw efforts for Irish patriots were not overlooked by the Irish. When the Abbey Theatre opened, its first three offerings were three Shavian plays, *Widowers' Houses, John Bull's Other Island,* and *Arms and the Man.* Other Shaw plays followed for that season. "The repatriation" of G. B. S. was complete.

1686 Weintraub, Stanley. "A Patchwork Self-Portrait, 1898-1950," SHAW, AN AUTOBIOGRAPHY, 1898-1950, selected by Stanley Weintraub (NY: Weybright and Talley, 1970; Lond: Reinhardt, 1971), pp. vii-ix, 263-96.
Shaw furnished sufficient material to construct a patchwork self-portrait of his life. He often was publicly silent on personal matters and wrote a good deal on subjects he wished to inflate. He wrote almost nothing about his marriage; his changing politics were another kind of blind spot. As is appropriate for a man of ideas, Shaw's autobiographical writings emphasize the progress of his mind.

1687 Weintraub, Stanley. "Shaw's LEAR," ARIEL, A REVIEW OF INTERNATIONAL ENGLISH LITERATURE, I (1970), 59-68.
Shaw made numerous references, all rather late in his life, to *Heartbreak House* as his KING LEAR play, in spite of the sub-title reference to Chekhov. When asked about its meaning, his stock reply was, "How should I know? I am only the author." The Shaw of 1914-18, confronted with a sense of helplessness and futility of the war years, wrote *Heartbreak* while within that frame of mind. The pessimism and near-nihilism of KING LEAR is indeed reverberated here in *Heartbreak*, but the outlook is, nevertheless, also radically different from LEAR.

1688 Zimbardo, Rose. "Introduction," TCIMB, pp. 1-15.
Taking the clue from Shaw, who subtitled *Major Barbara* "a discussion in three acts," but missing the irony, critics have focused upon the issues and have ignored the form, the pattern, the art of the play. The play, as Shaw claimed, "allows the expression of tragic truth within a comic design" and should therefore be seen as a conflict between the tragic view of man as superior to the world and its comic counterpart that man is its servant. The comic design in *Barbara* is not linear but cyclical: Barbara and Cusins replace Lady Britomart and Undershaft as the new generators in the ever upward advancement of the Life Force. Undershaft, the Dionysus, the tragic god, comes to his fullest expression, only to fall before the god reborn, the next Andrew Undershaft. The education of both Barbara and Cusins is to recognize that the spirit of the universe is will, and their choice is nothing other than the realization of their vital beings.

447

1689 Zimbardo, Rose (ed). TWENTIETH CENTURY INTER-
PRETATIONS OF MAJOR BARBARA (Englewood Cliffs, NJ:
Prentice-Hall, [Spectrum Books], 1970).
Table of contents, abstracted under date of original
publication: Rose Zimbardo, "Introduction" (1970); Martin
Meisel, from SHAW AND THE NINETEENTH CENTURY THEATER
(1963); Joseph Frank, "Shaw's 'Divine Comedy'" (1956);
Anthony S. Abbott, from SHAW AND CHRISTIANITY (1965);
Bernard Dukore, "The Undershaft Maxims" (1966); Margery M.
Morgan, "Major Barbara" (1970); Fred Mayne, from THE WIT
AND SATIRE OF GEORGE BERNARD SHAW (1967); Eric Bentley
from BERNARD SHAW (1947, 1957); Harold Fromm, from BERNARD
SHAW AND THE THEATRE IN THE NINETIES (1967); Francis
Fergusson, from THE IDEA OF A THEATER (1949); Donald
Costello, from THE SERPENT'S EYE: SHAW AND CINEMA (1965).

1971

1690 Adams, Elsie B. BERNARD SHAW AND THE AESTHETES
(Columbus: Ohio State UP, 1971).
[The book is divided into three major sections: Shaw and
the Moral Aesthetes; Shaw and the *fin de siècle*
Aestheticism; and the Aesthete and the Shavian Artist.

[Ms. Adams agrees with Holbrook Jackson's position of the
1890's that Shaw belongs to a movement of "art for life's
sake." She examines Shaw's relationship to two distinct
groups of aesthetes, that group which viewed the purpose
of art as essentially a moral one (Ruskin, Rossetti, the
Pre-Raphaelites, and Morris); and that group which
divorced the purpose of art from morality (Swinburne,
Whistler, Pater, Moore, Wilde, Beardsley, and Symons.)]

Shaw is sympathetic with much of Ruskin's and Morris's
thoughts on art, for like them he believed art was both
the reason for and result of social or moral change.
Shaw's utopia is not one of sensuous beauty but of
contemplation where art is abandoned with the toys of
childhood. The sense of the religious mission of the
theater is the key to understanding Shaw's reference to
Plays Pleasant as Pre-Raphaelite dramas, for like medieval
art they arise out of a genuine religious impulse.
Candida, for example, is a modern mystery play of Madonna
and Child.

Shaw's position is that art must ultimately serve a moral purpose, but not conventional morality; in fact, art is to be in opposition to conventional morality. In this regard, he shares with the *fin-de-siècle* aesthetes their desire to shock the public, seeking not a withdrawal but a change in society and ultimattely a change in the nature of humankind. He is not adverse to style, for he is, after all, a highly conscious artist, and his dramas should not be mistaken for formlessness. Like Wilde, Shaw maintains that life imitates art. His regret is that the art imitated is too often a shabby one.

Shaw's depiction of the aesthete in his novels and early plays is often contrasted with the expressor of Shavian values to make the contrast favorable to the latter. His artist is indifferent to convention and unscrupulous in his use of others for his own purpose, often being totally misunderstood by the public.

Shaw owes more to the Aesthetes than he acknowledged and probably more than he was aware of. Though his final faith in the power of thought transcends all sensory appeals, includingg the sensory appeal of art, no aesthete could have placed more emphasis on the place of art in man's life than Shaw did. His role as poet-prophet was to provide a "magic mirror . . . to reflect your invisible dreams in visible pictures."

1691 Albert, Sidney P. "The Price of Salvation: Moral Economics in *Major Barbara*," MD, XIV (Dec 1971), 307-23.
Major Barbara, as Shaw contended, could not have been written by an economic ignoramus, but what does that play tell us about the influence economics exerts on "life, character, and human destiny"?

In the first act the economic concerns of the family become the vehicle for viewing the moral, political, and religious structure of society. The serious challenges to Undershaft's crass materialism come from Barbara's genuine morality and religious dedication and Cusins's needs of the intellect and culture. The play progresses from domestic economy to the more complicated moral economics of religious charity, sin, and redemption in the second act. This act drives home the lesson that punishment breeds forgiveness, and both undermine morality. The third act takes up the larger issue of the rearrangement of men and society and centers upon "the interview" between Undershaft and Cusins in which the discussion moves from practical, economic considerations to their moral implications. Undershaft is morally neutral, not so Cusins and Barbara. Money remains "the price of Salvation" for him, but for Cusins and Barbara the sale of their souls is "for reality and for power" beyond themselves.

1692 Albert, Sidney P. "Reflections on Shaw and Psychoanalysis," MD, XIV (Sept 1971), 169-94.
Arthur Nethercot in "Bernard Shaw and Psychoanalysis" (1969) has performed a valuable service in introducing Shaw's relation to psychoanalysis, but it is incomplete; he misunderstands Shaw's assessment of Freudian psychoanalysis, and he underestimates Shaw's own contribution. [Evidence from Shaw's writing is presented to argue that Shaw knew of Freud at least by 1911. Citing Shaw's letters and prefaces, Albert shows that Shaw was not without some sympathy with Freud as an iconoclast, though he regarded most Freudians with his usual scepticism.] Freud (persuaded to read it by Ernest Jones) had occasion to draw on *Man and Superman*. Jones regarded *The Revolutionists' Handbook* highly; he cited *Caesar and Cleopatra* in PSYCHOPATHOLOGY OF EVERYDAY LIFE and again brought Shaw to Freud's attention. Ultimately Freud's attitude toward Shaw was derogatory, though Jones found much in Shaw's writings that was valuable. Shaw fortunately is a better psychologist because he is less a Freudian; he is always weakest when his thought is based on a particular school or system.

1693 Anderson, Jarvis Lynn. "The Artist Figure in Modern Drama," DAI, XXXII (1971), 6594A. Unpublished dissertation, University of Minnesota, 1971.

1694 Austin, Don. "The Structural Meaning of *Man and Superman*," SHAVIAN, IV (Spring 1971), 127-29.
The scene and act structure of *Man and Superman* points out the growing awareness of the hero. Each act concludes with a revelation to Tanner of his relationship to Ann. Each revelation moves toward a reconciliation between Tanner and Ramsden. As Tanner moves from illusion to reality, the play moves from present to future. This complexity promotes and parallels the conflict between youth and age and Tanner's growing awareness. The ultimate reality of the play is that woman is the Superman.

1695 Balashov, P. S. "Bernard Shou i idealy Oktíabría" (Shaw and the Ideals of October 1917, IZVESTIÍA AKADEMII NAUK SSSR: SERIÍA LITERATURY I ÍAZYKA (Moscow), XXX (1971) pp. 27-39.
Engels wrote of Shaw (1892) as "a paradoxical belles-lettrist, talented and sharp-witted, but worthless as an economist or politician." Like the plays, Shaw's journalism of the twenties is full of bitter reflections on World War I and the future of bourgeois civilization. Analysis of Shaw's work in this period clearly demonstrates that his criticism of bourgeois society has taken on new, more destructive forms, which in turn explains the emotional atmosphere of the major plays of this period: *Back to Methuselah, Saint Joan,* and *The Apple Cart,* for which *Heartbreak House,* with its satirical and lyrical opening, prepared the way. In 1941, Shaw wrote to A. Fadeev (letter is in the Archives of the Foreign Commission of the Union of Writers of the USSR), "When Russia destroys Hitler, she will become the spirtual center of the world." The ideals of Socialism aroused Shaw's enthusiasm, though his views on the way in which social antagonisms should be resolved were wrong. However, Shaw saw the humanistic character of the October Revolution, with its just and humane relations between people. [In Russian.]

1696 Balashov, P. S. "Posleslovie" (Afterword) in NOVELLI (Tales) by G. B. Shou (Moscow: Khudozhestvennaía literatura, 1971), pp. 210-23.
[Not seen.] [In Russian.]

1697 Bantaş, Andrei. PAGINI ALESE. SHAW DESPRE SINE ŞI DESPRE ALŢII (Selected Works. Shaw about Himself and about Others.) (Bucharest: Minerva, 1971).
[An introduction, not seen.] [In Romanian.]

1698 Barghel, Virginia. "Prefaţa, Prescurtarea Textului, Notele Explicative şi Vocabularul" (Preface, Abbreviated Text, Explanatory Notes, and Vocabulary), PYGMALION by G. B. Shaw (Bucureşti: Editura Didactica şi Pedagogica, 1971), pp. 7-12, 125-42, passim.
Shaw wrote about 50 plays in which he crushes the false bourgeois idols and values of the England of his time. *Pygmalion* stresses the profoundly moral idea of the development of personality through education. [In Romanian. Shaw Text and Chronological Table in English.]

1699 Bastable, Adolphus (pseud). "Our Theatres in the Seventies," SHAVIAN, IV (Spring 1971), 130-35.
The choice of *Major Barbara* at the Aldwych is inspired because of the new conservative government's apparent intention to adhere to its principles by making money at the expense of its principles. The issues Shaw raised in 1905 are with us today. The brilliance of the production lay in the clear expression of Shaw's ideas with no sacrifice of his wit. *Arms and the Man* suffered a setback when Laurence Harvey broke his leg and could play Sergius only toward the end of the run; anyone can play Bluntschli. Angela Pleasance made a brave try at *Saint Joan* at the Mermaid Theatre.

1700 Berner, S. S. "Stilicheskoe ispol'zovanie razgovornoĭ rechi v p'ese Bernarda Shou *Pigmalion*" (Stylistic Use of Colloquial Speech in *Pygmalion*), IZVESTIĬA VORONEZHSKOGO PED. INST. (Voronezh), III (1971), 3-17.
[Not seen.] [In Russian.]

1701 Best, Brian Stanley. "Development of Bernard Shaw's Philosophy of the Responsible Society," DAI, XXXII (Dec 1971), 3292A. Unpublished dissertation, University of Wisconsin, 1971.

1702 Bevan, Earl Dean, (ed). A CONCORDANCE TO THE PLAYS AND PREFACES OF BERNARD SHAW (Detroit: Gale Research Co., 1971).
[The CONCORDANCE extends to ten volumes and is based upon the Constable STANDARD EDITION of Shaw's plays and Prefaces. It omits the novels, criticism, letters, and political writings of Shaw. It is unfortunate that the publication of the CONCORDANCE preceded the Bodley Head edition of Shaw's plays and Prefaces, a more definitive edition than the STANDARD EDITION. It still remains, however, an extremely valuable source for Shavian research.]

1703 Bevan, Earl Dean. "The Making of a Shaw Concordance," DAI, XXXII (Oct 1971), 2081-82A. Published dissertation, University of Kansas, 1971, pub as A CONCORDANCE TO THE PLAYS OF BERNARD SHAW (1971).

1704 Bevan, Earl D. "A Shaw Concordance," MD, XIV (Sept 1971), 155-68.
The advent of computers has greatly assisted in the making of concordance. The present SHAW CONCORDANCE (1971) is the largest of its kind now in existence. It is limited to the plays and Prefaces and is based upon the Constable Edition of 1930-1938, rounding it out with the two later volumes containing *Buoyant Billions*, *Farfetched Fables*, *Shakes Versus Shav*, *Geneva*, *Cymbeline Refinished*, and *In Good King Charles's Golden Days*.

1705 Bowman, David H. "Shaw, Stead, and the Undershaft Tradition," ShawR, XIV (Jan 1971), 29-32.
W. T. Stead's MR. CARNEGIE'S CONUNDRUM contains major ideas that appealed to Shaw and eventually found their way in *Major Barbara*. Central among them is Shaw's dramatization of the Undershaft Tradition, the infusion of new blood into the business by rejecting the conventional family inheritance, the link-up with the Salvation Army in portraying conflict between Jehovah and Mammon, and Andrew Carnegie himself as the model for Undershaft in which the former's Gospel of Wealth is transformed into the latter's religion of a millionaire. Carnegie's ideas and Stead's crusades were seminal in the composition of *Major Barbara*.

1706 Boza Masvidal, A. "La dramática de Shaw y Pirandello" (The Drama of Shaw and Pirandello), RAGIONI CRITICHE, I (1971), 111-30.
[Not seen.] [In Spanish.]

1707 Bradbury, Malcolm. THE SOCIAL CONTEXT OF MODERN ENGLISH LITERATURE (Oxford: Basil Blackwell, 1971), pp. xxxi, xxxiv, 52, 85, 89, 142, 149, 151, 158-59, 209.
Shaw was one of those writers of the age of transition who managed to mediate seriousness and popularity. He was very successful from a commercial point of view.

1708 Bringle, Jerald E. (ed). BERNARD SHAW, PASSION PLAY: A DRAMATIC FRAGMENT, 1878 (Lond: Bertram Rota, 1971).
In February of 1878, when Shaw was 22 years old, he drafted a dramatization of Jesus. He abandoned the writing before its completion and made one short reference to it in *Sixteen Self Sketches*: "Virtually my first works were in the five novels I wrote from 1879-83, which nobody

would publish. I began a profane Passion Play, with the mother of the *hero* represented as a termagant, but never carried it through." The text is based upon the first and only copy of Shaw's 49 page holograph, written in blank verse, dated, but left untitled ["Passion Play," BM Add MSS 50593].

1709 Bringle, Jerald E. "The First Unpleasant Play by Bernard Shaw: An Analysis of the Formation and Evolution of *Widowers' Houses*," DAI, XXXII (1971), 3294A. Unpublished dissertation, New York University, 1969.

1710 Brodie, Alexander H. "A Hitherto Unrecorded Shaw Edition," BOOK COLLECTOR, XX (1971), 531-33. [Note 344 refers to a hitherto unrecorded edition of Shaw plays. Correspondence between Shaw and the Army authorities regarding this projected publication of the Forces Edition will be found in TORCH: THE JOURNAL OF THE ROYAL ARMY EDUCATIONAL CORPS, IV (April 1961), 11-14. (Not seen.)]

1711 Brown, G. E. GEORGE BERNARD SHAW (Lond: Evans Brothers Limited, 1970; NY: Arco Publishing Company [Arco Literary Critiques], 1971).
[Brown organizes his book into seven chapters. The first chapter presents the prospective for the other chapters, that is, to demonstrate how Shaw's plays work dramatically. Chapter two takes up the early plays which, while never too popular, have been successfully revived because Shaw uses a strong central situation and surrounds it with superficial trimmings which attract the casual theater-goer. These early plays are flawed by the clumsiness in the contrivance of exits and entrances and the plots are furthered by too much coincidence. Chapter three deals with Shaw's concept of Creative Evolution and the plays that rely upon it, namely, *Man and Superman, Back to Methuselah,* and *The Simpleton of the Unexpected Isles*. These plays demonstrate that Shaw is not interested merely in presenting problems, but in solving them through self-awareness and self-knowledge. They are plays that deal with the eternal interest of the philosopher's stone which enables men to live forever. Chapter four takes up the religious plays, *Major Barbara, Androcles and the Lion,* and *Saint Joan*. Shaw's interest in religious beliefs centers on its effect upon human conduct. Chapter five examines certain comic techniques,

such as paradox, comic character, and the anti-English joke as they are employed in *Caesar and Cleopatra, The Doctor's Dilemma,* and *Heartbreak House.*

Chapter six examines characterizations in such plays as *You Never Can Tell, Pygmalion, O'Flaherty V.C., Apple Cart, Geneva, Too True to Be Good.* Chapter seven, the final chapter, deals with such prose compositions as *The Intelligent Women's Guide to Socialism, Everybody's Poetical What's What,* the *Adventures of the Black Girl in Her Search for God,* and, of course, the Prefaces which often cost Shaw more labor than the plays themselves and do contain his personal views.]

1712 Cary, Richard. "Shaw Reviews SATAN THE WASTER," COLBY LIBRARY QUARTERLY, IX (1971), 335-47. In the summer of 1920, Vernon Lee, (Violet Paget) published a three-part work entitled SATAN THE WASTER: A PHILOSOPHIC WAR TRILOGY. Similar to many of Shaw's published works, Lee's publication contained a lengthy prologue, notes, and epilogue beside the "allegorical puppet-show" itself. Shaw's review in the NATION was favorable to Lee but only at the expense of Lloyd George, then Prime Minister. Lee's response to the review was one of gratitude, missing Shaw's subtle rhetorical purpose of praising her only to censure Mr. George. She must have realized that her response was far too grateful, for within a year she let fly a barrage of taunts at Shaw in a review of his play, *Back to Methuselah.* Their final exchange came when Miss Willis, a friend of Lee's, requested permission to reproduce Shaw's NATION review for a reissue of SATAN THE WASTER in 1930.

1713 Casper, Vivian C. "Shaw's Plays in the Light of Theories of Comic Form: An Increasing Linear Vision," DAI, XXXII (Oct 1971), 2083A. Unpublished dissertation, Rice University, 1971.

1714 Clemens, Cyril. "Bernard Shaw Meets Mark Twain," MARK TWAIN JOURNAL, XVI (Winter 1971), 22. [On the back page a letter to Cyril Clemens from Shaw is reprinted. In it Shaw recounts having met Mark Twain twice. Shaw recalls that he had stayed for lunch and told stories of the old Mississippi shopkeepers. Shaw acknowledged that they got along perfectly, as if they had known each other all their lives.]

1715 Codignola, L[uciano]. DUE MOMENTI DELLA CRISI DEL NATURALISMO TEATRALE: J. A. STRINDBERG, G. B. SHAW, DISPENSE DEL CORSO DEL PROF. L. CODIGNOLA (Two Moments of Crises in the Naturalistic Theater: J. A. Strindberg, G. B. Shaw, Course Notes of Prof. L. Codignola) (Urbino: Libreria Moderna Universitaria, 1971), pp. 93-149, 150-52.
For 50 years Shaw has been considered a revolutionary, but few have any idea why. He was a rebel outside the theater in his attitude toward the Boer War and World War I. [Comments of Shaw-without critical comment or amplification from the author--on *Caesar and Cleopatra, John Bull's Other Island, Man and Superman, The Doctor's Dilemma, Androcles and the Lion, Heartbreak House,* and *Saint Joan.* Biography. Of no value except as evidence of the very simple scholarship provided to Italian students.] [In Italian.]

1716 Cole, Margaret. THE LIFE OF G. D. H. COLE (Lond: Macmillan; NY: St Martin's P, 1971), pp. 37, 50, 51, 74, 75-76, 86, 90n, 117, 125, 127, 221, 223, 224.
[Shaw's appearance in the life of G. D. H. Cole, especially in relation to Fabian Society activities.]

1717 "The Comedy of an Unexpected Gentleman," SHAVIAN, IV (Spring 1971), 123-26.
A Fantasia in the Shavian Manner on Contemporary Themes. [A parody of Shaw.]

1718 Crane, Gladys. "Shaw's Comic Techniques in *Man and Superman*," ETJ, XXIII (March 1971), pp. 13-21.
Though *Man and Superman* has long been a favorite subject for critical analysis in which the focus of attention is on the philosophy of the play, a study of the techniques producing that humor is equally rewarding. Ann is not a typical "pursuing heroine," but is rather a woman with "superb control of her pursuing impulses." Contrast this control with Tanner's illusions of self-control, and the opportunities for comedy are apparent. Such character contrast and character self-delusion are also to be seen within the ironic focus of a comedy of manners. Shaw understood the basic sources of humor and applied them to the structure and characterization of *Superman* with superb skill.

1719 Crompton, Louis, with the assistance of Hilayne Cavanaugh (eds). "Introduction," THE ROAD TO EQUALITY: TEN UNPUBLISHED LECTURES AND ESSAYS, 1884-1918, by Bernard Shaw (Bost: Beacon P, 1971), pp. ix-xxxvi.

For 66 years, Shaw made social equality his major concern, devoting well over a thousand public lectures and essays to this theme. While he felt that equality of income was too radical for the Fabians in the 1890's, he was convinced that it was the next logical step to take after nationalization of land-ownership and industry. After the First World War, Shaw became increasingly concerned with the idea of the redistribution of income. Four main currents shaped nineteenth-century Socialism in England-- Utopian, Christian, Marxist, and Fabian, and to understand Shaw it is necessary to grasp his relationship to each. The least influential upon Shaw was Utopian Socialism. Shaw was much more amenable toward Christian Socialism because, like Carlyle and Ruskin, he believed that social instincts must rest on religious convictions. With Marx, Shaw ran into intellectual difficulty: Shaw abandoned Marx's economic theories because he was not a determinist at all. Shaw became a student of "the law of economic rent" and the so-called "non law of wages," and Henry George was his tutor. Shaw believed that inequalities could be dealt with by having the state correct rents for the public coffers, eventually expropriating the landowning class.

1720 Crompton, Louis, and Hilayne Cavanaugh (eds). "Shaw's 1884 Lecture on TROILUS AND CRESSIDA," ShawR, XIV (May 1971), 48-67.

This hitherto unpublished lecture which Shaw prepared on Shakespeare's TROILUS AND CRESSIDA for the New Shakespeare Society, founded by Frederick James Furnival in 1874, was read to the group in Shaw's absence by Miss Grace Latham on 29 February 1884.

After first giving a summary of the plot, Shaw systematically investigates its date of composition, its generic classification, its moral tone, its authenticity of authorship, and its literary sources. He concludes that the "date is within a year either way of 1600; that it should be classed as a history; that its moral is pessimistic; that it was written, with the possible exception of less than 20 lines, by Shakespeare; and that it was inspired by Chapman's ILIADS and founded partly on them and partly on the TROYLUS AND CRYSEYDE of Chaucer." The value of the lecture, as observed by the editors, is that it is "the fullest account we have of Shaw's theory of Shakespeare's development as a pessimist."

1721 Dawick, John. "Stagecraft and Structure in Shaw's Disquisitory Drama," MD, XIV (Dec 1971), 276-87.

The ultimate vision behind Shaw's drama is the desire to be free from the restrictions of matter, the desire for the vortex of pure intelligence. Shaw's dramaturgical materials were those of the nineteenth century, but he wished to free them to form new patterns. His new theater demanded a high degree of technical skill. *Getting Married, Misalliance* and *Heartbreak House* demonstrate this and also reveal "a progression from analytic to emblematic structure." The pattern of *Getting Married* "reflects the logical progression of its debate rather than its emotional development." In *Misalliance* Shaw used violent stage-business to show the need of a society that was bored with talk to find some escape. In *Heartbreak* atmosphere and rhythm create an emblematic pattern of the English ship of state drifting on the rocks of World War I.

1722 Dearden, James S. "*Ruskin's Politics* by Bernard Shaw," BOOK COLLECTOR, XX (1971), 335-46.

On 13 February 1918 a group of Ruskin's admirers formed the Ruskin Centenary Council, and Shaw was invited to be a member. His name was on the lecture list for Friday, 21 November 1919, but attendance was limited to holders of season tickets. The subsequent collection of these lectures for publication did not include Shaw's since it was intended for its own separate publication, which Shaw was not made aware of until sometime later. J. Howard Whitehouse supervised its publication, first under the printer Arthur J. Matthews, whose work was not satisfactory, so Whitehouse tried to interest the Caledonian Press, but that came to nought. Whitehouse then approached the Oxford University Press, which published 2000 copies: 500 were bound in September 1921 in quarter holland and grey paper boards. Over half of the first edition remains in stock at Bembridge, but it is virtually impossible to differentiate between copies of the first and second impression of the first edition.

1723 Dench, Judi. "Barbara and I," SHAVIAN, IV (Spring 1971), 120-22.

Both Shakespeare and Shaw demand total absorption by the
actors. Shaw's one fault is that he demands a great deal
from the audience. Barbara is, indeed, no match for
Undershaft. The play may be different today from its
appeal in 1905, because there was much more spiritual
commitment then.

1724 Denninghaus, Friedhelm. DIE DRAMATISCHE
KONZEPTION GEORGE BERNARD SHAWS. UNTERSUCHUNGEN ZUR
STRUKTUR DER BÜHNENGESELLSCHAFT UND ZUM AUFBAU DER
FIGUREN IN DEN STÜCKEN SHAWS (George Bernard Shaw's
Dramatic Concept. Studies in the Structure of Stage
Society and Characters in Shaw's Plays) (Stuttgart,
Berlin, Köln, Mainz: Kohlhammer, 1971); Russian
trans: F. Denninkhaus, TEATRALNOE PRIZVANIE SHOU
(Moscow: "Progress," 1978); part trans by John J.
Weisert, "Determinism and Voluntarism in Shaw and
Shakespeare," ShawR, XX (Sept. 1976), 120-31.
With Shaw's plays occurred a basic change in the history
of English drama. For the first time he made society the
subject of his plays; his drama is socially deterministic.
Shaw's deterministic concept is largely derived from his
studies of Karl Marx, but also influenced by Shelley and
Ibsen. Detailed analyses of his plays show how his char-
acters are determined by social forces, not only in his
Plays Unpleasant but also in plays like *Saint Joan, Arms
and the Man, Pygmalion, Getting Married,* and *John Bull's
Other Island.* Shaw's characters are not individuals but
representatives of social classes; they are "personifications of social conditions," as Marx wrote in DAS KAPITAL.
Even characters which appear free and independent, like
Vivie Warren or Saint Joan, are socially determined; they
represent a new class which develops in the womb of the
old societal structures. *Pygmalion* is an ideal show piece
of the deterministic drama in which a character is changed
by changing his social position. With Eliza, Shaw also
shows that the formation of a character is the result of a
dialectic interaction between natural characteristics and
social determination, the latter being the more decisive
factor. At the basis of Shaw's social determination is
economic determination. An analysis of *John Bull* shows
that the economic development in this play follows exactly
the laws of Marxist dialectics. Shaw's socially deterministic drama is in sharp contrast to Shakespeare's individualistic drama, which is centered on great individuals
as well as problems and conflicts considered eternally
human. *Joan* represents his most thorough discussion of
Shakespeare's art and philosophy. As in Karl Marx's
teachings, there is a utopian component of Shaw's socially

deterministic drama. His dream of a better future finds dramatic expression in *Back to Methuselah*. The deterministic and eschatological concept of history, so apparent in Shaw's work, can be traced back to the Romantics, even to the Greeks; but more specifically again to Karl Marx and Shelley. The perfect combination of the artistic and deterministic elements, however, Shaw found in Richard Wagner's RING OF THE NIBELUNGS. Although content takes precedence over form, Shaw sets out to find new forms for the modern scientific theater. His most important formalistic innovation is the discussion play, in which important social, moral and economic problems affecting the whole society, not merely individuals, are discussed. These problems can best be discussed in prose, and not in verse (this in sharp contract to T. S. Eliot's DIALOGUE ON DRAMATIC POETRY). Public address and its rhetorical devices supplant the monologue of the individualistic drama. Shaw's most important innovation can be seen in his portrayal of characters. He is not interested in man's eternal nature but in his changeability. His characters are full of contradiction, imposed on them by the environment in which they live. Shaw's characters can be classified by the degree of awareness they possess of these contradictions. Shaw's socially deterministic dramatic concept anticipates in many respects that of Bertolt Brecht, the famous German Marxist playwright. [In German.]

1725 Dervin, Daniel A. "George Bernard Shaw and the Uses of Energy," DAI, XXXII (1971), 425A. Unpublished dissertation, Columbia University, 1970.

1726 Downer, Alan S. "Shaw's First Play," SHAW: SEVEN CRITICAL ESSAYS, ed by Norman Rosenblood (Toronto and Buffalo: U of Toronto P, 1971), pp. 3-24.
There are certain keys to Shavianism in Shaw's note to William Archer accompanying *Rheingold*: "a series of consecutive dialogues in which an idea is prepared and developed; no idea of how the action will proceed beyond the point reached; a plot spells ruin for a play; a romantic notion brought into contact with real life." *Widowers' Houses* was a failure because it is bound by a plot, and the audience was not prepared for its Shavian elements; it is promising because Shaw proved he could create a vehicle that would perform its assigned functions. *Getting Married* is the first completely Shavian play. It is related to THE WAY OF THE WORLD. In

his Preface to *Three Plays by Brieux*, Shaw summarizes the
principles of Shavian drama.

1727 Dukore, Bernard. BERNARD SHAW, DIRECTOR
(Seattle: U of Washington P, 1971).
[Dukore first analyzes Shaw's theoretical and critical
pronouncements on drama and then examines his practices.
The theoretical ideas are culled from reviews, essays,
letters, prefaces, whereas the practical are culled from
Shaw's rehearsal notes and, of course, from the plays
themselves. Chapter one, "Theatre Background and
Experience," reveals that Shaw was versatile in every
aspect of a theatrical production. Chapter two, "The
Director: Goals and Groundwork," shows that in order to
produce the effect he wanted, to save time, Shaw
meticulously prepared every detail of production in
advance of his rehearsals with the actors. Chapter three,
"General Directing Practices," reveals that Shaw's first
directing practice was to read the play to the entire
company. The time needed to direct a play was four weeks:
one week for blocking the action, two weeks for
memorizing, one week for dress rehearsal. Chapter four,
"The Actor," shows that Shaw's resources as an acting
coach were astonishingly varied. He aimed at realism, but
he also wanted theatrical effectiveness. Chapter five,
"Stage Effects and Stage Effectiveness," concentrates on
Shaw's use of all the available techniques to achieve the
effectiveness of the scene and of the play. Shaw used the
techniques as a means of illuminating thematic aspects of
the play, not as substitutes for the effects intended by
the author. Chapter six, "Technical Elements of
Production," develops the notion that Shaw was vitally
concerned with the technical aspects of the theater. He
knew that to disregard them could destroy the illusion of
reality. He kept abreast of advancements in stage
technology. The final chapter, "Business of the Theatre,"
concludes that Shaw was "a complete man of the theatre,"
that all elements of play production fell within his
directional jurisdiction. Extensive bibliography.
Illustrated with sketches for costumes and sets.]

1728 Dukore, Bernard F. "The Middleaged Bully and
the Girl of Eighteen: The Ending They 'Didn't'
Film." Shaw R, XIV (May 1971), 102-6.
"I absolutely forbid . . . any suggestion that the middleaged bully and the girl of eighteen are lovers," Shaw
cabled the Minneapolis Civic Theatre in 1948 when they had
requested permission to modify the ending of *Pygmalion*.

The variations in the film versions of the play were accomplished without Shaw's approval. An examination of the original screenplay, housed at the Academic Center Library of the University of Texas, Austin, explicitly shows that Shaw's intentions were circumvented by others and that the romantic ending of bringing Eliza and Higgins together is also a contradiction of the suggestions and expectations of the play itself.

1729 Dukore, Bernard F. "Shaw on HAMLET," ETJ, XXIII (May 1971), 152-59.
Early in his career, Shaw made a name for himself by means of his astute criticism of Shakespeare. It is clear from the sheer energy he spent on this criticism that he highly esteemed the Bard. Although he called KING LEAR Shakespeare's greatest tragedy, he nevertheless asserted that the original morality of HAMLET sets that work above all others. His conflict arises not because he is irresolute, but because he has, in a sense, rejected a role expected of him, having evolved beyond it. Mosaic morality has given way to a Christian one.

Shaw characteristically places Shakespeare on the second level of literature and elevates Ibsen to the first.

1730 Egrí, Péter. "A Shaw-drámák Intellektuális Szatirájának Kibontakozása, II Közlemény (The Evolution of Intellectual Satire in Shaw's Plays, Part II), FIOLÓGIAI KÖZLÖNYI, XVII (1971), 51-70.
Superman as munitions manufacturer: *Major Barbara*. Superman as artist and physician: *The Doctor's Dilemma*. Superman as cheated horse-thief: *The Shewing-up of Blanco Posnet*. The differences between Shakespeare's mind and Shaw's: *The Dark Lady of the Sonnets*. Shaw is Shakespeare in reverse. Between two worlds: *Androcles and the Lion*. Turning the myth against the happy ending: *Pygmalion*. The crisis of World War I (Chekov and Shaw): *Heartbreak House*. Approaching Shakespeare and Brecht: *Saint Joan*. Political Utopia: *The Apple Cart*. Decadence: *Too True to Be Good*. The denouement of fascist dictatorship: *Geneva*. *Shakes vs. Shav*. [In Hungarian.]

1731 [Evans, T. F.] "Editorial," SHAVIAN, IV (Spring 1971), 117-19.
The present British government wants to return to free capitalism, summed up by Shaw as a "paper utopia." Shaw

complained that sex was the only subject theater managers thought worth writing plays about; the same is true today.

1732 Evans, T. F. "Intellectually Coherent Drama," SHAVIAN, IV (Spring 1971), 140-43.
[Review of THE BODLEY HEAD BERNARD SHAW: COLLECTED PLAYS WITH THEIR PREFACES, Vol I, 1970.] Even the experienced Shavian will find new material here.

1733 Forter, Elizabeth T. (ed). MAJOR BARBARA by Bernard Shaw (NY: Appleton-Century-Crofts [Crofts Classics], 1971).
[This inexpensive, paperback edition of *Major Barbara* contains an introductory essay by the editor on general aspects of the play.]

1734 Ganz, Arthur. "The Ascent to Heaven: A Shavian Pattern (Early Plays, 1894-1898)," MD, XIV (Dec 1971), 253-63.
From the first Shaw's plays embody both Romantic optimism and Romantic disillusion. The optimistic vision underlies Creative Evolution, but this theory is also pessimistic, for its end is a withdrawal from the human condition into self-contemplating intellect. The pattern of the pessimistic vision is an ascent to heaven, sometimes literal, sometimes figurative. *Mrs. Warren's Profession* establishes this pattern: in reaction to her education, Vivie rejects art, society, and love as tainted and withdraws to that "heaven" of pure numerical calculation, which anticipates the pure intellect of the Ancients in *Back to Methuselah*. In *Arms and the Man*, the optimistic Shaw triumphs. Marchbanks in *Candida* leaves human life behind. Dick Dudgeon in *The Devil's Disciple* literally chooses death; Anderson is committed to life and its illusions; but Burgoyne, prefiguring Caesar, is both in the world and beyond it.

1735 Goldberg, Michael K. "Shaw's Dickensian Quintessence," Shaw R, XIV (Jan 1971), 14-28.
By his own admission, Shaw borrowed heavily from Dickens for the themes, characters, and episodes in his plays. That debt took two essential forms, the one deriving from the great social themes and the other from the technical artistry. So many of Shaw's characters have their counterparts in Dickens, for example, Dick Dudgeon in Sydney Carton, Bill Walker in Bill Sikes, Mangan in Mr.

Merdle. Similarities of episodes and themes are also apparent: for example, the central episode in *The Devil's Disciple* recalls Sydney Carton's self-sacrificing art in A TALE OF TWO CITIES, and *Mrs. Warren's Profession* and *Major Barbara* both echo Dickens' attack on the mercantile ethos in HARD TIMES.

Shaw always applauded Dickens's social satire while deriding his sentimental heroics and contrived happy endings. His critical writings on Dickens show a definite appreciation for the later works, not so surprising in that Dickens's later works clearly reflect the social consciousness of Carlyle, whose teachings greatly influenced Shaw's own social thought.

Shaw's views of Dickens was determined by temperamental as well as ideological differences, but for all the dissimilarities between them, if Dickens had not existed, Shaw would have had to invent him.

1736 Gregory, Lady Augusta. COOLE, Completed from the manuscript and edited by Colin Smythe, with a Foreword by Edward Malins (Dublin: Dolmen P [Dolmen Editions X], 1971), pp. 7, 43, 44, 54-55.
[Expanded version of COOLE published in 1931. Anecdote of Shaw photographing Lady Gregory, and the text of a Shaw poem.]

1737 Griffith, Benjamin W. "Lydia and the Lady from Zurich: The Birth of a Shavian *Bon Mot*?" NOTES ON CONTEMPORARY LITERATURE, I (May 1971), 14-15.
Shaw's witty answer to the proposal of the lady in Zurich: "You have the greatest brain in the world, and I have the most beautiful body; so we ought to produce the most perfect child."--"What if the child inherits my body and your brains?" may have its source in *Cashel Byron's Profession*, in the children of Lydia and Cashel. The lady in Zurich may be apocryphal.

1738 Gŭlŭbova, S., and Ivan Gŭpchev. LETOPIS NA NARODNIĬA TEATR "IVAN VAZOV" 1904-1970 (Chronicle of the "Ivan Vazov" National Theater 1904-1970) (Sofia: Nauka i iskustvo, 1971).
[*Caesar and Cleopatra, Androcles and the Lion, Arms and the Man, Saint Joan, The Devil's Disciple, Mrs. Warren's Profession,* and *Candida* at the "Ivan Vazov" Theater, along with reviews.] [In Bulgarian.]

1739 Hatcher, Joe B. "Shaw the Reviewer and James's GUY DOMVILLLE," MD, XIV (Dec 1971), 331-34.
The Haymarket Theatre produced GUY DOMVILLE on 3 January 1895, and Shaw's review for the SATURDAY REVIEW appeared a few days later. In spite of Shaw's firm commitment to the "Ibsenite Spirit," which he saw lacking in James's play, he is nevertheless complimentary. He saw in that play ideas that deserved respect and not the deplorable reception it received from the audiences which jeered its author off the stage. The audiences, as Shaw pointed out, ascribed love as the sole motivation of every action and could not understand a man who acted according to his dedication to the church. Shaw may have responded differently had the audiences not behaved so boorishly, for he would not tolerate bad manners and he had a strong tendency to come to the defense of the underdog. A close reading of this review as well as others will reveal "a very sensible and fair dramatic critic.

1740 Helsztyński, Stanisław. "O Bernardzie Shaw w Polsce Uwagi Luźne" (Some Observations about Bernard Shaw in Poland), POLSKIE DEBIUTY BERNARDA SHAW, (Polish Early History of Bernard Shaw) by Stanisława Kumor (Warsaw: Wydawnictwa Uniwersitetu Warszawskiego, 1971), pp. i-xi.
[An "eyewitness" view of the early history of Shaw in Poland.] [In Polish.]

1741 Hiller, Wendy. "Portrait of Pascal," ShawR, XIV (Jan 1971), 33-36. [A review of THE DISCIPLE AND HIS DEVIL, by Valerie Pascal (1970).]
"'As a person very close to many of the incidents described in the biography, I will correct only the inaccuracies for the sake of the Shavian record. These include the statement that at a dinner at Pinewood Studios Shaw drank his own health and then walked out, that Gabriel Pascal "wrangled" about my playing the part in *Major Barbara*, and that everyone made big money in *Pygmalion* except Gabriel.'"

1742 Hirsch, Foster Lance. "The Edwardian Drama of Ideas," DAI, XXXII (1971), 3306A. Unpublished dissertation, Columbia University, 1971.

1743 Hoppe, E. O. "Shaw and the Camera," BOOKS AND BOOKMEN, XVI (June 1971), 18-19.

Shaw, after seeing Hoppe's one-man show of portraits of famous men in the Goupil Gallery in London, sent him a postcard with one line: "Your show is incomplete--GBS." Shortly afterwards arrangements were made for Shaw to come to Millais' House for a sitting. This was one of the first of many pictures taken, for Shaw was by no means camera-shy. He was himself occupied with photography. [Two Hoppe photographs of Shaw.]

1744 Houghton, Norris. THE EXPLODING STAGE, AN INTRODUCTION TO TWENTIETH CENTURY DRAMA (NY: Weybright and Talley, 1971), pp. 3-5, 7-8, 15, 22, 88-97, 138, 161, 165, 167, 183, 214, 242, 250.
It does not matter whether the critics who regard Shaw as a crusader or those who regard him as an artist are right. You can look for what you please and be satisfied. As a playwright he doesn't fail. He chose comedy because it carries didacticism with better grace than other kinds of drama. *Heartbreak House* is a discussion about life. There is no plot. It is a tone poem whose chords sound almost unbearably familiar today. *Man and Superman* is his climactic comedy on the duel between the sexes. *Saint Joan* is probably Shaw's greatest play.

1745 Hoy, Cyrus. "Shaw's Tragicomic Irony: From *Man and Superman* to *Heartbreak House*," VIRGINIA QUARTERLY REVIEW, XLVII (1971), 56-78.
Satire and romance, while contrary to each other, do in fact complement each other in various ways. In *Man and Superman, Major Barbara,* and *Heartbreak House*, Shaw deftly uses the contrivances of romance and satire to depict the conflict between real life and the romantic imagination.

Insofar as *Heartbreak* focuses on the process of Ellie Dunn's education, it follows the traditional comic movement in which a young innocent is initiated into the ways of the world and thus comes to a fuller knowledge of himself. That movement, however, is not without its satiric implications, for instead of being delivered from the illusions of romance, Ellie is confirmed in them, and so by the end of the play, she is back where she began with this difference: instead of being in love with love, she is in love with death.

The synthesis of culture and power represented in the marriage of Barbara and Cusins in *Barbara* is seen in *Heartbreak* to have disintegrated. What *Superman* has in common with *Heartbreak* is the theme of the pursuit of

happiness and its power to corrupt the will to action.   In
the former play, the incongruous follies and perversities
of man are acknowledged but are dismissed as curable
lapses along life's evolutionary way.   In the ending of
Heartbreak, the bombs represent a welcome intrusion of
violence into an over-cultured society that has come to
bore them all profoundly, as Don Juan is bored by hell.
The residents of Heartbreak House, unlike Don Juan, seem
to have given up life's struggle upward and have become
fascinated with death.

1746 Hugo, Leon.   BERNARD SHAW, PLAYWRIGHT AND
PREACHER (Lond: Methuen, 1971).
[This book is organized so as to present Shaw as both
teacher and dramatist.   The first three chapters follow
the mainstream of Shaw's philosophy, revealing a cohesive
progression of Shavian ideas.   The second part, chapters
four through eight, present an assessment of Shaw the
dramatist.   The purpose here is to create a cumulative
portrait of Shaw's dramas.   The third part, chapter nine,
is a synthesis, entitled "Artist-Philosopher."   The plays
discussed at any length are: *The Apple Cart, Caesar and
Cleopatra, Candida, Heartbreak House, Major Barbara, Man
and Superman,* and *Saint Joan.*]

1747 Hugo, Leon.   "*Major Barbara* at the Court,"
UNISA ENGLISH STUDIES, IX (1971), 1-6.
During the Vedrenne-Barker season at the Royal Court
Theatre from 1904-1907, Shaw was practically dramatist-in-
residence with 11 of his plays undergoing production.   The
most controversial of them was *Major Barbara.*   As his
correspondence reveals, Shaw had a great deal of difficulty finishing the play and there was concern whether the
Salvation Army would demand censorship.   On the contrary,
the Army was delighted with the play.   When it was first
performed, 28 November 1905, the press assailed it, especially THE MORNING POST, which also carried a full column
of the correspondence on the play.   While not a major
success, the play did arouse considerable interest.

1748 Hung, Josephine Huang.   "The Candida Character
in Kuan Han-ching's THE RIVERSIDE PAVILION," PRO-
CEEDINGS FROM THE INTERNATIONAL COMPARATIVE LITERA-
TURE CONFERENCE HELD 18-24 JULY AT TAMKANG COLLEGE
OF ARTS AND SCIENCES, TAIPEI, TAIWAN, REPUBLIC OF
CHINA, TAMKANG REVIEW, II-III, ed by Yen Yuan-shu
(Oct 1971-April 1972), 295-308.

Though THE RIVERSIDE PAVILION was written in the thirteenth century and though Chinese and Western drama can hardly be compared, the heroine of Kuan Han-ching's play is like Candida. Both women are unconventional in mind and action, and both must choose between her husband and another man.

1749 Hunningher, B. "Shaw en Brecht. Wegen en grenzen van socialistisch theater" (Shaw and Brecht. Ways and Limits of Socialist Theater), FORUM DER LETTEREN, XII (1971), 173-90.

Brecht, who knew Shaw's dramatic works only incidentally, wrote an ovation for Shaw's birthday in 1926. Both had a similar point of departure in their works: both strove for a new man within a new community. Their respective theater work had to be didactic and at the same time urge change. From there their work went in different directions. Each had his own particular brand of Socialism. Shaw felt that man had been given unlimited possibilities for finding fulfillment in life. Not the ignorant masses but a parliamentary system should see to the growth of society. For Shaw the virtuous worker contrasted with the unscrupulous capitalist was pure melodrama (Mrs. Warren/Vivian). No income without work was Shaw's revolutionary contribution. Possessions alone do not provide fulfillment (Marchbanks). It is the free will which serves as Shaw's societal cornerstone. One must do God's work without striving for material gain (Major Barbara). Only man can do it, and that is the reason for his existence. Brecht, like Shaw, was shocked by World War I. He hated the society which had made the mass-killing possible. His folk-ballads expressed this and later formed an integral part of his theater. While Shaw accepted the theater as he had found it (although he used it inversely for shock effect), Brecht developed his own form of epic theater. He did not seek applause or praise, but rather wanted to provoke his audience. Brecht, as opposed to Shaw, did not have the slightest faith in the individual, from whom nothing can or should be expected. Brecht, like Shaw, read DAS KAPITAL, and felt that Marxism was the salvation of all mankind. It did not result in a high level of creativity as was the case in Shaw's work. When one examines their respective work, Shaw reveals himself to be a more efficient Socialist than Brecht. [In Dutch.]

1750 Irving, Laurence. "The Death of Henry Irving," CORNHILL MAGAZINE, No. 1069 (Autumn 1971), 1-10.

[Account of the controversy aroused over a "gauche" Shaw article in DIE NEUE FREIE PRESS of Vienna about Henry Irving after his death.]

1751 Kantorovich, I. B. "Kharaktery i konflikt *Pigmaliona* B. Shou" (Characters and Conflict in B. Shaw's *Pygmalion*), UCHENYE ZAPISKI SVERDLOVSKOGO PED. INSTITUTA (Sverdlovsk), CXLIX (1971), 3-18.
Shaw makes Eliza's transformation convincing--from flower-girl to pupil to lady, though she remains the same throughout inwardly and retains human dignity. Shaw believed that gentlefolk and the poor are no different, providing they are genuine people. However, Shaw considered poverty a curse, even a crime. The transformation of Alfred Doolittle was intended to act upon the intellect and commonsense of the audience and to reflect upon common problems of contemporary life, as his characters do in the play. Thus the dramatic conflict in *Pygmalion* takes on an ideological and aesthetic aspect, a conflict between the creative approach to life and the creation of a new individual, with the venality of bourgeois civilisation and the inhuman nature of contemporary bourgeois society. The theme of *Pygmalion* is the difficult process of the mutual education of Eliza and Higgins, as Higgins admits. The composition of the play is close to that of the "well-made play," but Shaw's purpose was to make his audience think, invite them to participate in the discussions on stage and continue them afterwards. He used many situations and other accessories of "romantic comedy," but he parodies them. *Pygmalion* is highly intellectual, having little in common with the 'romantic comedy' of the late nineteenth century. [In Russian.]

1752 Kinyon, Frank J. "Bernard Shaw and the Irish Question," DAI, XXXI (Feb 1971), 4168A-69A. Unpublished dissertation, University of Nebraska, 1970.

1753 Knepper, B. G. "Shaw's Debt to THE COMING RACE," JOURNAL OF MODERN LITERATURE, I (1971), 339-53.
Shaw rarely gave credit to his many literary influences, but he did acknowledge Bulwer Lytton's THE COMING RACE as having a great influence upon him. The most important influences from Lytton are the political and social theories that underscore Shaw's plays; for example, the superior race, the Vril-ya, which Shaw acknowledged he

drew upon for his characterization of the Ancients in *Back to Methuselah*. Shaw refined and expanded many of the themes he took from Lytton adapting them to his own evolutionary concepts in his own ironic and intelligent style.

1754 Kumor, Stanisława. POLSKIE DEBIUTY BERNARDA SHAW (Polish Early History of Bernard Shaw), (Warsaw: Wydawnictwa Universitetu Warszawskiego, 1971). This work is an outline of the Polish history of Shaw and an attempt to show the impact of Shaw's works on Polish culture. An analysis of the relevant [Polish] material shows that Shaw did not worship dictators, and his Superman shares only the name of Nietzsche's Übermensch. With the reality of national independence Shaw gained popularity. Stage production was expert, especially by Arnold Szyfman at the Teatr Polski, preparing for the premiere of *The Apple Cart*. Shaw, along with Conrad and Chesterton, forced the Polish reader to range widely in English literature. Florian Sobieniowski's translations are faithful if not faultless. Although during World War II conservative elements were discouraged by his pro-Soviet views, after the war he became a patron in the State. [In Polish with Summaries in English and Russian.]

1755 Laden, Alice. THE GEORGE BERNARD SHAW VEGETARIAN COOK BOOK IN SIX ACTS, ed and adapted by R. J. Minney (NY: Taplinger, 1971 [2?]); adapted and rptd., Minney, R. J., "George Bernard Shaw's Vegetarian Recipes," HARPER'S BAZAAR, No. 3119 (Oct. 1971), 151-53.
Poverty probably provided the initial stimulus for Shaw's becoming a vegetarian at 25 in spite of his attribution to Shelley's THE REVOLT OF ISLAM. Shaw's mother was indifferent to his tastes, but his wife provided meals that were varied and appetizing. After Mrs. Shaw's death in 1943, Mrs. Alice Laden, her nurse, agreed to stay on as housekeeper. Shaw constantly ate sweets, even plain sugar and honey. All the recipes conform to Shaw's particular requirements. [A collection of recipes for vegetarian dishes served to Shaw. Photographs.]

1756 Lambert, J. W. "Plays in Performance, London," DRAMA, C (Spring 1971), 15-30.
The confrontation between the life of the senses and the life of the mind in *Mrs. Warren's Profession* is unfair;

even Shaw cannot prevent the senses from winning in terms of humanity. [Photograph.]

1757 Lambert, J. W. "Plays in Performance, London," DRAMA, CI (Summer 1971), 14-29.
Captain Brassbound's Conversion is Shaw not really on form, and it needs to be projected with panache and finesse.

1758 Lambert, J. W. "Plays in Performance, London," DRAMA, CII (Autumn 1971), 15-29.
John Bull's Other Island is one of Shaw's finest plays. *The Devil's Disciple* is dull without cool melodramatics. [Photograph of *John Bull*.]

1759 Larson, Gale K. "*Caesar and Cleopatra*: The Making of a History Play," ShawR, XIV (May 1971), 73-89.
Shaw was determined to write a play about Julius Caesar depicting his human strengths instead of the human weaknesses he discerned in Shakespeare's treatment. Shaw, therefore, carefully selected those historians whose concept of Caesar is more attuned to his own views. Plutarch is discarded for Theodore Mommsen, the nineteenth century German historian. Viewing history as an art, Shaw imagines the details and accessories of history as would a playwright, that is, making a scene visual, a character alive, and a conflict dynamic. Somewhere between Shaw's rather flippant claim for "historical divination" and a scrupulous use of historical sources lies Shaw's view and use of history.

1760 Leary, Daniel J. "How G. B. Shaw Destroyed His Irish Biographer," COLUMBIA LIBRARY COLUMNS, XXI (1971), 3-11.
Between 1910 and 1923, Professor Thomas Demetrius O'Bolger, an English teacher at the University of Pennsylvania, attempted to write a biography of Shaw that took into account the psychological conditions Shaw experienced as a child and a man. Because there were many aspects of his own family experience about which Shaw felt either shame or repugnance, he made many efforts at both impeding the progress of O'Bolger's work and, when it had been completed, blocked its publication. Shaw was a man with two selves, the public GBS and the private Bernard Shaw. He had always attempted to keep them separate, and

O'Bolger's book attempted to link the two, or rather to explain why Shaw felt it necessary to maintain a public image separate from his private one. It also attempted to explain the influence of this attitude on the plays of Shaw. It seems that Shaw felt threatened by O'Bolger's work, and that his reaction, of attempting to stifle in any way possible the publication of the work, did in fact succeed to such a great extent that it in part caused O'Bolger to die young, cursing Shaw, having failed at getting his biography published. B. C. Rosset, author of SHAW OF DUBLIN: THE FORMATIVE YEARS (1964), states that O'Bolger's biography is "trenchant, shrewd, sensitive yet petulant, bitter and even savage at times . . . . [However, it] deserves to join the assemblage of major biographies."

O'Bolger's dissertation, "The Real Shaw," as well as the untitled biography, are housed in the Houghton Library at Harvard University.

1761 Leech, Clifford. "Shaw and Shakespeare," SHAW: SEVEN CRITICAL ESSAYS (Toronto and Buffalo: U of Toronto P, 1971), pp. 84-105.
Shaw has lasted on the stage quite long. In the Preface to *Three Plays for Puritans*, Shaw claimed only that we were better historians, social critics, and scientists than the men in Shakespeare's day. Shaw reflected his world without much liking it, and he is at his best, not preaching his own gospel, but seeing the way men respond to the perennial demands in their own context. Unlike Helena in ALL'S WELL THAT ENDS WELL, Ann in *Man and Superman* has no kings and is on her own. Hypatia in *Misalliance* seven years later is even more direct. If Shaw uses all the old dramatic tricks, it is also true that Shakespeare works with debate in Shaw's manner as in LOVE'S LABOUR'S LOST. Shaw's mind worked best when he was distracted from the coherence of his arguments and produced a character like Eliza's father in *Pygmalion*. One might conclude that Shaw "believed in argument, but Shakespeare did not . . . . Shakespeare reached his highest level in Tragedy, Shaw in argumentative comedy."

1762 Lewis, Anthony. "The Dream of Efficiency," NYT, 22 May 1971, p. 31.
If Shaw could see the pain and hope of Britain's romance with the European Community, he might see parallels to Ireland's history "in the choice between being one's self apart and being part of something larger." It is not

always possible to be sure which side Shaw is on. In *John Bull's Other Island* Keegan foresees only ruin from efficiency, but in *Major Barbara* Shaw seems to extoll efficiency. *John Bull* at the Mermaid seems relevant: England will not be happy playing the part of an Ireland looking backward.

1763 Lindblad, Ishrat. "Creative Evolution and Shaw's Dramatic Art, with Special References to *Man and Superman* and *Back to Methuselah*." Unpublished dissertation, University of Upsala, Sweden, 1971.

1764 McCollom, William G. THE DIVINE AVERAGE. (Cleveland: Case Western Reserve UP, 1971), pp. 198-212.
[Part I treats the theoretical aspects of the nature of comedy; Part II makes application to specific plays. Chapter 11 is devoted to "Shaw's Comedy and Major Barbara."] In *Major Barbara* the conflict is between the comedy of its people and the intolerable state of modern society. The total effect is that of a problem comedy, in which the ending offers a hopeful, though hypothetical, solution. Each of the four divisions of the play opens with deceptively amusing dialogue and moves toward more overtly serious conflict.

Undershaft's complex moral passion is discernible--he regards himself as custodian of power held ready for one who will use it rightly. In addition to being a Dionysus and a Machiavelli, he is also a Moses who cannot enter the Promised Land. The higher levels of consciousness must therefore persist in Barbara and Cusins.

1765 McInerney, John M. "'Shakespearean' Word-Music as a Dramatic Resource in Shaw," Shaw R, XIV (May 1971), 90-94, 99.
Shaw's critical writings on Shakespeare and his dramatic practice demonstrate that he carefully orchestrated his own use of evocative language so as to serve his ideological causes. Shaw does not remove emotion from the theater as so often has been charged, but he artfully designs his characters' speeches so as to achieve the emotional effects he wants.

1766 Macksoud, S. John, and Ross Altman. "Voices in Opposition: A Burkeian Rhetoric of *Saint Joan*,"

QUARTERLY JOURNAL OF SPEECH, LVII (April 1971), 140-46.
Though Joan is French and fighting English imperialism, she espouses the values of Post-World War I England, Nationalism and Protestantism. She becomes sympathetic to the audience, and by a kind of halo effect she makes the audience tolerant of heresy, reminding them that their orthodoxy was once heresy. Joan's equating her "voices" with common sense and her womanliness also increase's her appeal to the audience, which comes to see that being French or English is irrelevant as compared with participating in Joan's execution. Joan's judges are not vicious, but mistaken, necessarily . . . , that is by Kenneth Burke's definition in THE PHILOSOPHY OF LITERARY FORM, they are *comic* fools. But if Joan were not condemned as a heretic, she would never have been canonized. The title, *Saint Joan*, is a rhetorical strategem to admonish audiences not to make the double mistake of her executioners, of excessively praising or condemning her.

1767 Mahony, Patrick. "Shaw Revisited," CORANTO, VII (1971), 25-28.
Shaw wanted to disturb the smugness of current ideas, and he chose ironic raillery as his weapon. He seems mild by contemporary standards. [Account of an interview with Shaw.]

1768 Matoba, Junko. "Bernard Shaw: Artist as Propagandist", SEISHINJOSHIDAIGAKU RONSO (Tokyo), No. 37 (June 1971), 61-74.
The core of Shaw drama is characterized by the method of contrast and inversion.

1769 Meisel, Martin. "Shaw and Revolution: The Politics of the Plays," SHAW: SEVEN CRITICAL ESSAYS, ed by Norman Rosenblood (Toronto and Buffalo: U of Toronto P, 1971), pp. 106-34.
Shaw's plays are designed to effect in the audience a permanent change in consciousness, but there is an apparent discrepancy "between what they seem to persuade to and the Fabian strategies aimed at social change." *Widowers' Houses* does not go beyond disposing an audience to make a revolution. *Mrs. Warren's Profession* creates the sense of the inadequacy of alternatives to revolution, and *The Philanderer* shuts out the alternative of escape even more directly. The *Pleasant Plays* and *Plays for*

Puritans "present a radical criticism . . . of the sustaining ideals, of contemporary . . . society." Apocalyptic revolutionary violence is explicit in the plays for the first time in *Major Barbara*. Apocalypse itself comes at last in *Heartbreak House*. The source of apocalyptic expectation is in the gospels; in both, Judgment is the last act in a drama of salvation. *Heartbreak* is not the end of Shaw's anti-Fabianism in drama, and after it, there is no longer any discrepancy between Shaw's plays and his politics.

1770 Melchinger, Siegfried. GESCHICHTE DES POLITISCHEN THEATERS (A History of the Political Theater) (Velber: Friedrich Verlag, 1971), pp. 312-13, 315-20, 371-72.
Shaw, Oscar Wilde and Edward Gordon Craig tried to destroy the Victorian way of thinking. Shaw was a rebel, but as a playwright he managed not to break the rules of the game. His satire recalls the satire of Aristophanes. [Briefly portrays *Mrs. Warren's Profession* and *Arms and the Men*.] [In German.]

1771 Merritt, James D. "Shaw and the Pre-Raphaelites," SHAW: SEVEN CRITICAL ESSAYS, ed by Norman Rosenblood (Toronto and Buffalo: U of Toronto P, 1971), pp. 70-83.
Shaw admired some of the pre-Raphaelite painters, especially Ford Madox Brown, for their realism. And the Morris household had a considerable effect on Shaw, though it was Shaw who influenced Morris's economic theories. *Candida* is based on the pre-Raphaelite Movement, which he regarded as a model for Christian Socialism. The drama lies in the revolt of pre-Raphaelitism against itself. Morell like Millais permitted "their private comforts to blind them to the ideals of their respective -isms." Marchbanks personifies the aspect of pre-Raphaelitism that wished for escape from reality. Candida is the mysterious force, Life, that initiates revolt.

1772 Metwally, Abdalla A. STUDIES IN MODERN DRAMA (Beirut: Beirut Arab University, 1971).
[Metwally assesses the dramatic works of Ibsen, Shaw, Synge, Eliot, and O'Neill. The essay on Shaw concentrates on *Man and Superman*, considered "the fourth play for Puritans," which demonstrates Shaw's technical virtuosity in weaving the interlude in Hell with the main fabric of the comedy.]

1773 Mills, Carl Henry. "Shaw's Debt to Lester Ward in *Man and Superman*," Shaw R, XIV (Jan 1971), 2-13.
In the dream sequence of *Man and Superman*, Shaw has Don Juan present a succinct summary of the then controversial "gynaeocentric theory," in which the female sex is viewed as the primary species and the male, secondary. This theory has its genesis in the work of Lester Ward, as attested to by the leading feminists at the turn of the century. Most of Shaw's major ideas depend upon and develop from Ward's gynaeocentric theory. He transforms the bland, scientific style of Ward's theory into the Shavian style of wit and vitality.

1774 Mundell, Richard Frederick. "Shaw and Brieux: A Literary Relationship," DAI, XXXII (Sept 1971), 1522A. Unpublished dissertation, University of Michigan, 1971.

1775 Myers, Charles Robert. "Game-structure in Selected Plays," DAI, XXXII (Sept 1971), 1676-77A. Unpublished dissertation, University of Iowa, 1971.

1776 Nathan, Rhoda B. "Bernard Shaw and the Inner Light," Shaw R, XIV (Sept 1971), 107-19.
Shaw is indebted not only to Puritan thought but also to Quaker thought. He had knowledge of and a familiarity with the JOURNALS OF GEORGE FOX, a noted Quaker of the 17th Century. Many of his plays have characters who are Quakers in thought and action. As further evidence for this indebtedness, Shaw himself confided to his friend and neighbor, Stephen Winsten, that he was a Quaker "by temperament" if not "by faith."

1777 Nelson, Raymond S. "The Quest for Justice in *Captain Brassbound's Conversion*," IOWA ENGLISH BULLETIN YEARBOOK, XXI (Fall 1971), 3-9.
Shaw set out in *Captain Brassbound's Conversion* to define justice as something more than revenge and punishment, but what Shaw had in mind is not as simple as what he did not have. "Duty" is untrustworthy and must be abandoned, and so must "self", to achieve independence. Society must be reconstituted on tolerance, freedom, kindness, and responsibility, on the New Testament. Justice must be based on actual life and avoid abstraction. Shaw is optimistic about human behavior. No misdeeds can be undone, and men must carry guilt forever. This awareness

will make men more responsible. Finally, Shaw's idea of justice is based on the belief that men will cultivate their own gardens. Shaw never abandoned the quest for justice outlined in *Brassbound*.

1778 Nelson, Raymond S. "Responses to Poverty in *Major Barbara*," ARIZONA QUARTERLY, XXVII (Winter 1971), 335-46.
All too often Shaw has been characterized as the irreverent iconoclast, and his own spirit of religion has been ignored. In *Major Barbara* Shaw combines the mystical and practical elements of religion. He treats the problem of poverty in full detail, accepting Samuel Butler's proposition that poverty is a crime. The strategy of the play is the responses of the major characters to men in dire need. Undershaft's method of dealing with poverty is drastic but realistically the most permanent course. The others are futile.

1779 Nickson, Richard. "The Art of Shavian Political Drama," MD, XIV (Dec 1971), 324-30.
Many critics and readers misconstrue Shaw's treatment of political matters in his later dramas and fail to recognize that throughout his life he remained fundamentally an artist who rendered the social system as he saw it, not as he would like to see it. He saw that system from a definite standpoint--a Socialist's view. His later plays do demonstrate the need for social reconstruction, but he did not succeed in dramatizing Socialist solutions to social problems because he did not even attempt to do so.

1780 Novick, Julius. "Daddy, What's a Philanderer?" NYT, 4 July 1971, II, p. 5.
The Philanderer at Niagara-on-the-Lake is topical all over again. It is a sort of sketch for *Man and Superman*. The Shaw Festival devotes itself to drawing-room comedy and appeals greatly to the stodgy audience. Yet Shaw was a revolutionary. The festival maintains a balancing act between its audience and its playwright.

1781 Obraztŝova, A. G. "Pis'ma Bernarda Shou" (Bernard Shaw's Letters) and "Primechaniĩa" (Notes), in PIS'MA (Letters) by Bernard Shou (Moscow: "Nauka," 1971), pp. 307-33 and 338-96.
[Not seen.] [In Russian.]

1782 O'Casey, Eileen. SEAN, ed with an "Introduction" by J[onathan]. C[ourtney]. Trewin (Lond: Macmillan, 1971; NY: Coward, McCann & Geoghegan,
1972), pp. 19, 21, 72, 84-85, 86, 87, 100-1, 106,
107-8, 111, 113, 125, 134, 144-45, 156, 161, 162,
171, 172, 177-78, 185-86, 201, 205, 206-10.
[Memories of Shaw's "staunch" friendship with O'Casey.]

1783 Parker, R. B. "THE CIRCLE of Somerset
Maugham," SHAW: SEVEN CRITICAL ESSAYS, ed by Norman
Rosenblood (Toronto and Buffalo: U of Toronto P,
1971), pp. 36-50.
Superficially there are enough resemblances between Shaw
and Maugham to include THE CIRCLE in the repertory of the
Shaw Festival. But seeing them together reveals how
different they really are. The contrast is in Shaw's
favor. Maugham always spoke of Shaw with great respect
because he made even more money than Maugham. But because
Shaw's plays are more than entertainments, they make
nonsense of Maugham's cynical formula for successful
drama. Therefore Maugham suggests that Shaw's ideas were
not really original and he pandered to the English
prejudice against sexual passion. But Maugham's plays are
not so cynically formulaic as they may seem.

1784 Peel, Marie. "Women's Lib in Lit," BOOKS AND
BOOKMEN, XVII (Nov 1971), 14-17.
While MRS. WARREN'S PROFESSION is "a very forceful and
effective play," "Vivie Warren is much less forward-
looking than her mother. I doubt if she would support
women's lib now."

1785 Portîanskaîâ, N. A. "Bernard Shou i ir-
landskaîâ demokraticheskaîâ drama" (Shaw and Irish
Democratic Drama). Dissertation, Moscow, 1971.
[In Russian.]

1786 Pravdev, Nikolai. "Shou i Gorki v Burgaskiîâ
teatur" (Shaw and Gorky at the Burgaski Theater),
TEATUR (Sofia) V (1971) 38-43.
Gorky and Shaw are our contemporaries as well as classics
of world dramaturgy. This season (1971), the Burgaski
Theatre has produced *The Devil's Disciple* and *The Lower
Depths*, raising the question of which writer surpasses the
other. The former has been produced many times in
Bulgaria. Shaw's work is something enormous--he was a

master of paradox, a politician, philosopher, and
revolutionary. Now the producer has shifted the center of
gravity of the play to a farcical, grotesque, vaudeville
level, away from satirical comedy and melodrama. On the
other hand, Gorky's play is taken very seriously,
according to the tradition of the Bulgarian theater. [In
Bulgarian.]

1787 Price, Joseph G. "The Mirror to Nature:
Shaw's TROILUS AND CRESSIDA Lecture," Shaw R, XIV
(May 1971), 68-72.
Shaw's 1884 lecture on TROILUS AND CRESSIDA anticipated
the general response of twentieth century critics in that
Shaw had pointed to that play as Shakespeare's most
realistic play, whose moral is the pessimistic exposure of
human folly. Shaw's insights into the characters and
scenes underscore the truly critical merit of his lecture.

1788 Radford, Frederick Leslie. "The Idealistic
Iconoblast: Aspects of Platonism in the Works of
Bernard Shaw," DAI, XXXII (July 1971), 450-51A.
Unpublished dissertation, University of Washington,
1971.

1789 Raknem, Ingvald. "Bernard Shaw: Saint Joan,"
JOAN OF ARC IN HISTORY, LEGEND AND LITERATURE.
(Oslo: Universitetsforlaget, 1971), pp. 180-203.
The facts of history are highly important, yet of greater
significance is what one makes of the facts. *Saint Joan*
is the work of a dramatist with very definite preconceived
notions: he refuses to accept the past as different from
the present. He could make his characters intelligible
only by "modernizing" them. He was ignorant of all
primary sources and chose instead to see Joan, to
interpret her life and events, in the light of his own
personal philosophy of life, that of Creative Evolution.
His play can be said to be an interpretation of the
historical events and characters, but not a faithful
representation of them. The spirit of fifteenth-century
France does not pervade the play. He misrepresented
Joan's antagonists, sacrificing obvious truths to obtain
dramatic and theatrical effects. He turned Joan into a
twentieth-century rationalist, completely disregarding the
intense religiosity of her nature. He has distorted the
Dauphin beyond recognition, and his characterization of
Cauchon is utterly wrong. Along with others I do not

believe the play will live by virtue of its historical truth.

1790 Reardon, Joan. "*Caesar and Cleopatra* and the Commedia dell' Arte," Shaw R, XIV (Sept 1971), 120-36.
Shaw refers to the Harlequin tradition in his Preface to *Three Plays for Puritans*, and one can see recognizable "commedia" types in the Egyptian and Roman characters in *Caesar and Cleopatra*. Through the use of repetitious patterns of action, variations of one "master-servant" relationship, recognizable character types, all aspects of the "commedia dell' arte," Shaw develops his twofold themes of dominion and revenge. The comic episodes or turns are frequent throughout the play. Caesar is a striking composite of the many comic figures of the "commedia dell' arte," such as Harlequin, Pierrot, Scapio, Capitano, and Pantalone.

1791 Redmond, James. "Günther Grass: A Kashubian G. B. S.," MD, XIV (May 1971), 104-13.
"Günther Grass is a thorough-going Shavian." Like Shaw, Grass is a Fabian; he stands alone, rejecting authority; his desire is to bring reason to bear on politics; he is ambivalent about the concept of the hero.

1792 Redmond, James. "To the Editor: SHAW--'THE CHUCKER OUT'" [1969], TLS, 26 Feb 1971, p. 244; Allan Chappelow, "To the Editor: Shaw's Policies," TLS, 23 April 1971, pp. 476-77; James Redmond, "To the Editor: Shaw's Politics," TLS, 7 May 1971, p. 535; Allan Chappelow, "To the Editor: Shaw's Politics," TLS, 4 June 1971, pp. 6, 9.
The reviewer of Allan Chappelow's SHAW--"THE CHUCKER OUT" gave high praise to the book, which it justly deserves, but there is a major misrepresentation of Shaw which permeates the central part of the work. Shaw is presented as a Socialist-democrat in appearance but in actuality is a "ruthless fascist ready to spring." In fact, Shaw was arguing in his letter to P. Palme Dutt for publication in LABOUR MONTHLY (subsequently published July 1941), against any concept of Socialism that might seem to accept totalitarianism in exchange for better working conditions. To argue the obverse is to distort Shaw's position.

Chappelow's Rejoinder:
The misrepresentation of Shaw's position is Mr. Redmond's;
I stand on what I wrote. Shaw in his last 30 years was
"highly critical of British democracy and decidedly
sympathetic to autocratic forms of government." It is
patently wrong to class Shaw as a Socialist-democrat.
Shaw was more anti-democratic than he was pro fascist.
When Shaw talked about "a sense of freedom," he was
contrasting two ways of life as he saw them, the British
with its long hours of work, slavery to capitalism, a
delusive freedom limited to speech, and the "Socialist,"
with shorter hours and more leisure, 'under complete State
regulations of people's lives and thought.'"

Redmond's Reply:
In this matter of Shaw's position, there is no scope for
an honest difference of opinion: "One of us is right and
the other is wilfully wrong." In my opinion Mr.
Chappelow's position is "thoroughly wrong."

Chappelow's Reply:
Throughout my book I demonstrate that since the 1920's
Shaw increasingly advocated totalitarian types of
government. Mr. Redmond is alone in his objection and he
and I "must agree to differ on this matter."

1793 Ricciardi, Joseph.   "Shakespeare versus Shaw,"
ISh, X (Fall 1971), 10.
[Poem.]

1794 Rix, Walter Torsten.   "Forschungsbericht:
Nietzsches Einfluss auf Shaw. Ein Beitrag zum Ver-
ständnis der Shawschen Geisteswelt" (Research
Report: Nietzsche's Influence on Shaw. A Contribution to the Understanding of Shaw's Philosophy),
LITERATUR IN WISSENSCHAFT UND UNTERRICHT, II (1971),
124-39.
An examination of relevant German and English secondary
sources from the years 1898 to 1970 shows that most of
them agree that Nietzsche had an impact upon Shaw. But
they vary as to the extent of that influence. The studies
are generally confined to thematic parallels between
Nietzsche and Shaw, such as the superman ideal, the moral
value system and the relation between the sexes. Further
research should concentrate on greater clarification and
detailed text analyses between respective Shaw texts and
those English translations of Nietzsche available to Shaw.
[In German.]

GEORGE BERNARD SHAW

1795 Roberts, Vera Mowry. THE NATURE OF THEATRE (NY, Evanston, San Francisco, Lond: Harper & Row, 1971), pp. 5, 20, 68, 106, 107-8, 122, 168, 197, 205, 318, 382, 450.
[Shaw's plays used to illustrate aspects of the stage.]

1796 Rodríguez-Seda, Asela. "Shaw in the Hispanic World: A Bibliography," MD, XIV (Dec 1971), 335-39.
[A bibliography concerning Shaw in Spain and Latin American to correct the impression that Shaw is unknown there.]

1797 Romm, A. S. "Drama Bernarda Shou *Nazad k Mafusaila*: k probleme Lenin i Shou" (Shaw's Drama *Back to Methusellah*: On the Lenin-Shaw Problem), UCHENYE ZAPISKI LENINGRADSKOGO PEDAGOGICHESKOGO INSTITUTA IM. GERTSENA (Leningrad) CCCCXLII (1971), 203-35.
Shaw's attempts to establish scientifically his concepts of Creative Evolution failed, as he often contradicted himself. Like most artists, he was a philosopher when he was writing plays, not when constructing metaphysical concepts. Despite his creative potential, Creative Evolution as a scientific philosophical idea does not bear criticism. Sending a copy of *Back to Methuselah* to Lenin, Shaw hoped to find him a well-wisher, but Lenin's pencilled notes in his copy show he was sceptical about Creative Evolution as "the only original, scientific religion," and ironical about Shaw's overestimation of the intellectual factor in economic and political life. But Lenin supported Shaw's satire and hostility towards capitalism. Lenin's objectivity enabled him correctly to evaluate one of the most original and daring of Shaw's works. [In Russian.]

1798 Rosenblood, Norman, "Introduction," SHAW: SEVEN CRITICAL ESSAYS, ed by Norman Rosenblood (Toronto and Buffalo: U of Toronto P, 1971), pp. xi-xiv.
Current Shaw criticism is as wide as Shaw's interests, and therefore, it is difficult to detect a mainstream.

1799 Rosenblood, Norman (ed). SHAW SEVEN CRITICAL ESSAYS (Toronto and Buffalo: U of Toronto P, 1971).
Table of contents abstracted separately under author's name: Alan S. Downer, "Shaw's First Play"; Stanley

Weintraub, "Genesis of a Play: Two Early Approaches to
Man and Superman"; R. B. Parker, "THE CIRCLE of Somerset
Maugham"; Warren Sylvester Smith, "Bernard Shaw and the
London Heretics"; James D. Merritt, "Shaw and the Pre-
Raphaelites"; Clifford Leech, "Shaw and Shakespeare";
Martin Meisel, "Shaw and Revolution: The Politics of the
Plays."

1800 Rowell, George (ed). "Introduction," VICTORIAN
DRAMATIC CRITICISM (Lond: Methuen, 1971), pp. xiii-
xxv.
Shaw with Dryden made the only substantial contribution of
an English dramatist to dramatic criticism. He is his own
John the Baptist.

1801 Schwanitz, Dietrich. GEORGE BERNARD SHAW:
KÜNSTLERISCHE KONSTRUKTION UND UNORDENTLICHE WELT
(George Bernard Shaw: Artistic Construction and
Disorderly World) (Frankfurt: Thesen Verlag
Vowinkel, 1971).
This book examines those elements in Shaw's plays which
connect it with modern drama. Shaw questioned conventional society and conventional drama and experimented
with new forms. His early plays, although still using the
form of the conventional well-made play, already produce
new stylistic features in their efforts to critize conventional society. In his later plays, Shaw gradually dis-
cards the restrictions of the well-made play. Stages in
this development are the historical and dream montage, and
paralleling of disparate ideas and discussion plays. The
increasing tendency towards the fantastic, especially in
the utopian plays, is generally harnessed by theme and
allegorical references. This tendency is particularly
evident in his later plays. One particularly modern
feature of Shaw's plays is the principle of montage. Shaw
manages to bring together the most disparate elements in
themes and characters; he combines different historical
time levels (*Caesar and Cleopatra, Saint Joan*); he compares concepts and elements of the most incongruent and
heterogeneous nature (as seen from a traditional view
point); and he recharges traditional concepts with new
meanings. By combining heterogeneous elements Shaw breaks
through the staleness of conventional society and drama,
thus bringing into focus their hollowness and lack of
purpose. To bring a new order to the chaotic and disorderly world, he introduces the principle of the Life
Force. It transcends reality; all disparate elements,
whether historical, ideological or utopian, lose their

disparity in the face of this Life Force. But behind Shaw's positive affirmation of the Life Force the disorderly world remains visible. Without his positive affirmation, Shaw's utopian drama would only be a step away from the theater of the absurd. Shaw's plays are very modern in their attempt to solve the philosophical and artistic problems of our times. [In German.]

1802 Scriabine, Vera. *"The Philanderer,"* ISh, X (Fall 1971), 6.
The Philanderer at Niagara-on-the-Lake is well done.

1803 Severns, James George. "Structural Dialectic in the Earlier Plays of Bernard Shaw," DAI, XXXII (Sept 1971), 1683A. Unpublished dissertation, University of Iowa, 1971.

1804 Shatzky, Joel Lawrence. "Shaw, Barker and Galsworthy: The Development of the Drama of Ideas: 1890-1910," DAI, XXXI (1971), 4180A. Unpublished dissertation, New York University, 1970.

1805 Shinkuma, Kiyoshi. GEORGE BERNARD SHAW: A DRAMATIST OF CONSCIENCE (Seto: Nagoya Gakuin Univ., 1971).
[Discusses the problem of money and conscience in *Widowers' Houses, Mrs. Warren's Profession* and *Major Barbara.*]

1806 Shinkuma, Kiyoshi. "On the Problems of Marriage in the Plays of G. B. Shaw," NAGOYA GAKUIN-DAIGAKU RONSHU (Seto), VIII (Dec 1971), 457-83.
Shaw's ideas on marriage are best summed up in *Getting Married,* in which he tried to make people realize many unreasonable aspects of the marriage law then current. [In Japanese.]

1807 Sidhu, Charan Dass. "The Pattern of Tragicomedy in Bernard Shaw," DAI, XXXI (1971), 5375A. Unpublished dissertation, University of Wisconsin (Madison), 1970.

1808 Sidnell, M. J., "Hic and Ille: Shaw and Yeats," THEATRE AND NATIONALISM IN TWENTIETH-CENTURY IRELAND, ed by Robert O'Driscoll (Toronto: U of Toronto P, 1971).
A series of unpublished letters between Bernard Shaw and W. B. Yeats makes clear their personal and literary relationship and in particular an airing of the issues bearing on the rejection of *John Bull's Other Island* for production at the Abbey Theatre. In 1901, with the Irish Literary Theatre well launched, Yeats asked Shaw to come to Ireland and help "stir things up still further." Shaw did not come and he refused Yeats's request to allow the Irish Litearary Theatre to perform *The Man of Destiny.* Instead, in 1904 Shaw agreed to make a patriotic contribution to the repertory of the Irish Literary Theatre. *John Bull* was the result. Yeats was displeased with the play and, after asking Synge and William Fay for their opinions, wrote a long, basically unfavorable response to Shaw. The play was not performed at the Abbey--that is, not until 1916. The mutual admiration and respect that survived in Shaw and Yeats, despite the rejection of *John Bull*, is their recognition that each of them had a role to play, albeit different, and that they were somewhat complementary figures of a common ancestor, Jonathan Swift.

1809 Simon, Elliott Martin. "The Theatrical Evolution of the Edwardian Problem Play: A Study of the Changes in the Dramatic Conventions of English Melodrama 1890-1914," DAI, XXXI (1971), 4180A-4181A. Unpublished dissertation, University of Michigan, 1970.

1810 Smiley, Sam. PLAYWRITING: THE STRUCTURE OF ACTION (Englewood Cliffs, NJ: Prentice-Hall [Prentice Hall Series in Theatre and Drama], 1971), pp. 13, 49, 50, 53, 54, 59, 74, 93, 95, 97, 105, 106, 108, 113, 123-26, 136, 151, 158, 167, 191, 204, 213, 216.
[Shaw's play's used to illustrate the principles of writing plays.]

1811 Smith, J. Percy. "Bernard Shaw's First Critic," UNIVERSITY OF TORONTO QUARTERLY, XL (1971), 300-15.
In 1878 Shaw read a new novel entitled CHEER OR KILL and wrote a criticism of it and sent it to its author, Elinor

Louise Huddart. That criticism began a correspondence that lasted until 1894 in which 178 letters were kept by Shaw. Shaw's correspondence with Huddart often bordered on the cruel, showing indifference to the ordinary ranges of human feeling. What did Shaw gain from this relationship? Possibly an understanding of the intelligent woman's lot in Victorian society, a situation of increasing concern for Shaw. There are at least three other ways in which the relationship was important for Shaw: first, she provided him with an audience; second, she served as his critic; and third, she gave him encouragement. Her role as critic of Shaw's novels is similar to her role as audience: she engaged him in discussions of novel-writing, forcing him to examine and defend his ideas and techniques. While Shaw kept her letters, none of Elinor's descendants knew about his letters and were astonished to learn of her novel-writing.

1812 Smith, Warren Sylvester. "Bernard Shaw and the London Heretics," SHAW: SEVEN CRITICAL ESSAYS, ed by Norman Rosenblood (Toronto and Buffalo: U of Toronto P, 1971), pp. 51-69.
The heretical societies of London were the "practicum" of Shaw's education. They provided him with forums to develop his skills as speaker and a committee man, and they helped resolve his concerns about religion and society. Shaw joined all sorts of societies, but he was unique in that he developed his own theology.

1813 Stone, Susan Beth Cole. "Myth and Legend in the Drama of Bernard Shaw," DAI, XXXI (1971), 4796A. Unpublished dissertation, University of Colorado, 1970.

1814 Sühnel, Rudolf. "Eine Betrachtung über die englischen Klassiker der Moderne" (A View of the English Classical Writers of the Modern Age), ENGLISCHE DICHTER DER MODERNE. IHR LEBEN UND WERK (Modern English Writers. Their Life and Work), ed by Rudolf Sühnel and Dieter Riesner (Berlin: Erich Schmidt, 1971), pp. 1-15.
Shaw, who favors the drama of thought, is a writer in the traditions of the satirist Ben Jonson, the moralist Molière, the humorist Dickens and the critic of society Ibsen. His strength is the combination of English sobriety and Puritanism (influenced by Bunyan, Wesley and

General Booth) and Irish fantasy and wit (influenced by Swift, Congreve and Wilde). [In German.]

1815 Tedesco, Joseph Santo. "The Theory and Practice of Tragicomedy in George Bernard Shaw's Dramaturgy," DAI, XXXII (Nov 1971), 2711A. Unpublished dissertation, New York University, 1971.

1816 Turner, Justin G. "Serendipity and George Bernard Shaw," MANUSCRIPTS, XXIII (1971), 140-41.
In 1926 a Shaw collector, identified only as Mr. Samuel, had acquired some early Shaw pamphlets from the 1880's and wrote Shaw asking if he would autograph them. He received no reply. Then late in the 1930's a friend informed him that the American Art Galleries (now Parke-Bernet) had his letter to Shaw with the latter's comment on it for sale for $45. Mr. Samuel got his letter back on which Shaw had scrawled his displeasure upon hearing that scarce books and pamphlets which he had presented to friends had subsequently been put up for sale. The letter is now in the Dartmouth College Library.

1817 Tyson, Brian F. "Shaw among the Actors: Theatrical Additions to *Plays Unpleasant*," MD, XIV (Dec 1971), 264-75.
In 1897 Shaw began, prior to publication, extensive revisions to his first three plays. He expanded stage directions to describe fully the characters. Dissatisfied with contemporary actors, he wished to make his plays "actor-proof." He did, however, have the examples before him of several great actors. Shaw's experience as a drama critic helped him to make the most significant revisions in the text of *Widowers' Houses, The Philanderer,* and *Mrs. Warren's Profession.* He used the skills of talented actors, Janet Achurch especially, to improve the climaxes of these three plays.

1818 Wall, Vincent C. "*Captain Brassbound's Conversion*," ISh, X (Fall 1971), 6.
Captain Brassbound's Conversion at the Cambridge Theatre, London, is a poor play, badly acted.

1819 Weintraub, Stanley. "G.B.S. Borrows from Sarah Grand: THE HEAVENLY TWINS and YOU NEVER CAN TELL," MD, XIV (Dec 1971), 288-97.

On three different occasions Shaw in 1895 went out of his way to praise Sarah Grand's three-volume novel THE HEAVENLY TWINS (1893). At this time he was at work on YOU NEVER CAN TELL, which treats the grave themes of Grand with such lightness that its apparent relationships to the tripart novel have gone unnoticed. Yet the themes are the same: parent-child relationships, the equality of women in society, and the power of the sex instinct. Grand's novel is long forgotten, but much of it survives in Shaw's play.

1820 Weintraub, Stanley. "Genesis of a Play: Two Early Approaches to *Man and Superman*," SHAW: SEVEN CRITICAL ESSAYS, ed by Norman Rosenblood (Toronto and Buffalo: U of Toronto P, 1971), pp. 25-35.
Shaw felt he would never see a satisfactory performance of Mozart's DON GIOVANNI. In 1887 he tried in a short story to work out his own version of the myth. This story bears remarkable resemblance to the Hell scene of *Man and Superman*. But John Tanner's ancestry is owed as much to Sidney Trefusis of *An Unsocial Socialist* as to the Don. The short story and novel both helped determine the form one of the century's greatest plays.

1821 Weintraub, Stanley. JOURNEY TO HEARTBREAK: THE CRUCIBLE YEARS OF BERNARD SHAW, 1914-1918 (NY: Weybright and Talley, 1971); part rptd in INTELLEC-TUAL DIGEST, II (Nov 1971), 29-36, 79-80.
[A selective biography, concentrating on Shaw's difficult and painful years during World War I. Shaw had weathered the controversy of the war years, but as Weintraub aptly puts it, "the failure of what he felt was his greatest play [*Heartbreak House*] in his own lifetime was heartbreak enough."]

1822 Weintraub, Stanley (ed). "SAINT JOAN" BY BERNARD SHAW (Indianapolis and NY: The Bobbs-Merrill Company [The Bobbs-Merrill Shaw Series], 1971).
[Text of *Saint Joan* with Introduction, Shaw Chronology, Joan of Arc Chronology, Shaw letters about Joan, a BBC radio talk, the "Burning Scene" written for the unused film version, extracts from the English translation of trial transcript that Shaw used, Bibliography, Illustrations, and Shavian Comments.]

1823 White, William.   "G. B. Shaw on Whitman,"
AMERICAN NOTES AND QUERIES, IX (1971), 122.
In Louis Untermeyer's edition of THE POETRY AND PROSE OF
WALT WHITMAN, Shaw is quoted as saying, "Whitman is a
classic . . . curious that America should be the only
country in which this is not as obvious as the sun in the
heavens." The source for this remark remains obscure
after many hours of researching. Any knowledge of its
source would be appreciated.

1824 Wilkenfeld, Roger B.   "Perpetual Motion in
Heartbreak House," TEXAS STUDIES IN LITERATURE AND
LANGUAGE, XIII (Summer 1971), 321-35.
Heartbreak House is concerned with the twin themes of
knowledge and identity. Its verbal action moves through
two basic paradigms: who individuals say they are or are
not, and who others say those individuals are or are not.
When Randall Utterword appears and announces to Captain
Shotover, "But I'm afraid you don't know who I am,"
Shotover responds, "Do you suppose that at my age I make
distinctions between one fellow creature and another?"
Here is the major theme of the play. In Act I, all the
visitors to Heartbreak House try to make distinctions by
proclaiming their independent identities. But thereafter
it becomes a game of exposing the poses in order to discover the "man under the pose." Heartbreak House proves
to be an environment sustaining life, and only Mangan and
Billie Dunn, who seek to flee its analytical confines, are
destroyed by the bombs, which thereby make the
"distinctions" Shotover refused to make. The others,
relinquishing the former inclination to manipulate, are
transformed into the desire to feel that they have become
"members one of another." The ending provides a sense of
healthy, integrated pluralism: "It we who have survived."

1825 Wisenthal, J. L. "The Cosmology of *Man and
Superman*," MD, XIV (Dec 1971), 298-306.
The prevalent Shavian view is to see the religious element
of *Man and Superman* only in the detachable Hell scene of
Act III, but in truth the entire play underscores that
religious element, showing the relationship between hell,
heaven, and earth, though the Hell Scene is indeed the key
to the symbolic nature of the play. The values implicit
in the conflicting states of being, hell, heaven and
earth, are resolved in the marriage of Anne and Tanner,
which contributes towards evolutionary progress. Like

E V E R Y M A N this play too is about "the proper purpose of life, expressed in terms of hell, heaven, and earth."

1826 Zarifopol, Paul. "Shaw, Wagner si dificult-ătile criticii" (Shaw, Wagner and the Difficulties of Criticism), P E N T R U A R T A L I T E R A R A (Speaking of Literary Art) (Bucharest, Minerva I, 1971), pp. 273-76.
[The commentary considers the question whether Shaw's music criticism of Wagner is historicist or not. French exactitude is contrasted with the German tendency to become lost in detail.] Shaw is frantically simple in his desire to show that all Wagner's grand opera is the result of his having broken with the liberal-Socialist ideology of the bourgeoisie after 1848. Happily Shaw's mind is too alert to submit to systems, and he writes with candor and amusing nonchalance. [In Romanian.]

1972

1827 A[malric], J[ean]-C[laude]. "Shaw (George Bernard)," L'ENCYCLOPAEDIA UNIVERSALIS, v. IV (Paris: E. U. France S.A., 1972), 942-43.
[Biography, Social Reformer and Critic, Dramatist, Art and Humor in the Service of Ideas, Bibliography, and "Correlats": Ibsen, Socialism, Victorian Age, H. G. Wells.] [In French.]

1828 Anderson Imbert, Enrique. "*Pigmalion* y el cine" (*Pygmalion* and Film) LA FLECHA EN EL AIRE (The Arrow in the Air) (Buenos Aires: Gure, 1972), pp. 268-73.
Even though Shaw first opposed the filming of his plays, he later cooperated with the directors. *Pygmalion*, a philosophical comedy, became a great film, and for some, even better than the play. [In Spanish.]

1829 Anderson Imbert, Enrique. "Shaw y su tiempo" (Shaw and His Time) LOS DOMINGOS DEL PROFESOR (The Sundays of the Professor) (Buenos Aires: Gure, 1972), pp. 127-83.
[Although written in 1946, this book was first published in 1972. Brief biography of Shaw with analysis of his drama.] Shaw's dramatic production can be seen as a

pyramid: a wide economic base with an apex directed
toward the moral ends of conduct.   In contrast with
Ibsen's plays, Shaw's offer solutions: the evil is
capitalism, the remedy is Socialism. [In Spanish.]

1830 Anderson, Verily. THE LAST OF THE ECCENTRICS,
A LIFE OF ROSSLYN BRUCE (Lond, Sydney, Auckland and
Toronto: Hodder and Stoughton, 1972), p. 242.
[Kathleen Scott in a letter writes of sculpturing Shaw.]

1831 Anniah Gowda, H. H. DRAMATIC POETRY FROM
MEDIEVAL TO MODERN TIMES (Madras: Macmillan, 1972),
pp. 31, 144, 195-96, 215, 219, 227, 255-63, 269,
272, 275-78, 310, 319, 325, 343, 351, 354, 358.
Shaw is three-quarters anti-poetic, but still one-quarter
poet. He used the word poetry to signify the purely
aesthetic and that which is alienated from utility and
morality, as illustrated in the *Don Juan in Hell* episode
of *Man and Superman*. But though Shaw's art is logical,
his philosophy is not. Shaw underestimated the poetry in
Ibsen just as he underestimated the morality in
Shakespeare. The mechanization of style in Shaw's plays
alienates them from poetry. Shaw's power as a poet lies
in his power to create symbols and his devotion to music.

1832 Bastable, Adolphus (pseud). "Our Theatres in
the Seventies," SHAVIAN, IV (Winter 1972-73), 222-
26.
[A brief history and review of current production of *The
Doctor's Dilemma* and also of Ibsen's THE MASTER BUILDER
with reference to Shaw's own views.]

1833 Benstock, Bernard. "Four British Writers,"
CONTEMPORARY WRITERS, XIII (Winter 1972), 116-28.
[A review of criticism including SHAW: SEVEN CRITICAL
ESSAYS, ed by Norman Rosenblood (1971).] Contemporary
criticism focuses on ideas in Shaw's drama. Rosenblood's
is a minor collection although Martin Meisel adeptly
accounts for the dichotomy in Shaw between Fabian
gradualism and apocalyptic change.

1834 Bentley, Eric. THEATRE OF WAR, COMMENTS ON 32
OCCASIONS (NY: Viking P, 1972), pp. x, 3-21, 62,
63n, 66, 100, 101, 104, 113, 118, 147, 148, 158,

163, 183-211, 246, 260, 285, 290, 327, 359, 360, 389, 399n, 413.
[Reprints essays, mostly from the 1960's, that mention Shaw, including "Bernard Shaw," "Ibsen, Shaw, Brecht," and "The Making of a Dramatist."]

1835 Bergman, Herbert. "Comedy in *Candida*," SHAVIAN, IV (Spring 1972), 161-69.
Candida's success owes less to its serious than to its comic elements. Shaw makes use of the mechanical personality in Morell and Eugene. Eugene is also an exaggeration of the type of poet. He is comic because his conception of Candida varies so much from the actuality. His actions and those of Candida, Burgess, and Lexy are incongruous. Candida makes ironic remarks. Shaw uses mechanical action for comic effect.

1836 Bergquist, Gordon N. "War and Peace in the Prose and Plays of Bernard Shaw," DAI, XXXIII (1972), 2315A. Dissertation, University of Nebraska, 1972, published as THE PEN AND THE SWORD: WAR AND PEACE IN THE PROSE AND PLAYS OF BERNARD SHAW (Salzburg, Austria: Institut für Englische Sprache und Literatur [Poetic Drama and Poetic Theory], 1977).

1837 Bogard, Travis. CONTOUR IN TIME, THE PLAYS OF EUGENE O'NEILL (NY: Oxford UP, 1972), pp. xiii, 7, 16, 32, 33n., 57, 171, 172, 215, 288, 295-96, 358, 383.
[Passing references to Shaw.]

1838 Brack, O. M. Jr. "Miss Gambogi and the Terry-Shaw Correspondence," PAPERS OF THE BIBLIOGRAPHICAL SOCIETY OF AMERICA, LXVI (Third Quarter 1972), 277-89.
Because of deletions and revisions in Shaw's printed letters, texts of all editions earlier than that of Dan H. Laurence are doubtful.

1839 Bradbury, Ray. "From Stonehenge to Tranquility Base," PLAYBOY, XIX (Dec 1972), 149, 323-24.
"Neither Shaw nor I . . . is here to celebrate the defeat of man by matter, but to proclaim his high destiny."

1840 Bradbury, Ray. "Introduction," THE WONDERFUL
ICE CREAM SUIT AND OTHER PLAYS (Toronto, Lond, NY:
Bantam Pathfinder Editions, 1972), pp. vi-xiv.
Shaw deserved to be the patron saint of the American
Theater.

1841 Bridgwater, Patrick. NIETZSCHE IN ANGLOSAXON-
RY, A STUDY OF NIETZSCHE'S IMPACT ON ENGLISH AND
AMERICAN LITERATURE (Leicester: Liecester UP,
1972), pp. 10, 14, 15, 30, 39, 55, 58-66, 68, 73,
91, 126, 171, 184.
Shaw *wrongly* enjoys the popular reputation of having been
influenced by Nietzsche because of his use of the word
Superman. Chesterton was one of the first critics to link
Shaw and Nietzsche. Shaw recognized Nietzsche as a fellow
iconoclast, but the context in which his own superman
appears demonstrates that he has little to do with the
"lyrical Bismarck." Oswald Spengler made the same error
as Chesterton. In social and political terms, Shaw
regarded Nietzsche as inept. Shaw's word *Superman*
replaced the word *Overman* used by early translators.
[Especially interesting.]

1842 Bryden, Ronald. "Sage on Wheels," NStat,
LXXXIII (7 July 1972), 22-23.
[A review of Shaw's *Collected Letters 1898-1910*, ed by Dan
H. Laurence (1972).] Laurence's edition reveals the depth
of Shaw behind his mask. Shaw's disappointment in his
personal life perhaps made the great comedies possible.
The Philanderer and *Man and Superman* mocked the type of
courtship of his early affairs, and *Saint Joan* implies
that "it is better to burn than marry." Shaw at this time
experienced loneliness and "solitary joy," comparable to
what occurs in *Heartbreak House.*

1843 Casson, John. LEWIS AND SYBIL, A MEMOIR (Lond:
Collins, 1972), pp. 12, 14-15, 66, 84, 92, 101, 105,
110, 112-27, 129-33, 135-38, 142, 143, 145-46, 147,
148, 150-52, 154, 163-64, 166, 170-71, 178, 179,
182, 196, 204, 206, 218, 224, 230, 235, 237, 253,
271, 275, 277, 289, 297, 301, 304, 306, 322, 323,
336.
[Shaw and Sybil Thorndike and especially *Saint Joan.*]

1844 Caute, David. THE ILLUSION, AN ESSAY ON
POLITICS, THEATRE AND THE NOVEL (NY, Evanston, San

Francisco, Lond: Harper & Row, 1972), pp. 24, 58, 100-1, 120, 202-3.
Shaw's "preoccupation with *what* he wanted to say and his eclectic approach to *how* he said it--placed a package of dynamite on the pedestal of an apparently impregnable form of realist public drama." [No index.]

1845 Cole, Susan A. "The Utopian Plays of George Bernard Shaw: A Study of the Plays and Their Relationship to the Fictional Utopias of the Period from the Early 1870's to the Early 1920's," DAI, XXXII (1972), 6966A-67A. Unpublished dissertation, Brandeis University, 1972.

1846 Collis, John Stewart. "The Second Half," SHAVIAN, IV (Spring 1972), 184-87.
[Essay-review of SHAW: AN AUTOBIOGRAPHY 1898-1950 selected from his writings by Stanley Weintraub (1970); includes a comparison of Shaw with Tolstoy.]

1847 Cookson, Tommy. "Introduction," SHAW (Lond: Edward Arnold [The Portrait Series], 1972), pp. 3-13.
[General Survey of Shaw's Life and Career.]

1848 Cookson, Tommy. SHAW (Lond: Edward Arnold [The Portrait Series], 1972).
[A play intended for reading made up largely of Shaw's own words and those of some of his contemporaries like Chesterton, Archer, and Ellen Terry plus some explanation by a Narrator. Intended for schools.]

1849 Crouch, Isabel M. "Joan of Arc and Four Playwrights: A Rhetorical Analysis for Oral Interpretation," DAI, XXXIII (1972), 843A. Unpublished dissertation, University of Southern Illinois, 1972.

1850 Dietrich, Richard F. "Introduction," AN UNSOCIAL SOCIALIST BY BERNARD SHAW (NY: W. W. Norton [The Norton Library], 1972), pp. v-ix.
Shaw's novels are about a new spirit arising from the Victorian ethos and rebelling against the standard of the day. The novels proceed in a dialectic. In *An Unsocial Socialist* Shaw has discovered the way in the person of

Sidney Trefusis to save the world as a clown-prophet. The
novel expresses Shaw's lifelong attempt to make romance
out of his quest for reality.

1851 Duerksen, Roland A. "Shelleyan Witchcraft:
The Unbinding of Brassbound," Shaw R, XV (Jan 1972),
21-25.
Captain Brassbound's Conversion owes much to Shaw's study
of Shelley's THE WITCH OF ATLAS. Lady Cicely frees
Brassbound just as the Witch liberates Truth.

1852 Dukore, Bernard F. "THE MADRAS HOUSE Prefin-
ished," ETJ, XXIV (May 1972), 135-38.
When Granville Barker was too busy directing and casting a
London repertory theater to finish THE MADRAS HOUSE, Shaw
wrote the ending to Act III. Barker "was infuriated" and
finished it himself. [The text of Shaw's version appears
in the article.]

1853 Edel, Leon. HENRY JAMES, THE MASTER: 1901-
1916 (Phila and NY: J. B. Lippincott, 1972),
pp. 106, 187, 334, 370, 372-76, 378, 497, 537.
[James's and Shaw's debate over James's dramatization of
his own story, OWEN WINGATE, as THE SALOON.]

1854 Egan, Michael. "Introduction," IBSEN (Lond and
Bost: Routledge and Kegan Paul, 1972), pp. 3, 8-9,
18, 21, 23, 24, 37.
[References to Shaw as a critic of Ibsen.]

1855 Evans, T. F. "Counting the Words," SHAVIAN, IV
(Winter 1972-73), 218-21.
[Essay on A CONCORDANCE TO THE PLAYS AND PREFACES OF
BERNARD SHAW, compiled and edited by E. Dean Bevan
(1972).]

1856 Farmer, Philip José. TARZAN ALIVE (Garden
City, NY: Doubleday, 1972), pp. 7, 108, 218, 219,
220, 221, 234, 239, 240, 245, 282, 283.
Shaw used the story of the fifth duke of Greystoke,
disguised, in *An Unsocial Socialist*.

1857 Farooqui, Khalida Saleem. "Reflections upon War and Humour in G. B. Shaw's *Arms and the Man*," ARIEL (Dept. of English, Univ of Sind), I (1972), 26-32.
[Not seen.]

1858 Feingold, Michael. "Notes on a Minor *Major Barbara*, NYT, 9 July 1972, II, pp. 1, 4.
The production of *Major Barbara* at Stratford, Connecticut is imperfectly executed. The actors sum up everything Shaw is accused of: he is all talk and he is dated. Shaw interrupts his talk with three kinds of action: comic, violent, and that of the mind.

1859 Felstiner, John. THE LIES OF ART: MAX BEER-BOHM'S PARODY AND CARICATURE (NY: Alfred A. Knopf, 1972), pp. 76, 77, 81, 83-90, 90-94, 105, 116-26, 132, 136, 141, 151, 157, 163, 208.
Beerbohm felt Shaw was not an artist, but his criticism of Shaw as a dramatist is still the best of its time. If the Shaw the playwright did not take hold of Beerbohm, Shaw the personality did; there are more caricatures of Shaw than of anyone else other than Beerbohm himself and King Edward.

1860 Friel, Brian. "Plays Peasant and Unpeasant," TLS (17 March 1972), 305-6.
Shaw is not an Irish playwright.

1861 Fry, Roger. LETTERS OF ROGER FRY, ed, with an Introduction by Denys Sutton, 2 vols (Lond: Chatto & Windus; NY: Random House, 1972), pp. 52, 120, 267n, 361, 363n, 411, 572, 633-34.
[References to Shaw in letters to others and a letter to Shaw. Index incomplete.]

1862 Gal'perina, L. I. "Opyt stilisticheskogo ana-liza sintaktichheskikh sredstv individualizatsii rechi personazheĭ: na materiale p'esy B. Shou *Maior Barbara*" (Attempt at Stylistic Analysis of Syntatic Means of Individualizing Speech of Characters: On Material from *Major Barbara*), TRUDY KIRGIZKOGO UNI-VERSITETA (Frunze), VI (1972), 57-67.
Analysis based largely on the utterances of Lady Britomart indicates that the use of syntactic means in the speech of

personages individualizes their own traits: peculiarities
of character, their relationship with their surroundings,
manners, etc. This seems to counter the accepted belief
that Shaw was too concerned with ideas and discussion to
differentiate between the speech of his characters, though
he of course wrote primarily to express ideas. [In
Russian.]

1863 Gaskell, Ronald. DRAMA AND REALITY: THE
EUROPEAN THEATRE SINCE IBSEN (Lond: Routledge &
Kegan Paul, 1972), pp. 17, 23, 25, 28, 30, 33, 34,
63.
[Shaw as illustration in discussion of modern drama.]

1864 Gelber, Norman. "The *Misalliance* Theme in
Major Barbara, Shaw R, XV (May 1972), 65-70.
Despite the importance of the "misalliance" theme in *Major
Barbara*, it is frequently neglected. This theme is an
important one in nineteenth-century romantic comedy and
also an important social issue. The Edwardians regarded
their society as open, which Shaw questioned. The
misalliance of Lady Britomart and Undershaft is in trouble
because each misunderstands his position in the eyes of
the other and also overlooks some aspect of the social
reality.

1865 Gielgud, John. DISTINGUISHED COMPANY (Lond:
Heinemann, 1972), passim.
[Many references to productions of and performances of
Shaw's plays.]

1866 Gill, Richard. HAPPY RURAL SEAT: THE COUNTRY
HOUSE AND THE LITERARY IMAGINATION (New Haven,
Connecticut and Lond: Yale UP, 1972), pp. 13, 135-
40, 143, 147, 157, 167, 234, 237, 247, 276.
Heartbreak House anticipated the exposure of the stately
home by Aldous Huxley, Victoria Sackville-West, Evelyn
Waugh, D. H. Lawrence and Christopher Isherwood.
Throughout the play the house functions both
metaphorically and literally. The characters and the
house are complicated and ambivalent; potential tragedy
modulates into farce.

1867 Gillespie, George. "Illustrations," SHAW, ed
by Tommy Cookson (Lond: Edward Arnold [The Portrait

497

Series], 1972), pp. 16, 28-29, 34-35, 39, 42-43, 51, 70, 74-75, 83, 93.
[Drawings of Shaw, characters from the plays, and others.]

1868 Gillie, Christopher. LONGMAN COMPANION TO ENGLISH LITERATURE (Lond: Longman, 1972), pp. 178, 212, 262-63, 783.
A talent for rhetoric and a delight in ideological conflict are characteristic of Shaw; "though most of his propaganda is out of date, his art still holds his plays on the stage." [A survey of Shaw's life and works.] Shaw was the first dramatist who realized that the reading public for plays was larger than the theater-going public; therefore he wrote long prefaces to his plays.

1869 Glicksberg, Charles I. "Shaw the Social Prophet," LITERATURE AND SOCIETY (The Hague: Nijhoff, 1972), pp. 83-92.
Shaw the artist was in conflict with Shaw the prophet. He does not hesitate to sacrifice Dubedet, the scoundrel, in *The Doctor's Dilemma* for the sake of the mediocre Doctor Blenkinsop. Shaw felt that what mattered in Ibsen was his message. The solution to the slum problem in *Widowers' Houses* is the reconstruction of society. *Mrs. Warren's Profession* may not have brought about social reform, but it served as the agent of moral enlightenment. *Major Barbara* outlives its period because it achieves universality of theme. Literature serves a higher function than social reform.

1870 Grazhdanskaîa, Zoîa T. "V. I. Lenin i B. Shou" (V. I. Lenin and B. Shaw), UCHENYE ZAPISKI MOSKOV-SKOGO OBLASTNOGO PEDAGOGICHESKOGO INSTITUTA (Moscow), CCLVI (1972), 3-10.
Shaw's copy of *Back to Methuselah* which he inscribed and sent to Lenin is preserved in the Archives of Marx-Leninism of the Central Committee of the Communist Party of the Soviet Union. Shaw believed that Lenin never received it, but the copy has copious annotations by Lenin, positive and negative. [In Russian.]

1871 Gussow, Mel. "Stage: Bergman Tour," NYT, 18 April 1972, p. 55.
Shaw's contribution, *Captain Brassbound's Conversion*, is less than Ingrid Bergman's.

1872 Harrington, John (ed). MALE AND FEMALE:
IDENTITY (NY, Lond, Sydney, Toronto: John Wiley
[Perception in Communication], 1972), pp. 85-87.
[Selection from the Preface to *Getting Married* with
questions.]

1873 Henderson, Robert M. D. W. GRIFFITH, HIS LIFE
AND WORK (NY: Oxford UP, 1972), p. 268.
[Anecdote concerning Shaw as scenario writer for D. W.
Griffith.]

1874 Hewes, Henry. "Shavian Cream," SRL, LV (5 Aug
1972), 60.
Misalliance tops the list of Shaw revivals in North
America. [Review of Niagara-on-the-Lake production.]

1875 Houseman, John. RUN-THROUGH, A MEMOIR (NY:
Simon and Schuster, 1972), pp. 91, 131, 289, 328,
343, 350, 481.
[The Mercury Theatre and Shaw, *Heartbreak House* in
particular. Photograph.]

1876 Hugo, L[eon] B. "*The Doctor's Dilemma* at the
Court Theatre," UNISA ENGLISH STUDIES, X (1972), 29-
33.
The Vedrenne-Barker seasons at the Court Theatre
revolutionized English drama, and Shaw was the third
partner in the undertaking. Shaw had accused Ibsen of
using death on the stage for morbid reasons. William
Archer, defending Ibsen accused Shaw of not being able to
confront death on the stage. The deathbed scene in *The
Doctor's Dilemma* was Shaw's answer. At the same time that
Shaw was busy with the production of *Dilemma*, he put down
H. G. Wells, who was attempting to topple the hierarchy of
the Fabian Society.

1877 Hugo, Leon. "G. B. S. in Cape Town," LANTERN,
XXII (Dec 1972), 24-26, 84-89.
When Shaw arrived in Cape Town in 1932, he was not given a
civic welcome, annoying the local Fabians. He was
interviewed and photographed often, with both still and
moving picture cameras. [Excerpts from Shaw's
pronouncements and several photographs and one drawing of
him are here reproduced.] He enjoyed sightseeing and
swimming. He was attacked on religious grounds by Father

Vassall-Phillips, to which he replied. [Shaw's reply is reproduced.] He defended Bolshevik Communism in an address and attacked the position of blacks.

1878 Hulban, Horia. "Notes on Style and Substance in Shaw's *Pygmalion*," ANALELE ŞTIINŢIFICE ALE UNIVERSITĂŢIL IAŞI, LING, XVIII (1972), 127-35.
Pygmalion must be followed on four levels at least: 1) didactic, the problem of phonetics, 2) the reversed myth, 3) social, and 4) dramatic. Shaw contributed to the development of the Pygmalion motif in the artist's triumph over nature, the punishment of the misogynist bachelor, and the education of Galatea. The linguistic structure of the play is in perfect agreement with the dramatic structure, showing Shaw's dramatic art and opening the way for a dialectical and social variant of the English language on the stage. [Summary in Romanian.]

1879 Hynes, Samuel. "'Mr. Pember's Academy'," EDWARDIAN OCCASIONS, ESSAYS ON ENGLISH WRITING IN THE EARLY TWENTIETH CENTURY (NY: Oxford UP, 1972), 191-208.
[Shaw and the Academic Committee, an attempt at a literary academy.]

1880 Johnson, Betty Freeman. "Shelley's CENCI and *Mrs. Warren's Profession*," ShawR, XV (Jan 1972), 26-34.
Shaw was in charge of the Shelley Society's press relations for their production of THE CENCI, and in his review he pronounced the play unworthy of Shelley, "second-hand Shakespere." Five years later he was involved in an attempt to revive the play. The most obvious link between Shelley's play and Shaw's is the theme of incest. A more significant link is the action common to both plays of the attempt of one person, a parent, to dominate the will of another. Both plays "feature emotional confrontation scenes and the pronouncement of a parental curse."

1881 Kantorovich, I. "Dzorzh B. Shou. *Pis'ma* sos. A. G. Obraztsova," (George B. Shaw. *Letters*, A. G. Obraztsova [comp], NOVII MIR (Moscow), XLVIII (1972), 284-85.
The epistolary remains of Shaw are colossal, but little has been published in Russian translation, aside from

single items addressed to Russian cultural activists. In his letters, Shaw deals with the theater, war, and his attitude to the Soviet Union. [In Russian.]

1882 Kantorovich, I. "Iz naslediîa Bernarda Shou" (Shaw's Heritage), INOSTRANNAIÂ LITERATURA (Moscow), No 8 (1972) 261-63.
Few of Shaw's letters have been published hitherto in the Soviet Union. Two addressed to L. N. Tolstoi were published in 1911. This collection [*Pis'ma* Sos. A. G. Obraztsova (1971) (Not seen)] covers the years 1892-1949. The introduction and notes by Obraztsova assist the reader to find his way in this complex and sometimes contradic- tory material. It is a pity that Shaw's attitude to the plays of Shakespeare is not reflected. [In Russian.]

1883 Kantorovich, I. "Osvoenie Shou," (Acclimatiza- tion of Shaw), TEATR (Moscow), II (1972), 53-58.
Too True to Be Good was translated into Russian soon after Shaw's visit in 1931 and produced at the Sverdlovsk Dramatic Theater but without success. The same theater has now (1971) produced *Saint Joan*, a bold experiment which must be approached attentively. The play is of interest not only to students of the Middle Ages. Two dangers arise in production: it can be overly modernized, and tradition and convention can be too harmoniously com- bined. Unfortunately, the producer at the Sverdlovsk Theater uses costumes of operatic splendor, which contra- dict the style of the production. The text has been cut, and the Epilogue omitted, though it is essential in defining the social structure of the conflict. The only play of Shaw's successfully produced in the Soviet Union in the thirties and forties was *Pygmalion* at the Malyi Theater (Moscow) in 1944. In the late forties and early fifties, only *Pygmalion* and *The Devil's Disciple* were produced. The centenary marked a new period for Shaw's plays, with productions in Moscow, Leningrad, Tallin (Estonian SSR) *Heartbreak House, Saint Joan,* and *Caesar and Cleopatra*). At the end of the sixties, *The Million- airess* and *Arms and the Man* were produced in 15 theaters, averaging two years for a play: at this rate, half of all Shaw's plays will have been produced in the USSR by the year 2000. [In Russian.]

1884 Kapp, Yvonne. ELEANOR MARX, VOLUME I: FAMILY LIFE, 1855-1883 (Lond: Lawrence and Wishart; NY:

Pantheon Books, 1972), pp. 173n, 192, 259, 265, 270-1.
[Shaw's early relationship with Eleanor Marx, after meeting her in the British Museum reading room.]

1885 Kenny, Brother Brendon. "Shaw's Theater: Upsetting the Applecart of Government," ENGLISH JOURNAL, LXI (May 1972), 670-72, 684.
The Applecart has the advantage for the high school class in that it broaches the theory of government devoid of our modern prejudices of war and race.

1886 Kerr, Walter. "Ravishing Bergman, Ravished Shaw," NYT, 23 April 1972, II, pp. 1, 10.
The production of *Captain Brassbound's Conversion* is a stock company one to provide Ingrid Bergman an opportunity to glow. Shaw throws away his scenes, and the director finishes the job. [Photograph.]

1887 Kerr, Walter. "Shaw's Not Wilde," NYT, 9 April 1972, II, p. 3.
Misalliance always totally occupies itself with whatever comes to mind at the moment. The Roundabout Theater's revival is a good amateur try. Shaw is not Oscar Wilde: he did not write epigrams or jokes on people; he wrote attitudes.

1888 Krajewska, Wanda. "Dramat Angielski w Repertuarze Teatrów Polskich w Okresie Młodej Polski (1885-1918)" (English Drama in the Polish Theaters in the Time of Young Poland), KWARTALNIK NEOFILOLOGICZNY, XIX (1972), 21-51.
The most popular contemporary playwrights were Wilde and Shaw, though because their plays were performed as domestic Polish comedies, they were misunderstood. Shaw was treated better as a kind of Ibsen, and productions of his plays revealed new dramatic techniques. [Includes a list of English plays staged in Polish theaters in 1885-1918.] [In Polish with a summary in English at the conclusion.]

1889 Krajewska, Wanda. RECEPCJA LITERATURY ANGIELSKIEJ W POLSCE W OKRESIE MODERNIZMU (1887-1918) (Reception of English Literature in Poland in the

Modernism Period [1887-1918]) (Wroclaw: Ossolineumm, 1972), pp. 192-97.
The first mention of Shaw's work in Poland occurred in 1898, when J. Plonski writing in ZYCIE (Cracow) pointed out that few worth-while plays were being produced in London, and that Shaw's were more welcome in the US and provinces. L. Szczepanski (1898), reviewing a production of Pinero's THE PRINCESS AND THE BUTTERFLY in Cracow, remarked on Shaw's reforms in the English theater and his introduction of Ibsen. Later notices of Shaw productions in London were plot summaries. In Poland, the first production was *The Devil's Disciple* (Lwow, Poznan, 1903), concentrating on the aspect of the struggle for independence. *Arms and the Man* (1904) was chosen for political reasons. But texts were not published and producers had no access to prefaces or stage-directions, so they allowed themselves considerable liberties. Not for several years was Shaw recognized as a "laughing philosopher." After the 1905 Revolution, Shaw became of interest in Poland as a Socialist agitator and social reformer, and he was written about in the left-wing magazines. This led to productions of *Mrs. Warren's Profession* and *Widowers' Houses.* His work was mainly known in Poland through German translations and criticism; little was known of his ideas on art or his theater criticism. [In Polish.]

1890 Kronenberger, Louis. THE LAST WORD: PORTRAITS OF FOURTEEN MASTER APHORISTS (NY: Macmillan; Lond: New York Collier Macmillan, 1972), pp. 205-24.
[Brief biography, including many Shavian aphorisms, followed by a listing of aphorisms.]

1891 Kunzinš, Kārlis. LATVIEŠU TEATRA VĒSTURE (1901-1940) (History of the Latvian Theater [1901-1940]) Vol II (Riga: "Liesma," 1972), pp. 413-16.
Productions in Latvia of: *Widowers' Houses, Captain Brassbound's Conversion, The Devil's Disciple, Pygmalion, Arms and the Man, Candida, Saint Joan,* and *You Never Can Tell.* [In Latvian.]

1892 Logo, Mary M. (ed). IMPERFECT ENCOUNTER, LETTERS OF WILLIAM ROTHENSTEIN AND RABINDRANATH TAGORE 1911-1941 (Cambridge, Massachusetts: Harvard UP, 1972), pp. 42, 111, 127n, 264n, 341, 342n.
[Passing references to Shaw.]

1893 Lambert, J. W. "Plays in Performance, London," DRAMA, CIV (Spring 1972), 14-32.
Geneva is minor Shaw.

1894 Larik, K. M. "Bernard Shaw as a Dramatist," ARIEL (Dept. of English, Univ of Sind), I (1972), 33-38.
[Not seen.]

1895 Laurence, Dan H. "Bernard Shaw and the American Theater: A Projected Study," ISh, XI (Fall 1972), 1-4.
[Plan for a book-length study of Shaw's relations with the American Theater.]

1896 Laurence, Dan H. "Introduction," BERNARD SHAW, COLLECTED LETTERS 1898-1910, ed by Dan H. Laurence (NY: Dodd, Mead, 1972), pp. xi-xviii.
"Shaw wrote to be understood . . . and the letters contain some of the most lucid writing in the English language since Swift." He was perenially youthful, and his epistolary art was comic.

1897 Lawrence, Kenneth. "Bernard Shaw: The Career of the Life Force," MD, XV (Sept 1972), 130-46.
Shaw's desire for a utilitarian theater led him to a drama of ideas, which was reinforced by his contentiousness, his evangelism, and his dramatic conceptions. Further, *Man and Superman, Back to Methuselah,* and *The Simpleton of the Unexpected Isles* are thesis plays, distinguished by dialectical structure and subordination to argument. To gain a clearer understanding of Shaw's thesis drama it is necessary to consider his use of Plato, whose dialectical method is a prototype of Shaw's. All the forms that the Life Force assumes in *Superman* are dialectical derivatives of its goal: a better species. World War I changed Shaw's view of the Life Force. Creative Evolution needed more time than the life of a single man. Plato can be seen behind the scenes of *Methuselah*. Although *Simpleton* is a weaker play, its dialectic is not exclusively simple Hegelianism. Shaw perhaps introduces the angel to judge the drama of ideas as well as the Life Force, but the play ends hailing the Life to come. [A detailed comparison of Shaw and Plato: specific ideas as well as dialectic technique.]

1898 Lazenby, Walter. ARTHUR WING PINERO (N Y: Twayne [TEAS], 1972), pp. 18, 19, 21, 22, 45, 89, 107, 111, 116, 128, 131, 149, 150, 155.
[Passing use of Shaw as basis for measuring Pinero's achievement.]

1899 Leary, Daniel J. "About Nothing in Shaw's *The Simpleton of the Unexpected Isles*," ETJ, X XIV (May 1972), 139-48.
The Simpleton of the Unexpected Isles (as well as all the late plays from *The Apple Cart* to *Farfetched Fables*) anticipates future dramatic developments and shows Shaw's "impatience with old forms." *Too True to Be Good* and *Heartbreak House* dramatize absurdist encounters with moral and mental nakedness, and *Simpleton* epitomizes the stripping of illusions so that the play's central issue is Nothing and its dominant structural feature is the unexpected. Shaw rejects the dialectic frame in both *Simpleton* and *Back to Methuselah* although a tension between opposites exists in each. The rejection is "not as promising" in *Simpleton* as in *Methuselah*. Shaw also questioned his prophetic stance toward Creative Evolution in the prefaces to *On the Rocks* and *The Six of Calais*. Nevertheless, Shaw's characters have a positive response to their heightened sense of Nothingness. ["On Church Going" is cited to compare Iddy's response to Shaw's own.]

1900 Leary, D. J. "Shaw's Blakean Vision: A Dialectic Approach to *Heartbreak House*," M D, X V (May 1972), 89-103.
Ariadne provides the clue to understand *Heartbreak House* when she says that "there are only two classes in good society in England: the equestrian classes and the neurotic classes." Blake's writings can show Shaw's connection with "the mythopoetic content of English art." The dialectic quest of *Heartbreak* "is for a synthesis of Heartbreak House and Horseback Hall." Heartbreak echoes *Man and Superman* and anticipates *Back to Methuselah*. The characters are both individual and archetypal. The play deals with tragic confusion and the search for identity. The archetypal aspects can be approached through Blake's four archetypes and seem to be derived from THE FOUR ZOAS. "As in Blake's myth, the movement has been from the center to circumference, from individual to universal man."

1901 Leary, Daniel J. "Shaw? Why Not!" PROMETHEAN, X X (1972), 80-89.

[This essay is an extended description of Leary's difficulties presenting Shaw as "relevant" to his students. Because the open-ended "Why Not?" was shared by both students and Shaw, "Why Not?" became the focal point of the course.]

1902 Lichtheim, George. EUROPE IN THE TWENTIETH CENTURY (NY and Washington: Praegar, 1972), pp. 23, 45-46, 50, 92, 148, 185, 188, 197.
[Shaw and Socialism.] Shaw played the role of intellectual rebel. His misfortune was that after 1914 he no longer had much to say. His faith degenerated into eulogy of dictators. He was more effective as social critic and champion of the Ibsenite new woman than in the role of prophet.

1903 Lillie, Beatrice. EVERY OTHER INCH A LADY (Garden City, NY: Doubleday, 1972), pp. 241-46.
[Beatrice Lillie playing Sweetie in *Too True to Be Good*. [Not indexed.]

1904 Little, Stuart. OFF-BROADWAY: THE PROPHETIC THEATRE (NY: Coward, McCann & Geoghegan, 1972), pp. 32, 75, 94, 116, 139, 142, 143.
[Shaw and Off-Broadway.]

1905 Mabley, Edward. DRAMATIC CONSTRUCTION: AN OUTLINE OF BASIC PRINCIPLES (Phila and NY: Chilton Book Company, 1972), pp. 153-72.
Analysis of *Pygmalion*. Premise. Synopsis. Protagonist and Objective. Obstacles. Crises and Climaxes, Theme. Resolution. Opening. Unity. Exposition. Characterization. Development. Dramatic irony. Preparation. Activity. Dialogue. Plausibility.

1906 McDowell, Frederick P. W. "GBS: *Passion Play*," Ish, XI (Fall 1972), 6-7.
Shaw's *Passion Play*, edited by Jerald E. Bringle (1971) provides an interesting contrast between Jesus and Judas.

1907 McElderry, Bruce R., Jr. MAX BEERBOHM (NY: Twayne [TEAS], 1972), passim.
[Biographical information concerning Beerbohm's succeeding Shaw as drama critic of the SRL; survey of Beerbohm's

estimate of Shaw's plays; description of Beerbohm's parodies and caricatures of Shaw.]

1908 McIlwaine, Robert S. "The Intellectual Farce
of Bernard Shaw," DAI, XXXII (1972), 4751A. Unpublished dissertation, Duke University, 1971.

1909 McNicholas, Sister Mary V., OP. "*The
Quintessence of Ibsenism*: Its Impact on the Drama
of Eugene Gladstone O'Neill," DAI, XXXII (1972),
5238A. Unpublished dissertation, University of
Indiana, 1971.

1910 Makusheva, S. P. "Karikatura iâk zasib satiri
u tvorakh Bernarda Shou" (Caricature as a Means of
Satire in Shaw's Works), INOZEMNA FILOLOGIIA
(L'viv), No 29 (1972), 127-33.
Shaw's satirical work includes literary caricatures
associated with the transitory period of capitalism at its
peak after World War I (Imperialism). The social themes
which dominated his work before WW II give way to political themes, and Shaw expresses his socio-political ideas
by means of paradox, sarcasm, grotesque buffoonery and
caricature. Examples occur in *The Apple Cart* performed in
Moscow in 1951, *Man and Superman, Back to Methuselah* and
Too True to Be Good performed in Moscow in 1952. [In
Ukrainian.]

1911 Mathison, Imogene. "Responses of College
Sophomores to Three Plays," DAI, XXXIII (1972),
1983A. Unpublished dissertation, Florida State
University, 1972.

1912 Matoba, Junko. "Shaw Versus Shakespeare,"
SEISHIN JOSHIDAIGAKU RONSO (Tokyo), No. 41 (Dec
1972), pp. 1-14.
Shaw's criticism of Shakespeare, the major themes of which
are "deflation of the Bard's philosophy and praise of his
word-music," is rather unpopular even among sympathetic
critics. However, the point would be to know "the reasons
why he had to talk of Shakespeare in that way." As a
Shakespeare critic he is unique "not because of insight or
his wide knowledge of the Bard but because there has never
been a writer who had devoted so many of his pages to

Shakespeare and yet all the time was talking of himself and of his dramaturgy."

1913 Meier, Paul. LA PENSÉE UTOPIQUE (Utopian Thought) (France: Edition Sociales, 1972). [Not seen. See Meier, Paul. WILLIAM MORRIS: THE MARXIST DREAMER (1978).] [In French.]

1914 Mikhail, E. H. A BIBLIOGRAPHY OF MODERN IRISH DRAMA 1899-1970 (Seattle: U of Washington P, 1972). [A comprehensive bibliography of general studies of Irish Drama, including Shaw's plays.]

1915 Misiolek, E. WSTEP DO GEORGE BERNARD SHAW PIGMALION (Introduction to Bernard Shaw's *Pygmalion*) (Warsaw: PIW, 1972). [Not seen.] [In Polish.]

1916 Morgan, Margery M. THE SHAVIAN PLAYGROUND (Lond: Methuen, 1972); rptd (Lond: Methuen [University Paperback], 1975). [Illustrated, especially with production photographs. Chapter 5 appeared originally as the Introduction to YOU NEVER CAN TELL (1967); a variant form of Chapter 8 appeared in Zimbardo, Rose (ed). TWCIMB (1970); Chapter 11 and part of Chapter 17 appeared as "Bernard Shaw on the Tightrope," MD (1962) and "Two Varieties of Political Drama," SHAVIAN (1962); Chapter 13 appeared as "*Back to Methuselah*: the Poet and the City," ESSAYS AND STUDIES, New Series, XIII (1960); rptd in Kaufman, R. J. (ed). G. B. SHAW (1965). Abstracted under date of first publication.]
The Novels: Shaw's novels anticipate the plays. Instead of correcting characterization by greater realism and subtlety, Shaw sets attitude against attitude from outside, a technique more suited to the stage. Socialist Drama: *Widowers' Houses* is not very like the well-made play, Augier's CEINTURE DOREÉ, it started from; the real originality is in the dramatic tension resulting from the Socialist logic in conflict with private emotion. The tension and conflict in *The Philanderer* arise from Shaw's recognition that there is danger in reason and the suppression of feeling. In *Mrs. Warren's Profession*, Shaw transferred the shame associated with prostitution to business. But Vivie chooses an equally bad alternative: "the puritan's retreat from life into abstractions."

Tales for the Nursery: What Shaw found amusing as a boy is what Shaw took as the basis of his plays. *Arms and the Man* suggests "a puppet play for human actors." All of Shaw's plays deal with parental, repressive authority. Like *Caesar and Cleopatra* it illustrates the growth from a primitive state of nature to a more civilized condition. *Captain Brassbound's Conversion* adapts two Shakespearian roles: Shylock and Portia. Androcles is "the clown encountering the pantomine lion," and the childish delight is analogous to paradisal joy. The Virgin Mother: The conflicts in *Candida* between Marchbanks and Morrell are not resolved by the conclusion; they are "only distanced and stilled in an aesthetic transformation." The "Woman Question" of the play is created by Candida's representing both the actual woman and the ideal.

Verbal Heroics: The crux of *Man and Superman* is the relation of the Hell scene to the rest of the play, yet Shaw as a practical man of the theater knew it must be detachable. He is "more artist than philosopher" in *Superman*.

Problem Plays: The theme of *The Doctor's Dilemma* is abstractly conceived, and the action is organized syllogistically. *Pygmalion* examines the social question: "what creates 'the deepest gulf that separates class from class and soul from soul?'"

The Greek Form Again: *Getting Married* has an affinity with the classical burlesque. Shaw has tried to revive the ritual origins of comedy. Shaw's Dream Play, *Heartbreak House*, is "the underworld of dreams and symbols."

The Histories: Historical drama is costume drama. The conventions of historical drama in *The Devil's Disciple* allowed Shaw his search for an heroic image. Shaw worked wiwthin the facts of historical authority, as in *Caesar*, and those facts disciplined his imagination. Shaw, unlike Shakespeare, avoided tragedy in *Caesar* and in *Saint Joan* partly by use of the pantomime conventions.

Farewell to Platonism: *Too True to Be Good* is Shaw's rejection of the saving power of reason and of the law.

Eschatological Plays: Shaw always expressed contempt for mere talk, and this contempt turned on parliamentary democracy. *On the Rocks* attacks both the proletariat and the aristocracy, arguing for benevolent tyranny. Finally it rejects this tyranny in a call for revolution. Shaw included the possibility of violent insurrection within "the inevitability of gradualness" in the 1928 *The Intelligent Woman's Guide* and "The Transition to Social Democracy." *The Simpleton of the Unexpected Isles* revives both the eighteenth century oriental fable and the eighteenth century tradition of reason.

Late Burlesques: The moment in history of *In Good King Charles's Golden Days* is a pause between the absolutism of Charles I and the demogoguery of Titus Oates, and this represents the modern choice between Fascist tyranny and mob rule. *Geneva* is Shaw's most Aristophanic play, and he brought caricatures of actual people on stage.

The Shavian Muse--In Conclusion: "Shaw has been more underestimated after his death than he was overestimated in his lifetime." Epifania Ognisanti di Parerga of *The Millionairess* is the "Shavian muse unveiled." Shaw was "one of the nineteenth century's most effective contrivances for transcending its limitations and growing into a new world of values."

1917 Nelson, Raymond S. "*Back to Methuselah*: Shaw's Modern Bible," COSTERUS (Amsterdam), V (1972), 117-23.
Back to Methuselah is Shaw's attempt to make an iconography for the new religion of the twentieth century, which already exists. It is an elaboration of convictions that had been developing a lifetime. It begins with the fall and ends in redemption. Man deteriorates through a neglect of responsibilities, and his lifespan shrinks. But man can be redeemed through creative evolution. He must save himself because he is limited to self creation, and there is no forgiveness through vicarious suffering. These ideas appear as early as *Major Barbara, Androcles and the Lion,* and *Man and Superman,* and Eric Bentley is wrong when he thinks Shaw changed his mind by the time of *Methuselah.* Shaw believed the dogma of *Methuselah* but does not accept its "literal truth."

1918 Nelson, Raymond S. "*Mrs. Warren's Profession* and English Prostitution," JOURNAL OF MODERN LITERATURE, II (Third Issue 1971-72), 357-66.
The germ idea of *Mrs. Warren's Profession* came from Maupassant's YVETTE through Janet Achurch's play MRS. DAINTY'S DAUGHTER. As the cities grew in the nineteenth century, the number of prostitutes mounted. Conditions were bad on the continent as well as in England. There

were chains of brothels employing English girls.   Mrs.
Mary Jeffries maintained a series of brothels, and she was
impossible to prosecute.   *Mrs. Warren* was, therefore,
bound to touch the consciences of the playgoers.   Shaw's
explanation for the hordes of women employed as
prostitutes is need, and the evidence suggests he was
right, though William Booth, agreeing with William Logan,
argued there were other reasons.   Shaw's analysis is
identical with the Socialist point of view.

1919 Nelson, Raymond S.   "Shaw's Heaven, Hell, and
Redemption," COSTERUS (Amsterdam), VI (1972), 99-
108.
Man and Superman still provides the best understanding of
Shaw's heaven and hell, which bears little resemblance to
traditional ideas of these places.   They are states of
soul.   Shaw, following Carlyle, concluded that the pursuit
of happiness and pleasure was hell.   Though heaven is not
portrayed, it is the antithesis of hell, where mind is
preferred to body and reality is mastered.   It is a place
of work as well as one of contemplation.   The word
"honor" as used by the devil and by Tanner has different
meanings and should not be confused.   Individual salvation
is meaningless to Shaw.   The Life Force is larger than any
individual's comprehension.   Salvation is possible only in
an improved race.

1920 Nelson, Raymond S.   "Wisdom and Power in
Androcles and the Lion," YEARBOOK OF ENGLISH
STUDIES, II (1972), 192-204.
The farcical elements of *Androcles and the Lion* are so
insistent that Shaw's themes of religious persecution and
religious faith are obscured.   The central idea of the
play is the marriage of wisdom and power.   *Major Barbara*
represents a slightly different treatment of this theme.
Cusins, armed with wisdom, is prepared to assume power.
The ideas represented by Lavinia and Androcles make up the
wisdom of Androcles.   Rome represents Imperial power.
Rome disintegrated because power was uninformed by
religious faith.

1921 Nethercot, Arthur H.   "Who *Was* Eugene
Marchbanks?" ShawR, XV (Jan 1972), 2-20.
The question of Marchbanks's identity was started by
Oliver Elton, who described in a review the actor who
played Marchbvanks as "got up to look like Shelley."
[Includes a review of the Shelley-Marchbanks tradition.]

Henderson in the Shaw biography suggests as models also 1) Shaw's youthful character, 2) the Celtic Renascence, especially Yeats, and 3) Ibsen. The idea of the influence of pre-Raphaelitism is also raised but rejected on Shaw's authority. DeQuincy was suggested by Shaw, though some critics feel this was an attempt to disguise his own self-portrait. Shaw's attitude toward Yeats would seem to rule out him as the model for a serious male character. The controversy over the model for Marchbanks focuses on the speeches between Marchbanks and Morell in Act II. But because of the description of Marchbanks at his entrance and because of verbal echoes from the poems, Shelley must be the chief model.

> **1922** Novick, Julius. *"Major Barbara*: Major Shaw," HUMANIST, XXXII (21 Nov 1972), 35-36.

Although *Major Barbara* had a "fainthearted revival" at the American Shakespeare Festival Theatre in Stratford, Connecticut, the play is prophetic and "relevant." Perivale St. Andrews is prosperous middle-class America, where physical needs are met making possible a spiritual regeneration. Shaw successfully dramatizes ideological debate.

> **1923** Ogiso, Masafumi. "Ogai to Shaw" (Ogai and Shaw), JISSEN EIBEI BUNGAKU (Jissen Women's Junior College, Tokyo), I (Jan 1972), 39-50.

Judging from many comments on Shaw scattered in his voluminous writings, it is clear that Ogai Mori (1862-1922) had a great interest in Shaw. His sources of information were chiefly German publications. When he translated *The Shewing-up of Blanco Posnet* into Japanese in 1910, it was Siegfried Trebitsch's German version, not Shaw's original, that he used as the text. He did not translate one phrase into Japanese, because it betrayed in his eyes Shaw's blasphemous idea. Interestingly this phrase exists only in Trebitsch's version, not in Shaw's published edition (1911). This fact and further examination reveal that the 1911 edition differs considerably in some parts from the 1909 version which is the original text of the German version. [In Japanese.]

> **1924** Okumura, Saburo. "Shaw to Genjitsu -Shaw Engeki no Tenkai-" (Shaw and Reality--Development of Shavian Drama), JINBUN KENKYU (Osaka Municipal University, Osaka), XXIV (Nov 1972) 601-20.

Shaw's drama is basically a comedy of disillusionment.
[On Shaw's sense of reality or his method of grasping
reality.] [In Japanese.]

1925 "Our Theatres in the Seventies," SHAVIAN, IV
(Spring 1972), 178-83.
[A brief history and review of current productions of *John
Bull's Other Island, Major Barbara, Caesar and Cleopatra,
Captain Brassbound's Conversion,* and *The Devil's Disciple.*]

1926 "Palmer, D. J. "Drama," THE TWENTIETH CENTURY
MIND: HISTORY, IDEAS, AND LITERATURE, I: 1900-
1918, ed by C. B. Cox and A. E. Dyson (Lond, Oxford
and NY: Oxford UP, 1972), pp. 468-72.
Because Shaw's aims in dramatic reform were an integral
part of his social analysis, he was the most radical
champion of the "new drama." Instead of discarding the
old stage tricks, he used them to new purpose. Because
Shaw's plays are polemical and his polemics are dramatic,
he is subject to two sources of misunderstanding. His
best plays were written by the time of *Saint Joan.* One
might expect his use of the Nietszchean Superman and the
Life Force to date his work, but *Man and Superman,* where
they appear most prominently, has survived better than
most. The theme of emancipation which is a radical issue
in *Superman* is treated in individual terms in *Pygmalion.*
The first wave of modern drama is over with the apocalyptic vision of *Heartbreak House.*

1927 Parker, William. "Broadbent and Doyle, Two
Shavian Archetypes," ASPECTS OF THE IRISH THEATRE
(Paris: Editions Universitaires [Cahiers Irland-
ais], 1972), pp. 39-49.
The Englishman's love for Blockheads created the success
with English audiences of Tom Broadbent in *John Bull's
Other Island.* Larry Doyle exposes the wrong-headedness of
Broadbent's ideas but does not take much positive action;
Broadbent acts and succeeds. They are complementary
characters.

1928 Pearson, Michael. THE AGE OF CONSENT,
VICTORIAN PROSTITUTION AND ITS ENEMIES (Newton
Abbot: David & Charles, 1972), pp. 122, 156, 212,
216 [The 5£ VIRGINS (NY: Saturday Review Press,
1973)?].

[Brief references to Shaw's comments on William Thomas Stead.]

1929 Peart, Barbara. "Shelley and Shaw's Prose," Shaw R, X V (Jan 1972), 39-45.
Shaw used ideas and textual material from Shelley's writing on religion for "On Miracles, a Retort," the Prefaces to *Androcles and the Lion* and *Back to Methuselah*, "A Catechism on My Creed," and "On Ritual, Religion, and the Intolerableness of Tolerance." [Illustrated with parallel passages from Shaw and Shelley.]

1930 Pedersen, Lisë B. "Shavian Shakespeare: Shaw's Use and Transformation of Shakespearian Materials in His Drama," D AI, X X XII (1972), 6998A. Unpublished dissertation, Louisiana State University, 1971.

1931 Perry, George. "The Man Who Staged the War," SUNDAY TIMES MAGAZINE (Lond), 16 April 1972, p. 48; rptd in Shaw R, X V (Sept 1972), 104-9.
[Brief history of how Robert Cedric Sherriff came to write JOURNEY'S END. Reproduces Shaw's letter to Sheriff suggesting it be performed.]

1932 Pitman, Sir James, K. B. E. "'Av We Eny 'Oap Fu' Bettr Speling? Yes--Within Limits," CONTEMPORARY REVIEW, CCXXI (Aug 1972), 88-94.
[Essay arguing for variant spelling.] Shaw wanted a new alphabet, not spelling reform.

1933 "Public Shaw and Private Shaw," TLS, 4 Aug 1972, pp. 917-18.
[Review of Bernard Shaw, COLLECTED LETTERS 1898-1910 (1972); THE BODLEY HEAD BERNARD SHAW, Vol IV (1972); Margery M. Morgan, THE SHAVIAN PLAYGROUND (1972); Louis Crompton, SHAW THE DRAMATIST (1969); Leon Hugo, BERNARD SHAW: PLAYWRIGHT AND PREACHER (1971).] It seems obvious that there was a causal relationship between Shaw's marriage in 1898 and the burst of creative activity that followed. Charlotte was a barricade between Shaw and sex. All of Shaw's activities get into the letters, but the letters are rarely intimate. Shaw's truthtelling and reasonableness must have been trying. Shaw's plays cannot be reduced to a relationship with the life or to their

ideas either, because the interaction of the ideas is not logical. [Photographs.]

1934 Quinton, A. M. "Social Thought in Britain," THE TWENTIETH CENTURY MIND: HISTORY, IDEAS, AND LITERATURE, I: 1900-1918, ed by C. B. Cox and A. E. Dyson (Lond, Oxford and NY: Oxford UP, 1972), pp. 114-15, 122ff.
In *Socialism and Superior Brains* Shaw exposed the weakness of W. H. Mallock's defense of capitalist distribution of wealth. Shaw's theoretical contribution to Fabianism is his combination of Henry George's moral attitude to unearned increment on land with the economist's concept of rent cover. The Fabian attitude toward the Boer War is applied to Ireland in *John Bull's Other Island*. Shaw deviated from the Fabians finally. The contempt for democracy in *The Applecart* went far beyond their lack of enthusiasm for popular government. In *Man and Superman* and *The Revolutionist's Handbook* Shaw transcended Fabianism: human beings and not institutions need to be reformed.

1935 Raud, V. "Pilguheit G. B. Shaw'elule ja loomingule" (A Glance at G. B. Shaw's Life and Work), G. B. SHAW: NAIDENDID (G. B. Shaw: Plays) (Tallinn, 1972), 536-43.
[Not seen.] [In Estonian.]

1936 Richardson, Betty Hoyenga. "Anatomizing GBS: A Survey of Recent Shaw Scholarship," PAPERS ON LANGUAGE AND LITERATURE, VIII (1972), 211-23.
Shaw recorded the social, religious, political and dramatic events and ideas of the nineteenth and twentieth centuries, so it is hardly surprising that there are few comprehensive interpretations of Shavian drama. The torrent of works gives evidence for the possibility of a Shaw revival. [Survey of Shaw criticism.]

1937 Roberts, Warren. "Modern Literary Materials at the University of Texas: Their Scope and Usefulness," JOURNAL OF MODERN LITERATURE, II (Third Issue 1971-72), 329-41.
[Brief description of Shaw materials at the University of Texas in the context of the Library's development.]

1938 Robinson, Gabrielle Scott. "Beyond the Waste Land: An Interpretation of John Whiting's SAINT's DAY," MD, XIV (Feb 1972), 463-77.
Whiting may have copied *Heartbreak House* for his SAINT'S DAY.

1939 Roby, Kinley E. "The Four Mile Radius," Shaw R, XV (Sept 1972), 119-26.
[Essay--review of BERNARD SHAW'S NONDRAMATIC LITERARY CRITICISM, ed by Stanley Weintraub (1972).] Shaw's belief that "the past does not predict the future and that human experience has a purpose" conditioned his attitudes toward all art. Shaw was amazingly consistent in his attitudes toward the function of literature, but also very limited. His nondramatic criticism is not a significant part of his total writing, but it is important and still has its adherents.

1940 Roby, Kinley E. A WRITER AT WAR: ARNOLD BENNETT, 1914-1918 (Baton Rouge: Louisiana State UP, 1972), pp. 7, 22, 24, 51n, 52-54, 106n, 180, 181, 185, 186, 214, 215, 218.
[Bennett's clash with Shaw over *Common Sense about the War*.]

1941 Rodenbeck, John von B. "Bernard Shaw's Revolt against Rationalism," VICTORIAN STUDIES, XV (June 1972), 409-37.
Confusion over Shaw's idea of reason results largely from the ambiguity of the term in the Victorian period. Shaw was influenced by Victorian rationalism but finally rejected it. *Immaturity* and *The Irrational Knot* were written before his revolt. Shaw's anti-rationalism is evident in his ideas of history and society and in his art, and it emerges especially through the influence of Carlyle, Wagner, and Shelley; *Cashel Byron's Profession*, however, shows Shaw's independence from them. *Love among the Artists* and *The Doctor's Dilemma* are early signs of Shaw's conversion to anti-rationalism particularly in his use of the "naive hero," a development he finds inevitable according to the preface to *The Perfect Wagnerite*. [*Saint Joan, Man and Superman, Caesar and Cleopatra,* as well as *An Unsocial Socialist* and *You Can Never Tell* are also cited for their naive heroes.] Seeing nature as "dynamic," Shaw rejected the static, doctrinal aspect of Victorian rationalism in the preface to *Farfetched Fables*. His own view was that, in the course of man's development,

any progress was likely the result of irrational passions, as he indicates in the preface to *Back to Methuselah* and *Sixteen Self-Sketches*, and he emphasizes the unconscious in *The Revolutionist's Handbook*. Marx was also essential to his revolt and to the formation of Fabian Socialism as Shaw reveals in his letters, *Autobiography*, and *Essays in Fabian Socialism*. Shaw rejected neo-Hegelianism (a rationalist idealism) in *The Quintessence of Ibsenism*. [*Heartbreak House* is also cited to support this point.]

1942 Rodgers, W. R. IRISH LITERARY PORTRAITS: W. B. YEATS, JAMES JOYCE, GEORGE MOORE, GEORGE BERNARD SHAW, OLIVER ST. JOHN GOGARTY, F. R. HIGGINS, AE (Lond: British Broadcasting Corporation, 1972; NY: Taplinger, 1975), pp. 116-41.
[Broadcast conversations about Shaw with Sean O'Casey, St. John Ervine, Denis Johnston, Lord Glenavy, Frank O'Connor, Lady Hanson, Sean Macreamoinn, William Meegan, Mrs. Tyrell, Mr. Fry, Mr. Kerwan, Father Leonard, Dr. Bodkin, Shelagh Richards, Austin Clarke, Lady Thomson, Pearse Beasley and Oliver Gogarty. Anecdotes and speculation about Shaw's childhood, youth, and various character. First broadcast in Sept 1954.]

1943 Romm, A. S. SHOU--TEORETIC: UCHEBNYE SPOSOBIE (Shaw the Theoretician: Scholarly Methods) (Leningrad: State Pedagogical Institute, 1972).
Shaw's art was born in the heart of "intellectualism" and was one of the most daring attempts to solve the problems of "intellectualism", either as comedy or tragicomedy. It is from these efforts that his intellectual interest in the drama emerged. His main aim to was to establish conditions of life compatible with the best aspects of man's nature and thus liberate man's creative possibilities. His politics and sociology were means to this, and his ethics are a direct continuation of both. It was the duty of art to arouse human thought from lethargy. Although the English drama at the end of the nineteenth century was anti-intellectual, and melodrama reigned, the theater stimulated Shaw, and Ibsen's influence helped him find himself as a dramatist. [In Russian.]

1944 Rouby, Jason.   "The Adventures of My Fair Philologist," BAKER STREET`JOURNAL, XXII (Sept 1972), 135-39.

[Has not a whit to do with Shaw but quite a lot to do with Holmes and Henry Higgins.]

1945 Roy, Emil. BRITISH DRAMA SINCE SHAW (Carbondale and Edwardsville: Southern Illinois UP; [Crosscurrents/Modern Critiques] Lond and Amsterdam: Feffer & Simons, 1972), pp. 1-20, 21-24, 38, 39, 44, 45, 56, 70, 86, 95, 98, 100, 125, 129.

Shaw's dominance of modern high comedy is undisputed. O'Casey stands above Shaw's other imitators, and he is in harmony with Shaw's thought. Shaw's concepts were derived chiefly from his cheerful temperament. What counts in the plays is the passion with which the characters identify their integrity with ideas; his dramatic practice is traditional. He avoids ambiguity and also frequently considers values with no references to non-dramatic reality. For the first two decades Shaw exploits the same enlightened drawing-room as Oscar Wilde. [Analysis of *Major Barbara* to set out variations on traditional comic motifs.] The more lasting, possibly crippling, ties bind son to mother, daughter to father. Resistance heightens the determination of the young ladies, and the young man's vitality is measured by his capacity to resist and to attack father figures. The anti-comic society is symbolized by father figures, usually at the moment when the children are about to break into adulthood. The fathers do not acquiesce in any incestuous attachment; they assist the younger rival. The young hero is defeated by assimilation. The father-figures divert oedipal feelings away from younger women at the cost of a heightened drive toward death. Their proliferation casts doubt on any legitimate center of authority. The overpossessive matriarchs drive their exhausted husbands away and create artist-philosophers of their sons. Shaw's admiration for women's passion, tenacity and vitality is qualified by his distrust of their impersonality, their contempt for abstractions, and their faithlessness. *Heartbreak House* is a turning point as well as a culmination in Shaw's career, which "is increasingly marked by his tendency to locate his 'basis in reality' in 'the attitudes of the ironist.'" It dramatizes the impact of a milieu upon a group. *Saint Joan* pits an obsessed heroine against institutions. Joan transforms the Dauphin into a King. When she chooses an absurd death, she regains her free will. Only Wilde among Shaw's contemporaries rivalled his genius, though he never approached Shaw's aspirations.

1946 Schoeps, Karl-Heinz J. "Bertolt Brecht und Bernard Shaw: Eine Untersuchung von Einflüssen und Parallelen" (Bertolt Brecht and Bernard Shaw: An Investigation of Influences and Parallels), D AI, X X X II (1972), 6452A-6453A. Dissertation, University of Wisconsin, 1972, published as BERTOLT BRECHT UND BERNARD SHAW, 1974.

1947 Schults, Raymond L. CRUSADER IN BABYLON, W. T. STEAD AND THE PALL MALL GAZETTE (Lincoln: U of Nebraska P, 1972), pp. 2, 38, 59n, 188, 237n, 240.
[Brief references to Shaw in relation to W. T. Stead.]

1948 Searle, William. "Shaw's Saint Joan as 'Protestant,'" Shaw R, X V (Sept 1972), 110-16.
In *The Perfect Wagnerite* Shaw identifies Protestantism with any protest against authority that tries to impose its will on man. In a letter he implies that irrationalism is "an inseparable feature of the Protestant mentality." The Church in *Saint Joan* then can be identified with the modern materialist world in their dependence upon rationalism and rejection of personal inspiration. But Shaw was skeptical that even the most inspired of leaders could induce men to make necessary reforms. Further, Joan is "quite as much of an absolutist as her judges," and Shaw "was unable to provide an objective criterion for determining the proper limits of toleration."

1949 Sen, Taraknath. "Shaw" and "'The Man of the Century': BERNARD SHAW: HIS LIFE, WORK AND FRIENDS" A LITERARY MISCELLANY (Calcutta: Rupa, 1972), pp. 43-47, 48-100.
[Not seen.]

1950 Shamshurin, A. "Bernard Shou v SSSR" (Bernard Shaw in the USSR), LITERATURNAIA ROSSIIA (Moscow), X X II (1972), 24.
[Not seen.] [In Russian.]

1951 Shinkuma, Kiyoshi. "Shavian Irony nitsuite" (On Shavian Irony), NAGOYAGAKUINDAIGAKU RONSHU (Seto), IX (June 1972), 29-56.
Shavian irony is directed not against individual but against social evil. Shaw's intention is to make people

uncomfortable rather than amused. The ending of *Major Barbara*, apparently an easy-going solution, is a typical example. [In Japanese.]

1952 Skelton, Robin. "Jack Coughlin: Irish Portraits," MALAHAT REVIEW, XXII (April 1972), 63-72.

"We can see in the Shaw portrait [here reproduced] an evocation of the playwright's delicacy and sharpness of wit."

1953 Smiley, Sam. THE DRAMA OF ATTACK, DIDACTIC PLAYS OF THE AMERICAN DEPRESSION (Columbia: U of Missouri P, 1972), pp. 5, 8, 87, 145-46, 203-4.

Shaw is one of the best didactic playwrights because he entertained.

1954 Sokolov, Raymond A. "The Pygmalion Approach to Nuts and Vegetables," NYT Mag, 16 July 1972, p. 28.

[Several Shaw vegetable recipes as remembered by his cook, Alice Laden.]

1955 Stansky, Peter, and William Abrahams. THE UNKNOWN ORWELL (NY: Alfred A. Knopf, 1972), pp. 58, 99, 105, 106, 120, 121, 136.

Shaw was one of Orwell's favorite authors.

1956 Stein, Walter. "Drama," THE TWENTIETH CENTURY MIND: HISTORY, IDEAS, AND LITERATURE, II: 1918-1945, ed by C. B. Cox and A. E. Dyson (Lond, Oxford and NY: Oxford UP, 1972), pp. 417-25.

It is open to question whether Shaw continues to be important to us. Two aspects of his work, his beliefs and his theatrical paradox and verbal clowning, are crucial. *Heartbreak House* is unmatched by anything else in Shaw's canon, but it is defectively brittle. It is superficial when compared with Chekov and trivial and confused when compared with Jonson, Aristophanes, or Molière. The 'heartbreak' is not measured in the play, and it is "transcended without taking its measure" in *Back to Methuselah*. What is taught in these plays is a "sell-out of human values." But in the plays like *Man and Superman* and *Pygmalion* Shaw demonstrated a comic creativeness. The drama where he charted the metaphysical depths is inadequate.

1957 Stinton, Colin. "The Shaw Festival," PLAYERS,
XLVII (Aug-Sept 1972), 292-99.
[Brief history of the Shaw Festival at Niagara-on-the-
Lake, Ontario.]

1958 Stokes, John. RESISTIBLE THEATRES: ENTERPRISE
AND EXPERIMENT IN THE LATE NINETEENTH CENTURY (Lond:
Paul Elek Books; NY: Barnes & Noble, 1972), pp. 7,
11, 12, 15-18, 22, 25, 75, 115, 128, 139, 144-48,
151, 178, 180.
Not surprisingly *The Quintessence of Ibsenism* is more
reminiscent of Shaw's work than Ibsen's. What is
important is the conflict between Ibsen's principles and
Clement Scott's. Shaw's interest in Ibsen is based on his
ability to show ideas in action. Shaw's plays are
essentially argument, where discussion and action are
involved in each other. Pinero and Jones, though they
followed Ibsen's lead in treating controversial subjects,
are the opposite of Shaw. They preserve the morality as
well as the form of the conventional play.

Shaw was dissatisfied with George Moore's THE STRIKE AT
ARLINGFORD, claiming the 'strikology' was inaccurate.
Comparisons between Moore's play and *Widowers' Houses* were
inevitable, with Moore's play defended as being more
human, Shaw's, more accurate sociologically. It cannot be
denied that Shaw's theatricality is effective, but it
discloses only truths that have always existed, which is
what Shaw means by realism.

1959 Sullivan, Kevin. OSCAR WILDE (NY and Lond:
Columbia UP [Columbia Essays on Modern Writers],
1972), pp. 4, 22, 33-34.
[Shaw comments on Wilde.]

1960 Sutherland, Don. "Shaw and Wittgenstein. An
Imaginary Conversation," SHAVIAN, IV (Winter 1972-
73), 215-17.
[Comic dialogue between Shaw and Wittgenstein in which
Shaw talks Wittgenstein into silence.]

1961 Sykes, Christopher. NANCY, THE LIFE OF LADY
ASTOR (NY, Evanston, San Francisco, Lond: Harper
and Row, 1972), pp. 283, 294-301, 306-9, 321, 324-
48, 350, 353, 357, 384, 400-3, 411-12, 423-24, 443-

44, 448, 454-57, 464, 466-67, 469-71, 473-79, 489-92, 497-502.
The very deep friendship between Nancy Astor and Shaw was an improbable one, though Shaw always liked pretty women; they were both famous, and both were actors. Nancy used Shaw for political reasons, but he supported her causes. Through Shaw Nancy's friendship with T. E. Lawrence intensified. [An account of the Astors's journey to Russia with Shaw.] Shaw showed the depth of his feeling and sincerity of his friendship in the crisis over Nancy's son, Bobbie. He persuaded Nancy to sit to the sculptor, Kisfalud de Strobl. He defended Nancy and the Cliveden set against charges of pro-Nazism. She made every effort to insure Shaw's comfort in his old age during the war. [Illustrated with photos of Shaw. Extensive quotation from Shaw-Nancy Astor correspondence.]

1962 Taranow, Gerda. SARAH BERNHARDT, THE ART WITHIN THE LEGEND (Princeton, NJ: Princeton UP, 1972), pp. 45, 56, 57, 65, 103, 104, 242, 244-47.
[Shaw on acting.]

1963 THEATER IN DER ZEITENWENDE: ZUR GESCHICHTE DES DRAMAS UND DES SCHAUSPIELTHEATERS IN DER DEUTSCHEN DEMOKRATISCHEN REPUBLIK 1945-1968 (Theater in an Age of Transition: On the History of the Drama and the Stage in the German Democratic Republic 1945-1968), ed by Werner Mittenzwei (Berlin: Henschelverlag Kunst und Gesellschaft, 1972), 2 vols, vol I, pp. 154, 211, 278; vol II, pp. 242, 243.
Shaw's *Pygmalion* is one of the most popular plays with the audience of the German Democratic Republic. Peter Hacks, the German playwright, seems to be a disciple of Shaw. [In German.]

1964 Thomas, Frank. LAST WILL AND TESTAMENT, WILLS ANCIENT AND MODERN (NY: St. Martin's Press, 1972), pp. 11, 92, 138-40.
[Description of Shaw's Will and how the bequests were carried out.]

1965 Tunney, Kieran. TALLULAH--DARLING OF THE GODS (Lond: Secker & Warburg, 1972), pp. 11, 15, 54, 68, 94-95, 128-9, 131-35, 138, 208.
[Shaw and the author as well as Tallulah Bankhead.]

1966 Waldau, Roy S.   VINTAGE YEARS OF THE THEATRE
GUILD, 1928-1939 (Cleveland and Lond: Press of Case
Western Reserve U, 1972), pp. 4, 8, 9, 13, 15, 17,
19, 21, 22, 24, 26, 27, 29, 30, 36, 39, 40, 41, 42,
54, 55, 56, 71-76, 89, 106, 110, 111, 112, 113, 135,
136, 138, 141, 151, 153, 190, 197, 198, 200, 202,
209, 210, 228, 231-32, 235, 237, 241, 245, 248, 249,
254, 274, 275, 298-99, 303, 304, 310, 324-25, 338,
341, 343, 345, 372, 378, 379, 387.
[Shaw and the Theatre Guild.   Photographs.]

1967 Walker, John.   "Bernard Shaw and Don Roberts,"
Shaw R, XV (Sept 1972), 94-103.
There are many parallels in the lives of Shaw and Robert
Bontine Cunninghame Graham (Don Roberts).   Though Shaw
admired Graham, the admiration was not returned.

1968 Wasserman, Marlie P.   "Vivie Warren: A
Psychological Study," Shaw R, XV (May, 1972), 71-75.
Few critics have even acknowledged Shaw's use of
psychology, and there is no psychological study of Vivie
Warren.   Although Shaw was ignorant of Freud and
psychoanalysis when he wrote *Mrs. Warren's Profession*, he
instinctively understood the effects of institutional life
upon Vivie.   She failed to learn to love and has developed
egoism in its place.

1969 Watson, Barbara Bellow.   "Introduction to the
Norton Library Edition," A SHAVIAN GUIDE TO THE
INTELLIGENT WOMAN (NY: W. W. Norton, 1972) [orig
pub without intro NY: W. W. Norton and Lond:
Chatto & Windus, 1964], pp. 3-6.
Eight years ago, Shaw's views on women were much needed
but unlikely to be understood if taken piecemeal and out
of context.   Now, Shaw's opinions are even more needed and
can be seen to be even more important.   The hazards of
reading Shaw, moreover, have increased.   For Shaw, women's
rights were merely human rights, irrespective of gender,
and terms like "feminism" and "women's liberation" are
abstractions that get in the way of understanding Shaw.
Shaw's clarity about basic issues, that there is really no
such thing as adultery for example, are more valuable now
than ever.   Shaw did, however, seem to believe in the
slight superiority of women, a condition apparently
demanded by higher civilizations.   After all is said,
however, perhaps Shaw's greatest value lies not in his
ideas but in the spirit that pervades his work, that

spirit that enables Ellie Dunn in *Heartbreak House* to glimpse a vision of "life with a blessing."

1970 Watson, Barbara Bellow. "Introduction," *An Unsocial Socialist*, by Bernard Shaw (NY: W. W. Norton [The Norton Library], 1972, pp. xi-xiv.
Shaw would not write long about anything without introducing his view of women. He perceived that women are human beings. But a man is the hero of *An Unsocial Socialist*, and he is a cad in deed, though a philosopher in his reasons. The brutality of Trefusis is to liberate women, which is no comfort to his wife, though it may begin her freedom. But Agatha Wylie is a true match for the Shavian hero, and the whole liberation movement could be reconstructed from her.

1971 Webster, Margaret. DON'T PUT YOUR DAUGHTER ON THE STAGE (NY: Alfred A. Knopf, 1972), pp. 11-12, 66, 86, 196-97, 258, 276-78, 282, 286, 289, 305-6, 327-28, 349, 371, 376.
[Recounts briefly the circumstances of Margaret Webster's directing Shaw plays.]

1972 Weintraub, Rodelle. "Shaw's Jesus and Judas," Shaw R, XV (May 1972), 81-83.
[Review of PASSION PLAY. A DRAMATIC FRAGMENT, 1878, by Bernard Shaw, edited by Jerald E. Bringle (1971).] Shaw's Jesus joins the Jesuses of other modern plays. Jesus suffers from a generation gap, and Judas has little difficulty tempting him away from home. The discussion between Judas and Jesus parallels that between Shaw and Father Addis in 1878. Shaw is Jesus but also Judas; the play parallels Shaw's own experience.

1973 Weintraub, Stanley. "*Heartbreak House*: Shaw's LEAR," MD, XV (Dec 1972), 255-65.
Like his Cleopatra play, Shaw offered his KING LEAR not in competition with Shakespeare but as commentary. Shaw regarded *Heartbreak House* as his greatest play. He first pointed publicly to the relationship between his play and LEAR in 1949 in the puppet play *Shakes vs. Shav*. Privately he had already in 1917 hinted as much to Lillah McCarthy. He was very reluctant to release the play or even permit anyone to read it. Shaw regarded LEAR as Shakespeare's masterpiece, yet he objected to Gloucester's despair. Shaw admired in LEAR the actual interweaving of

tragic and comic. Heartbreak contains textual echoes of
LEAR. Ellie, Hesione and Ariadne are modern embodiments
of Lear's daughters. Lear resigns his power to his
daughters, but Shotover is very much in control, and
unlike Lear, understands his daughters. Happiness, which
Lear craves, is detested by Shotover. Shaw is less
despairing than Shakespeare, and "Shotover is a
Bunyanesque hero."

1974 Weintraub, Stanley. "Introduction. Bernard
Shaw: The Social Critic as Literary Critic,"
BERNARD SHAW'S NONDRAMATIC LITERARY CRITICISM
(Lincoln: U of Nebraska P [Regents Critics Series],
1972), pp. ix-xxvii.
Shaw was modest about his nondramatic criticism, which
furnishes Shavian insights into other writers as well as
it reflects his own creative methods and motives. Most of
it was done anonymously, but especially after the early
period where the motivation was cash, it is remarkably
consistent. [There follows a description of Shaw's
criticism, citing particular characteristics, essays, and
authors.]

1975 White, Terence de Vere. THE ANGLO-IRISH (Lond:
Victor Gollancz, 1972), pp. 31-37, 50, 181, 189,
197.
[Shaw as a source for the definition of Irishness.]

1976 Williams, Raymond. "Social Darwinism," List,
LXXXVIII (23 Nov 1972), 696-700.
Shaw held a naive notion of Creative Evolution. In *Back
to Methuselah* Shaw apparently believed that man's proper
goal was to become "pure intelligence."

1977 Wilson, Colin. "Shaviana," BOOKS AND BOOKMEN,
XVII (April 1972), 32-33.
[Review of SHAW THE DRAMATIST, by Louis Crompton, THE
SHAVIAN PLAYGROUND by Margery M. Morgan (1972).] Shaw is
at last getting the recognition he never had during his
lifetime. Shaw alive was controversial and then a bore.
The swing in Shaw's favor has been slow. This new
recognition is not altogether a good thing, if the
American academic world gets hold of him.

1978 Wilson, Colin. "Shaw in His Letters," BOOKS AND BOOKMEN, XVII (Sept 1972), 26-27.
[Review of BERNARD SHAW: COLLECTED LETTERS 1898-1910, ed by Dan H. Laurence (1972); and BERNARD SHAW, HIS LIFE, WORK, AND FRIENDS, by St. John Ervine (1956).] H. G. Wells's attacks imply that Shaw was a sham, not to be taken seriously. Shaw's letters show him to be good-natured and cheerful. The real test of any critic of Shaw is his opinion of the last act of *Back to Methuselah*.

1979 Wilson, Donal Stuart. "Shaw on the Production of Shakespeare," DAI, XXXIII (1972), 1880A. Unpublished dissertation, University of California, Los Angeles, 1972.

1980 Wisenthal, J. L. "The Underside of Undershaft: A Wagnerian Motif in *Major Barbara*," ShawR, XV (May 1972), 56-64.
Passages written by Shaw for *The Perfect Wagnerite* in 1907, the year *Major Barbara* was published, connecting Alberic with modern manufacturing giants and also suggesting the solution to the dilemma of capitalism by having Siegfried learn Alberic's trade links Wagner with the Shaw play. But the parallels are deeper: Undershaft is more like Wotan than Alberic, benevolent, but limited in accomplishment. Undershaft in persuading Cusins and Barbara to join his foundry is like Wotan's calling a new race into being, and both hasten their ruin, though Shaw leaves "the final outcome uncertain."

1981 Woodeson, John. MARK GERTLER, BIOGRAPHY OF A PAINTER, 1891-1939 (Lond: Sidgwick & Jackson, 1972), pp. 113-14, 170.
Gertler hated *The Doctor's Dilemma*, especially the portrayal of the "artist part."

1982 Zdrenghea, Mihai. "Means of Expressing the Idea of Superlative in English," STUDIA UNIVERSITATIS BABES-BOLYAI. SERIES PHILOLOGIA, XVII (1972), 123-30.
[Use of *Arms and the Man* for examples of the superlative in English.]

1973

1983 Albert, Sidney P. "Counselor to the World,"
ShawR, XVI (Jan 1973), 33-37.
[Essay-review of BERNARD SHAW: COLLECTED LETTERS 1898-
1910, ed by Dan H. Laurence (1972).] "Since Shaw's
private life was inextricably bound up with his public
life, and since his interests, involvements, and professional activities projected him prominently into the historical currents and movements of the day, . . . his
letters embrace a cosmos of topics."

1984 Alterescu, Simion (ed). ISTORIA TEATRULULUIÎN
ROMANIA 1919-1944 (History of the Theater in Romania
1919-1944), (Bucharest: Academia de Ştinţe, 1973),
III, 564.
[Shaw plays in translation (Romanian and French) and
adaptation on the Romanian stage.] [In Romanian.]

1985 Andrews, Katherine. "The Necessity to Conform:
British Jingoism in the First World War," DALHOUSIE
REVIEW, LIII (Summer 1973), 227-45.
[Shaw's Preface to *Heartbreak House* and *What I Really
Wrote about the War* used as evidence in describing the
unreasonable attitude of British writers toward Germany
during World War I.]

1986 Ayrton, Michael. "A Performance of *Saint
Joan*," FABRICATIONS (Lond: Secker and Warburg,
1972), pp. 43-51.
[A long (fictional?) anecdote about an unknown actor
playing Gilles de Rais in a repertory performance of *Saint
Joan*, who interpolated a speech in the Epilogue attacking
Shaw and defending de Rais.]

1987 Bailey, J. O. "Shaw's Life Force and Science
Fiction," ShawR, XVI (May 1973), 48-58.
Shaw's plays are not science fiction but are religious
dramas of the Life Force. Yet they used the devices of
science fiction. [Brief sketch of the bases of Shaw's
Life Force.] Wells's TIME MACHINE, which is Darwinism,
contrasts with Shaw's views. Splitting mankind into

opposing species, the possibility of eternal life on earth, a traveller from the present, creation without sex, automata, a beautiful environment, the mechanisms of walkie-talkie and two-way television, new species are all imaginative contrivances of science fiction used by Shaw. [Many works that Shaw might have read are cited.] Now writers of science fiction derive ideas from Shaw, though not always with Shaw's seriousness of purpose.

1988 Bain, Carl E. "A Preface to Drama," in DRAMA (NY: W. W. Norton, 1973), pp. xiii-xxx, esp xxiv-xxvii.
Shaw's characteristic method is satirric. He uses a parodistic method in structuring his plays. His tendency to down-grade sexual relationships often makes his characters bland. At his best he presents a witty and elegant expression of his unique vision.

1989 Balthasar, Hans U. von. "[Maschere Nude:] George Bernard Shaw" ([Naked Masks:] George Bernard Shaw), THEODRAMATIK, I: PROLEGOMENA (Einsiedeln: Johannes, 1973), pp. 216-26.
[Not seen.]

1990 Barker, Dudley. G. K. CHESTERTON, A BIOGRAPHY (NY: Stein and Day, 1973), pp. 15, 42, 57, 117, 126, 131-32, 151, 163, 171, 175-76, 181-87, 197-98, 210, 214, 221-24, 227, 235, 250, 262, 264, 272, 276-78, 286-87.
[Account of the year after year Shaw-Chesterton debate in print, on the platform, and on radio.]

1991 Barnes, Clive. "Stage: *Don Juan in Hell* at 70," NYT, 16 Jan 1973, p. 33.
I do not regard Shaw as one of the great dramatists of the century. When Shaw scores, he often plagiarizes.

1992 Barr, Alan P. VICTORIAN STAGE PULPITEER, BERNARD SHAW'S CRUSADE (Athens: U of Georgia P, 1973).
[The beginning surveys nineteenth-century Christian attitudes.] Shaw's father's humorous hypocrisy, his mother's antagonism, and his uncle's Rabelaisian irreverence were the major personal influences on his religious formation. The protestant Church in which he was baptized

was repugnant to him. He embraced the spirit of rationalism. Music, literature, and painting offered a way when
he had exhausted rationalism. Shaw, Yeats and Joyce all
dealt with religious problems, readjusting the views they
inherited. From the beginning Shaw attempted to affirm
the mystical in man, and he was a moralist. He sought an
answer to the questions of the purpose of life, and his
focus was on life on earth, reconciling religion with
science and history. A set of uniform beliefs was necessary to counteract anarchy, and it must be "flexible,
credible, and fed on continual controversy." Shaw dismissed all existing religions, including the atheist's
faith. In *The Black Girl in Her Search for God* he
attempted to free the Bible from all its sacred superstition. He rejected the salvationist attitudes of religion;
and he indicted Pauline Christianity in *Androcles and the
Lion* and *Major Barbara*. *Crude Criminology* express Shaw's
contempt for the entire penal system. The individual,
rationalist position is exemplified by St. Joan. Shaw
wished men to leave sin, guilt, and cruelty behind, to
revitalize Christianity. Shaw's religion, Creative Evolution, is more a philosophical disposition than a particular religious formulation. It is largely a reaction
against Darwinism. The Life Force is God, and very much
like Blake's "Somebodaddy." The religious man, like Don
Juan in *Man and Superman*, aligns himself with the world's
purpose. *Back to Methuselah* is Shaw's attempt to create
legends for his religion, assimilating the symbols,
language and figures from other religions. Shaw recognized that he was a serious moral artist, and to achieve
success as such he needed to call attention to himself,
which he did by creating a public persona: G. B. S. Shaw
mastered the literary tradition; his "creative reading" of
other writers was in the service of making a point. Shaw
saw himself in Bunyan, but his attempts to Shavianize
PILGRIM'S PROGRESS failed. His criticism of Shakespeare
is dramatically sound, but he was also campaigning for
Ibsen against Shakespeare. He saw Ibsen only as a reformer, not as a poet. He identified with the youthful
Wagner. It is unclear whether or not Shaw was influenced
by Nietzsche. Shaw was always didactic, most clearly in
the prefaces to his plays. The plays brilliantly
translate his vision onto the stage. [Bibliography. Well
documented.]

1993 Bermel, Albert. CONTRADICTORY CHARACTERS: AN
INTERPRETATION OF THE MODERN THEATRE (NY: E. P.
Dutton, 1973), pp. 44n, 185-206, 281, 288.

In *Saint Joan* emphasis must be placed on the person, not the saint. Joan must be conceived as a "heroic nuisance," prodding her fellow men beyond their limit and as a shrewd tactician capable of threatening the church and political structure. Joan derives her force from characters' attributing power to her, and she wins support by flattery and appeals to self-interest. Rashness and vanity cause her decline, but in choosing to die she transcends her fraility and becomes a redeemer. The Epilogue is necessary for the play's unity and to relate the past to current affairs; an intrusion in *Man and Superman* functions similarly. Granting Joan's rightness in retrospect, the world refuses, nevertheless, to tolerate a Superman like Joan. [*The Quintessence of Ibsenism* is cited to explain Ibsen's choice for a "masculine genius." Reference to *Heartbreak House* supports the view that the entire play, rather than any single character, is the playwright's spokesman.]

1994 Berst, Charles A. BERNARD SHAW AND THE ART OF DRAMA (Urbana, Chicago and Lond: U of Illinois P, 1973). "*Arms and the Man*: The Seriousness of Comedy," rptd from MODERN LANGUAGE QUARTERLY (June 1966); "*Mrs. Warren's Profession*: Art over Didacticism," rptd from A JOURNAL OF ENGLISH LITERARY HISTORY (Sept 1966); "*Major Barbara*: Giving the Devil His Due," rptd from PUBLICATIONS OF THE MODERN LANGUAGE ASSOCIATION (March 1968); "*Caesar and Cleopatra*: An Anatomy of Greatness," rptd from JOURNAL OF ENGLISH AND GERMANIC PHILOLOGY (Jan 1969), all abstracted under date of first publication.
This book deals with Shaw's plays individually and as artistic achievements.

Shaw's attitudes toward Candida changed from near adulation to implying that she was a female counterpart of Ibsen's Torvald Helmer. His ambivalence reflects an ambivalence in the play. One view of the play sees the resolution of the conflicts by Candida's wisdom. A second view sees Marchbanks exposing the shallow philistinism of Candida and Morell. A third neglected view sees Morell showing up the lack of social integrity and personal humaneness in Candida and Marchbanks. The vitality of Shaw's dramaturgy lies in the interaction of all these perspectives. But Morell is most important; his values are most carefully examined, and he survives with his strengths all the more apparent.

Shaw's Life Force concept is probably most frequently
referred to and also most generally misunderstood. When
Shaw's own dialectic and dramatic qualifications are taken
into account, he is seen "as a poetic theorizer dealing
metaphorically with a highly personal and tentative
hypothesis." The Life Force philosophy applies only
obliquely to *Man and Superman*, and the weight of the
metaphysics seems excessive without the hell scene. Each
element of the play is both qualified and vitalized by the
others. Act III is both extraneous and central to the
play. Two levels of consciousness serve as a sumliminal
complement to the dialectical voices. The one provides a
comic link connecting the scene with the trumpery story,
while the other provides an oversoul, exploiting the
ironies between drama and life and searching for a
direction between the ironies. Only this last is less
than successful. The philosophy seems more dramatic than
sound. In *Androcles and the Lion* Shaw is trying something
new. Fable, parody, and parable interact. The play
points up the discrepancy between conformist religion and
spiritual individualism.

In *Pygmalion* Shaw combined pure fancy with mythical
associations and a keen social and spiritual sensibility,
which most critics overlook because they stress one
element at the expense of the others. Everything in the
play aims at an archetypal pattern of the soul's awakening
to true expression. The phonetic lesson is secondary to
Shaw's pointing out the hollowness of social distinctions.
Shaw in *Heartbreak House* places the dreamy society within
an all-encompassing dream. The play is about the despair
of a sensitive consciousness facing the horror of social
and historical realities. It is as much Strindbergian as
Chekhovian. The dream quality is counterpointed by the
active Shavian intellect. *Saint Joan* tests and
strengthens the saint's legend by subjecting it to
irreverent skepticism and rationalism. Shaw's Preface
clarifies the elements of his approach: the uniqueness of
Joan, his artistic-historical viewpoint, and the allegory.
Joan thinks of people as individuals, but this is her
weakness as well as her strength because she fails to see
the abstractions behind the individuals. Joan and Caesar
are alike, but since she has not compromised herself, her
tragedy is less personal. "Shaw's vision compounds
itself, finally, into a six-fold view--historical,
allegorical, mundane, spiritual, tragic, and comic."
Aesthetically the Epilogue is a pastiche, immortalizing
Joan's relationship with man and refuting any possibility
that modern man is spiritually more enlightened than
Joan's contemporaries.

Shaw's best plays "have a classical quality as they achieve the depth, complexity, economy, and coherence of fine dramatic poetry." [Bibliography. In spite of verbosity and turgidity, this book has some interesting insights.]

1995 Betts, Ernest. THE FILM BUSINESS: A HISTORY OF BRITISH CINEMA, 1896-1972 (Lond: George Allen & Unwin, 1973), pp. 129-30, 153, 166-67.
[Shaw and the movies.]

1996 Blackett, Monica. THE MARK OF THE MAKER: A PORTRAIT OF HELEN WADDELL (Lond: Constable, 1973), pp. 91, 92-93, 118-19, 120, 139, 171, 177-78, 202.
Shaw read Helen Waddell's play THE ABBÉ PRÉVOST; he promised his help but apparently forgot. Mrs. Shaw liked PETER ABELARD and "persuaded" Shaw to read it. Waddell recognized that Shaw had the "kindest heart in the world" when she saw him waiting so tenderly on the failing Mrs. Shaw. Waddell wrote Mrs. Shaw's obituary for the TIMES, which contained some awkward misprints, about which Shaw wrote very kindly.

1997 Bradbury, Ray. "Interview with Ray Bradbury. Interviewers: Paul Turner and Dorothy Simon," VERTEX, I (APRIL 19793), 24-27, 92-94.
I'm a big Shaw fan; *Don Juan in Hell* is one of the great plays.

1998 Bradbury, Ray. "Shaw as Influence, Laughton as Teacher," ShawR, XVI (May 1973), 98-99.
Shaw and Shakespeare should be the patron saints of the American theater. Charles Laughton introduced them to me.

1999 Brecht, Bertolt. ARBEITSJOURNAL. ERSTER BAND 1938 - 1942 (Working Diary. First Volume 1938 - 1942) (Frankfurt: Suhrkamp, 1973), pp. 189, 199.
The influence of the European workers' movement on the stage is characteristic of European naturalism (e.g. of the works of Shaw). In Shaw's plays the major theme appears in the characters' discussions or in the preface. [In German.]

2000 Brockett, Oscar G., and Robert R. Findlay.
CENTURY OF INNOVATION: A HISTORY OF EUROPEAN AND
AMERICAN THEATRE AND DRAMA SINCE 1870 (Englewood
Cliffs, NJ: Prentice-Hall, 1973), passim, especial-
ly 111-17.
[Brief survey of Shaw's career in the theater. Reference
to some significant productions. Photographs.]

2001 Brophy, Brigid. PRANCING NOVELIST: A DEFENSE
OF FICTION IN THE FORM OF A CRITICAL BIOGRAPHY IN
PRAISE OF RONALD FIRBANK (Lond: Macmillan, 1973),
pp. 9, 32, 35, 73, 81, 192, 196, 205, 232, 249, 254,
304, 338, 370, 406, 465, 487, 497-500.
Because Shaw is the next literary giant after George
Eliot, and because he was not a successful novelist, the
novel seemed dead. Firbank, like Shaw and perhaps
borrowing from Shaw, used odd spellings and used the
exclamation mark to indicate reaction in dialogue. Again
like Shaw, Firbank created a public persona as protection.
Shaw was possibly the example that inspired Firbank's plea
for a fair division of work and pleasure between the
sexes. He learned also to use stage directions to make
plays readable. *Heartbreak House* is probably the source
of the pastoral third act of THE PRINCESS ZOUBAROFF as
well as of its Russianness and the merger between "lyrical
mood and programmatic social design." Shaw's influence is
felt in SANTAL in the use of vegetarianism.

2002 Butler, Ivan. CINEMA IN BRITAIN: AN ILLUS-
TRATED SURVEY (South Brunswick and NY: A. S.
Barnes; Lond: Tantivy, 1973), pp. 125, 141, 160-61.
[*Pygmalion, Major Barbara* and *Caesar and Cleopatra* in the
movie versions.]

2003 Cahill, Susan and Thomas. A LITERARY GUIDE TO
IRELAND (NY: Charles Scribner's Sons, 1973), pp. 6,
69, 71, 102, 111, 112, 149, 255, 263-64, 280, 288,
312.
[Irish places associated with Shaw, either through life or
literature.]

2004 Chappelow, Allen. "Photographing the Chucker-
Out," FORUM (Houston), II (1973), 50-53.
[Extended anecdote about how Chappelow was permitted to
photograph Shaw, and Shaw's interest in the camera, and
the resulting photographs. Photographs.]

2005 Christopher, J. R. "Methuselah, Out of Heinlein by Shaw," Shaw R, XVI (May 1973), 79-88.
Robert A. Heinlein's FUTURE HISTORY is influenced by *Back to Methuselah*. His thematic organization is similar to Shaw's, the question of length of life.

2006 Clurman, Harold. "Theatre," NATION, 1 Jan 1973, p. 86.
The reason audiences go to hear *Don Juan in Hell* is Shaw's dialogue is action.

2007 Cole, Susan Ablon, "The Evolutionary Fantasy: Shaw and Utopian Fiction," Shaw R, XVI (May 1973), 89-97.
Two categories of utopia appear at the end of the nineteenth century: technological and the kind that stresses the spiritual development of man, evolutionary. *Back to Methuselah* is one of the most thorough examples of the evolutionary utopia. It is distinguished from others like H. G. Wells's THE TIME MACHINE and Bulwer-Lytton's THE COMING RACE by elimination of the contemporary protagonist for audience identification and for unification and by no interest in presenting the actual life of the utopia. Shaw wished to create myth. Shaw derives his idea of evolution largely from Samuel Butler. The final development of Shaw's vision is a return of the Life Force to a state before it was imprisoned in man, a vision circular and antiprogressive. But Shaw identified realism with his utopian fantasy and disillusionment with wrong-headed romantic imagination, and this provides an insight into his optimism and the basis for his judgment of the work of others.

2008 Couchman, Gordon W. "Bernard Shaw and the Gospel of Efficiency," Shaw R, XVI (Jan 1973), 11-20.
The theme of the virtue of efficiency is a recurring one in Shaw's writing. He desired it in himself, admired it in government, especially the dictatorships of the thirties, and demonstrated it in Creative Evolution.

2009 Couchman, Gordon W. THIS OUR CAESAR: A STUDY OF BERNARD SHAW'S *CAESAR AND CLEOPATRA* (Paris: Mouton, 1973).
Analysis of Shaw's criticism of Shakespeare shows the Puritan basis for his *Caesasr and Cleopatra*. [Shaw's contributions to OUR THEATRES IN THE NINETIES and NEW

STATESMAN cited for support.] The Preface to *Three Plays
for Puritans* reveals Shaw's disdain for the "modern
romantic convention." Shaw's sources for *Caesar* include
Plutarch, Mommsen, and Froude; but he is mostly concerned
with unmasking Shakespeare's glamorized versions of the
lovers and presenting a disciplined hero (Caesar) in
response to the self-indulgent Antony. Shaw's "Puritan
polemic" is also exhibited in *Sixteen Self Sketches, Man
and Superman,* and the Preface to *Misalliance.* Cleopatra
learns under Caesar the difference between happiness and
greatness, a distinction paralleled in *The Man of Destiny,
Candida, Superman, Major Barbara,* and *Heartbreak House;*
however, Cleopatra contrasts with Shaw's other heroines
(with those from *Mrs. Warren's Profession, The Millionairess, You Never Can Tell, The Philanderer,* and *Saint
Joan*) who are more like Caesar in aggressiveness and
domination. Shaw's Caesar is efficient yet anti-mechanis-
tic, as is Bluntschli in *Arms and the Man.* [*The Perfect
Wagnerite, Back to Methuselah, Everybody's Political
What's What,* and Prefaces to *On the Rocks* and *Geneva* also
cited for a discussion of Shaw's "Great Men."] However,
Shaw's glorifying totalitarian states is intellectually
weak. He learned from Meredith and Bergson about the
comic spirit as *The Inca of Perusalem* shows. Shaw's
comedy in *Caesar* serves to ridicule "all things insular
and provincial." [Extensive bibliography.]

2010 Crane, Gladys M. "Shaw's *Misalliance*: The
Comic Journey from Rebellious Daughter to Conventional Womanhood," ETJ, XXV (Dec 1973), 480-89.
Hypatia Tarleton in *Misalliance* reverses the expectations
of middle-class society for women. Her vitality is like
Ann Whitefield's in *Man and Superman.* But her engagement
to Bentley is a measure of her lack of self-knowledge.
Her humor results from her interactions with the other
characters. Her primary motive is rebellion, but she
cannot be truly independent. She settles for economic
dependence on her father and an unfeeling marriage based
on money.

2011 Dace, Letitia, and Wallace Dace. THE THEATRE
STUDENT, MODERN THEATRE AND DRAMA (NY: Richards
Rosen P, 1973), pp. 46-49.
Shaw's superb comic skill can banish pity and fear from
the hearts of his audience--at least for the duration of
the play. [Conventional description of Shaw's drama.]

2012 Darlington, W. A. "Why Shaw Gave up Criticism," DAILY TELEGRAPH, 23 July 1973; rptd in ISh, XV (Fall 1976), 6-7.
Shaw was a great critic and a great dramatist who wrote plays to illustrate his critical doctrines.

2013 Deane, Barbara. "Shaw and Gnosticism," ShawR, XVI (Sept 1973), 104-22.
The Gnostic dualism of the struggle of mind and matter with the eventual triumph of mind is a clue to Shaw's religious thought. [There follows a summary of Gnostic thought as opposed to Christianity.] Shaw had contempt for the Theosophists, but he shared their belief in evolution. Shaw and the Gnostics both believed that man is inherently good in opposition to the idea of original sin, but the evidence concerning whether or not Shaw shared the Gnostic view that the flesh is inherently evil is contradictory. The version of the story of Adam and Eve Shaw used in *Back to Methuselah* is the Gnostic version and can be found in Mme. Blavatsky's THE SECRET DOCTRINE. Shaw shared with the Gnostics an identification of mind with spirit, and whatever interferes with the upward progress of the mind is evil. Shaw's Ancients are similar to Gnostic Therapeuts. Shaw has much in common with Gnostic Christology. Both Shaw and the Gnostics attempted to synthesize beliefs from many sources.

2014 Dukore, Bernard F. BERNARD SHAW, PLAYWRIGHT. ASPECTS OF SHAVIAN DRAMA (Columbia: U of Missouri P, 1973). Section of Part Two, Chap. III, on Caesar and Cleopatra, rptd from ETJ (May 1973); section of Part Two, Chap. IV, on *Major Barbara*, rptd from ShawR (Jan 1973), abstracted under date of first publication.
This book divides into two parts: "the first centers upon Shaw's theory, the second upon his practice."

In writing his plays, Shaw depended more on inspiration than logic. His sources were varied, but the major source was the life around him. Shaw's realism is in the psychology that lies beneath the surface. He attacked the well-made play, especially its plot. but Shaw was careful in his revisions, his attention to stage craft and historical authenticity, though not in the matter of style. Shaw usually submitted to the mechanical limitations of the stage. In his plays the conflict is created by "a conflict of unsettled ideals." Discussion is what distinguishes the modern play from the old-

fashioned. Art derives from doctrine and is didactic.
Shaw tries in his first acts "to furnish a complete social
and psychological *milieu*." Shaw's plays are unified by
theme. Shaw's plays are startlingly contemporary. He is
not a forerunner of the writers for the theater of the
absurd, but he does dramatize the abyss, and he was a
"protoexistentialist." He was closer to the theistic
existentialists than to the humanistic or atheistic in his
Creative Evolution. Shavian man is free, responsible for
his actions, and all that he may rely on. Shaw's
Socialism manifests itself in four ways: 1) "An underlying viewpoint," 2) "Destructive Criticism (dramatizations, with no explicit solutions, of the deficiencies of
capitalist society), 3) Socialist Parables," and 4)
"Socialism Explicit." [Discussion and illustration from
all the major plays.]

2015 Dukore, Bernard F. "Revising *Major Barbara*,"
Shaw R, XVI (Jan 1973), 2-10; rptd in BERNARD SHAW,
PLAYWRIGHT (1973).
Shaw's revisions of *Major Barbara* were the most drastic of
any he ever did. Comparing Act III, Scene 2 of the Derry
manuscript with the Standard Edition shows that Shaw's
revision falls into two categories: 1) strengthening
Barbara and Cusins, and 2) altering the structure of the
scene to dramatize the contrast between them and
Undershaft. Undershaft's conversion of Barbara and Cusins
"suggests not their defeat but their possible victory."

2016 Dukore, Bernard. "'Too Much of a Good
Thing'?--Structural Features of *Caesar and Cleopat-
ra*," ETJ, XXV (May 1973), 193-98 rptd in BERNARD
SHAW, PLAYWRIGHT (1973).
Like *Man and Superman, Caesar and Cleopatra* has a detachable third act, but should it be cut? Shaw himself regarded Act III as dispensable, though in the 1913 revival
with Forbes Robinson, Shaw restored it, writing a shorter
Ra prologue. The third act introduces Apollodorus. It is
an important thematic link and part of the pattern of
Cleopatra's development as well as preparation for
Caesar's failure in teaching her ideal queenship as well
as his failure in ideal kingship.

2017 Ellmann, Richard. GOLDEN CODGERS: BIOGRAPHI-
CAL SPECULATIONS (NY and Lond: Oxford UP, 1973),
pp. 119-20, 122-23.
[Brief references to Shaw and religion.]

2018 Elsom, John. EROTIC THEATRE (Lond: Secker & Warburg, 1973), passim.
[Some comments from Shaw about the connection between sex and the theater; the role of *Mrs. Warren's Profession* and *Man and Superman* along with the works of the naturalists in making a case against propriety; the position of the Preface of *The Shewing-up of Blanco Posnet* in the censorship argument. No documentation. Illustration of Granville Barker and Madge McIntosh as Frank and Vivie in *Mrs. Warren*.]

2019 Fleischer, Leonard. "The Uses of History in Twentieth Century British and American Drama," DAI, XXXIII (1973), 5171A. Unpublished dissertation, New York University, 1971.

2020 Fowler, Lois Josephs. "Women in Literature and the High School Curriculum," ENGLISH JOURNAL, LXII (Nov 1973), 1123-26.
Candida, Mrs. Warren's Profession, Caesar and Cleopatra, and any number of other Shaw plays depict women strong enough to be manipulative.

2021 Gibbs, A. M. "Yeats, Shaw and the Unity of Culture," SOUTHERN REVIEW: AN AUSTRALIAN JOURNAL OF LITERARY STUDIES, VI (Sept 1973), 189-203.
Shaw and Yeats each held ambivalent attitudes toward the other. But Shaw's view of an integrated culture expressed by Keegan in *John Bull's Other Island* is similar to Years's idea of Byzantium, and both were influenced by Blake and Shelley. It is perhaps oversimplifying to say that Shaw supported political commitment, whereas Yeats's conception involved withdrawal from political realities. Perhaps the major distinction between the two is that between comic and tragic.

2022 Gill, Stephen. "Shaw, the Suffragist," LITER-ARY HALF YEARLY, XIV (1973), 153-56.
Shaw's ambition was to see women economically and politically treated on a par with men. He wrote *Press Cuttings* for the women's suffrage movement. *Fanny's First Play* and *Getting Married* depict his continued interest in the women's cause.

2023 Glicksberg, Charles I. "Bernard Shaw and the New Love-Ethic," THE SEXUAL REVOLUTION IN MODERN ENGLISH LITERATURE (The Hague: Martinus Nijhoff, 1973) pp. xii, xvi, 33-34, 35, 45-58, 178.
Before Shaw could establish himself as a dramatist, he had to fight censorship, for the dramatist is restricted by taboos and cannot be too far in advance of his audience. Shaw hailed Ibsen as a social realist, and unlike Strindberg, he was sane in his sexual attitudes. He was a puritan at heart, but he counseled men to stop fooling themselves with lofty talk of love. He acknowledged sexual appetite but opposed its gratification at the expense of the female. Shaw was opposed to all censorship until the harm was proved. *Mrs. Warren's Profession*, for all its controversy, is chaste in its handling. He was not in sympathy with the romantic conception of love and felt that sexual passion was exaggerated. *Man and Superman* exposes the lie of love and marriage as everlasting bliss. *Back to Methuselah* carries to extremes the idea that the goal of the Life Force is philosophic man not bodily perfection. In *Androcles and the Lion* he dramatizes the trap that marriage sets. Shaw was fundamentally a rationalist in his approach to the sexual problem. [Judicious view of Shaw's ideas of sexuality in his social and dramatic context.]

2024 Goetsch, Paul. "Vorwort" (Preface), DAS ENGLISCHE DRAMA (English Drama), ed by Josefa Nünning (Darmstadt: Wissenschaftliche Buchgessel-schaft, 1973), pp. vii-xi.
[References to Shaw as dramatic critic and to his reception of Ibsen's plays.] [In German.]

2025 Gottesman, Ronald. UPTON SINCLAIR: AN ANNOTATED CHECK LIST (Kent State, Ohio: Kent State UP [Serif Series 24], 1973) items A378, A1354, A1356, A1414, A1927, A1947.
[A Checklist, including Sinclair on Shaw.]

2026 Gourlay, Logan. OLIVIER (Lond: Weidenfeld and Nicolson, 1973), pp. 26-27, 35, 42, 49, 76-77, 91-95, 116, 124, 128, 190-91,
[Anecdotes of Sir Lawrence Olivier's performances in *Arms and the Man*, *Caesar and Cleopatra*, and *The Devil's Disciple*, among others.]

2027 Green, Jonathan ed. CAMERA WORK: A CRITICAL ANTHOLOGY (Millerton, NY: Aperture, 1973), pp. 34, 93, 121, 126, 127, 167.
[References to Shaw. Shaw's portrait of Alvin Langdon Coburn. Edward J. Steichen portrait of Shaw.]

2028 "Greetings from Absent Friends," SHAVIAN, IV (Summer 1973), 276-79.
[Letters from Mrs. Warren, Jack Tanner, Tom Broadbent, Lady Britomart, and King Magnus concerning their present situation.]

2029 Hardwick, Michael. A LITERARY ATLAS & GAZETEER OF THE BRITISH ISLES (Newton Abbot: David & Charles, 1973), p. 51, 184.
[Guide with maps to locations associated with Shaw.]

2030 Hardwick, Michael and Mollie. THE BERNARD SHAW COMPANION (Lond: John Murray, 1973; NY: St. Martin's P, 1974).
Chronology of Shaw's works. Plots of the plays. Who's who. A sampler of quotations. The life of Shaw. [Photograph.]

2031 Harrison, N. J. "The New Alphabet," ISh, XII (Fall 1973), 6-7.
The Shaw Alphabet of 1962, though excellent in principle, does not pursue its logic fully. I have perfected it so that it is now fit for general use and have renamed it The New Alphabet. [Specimen of words in The New Alphabet.]

2032 Heinlein, Robert. "Heinlein on Science Fiction," VERTEX, I (April 1973), 46-49, 96-98.
[Quotes *Caesar and Cleopatra* to support the idea of change. Text of a speech given in 1941 at the Third World Science Fiction Convention, mimeographed at about that time (200 copies); an additional 100 printed later.]

2033 Hellman, Lillian. PENTIMENTO (Bost and Toronto: Little, Brown, 1973), pp. 201-2.
Shaw was needed to adapt L'ALOUETTE by Jean Anouilh; he wrote a fine play about Joan of Arc "without Mr. Anouilh's bubble glory stuff." Shaw's play is about "the miraculous

self-confidence that carried defeated men into battle
against all sense."

2034 HENDERSON, LESLIE M.   THE GOLDSTEIN STORY
(Melbourne: Stockland P, 1973), pp. 90, 101, 107,
159-67, 169, 175.
The basis of the literary friendship of Henry Hyde
Champion and Shaw was social reform. [Letters from Shaw
to Champion concerning productions of Shaw plays in
Australia.]

2035 Hill, John Edward. "Dialectical Aestheticism:
Essays on the Criticism of Swinburne, Pater, Wilde,
James, Shaw, and Yeats," DAI, XXXIII (1973), 3648-
49A.   Unpublished dissertation, University of
Virginia, 1972.

2036 Holden, David Franklin. "Analytical Index and
Annotated Bibliography to Modern Drama, Volumes I-
XIII," DAI, XXXIII (1973), 3649A. Unpublished dis-
sertation, University of Kansas, 1972.

2037 Hulban, Horia. "Stilul aforismelor lui G. B.
Shaw" (Style of G. B. Shaw's Aphorisms) ANALELE
ŞTIINŢIFIÇE ALE UNIVERSITĂŢII "AL. I. CUZA" DIN IAŞI
(S.N.) F. LITERATURA, XIX (1973), 81-89.
Shaw's aphorisms in the plays take the form of play on
words, metaphors, antonyms, expressing opinions, spiritual
non-conformity, analogies and paradoxes, for the purpose
of concise expression and subordinating form to idea in
order to make situations significant. [In Romanian.]

2038 Hummert, Paul A.   BERNARD SHAW'S MARXIAN
ROMANCE (Lincoln: U of Nebraska P, 1973).
Even in Shaw's first four novels the predisposition to
Marxist principles is evident; in *An Unsocial Socialist*
the impact of DAS KAPITAL is immediately apparent. As
Shaw makes clear in *Essays in Fabian Socialism*, he
strictly adhered to Marx's history of the development of
economics, though he rejecteed the solution of revolution.
In *The Quintessence of Ibsenism* he blends Ibsen and Marx.
Widowers' Houses reflects Shaw's interest in Socialism.
The Philanderer only indirectly reflects Socialism, but
Mrs. Warren's Profession reveals capitalism as the cause
of prostitution. *Candida, Arms and the Man, The Man of*

Destiny, and *You Never Can Tell*, are too pleasant to be really Shavian. In *The Sanity of Art*, in which Shaw answers Max Nordau's DEGENERATION, Shaw demonstrates that artists are those who will not submit to exploitation and who expose the industrial system. In *The Perfect Wagnerite* Shaw imparts only Wagner's ideas. In *Caesar and Cleopatra* Shaw's principal concern is the Marxist interpretation of history, as it is in *John Bull's Other Island*. *The Devil's Disciple* deals with Marx's priest. *Major Barbara's* religious theme embraced Shaw's most complete expression of Marxism to date. In *Androcles and the Lion* Shaw identifies Christ with Marxism. *Saint Joan* attacks the church's identification with the landed aristocracy. *Captain Brassbound's Conversion* is Shaw's first Marxist denunciation of the law. *The Doctor's Dilemma* indicts doctors as servants of the establishment. In *Misalliance*, however, Shaw softened his indictment of marriage to make it palatable to the West End audience. In *Pygmalion* Shaw skillfully submerged the Marxian indictment of marriage into the comedy. *Heartbreak House* demonstrates Shaw's impatience with Fabian gradualism. When Shaw completed *Man and Superman*, Creative Evolution is confined to the embellishments of the play: "Don Juan in Hell," *The Revolutionist's Handbook*, and *Maxims for Revolutionists*. Shaw returned to Creative Evolution 18 years later in *Back to Methuselah*. Religion and politics and economics underly *Methuselah*. In *The Intelligent Woman's Guide to Socialism and Optimism*, Shaw tempers his enthusiasm for Russia with Fabian reform. Shaw revisited Russia, and *The Apple Cart* and *Too True to Be Good* reflect his state of mind before his trip. *On the Rocks*, almost completely bereft of humor, condones even the bloodiest aspects of the Russian Revolution and expresses scorn for the Fabians. *The Rationalization of Russia* helps clarify the theme of purgation of capitalism of *The Simpleton of the Unexpected Isles*. *The Millionairess* looks like an aboutface, but actually Shaw is attempting to reconcile the role of the vibrant individualist (Epifania) with the communist state. In *Geneva* he castigates the international social evil of nationalism. The spirit of Marx pervades Act I of *Bouyant Billions*, and *Farfetched Fables* is a full summary of Shaw's principles.

2039 Iakubovich, V. "Nenuzhnyĭ bagazh prozy ili shkola pisatel'skogo masterstva: Romany B. Shou" (The Useless Baggage of Prose, or The School of Writing Mastery: Shaw's Novels) NEKOTORYE PROBLEMY ANGLIISKOI LITEARTURY (Some Problems of English Philology) (Piatigorsk: np, 1973), pp. 277-300.

The ideas and themes of Shaw's novels show he was a writer hostile to the "art for art's sake" theory. He was in the tradition of the English realist school. His criticism of the bourgeois world was not consistent owing to mistaken Fabian beliefs. The problems discussed in his novels (prejudices of bourgeois marriage, morals, class barriers, the need of radical social changes) were relevant to his time and developed in the plays. Autobiographical elements give way to deliberate typification of situations and characters. His use of language foreshadows the stage-directions and descriptions so important in the plays. [In Russian.]

2040 Inglis, Brian. ROGER CASEMENT (Lond, Sydney, Auckland, Toronto: Hodder and Stoughton, 1973), pp. 13, 147-48, 325-28, 330, 350-51, 363, 378, 379, 386, 397-99.
Casement's views of the relationships of Ireland to England were similar to those Shaw expressed in the preface to *John Bull's Other Island*. Casement's friends hoped Shaw's wife would put up the money for his defense. Shaw was a consistent critic of *Sinn Fein* and was one of the first to warn that execution of Casement would hand Ireland over to *Sinn Fein*. Shaw encouraged T. E. Lawrence to write a life of Casement. [Reprints part of Shaw's defense of Casement and his letter *Shall Roger Casement Hang* from the MANCHESTER GUARDIAN (22 JULY 1916).]

2041 Kagarlit͡skiĭ, I͡u. "Si͡urprizy Shou" (Shaw's Surprizes), TEATR (Leningrad), VII (1973), 99-101. Review of SHOU--TEORETIK, by A. Romm (1972).]
Shaw's main secret is that of his "life philosophy," which contains the key to his artistic method, and which he had in the most obvious place--his works, with their Prefaces. He cannot be understood without them. Yet Shaw always stressed his own originality and was so different that more than one scholar has been led astray. At one time, the phrase "critical realism of the nineteenth or twentieth century" was regarded as praise and became traditional. Now we speak simply of twentieth century realism. Yet Shaw learned from the writers of the nineteenth century, and also of the eighteenth century Enlightenment. Shaw suddenly exposed the bourgeois, with prophetic insight into the nature of capitalism because he read Marx. [In Russian.]

2042 Kagarlitski, Julius. "Bernard Shaw and Science Fiction: Why Raise the question?" Shaw R, XVI (May 1973), 59-66.
[Translated by Roger Freling from Russian.] Shaw rejected "mathematical analysis, the basis for the modern pure sciences, and Darwinism, the basis for the modern natural sciences. By exploring Shaw's relationship to science, we may illuminate science fiction, where scientific problems are social problems. Shaw carries the most ordinary truths to fantastic limits and creates paradoxes. As his writing uses fantasy more and more, it opposes science. In this he is like Swift, and also like Swift his desire is "to return to man the entire world." Further he attacks science as prejudice. Shaw attempted in his fantasy to create "a mythological work based on unconditional faith and intended to give rise to a kind of new religion." [Refers to *Back to Methuselah* as Shaw's chief fantasy.]

2043 Kamer, Hansrudolf. KÜNSTLERISCHE UND POLITISCHE EXTRAVAGANZ IM SPÄTWERK SHAWS (Artistic and Political Extravaganza in Shaw's Later Work) (Bern: Francke [Vol 73 of SCHWEIZER ANGLISTISCHE ARBEITEN (SWISS STUDIES IN ENGLISH)], 1973).
Shaw's later plays are little accepted, understood, and appreciated. His political views from the 1930's to the 1950's, especially his concept of the role of the state, provide the basis for the interpretation of his later plays. In view of his lifelong advocacy of socialism it is wrong to accuse Shaw of fascist learnings. Shaw's later plays show traits of Brecht's epic theater and influences of nineteenth century genres such as extravaganza, burlesque, and opera bouffe. Politically, Shaw was a pragmatist, a *Realpolitiker* and a moralist at the same time. But his reputation rests upon the quality of his whole dramatic work. His later works generally measure up to his earlier ones. "They explore and invent new dramatic dimensions for philosophic and parabolic purposes: They achieve this by the brilliant use of open allegory and symbolic action and setting." [In German, with summary in English.]

2044 Kantorovich, I. B. "Opyt sravnitel'nogo analiza *Gor'k'o no pravda* Shou s *Dobrym chelovekom iz Sychuani* Brekhta" (Attempted Comparison of Shaw's *Too True to Be Good* with Brecht's *Good Woman of*

Sechuan), NAUCHNYE ZAPISKI SVERDLOVSKOGO PED. INST.
(Sverdlovsk), CCIII (1973), 58-75.
[Not seen.] [In Russian.]

2045 Karrer, Wolfgang, and Eberhard Kreutzer. DATEN
DER ENGLISCHEN UND AMERIKANISCHEN LITERATUR VON 1890
BIS ZUR GEGENWART (Details of English and American
Literature from 1890 to the Present) (Munich:
Deutscher Taschenbuchverlag, 1973), pp. 12, 14, 15,
16, 18, 21, 22, 24, 72, 74, 79, 82, 88-89, 100, 111,
118, 124, 125.

2046 Kennedy, Andrew. "The Absurd and the Hyper-
Articulate in Shaw's Dramatic Language," MD, XVI
(Sept 1973), 185-92.
[Part of the chapter on Shaw from Andrew Kennedy, SIX
DRAMATISTS IN SEARCH OF A LANGUAGE (1974).]

2047 Kester, Dolores A. "Shaw and the Victorian
'Problem' Genre: The Woman Side," DAI, XXXIV
(1973), 2566A. Unpublished dissertation, University
of Wisconsin (Madison), 1973.

2048 Khanna, Savitri. "Shaw's Image of Woman,"
SHAVIAN, IV (Summer 1973), 253-59.
Shaw had little intimate contact with women and could not
learn that they are masqueraders. His ignorance led him
to argue in *The Quintessence of Ibsenism* that women were
not different from men. Starting from this wrong premise,
he concluded in *Mrs. Warren's Profession* that woman should
strive for economic independence. He underestimated
Nature's demands upon women by making children dependent
for so long. At the same time Shaw deserves women's
gratitude for his efforts toward their emancipation.

2049 Kidd, Walter E. BRITISH WINNERS OF THE NOBEL
LITERARY PRIZE (Norman: U of Oklahoma P, 1973), pp.
5, 7-8, 47, 67, 83-129, 204.
[Survey of Shaw's life, career, and ideas.]

2050 Komatsu, Motoya. "Bernard Shaw Kuronbomusume
no Kamisama Sagashi ni tsuite" (On *The Adventures of
the Black Girl in Her Search for God*), AKITA DAIGAKU

KYOIKUGAKUBU KENKYUKIYO (Akita), (Jinbunkagaku, Shakaikagaku) No. 23 (Feb 1973), 13-27.
The Adventures of the Black Girl in Her Search for God does not possess much literary value, but it is a highly interesting piece which throws light on Shaw's view of God, life and morality. [In Japanese.]

2051 Kosok, Heinz. "Drama und Theater im 19.Jahrhundert" (Drama and Theater in the 19th Century) DAS ENGLISCHE DRAMA (English Drama), ed by Josefa Nunning (Darmstadt: Wissenschaftliche Buchgesellschaft, 1973), pp. 349-402.
One of the main features of nineteenth-century literature is a gap between the stage and literary quality. Shaw was the first to bridge this gap. *Mrs. Warren's Profession* could be called the first modern drama, a precursor of twentieth century drama. [In German.]

2052 Lambert, J. W. "Plays in Performance, London," DRAMA, CX (Autumn 1973), 14-29.
Misalliance correctly, but unhelpfully, observes that the relationships between age and youth, for example, are baffling.

2053 László, Anna. HEVESI SÁNDOR [Alexander Hevesi] (Budapest: Gondolat, 1973), passim.
[Passing references to the director-translator Hevesi's relationship with Shaw.] [In Hungarian.]

2054 Leary, Daniel J. "The Ends of Childhood: Eschatology in Shaw and Clarke," ShawR, XVI (May 1973), 67-78.
In 2001 A.D. A SPACE ODYSSEY, THE CITY AND THE STARS, and CHILDHOOD'S END Arthur C. Clarke "poses the ultimate Shavian question: What is to become of man's creative energy when he has solved the problems of his animal needs and transcended his childish instinct toward irresponsible aggression?" Clarke's answer corresponds with Lilith's final speech in *Back to Methuselah.* Shaw juxtaposes "racial memory, present experience, and future hope" in *Methuselah.* Clarke manipulates the past in the light of modern astronomy. Shaw's views on biology are very modern; vide: Jung, Jacques Monod and B. F. Skinner. Both writers tell us "to live our lives according to our dreams."

2055 Le Bourgeois, John Y. "William Morris to George Bernard Shaw," DURHAM UNIVERSITY JOURNAL, LXV (March 1973), 205-11.
Shaw met William Morris in 1884. Shaw admired the older man, and as the text of thirteen letters from Morris to Shaw [here reproduced] demonstrate, the admiration was mutual.

2056 Levin, Gerald. "Shaw, Butler, and Kant," PHILOLOGICAL QUARTERLY, LII (Jan 1973), 142-56.
Shaw probably would have agreed with Kant that the only unqualified good is good will, but he differed from him in assuming that the suprasensible origin of the will guaranteed the goodness of its effects. Shaw's failure to distinguish between kinds of means resulted in part from his attachment to Lamarckian ideas. Shaw shared Butler's confusion of reason and instinct as in some sense instinctive. An important problem for Shaw was the reconciliation of vitality with moral consciousness and self-control. "For Kant man becomes a noumenal being by virtue of his thought in the realm of moral experience; he cannot, however, know more than the face of his moral freedom. Dick Dudgeon, Joan and Barbara Undershaft are ultimately imagined as noumenal beings existing in a kingdom of ends. But they are noumenal beings by virtue of their feeling alone." "Shaw's criticism of 'limited liability in morals,' in the preface to On The Rocks, is . . . explicable only on the assumption of an innate moral sense." In the thirties Shaw gave enough new thought to Houston Stewart Chamberlain's discussion of Kant and racial theories in FOUNDATIONS OF THE NINETEENTH CENTURY to repudiate the racial theory in the preface to The Millionairess. "Based on an insecure conception of reason and feeling and uncriticized assumptions, [Shaw's] voluntarism ended in intellectual contradiction and an escape from tragic insight into moral absolutes that, in the prefaces of the thirties, are feebly rationalized."

2057 Lorichs, Sonja, "The Unwomanly Woman," SHAVIAN, IV (Summer 1973), 250-52.
In his novels and plays Shaw speaks for the New Woman in opposition to the womanly woman, whose goal is marriage. In Mrs. Warren's Profession, he argues for women's education. This theme returns in Pygmalion. Barbara in Major Barbara and Fanny and Margaret in Fanny's First Play rebel against their repressive middle-class backgrounds. Edith and Lesbia of Getting Married refuse to marry. The Apple Cart points to a time when women will be active in

government. Shaw's Joan is the most unwomanly woman of all.

2058 Lorichs, Sonja. THE UNWOMANLY WOMAN IN BERNARD SHAW'S DRAMA AND HER SOCIAL AND POLITICAL BACKGROUND (Uppsala, Sweden: Acta Universitatis Upsaliensis [Studia Anglistica Upsaliensia], 1973).
[Published dissertation, Uppsala University.] [Brief critical survey.] The model for Shaw's modern woman was Nora from A DOLL'S HOUSE. [Survey of Victorian and Edwardian social and political background.] *Mrs. Warren's Profession* is Shaw's first play to present a full-length portrait of the Unwomanly Woman. Other plays that could be called immoral were presented on the London stage, but their heroines, unlike Shaw's, were womenly women. *Caesar and Cleopatra* demonstrates Shaw's concern for the education of women.

Critics trying to analyse Barbara of *Major Barbara* seem to be attracted by her "pious and sympathetic" character, but she may be in actuality a New Woman, who emancipates herself by revolt and becomes independent of her environment. [Brief examination of the history of the Salvation Army.]

The theme of marriage and divorce is the single problem of *Getting Married*. The question of economic dependence is crucial; violation of marriage laws meant ruin for the woman; love is irrelevant. [Brief history of English marriage laws, and survey of Shaw's views toward marriage.]

In *Fanny's First Play*, Fanny O'Dowda and Margaret Knox belong to Shaw's new type of heroine. [Brief survey of the suffragette struggle.] Shaw's only play about Suffrage is *Press Cuttings*. The theme of the middle-class girl who tires of an empty life is repeated in *Too True to Be Good* and *The Millionairess*.

Phonetics, along with class discrimination and woman's education, is the theme of *Pygmalion*. The solution to class distinctions is class circulation. [Brief survey of English education.] Shaw created in Eliza a modern woman, eager to learn. She intends to be independent and a loving wife as well. In *The Apple Cart*, Shaw created two unique career women. Annajanska in *The Bolshevik Empress* is an early version of Joan, the Unwomanly Woman who is a military leader.

Generally Shaw's drama is socially conditioned; therefore, it is natural that he should have written plays about women's position in society. Barbara is the one with whom Shaw is most involved personally. Joan is the genius. [Chronology. Bibliography.]

2059 McDowell, Frederick P. W. "Bernard Shaw: Biographical and Textual Scholarship," JOURNAL OF MODERN LITEARTURE, III (Feb 1973), 120-29.
Shaw provided some of the most valuable information about himself. His view was that he happened to things rather than the reverse; therefore, his biography is one of his mind and its influence on others. Everything he wrote is in a sense autobiographical. World War I is the most significant event in Shaw's life, extending his views about human nature and inducing a new disillusionment.

2060 Mackenzie, Norman and Jeanne. THE TIME TRAVELLER: THE LIFE OF H. G. WELLS (Lond: Weidenfeld and Nicolson, 1973; also publ. as H. G. WELLS (NY: Simon and Schuster, 1973), pp. 49, 62, 74, 102, 108, 109, 168, 171, 174, 177, 184-200, 204-220, 222, 223, 231-33, 240, 245-47, 250, 253-55, 277, 286-88, 297, 300-1, 309, 345, 347-49, 351-53, 358, 362-63, 382-85, 399, 422, 427.
Shaw's meeting with Joseph Conrad in Wells's company was not a success. Shaw was one of Wells's sponsors when he joined the Fabian Society. He supported Wells's attempt to reform the Society so long as he believed Wells was serious. But Shaw finally could not believe that Wells would cease playing the prophet, and he feared Wells would split the Society. Finally Shaw realized that "there was no chance of taming Wells into a Fabian asset." Shaw and Wells again quarrelled about the moral superiority of the Allies in World War I and about Russia. When Jane Wells was dying, Shaw was tactless and unsympathetic, claiming the cancer was the result of poor thoughts. Shaw attempted to restrain Wells in his quarrel with G. Herbert Thring, secretary to the Society of Authors. Shaw's final quarrel with Wells was over Soviet Russia and Wells' version of the Fabian Society rupture in EXPERIMENT IN AUTOBIOGRAPHY. [Photograph of Shaw.]

2061 Makusheva, S. P. "Listi i noveli Bernarda Shou" (Letters and Short Stories of Bernard Shaw), INOZEMNA FILOLOGIIA (L'viv), XXXI (1973), 162-65.

We know Shaw as a dramatist who struggled ceaselessly for justice, progress and intellect, so these books [PIS'MA (Letters) and NOVELI (Short Stories) (1971) (Not seen.)] come as a surprise. Obraztsova contributes an afterword and commentary on Shaw's epistolary style, showing them to be the most lyrical and intimate genre of his work. It is also surprising that Shaw was a master of the short story in composition and form. *The Adventures of the Black Girl in Her Search for God, Cannonfodder, The Serenade, The Emperor and the Little Girl,* and *Aerial Football* are highly paradoxical, anti-religious and anti-war in themes. [In Ukrainian.]

2062 May, Robin. A COMPANION TO THE THEATRE: THE ANGLO-AMERICAN STAGE FROM 1920 (Guildford and Lond: Lutterworth Press, 1973), pp. 15, 61-62, 201.
[Entries for *Saint Joan* and MY FAIR LADY. Very brief survey of stage appearances of Shaw plays.]

2063 Messervy, Fontell C. "For the Advanced: Shaw's *St. Joan*" (sic), DRAMATICS, XLIV (March 1973), 32-33.
Shaw's *Saint Joan* offers a challenge to advanced high school drama students.

2064 Mikhail, E. H. DISSERTATIONS ON ANGLO-IRISH DRAMA, A BIBILIOGRAPHY OF STUDIES 1870-1970 (Totowa, NJ: Rowman and Littlefield; Lond: Macmillan P, 1973), pp. 28-39. [Bibliography of dissertations on Shaw.]

2065 Mills, Carl Henry. "Shaw's Theory of Creative Evolution," ShawR, XVI (Sept 1973), 123-32.
Shaw's theory of Creative Evolution has been attackekd by the Darwinists on the one hand and systematic philosophers on the other. Now modern microbiology is opposed to it. Lamarck's truths: 1) that species vary under changing external influences, 2) that there is a fundamental unity in the animal world, and 3) that there is a progressive and perpetual development are the basis for Shaw's theory. Goethe's optimism also is important. The "ability of the independent life force to enter into matter is perhaps the most important concept that Butler and Shaw contributed to evolutionary thought." Shaw's theory is first dramatized in *Man and Superman*. One of the purposes of life is to subdue matter; death is the greatest obstruction to the

Life Force. To live 300 years is not impossible as Shaw
suggests in *Back to Methuselah.*

2066 Morsberger, Robert E. "The Winning of Barbara
Undershaft: Conversion by the Cannon Factory, or
'Wot prawce selvytion nah?'" COSTERUS (Amsterdam),
IX (1973), 71-77.
Major Barbara is a mediaeval "conversion drama" disguised
as a drawing-room comedy. Both Undershaft and Barbara
want to convert people to an awareness of their inner
strength and decency. Undershaft convinces Barbara that
the Salvation Army perpetuates poverty and the religion of
gunpowder and money sets men free. The last scene is not
so effective as it should be, partly because it is an
uneasy mixture of morality and Oscar Wilde. Undershaft's
purchase of Barbara and Cusins is never really examined in
the light of reality; the play ends on a false note.

2067 Nelson, Raymond S. (ed) "Introduction," "A
Bernard Shaw Chronology," "Selected Bibliography,"
"Note on the Text and the British Museum Manuscript," and "Notes," in *Candida, A Mystery,* by
Bernard Shaw (Indianapolis and NY: Bobbs-Merrill
[Bobbs-Merrill Shaw Series], 1973), pp. vii-xxxi,
passim.
Candida was not immediately accepted, probably because it
was a generation ahead of its time. Marriage is one of
its main themes, in terms of pre-Raphaelitism and "mystery
drama."

2068 Nicoll, Allardyce. ENGLISH DRAMA 1900-1930:
THE BEGINNINGS OF THE MODERN PERIOD (Cambridge:
Cambridge UP, 1973), 2, 5, 9, 27, 53, 70, 83, 85,
93, 121, 128, 137, 166-67, 180, 185, 200, 219, 220,
226, 276, 344-45, 350-62, 380, 390-92, 396, 400,
408, 414, 419, 420, 432, 941-43.
[Shaw's role in the history of the English theater 1900-
1930. Includes a Hand-List of Plays.]

2069 Novick, Julius. "You Can Tame Shaw to Death,"
NYT, 19 Aug 1973, II, pp. 1, 3.
The "Niagarafication" of Shaw has been going on for a
long time, and Shaw himself was not averse to becoming
fashionable. He is both revolutionary and an entertainer.
The Festival at Niagara-on-the-Lake regards him mainly as
an entertainer. The production of *You Never Can Tell* does

well by the comedy but misses the feeling. *Fanny's First Play* is minor, and the production is uneven.

2070 Okouchi, Toshio. BERNARD SHAW NO GEKI (Bernard Shaw's Dramas) (Tokyo: Gaku Shoboshuppan, 1973; rvsd ed 1979).
By making use of dramatic techniques of popular theater Shaw dramatized the subjects which were excluded from the traditional theater. Social protest was the keynote of his early plays, and the philosophy of the Life Force was the main theme in the middle plays. His later plays were political extravaganzas. [In Japanese.]

2071 Pervić, M. "George Bernard Shaw: *Kandida*" (George Bernard Shaw: *Candida*), POLITIKA (Belgrade), LXX (1973), 21612.
[Not seen.] [In Serbian.]

2072 Peters, Sally A. "Shaw: A Formal Analysis of Structural Development through an Examination of Representative Plays," DAI, XXXIV (1973), 3426A. Unpublished dissertation, Florida State University, 1973.

2073 Pliatskovskaia, N. "Telezha s iablkami" (*The Apple Cart*), TEATR (Moscow) I (1973), 84-85.
The Apple Cart at the Comedy Theatre, Leningrad, now produced for the first time in the Soviet Union is one of Shaw's most merciless plays. The object of his sarcasm was actual persons in British politics of the thirties, but this does not lessen the general idea of satire attacking bourgeois democracy and its political activists. [In Russian.]

2074 Quennell, Peter and Hamish Johnson. A HISTORY OF ENGLISH LITERATURE (Lond: Weidenfeld & Nicolson, 1973), pp. 492-94.
[A brief portrait of Shaw and his works.] Shaw's plays are easier to enjoy in the theater than in book-form. They have "little genuine creative substance." Shaw's conceit prevented him from becoming a genius.

2075 Redmond, James. "William Morris or Bernard Shaw: Two Faces of Victorian Socialism," THE VICTO-

RIANS AND SOCIAL PROTEST, A SYMPOSIUM, ed by J. Butt and I. F. Clarke (Newton Abbot, Devon: David & Charles; Hamden, Connecticut: Archon Books, 1973), pp. 156-76.
During the 1880s and 90s William Morris and Shaw worked together for Socialism. Beneath the surface, they embraced very different kinds of Socialism, though they both believed they belonged to the mainstream of British Socialism. Each spelled out the ideal Socialist community. Shaw gave modern expression to the Socratic concept of intellectual dominance, both politically and psychologically. Morris rejected this. Shaw's ideas are most clearly set out in *Back to Methuselah, The Simpleton of the Unexpected Isles,* and *Farfetched Fables.* His ideal is brought about by eliminating human emotion. The individual must be subordinated to the general good. Morris looked back; Shaw placed his Utopia in the future. The psychological differences between Shaw and Morris produced different versions of Victorian Socialism: one based on the repressive principle, and one on the pleasure principle.

2076 Sagittarius. "An Intelligent Woman Guiding the Shavians," SHAVIAN, IV (Summer 1973).
The women in Shaw's life were not good enough. He fought for women, but on the evidence from the plays, he believed that the "validity of a cause has nothing to do with the worth of the object." Shaw would today rebuke the misuse of woman-power.

2077 Salmon, Eric. "Shaw and the Passion of the Mind," MD, XVI (Dec 1973), 239-50.
Shaw's unique contribution to the theater is his "capacity for seeing the dramatic experience itself in terms of pure intellect." Shaw thought of his plays as performing the same function as a lecture, but this is true only of the minor plays. Shaw's characters are not psychologically realistic; they are "conventionalized, stylised devices designed by the plays which contain them . . . to serve as containers for various intellectual concepts." These concepts lie deep in human reality; therefore, the conflict among them is profoundly true. Because the action of the plays is in the mind, he chose plots of strong, overt action-- melodrama. *Man and Superman, Heartbreak House, Major Barbara,* and *Caesar and Cleopatra* are the finest examples of Shaw's balancing caricatured characters against intellectual complexity. *Saint Joan* is a major play, but it is faintly unsatisfactory because the

melodrama overwhelms the intellectual. *Superman* is the finest example of confidence in the powers of the human mind: *Heartbreak* is at the other extreme where the Life Force is called into question.

2078 Seymour-Smith, Martin. FUNK & WAGNALLS GUIDE TO MODERN WORLD LITERATURE (NY: Funk & Wagnalls; Lond: Wolfe Publishing, 1973), pp. 255-56.
Shaw was a superficial thinker and a third-rate creative writer. His importance as an Ibsenite revolutionary is exaggerated.

2079 Shimada, Kinji. "Akutagawa Ryunosuke to Eibungaku -Hikakubungaku Koen' " (Ryunosuke Akutagawa and English Literature--Lecture in Comparative Literature) NIHONBUNGAKU TO EIBUNGAKU (Japanese Litearture and English Literature), ed by Yoshie Okazaki 2nd Kinji Shimada (Tokyo: Kyoiku Shuppan Center, 1973), pp. 42-74; rptd as "*Kugutsushi* Zengono Igirisuteki Roshiyateki Zaigen" (The British and Russian Sources in Akutagawa around His *The Puppeteer*), in NIHON NIOKERU GAIKOKUBUNGAKU -HIKAKU-BUNGAKU KENKYU- (Foreign Literature in Japan - Studies in Comparative Literature), vol. 1, ed by Kinji Shimada (Tokyo: Asahi Shimbunsha, 1975), pp. 567-629.
Akutagawa was deeply influenced by four British writers: Browning, Morris, Shakespeare and Shaw. He learned much from Shaw's paradox. His HANKECHI (The Handkerchief) and ARUHINO OISHI KURANOSUKE (Oishi Kuranosuke on a Certain Day) are good examples. [In Japanese.]

2080 Shinkuma, Kiyoshi. "Shaw an Iconoclast," NAGOYA GAKUINDAIGAKU RONSHU (Seto), IX (March 1973), 215-39.
In *The Man of Destiny* Shaw tried to depict the hero not as a man of destiny but as a man of will and courage in order to destroy the idolatrous image of Napoleon. [In Japanese.]

2081 Simon, John. "*Don Juan in Hell*," NEW YORK, 29 Jan 1973, p. 58.
Shaw actually put ideas on stage, and he succeeded in making it diverting.

2082 Sirasek, L.   "George Bernard Shaw: *Zanat gospodje Voren*" (George Bernard Shaw: *Mrs. Warren's Profession*), VECER (Belgrade), XXIX (24 Dec 1973), 297.
[Not seen.]   [In Serbian.]

2083 Staud, Géza.   "Irodalmi és Színházi Működése" (Literary and Theatrical Work), HEVESI SANDOR, by Anna László (1973), pp. 343-422.
[An extensive bibliography, including Shaw.]   [In Hungarian.]

2084 Stein, Rita Louise.   "The Serious Comedy of St. John Hankin and Harley Granville Barker: A Study of Two Edwardian Contemporaries of Shaw," DAI, XXXIII (1973), 5750A-51A.   Unpublished dissertation, Columbia University, 1972.

2085 Stone, Susan C.   "*Geneva*: Paean to the Dictators?" ShawR, XVI (Jan 1973), 21-29.
Geneva supplies fuel for those who attack Shaw's blind devotion to dictators.   Shaw was not guilty of "absurd adulation" of the dictators; he was aware of their shortcomings though he recognized their achievements.   He overstated his case to achieve an impact on an unsympathetic audience.   Only two passages glorify Battler (Hitler); Shaw admired Hitler's rescuing the Germans from their position of humiliation of defeat.   Bombardone (Mussolini) provides the best evidence for Shaw's hero-worshipping, though Shaw undercuts his portrait as well. It is the Judge who most clearly represents Shaw's views.

2086 Ternik, E.   "Bernard Shou v Leningrade" (Bernard Shaw in Leningrad), NEVA (Moscow), No 2 (1973), 220.
On the occasion of Shaw's visit to Leningrad in Summer 1931, Academician Samoilovich said: "Despite Shaw's age, he has found it necessary to undertake a long journey to the country building Socialism." At the Leningrad railway station, Shaw was welcomed by representatives of Soviet and social organizations including Alexei Tolstoi. I guided him around the city, to museums, factories, rest homes for workers, and Shaw made a short speech on Lenin for a talking-film. [In Russian.]

2087 Tetzeli von Rosador, Kurt. "Shaws *Saint Joan* und die Historiker" (Shaw's *Saint Joan* and Historians), GERMANISCH-ROMANISCHE MONATSSCHRIFT, Neue Folge XXIII (Sept 1973), 342-55.
A closer examination of historians' reactions to Shaw's *Saint Joan* shows that there is a shift away from the demand that playwrights should strictly adhere to the facts and to conceding that artists have some freedom in the interpretation of historic materials. [In German.]

2088 Valency, Maurice. THE CART AND THE TRUMPPET, THE PLAYS OF GEORGE BERNARD SHAW (NY: Oxford UP, 1973).
The Green Years. [Biography, writing the novels, Fabianism, reviewing through 1898.] Shaw's Theater. [The Victorian Stage.] The Unpleasant Plays. It was either ambitious or naive of Shaw to attempt in England the style of unpleasant plays. [History of the writing, production and reception of *Widowers' Houses*. *Widowers' Houses* considered in the context of continental naturalism.] The difficulty in *Widowers' Houses* is that the reasoning is impeccable, but the characterization of Trench and the change of his position are not. [History of *The Philanderer*.] *The Philanderer* is a protest against the unreasonable possessiveness of women in love. [*Mrs. Warren's Profession* in the context of French and English thesis drama.] Shaw justifies Mrs. Warren's choice of profession, but not the profession itself. In Shaw the actions of the characters are not surprising; their reasons for acting are. The Pleasant Plays. [History of *Arms and the Man*.] *Arms* is a textbook well-made play. At this point Shaw realized that his success depended upon theatrical methods, and he developed a technique through which revelation of character coincides with the ideological development of the action. Sergius and Bluntschli (as types) haunt the plays of Shaw. [History of *Candida*, in the context of nineteenth century domestic comedies and pre-Raphaelitism.] Marchbanks is a first glimpse of the superman. [History of *The Man of Destiny* and *You Never Can Tell*.] *Never Can* is the first of Shaw's tragic farces. Plays for Puritans. [History of *The Devil's Disciple*, in the context of melodrama.] Dick Dudgeon's heroic self-sacrifice is according to the traditional formula; his motivation is new. [Dudgeon in the context of nineteenth century anarchism.] [History and context of *Caesar and Cleopatra*.] With *Caesar* Shaw embarked on a new course: it has no plot and no idea; it is based on characterization. [Discussion of Caesar as a superman in the context of Shaw's and nineteenth century thought.] [His-

tory and context of *Captain Brassbound's Conversion.*]
Brassbound is a 'demonstration of the power of genius to
organize its environment according to the principles of
its nature." By this time Shaw reached a modus vivendi
with the middle class; his hatred of its hypocrisy was
tempered by pity for its stupidity. [*Superman* in the
context of the revitalization of spiritual values in the
nineties, symbolism and symbolist drama, the English
idealists of the seventies, Scribean drama, Shaw's biography and the Don Juan myth.] Shaw's faith is most clearly
found in *The Revolutionist's Handbook.* [A survey of attitudes towards women in literature.] The vintage years.
John Bull's Other Island is flattering to nobody. [Exami-
nation of the stage Irishman.] Since the Prefaces were
written after the plays, the Preface to *Superman* is most
pertinent to *John Bull.* That Shaw did not destroy *How He
Lied to Her Husband* indicates to what degree he lacked
self criticism. [The economic context of *Major Barbara.*]
The question *Barbara* posed, is it better to sedate the
poor with dreams of heaven or wake them to the grim reality of life on earth, is answered before the play is over.
The Doctor's Dilemma exhibits an orthodox faith in modern
science. The question posed in *Dilemma* is: given a
choice, which type of human being is it advisable to
preserve? [The history of the question of the relation of
art to morality.] *Getting Married* is a plotless comedy,
much like a platonic dialogue. [Examines the psychological motivations of the characters of *Candida* and *Getting
Married.*] The intellectual genre launched by Shaw's discussion plays did not result in works of great distinction. The *Shewing-up of Blanco Posnet* is singularly
inept as a play. [Comparison with Tolstoy's THE POWER OF
DARKNESS.] *Misalliance* is a "tolerably dull entertainment." *Fanny's First Play* is very slight. *Overruled* is a
particularly innocuous farce. Discussion of religious
drama.] *Androcles and the Lion* extends the doctrine of
Barbara. *Pygmalion* is a play about the relation of speech
to class; it is a love story, and it is a play of *declassement.* [Discussion of plays of *declassement.*] There
is a disparity between Shaw the dramatist and Shaw the
novelist. Shaw violates the realism of the myth. [Shaw
and Mrs. Patrick Campbell, and World War I.] *Heartbreak
House.* The characters of *Heartbreak* are purely artificial. *Heartbreak* is first a "psychic cleaning establishment." [Comparison with Chekhov.] Shaw claimed the
Life Force had taken a hand in the composition of his
masterpiece, *Back to Methuselah.* It includes some of
Shaw's best scenes, but it is "so tedious as barely to
support the spectator's attention." Shaw does not seem to
believe his own facts; his faith was subject to change and

his religion is metaphor. [The facts of Saint Joan's life.] *Saint Joan* inaugurates a new tradition of historical drama: a modern interpretation of history, peopled with characters intelligible in modern terms. [Survey of the traditional patterns of Joan's story.] Shaw's tragedy derives from Hegel's notion that in a dynamic universe, it is tragic to stand firm. The matter of Shaw's shifting popularity hangs on the question of whether the drama of the intellect is absorbing or the springs of tragedy lie elsewhere. *The Apple Cart* illustrates Shaw's slow decline as a dramatist. His last plays did not shape themselves properly; he never had a secure sense of dramatic form. The Cart and The Trumpet. What we miss in Shaw's plays is a sense of reality. Nor is Shaw a poet. [Shaw's achievement, especially in the context of his fellow playwrights and his time.] "The sense of God as the vital stream from which we emerge as individuals, and with which--we inevitably merge--is central to his work . . . . The idea is sheerest poetry and comes as close to truth as one needs to come in order to write plays." [Agreement or not with Valency's conclusions does not change the importance of this book. Its value derives partly from its success in judging Shaw not on the significance of his sources or the truth of his ideas, but as a dramatist in the context of his intellectual, theatrical and social ambience. Also, Valency's erudition, generous tone, and very graceful writing should be noted.]

2089 Vlodavskaia, I. A. "S. Butler i B. Shou" (Samuel Butler and Bernard Shaw), FILOLOGICHESKII NAUKI (Moscow), No 5 (1973), 44-53.
Shaw's reading of Samuel Butler's work was decisive in forming his own philosophical doctrine, but so also was the work of William Morris, L. Tolstoi and others, though it also increased the contradictions in his own outlook and work. Both shared an attitude of rebellion and hatred of the Church and religion, scientific orthodoxy, and despotism. Shaw's doctrine of the Life Force was not as direct as Butler's, whose outlook was more limited. [In Russian.]

2090 Wall, Vincent. BERNARD SHAW, PYGMALION TO MANY PLAYERS (Ann Arbor: U of Michigan P, 1973).
[A record of Shaw's relationship with the actors and especially the actresses who appeared in his plays. The point of view is that Shaw was creating a new kind of theater as he wrote his plays, and his working so closely with the actors provided a special opportunity to develop

a new theatrical style, s well as to act as mentor to a series of young women. Illustrated.]

2091 Weimer, Michael. "The Well-Tempered Performance: Shaw as a Critic of Music," YALE/THEATRE, IV (Summer 1973), 15-19.
Shaw the future dramatist is clearly visible beneath Shaw the music critic; he reviewed music as a theatrical situation. He was always antiformalist, feeling the creative genius of the composer must be served. Shaw recognized the advantages in conveying feeling of performed music over the spoken word, yet he respected controlled feeling. But he saw the real task of the critic to be the education of the public.

2092 Weintraub, Stanley. "*Don Juan*: A Timeless Play," NEW YORK SUNDAY NEWS, 14 Jan 1973, p. 14.
Don Juan in Hell is *the* twentieth century play.

2093 Weintraub, Stanley. "Four Fathers for Barbara" DIRECTIONS IN LITERARY CRITICISM. CONTEMPORARY APPROACHES TO LITERATURE, ed by Stanley Weintraub and Philip Young (University Park and Lond: Pennsylvania State UP, 1973), pp. 201-10.
Shaw was seldom as specific about the real-life models for characters as he was for those of *Major Barbara*. He suggested the play might be called *Andrew Undershaft's Profession*, and the profession was crucial for Shaw. Charles McEvoy, Alfred Nobel, Sir Basil Zaharoff and Fritz Krupp were models for Undershaft. For Krupp, life followed art when there was no male heir to the munitions wealth and power, and the succession fell to his daughter Bertha (1902) with another daughter, Barbara, disinherited. Bertha married a scholarly, obscure diplomat, hand-picked by the Kaiser, who took the name Krupp. Andrew Carnegie may have been in Shaw's mind for the Undershaft philanthropic philosophy, as well as George Cadbury and Ebenezer Howard. But the four fathers for Barbara are only a beginning to understanding Shaw's most complex play.

2094 Weintraub, Stanley. "Gleaning the Shaw Archives," SOUTH ATLANTIC QUARTERLY, LXXII (Winter 1973), 149-53.
Unfortunately the vast amount of Shaw material is being published unsystematically. Although THE CHUCKER-OUT

edited by Allan Chappelow (1969) and collected by him from
material particularly from the British Museum is poorly
organized, it is a vital Shaw source book.

2095 Weintraub, Stanley. "Introduction," "Notes on
the Critics," and "A *Saint Joan* Checklist," StJFYA,
pp. 3-7, 247-48, 249-55.
Criticism of *Saint Joan* generally has sustained Shaw's
high opinion of the play, although "with reservations
based upon everything from religion and politics to
rhetoric and polemics." The still-controversial Epilogue
may have been the basis of Shaw's conception. *Joan* shows
Shaw on the upswing from the bitterness of World War I.
Shaw as usual refused to cut the play to fit Broadway. It
was a popular success, and to it Shaw probably owed the
Nobel Prize. Fifty years of criticism are but a
beginning.

2096 Weintraub, Stanley (ed). SAINT JOAN FIFTY
YEARS AFTER 1923/24-1973/74 (Baton Rouge: Louisiana
State UP, 1973).
Contents, abstracted under date of first publication:
Weintraub, "Introduction" (1973); Walter Tittle, "Mr.
Bernard Shaw Talks about St. Joan," OUTLOOK (1924); James
Graham, "Shaw on *Saint Joan*," NYT (1924); Luigi
Pirandello, ["Bernard Shaw's *Saint Joan*"] "Pirandello
Distills Shaw," NEW YORK TIMES SUNDAY MAGAZINE (1924);
Jeanne Foster, ["A Super-Flapper"] TRANSLATIC REVIEW
(1924); Desmond MacCarthy, "*St Joan*: The Theme and the
Drama," NStat (1924); Edmund Wilson, ["*Saint Joan*: The
Unexpected in Shaw"] "Bernard Shaw since the War," NEW
REPUBLIC (1924); J. van Kan, "Bernard Shaw's *Saint Joan*:
An Historical Point of View," FORTNIGHTLY REVIEW (1925);
Johan Huizinga, ["Bernard Shaw's Saint"] "Bernard Shaw's
Heilige," DE GIDS (1925); John Mackinnon Robertson, "Mr.
Shaw and The Maid,'" from MR. SHAW AND "THE MAID" (1925);
T. S. Eliot, "Shaw, Robertson and 'The Maid,'" CRITERION
(1926); Charles Sarolea, "Has Mr. Shaw Understood Joan of
Arc?" ENGLISH REVIEW (1926); Edith J. R. Isaacs,
["Argumentative Martyrs"] "Saints and Lawmakers," TAM
(1936); Alick West, "*Saint Joan*: A Marxist View," from
GEORGE BERNARD SHAW: "A GOOD MAN FALLEN AMONG THE
FABIANS" (1950); Arland Ussher, "Joan As Unhappy
Trotskyist," from THREE GREAT IRISHMEN: SHAW, YEATS,
JOYCE (1952); E. J. West, "*Saint Joan*: A Modern Classic
Reconsidered," QUARTERLY JOURNAL OF SPEECH (1954); T. C.
Worsley, "An Irish Joan," NS & Nation (1954); Louis L.
Martz, ["The Saint as Tragic Hero"] "The Saint as Tragic

Hero: *Saint Joan* and MURDER IN THE CATHEDRAL," from
TRAGIC THEMES IN WESTERN LITERATURE (1955); Hans Stoppel,
"Shaw and Sainthood," ENGLISH STUDIES (1955); John
Fielden, "Shaw's *Saint Joan* as Tragedy," TWENTIETH CENTURY
LITERATURE (1957); J.I.M. Stewart, "That Sure Mark of
Greatness: *Saint Joan* and Its Imperfections," from "Shaw"
in EIGHT MODERN WRITERS (1963); Daniel C. Gerould, "*Saint
Joan* in Paris," Shaw R (1964); A. Obraztsova, "A People's
Heroine," from DRAMATURGICHESKII METOD BERNARDA SHOU
(1965); Weintraub, "Bernard Shaw's Other Saint Joan,"
SOUTH ATLANTIC QUARTERLY (1965); A. N. Kaul, ["Shaw's
Joan: The Hero as Saint"] "George Bernard Shaw: From
Anti-Romance to Pure Fantasy," from THE ACTION OF ENGLISH
COMEDY: STUDIES IN THE ENCOUNTER OF ABSTRACTION AND
EXPERIENCE FROM SHAKESPEARE TO SHAW (1970); Weintraub,
"Notes on the Critics," (1973); Weintraub, "A *Saint Joan*
Checklist (1973).

2097 Williams, George G[uion]., assisted by Marian
and Geoffrey Williams. GUIDE TO LITERARY LONDON
(Lond: B. T. Batsford, 1973), pp. 13, 15, 80, 94,
137, 145, 147, 168, 213, 229, 239, 265, 316, 333,
364.
[Literary Tours of London.]

2098 Wilson, Colin. THE OCCULT, A HISTORY (NY:
Random House, 1971; rptd NY: Vintage Books, 1973),
pp. 63, 135, 139, 291, 311, 336, 359, 392, 404, 539,
541, 563, 569, 570, 576.
[Passing references to Shaw and his works in a history of
human consciousness other than the normal waking sort.]

2099 Worth, Katharine J. REVOLUTIONS IN MODERN
BRITISH DRAMA (Lond: G. Bell & Sons, 1972), pp. 5,
6, 9, 67, 73-78, 84, 101-5, 115, 171-72.
John Osborne is one of Shaw's heirs. WEST OF SUEZ is
Heartbreak House updated. THE ENTERTAINER also has strong
affinities with *Heartbreak*, though Shaw relies more on the
reason of the audience. Luther is Osborne's equivalent to
Saint Joan. Osborne supplies the missing, unreasonable
notes in the Shavian debate. *Mrs. Warren's Profession*
foreshadows UNDER PLAIN COVER. Shaw subverted realism
within the convention of realism itself to shock the
audience, as in *The Simpleton of the Unexpected Isles*.
Too True to Be Good brings the stage illusion out in the
open. But for Shaw, analysis prevails.

1974

2100 Adams, Elsie. "Feminism and Female Stereotypes in Shaw," Shaw R, XVII (Jan 1974), 17-22; rptd in FF. Shaw has created unusual and powerful fictional women, but in departing from the nineteenth century stereotypes, he presents familiar types from Western Literature: temptress, goddess, mother, and the "emancipated" woman. In contrast with such treatment in his plays, his political statements challenge tradition. [The essay illustrates the types of women from Western Literature from the Gallery of Shaw's women characters.]

2101 Anthony, Piers (pseud of Piers Jacob). TRIPLE DETENTE (NY: Daw Books, 1974), pp. 40, 45, 61, 64, 72, 73, 76, 88, and passim.
[Science fiction novel that uses *The Revolutionist's Handbook and Pocket Companion*. Not seen.]

2102 Anzai, Tetsuo. "Mittsu no Doramatsurugi-- Shakespeare, Ibsen, Shaw" (Three Types of Drama- turgy--Shakespeare, Ibsen and Shaw), EIGUNGAKU TO EIGOGAKU (Sophia University, Tokyo), No. 10 (March 1974), 33-46.
From the viewpoint of the handling of Time there are three types of dramaturgy in European drama. The first is exemplified in Greek tragedy, in which the past governs the present and the action of the play always advances back to the past, not forward to the future. The second type is seen in the medieval mystery plays, where Time never runs back to the past. Time is linear in the second, while it is circular in the first. We may add the third type, which can be seen in the moralities and in many plays of Shakespeare and Beckett.

Almost all of Shaw's plays have the characteristics of the second type. [In Japanese.]

2103 Appia, H. "A propos de *Pygmalion*, George Bernard Shaw phoneticien" (Apropos *Pygmalion*, George Bernard Shaw the Phonetician), ÉTUDES ANGLAISES, XXVII (Jan-March 1974), 45-63.

Shaw's friends, Lecky, Bell, and Ellis, his association with R. Bridges in the phonetics battle, his work as chairman of the Advisory Committee on Spoken English at the B.B.C., his alphabet and his bequest to realize it, and *Pygmalion* all illustrate the preoccupation of Shaw with aspects of language that sociolinguists are now carefully studying. [Illustration of the Shaw alphabet and cover portrait.] [In French.]

2104 Aquino, John. "Shaw and C. S. Lewis's SPACE TRILOGY," Shaw R, XVII (Jan 1975), 28-32.
Although *Back to Methuselah* has never been very successful on the stage, it has had much influence on other works, most especially C. S. Lewis's SPACE TRILOGY (OUT OF THE SILENT PLANET, 1941; PERELANDRA, 1944; THAT HIDEOUS STRENGTH, 1946). In THE SCREWTAPE LETTERS, Lewis equates Shaw and the Life Force of *Man and Superman* with the Devil. In the SPACE TRILOGY, the character Weston is identified with Shaw, and some of his speeches are a rephrasing of Shaw's Life Force in *Methuselah* in order to refute it. Without knowledge of this, much of the trilogy is without reference.

2105 Bentley, Nicolas. EDWARDIAN ALBUM: A PHOTO-GRAPHIC EXCURSION INTO A LOST AGE OF INNOCENCE (Lond: Weidenfeld and Nicolson, 1974).
[Photograph of Shaw.] Shaw is the leading "anti-establishment figure of the day."

2106 Berst, Charles A. "The Craft of *Candida*," COLLEGE LITERATURE, I (Fall 1974), 157-73.
Half-truths--that Shaw is an intellectual playwright who wrote plays of ideas, that his characters are only his mouthpieces, that his structures are loose, and that his dialogue expands for its own sake--persist. "In *Candida* emotions and characterization are far more important than ideas, the characters are complex individuals greatly removed from Shaw, the structure is extremely tight, and the dialogue is masterfully concentrated.

2107 Böll, Heinrich. "George Bernard Shaw: an Herbert Wehner" (George Bernard Shaw: to Herbert Wehner), Ulrich Greiwe (ed), ALARMIERENDE BOT-SCHAFTEN, ZUR LAGE DER NATION (Alarming Tidings, On the Situation of the Nation) (Munich: Desch, 1974); rptd in Heinrich Böll, EINMISCHUNG ERWÜNSCHT (Suit-

able Mingling) (Köln: Kiepenheuer & Witsch, 1977),
pp. 148-56.
[Not seen.] [In German.]

2108 Brainerd, Barron, and Victoria Neufeldt. "On
[Solomon] Marcus' Methods for the Analysis of the
Strategy of a Play," POETICS, X (1974), 31-74.
[Brief commentary on *Caesar and Cleopatra* in the light of
Solomon Marcus's method put forward in POETICA MATHEMATICA
(Bucharest: Editura Acad. Rep. Soc. Romania, 1970) and
"Ein Mathematisch-linguistiches Dramenmodell" (A
Mathematical-linguistic Drama Model), ZEITSCHRIFT FÜR
LITERATURE WISSENSCHAFT UND LINGUISTIK I, 139-52.]

2109 Bryden, Ronald. "Pygmalion," P&P, XXI (June
1974), 30-31.
Pygmalion is so modern, Shaw seems to have been a prophet.
Eliza could be any former British colony with a crippling
legacy and refusing to stand on its own feet. [A review
of the play with Diana Rigg and Alec McCowen, praising the
production and comparing Shaw's play with MY FAIR LADY to
the latter's disadvantage. Illustrated.]

2110 Burgess, Anthony. "PLAYBOY Interview: Anthony
Burgess," PLAYBOY, XXI (Sept 1974), 69-86.
If America came back to the monarchical principle, Shaw's
prophecy in *The Apple Cart*, which nobody dares perform,
might be fulfilled. America comes back to England, and
all power moves to Washington.

2111 Chernikova, I. K. "Kharakter T͡sezari͡a v
'istorii' Shou T͡zezar' i Kleopatra" (The Character
of Caesar in Shaw's "History" *Caesar and Cleopatra*),
NAUCHNYE TRUDY SVERDLOVSKOGO PED. INSTITUTA
(Sverdlovsk), CCXVIII, (1974), 62-78.
Shaw sought to make Caesar an ideal, progressive political
activist-realist, fighting for the achievement of his
political program. His Caesar is the wise State activist,
politician and diplomat in peace-time, propagating Rome's
more developed civilization, seeking (like a Fabian) to
elevate the Egyptians to the cultural level of the Romans.
But the historical character in the play is woven from
contradictions, and his portrait depicts the profound
contradictions in the positive program of Shaw himself.
[In Russian.]

2112 Ciarletta, Nicola. AGNUS VOLONTARIO: DALLA
"PERSONA" ALLA PERSONA (Voluntary Lamb: From Char-
acter [Mask?] to Person) (Rome: Bulzoni, 1974).
[Not seen.   On *Man and Superman*, pp. 225-29; on *Saint
Joan*, pp. 312-17.] [In Italian.]

2113 Clurman, Harold. THE DIVINE PASTIME (NY:
Macmillan; Lond: Collier Macmillan, 1974), pp. 1,
2, 4, 5-6, 7, 14, 33, 34, 40, 41, 60, 91, 92, 102,
104, 116, 130, 175, 188, 193, 194, 195, 201, 202,
244, 307.
[A collection of essays and occasional pieces that
appeared from 1946 to 1974, which make passing reference
to Shaw.]

2114 Clurman, Harold. ALL PEOPLE ARE FAMOUS:
INSTEAD OF AN AUTOBIOGRAPHY (NY and Lond: Harcourt
Brace Jovanovich, 1974), pp. 7, 31, 57, 71, 227,
250, 261, 263.
[Several anecdotes about Shaw and his work.]

2115 Cole, Margaret. "H. G. Wells and the Fabian
Society," EDWARDIAN RADICALISM 1900-1914:   SOME
ASPECTS OF BRITISH RADICALISM, ed by A. J. A. Morris
(Lond and Bost: Routledge & Kegan Paul, 1974), pp.
97-98, 100, 103-4, 109, 111.
[An account of the row between H. G. Wells and the Fabian
Society much less sympathetic to the idea that Wells was
the genuine radical defeated by the reactionary Shaw,
Sidney and Beatrice Webb and Edward Pease than is usually
accepted.]

2116 "The Cowboy Picture," TIMES LITERARY SUPPLE-
MENT, 17 May 1974, p. 518.
[A photograph heading review of G. K. CHESTERTON, A
CENTENARY APPRAISAL, ed by John Sullivan, showing Shaw
among Lord Howard de Walden, William Archer, J. M. Barrie,
and G. K. Chesterton from a film devised by Barrie.]

2117 Crane, Gladys M. "Shaw and Women's Lib,"
ShawR, XVII (Jan 1974), 23-31; rptd FF; pp. 174-84.
Shaw's creation of women characters who were not
stereotypes was his blow for women's emancipation. Shaw's
heroines have in common with today's liberated women the
struggle to free themselves from stereotyped roles. They

are at odds with society, and they are superior to the male characters. Epifania Fitzfassenden in *The Millionairess* is economically independent and thereby has power over others, but she is not fully liberated because she values people according to their wealth. Lesbia Grantham in *Getting Married* rejects the traditional role of wife and mother, but she has nothing better. Vivie Warren of *Mrs. Warren's Profession* and Lina Szczepanowska of *Misalliance* are fully liberated. Both are attractive enough to have the choice of marriage or career; both are intelligent; both are economically independent. Joan of *Saint Joan* represents complete fulfillment and self-realization.

2118 Curtis, Anthony (ed). THE RISE AND FALL OF THE MATINEE IDOL (NY: St. Martins P, 1974), passim. [A collection of essays by various hands on the subject of those magnetic actors of the past 75 years called matinee idols, with references to Shaw and his plays.]

2119 Dargan, O. P. "Shaw through Indian Eyes," SHAVIAN, IV (Winter 1974), 297-99. Indian popular opinion is enthusiastic about Shaw's austere living. Indian teachers reject Shaw as a man who ridiculed the great things of life. A third opinion held by serious students of Shaw admires Shaw's works on the basis of the resemblance between them and traditional Indian thought.

2120 Davies, Robertson. "*Man and Superman*," TLS, 15 Feb 1974, p. 158. A mistake in the "Epistle Dedicatory" to *Man and Superman*, 'mille etre' for 'mille e tre', has been perpetuated in the Bodley Head Edition of 1971.

2121 Doherty, Brian. NOT BLOODY LIKELY, THE SHAW FESTIVAL: 1962-1973. (Canada: J. M. Dent (Canada), 1974). [History of Shaw Festival at Niagara-on-the-Lake, lavishly illustrated with photographs, especially of production.]

2122 Dolis, John J., Jr. "Bernard Shaw's *Saint Joan*: Language Is Not Enough," MASSACHUSETTS STUDIES IN ENGLISH, IV (Autumn 1974), 17-25.

The problem of language is central to *Saint Joan*. Joan's mistake is thinking that language is the sole basis for understanding between humans. She is a very convincing talker, but words bring about only misunderstanding. She uses language as a means of action rather than accepting the action inherent in the words; she confuses her will with the will of God. A complete understanding of her vision requires more than words, and at the end it is communicated to all, through gesture, not language.

2123 Drabble, Margaret. ARNOLD BENNETT: A BIOGRAPHY (Lond: Weidenfeld and Nicolson; NY: Alfred A. Knopf, 1974), pp. 87, 208, 210, 216, 241, 249, 253-54, 270, 284, 293-94, 298, 326, 354.
[References to Shaw's relations with Arnold Bennett.] Shaw had written *Annajanska* for Lillah Macarthy because she needed work to cheer herself up from the unhappiness of a foundering marriage. Beaverbrook said that *Saint Joan* was the greatest play that he had ever seen. Bennett did not like *Back to Methuselah* and fell asleep during the performance. He consoled Shaw for the bad performances of *Man and Superman*. Shaw on the occasion of the unveiling of a plaque at Bennett's birthplace praised him as one of the first writers to appreciate provincial life.

2124 Dukore, Bernard F. "*Widowers' Houses*: A Question of Genre," MD, XVII (March 1974), 27-32.
Shaw thwarts the audience's expectations. *Widowers' Houses* is like melodrama, the well-made play, and romantic comedy, but it is also different from all three. When Shaw allows Sartorius, the villain of conventional melodrama, "to justify himself under the existing social framework," Shaw indicts the audience. The features of the well-made play are employed only to be ignored or mocked. When the "hero" and "heroine" are united at the play's conclusion, the effect is to parody romantic comedy, the triumph of "dark forces" in the form of the happy ending. Shaw "delights disturbingly."

2125 Gielgud, John. EARLY STAGES (NY: Taplinger, 1974), xi, 4, 6, 46, 110-11.
[Anecdote of Shaw's reading and acting out *Arms and the Man*.]

2126 Goldstein, Malcolm. THE POLITICAL STAGE (NY: Oxford UP, 1974), passim.

[Brief mention of the appearance of Shaw's plays on the American stage.]

    2127 Green, Benny. "Benny Green on the Flaws in the
    Shavian Solution," Spec, CCXXXIII (10 Aug 1974),
    178-79.
Sexual passion and worldly envy are both missing from
Shaw's works, which shows that many problems deemed
insoluble are not problems or can easily be resolved.
Shaw's answer to the possible annihilation of man is the
wishful thinking of eugenics. [Review essay of the Bodley
Head *Plays and Prefaces of Bernard Shaw*; JOURNEY TO
HEARTBREAK, THE CRUCIBLE YEARS OF BERNARD SHAW 1914-1918,
ed by Stanley Weintraub (1971); and BERNARD SHAW AND THE
ART OF DRAMA, by Charles Berst (1973).]

    2128 Greer, Edward G. "Political Ploys and Plays,"
    DRAMA, CXIV (Autumn 1974), 27-32.
[A survey of American political drama, suggesting that the
importation of Shaw's plays influenced the generation of
S. N. Behrman, Philip Barry, and Robert Sherwood.]

    2129 Havighurst, Alfred F. RADICAL JOURNALIST: H.
    W. MASSINGHAM (Lond and NY: Cambridge UP. [Con-
    ference on British Studies Biographical Series],
    1974), passim.
[Shaw's friendship, personal and professional, with
Massingham, with many quotations from Shaw.]

    2130 Henderson, Lucile Kelling. "Shaw and Woman: A
    Bibliographical Checklist," ShawR, XVII (Jan 1974),
    60-[66]; expanded and rptd in FF.

    2131 Hess, Hans. GEORGE GROSZ (UK: Studio Vista;
    NY: Macmillan, 1974), p. 121.
[Costume Study of the Emperor for *Androcles and the Lion*.]

    2132 Jenkins, Alan. THE TWENTIES (NY: Universe
    Books, 1974), pp. 84, 89, 114, 115, 135, 188, 196,
    198, 201, 238.
[Shaw and the events of the Twenties. Photograph of
Prince Paul Trubetzkoy's portrait bust of Shaw.]

2133 Kantorovich, I. B.   "Polozhitel'nyi geroĭ v 'zhestokoi melodrame' Shou" (The Positive Hero in Shaw's "Cruel Melodrama"), NAUCHNYE TRUDY SVERDLOV-SKOGO PED. INSTITUT (Sverdlovsk), CCXVIII (1974), 62-79.
For all his external unlikenesses, Blanco Posnet is reminiscent of Marchbanks in his uncompromising attitude towards the falsity of surrounding society, helplessness in his struggle with surrounding evil, and his daring flights of thought in search for truth and fervent love of humanity. These traits are all confirmed in the dramatic action. The contrast between the two Posnet brothers reveals Blanco as disinterested and possessing humanistic ideals. The idea that man is naturally good but disfigured by the world of property and profiteering was confirmed by Renaissance Humanists. Shaw modernized the idea somewhat. His positive heroes are, by Creative Evolution, the predecessors of a generation permeated with the ideals of true humanists. Because of this ideal, Blanco Posnet emerges from a situation in which everyone is against him. But the positive hero of this "miniature melodrama" cannot be reduced to the traditional "little man," nor to his near equivalent, the "plain man." [In Russian.]

2134 Kelley, Nora.   "A Sketch of the Real Lucy Shaw," ISh, XIII (Fall 1974), 12.
Lucy Shaw was an exceptional woman. It is possible to detect a tender note in Shaw's words about Lucy.

2135 Kemp, Peter. MURIEL SPARK (Lond: Paul Elek, 1974; NY: Barnes & Noble, 1975), p. 94.
[Quotation from postcard, signed G.B.S. from THE PRIME OF MISS JEAN BRODIE.]

2136 Kenny, Herbert A. LITERARY DUBLIN, A HISTORY (NY: Taplinger; Dublin: Gill & Macmillan; Lond: Macmillan, 1974), pp. 15, 18, 98, 115, 166, 173, 178, 184, 196-98, 210-12, 222, 233, 239, 320.
[Brief biographical reference to Shaw. Illustrated with a drawing by Charles Carrol after the Karsh photograph.]

2137 Kerr, Walter.   "A *Devil's Disciple* Unencumbered by Shaw," NYT, 18 Aug 1974, II, p. 1.

The Devil's Disciple is becoming a better play every year. Until The Niagara-on-the-Lake production the two elements of mockery and melodrama did not mix, because we do not apologize for melodrama any more and because we are not waiting to hear Shaw say anything new. It is all Shaw now. Nothing similar will happen to *Too True to Be Good*. The production of *The Admirable Bashville* has missed the point of the parody of Shakespeare.

2138 Kleinhans, Charles Nelson. "Toward a Generic Definition of Late Nineteenth Century Farce: Courteline, Feydeau, Pinero, Wilde, Shaw and Jarry," DAI, XXXIV (1974), 5180A. Unpublished dissertation, Indiana University, 1973.

2139 Lambert, J. W. "Plays in Performance, London," DRAMA, CXIX (Autumn 1974), 36-55.
[Review of an indifferent production of *Pygmalion*. Photograph.]

2140 Langhorne, Elizabeth. NANCY ASTOR AND HER FRIENDS (NY and Washington: Praeger, 1974), pp. 36, 56, 112-15, 119, 121-23, 132, 136, 138, 141-42, 146-49, 203, 235, 244-46, 249, 253-54, 258, 260.
[Describes Shaw's friendship with Nancy Astor. Illustrated with photos of Shaw.]

2141 Langner, Lawrence. "Saint Bernard and Saint Joan," ShawR, XVII (Sept 1974), 114-23.
[A brief play that parodies *Saint Joan* with an introduction of Stephen Grecco summarizing Shaw's and Langner's discussion over the length of *Joan*.]

2142 Larson, Gale K. (ed). *Caesar and Cleopatra*, by Bernard Shaw (Indianapolis and NY: Bobbs-Merrill [Bobbs-Merrill Shaw Series], 1974).
[Text of *Caesar and Cleopatra* with Introduction, Chronology, Bibliography, Notes, Illustrations, and Shavian Reviews and Comments.]

2143 Laurence, Dan H. "What's Your Opinion, Mr. Shaw?" LIBRARY CHRONICLE, ns No 8 (Fall 1974 [1976]), 53-59.

[Shaw's solutions for the problem of satisfying the demands of journalists while protecting his privacy and himself from misquotation. Illustrated with letters and postcards.]

2144 Lefcourt, Charles R. "*Major Barbara*: An Exercise in Shavian Wit and Wisdom," ENGLISH RECORD, XXV (Spring 1974), 27-29.
Shaw grows more relevant, especially in Freshman classes. [Discussion of reaction of students to a first reading of Shaw and possible assignments for them.]

2145 Lindblad, Ishrat. "*Household of Joseph*: An Early Perspective on Shaw's Dramaturgy," Shaw R, XVII (Sept 1974), 124-38.
The fragment of the juvenile verse play, *Household of Joseph* reveals Shaw launching his lifelong attack on orthodox Christianity and the institution of the family. It also contains thinly disguised autobiographical material. Since the manuscript is dated February 1878, it proves Shaw had turned to playwriting earlier than his failure as a novelist. Both Jesus and Judas are realists, and one of the ways they reveal themselves is through their tendency to philander. But Jesus is a poet, and Judas is Shaw's real protagonist. Shaw later in his prefaces identified Jesus with the rebel's role, although he never again put him in the play. The pattern of the friendship between the poetic Jesus and the rational philosopher Judas is one that continued to appear in the early plays. Although JESUS CHRIST SUPERSTAR and GODSPELL allow for the idea of a rebellious Jesus, *Household* differs from them in that Shaw does not idealize Jesus as an extraordinary man; following the Biblical story, but inventing incidents, Shaw attempts to pull the pedestal from under Jesus' feet.

2146 Lutz, Jerry. PITCHMAN'S MELODY: SHAW ABOUT "SHAKESPEAR" (Lewisburg, Pennsylvania: Bucknell UP, 1974).
Putting Shakespeare to Use. Shaw related Shakespeare to his own life, his background, love, death of relatives and personal income, but it was to satisfy his ego, not to illuminate his biography. In redrawing the characters of *Caesar and Cleopatra*, Shaw did not claim to be a better playwright than Shakespeare, though he had little respect for Shakespeare's moral philosophy. Shaw's Principles of Criticism. His criticism of Shakespeare was determined by

the prevailing attitude of mindless adoration. In the Preface to *Overruled* Shaw said that a play should reflect life, but he was not consistent; in "The Author's Apology" to *Mrs. Warren's Profession* he argued that drama is the presentation of a parable to teach the audience. In 1939 in *Our Theatres in the Nineties* he explained that he would have been kinder to Shakespeare if he had not been so taken up with promoting Ibsen and Wagner. Music and thought: Shakespeare vs. Ibsen. Shaw could not resist making fun even at the expense of Ibsen as he does in *The Philanderer*. Shaw went overboard in praising Brieux and was deceived by Brieux's social criticism into believing that Brieux was a good playwright. In the Preface to *Back to Methuselah* Shaw accused Ibsen of pessimism. Shaw did not write plays on the Ibsen model but went back to the classical style. In spite of his written antagonism to Shakespearean music, Shaw was a word-musician in his own plays. But Shaw felt that Shakespeare was the supreme dramatic musicmaker, and that productions of Shakespeare should appeal musicmaker, and that productions of Shakespeare should appeal primarily to the ear, not to the mind. Shakespeare has two major deficiencies: he wrote no prefaces and there are few stage directions. Shakespearean Production. Shaw's best criticism is of the production of Shakespeare's plays. Shaw admired William Poel, the originator of the Elizabethan revival in staging, especially for his efforts to restablish the precedence of the playwright over the actor and the scene painter. But Shaw ignored Poel's defects. He found his ideal actor in Poel's production of RICHARD II, Harley Granville Barker. Shaw said that the author could learn about his characters from the actors, but he never mentioned an actor who taught him anything. [Shaw's views on contemporary actors.] The Exposure Exposed. Shaw's Shakespearean criticism tells us more about himself than about Shakespeare. By his own definition Shaw was an "original thinker," one who criticized the accepted ideas of his time, but not one who originated new ideas. He denied his originality in dramatic technique. The construction of his plays was influenced by music. Shaw wanted the moderns, himself and Ibsen, to take their place beside Shakespeare, not replace him.

2147 McCauley, Jamie Caves. "Kipling on Woman: A New Source for Shaw," ShawR, XVII (Jan 1974), 40-44; rptd in FF.
"Rikki-Tikki-Tavi," the name of the mongoose in Kipling's THE JUNGLEBOOK, is the source of Ann's diminutive for Octavius in *Man and Superman*, but Shaw has more in common

with Kipling's book than the name. Kipling comes close to
anti-Darwinism in history, suggesting a purpose in the
universe. He shows the male dominated by the female, who
is driven by a desire to nurture her young. Kipling
alludes to Nag the cobra in a later poem entitled THE
FEMALE OF THE SPECIES, which is a sort of poetic version
of the philosophy in *Superman*. Although Kipling's ideas
on the male-female relationship are commonplaces of the
time, Shaw's ironic use of the name "Ricky-Ticky-Tavy"
cannot be coincidental.

2148 McDowell, Frederick P. W. "Bernard Shaw:
Writer of 'The Grand School,'" JOURNAL OF MODERN
LITERATURE, III (April 1974), 1039-44.
Shaw's letters are almost inexhaustible for their
significance to the student of Shaw and of Edwardian
literature and culture. [Review-essay of BERNARD SHAW:
COLLECTED LETTERS, 1898-1910, ed by Dan Laurence (1972).]

2149 McDowell, Frederick P. W. "George Bernard
Shaw," JOURNAL OF MODERN LITERATURE, III (Feb 1974),
772-78.
[Review essay of Shavian scholarship and criticism.]

2150 Manvell, Roger, CHAPLIN (Bost and Toronto:
Little, Brown [The Library of World Biography],
1974), pp. 15, 163-64, 181, 183, 206, 223.
[References to Shaw and Chaplin.]

2151 Mason, Michael. "*Caesar and Cleopatra*: A
Shavian Exercise in Both Hero-Worship and Belittle-
ment," HUMANITIES ASSOCIATION REVIEW, XXV (Winter
1974), 1-10.
Caesar is Shaw's full-length portrait of political genius.
In order to avoid idolatry, Shaw emphasizes Caesar's
foibles. But he stabilized the Roman world and prepared
for imperial destiny. He is above pettiness, genuinely
original, always in control of himself. But Shaw is
pessimistic: Caesar's achievements in Egypt will be
undone by his assassination and Cleopatra's infatuation
for Antony. Shaw portrayed Cleopatra as an unstable and
uneducated woman, but this is false and done only to increase Caesar's stature.

2152 Mason, Michael. "*Captain Brassbound's Conversion*: A Coat of Many Colours," SIGNUM, I (May 1974), 23-29.
The inspiration for *Captain Brassbound's Conversion* is from Ellen Terry, Shelley's THE WITCH OF ATLAS, Cunninghame Graham's MOGREB-EL-AKSA, Mary Kingsley and her TRAVELS IN WEST AFRICA, and Edward John Eyre and the land problems in the West Indies.

2153 Mattus, Martha Elizabeth. "The 'Fallen Woman' in the *fin de siecle* English Drama: 1884-1914," DAI, XXXV (1975), 4738A. Unpublished dissertation, Cornell University, 1974.

2154 Meredith, Burgess. "A Marchbanks Fondly Recalls His Candida," NYT, 16 June 1974, II, p. 3.
[Meredith remembers Katharine Cornell with whom he played in *Candida* in 1942.]

2155 Mikhail, E. H., and John O'Riordan (eds). THE STING AND THE TWINKLE, CONVERSATIONS WITH SEAN O'CASEY (Lond: Macmillan P; NY: Barnes and Noble, 1974), pp. 3, 4, 5, 16, 21, 30, 43, 44, 46, 53, 62, 66-67, 68-69, 75, 76, 83, 84, 85, 87, 101, 105, 107, 116, 124, 131, 133, 153, 160.
[Comments about O'Casey, citing Shaw, by: Lady Gregory, Constance Vaughan, George Walter Bishop, Leslie Rees, J. L. Hodson, Bosley Crowther, Maurice Brown, Dom Wulstan Phillipson, O.S.B., Boris Izakov, Robert Emmett Ginna, Joseph Stein, Saros Cowasjee, W. J. Weatherby, Niall Carroll, John O'Riordan, and David Krause.]

2156 Mix, Katherine Lyon. MAX AND THE AMERICAS (Brattleboro, Vermont: Stephen Greene P, 1974), pp. 20, 44, 45, 78-80, 86, 92, 158.
[Shaw's relations with Max Beerbohm and James Gibbons Huneker.]

2157 Mouton, Janice Malmsten. "Joan of Arc on the Twentieth-Century Stage: Dramatic Treatments of the Joan of Arc Story by Bertolt Brecht, George Bernard Shaw, Jean Anouilh, Georg Kaiser, Paul Claudel, and Maxwell Anderson," DAI, XXXV (1974), 3693A. Unpublished dissertation, Northwestern University, 1974.

2158 Nathan, Rhoda B. "The Shavian Sphinx," ShawR, XVII (Jan 1974), 45-52; rptd in FF.
The idea of woman as sphinx is neither new nor exclusive to Shaw. He combined the malign, female Greek sphinx with the benign, awe-inspiring Egyptian sphinx. The essence of both sphinxes is mystery and enigma. Not all Shaw's heroines are sphinxes. Cleopatra is not. Shaw's sphinx embodies female wisdom. Candida possesses the necessary power, charm, and authority. Hesione Hushabye of *Heartbreak House* and Ann Whitefield of *Man and Superman* are more siren than sphinx, but they are true sphinxes. Jennifer Dubedat of *The Doctor's Dilemma* is a mini-sphinx. Mrs. George of *Getting Married* is "the *echt* sphinx of the Shavian canon."

2159 Nickson, Richard. "G.B.S. Versus U.S.A.," ISh, XIII (Fall 1974), 13.
Americans are rabidly anti-Shavian. [Humorous survey of American attitudes toward Shaw.]

2160 "No Consummmation," List, XCII (14 Nov 1974), 638.
Shaw really believed that "words, which he could control, were preferable to reality, which he could not." [Report of Bernard Levin broadcast at Ayot St. Lawrence. Photograph.]

2161 Obraztŝova, Anna Georgeievna. BERNARD SHOU I EVROPEĬSKAIÂ TEATRAL'NAIÂ KUL'TURA (Bernard Shaw and European Theatrical Culture) (Moscow: "Nauka," 1974).
For Shaw, the theater and drama were weapons for enlightening and improving mankind. Innovative actors and producers were essential in this process. In his search for "heroic" players, Shaw had dealings with Mrs. Campbell, Granville Barker and numerous others. Both Shaw and Stanislavskii were reformers in the theater, though Stanislavskii did not introduce Shaw's plays into the Soviet Union, and indeed they occupied diametrically opposed positions. However, both protested during the first decade of the twentieth century against injustices in social reality and in art. Both sought to widen the aesthetic possibilities of the theater. The synthesis of drama and music was one of the complex processes which occurred at the end of the nineteenth century. Shaw regarded himself as a student of Wagner as well as of Ibsen, and composition is an important element in his

dramaturgy, i.e. the organization of many layers of discussion, though the one-act plays have their own laws. He was concerned with tempo, rhythm contrast and set pieces, such as duets.

Brecht frequently called Shaw his teacher. Brecht and Shaw believed that Socialist transformation was essential and that the theater was a tribune for the propagation of ideas. [In Russian.]

2162 Okumura, Saburo. "Pinero no Tanqueray no Gosai--Igirisukindaigeki no Ichi Keitai" (Pinero's THE SECOND MRS. TANQUERAY--a Type of Modern English Drama), JINBUN KENKYU (Osaka Municipal University, Osaka), XXVI (Oct 1974), 268-86.
Shaw wrote *Mrs. Warren's Profession* as a corrective to Pinero's SECOND MRS. TANQUERAY. His intention was to revitalize characters who were dwarfed by Pinero. [In Japanese.]

2163 Parker, John, MP. "The Search for Jessie Holliday: An Historical Account," SHAVIAN, IV (Summer 1974), 284-90.
[An account of the search to identify Jessie Holliday (1884-1915), who was an ardent admirer of Shaw, had done a water color and many sketches of Shaw, and had named her son Shaw.]

2164 Peart, Barbara. "DeQuincey and Marchbanks," ShawR, XVII (Sept 1974), 139-40.
The incident in *Candida* where Marchbanks thought he could not get any money on a seven day bill until the seven days were up is based on an anecdote reported in David Masson's DE QUINCEY. The name "Marchbank" is discussed in a lengthy footnote in De Quincey's AUTOBIOGRAPHY 1785-1803. Marchbanks is also modelled on the young Shaw, Yeats, and Shelley.

2165 Pedersen, Lisë. òShakespeare's THE TAMING OF THE SHREW vs. Shaw's *Pygmalion*: Male Chauvinism vs. Women's Lib?" ShawR, XVII (Jan 1974), 32-39; rptd in FF.
Pygmalion seems deliberately to challenge and contradict THE TAMING OF THE SHREW. Petruchio and Higgins are both bullies. Petruchio resorts to physical abuse in order to "tame" Kate. Higgins bullies Eliza because he bullies

everyone. Kate's test is her response to her husband's order; Eliza's test is her success at impersonating a duchess. In each there is a wager on the outcome, and both women pass with ease. Christopher Sly and Alfred Doolittle are parallel in that both imply a commentary on the major plot as they are transformed socially. In June 1888 Shaw wrote a letter to the PALL MALL GAZETTE signed Horatia Ribbonson asking a boycott of SHREW because Petruchio was a money-hunting bully who tamed his wife by breaking her spirit. The differences between SHREW and *Pygmalion* are in "the methods by which the woman is transformed and in the final attitudes of the man and the woman toward each other." Both women must gain self-control. Eliza recognizes at the end that she, like Higgins, had been unable to control herself, and that Pickering, not Higgins, has set her a good example for good behavior. Kate submits to Petruchio, but Eliza exults in being free from Higgins's domination, and Higgins shares her view. Shaw dramatized his criticism of Shakespeare, that he had failed to create a morality opposed to the conventional one of his time.

2166 Perry, George. THE GREAT BRITISH PICTURE SHOW, FROM THE 90s TO THE 70s. (NY: Hill and Wang, 1974), pp. 10, 52, 58, 65, 83, 84, 89, 110-11, 201-2, 274.
[Shaw and the movies: *How He Lied to Her Husband, Pygmalion, Major Barbara, Caesar and Cleopatra, Androcles and the Lion, The Millionairess,* and *The Devil's Disciple.*]

2167 Petzold, Dieter. "Aspekte des Dramas: George Bernard Shaw, *Saint Joan*" (Aspects of the Drama: George Bernard Shaw, *Saint Joan*), EINFÜHRUNG IN DAS STUDIUM DER ENGLISCHEN LITERATUR (Introduction to the Study of English Literature), ed by Jobst-Christian Rojahn (Heidelberg: Quelle & Meyer, 1974), pp. 104-20.
[An introduction to the analysis of drama. Discusses the following aspects of *Saint Joan*: unity of action, plot as structural action, the logical connecting of the parts of action, the ways of characterizing, 'real' persons vs. types, language and the producing of illusion, language as a medium of character, unity of time, the producing of suspense, the presentation of the past in the drama, analytical drama, anachronism.] [In German.]

2168 Quinn, Martin. "Dickens and *Misalliance*," ShawR, XVII (Sept 1974), 141-43.
Shaw's personal involvement with Dickens emerges through the many allusions and references in the Preface to *Misalliance*, "Parents and Children."

2169 Ray, Gordon. H. G. WELLS AND REBECCA WEST (New Haven: Yale UP, 1974), pp. 1, 2, 27, 98, 175.
[Brief references to Shaw.]

2170 Redmond, James. "A Misattributed Speech in *Man and Superman*," TLS, 18 Jan 1974, 60.
Despite the care that Shaw took over the printing of *Man and Superman*, he allowed one awkward corruption to appear in the first act in the second half of a speech attributed to Octavius. It clearly should be spoken by Ann.

2171 Riewald, J. G. (edited with introduction). THE SURPRISE OF EXCELLENCE: MODERN ESSAYS ON MAX BEERBOHM (Hamden, Conn: Archon Books, 1974), passim.
Essays are organized under various titles, accompanied by a bibliographical note. Contents abstracted under year of first publication. Essays with only passing use of Shaw's name are not listed. Guy Boas, "The Magic of Max," BLACKWOOD'S MAGAZINE, CCLX (Nov 1946), 341-350; Edmund Wilson, "An Analysis of Max Beerbohm," NY (1 May 1948), 80-86; Katherine Lyon Mix, "Max on Shaw," ShawR, VI (Sept 1963), 100-104; Edmund Wilson, "A Miscellany of Max Beerbohm," originally "Meetings with Max Beerbohm," ENCOUNTER, XXI (Dec 1963), 16-22; W. H. Auden, "One of the Family," NY (23 Oct 1965), 227-244; Bruce R. McElderry, Jr., "Max Beerbohm: Essayist, Caricaturist, Novelist," ON STAGE AND OFF: EIGHT ESSAYS IN ENGLISH LITERATURE (1968), pp. 76-86.

2172 Robinson, Gabriele Scott. "The Shavian Affinities of John Whiting," ShawR, XVII (May 1974), 86-98.
John Whiting encountered Shaw twice; once as a child at a luncheon and once at the beginning of WW II, windowshopping in Piccadilly. [A comparison of Whiting's character, ideas, dramatic techniques with those of Shaw.]

2173 Rodriguez-Seda, Asela C.   "George Bernard Shaw
in the Hispanic World: His Reception and Influence," DAI, XXXIV (1974), 7779A.   Unpublished dissertation,   University   of   Illinois   (Urbana-
Champaign),   1973.

2174 Schoeps, Karl-Heinz.   BERTOLT BRECHT UND
BERNARD SHAW (Bertolt Brecht and Bernard Shaw)
(Bonn: Bouvier [Studien zur Germanistik, Anglistik
und Komparatistik, 26], 1974).
There is no question that Brecht was familiar with most if
not all of Shaw's plays, since they constituted a large
part of Germany's theater fare before 1933, especially in
Berlin,   where   Brecht   had   lived   since   1924.   Brecht
referred   to Shaw on several occasions,   but his most
outstanding testimony of his indebtedness to Shaw is his
"Ovation for Shaw," written in 1926 as part of a
congratulatory address for Shaw's seventieth birthday.
Unquestionably there are many elements in Shaw's work for
which Brecht had no use.   But both playwrights were
vociferous social critics whose writings were intended to
bring about change in the society in which they lived.   To
this end they used similar dramatic techniques and themes
and drew upon similar traditions.   For both Brecht and
Shaw the stage became a forum for political instruction.
But to make their message more palatable to the
theatergoer,   they generally presented it in a very
entertaining way.   Aristotelian catharsis and empathy,
which stood in the way of the learning process they hoped
to start in the mind of the spectator, were replaced by
anti-illusionary or so-called alienation effects.   Both
Brecht and Shaw were also keenly aware that in using this
method   they   were   following   a   long   tradition;   they
repeatedly referred to Aristophanes, Beaumarchais, Gay,
Molière, Shelley, Swift, and particularly Shakespeare.
The theater of their own day and the bible provided them
with ample material to shape their own plays--mostly in
the form of counter-convention.   Despite many differences
between Brecht and Shaw, we can be sure that Brecht was
influenced by Shaw's work--not in a narrow, positivistic
sense, but in the form of catalytic impulses originating
from new and pioneering concepts.   In the works of Shaw,
Brecht found a confirmation of his own ideas about drama,
particularly during the incubation period of his epic
theater in the late 1920's.   [In German.]

2175 Schoeps, Karl-Heinz.   "Epic Structures in the
Plays of Bernard Shaw and Bertolt Brecht," ESSAYS ON

BRECHT, THEATER AND POLITICS, ed by Siegfried Mews and Herbert Knust (Chapel Hill: U of North Carolina P [U of North Carolina Studies in the Germanic Languages and Literatures], 1974), pp. 28-43.

2176 Schotter, Richard David. "Shaw's Stagecraft: A Theatrical Study of *Pygmalion*," DAI, XXXIV (1974), 5991A. Unpublished dissertation, Columbia University, 1970.

2177 Sidnell, Michael J. "*Misalliance*: Sex, Socialism and the Collectivist Poet," MD, XVII (June 1974), 125-39.
In Shaw's plays the voice of the playwright is heard so strongly along with the characters's that it is a principle of construction. In *Misalliance* Hypatia's "Papa: buy the brute for me" climaxes the plot and also couples sex and Socialism. The word "brute" reminds the audience it is still in the carnal era and is part of the animal imagery of the play. Johnny is the complacent animal. Bentley and Lina are people of the future, advanced in the evolutionary process, and with whom nature will eventually catch up. Hypatia and Percival are a "realistic accommodation with present norms." [Contains a digression on the difference between Shaw and Zamyatin's WE on the one hand and Huxley's BRAVE NEW WORLD and Orwell's 1984 on the other: Shaw appreciates the positive possibilities of the race for reason and detachment.]

2178 Smith, J. Percy. "*You Never Can Tell*: Shaw and the Melting Mood," WASCANA REVIEW, IX (Fall 1974), 25-41.
Shaw's choice of comedy was partly a matter of taste and talent, but it was also supported by philosophical insights. He had little patience with laughter of the "mere ribtickling variety." Shaw recognized that *You Never Can Tell* could be seen as farce. The opening situation of family divisions is not inherently or necessarily comic; the accidental opportunity for reconciliation allows for the comic spirit. At the end of Act II, in what ought to be a *moving* episode, Gloria recognizes the sterility of her rational education, and Valentine understands that nothing in his past has prepared him for the depth of his feeling. For each it is a moment of perception of coming fulfillment and also of loss--of freedom. If we are not in the melting mood at the play's conclusion, the play has failed. This mixture

of laughter and tears goes beyond Meredithian and Bergsonian views of comedy to Shakespeare's "tender laughter
of reconciliation." Shaw lacked anything like the Elizabethan world view that Shakespeare could depend on. That
he constructed his own Shavian world-picture is the mark
of his genius. Shaw's world-picture contains the element
of possibility, and that contributes to the quite un-
Shakespearian tone of his comedies.

2179 Smith, T[homas]. W. NOTES ON BERNARD SHAW:
HEARTBREAK HOUSE (Bath: James Brodie, [Notes on
Chosen English Texts], n.d. [1974?]).
[Study notes.]

2180 Somers, John Wilmot. "The Sources and
Aesthetics of Modern Drama," DAI, XXXV (1974),
1287A. Unpublished dissertation, University of
Missouri, 1973.

2181 Tetzeli, Kurt von Rosador. "The Natural
History of *Major Barbara*," MD, XVII (June 1974),
141-53.
Major Barbara derives its consistency from Shaw's theory
of history. His "view of history as natural history leads
to an analysis of the nature of man and society in socio-
economic and metabiological or religious terms"; "while
the socio-economic dimension of man and society is fully
drawn, the metabiological side is, owing to its future
perspective, treated less extensively, thus connecting
social actuality and possible biological advance, present
diagnosis and future hope only briefly and rather
tentatively."

2182 Trebilcock, Clive. "Radicalism and the
Armament Trust," EDWARDIAN RADICALISM 1900-1914:
SOME ASPECTS OF BRITISH RADICALISM, ed by A.J.A.
Morris (Lond and Bost: Routledge & Kegan Paul,
1974), pp. 180-201.
Dramatic license might be allowed Shaw in his hyperbolic
attack on the armament industry in *Major Barbara*, but
there is no excuse for others who claimed that the government was under control of the Armament Trust.

2183 Turco, Alfred, Jr. "Ibsen, Wagner, and Shaw's
Changing View of Idealism," ShawR, XVII (May 1974)

78-85; rptd as part of Chap 3, SHAW'S MORAL VISION
(Ithaca, NY and Lond: Cornell UP, 1976), pp. 108-
19.
Critics who judge *The Quintessence of Ibsenism* and *The
Perfect Wagnerite* as attempts to read Socialism into Ibsen
and Wagner are unfair. *Wagnerite* is the ideological
successor to *Quintessence*. Wagner's giants, gods and
heroes are the equivalent of Philistines, idealists, and
realists. The dwarfs are really a perversion of human
nature. *Wagnerite* is important to understand Shaw's
development. In *Quintessence* Shaw lumped all kinds of
idealism together; in the *Wagnerite* he distinguishes
between Frika and Loki, symbolizing the "Lie that must
. . . hide the truth," and Wotan, symbolizing "action
seeking to realize ideals in deeds." Shaw's earliest
dramas "subverted all forms of idealistic aspiration," but
in the dramas of the mid and late 1890's a change is
discernible in characterization: Marchbanks, Dick Dudgeon
and Caesar represent man caring more about Life, but less
about their own lives. Shaw measured Ibsen's characters
by the life they have risen above, but Wagner's by the
life they fall short of. "The idealist's tragedy [is]
more compelling than the realist's triumph." This
reflects Shaw's growing doubts about immediate solutions
for the world's problems.

2184 Twain, Mark. "Mental Telegraphy?" ShawR, XVII
(May 1974), 69-70.
[The beginning of an article by Samuel Clemens on the
similarity between his "The Late Rev. Sam Jones's
Reception in Heaven" and Shaw's "Aerial Football, the New
Game." Published for the first time and followed by
Shaw's story.] Shaw must have gotten the incidents for
his story out of my head by "thought-transference" because
we did not talk of my article. I believe in mental
telegraphy.

2185 Usigli, Rodolfo. CONVERSACIONES Y ENCUENTROS
(Conversations and Encounters) (Mexico: Organiza-
ción Editorial Novaro, 1974). [Not seen.] [In
Spanish.]

2186 Watson, Barbara Bellow. "The New Woman and the
New Comedy," ShawR, XVII (Jan 1974), 2-16; rptd in
FF.
When Shaw thinks about women, he makes no assumptions.
This change in the treatment of women changed the struc-

ture of comedy. Instead of the conflict of the individual
with social institutions, Shaw presents the conflict between the "individual woman's humanity and the rigidity of
the sex role assigned to her." Women are subversive
rebels. In *Captain Brassbound's Conversion* Lady Cicely
escapes marriage. Eliza in *Pygmalion* is not swept into
Professor Higgins's arms; she finds herself. In *Getting
Married* the argument demonstrates a woman's "need to preserve a self in spite of marriage." *Man and Superman*
seems to be a problem for feminists. But Ann explains
that she can be herself, not an idea, married to Jack
because he has no illusions about her. Ann is devious
only because society insists she be. To assume that
Shaw's polar mother-woman and artist-man is an eternal
principle is wrong. The heroine of *The Millionairess* is
the incarnation of the radical woman. The women in
Village Wooing and *Too True to Be Good* are even more to
this point. Joan's martyrdom in *Saint Joan* results from
her conflict with the illogical woman role. In *Major
Barbara* the woman's story is primary. The interesting
question in *Candida* is *why* she makes her choice. Although
the dominance of the women in *Heartbreak House* is one of
the signs of decadence, it is healthier than the male
submission. The main idea in *The Apple Cart* is really a
variant on the theme of feminine rebellion: Magnus's role
of king does not fit him as a man. In *The Quintessence of
Ibsenism* Shaw recognized that "the woman's revolt would
come first because the woman's enslavement was more complete," and that she would be a model for revolting
against roles.

2187 Wearing, J. P.   THE COLLECTED LETTERS OF SIR
ARTHUR PINERO (Minneapolis: U of Minnesota P; Lond:
Oxford UP, 1974), pp. 12-13, 169, 209, 214-15, 216-
27, 234-38, 240-48, 251, 260-61, 266, 289.
Pinero and Shaw got to know each other through their work
for the Society of Authors, but though they shared
business and professional concerns, their relationship was
never close. [Letters to Shaw and also mentioning Shaw.]

2188 Weightman, John.   "Art Versus Life," ENCOUNTER,
XLIII (Sept 1974), 57-59.
Seeing the revival of *Pygmalion* and productions of David
Storey's LIFE CLASS and Tom Stoppard's TRAVESTIES raises
the questions "What is art? What is life? Does the term
'realism' make any sense?" *Pygmalion* is stagey, but
stageyness "is a way of being realistic by unrealistic
means." Shaw shows the real-life art product, Eliza,

transcending the artist, Higgins. She becomes a whole person but the end does not quite ring true. Shaw could not believe in a full physical and intellectual relationship, and therefore his play is a notch below Molière's L'ECOLE DES FEMMES.

2189 Weiler, Peter. "William Clarke: The Making and Unmaking of a Fabian Socialist," JOURNAL OF BRITISH STUDIES, XIV (Nov 1974), 77-108.
Clarke shared the views of Fabians like Shaw concerning the "nouvelle couche sociale," but disagreed with Shaw about ultimate ethical and philosophical aims.

2190 Weimer, Michael. "Shaw's Conversion Plays, 1897-1909," DAI, XXXIV (1974), 7253A. Unpublished dissertation, Yale University, 1973.

2191 Weintraub, Rodelle. "The Gift of Imagination. An Interview with Clare Boothe Luce," Shaw R, XVII (Jan 1974), 53-59; rptd in FF.
I began to read Shaw when I was fourteen, and he fixed in my mind the idea that I wanted to be a playwright. [Mrs. Luce recalls a meeting with Shaw and her appearance as Candida.] No women comparable to Shaw's female characters exist in the American theater. Shaw was a weak political philosopher but a great playwright.

2192 Weintraub, Rodelle. "'Mental Telegraphy?': Mark Twain on G.B.S.," ShawR, XVII (May 1974), 68.
[A brief description of Shaw's meeting with Samuel Clemens and the resemblance between Shaw's "Aerial Football, the New Game," and Clemens's THE LATE REV. SAM JONES'S RECEPTION IN HEAVEN, both of which appeared after the meeting.]

2193 W[eintraub], S[tanley]. "Shaw, George Bernard," ENCYCLOPEDIA BRITANNICA, Macropaedia, XVI (Chicago et al: Encyclopaedia Britannica, 1974.) 655-59.
Shaw is the most significant British playwright since the seventeenth century; he is more than the best comic dramatist of his time; some of his greatest works are unmatched by his stage contemporaries for their high seriousness and prose beauty. [Biography and career. Major works and Bibliography.]

2194 Weintraub, Stanley. WHISTLER: A BIOGRAPHY
(NY: Weybright and Talley, 1974), pp. 103, 182-83,
215, 312, 325, 326, 366.
Shaw may have borrowed Rosetti's attitude toward patrons
for Dubedat in *The Doctor's Dilemma*. Shaw based some of
his characters in *Immaturity* on the Lawson family. He
felt Whistler's lawyer in the Ruskin case had bungled in
not claiming damages on "the basis of loss to his
commercial" reputation. [Unfavorable Shaw comment on
Whistler's exhibit, "Notes, Harmonies, and Nocturnes" and
of a William Stott nude.]

2195 Wharton, John F. LIFE AMONG THE PLAYWRIGHTS,
BEING MOSTLY THE STORY OF THE PLAYWRIGHTS PRODUCING
COMPANY, INC. (NY: Quadrangle, 1974), pp. 148,
190, 204, 232, 252, 258, 269.
[Shaw as illustration.]

2196 Whitehead, Graham G. R. "The Craftsmanship of
Sean O'Casey," DAI, XXXIV (1974), 5377A. Unpublished dissertation, University of Toronto, 1972.

2197 Willett, John. "The High Art of Low Satire,"
TLS, 13 Dec 1974, p. 1410.
[Essay-review of GEORGE GROSZ by Hans Hess and GEORGE
GROSZ by Beth Irwin Lewis which reproduces Grosz's designs
for Shaw's *Caesar and Cleopatra*.]

2198 Williams, Jay. STAGE LEFT (NY: Charles
Scribner's Sons, 1974), pp. 6, 10, 12, 18, 102-4,
120, 185, 232, 234, 243.
[Brief references to Shaw's relations with the Theatre
Guild, the Provincetown Playhouse and the Federal
Theatre.]

2199 Williamson, Audrey. "Shaw's Evolution," Spec,
CCXXXIII (24 Aug 1974), 229.
Shaw's speculation of the evolution of man towards the
Superman is a case of, if not a derivation from, at least
a parallel to LaMettrie in L'HOMME MACHINE. [Response to
Benny Green on the Flaws in the Shavian Solution, Spec
CCXXXIII (10 Aug 1974), 178-79.]

2200 Wisenthal, J. L. THE MARRIAGE OF CONTRARIES:
BERNARD SHAW's MIDDLE PLAYS (Cambridge, Massachusetts: Harvard UP, 1974).
I. Introduction. From the very earliest Shaw saw the
world in terms of contraries. His usual practice is to
present his characters fairly from their point of view
complementing others of equal validity. Shaw's
perspective is also evolutionary, a continual becoming.
II. *Man and Superman*. *Superman* along with the
Revolutionist's Handbook is concerned with Vital Economy.
Acts, I, II, and IV deal with the sexual aspect; act III
with the philosophical; the *Handbook* with the political
and social. The three points of view: diabolic (the
Devil and the Statue), the angelic (Juan), and the earthy
(Ana) are related to the three types of people discussed
in *The Quintessence of Ibsenism*. Tanner's union with Ann
offers hope for biological and social progress. The main
suggestion of the *Handbook* is that for the present we
should allow the Life Force to work its instinctive way.
III. *Major Barbara*. The aspect of *Barbara* which Shaw
wished his readers to consider is the economic one. This
is similar to *Mrs. Warren's Profession*: the greatest evil
is to be poor. But this is misleading; in reality it is
about power. Undershaft is contradictory toward Barbara
and Cusins; he wishes them both to submit to him and to
supplant him by bringing about a new order. Neither
Barbara nor Cusins can achieve much alone; they must fuse
with Undershaft. IV. *John Bull's Other Island*. This is
the first of Shaw's plays in which characters are overtly
symbolic. It is about the Irish national temperament in
contrast with the English. Broadbent inhabits the world
of the Flesh. He is invulnerable to intellectual opposition, a weakness as well as strength and source of vitality. Keegan, the Irishmen, is not of this world. Doyle,
the Irishman living in England, lies between the two
extremes. The ideal union of facts and dreams would be
between Broadbent and Keegan. But Broadbent's victory may
be only temporary. V. *The Doctor's Dilemma* and
Pygmalion. In these plays there is a choice between a
character who embodies perfection of work (Debedat and
Higgins) and other characters who possess qualities he
lacks. The idea that there is something inhuman and anti-
social about the man who is dedicated to his work is found
frequently in Shaw's writings. Higgins is also an artist,
who regards other people not in human terms but as so much
stone to be used for his higher purposes. The play ends
with no clear victory for either Eliza's warm human qualities or Higgins's cold professional ones. VI. *Misalliance*. There is an opposition between body and brain,
energy and thought, in the play. The superficial theme is

the incompatibility of parents and children; the subtler
theme is the exhaustion of the two ruling classes: the
capitalist middle class and the aristocracy. There is no
hope to be found in a union of these two classes symbolized by a marriage between Bentley and Hypatia. VII.
Heartbreak House. Heartbreak House is a Palace of Lies
where trhe truth cannot be suppressed. "Heartbreak" has
different meanings when applied to different people in the
play. Ellie's marriage to Shotover is a union of
opposites: youth and age; another union of opposites is
the business relationship between Dunn and Mangan. But
the union that is most needful, between power and culture,
is not there. VIII. *Saint Joan*. This play combines
fidelity to the historical records with contemporary relevance. Joan in the records of the trial is a Shavian
character. The principal representatives of restraint are
the Judges, but they are other than hateful monsters. The
Idealist can do great harm while acting in a noble manner.
The real miracle is human genius and its capacity to
influence people. Joan combines heavenly vision and
earthly good sense. In *Superman* and *Barbara* this combination leads to success, but Joan is not completely successful. The most pessimistic reason for Joan's failure
is that the superior person and the ordinary world cannot
live together. IX. *Back to Methuselah*. In the final
section of the Preface Shaw expresses the view that
Methuselah would be his last work and implies that it is
his first work of real significance. The central idea of
the play is that we do not live long enough to become
mature, and this had a personal application for Shaw.
Also it expresses the feeling arising from the war that it
is doubtful that the human animal is capable of saving
himself. In the early plays, the Word must be made Flesh.
In the final play *As Far as Thought Can Reach*, the highly
evolved achieve independence of the world around them and
their struggle is with their own bodies. In *Methuselah*
Shaw does not give ideas the freedom to enter into conflict with each other, but he arranges beforehand for
ideas to which he has committed himself to triumph.
Because it lacks dialectical tension it looks to the later
plays. Its relative artistic failure results from the
break-down of the balancing of contraries.

2201 Wittman, Robert. CANDIDA OR WHAT SHAW REALLY
MEANT (Hicksville, NY: Exposition P, 1974).
[A "version" of *Candida* with Shaw's text intermingled with
Wittman's "Freudian" text explaining what Shaw really
meant.]

2202 Woodcock, George. WHO KILLED THE BRITISH EMPIRE, AN INQUEST (NY: Quadrangle/The New York Times Book Co., 1974), pp. 132, 231, 243.
[Shaw as evidence of the mutual cultural advantages of Irish union with England and of the Fabian view of Colonialism.]

1975

2203 Adams, Elsie B. "Shaw's *Caesar and Cleopatra*: Decadence Barely Averted," ShawR, XVIII (May 1975), 79-82.
The fourth act of *Caesar and Cleopatra* is akin to the decadent literature of the 1890's. Throughout the play there is both verbal and physical violence. Generally decadence is characterized by themes of impending death and destruction and a response of luxurious appreciation of the twilight scene. The banquet scene takes place at twilight. There is a lavish banquet. Caesar and Cleopatra are gorgeously dressed. Caesar woos her, becoming lover and poet. Pothinus is killed. Then Shaw shifts the emphasis to the moral issues raised by the killing and makes his point the contrast between vengeance and clemency.

2204 Ahrens, Rüdiger. "Einleitung" (Introduction), ENGLISCHE LITERATURTHEORETISCHE ESSAYS 2: 19. UND 20. JAHRHUNDERT (English Essays of Literary Theory 2: 19th and 20th Centuries), ed by Rüdiger Ahrens (Heidelberg: Quelle & Meyer, 1975), pp. 9-25, 209-28.
Shaw fights against art for art's sake and wants to restore the lost connection between art and life. He favors a moralistic realism. [Reprints Shaw's essays "Fiction and Truth" (1887) and "The Problem Play" (1895), providing annotations (explains difficult words and briefly introduces the authors referred to in Shaw's essays). Gives a brief biographical sketch.] [Introduction in German, biographical sketch, Shaw's essays and annotations in English.]

2205 "The Arms Dealers: Guns for All," TIME, 3
    March 1975, p. 34.
[Essay on the arms trade using Undershaft from *Major
Barbara* as the point of departure.]

2206 Balint, Stefan (ed). TEATRUL NATIONAL--CRAIOVA
    1850-1975 (The Craiova National Theater 1850-1975)
    (Craiova?: no publisher, no date).
Pygmalion was produced at the National Theatre, Craiova
(Moldavia) in 1945/6 and 1959/60 seasons: *The Devil's
Disciple* in 1956/7, and *Caesar and Cleopatra* in 1968/9.
[In Romanian.]

2207 Bermel, Albert. "Jest and Superjest," ShawR,
    XVIII (May 1975), 57-69.
When Mendoza in *Man and Superman* sets Jack Tanner apart by
telling him that his tragedy is to have gained his heart's
desire, he is more shrewd and penetrating than those
critics who take Tanner at face value. Does Tanner
represent Creative Evolution? He has been infected with
the Life Force since childhood, and his conflict with Ann
is an internal conflict. How well does Tanner's alter-ego
Don Juan fit the role of Superman? Juan has the advantage
over Tanner of knowledge of himself and awareness that the
better life will come not from changing the system but
from escaping the system and changing oneself.1

It is necessary to distinguish between the characters of
the Hell scene and those of the four act comedy which
encloses it. Tanner has too many defects to qualify as
the incipient Superman, but Juan is an incorporeal spirit
in a poetic-fantastic dream. Juan is a mockery of the
Superman.

Shaw revealed in his plays his skepticism about the Superman's coming into existence: 1) mankind has the handicap
of having too far to go; 2) through the millenia, man has
remained morally static; and 3) when an extraordinary man
does appear, mankind does not acknowledge his superhuman
qualities. Shaw may view man's chances of his transcending himself with skepticism but not with gloom.

2208 Bowman, David. "Bernard Shaw Discovers
    Melodrama," INTERPRETATIONS, VII (1975), 30-37.
Shaw's plays failed when they tried to be original, and
they failed when they tried to imitate the prevailing

taste of the London stage. *Widowers' Houses, The Philanderer,* and *Mrs. Warren's Profession* were more indictment-by-essay than drama. *Arms and the Man* was more successful as theater for entertainment. With the exception of *Candida* Shaw's next three plays failed to come off. The remedy for his plays was to be stagey. The melodramatic *Devil's Disciple* and *Caesar and Cleopatra* allowed him to retire from journalism and devote the rest of his life to drama.

2209 Bowman, David. "The Eugenicist's Handbook," ShawR, XVIII (Jan 1975), 18-21.
Eugenics is the major topic of *Man and Superman* and the sole subject of the *Revolutionist's Handbook.* Shaw's association with Karl Pearson and Francis Galton shapes the scientific message of the play. Pearson is best remembered for applying the calculus of probability to biological data, biometry. He was the leading disciple of Galton, the father of eugenics. During September-October, 1901, the TIMES published three letters of Shaw that show collaboration with Pearson. Galton's ideas of breeding for human improvement was an intellectual commonplace. But Shaw went beyond Galton and Pearson in his ideas concerning Human Breeding.

2210 Brien, Alan. *"Too True to Be Good,"* P&P, XXIII (Dec 1975), 22-23.
[Not entirely favorable review of Royal Shakespeare Company production.] Shaw had much in common with W. S. Gilbert as a plot-maker, but *Too True to Be Good* encompasses too many diverse styles: operetta, broad comedy, and German expressionism. The message is buried under stale stage tricks; the message is true, but the play gets in the way.

2211 Brown, Geoff. *"On the Rocks,"* P&P, XXIII (Oct 1975), 37.
On the Rocks seems quaint.

2212 Browne, Terry W. PLAYWRIGHT'S THEATRE, THE ENGLISH STAGE COMPANY AT THE ROYAL COURT THEATRE (Lond: Pitman Publishing, 1975), pp. 4, 14, 66, 104, 107, 110, 114, 118, 126.

[Shaw's role in the founding of the English Stage Company
(The Royal Court under Vedrenne-Barker). List of plays.
Financial tables.]

2213 "The Buffoon" and "The Spring-Heeled Marcher,"
NEW EDINBURGH REVIEW (1975).
[Two issues devoted to Shaw. Not seen.]

2214 Campbell, Margaret. DOLMETSCH, THE MAN AND HIS
W O R K (Lond: Hamish Hamilton, 1975), pp. 55, 58-60,
64, 69, 75, 78-80, 81, 82, 85, 87, 92, 96, 99, 101,
114, 119, 130, 133, 136, 139, 140, 144, 149, 150,
169, 176, 194, 214, 222, 223, 254, 276, 280, 281,
297.
Shaw and his account of a meeting of the Incorporated
Society of Musicians (1893), and his approval of Arnold
Dolmetsch's "old" music on old instruments.   [Shaw's
approving criticism of Arnold Dolmetsch's crusading.]

2215 Carpenter, Charles A.   "Sex Play Shaw's Way:
Man and Superman," ShawR, XVIII (May 1975), 70-74.
Shaw felt the English theater needed a play that openly
exhibited and discussed sex and so gave it *Man and Superman*.   But the play does not affront the Puritan side of
the audience.   The result is a sex play that is valid in
his terms and viable in his generation's.   The most
backward-looking element is its moral basis.   Tanner resists Ann by his moral passion, and she wins him only
after she ceases to provoke it.   She is ennobled by her
love for him.   But the play is almost free of sexual play
and language.   There is one sexual pun: Ann's remark,
"You very nearly killed me, Jack" during the climactic
seduction scene.   Since the Life Force is the seducer in
the Shavian universe, Shaw had introduced "the sexiest
concept in Western drama and show[n] it going all the
way."

2216 Cassirer, Peter.   "Hur gick det sedan för Eliza
Doolittle?   En studie i dramats semiotik" (How Has
It Gone Since for Eliza Doolittle?   A Study of
Semiotics in the Play), TIDSK RIFT FÖR LITTERATURVE-
TENSKAP, IV (1975), 33-51.
[Not seen.]   [In Swedish.]

2217 Christopher, Joe R. "Lazarus, Come Forth from That Tomb!" RIVERSIDE QUARTERLY, VI (Aug 1975), 190-97.
Although the conclusion of *Back to Methuselah* has little to do with Robert Heinlein's TIME ENOUGH FOR LOVE: THE LIVES OF LAZARUS LONG, setting, costume, names, and the emphasis on children are reminiscent of Shaw.

2218 Churchill, R. C. (comp and ed). A BIBLIOGRAPHY OF DICKENSIAN CRITICISM 1836-1975 (NY and Lond: Garland Publishing, 1975), pp. 21, 22, 26, 36, 86, 89, 95, 96, 101, 102, 105, 107, 109, 115, 119, 120, 137, 161, 199, 201, 208, 209, 214, 224, 231, 240, 241, 255, 257, 275.
[Bibliography that contains Shaw criticism of Dickens as well as criticism of Shaw and Dickens.]

2219 Cook, Chris. SOURCES IN BRITISH POLITICAL HISTORY, 1900-1951 (NY: St. Martin's P, 1975), vol I, pp. 95-96; vol V, pp. 177-79.
[A guide to papers, including those of Shaw, in the archives of Societies and in private hands.]

2220 Cottrell, John. LAURENCE OLIVER (Englewood Cliffs, NJ: Prentice-Hall, 1975), pp. 6-7, 28, 39, 43, 55, 95, 182, 246, 331, 390, 398.
[Anecdotes.]

2221 Crawford, Fred D. "Journals to Stella," ShawR, XVIII (Sept 1975), 93-109.
Both Shaw and Swift found an outlet for their emotions in their correspondence. [An examination of the parallels and some differences between Shaw's letters to Ellen Terry, Mrs. Patrick Campbell and Florence Farr and Swift's correspondence with Jane Waring, Esther Vanhomrigh and most importantly Esther Johnson.]

2222 Dalrymple, Jean. FROM THE LAST ROW (Clifton, NJ: James T. White, 1975), pp. 62, 77, 84-86, 103, 105, 113, 129, 217.
[The New York City Theatre Company's productions of Shaw plays, and Jean Dalrymple's story of the beginnings of the transformation of *Pygmalion* into MY FAIR LADY.]

2223 Davies, Marion. THE TIMES WE HAD: LIFE WITH WILLIAM RANDOLPH HEARST, ed by Pamela Pfau and Kenneth S. Marx (Indianapolis and NY: Bobbs-Merrill, 1975), pp. 138-43.
[Anecdotes of the visit by Shaw to California in 1932. Photographs.]

2224 Davies, Stan Gébler. JAMES JOYCE, A PORTRAIT OF THE ARTIST (NY: Stein and Day, 1975), pp. 45n, 50n, 129n, 156n, 157, 206, 211, 234n, 235, 237, 238, 265, 292.
[Passing references to Shaw.]

2225 DeMoss, Virginia. "The Probable Source of Eliza Doolittle's Plumed Hat in Shaw's *Pygmalion*," N&Q, XXII (May 1975), 203.
It is probable that the hat Eliza wears in Act II of Shaw's *Pygmalion* was suggested by an eighteenth century production of Rousseau's opera, PYGMALION.

2226 Dervin, Daniel. BERNARD SHAW, A PSYCHOLOGICAL STUDY (Lewisburg, Pennsylvania: Bucknell UP; Lond: Associated U Presses, 1975).
[A layman's Freudian study of Shaw and his plays, with parallels between Freud and Shaw. The first half subordinates literary values to clinical observations; the second half reverses this orientation. Plays are examined as combinations of structure and Energy. Documentation and bibliography. Remarkably sensible and sensitive and for the most part free of cant and jargon. Table of contents accurately describes the pattern of the book: "The Superfluous Child," "Impecunious Son," "Fatherless Fellow," "Ibsenite," "Unpleasant Plays and Melodramas," "Man and Superman," "Discussion Plays," "Heartbreak House and After."]

2227 Dombrowski, Eileen. "Shaw's Mozartian Ana: DON GIOVANNI and *Man and Superman*," SHAVIAN, V (1975), 15-21.
Shaw's Ana is a direct adaptation of the Mozartian original. Both are preoccupied with decorum. Both pursue men. Zerlina and Donna Elvira also contribute to Shaw's characterization of women, in that all control their chosen mates.

2228 Esslinger-Carr, Pat M. "The Epilogue One More Time: Shaw and the Tragedy of Waste," WESTERN HUMANITIES REVIEW, XXIX (Summer 1975), 292-95.
The epilogue to *Saint Joan* is necessary to the peculiarly Irish view of tragedy, where the useless effort and fruitless martyrdom of Irish patriots becomes a monumental waste.

2229 Evans, T. F. "The Age of Bernard Shaw," KIPLING JOURNAL, XLII (Dec 1975), 6-11.
[A talk by Evans to the Kipling Society on 17 Sept 1975 reported by J. H. McGivering.] It is possible to speak of "The Age of Bernard Shaw," and Kipling, although a writer of gifts, does not fit into that Age.

2230 Evans, T. F. "Notes from London," ISh, XIV (Fall 1975), 5.
The National Theatre at the Old Vic is performing an excellent production of *Heartbreak House*.

2231 Evans, T. F. "Notes from London," ISh, XIV (Winter 1975/76), 32.
On the Rocks at the Mermaid Theatre is still timely. *Too True to Be Good* by the Royal Shakespeare Company at the Aldwych Theatre shows there is more in Shaw than anyone guessed.

2232 Fabrikant, Geraldine. "The Photographs of Gisèle Freund," MS, III (March 1975), 60-65, 89-90.
[Photograph of Shaw.] Shaw insisted that his entire beard be included in the photograph. Freund tried to capture Shaw's arrogance. When the photograph was developed, a part of the beard was cut off. She could not send it to Shaw; instead she sent it to H. G. Wells, who liked it very much. Shaw had posed on the recommendation of James Joyce.

2233 Farson, Daniel. THE MAN WHO WROTE DRACULA, A BIOGRAPHY OF BRAM STOKER (Lond: Michael Joseph Ltd, 1975), pp. 45, 177-78.
[The story of Shaw's review of Henry Irving's performance of RICHARD III, which apparently suggested that Irving was drunk. Irving never forgave Shaw, and the negotiations over *The Man of Destiny* came to nothing.]

2234 Feuer, Lewis S. IDEOLOGY AND THE IDEOLOGISTS
(NY and Lond: Harper & Row, 1975), pp. 4, 36-37,
119-20, 129, 144-45, 162-63.
[Shaw and revolution, Nietzsche, dictatorship, and anti-
Semitism.]

2235 Ford, Eric. "G. Bernard Shaw: Ehrenburger
Dieser Stadt: 1950.   Eulenspiegel and Mölln,
Western Germany," SHAVIAN, V (1975), 14, 22.
[Account of how Shaw's head in bas relief appears on the
walls of the Rathaus of Mölln.]

2236 Frank, Joseph. "Exile and the Kingdom: The
Incipient Absurdity of Milton and Shaw," MOSAIC, IX
(Fall 1975), 111-21.
Heartbreak House offers none of comedy's or Shaw's usual
creative hopes; it is Shaw's alienation from Shaw. The
theme is sterility. Shaw is "exiled" from the major
thrust of his own work and anticipates a Camusian view of
the universe.

2237 Freeman, Ronald E. "Victorian Bibliography for
1974," VICTORIAN STUDIES, XVIII (June 1975), 590-91.
[Bibliography with a section devoted to Shaw.]

2238 Fyfe, H. Hamilton. "Brieux and Bernard Shaw,"
ISh, XIII (Winter 1975), 24-25.
Shaw is superior to Brieux because he refused to "bow
before the tyranny of the story-telling system."

2239 Gilenson, Boris. "New Contributions to Soviet
Studies of Shaw's Works," trans by David Marks,
SOVIET LITERATURE, VII (1975), 162-66.
Soviet interest in Shaw is as alive today as ever.
[Survey of Shavian scholarship and publishing in the
Soviet Union.]

2240 Gillie, Christopher. MOVEMENTS IN ENGLISH
LITERATURE 1900-1940 (Lond and NY: Cambridge UP,
1975), pp. 6, 22, 78, 114, 164-70.
Shaw exerted a retarding influence on the English theater
because he offered a bad critical influence and his own
achievement was too idiosyncratic to be a creative

influence. The art of Shaw's dramatic writing is distinct from the craft as can be seen in *The Doctor's Dilemma*. The art comes out in the use of language; the craft in his travesty of nineteenth century stock theater.

2241 Grebanier, Bernard. THEN CAME EACH ACTOR (NY: David McKay, 1975), pp. 37, 58, 262, 275, 276, 280, 295, 296, 300, 306-7, 308, 311, 312, 313, 315, 328, 332, 334-35, 336, 338-39, 371, 376, 381, 383, 384, 385, 386, 387, 388, 389, 390, 396, 418-19, 431, 432, 441, 443, 456, 457, 459.
[Shaw and Shakespearean actors and acting.]

2242 Green, Ronnie Lloyd. "The Comic Vision: Patterns of Initiation," DAI, XXXV (1975), 8063A. Unpublished dissertation, Wayne State University, 1974.

2243 Greiner, Norbert. "G. B. 'Owlglass' Shaw: A Biographical Footnote," N&Q, XXII (May 1975), 203-5. Shaw was offered by the Mayor of Moelln (West Germany) the name of honorary Til Eulenspiegel, which he accepted.

2244 Greiner, Norbert. "Mill, Marx and Bebel: Early Influences on Shaw's Characterization of Women," ShawR, XVIII (Jan 1975), 10-17; rptd in FF. Shaw had read Mill's THE SUBJECTION OF WOMEN when attending the meetings of the Zetetical Society and discovered what would become for him a major thesis, that "woman's nature" was an artificial construct of Capitalism. The COMMUNIST MANIFESTO's definition of the family as an artificial institution is also valid for Shaw. There are many striking parallels between August Bebel's DIE FRAU UND DER SOZIALISMUS and Shaw, that it might have served as a direct source for Shaw. A test for Shaw of an author's moral and political realism was his characterization of women.

2245 Gurewitch, Morton. COMEDY: THE IRRATIONAL VISION, (Ithaca & Lond: Cornell UP, 1975), pp. 94-95, 107n, 117, 234-35.
Shaw's achievement in comedy is the expulsion of error, not the discovery of certain truth. In *Major Barbara*, Undershaft recommends that all worn-out ideas by which we

live ought to be thrown off.   But although he declares
that killing "is the final test of conviction," he has not
himself murdered anyone.   Barbara is convinced the
citizens of Undershaft's workers utopia are eager for the
salvation of their souls, though she may discover that
being well fed is as great an enemy of the soul's
redemption as hunger.   Cusins sees through humanism to
the necessity of joining power to grace.   There is one
enormous qualification: Shaw has pointed out that social
and moral ideas go out of date; therefore they may lose
their relevance in literary works too.

Shaw uses the farcical fool as an "aide-de-camp" to a
witty critic;   clowning is a sign of intellectual liveliness.

2246 Harrison, Rex.   REX, AN AUTOBIOGRAPHY (NY:
William Morrow, 1975), pp. 23, 25, 69-71, 155, 159-
62, 185.
[Anecdote of Shaw's filming an introduction for Americans
to *Major Barbara*.   Photograph of Shaw.]

2247 Harrison, Rosina.   ROSE: MY LIFE IN SERVICE
(Lond: Cassell; NY: Viking P, 1975).
[The impressions of the maid of Nancy, Lady Astor.]   Shaw
was Lady Astor's greatest literary friend.   [Photograph.]

2248 Hartnoll, Phyllis.   WHO'S WHO IN SHAW.   With a
Foreword by W. A. Darlington [not abstracted]   (NY:
Taplinger, 1975).
[An alphabetical descriptive directory of all the
characters in Shaw, followed by "The Characters--play by
play."]

2249 Hayman, Ronald.   THE FIRST THRUST, THE
CHICHESTER FESTIVAL THEATRE (Lond: Davis Poynter,
1975), pp. 36, 41, 75, 125, 157, 163, 169, 206, 209,
212, 213.
[History of the Chichester Festival Theatre with
descriptions of productions of Shaw plays: *Saint Joan,
Heartbreak House, Arms and the Man, Caesar and Cleopatra,*
and *The Doctor's Dilemma.*]

2250 Higham, Charles. KATE, THE LIFE OF KATHARINE HEPBURN (N Y: W. W. Norton, 1975), passim.
[Brief description of Hepburn's turning down the role of Epifania in *The Millionairess*, finally playing it in London and New York as well as in the movies.]

2251 Hirota, Norio. "Bernard Shaw no Buntai" (Bernard Shaw's Style), WASEDA SHOGAKU (Tokyo), No 252/3 (Dec 1975), 101-24.
[Surveys the characteristics of Shaw's style using chiefly *Man and Superman*.] [In Japanese.]

2252 Holroyd, Michael. "Bernard Shaw y el problema inglés" (Bernard Shaw and the English Problem), REVISTA DE OCCIDENTE, No 2 (Dec 1975), 16-24.
[Not seen.] [In Spanish.]

2253 Hyde, H[arford]. Montgomery. OSCAR WILDE (N Y: Farrar, Straus and Giroux, 1975), pp. 37, 113n, 125, 142n, 143, 151, 172, 181, 207, 271, 307, 336n, 383, 388.
[Passing references to Shaw in a biography of Wilde.

2254 Iakovlev, S. S. "Shou i Pristli" (Shaw and Piestley), REALIZM V ZARUBEZHNYKH LITERATURAKH (Realism in Foreign Literatures), (Saratov), IV (1975), 51-66.
A new genre of tragic farce, arousing accusatory laughter, appeared in the West in the twenties, caused by the contradictions inherent in the capitalist world between the two wars. Shaw's satirical cycle of plays and political extravaganzas are examples. In his early plays criticising capitalism, Shaw believed it might be transformed, but later his disillusion with capitalist reality intensified, though his tragedy was almost blended with irony. The satire characteristic of Shaw is dulled in Priestley's plays though Shaw's sardonic laughter is sometimes to be heard in them. [In Russian.]

2255 Ichikawa, Matahiko. WARAU TETSUJIN BERNARD SHAW (Laughing Philosopher Bernard Shaw) (Tokyo: Wasedadaigaku Shuppanbu, 1975).

The militarism that raved in Japan for many years could be responsible for the relative unpopularity of Shaw among the general public. Now militarism, which is incompatible with Shaw's ideas and comedy, is dead. It is high time we tried to revaluate and rediscover Shaw. [A good introduction.] [In Japanese.]

2256 Jenckes, Norma Margaret. *"John Bull's Other Island:* A Critical Study of Shaw's Irish Play in Its Theatrical and Socio-Political Context," D AI, X X X V (1975), 4526A. Unpublished dissertation, University of Illinois (Urbana-Champagne), 1974.

2257 Jenckes, Norma. "The Rejection of Shaw's Irish Play: *John Bull's Other Island,"* EIRE, X (Spring 1975), 38-53.
Shaw did not need to be urged by William Butler Yeats; he volunteered a play for the Abbey Theatre. *John Bull's Other Island* attacked the basic tenets the Abbey was seeking to promote in Ireland; it neither flatters the Irish past, nor does it depend upon "warm emotion." It disparages the Celtic Twilight. The Shaw-Yeats antipathy extended beyond the Abbey's rejection of Shaw's play. Generally Irish critics have condemned the play, concluding that Shaw was too remote from his native land to portray it truly, though some close to the events considered the rejection of *John Bull* a mistake.

2258 Jenkins, Simon. LANDLORDS TO LONDON: THE STORY OF A CAPITAL AND ITS GROWTH (Lond: Constable, 1975), pp. 192-93.
[The role of Shaw's writing in the STAR in the early program of the London County Council.]

2259 Johnson, Ann. "Review of Vincent Wall, BERNARD SHAW, PYGMALION TO MANY PLAYERS [1973]," COMPARATIVE DRAMA, IX (Spring 1975), 92-95.
Shaw was obsessed with instructing his actors because the musical qualities of his plays made unusual demands on them. He created a new idea of the director's role.

2260 Johnson, Josephine. FLORENCE FARR, BERNARD
SHAW'S 'NEW WOMAN' (Totowa, NJ: Rowman and Little-
field, 1975), passim.
[A biography of F. Farr with many references to Shaw.
Illustrated. Weak documentation.]

2261 Kalem, T. E. "A Tale of Two Stratfords," TIME,
30 June 1975, pp. 66, 68.
[Review of *Saint Joan* at Stratford, Ontario.] Joan's real
vision is of the age of democracy, and her voices are the
voice of the downtrodden masses. But she escapes Shaw's
didacticism, which is why audiences love her. [Photo-
graph.]

2262 Kauffmann, Stanley. "A Life in the Theatre,"
HORIZON, XVII (Autumn 1975), 80-85.
[A brief survey of Henry Granville-Barker's theatrical
career.] In 1899 when Barker was 22 he read a minor role
in a copyrighting performance of *Caesar and Cleopatra* and
met the 43 year old Shaw. Barker's performances in
*Candida, Man and Superman, John Bull's Other Island, Major
Barbara,* and *The Doctor's Dilemma* helped to change Shaw
from a "published but rarely performed dramatist into a
famous theatre artist." He influenced Shaw because Shaw
had him in mind when writing certain roles. Shaw loomed
largest in the list of plays performed by the Barker-
Vedrenne management of the Royal Court Theatre. Barker is
the best playwright influenced by Shaw; he joined the
Fabian Society under Shaw's influence, and probably partly
in imitation of Shaw married a rich wife, Helen
Huntingdon, divorcing Lillah McCarthy and bringing about a
breach with Shaw. [Illustrated.]

2263 Kazantsakis, M. N. "The Homeric G. B. S.,"
ShawR, XVIII (Sept 1975), 91-92.
[Originally a broadcast, aired in 1946 on Shaw's ninetieth
birthday by the B. B. S. Overseas Service.] If Homer and
not Jehovah had created the world, Shaw would have been an
Olympian god. Shaw reveals himself in three personalities: Revolutionary, Prophet, and old grandfather. He
would have asked to be "the world's spiritual dictator."

2264 Kennedy, Andrew K. SIX DRAMATISTS IN SEARCH OF
A LANGUAGE, STUDIES IN DRAMATIC LANGUAGE (Lond and
NY: Cambridge UP, 1975), pp. 38-86 and passim.

Shaw never decided whether 'art' was an essential element of drama or "a by-product of having something urgent to say." This affected all his work. His idea of 'conviction' worked against the dialectic of opposed attitudes expressed in dialogue. It worked against the idea of a play's possessing a disciplined form. And it eliminated the possibility of static or inner drama. Shaw viewed the theater as a temple, "where the sermon is more important than my liturgy." He wished to exploit the music in words, by which he meant the "energies of the aria and vocal ensemble" to be created in rhetoric. Although music is one of the chief means of emphasizing meaning in his plays, Shaw seems to distrust it so that he must make the words mean something explicit. The result is over-rationalized, a "word-flood." Shaw only gradually recognized that his language was not naturalistic, but was instead rhetorical, though he could not distinguish between naturalism as a style and as an ideology. Shaw's plays are expressions of "verbal theatricality" rather than "spoken action." Tension results from the pull between verisimilitude and rhetoric. [Language in *Major Barbara*, *Heartbreak House* and *Village Wooing* is examined to make the point.] Shaw uses direct parody [Dialogue from *Arms and the Man* is examined] of language to debunk a foolish attitude. He employedd conscious self-parody [*Man and Superman*] where the characters are unconscious, but Shaw is aware: "manifesto and windbaggery in one breath." Shaw used pastiche 1) to express some true feeling with which the audience could empathize or 2) to create a poetry of the theater. *Saint Joan* is a chronicle play, having several styles, and its unity depends upon one style illuminating another ironically. Shaw's "dramatic language is inseparable from a relativist vision that works in several styles," yet Shaw was unable to control his styles and language fully. After the First World War Shaw glimpsed the need to break the old language down in order to accommodate a new experience, but he "used the old dramatic language to defend himself from the need to renew it" [language from *Too True to Be Good* is analyzed]. [There follows an "Appendix: Notes on Shaw's use of the word 'absurd.'"] [Original and essential.]

2265 Kingston, Jeremy. "*Heartbreak House*," P&P, XXII (April 1975), 20-21.
John Schlesinger's direction of *Heartbreak House* is clean and clear. Shaw was right to regard it as his best. [Photographs.]

2266 Kissel, Iuriĭ Ĩakovich. OKAZAL'NOE ISPOL'ZOV-
ANIE FRAZEOLOGICHESKIKH EDINITS V PROIZVEDENIAKH
BERNARDA SHOU I O. UAĨLD (Occasional Use of Phraseo-
logical Units in the Works of Bernard Shaw and O.
Wilde) (Voronezh: University, 1975).
[Not seen.] [In Russian.]

2267 Lago, Mary M., and Karl Beckson (eds). MAX AND
WILL. MAX BEERBOHM AND WILLIAM ROTHENSTEIN, THEIR
FRIENDSHIP AND LETTERS 1893-1945 (Cambridge, Mass:
Harvard UP 1975), pp. 6-7, 39, 40, 46, 48n, 101,
130-31, 132, 164, 165n, 167, 168, 171, 173.
[Shaw in the letters of Beerbohm and Rothenstein.]

2268 Lambert, J. W. "Plays in Performance, London,"
DRAMA, CXVII (Summer 1975), 37-55.
John Schlesinger's production of *Heartbreak House* was
immensely satisfying, except for a tendency to isolate
certain set pieces and interrupt the play's flow. Shaw
might not have relished the turning of Jennifer and
Dubedat into a pair of tricksters as has been done in the
Mermaid *Doctor's Dilemma*, but it did add another dimension
to the play. [Photograph of *Heartbreak*.]

2269 Lambert, J. W. "Plays in Performance, London,"
DRAMA, CIX (Winter 1975), 40-58.
Too True to Be Good at the Aldwych has received rapturous
reviews, but it is a production which lacks faith in the
play. *On the Rocks* is unnerving in the number of
parallels with present day. [Photographs.]

2270 Laurence, Dan H. "Introductory Comments,"
CLASSIC THEATRE: THE HUMANITIES IN DRAMA, ed by
Sylvan Barnet, Morton Berman, and William Burto
(Bost: Little, Brown, 1975), pp. 640-42.
Shaw was a castigator of morals by ridicule, and in *Mrs.
Warren's Profession* he exposes the hypocrisies, cant, and
illusions of the Victorian world. Against these
pretensions stands Vivie Warren. Although the play is an
early one, it is a notable theatrical achievement.

2271 Laurence, Dan H. "A Joan for This Season,"
STRATFORD FESTIVAL [Program for the twenty-third
season of the Stratford, Canada Festival.] (1975),
n.p.

Shaw depicted as conscientiously as he could the irreconcilable conflict between Joan and her judges; he has
portrayed Joan as a living woman.

2272 Laurence, Dan H.   "Shaw, Books, and Libraries,"
PAPERS OF THE BIBLIOGRAPHICAL SOCIETY OF AMERICA,
LXIX (1975), 465-79; rptd with line drawing of Shaw
self-portrait (Austin: Humanities Research Center,
University of Texas at Austin [Bibliographical Monograph, no 9], 1977).   [Slightly revised text of
paper read at meeting of the Bibliographical Society
in New York, 24 Jan 1975.]
Shaw worked in the Reading Room of the British Museum,
starting in 1880, daily for eight years. He wrote a poem
(text herein reprinted) about Violet Beverly, whose
presence in the Reading Room next to him was distracting.
He became a disciple of William Morris in book design but
did not collect books. He despised keeping letters and
mementos, though he presented some manuscripts as gifts to
the British Museum. He felt LADY CHATTERLEY'S LOVER
should be required reading for marriageable girls. T. E.
Hanley gave the University of Texas five huge cartons of
scraps gathered by his secretaries. All his life Shaw was
a benefactor of libraries, and the bulk of his estate went
to R.A.D.A., the National Gallery of Ireland, and the
British Museum library because they represent what the
public ought to want and don't.

2273 Laurie, Douglas.   *"On the Rocks,"* ISh, XIV
(Winter 1975/76), 26.
On the Rocks at the Mermaid Theatre is still timely. Shaw
is in top form, and the audience enjoys the play in spite
of the theme of political chaos.

2274 Lindenberger, Herbert. HISTORICAL DRAMA, THE
RELATION OF LITERATURE AND REALITY (Chicago and
Lond: U of Chicago P, 1975), pp, 2, 9, 18, 21, 41,
48, 50, 51, 66, 67, 72, 106, 107, 127, 140, 141,
146, 176n, 181.
[Shaw and the history play: *Caesar and Cleopatra, The Man
of Destiny,* and *Saint Joan.*]

2275 Lindsay, Jack. WILLIAM MORRIS, HIS LIFE AND
WORK (Lond: Constable, 1975), pp. 205, 212, 270,

275, 279, 288, 290, 295, 296, 303, 304, 309, 323, 325, 327, 334, 354, 359, 360.
[Shaw's role in William Morris's biography.

2276 Lorichs, Sonja. "Two Mother Characters in Bernard Shaw's Drama," SHAVIAN, V (1975), 5-8.
Mrs. Warren and Lady Britomart have traits in common. Both women are domineering. Shaw has some sympathy for Mrs. Warren; the delineation of Lady Britomart is ironical from the beginning.

2277 Macainsh, Noel. "Baylebridge, Nietzsche, Shaw: Some Observations on the 'New Nationalism,'" AUSTRALIAN LITERARY STUDIEDS, VII (Oct 1975), 141-59.
The source of the particular amalgam of religion, evolution, and eugenics advanced in William Baylebridge's NATIONAL NOTES (1913) can be found in Shaw rather than Nietzsche. Baylebridge alludes to Shaw's discussion in *The Revolutionists' Handbook* of the role of contraceptives in combining pleasure with sterility. [Very brief reference to Shaw.]

2278 MacDermott, Norman. EVERYMANIA, THE HISTORY OF THE EVERYMAN THEATRE, HAMPSTEAD, 1920-1926 (Lond: Society for Theatre Research, 1975), pp. viii, 1-5, 11, 12, 23, 24, 27, 30, 31, 32, 35, 36, 39, 40-48, 54, 56-58, 63, 64, 65-67, 69, 89, 94, 103, 107, 108, 109.
[Shaw and his plays in the history of the Everyman Theatre. Includes the text of a Shaw address on *The Present Predicament of the Theatre*, photographs, Cast Lists and Critics and Calendar of Productions.]

2279 Maiskiĭ, Ivan. "Bernard Shou: *Dilemma doktora*" (Bernard Shaw: *The Doctors' Dilemma*), INOSTRANNAIA LITERATURA (Moscow), No. 6 (1975), 165-6.
Without Shaw's plays it is difficult to imagine the work of our theaters, producers and players. His work is the more valuable in that it was in many ways permeated with the progressive ideas of his time and the struggle against social injustice. In *The Doctor's Dilemma*, Shaw attacks all forms of inequality of women and stresses ideas of humanity and justice. His works are an important example of critical realism. The play is only known to us in pre-revolutionary translations. [In Russian.]

2280 Makusheva, S. R. "Muzika v p'esakh B. Shou" (Music in Shaw's Plays), INOZEMNA FILOLOGIIA (Lv'iv), No 38 (1975), 125-34.
Analysis of the musical fragments in Shaw's plays shows they were used to heighten satirical or ironical effect in the revelation of character and situations. Examples occur in *Caesar and Cleopatra, Man and Superman,* and *Saint Joan.* [In Ukrainian, with English summary.]

2281 Malmi, Carol Lea. "The Royal Court Theatre 1904-1907," DAI, XXXV (1975), 6849A. Unpublished dissertation, Northwestern University, 1974.

2282 Mander, Raymond, and Joe Mitchenson. THE THEATRES OF LONDON (Lond: New English Library, 1975), pp. 280-82.
[About the Shaw Theatre, which takes its name from Shaw.]

2283 Mason, Philip. KIPLING, THE GLASS, THE SHADOW AND THE FIRE, (NY, Evanston, San Francisco, Lond: Harper & Row, 1975), passim.
[Kipling contrasted with Shaw among others; Kipling's UNPROFESSIONAL compared with *The Doctor's Dilemma.*]

2284 Masumoto, Masahiko. "Bernard Shaw," OBEISAKKA TO NIHON KINDAIBUNGAKU, EIBEIHEN II (European and American Writers and Modern Japanese Literature, Anglo-American II) ed by Koji Fukuda, Takehiko Kenmochi and Koichi Kodama (Tokyo: Kyoiku Shuppan Centre, 1975), pp. 256-89.
Shaw's name became very popular in 1910's through 1920's among Japanese intellectuals. But it can not be observed that he exerted a deep influence over them. The reasons would be: 1) they failed to enjoy Shaw's comedy, because it was so different from the traditional Japanese drama; 2) the early introduction of Shaw into Japan often emphasized philosophical aspects of Shaw and tended to forget his dramatic merits; 3) Shaw was too much in the centre of journalistic and gossipy news; and 4) Japanese translations were often not suitable for presentation. [On Shaw's reception and fate in Japan in the period of 1890's through 1940's.] [In Japanese.]

2285 Morgan, Margery M. "Shaw," ENGLISH DRAMA (EXCLUDING SHAKESPEARE), ed by Stanley Wells (Lond:

Oxford UP [Select Bibliographical Guides], 1975) pp. 231-47.
Shaw criticism still follows the lines laid down by early reviewers. [There follows a survey of criticism and a bibliography.]

2286 Narumi, Hiroshi and Masahiiko Masumoto, Ryoichi Nakagawa, Yoshikazu Mizuno and Matahiko Ichikawa. "Shaw to Nihon" (Shaw and Japan), GBS (Tokyo), No. 4 (Nov 1975), pp. 3-7.
[Summary of the symposium held 7 Dec 1974. Discussed topics: 1) history of Shaw's introduction into Japan; 2) his views of Japan; 3) his influences; and 4) Shaw and modern Japanese drama.] [In Japanese.]

2287 Nelson, Raymond S. "Shaw's Heaven and Hell," CONTEMPORARY REVIEW, CCXXVI (March 1975), 132-36.
Although *Back to Methuselah* is Shaw's ultimate formulation of a twentieth century religious faith, the earlier *Man and Superman* still provides the best insight into Shaw's conceptions of Heaven and Hell. They are not actual places but states of soul. The pursuit of happiness, as for Carlyle, is one of the marks of Hell, because it leads to will-lessness. Although Heaven is not portrayed, it is the place of the mind and, as it was for Carlyle, a place of work.

2288 Nicoll, Allardyce. "English Drama 1900-1945," ENGLISH DRAMA (EXCLUDING SHAKESPEARE), ed by Stanley Wells (Lond: Oxford UP [Select Bibliographical Guides], 1975), pp. 273-74.
Shaw is the "true theatrical colossus of the time," 1900-1945. He sought to appeal to the reading public as well as the play-going one.

2289 Novick, Julius. "A New Director Brings Change to Stratford," NYT, 29 June 1975, II, p. 5.
Pat Galloway as Joan at Stratford, Ontario does not blaze.

2290 Novick, Julius. "This *Devil's Disciple* Makes Shaw Look Very Good Indeed," NYT, 19 Oct 1975, II, p. 5.
The Niagara-on-the-Lake Shaw Festival has shipped south *The Devil's Disciple* as a Bicentennial present. Shrewdly

Shaw varies his melodrama with high comedy.   The entire production is a vindication of Shaw.

2291 O'Casey, Sean.   THE LETTERS OF SEAN O'CASEY, 1910-41, vol I, ed by David Krause (NY: Macmillan, 1975), passim.
[Includes letters to Shaw and his wife, letters from Shaw and his wife, and many references to and quotations from Shaw and his works throughout.   Illustrated with a photograph of O'Casey and Shaw.   Thoroughly indexed.]

2292 O'Connor, Gary.   *"Doctor's Dilemma,"* P&P, XXII (July 1975), 35.
Robert Chetwyn's production of *The Doctor's Dilemma* is good, and the play is not dated.   [Photograph.]

2293 Palmer, Lilli.   CHANGE LOBSTERS--AND DANCE, AN AUTOBIOGRAPHY (NY: Macmillan, 1975; first published as DICKE LILLI--GUTES KIND [Zürich: Droemer Knauer Verlag, 1974]), pp. 195-205.
[An account of a meeting with Shaw before Palmer played Cleopatra.]

2294 Penev, Pencho.   ISTORIIA NA BULGARSKIIA DRAMA-TICHESKI TEATR (History of the Bulgarian Dramatic Theater) (Sofia: Nauka i izkustvo, 1975).
Candida was produced in Sofia at the Bulgarian National Theater in 1915, *Androcles and the Lion* in the 1924/5 season.   *Saint Joan* and *The Devil's Disciple* were in the repertoire of the National Theater in the 1930's.   Since World War II, *Mrs. Warren's Profession* has been in the repertoire of the National Theater with Olga Kircheva in the title role.   [In Bulgarian.]

2295 Porges, Irwin.   EDGAR RICE BURROUGHS: THE MAN WHO CREATED TARZAN (Provo, Utah: Brigham Young UP, 1975), pp. 462-63.
[Shaw's correspondence with William R. Thurston about Thurston's THE GREAT SECRET and THURSTON'S PHILOSOPHY OF MARRIAGE.]

2296 Potter, Robert.   THE ENGLISH MORALITY PLAY, ORIGINS, HISTORY AND INFLUENCE OF A DRAMATIC TRADI-

TION (Lond and Bost: Routledge Kegan Paul, 1975),
   pp. 1, 4, 225-28, 232.
When Shaw published *Man and Superman*, he let it be known
that he had seen William Poel's production of EVERYMAN and
was impressed. The connection between Ann Whitefield,
Shaw's Everywoman, and the character of Everyman is not so
obscure when it is remembered that the character was
played by a woman in Poel's production. Most important is
the portrayal of Ana's choice between Heaven or Hell in
the hell scene, which is like Everyman's discovery of his
true nature.

2297 Potter, Roseanne Giuditta. "The Rhetoric of
Seduction: The Structure and Meaning of Shaw's
Major Barbara," DAI, XXXVI (1975), 2853A. Unpub-
lished dissertation, University of Texas, 1975.

2298 Prideaux, Tom. LOVE OR NOTHING: THE LIFE AND
TIMES OF ELLEN TERRY (NY: Charles Scribner's Sons,
1975).
[Index; no documentation. One chapter, "The Paper
Courtship," deals superficially with the Shaw-Terry
correspondence; a few references to comments made by Shaw
relating to Terry's professional career, especially to
Terry's appearing in Shaw's plays.]

2299 Pullar, Philippa. FRANK HARRIS, A BIOGRAPHY
(NY: Simon and Schuster, 1976), pp. 121, 166n, 170,
174-75, 178-80, 190, 221n, 228, 230, 264, 296, 302,
322-23, 339, 346, 347, 348, 353, 358, 360-63, 380,
383, 391, 393-94, 396, 400, 406-7, 409, 410, 412.
[Shaw and Frank Harris.]

2300 Quinn, Martin Richard. "Dickens and Shaw: A
Study of a Literary Relationship," DAI, XXXV (1975),
7323A. Unpublished dissertation, Pennsylvania State
University, 1974.

2301 Quinn, Martin., "Dickens as Shavian Metaphor,"
ShawR, XVIII (May 1975), 44-56.
Shaw estimated that allusions to Dickens in his literary
works would outnumber all those to any other writer by a
ratio of four to one. Dickens became for Shaw a profound,
personal and conscious rhetorical tool. At the same time

Dickens was better known to Shaw's public than the Bible, Marx or Ibsen and therefore was surrogate for them. Shaw wrote an introduction to HARD TIMES and to GREAT EXPECTA- TIONS. He read Dickens very early in his life. [There follows a long compilation of metaphoric use of Dickensian allusions.] Shaw's entire generation had been influenced by Dickens and many of Shaw's friends and associates were enthusiastic appreciators. Even Shaw's biographers adopt Dickensian expressions. Shaw references to Dickens also became an atonement for the book he did not write. He was aware of anti-Dickens snobbery and sometimes was not im- mune to its influence as he faulted Dickens for his Phil- istinism, his inconsistency as a social critic and his philosophical limitations.

2302 Radford, Frederick L. "The Conspicuously Elusive Mr. Shaw," NINETEENTH CENTURY THEATRE RE- SEARCH, III (Spring 1975), 37-45. [Not seen.]

2303 Roby, Kinley E. "Stap Street to Robbins's Row," Shaw R, XVIII (Jan 1975), 2-5. Shaw's reading of Henry George and Marx only intensified the feeling of social justice already brought into being by his experience as a collecter of slum rents for Uniacki Townshend and Company. Edward, Prince of Wales, had been accused of maintaining a slum. In response, he became interested in working class housing. The newspapers also kept the unhappy details of the miserable housing condi- tions before the public in 1884. All of this provided Shaw with a theme and supporting material.

2304 Rodgers, W. R. "George Bernard Shaw," IRISH LITERARY PORTRAITS (Lond: British Broadcasting Corporation, 1972; NY: Taplinger, 1975, pp. 116-41. [Originally a BBC broadcast in 1954 of pre-recorded comments arranged by Rodgers of St. John Ervine, Sean O'Casey, Denis Johnston, Lord Glenary, Frank O'Connor, Lady Hanson, Sean Macreamoinn, William Meegan, Mrs. Tyrell, Mr. Fry, Mr. Kerwan, Father Leonard, Dr. Bodkin, Shelah Richards, Austin Clarke, L. A. G. Strong, Lady Thomson, Pearse Beasley, and Oliver Gogarty. Anecdotes and speculation about Shaw's childhood, youth, and various character.]

2305 Rodway, Allan. ENGLISH COMEDY, ITS ROLE AND NATURE FROM CHAUCER TO THE PRESENT DAY (Berkeley and Los Angeles: U of California P, 1975), pp. 39, 49, 54, 55, 82, 126, 211, 212, 217, 237-43.
Inversion is often found in Shaw's works. No nineteenth-century writer of comedy before Shaw had a guiding coherence of outlook, and Shaw achieved it by freezing his emotional assets. Shaw's comedies of ideas have not lasted well because the clarity and cleverness cannot disguise their crankiness. He had little faith in human rationality in general, hence he admired communism and fascism: they lent the people to organization by men of power. he is utilitarian in his heartlessness. His positive comedies (*Back to Methuselah*) are inferior to the negative, destructive ones because they provide an answer. *Widowers' Houses* is the best example of a positive comedy. *Heartbreak House* is more sensitive to human feelings, and probably it expressed more than Shaw intended. It does not resolve feeling and reason, but it is *aware* of them, achieving some depth.

2306 Roll-Hansen, Diderik. "Sartorius and the Scribes of the Bible: Satiric Method in *Widowers' Houses*," Shaw R, XVIII (Jan 1975), 6-9.
The scribes who "devour widows' houses" (Matt. 23.14, Mark 12.40) are smooth villains like Shaw's Sartorius, though both work within the law. But Shaw's satire cannot be accounted for only by the Scriptural title. He insisted that the "guilt of defective social organization" cannot be placed on individuals. The social system must be changed.

2307 Sal'perina, L. I. "O nektorykh sintaktiches-kikh parametrakh izucheniîa rechevoǐ kharateristiki personazheǐ. Na materiale p'esy Bernarda Shou *Major Barbara*" (On Some Syntactical Parameters in the Study of Verbal Characteristics of Persons. On Material of Shaw's *Major Barbara*), SBORNIK NAUCHNYKH TRUDOV MOSKOVSKOGO INST. INOSTRANNYKH ÎAZYKOV, LXXXIV (1975), 36-47.
[Not seen.] [In Russian.]

2308 Savchenko, S. V. "Tvorchǐ shliâkh Bernarda Shou. Do 80-richniîa z dnîa narozhdenniîa" (Creative Progress of Bernard Shaw. On the 80th Anniversary of His Birth), Z ISTORII ZARUBEZHNIKH LITERATUR

(On the History of Foreign Literature) (Kiev: 1975), pp. 105-30.
[An essay, reprinted, date and place unknown. Not seen.]
[In Ukrainian.]

2309 Scally, Robert J. THE ORIGINS OF THE LLOYD GEORGE COALITION, THE POLITICS OF SOCIAL IMPERIALISM, 1900-1918 (Princeton, NJ: Princeton UP, 1975), pp. 36-39, 50-51, 77.
[Shaw and the Fabian Society and the Boer War.]

2310 Schneede, Uwe M., Georg Bussmann and Marina Schneede-Sczesny. GEORGE GROSZ: LEBEN UND WERKE (George Grosz: Life and Works) (Stuttgart: Verlag Gerd Hatje, 1975), pp. 64, 90.
Grosz did the designs for a Berlin production of *Caesar and Cleopatra* in 1920 and for *Androcles and the Lion* in 1924. [In German.]

2311 Senart, Philippe. "La Revue Théâtrale: *Androclès et le Lion*," (Theater Review: *Androcles and the Lion*) NOUVELLE REVUE DES DEUX MONDES (Sept 1975), 700-1.
The Guy Rétoré production of *Androcles and the Lion* at the Theatre de l'Est Parisien is a rather racy mixture of QUO VADIS and LA BELLE HÉLÈNE. [In French.]

2312 Shaitanov, I. O. ISTORICHESKIE DRAMY BERNARDA SHOU. K VOPROSU OB EVOLIUTSII ZHANRA (Shaw's Historical Dramas: The Question of Evolution of a Genre) (Moscow: Moskovskiĭ gos. ped. institut im. V. I. Lenina, 1975).
[Published dissertation. Not seen.] [In Russian.]

2313 "Shaw, George Bernard," DER NEUE KNAUR (The New Knaur [Encyclopedia]) (München, Zürich: Droemer Knaur, 1975), vol VII, p. 5514.
[A brief survey of Shaw's life and works.] Shaw's prefaces are brilliant and emphasize his own points of view. [In German.]

2314 Silver, Arnold. "*The Millionaires's*: Confessional Comedy," SHAVIAN, V (1975), 4.

Shaw tries to satirize Epifania, but this competes with his admiration for her strength and reveals his divided outlook on the "boss" personality. Shaw uses memories of his marriage to Charlotte as material for Epifania's personal life. [Précis of a talk Silver gave in London.]

2315 Simon, John. "COLLECTED PLAYS WITH THEIR PREFACES," NEW YORK TIMES BOOK REVIEW, 2 Nov 1975, pp. 1-2.
Shaw has neither been eclipsed nor been firmly established as a respected writer. His reputation is still hounded by the animus of some of his most brilliant contemporaries, especially poets. But he had dazzling champions as well. The question is whether Shaw's ideology destroys his art. He was a bundle of contraries. As with Wilde, the paradox is basic to Shaw, though Shaw let it permeate every level of his drama. For the two major anxieties of man, love and death, Shaw devised the remedy of the Life Force, which all but prevents any sense of tragedy. Still even the desperate avoiding of love and death creates an "intensity that rises to the heights of a poetry of the prosaic," especially in *Heartbreak House* and *Saint Joan*. One of Shaw's triumphs is that his plays read as dramatically as they play. [Photograph.]

2316 Simon, John. SINGULARITIES, ESSAYS ON THE THEATER, 1964-1973 (NY: Random House, 1975), pp. 21, 49, 93, 103, 168, 178, 197, 198, 210-11.
[Mention of Shaw in essays, collected and reprinted.]

2317 Simon, John. UNEASY STAGES, A CHRONICLE OF THE NEW YORK THEATER, 1963-1973 (NY: Random House, 1975), pp. 80, 96, 234, 261, 267-68, 283-84, 380, 395-96, 428, 444, 445, 447-48.
[Shaw reviewed and mentioned in reviews, collected and reprinted.]

2318 Skidelsky, Robert. OSWALD MOSLEY (NY: Holt, Rinehart and Winston, 1975), pp. 58, 94, 133, 165, 237, 249, 277-78, 310, 313, 335n, 348-49, 476, 478, 500.
Change by Chamberlain's Social-Imperial Party was to be brought about by "an elite of heroic technicians: The "higher types' of Shaw's plays." For Mosley the League of Nations was like Shaw's vision of an organization of higher powers which would control the lower ones. In 1924

Mosley read *The Perfect Wagnerite*; he may have already
seen himself as the heroic Siegfried. From *Caesar and
Cleopatra* Mosley learned to dissimulate for pragmatic
reasons. Mrs. Mosley solicited Shaw's aid for Mosley's
candidature for the rectorship of Glasgow University.
[The text of Shaw's letter explaining why his support is
"superfluous" follows.] Although Shaw had no sympathy
with anti-Semitism and did not believe that Fascism could
succeed in England, he viewed both Fascism and communism
as collectivist ideologies revolting against capitalism.
Mosley supported the ideas of Creative Evolution in *Man
and Superman* and *Back to Methuselah*. He disagree with
Shaw's view in *Wagnerite* that Wagner's destruction of
Siegfreid in GÖTTERDÄMMERUNG was intolerable.

2319 Sklar, Sylvia, THE PLAYS OF D. H. LAWRENCE: A
BIOGRAPHICAL AND CRITICAL STUDY (Lond: Vision Press
Limited, 1975), pp. 25-28, 40, 51, 176, 198, 249.
D. H. Lawrence's feelings toward Shaw were always mixed.
Lawrence's plays have a slight Shavian flavor.

2320 Smith, Warren Sylvester. "Future Shock and
Discouragement: *The Tragedy of an Elderly Gentleman*," ShawR, XVIII (Jan 1975), 22-27.
Forty years before Alan Toffler conceived the term, Shaw
in *The Tragedy of an Elderly Gentleman* predicted that
people would die of an inability to comprehend and adjust
to a new environment. Shaw in 1920 saw fundamental change
in the life process as the only hope for man.
Prolongation of life and vitality could bring about the
needed alteration. *Elderly Gentleman* is not successful as
prediction. The real issue of the play is the gulf
between the longlivers and the shortlivers. We are the
shortlivers and the future does not lie with us and our
false and unreal world. The effect is to show the
audience how their world looks to more exalted eyes.
"This is the most debilitating kind of 'future shock'--one
that Toffler does not deal with--the realization that
one's life, one's life style, one's entire civilization,
may count for nothing in the larger scheme of things."

2321 Smith, Warren S[ylvester]. "G. B. Shaw at
119--Indications of Immortality," NYT, 2 Nov 1975,
II, pp. 1, 5.
Shaw's greatness is still debated. But his plays are
still performed and Shaw-inspired events continue to
flower. In spite of the quibbles of purists MY FAIR LADY

captured must of Shaw's wit and preserved the message that the Life Force aided by human effort can make a jump forward. [Statistical survey of Shaw productions, writing about Shaw, and Shaw societies.] Among Shaw's victories are: a restoration of a zest for language, making theater a place for thought, pioneering unconventional drama, feminism and vegetarianism. His major defeat is the failure to promote alphabet reform. The world Shaw worked for has not come about. [Illustrated.]

2322 Smith, Warren S[ylvester]. "Some Vital Statistics on GBS--Twenty-five Years after, 1950-1975," Shaw R, XVIII (Sept 1975), 90.
[A listing of numbers of productions of Shaw plays, books on Shaw, etc.]

2323 Steinhoff, William. GEORGE ORWELL AND THE ORIGINS OF 1984 (Ann Arbor: U of Michigan P, 1975), passim.
Shaw was a destroyer of values, and his Marxist hopefulness, without a spiritual life based on faith in the Divine, degenerated into praise for totalitarian dictators. Orwell thought of Shaw as one who wished to exert power, and that the hedonism in Shaw's Socialism was a threat. Shaw, like the pigs in ANIMAL FARM, expected to impose social benefits from above.

2324 Stone, Susan. "Biblical Myth Shavianized," MD, XVIII (June 1975), 153-63.
Back to Methuselah and *The Simpleton of the Unexpected Isles* re-work biblical myths in books for Shaw's own Bible of Creative Evolution. In "In the Beginning" Shaw uses the traditional myth of Adam and Eve to show the limitations of man and the introduction of social and economic evils into the world as well as man's potential for redemption. *Simpleton* uses the idea of the Judgment Day, but as a mark of the beginning of a new and better world, not as one of the end of the world. Judgment will be based on the social worth of the individual. The idea of the seriousness of judgment is all Shaw retains from the Christian myth. Responsibility for man is taken away from the supernatural and given to man.

2325 Stürzl, Erwin, and James Hogg. THE STAGE HISTORY OF G. B. SHAW'S SAINT JOAN (Salzburg: Inst.

für Englische Sprache und Literatur, University of Salzburg, 1975).
[Not seen.]

2326 Styan, J. L. DRAMA, STAGE AND AUDIENCE (Lond and NY: Cambridge UP, 1975), pp. 6, 10, 13, 35, 66, 99, 104, 144, 171-74, 206, 229.
Shaw called for a presentational style of acting. He thought of a play as if it were opera, asking for declamation. The direct perception of performance *per se* ensures the satirical shots finding their target. [Brief analysis of a patch of dialogue from *Man and Superman*.]

2327 Sutherland, James (ed). THE OXFORD BOOK OF LITERARY ANECDOTES (Oxford: Oxford UP, 1975), pp. 287, 302-7, 308.
[Eight anecdotes about Shaw; two others in which he is mentioned; fully documented.]

2328 Sutton, Max Keith. W. S. GILBERT (NY: Twayne [TEAS 178], 1975), pp. 80, 91, 112, 113, 124-25.
Shaw missed the point when he contrasted *Arms and the Man* with ENGAGED. He showed "bored contempt" for THE GONDOLIERS, but liked UTOPIA LIMITED. Shaw "objected that Gilbert did not take his paradoxes seriously" and considered Gilbertian irony "barren cynicism."

2329 Thiele, Vladimir. PAN SHAW A PAN TWAIN: VESELÉ HISTORKY ZE ŽIVOTA DVOU SLAVNÝCH SATIRIKŮ, IRONIJŮ A POSMĚVÁČKŮ (Mr. Shaw and Mr. Twain: A Humorous History from the Life of the Two Famous Satirists, Ironists, Mockers) (Prague: Melantrich, 1975).
[Not seen.] [In Czechoslovak.]

2330 Thomas, Gwyn. "Mr. Barrie and Mr. Shaw," List, XCIV (14 Aug 1975), 218-19.
J. M. Barrie and Shaw regarded their coming to London from the Celtic outback as natural. They were different from each other in almost every way. I thought it would be pleasant to dramatize them in 1911, just a brief time away from the exit of the Victorian-Edwardian world in 1914. [Explanation of the setting of Gwyn Thomas's TV play, THE GHOST OF ADELPHI TERRACE.]

2331 Trabskiĭ, A. Ĩa. (ed). RUSSKIĬ SOVETSKIĬ
TEATR 1921-1926 (Soviet Russian Theater 1921-1926)
(Leningrad: "Iskusstvo," 1975).
The Devil's Disciple was produced in Moscow at the Malyi
Theater in the 1924/25 season. A production of *Caesar and
Cleopatra*, using the pre-revolutionary costumes and sets
which were in storage, was also planned but not performed.
In 1922 V. E. Meierhold stated that the first production
at his Actors' Theater would be *Heartbreak House*, but it
was cancelled. *Saint Joan* had 30 performances in the
1924/25 season at the Moscow Kameralnyi Theatre (MKT) with
Tairov, who declared: "I consider *Saint Joan* an entirely
contemporary play . . . though Shaw spoiled it by his
enormous preface, developing ideas which do not at all
emerge from the play itself." *Caesar and Cleopatra* had 15
performances in the 1922/23 season at the Leningrad State
Pushkin Theatre, with eight more performances in the
1924/25 season. *Fanny's First Play* was included in the
current repertoire in the 1924/25 season because it was "a
protest against bourgeois mentality." *Pygmalion* was also
in the 1924/25 season with 12 performances. When *Joan* was
revived for the 1925/26 season, it ran for only two
performances. *Misalliance* was produced at the Leningrad
Bol'shoi Gorky Theater in the 1922 Summer season, with
five performances, and six more in the 1922/23 season.
Captain Brassbound's Conversion had 21 performances in
1923/24 season, and five more in the 1924/25 Winter
season. [In Russian.]

2332 Tynan, Kenneth. A VIEW OF THE ENGLISH STAGE
1944-63 (Lond: Davis-Poynter, 1975), pp. 11, 41,
81, 93, 108, 115-16, 123, 126, 139, 185, 245, 247,
255, 259-60, 273, 322, 358, 364, 366, 368-70, 373-
74, 379-80.
[A collection of reviews, including those of Shaw plays,
on the British stage. Many of these reviews were
collected earlier in CURTAINS (1961).]

2333 Vasilyevna, Larissa. "G.B.S. in the USSR,"
ANGLO-SOVIET JOURNAL, XXXVI (Dec 1975), 20-22.
[Shaw's appreciation of and appreciation by Russia,
especially Soviet Russia.]

2334 Walser, Robert, BRIEFE (Letters), ed by Jörg
Schäfer and Robert Mächler (Genf: Helmut Kossodo,
1975), pp. 262, 274-75, 410, 413.

[Passing references to Shaw (e.g., his remarks on children).] Shaw is an arrogant and stupid writer, but able to make excellent use of his stupidity. [In German.]

2335 Weigel, John A. COLIN WILSON (Bost: Twayne [TEAS], 1975), pp. 20, 23, 26, 36, 39, 42, 44-45, 53, 97, 110, 112.
[Shaw's influence on Wilson's life and writing.]

2336 Weightman, John. "The Mystery of *Heartbreak House*," ENCOUNTER, XLIV (May 1974), 39-41.
After seeing John Schlesinger's production of *Heartbreak House* at the Old Vic, I am dismayed to feel it is not so much a symbol of a collapsing civilization as of Shaw's deepest reaction to the uncertainties of the Shavian metaphysic when brought up against a great catastrophe. Shaw was unable to deal with the enormous evil of the war--he could only assemble his usual characters and put them through a series of theatrical tricks.

2337 Weintraub, Stanley. "Autobiography and Authenticity: Memoir Writing among Some Late Victorians," SOURCES FOR REINTERPRETATION: THE USE OF NINE-TEENTH-CENTURY LITERARY DOCUMENTS. ESSAYS IN HONOR OF C. L. CLINE (Austin: Department of English and Humanities Research Center, University of Texas at Austin, 1975), pp. 1-21.
[Snobby Price in *Major Barbara* as example of confession as theater. Erik Erikson's analysis (1956) of Shaw as example of relationship between confession and motive.] Shaw invented little about his life, usually telling the half-truth if not the whole truth. Sometimes he provided information, beyond anyone's desire to know, to throw the searcher off the scent or to preserve his public image. [An extended example of a Shaw confession from several sources.]

2338 Weintraub, Stanley. "Books Considered," NEW REPUBLIC (27 Dec 1975), 27-28.
"The Shavian industry notwithstanding, G.B.S. is surviving primarily as a sure-fire playwright."

2339 Weintraub, Stanley. "Exploiting Art: The Pictures in Bernard Shaw's Plays," MD, XVIII (Sept 1975), 215-38.

The art of Shaw's formative years remained a catalyst for his playwriting throughout his life, inspiring scenes and parody and appearing in the plays as part of the set or as a model for the set. [Illustrations of works used by Shaw.]

2340 Weintraub, Stanley, and Rodelle Weintraub. LAWRENCE OF ARABIA (Baton Rouge: Louisiana State UP, 1975), pp. 32-33, 35, 51-52, 68-74, 79, 81, 110, 117, 123, 127, 139, 151, 156.
[Shaw's suggested revisions of SEVEN PILLARS OF WISDOM and THE MINT; Lawrence as Private Meek in *Too True to Be Good.*]

2341 Wilpert, Gero von (ed). LEXIKON DER WELTLIT-ERATUR. BAND I: BIOGRAPHISCH-BIBLIOGRAPHISCHES HANDWÖRTERBUCH NACH AUTOREN UND ANONYMEN WERKEN (Dictionary of World Literature. Volume I: Bio-graphical-Bibliographical Glossary of Authors and Anonymous Works) (Stuttgart: Alfred Kröner, 2nd enlgd ed 1975), pp. 1487-88.
[A survey of Shaw's life and works.] Shaw is a witty, ironical and satirical dramatist. [In German.]

2342 Wilson, Edmund. THE TWENTIES, ed with an introduction by Leon Edel (NY: Farrar, Strauss and Giroux, 1975), pp. 55, 422-23, 426.
[Passing references to Shaw, expressing Wilson's admiration.]

2343 Wolfe, Willard. FROM RADICALISM TO SOCIALISM: MEN AND IDEAS IN THE FORMATION OF FABIAN SOCIALIST DOCTRINES (New Haven and Lond: Yale UP, 1975), pp. 109, 113-49, 228, 229, 236-37, 251-52, 260, 284-91, 296, 297, 310.
[Summary of Shaw's social, economic, and political development, climaxing in his "conversion" by Henry George.] Shaw soon outstripped George. He began as a land nationalizer, working on the CHRISTIAN SOCIALIST. He converted to Marxism. But perhaps Shaw's claims of the violence of his conversion are exaggerated, because it is based only on the first chapter of CAPITAL and is a very limited Marxism. Proudhon, Ruskin, and George are probably more important. Shaw then fought the system openly by preaching to anyone who would listen. His dependence on Proudhon lead him to Radical-individualist

utopianism, though he was in agreement with the Marxist idea of the need for revolution.   He was the natural ally of William Morris.   "At heart an Anarchist," Shaw supported Morris against H. M. Hyndman, whose style was Collectivism.   Shaw scholars do not generally agree, however, that Shaw was an Anarchist, both because he denied it later and because the title *How An Anarchist Might Put It* sounds tentative.   But Shaw's allowing the article to appear over his signature in the ANARCHIST makes the conclusion that he was "committed publicly" seem inescapable.   Still his closeness to orthodox Anarchism varied with the subject.   As he became more Malthusian, Shaw came more under the influence of Sidney Webb and farther from the Anglo-Marxists.   Because he was opposed to Hyndman, Annie Besant came to his defense.

Shaw was the last of the Fabian "Old Gang" to accept collectivism.   The change derived more from considerations of political activism than from ideology.   He rejected Proudhon and Anarchism, especially the individual variety.

2344 Yoder, Jon A.   UPTON SINCLAIR (NY: Frederick Ungar [Modern Literature Monographs], 1975), pp. 2, 6.
[Shaw's attempt to influence the Nobel Prize Committee in 1931 in Sinclair's favor.]

1976

2345 Amalric, Jean-Claude.   "George Bernard Shaw, du réformateur victorien au prophète édouardien. Formation et évolution de ses idées (1856-1910) (George Bernard Shaw, from Victorian Reformer to Edwardian Prophet.   Formation and Evolution of His Ideas [1856-1910])."   Published dissertation, Université de Paris-Sorbonne, 1976; pub under the same title (Paris: Didier, 1977).

2346 Andrecht, Ernst H.   SPRACHSOZIOLOGISCHE ASPEKTE IN DER DRAMATISCHEN SPRACHGESTALTUNG BERNARD SHAWS (Aspects of Sociological Language in Bernard Shaw's Formation of Dramatic Language) (Bern: Herbert Lang; Frankfurt/Main: P. Lang, 1976).
[Not seen.]   [In German.]

2347 Applebaum, Stanley (ed). THE NEW YORK STAGE, FAMOUS PRODUCTIONS IN PHOTOGRAPHS (N Y: Dover, 1976), pp. 22, 52, 57, 64.
[*Candida, Heartbreak House, Saint Joan*, and *Back to Methuselah*.]

2348 Ayling, Ronald. CONTINUITY AND INNOVATION IN SEAN O'CASEY'S DRAMA, A CRITICAL MONOGRAPH (Salzburg: Institut für englische Sprache und Literatur [Salzburg: Studies in English Literature (Poetic Drama & Poetic Theory)], 1976) pp. 12-13, 15, 18, 50, 52, 99, 146, 149-50, 169.
[Shaw in the artistic biography of Sean O'Casey.]

2349 Balice, Vincent. "Chesterton and Ibsen: A Misunderstanding," CHESTERTON REVIEW, II (Spring-Summer 1976), 215-25.
Chesterton in his writing on Ibsen followed too closely Shaw's thought, which was incorrect. He equated Ibsen with Shaw, and in attacking Ibsen was attacking Shaw. [See Charles Leland (1976) for a reply.]

2350 Ball, John, and Richard Plant. A BIBLIOGRAPHY OF CANADIAN THEATRE HISTORY, 1583-1975 (Toronto: Playwrights Co-op, 1976), items C406, C485, C487, G189 [Shaw Festival; Niagara-on-the-Lake; C376, C385, C394, C401, C431, C451, C474, C492, C503, C513, C534, I62, I64].

2351 Barnes, Clive. "Theater," NYT, 19 Feb 1976, p. 45.
Shaw is at his best as a political writer, and *Mrs. Warren's Profession* is Shaw at his best. Lynn Redgrave is marvellous as Vivie; Ruth Gordon is deplorable as Mrs. Warren.

2352 Barron, Neil, et al. ANATOMY OF WONDER: SCIENCE FICTION (N Y and Lond: R. R. Bowker, 1976), pp. 72-73.
[A bibliographical guide to *Back to Methuselah* and *Far-fetched Fables*.]

2353 Barzun, Jacques. "The Maid in Modern Dress," TLS, 19 Nov 1976, p. 1448.

[Review of William Searle, THE SAINT AND THE SKEPTICS (1976).] The loneliness of Shaw's God and Joan has nothing to do with pride. God is a powerful worker in the corner of the universe, and his loneliness results from there being relatively few Joans and Shaws around.

2354 Bedell, Jeanne Fenrick. "Towards Jerusalem: The Changing Portrayal of the Working Class in Modern English Drama 1900-1970," DAI, XXXVII (1976), 3635A. Unpublished dissertation, Southern Illinois University, 1975.

2355 Benstock, Bernard. PAYCOCKS AND OTHERS: SEAN O'CASEY'S WORLD (Dublin: Gill and Macmillan; NY: Barnes & Noble, 1976), pp. 3, 9, 12, 182, 288, 297. [Shaw in the biography of Sean O'Casey.]

2356 Berst, Charles A. (ed). "Bernard Shaw: Scholarship of the Past 25 Years, and Future Priorities. A Transcript of the 1975 MLA Conference of Scholars on Shaw," ShawR, XIX (May 1976), 56-72. [An evaluation of past scholarship, with some ideas about future needs and expectations.]

2357 Breyer, Heinrich. "München: Klaus Maria Brandauers 'Opfertod,' Shaws 'Arzt am Scheideweg' in Noelte-Inszenierung an den Kammerspielen" (Munich: Klaus Maria Brandauer's DEATH OF SACRIFICE, Shaw's *The Doctor's Dilemma* in a Production by Noelte at the Munich Kammerspiele), DIE BÜHNE (Vienna), No. 208 (Jan 1976), p. 22. [A review of a production of *The Doctor's Dilemma* at the Munich Kammerspiele.] Shaw's mixture of cabaret, satire, and sentimental cult of the genius can hardly be revived in our time. [In German.]

2358 Briden, E. F. "James's Miss Churm: Another of Eliza's Prototypes?" ShawR, XIX (May 1976), 17-21. Miss Churm from Henry James's "The Real Thing" may be an ancestor of Eliza Doolittle. [There follows an examination of "strikingly detailed anticipations of *Pygmalion*" in the James story.]

2359 Brown, Barbara Browning. "Qualities of Bernard Shaw's 'Unreasonable Man,'" DAI, XXXVII (1976), 981A. Unpublished dissertation, Ohio University, 1976.

2360 Bushko, David Arthur. "Arthur Bongham Walkley's Theory and Practice of Dramatic Criticism," DAI, XXXVII (1976), 981A. Unpublished dissertation, Columbia University, 1976.

2361 Carr, Pat M. BERNARD SHAW (NY: Frederick Ungar [World Dramatists], 1976).
[Sensible and sturdy introduction, both historical and critical, to Shaw's dramatic achievement: Shaw the Man. Fabianism and the Life Force. Shaw and Nineteenth Century Drama. Includes discussion of the major plays individually. Especially useful is the chapter "Shavian Drama Today." Chronology. Bibliography. Halftone illustrations from stage and film productions.]

2362 Černy, František, et al. DĚJINY ČESKÉHO DIVADLA (History of the Czech Theater), III (Prague: Academia věd, 1976).
Karel Mušek translated and produced *You Never Can Tell* at the Prague National Theater (1906), *Mrs. Warren's Profession* (1907), *The Philanderer* (1908), and *Pygmalion* (1913, with 60 performances). *Candida* was first produced at the Svanda Theater (Prague) in 1905, with a production in 1906 at the Prague National Theater. Mušek also directed productions at the National Theater of *Androcles and the Lion* (1915) and *Caesar and Cleopatra* (1917). *Pygmalion* had been produced there in 1913 (again in 1928). Amateur companies produced *Mrs. Warren* in 1911 and 1914, and *Pygmalion* (1914). [In Czech.]

2363 Chaillet, Ned. "Actors Company," P&P, XXIII (June 1976), 31.
Widowers' Houses is still timely in its assault on property speculators, but the production at the Actor's Company is weighted in the direction of pure entertainment.

2364 Chernikova, I. K. "Melodrama Bernarda Shou *Uchennik d'iavola*" (Shaw's Melodrama *The Devil's*

Disciple) NAUCHNYE TRUDY SVERDLOVSKOGO GOS. PED.
INSTITUTA (Sverdlovsk), CCLXXX (1976), 94-111.
The central conflict in *The Devil's Disciple*, as always in
Shaw's plays, is between life and false ideals.   The
conflict is made more profound and concrete by various
episodes and situations and is on several levels--family
relations, between Americans and British etc., but Shaw
sought to show the struggle and difficult victory of his
positive heroes in the eternal battle with falsehood and
dead ideals.   Shaw's use of melodrama affected the action
and specific gravity of the play, since Shaw retained the
essential element in all his plays--discussion.   He also
made use of realistic detail, which traditional melodrama
ignored.   He continued to develop the exposing of historical characters.   Although the main theme is religious by
nature, the play is not religious in the literal meaning
of the word, but is concerned with other human values.
Unlike conventional melodrama, Shaw sought to cause
laughter and surprise, rather than tears: to expose the
grasping policy of Great Britain, and his own concept of
religion.   [In Russian.]

2365 Chernikova, I. K. "*Sviataiā Ioanna* Bernarda
Shou: k voprosu o prirode zhanra," (Shaw's *Saint
Joan*:   The Question of the Nature of Genre),
NAUCHNYE TRUDY SVERDLOVSKOGO GOS. PED. INSTITUTA
(Sverdlovsk), CCLIX (1976), 83-101.
In creating the character of Saint Joan, Shaw followed
Shakespeareian tradition.   She can be compared to Julius
Caesar who gave voice to Shaw's Fabian program and was an
ideal individual in all respects.   Saint Joan is far from
such idealism, but a realistic, national character, who
lives according to the laws of heart and reason.   Unlike
Shakespeare, however, the "people" (folk) of Shaw act offstage, and we only hear their reactions.   The development
of historical drama in Shaw's work was closely connected
with the processes characteristic of nineteenth-century
European drama at the end of the century and is marked by
duality and contradictions.   [In Russian.]

2366 Clausen, Christopher. "Padraic Pearse: The
Revolutionary as Artist," Shaw R, XIX (May 1976), 83-
92.
To the reader of his journalism, Pearse may seem to be
Shaw's kind of Irishman, one who can face reality, and not
Yeats's kind, one who deals in symbols.   His actions led
greater writers, including Shaw, to reassess their
feelings about Irish nationalism.

2367 Cohn, Ruby. "Shaw *versus* Shakes," MODERN SHAKESPEARE OFFSHOOTS (Princeton: Princeton UP, 1976), pp. 241-42, 245, 321-39, 369, 392.

Against actors, Shaw exalted Shakespeare's text. As a champion of Ibsen, Shaw attacked Shakespeare's ideas. [Consideration of the Shakespeare "offshoots": *Caesar and Cleopatra*, the dramatization of *Cashel Byron's Profession, The Dark Lady of the Sonnets*, the burlesque scenes from MACBETH, *Cymbeline Refinished*, and *Shakes Versus Shav.*] Shaw's Shakespeare offshoots are less vigorous than his Shakespeare commentary.

2368 Conlon, Denis. "Chesterton: A Dramatist in Spite of Himself," CHESTERTON REVIEW, III (Fall/Winter 1976/77), 99-117.

In spite of Shaw's encouragement, Chesterton resisted writing for the theater. Finally Shaw's efforts were rewarded. In 1913 Chesterton's MAGIC was produced, for which Shaw wrote the curtain raiser *The Music Cure*. [Text of Shaw-Chesterton correspondence.]

2369 Cordell, Richard A. "Shavian Notes," ISh, XV (Fall 1976), 4.

The Broadway revival of *Mrs. Warren's Profession* is very alive and shows that Shaw refuses to date.

2370 Crawford, Fred D[ean]. "Shaw among the Houyhnhnms," ShawR, XIX (Sept 1976), 102-19.

Shaw in his version of Gulliver's fourth voyage attempts to avoid Swift's mistake of allowing the audience to evade the satire. In Part IV of *Back to Methuselah*, Shaw presents a small GULLIVER'S TRAVELS. The Elderly Gentleman is the most likely figure for audience identification, and he is ultimately reduced to misanthropy, like Gulliver. [There follows a detailed comparison between the Elderly Gentleman and Gulliver.] But the Elderly Gentleman is a tragic figure who asserts man's nobility in spite of his short-lived condition. Gulliver is a comic figure who absurdly regards himself as a Yahoo. The audience can identify with the Elderly Gentleman, but not with Gulliveer. In Part V, Shaw's satire is harder to ignore than Swift's because Ozymandias and Cleopatra-Semiramis are "so pointedly twentieth-century human beings with the universal limitations of modern man."

2371 Crawford, Fred Dean. "Swift and Shaw: Satiric Attitude and Influence," DAI, XXXVI (1976), 4503A. Unpublished dissertation, Pennsylvania State University, 1975.

2372 Dolby, William. A HISTORY OF CHINESE DRAMA (Lond: Elek Books; NY: Harper and Row [Barnes and Noble Import Division], 1976), pp. 104, 205, 208, 232, 280.
[Shaw and Mei Lanfang, the great Chinese classical actor, and Shaw's plays in China.]

2373 Dukore, Bernard F. (ed). "Introduction" and "Bibliography," 17 PLAYS: SOPHOCLES TO BARAKA (NY: Thomas Y. Crowell, 1976), pp. 512-18.
[Introduction to *Pygmalion*.]

2374 Dupré, Catharine. JOHN GALSWORTHY (Lond: Collins; NY: Coward, McCann & Geohegan, 1976), pp. 119, 121, 135, 147, 277.
[Galsworthy and Shaw considered as dramatists of the new theater of ideas.]

2375 Esslin, Martin. AN ANATOMY OF DRAMA (Lond: Temple Smith, 1976; NY: Hill and Wang, 1977), pp. 22, 29, 38, 98-99, 101-2.
Shaw demythologized his historical characters. He contributed much to the rise of left-wing thinking in Britain. And the uttering of the word *bloody* on the stage in *Pygmalion* marked a great change.

2376 Evans, T. F. "Introduction," SHAW, THE CRITICAL HÉRITAGE, ed by T. F. Evans (Lond, Henley and Bost: Routledge & Kegan Paul, 1976), pp. 1-38. Though the progress was not smooth, at his death Shaw was unchallenged as the leading English dramatist of the century. Many critics were unable to judge his plays solely as plays. Because of the loss of records of Constable & Co Ltd in the bombing during the war it is difficult to obtain accurate information about the publishing of the plays. With the publication of *Plays Pleasant and Unpleasant* Shaw made his first impact on the reading public. Critics became even more marked in drawing distinctions between what was and what was not dramatic in Shaw's plays after The Royal Court Theatre productions began. Shaw kept up a running exchange with the critics, and his plays provoked great discussion. Books on Shaw began to appear in the first decade of the century. World War I is a central point in Shaw's career, and his attitudes toward the war aroused a furor. The assumption was that Shaw was finished, and *Heartbreak House* and *Back to Methuselah* did little to advance his reputation. *Saint Joan*, however, became his best known work. After this his plays became increasingly political. The criticial response between the wars became more careful and detailed. Shaw in his early career was more established as a dramatist in the theater in America than in England. He was never so popular in Latin Europe as in Northern and Eastern Europe. The obituary and centenary tributes were uneven, focusing on the early plays and on the public man.

2377 Evans, T. F. (ed). SHAW, THE CRITICAL HERITAGE (Lond, Henley and Bost: Routledge & Kegan Paul, 1976).
Contents, abstracted under date of first publication: Evans, "Preface," "Acknowledgments," "Introduction," "Note on The Text" (1976); unsigned notice, DAILY TELEGRAPH (1892); [W. Moy Thomas] unsigned notice, DAILY NEWS (1892) J. T. Grein, letter, DAILY TELEGRAPH (1892); [William Archer] initialled notice, WORLD (1892); W. A., notice, ILLUSTRATED LONDON NEWS (1892); [A. B. Walkley] initialled notice, SPEAKER (1892); Oscar Wilde, letter to Shaw (1893); unsigned notice, STAR (1894); [William Archer] initialled notice, WORLD (1894); [A. B. Walkley] initialled notice, SPEAKER (1894); unsigned notice, ABERDEEN JOURNAL (1897); [Oliver Elton] unsigned notice, MANCHESTER GUARDIAN (1898); H. A. Jones, letter to Shaw (1898); Max Beerbohm, review, SATURDAY REVIEW (1898); unsigned notice, TIMES (1899); G. S. Street, "Sheridan and Mr. Shaw," BLACKWOOD'S MAGAZINE (1900); William Archer, notice, WORLD (1900); Arnold Bennett, "George Bernard Shaw," ACADEMY (1901); J. G. Huneker, review, MUSICAL COURIER (1901); G. K. Chesterton, "Man v The Superman," DAILY NEWS (1903); Max Beerbohm, "Mr. Shaw's New Dialogues," SATURDAY REVIEW (1903); [F. G. Bettany] unsigned review, ATHENAEUM (1903); [E. A. Baughan] initialled notice, DAILY NEWS (1905); [A. B. Walkley] unsigned notice, TLS (1905); William Archer, notice, WORLD (1905); Bertrand Russell, letter to Goldsworthy Lowes Dickinson, AUTOBIOGRAPHY (1967); W. B. Yeats, letter to Shaw, THE LETTERS OF W. B. YEATS (1954); [A. B. Walkley] unsigned notice, TIMES (1904); E. A. Baughan, notice DAILY NEWS (1904); William Archer, notice, WORLD (1904); Max

Beerbohm, "Mr. Shaw at His Best," SATURDAY REVIEW (1904);
Reginald Farrer, "Salted Pap," SPEAKER (1904); Francis
Prevost, article, EDINBURGH REVIEW (1905); unsigned
notice, NEW YORK HERALD (1905); unsigned notice, PALL MALL
GAZETTE (1905); unsigned notice, MORNING POST (1905);
BEATRICE WEBB, diary entries, OUR PARTNERSHIP (1948); J.
T. Grein, notice, SUNDAY TIMES (1905); William Archer,
notice, WORLD (1905); Alex M. Thompson, "The Sur-Passing
Shaw," CLARION (1905); Max Beerbohm, "Mr. Shaw's
Position," SATURDAY REVIEW (1905); Sir Oliver Large,
"*Major Barbara*, G.B.S., and Robert Blatchford," CLARION
(1905); Rupert Brooke, letters, THE LETTERS OF RUPERT
BROOKE (1958); John Galsworthy, letter to Mottram in R. H.
Mottram, FOR SOME WE LOVED (1956); unsigned notice,
MORNING POST (1906); Desmond MacCarthy, notice, SPEAKER
(1906); St John Hankin, article, FORTNIGHTLY REVIEW
(1907); [Joseph Knight] unsigned review, ATHENEUM (1907);
unsigned notice, YORKSHIRE POST (1907); unsigned notice,
TIMES (1907); [E. A. Baughan] initialled notice, DAILY
NEWS (1907); unsigned notice, MORNING POST (1907); Leo
Tolstoy, letter to Shaw, LIFE OF TOLSTOY ([1930]); H. G.
Wells, letter to Shaw undated; H. Hamilton Fyfe, notice,
WORLD (1908); Henry James, letter to Shaw, in THE COMPLETE
PLAYS OF HENRY JAMES (1949); James Joyce, "La Battaglia
fra Bernard Shaw e la Censura," Il PICCOLO DELL SERA
(1909); Max Beerbohm, Mr. Shaw's 'Debate,'" SATURDAY
REVIEW (1910); H. L. Mencken, "The New Dramatic
Literature," SMART SET (1911); George Herbert Mair, from
ENGLISH LITERATURE: MODERN (1911); John Jay Chapman,
"Shaw and the Modern Drama," HARPER'S WEEKLY (1913); E. A.
Baughan, initialled notice, DAILY NEWS (1913); Desmond
McCarthy, notice, NStat (1913); Dixon Scott, "The
Innocence of Bernard Shaw," BOOKMAN (1913); E.F.S.,
notice, WESTMINSTER GAZETTE (1914); Alex M. Thompson,
notice, CLARION (1914); [H. W. Massingham] initialled
notice, NATION (1914); John Palmer, "Mr. Bernard Shaw: an
Epitaph," FORTNIGHTLY REVIEW (1915); unsigned, "The
Philanderers," NATION (1919); unsigned, "The English
Marivaux," TLS (1919); [John Middleton Murry] "The Vision
of Mr. Bernard Shaw," ATHENAEUM (1919); unsigned notice,
DAILY TELEGRAPH (1921); [Naomi Royde-Smith] notice,
WESTMINSTER GAZETTE (1921); James Agate, notice, SATURDAY
REVIEW (1921); Sydney W. Carroll, notice, SUNDAY TIMES
(1921); Desmond MacCarthy, notice, NStat (1921); Lady
Gregory, diary entry, LADY GREGORY'S JOURNALS (1946); J.
C. Squire, review, OBSERVER (1921). Desmond MacCarthy,
review, NStat (1921); [R. Crompton Rhodes] unsigned
notice, BIRMINGHAM POST (1923); James Agate, notice,
SUNDAY TIMES (1924); Ashley Dukes, from THE YOUNGEST DRAMA
(1923); Alexander Woolcott, notice, NYHT (1923); unsigned

notice, STAGE (1924); Luigi Pirandello, "Pirandello Distills Shaw," NYT (1924); [A. B. Walkley] unsigned notice, TIMES (1924); James Agate, notice, SUNDAY TIMES (1924); Hubert Griffith, notice, OBSERVER (1924); [T. S. Eliot] "Commentary," CRITERION (1924); Robert de Flers, notice, LE FIGARO (1925); Rebecca West, "Interpreters of Their Age," SRL (1924); William Archer, "The Psychology of G.B.S.," BOOKMAN (1924); Robert Lynd, "G.B.S. as G.O.M.," BOOKMAN (1924); Émile Cammaerts, "Molière and Bernard Shaw," NINETEENTH CENTURY (1926); T. E. Lawrence, letter to William Rothenstein, THE LETTERS OF T. E. LAWRENCE (1938); Winston Churchill, article, PALL MALL (1929); [Ivor Brown] notice, MANCHESTER GUARDIAN (1929); H. W. Nevinson, notice, NEW LEADER (1929); W. B. Yeats, letters to Lady Gregory, in THE LETTERS OF W. B. Yeats (1954); St. John Ervine, "Mr. Shaw's Superb Pantomine," OBSERVER (1929); Harold J. Laski, "Is Democracy Breaking Down," List (1930); [Charles Morgan] notice, TIMES (1932); H. W. Nevinson, "Shakespeare's Rival," Spec (1932); George Orwell, letter to Brenda Salkeld, in THE COLLECTED ESSAYS, JOURNALISM AND LETTERS OF GEORGE ORWELL (1968); Osbert Burdett, article, LONDON MERCURY (1933); Lillah McCarthy, from MYSELF AND MY FRIENDS (1933); unsigned notice, MORNING POST (1933); Kingsley Martin, notice, NS & Nation (1933); unsigned notice, IRISH TIMES (1934); H. G. Wells, from EXPERIMENT IN AUTOBIOGRAPHY (1934); Bonamy Dobrée, "The Shavian Situation," Spec (1934); "The Encirclement of Mr. Shaw: Social Doctrines in a Dilemma," TLS (1936); Edmund Wilson, "Bernard Shaw at Eighty," ATLANTIC MONTHLY (1938); Alan Dent, notice, Spec (1938); Brooks Atkinson, notice, NYT (1940); James Agate, notice, SUNDAY TIMES (1939); Salvador de Madariaga, "G.B.S.: Domestic Mesphistopheles," List (1940); Harold Hobson, article, in ENGLISH WITS (1940); H. G. Wells, letter to Shaw, in G.B.S. 90 (1946); J. B. Priestley, "G.B.S. - Social Critic," in G.B.S. 90 (1946); Val Gielgud, "Bernard Shaw and the Radio," in G.B.S. 90 (1946), Dean Inge, "Bernard Shaw: Socialist or Rebel?" List (1946); [Jakob Welti] notice, ZÜRCHER ZEITUNG (1948); unsigned notice, TIMES (1949); H. N. Brailsford, reprint of broadcast talk, List (1949); Terence Rattigan, "Concerning the Play of Ideas," NS & Nation (1950); Obituary, TIMES (1950); Obituary, MANCHESTER GUARDIAN (1950); James Bridie, Obituary, NS & Nation (1950); "Sagittarius," "The Dean's Dilemma," NS & Nation (1950); Allan M. Laing, "G.B.S. in Heaven," NS & Nation (1950); Thomas Mann, "He Was Mankind's Friend," List (1951); Eric Bentley, "Shaw Dead," ENVOY (1951).

2378 Findlater, Richard (pseud). THE PLAYER QUEENS (Lond: Weidenfeld and Nicolson, 1976), pp. 128, 130, 132, 134, 139, 145, 146, 148-50, 153, 154, 156-59, 164-67, 170, 173, 179, 180, 186, 187, 199, 202, 203, 211, 212, 214.
[Shaw and Ellen Terry, Janet Achurch, Mrs. Patrick Campbell, Sybil Thorndike, Edith Evans, and Peggy Ashcroft.]

2379 Finneran, Richard J. (ed). ANGLO-IRISH LITERATURE, A REVIEW OF RESEARCH (NY: Modern Language Association of America, 1976), pp. 167-215, passim.
[Includes "Bernard Shaw" by Stanley Weintraub, abstracted separately.]

2380 Frank, Joseph. "Soph v. Shaw," Shaw R, XIX (May 1976), 93-94, 99.
"Tragedy of an Elderly Gentleman," Part IV of *Back to Methuselah* can be considered Shaw's OEDIPUS REX.

2381 Gibbs, A. M. "Comedy and Philosophy in *Man and Superman*," MD, XIX (June 1976), 161-75.
"This essay explores the relations between the philosophical themes expressed in the discussions in the play and Dream, and the meanings inherent in the action and in Shaw's manipulation of dramatic conventions. One of the main contentions is that although *Man and Superman* as a whole contains . . . pessimistic ingredients, . . . the optimistic views . . . are aligned with the victorious forces in the action . . . . I have found it useful to compare the basic patterns of the main and sub-plots with an account of the classical New Comedy which Northrop Frye presented in his ANATOMY OF CRITICISM."

2382 Gilbert, W. Stephen. "Revolutionary Revival," P&P, XXIII (Sept 1976), 24.
The Devil's Disciple, directed by Jack Gold, is a triumphant revival. [Photographs.]

2383 Gooch, Bryan N. S., and David S. Thatcher. MUSICAL SETTINGS OF LATE VICTORIAN AND MODERN BRITISH LITERATURE: A CATALOGUE (NY and Lond: Garland, 1976), pp. 644-47.
Catalogues the musical settings of Shaw's work: *Androcles and the Lion, Arms and the Man, Back to Methuselah, Caesar*

and Cleopatra, *The Devil's Disciple*, *Great Catherine*, *Heartbreak House*, *Major Barbara*, *Pygmalion*, *Saint Joan*, *The Six of Calais*, and *Widowers' Houses*.

2384 Gordon, Ruth. MY SIDE, THE AUTOBRIOGRAPHY OF RUTH GORDON (NY: Harper & Row, 1976), pp. 213, 380-81, 405, 471. [Anecdotes.]

2385 Gotthelf, Harold. "Normal Vision: A Study of Bernard Shaw's Satire," DAI, XXXVI (1976), 3730A. Unpublished dissertation, Columbia University, 1975.

2386 Graves, Richard Percival. LAWRENCE OF ARABIA AND HIS WORLD (NY: Charles Scribner's Sons, 1976), pp. 96, 97, 101, 103, 104, 107, 110.
[Shaw's friendship with Lawrence. Photographs.]

2387 Hark, Ina Rae. "Bernard Shaw and Victorian Satiric Inversion," DAI, XXXVI (1976), 4509A. Unpublished dissertation, University of California (Los Angeles), 1975.

2388 Higgs, Calvin T. "Shaw's Use of Vergil's AENEID in *Arms and the Man*," ShawR, XIX (Jan 1976) 2-16.
In *Arms and the Man* Shaw attempts to analyze the question: if the heroes of epic literature had been free to make individual decisions, would the result have been the same or chaos? The play is a kind of mock epic, but Shaw mocks on the thematic not the stylistic level. His first method is direct parallelism: Bluntschli and Raina and Aeneas and Dido. The second method is reversal, giving Dido's speech to Bluntschli, producing absurdity. The third method is omission, to create an anxiety level. [There follows careful analysis of Shaw and Vergil.] Destiny operates in both Shaw and Virgil, though Shaw brings it down to the human level. [Very perceptive and suggestive essay.]

2389 Higham, Charles. CHARLES LAUGHTON: AN INTIMATE BIOGRAPHY (Garden City, NY: Doubleday, 1976), pp. 8, 119, 157-60, 162, 164-66, 201, 203.
[An account of the reading performance, and Laughton's role in it, of *Don Juan in Hell*.]

2390 Holroyd, Michael. "G.B.S. and Ireland,"
SEWANEE REVIEW, LXXXIV (Winter 1976), 35-55.
In England Shaw was misunderstood; in Ireland unappreciated. So he became controversial and rich. Shaw's philosophy was so constructed as to obliterate the revulsion he felt for Dublin life. [Sketch of Shaw's Dublin life, with some emphasis on the role of Vanderleur Lee.]

2391 Holroyd, Michael. "Paradox of Shaw," BOOKS AND
BOOKMEN, XXI (May 1976), 14-15.
[Review of SHAW: THE CRITICAL HERITAGE ed by T. F. Evans (1975).] Shaw's humor was a handicap to his reputation, but it is also his vitality and the source of his true originality. Shaw's critics were right, especially in their judgment that he is verbose and too long, but their deductions are wrong.

2392 Holroyd, Michael. "The Wrongs of Copyright,"
TLS, 23 April 1976, p. 487.
There is no Shaw collection; there is a Shaw distribution.

2393 Hubenka, Lloyd J. "Introduction" and "Notes,"
BERNARD SHAW, PRACTICAL POLITICS (Lincoln and Lond: U of Nebraska P, 1976), pp. vii-xxv, and passim.
As Shaw's audiences increased, his political utterances became more disturbing to the Fabians. Yet the "repugnant" ideas were latent in his earlier political thought. Directly or not, the Fabians were influenced by Mill. Shaw never entirely adopted the Fabian line. The transcendentalists had a considerable influence on Shaw. He dismissed Labour and the Progressives. [Discussion of Shaw and equality of income.] Shaw admired the Bolshevik society, and he regarded liberty paradoxically.

2394 Hughes, Catharine. "Mrs. Warren's Profession,"
AMERICA, CXXXIV (13 March 1976), 208.
Even today Mrs. Warren's Profession is amusing in a good production, but a worse one than that at Lincoln Center would be hard to imagine.

2395 Kapp, Yvonne. ELEANOR MARX, VOLUME II: THE
CROWDED YEARS, 1884-1898 (Lond: Lawrence and Wishart; NY Pantheon Books, 1976), pp. 45-46, 58, 72, 102n, 103-5, 106, 114, 115, 195, 198, 231n, 249,

324, 355n, 380n, 474, 527, 545n, 547n, 658, 661n, 663.
[Shaw and Eleanor Marx and Edward Aveling, in the context of the Fabians and the theater, especially Ibsen.]

2396 Kauffman, Stanley. PERSONS OF THE DRAMA, THEATER CRITICISM AND COMMENT (NY, Hagerstown, San Francisco and Lond: Harper & Row, 1976), pp. 37, 77, 85, 141, 173, 212, 231, 305-26, 356, 377.
[Reprints "Bernard Shaw: Collected Letters 1874-1897," NEW REPUBLIC (27 Nov 1965) and "The Lives of Granville Barker," HORIZON (Autumn 1975), among other references to Shaw.]

2397 Kimura, Masami. "Shaw to Wickstead--Igirisu Shakaishugishisoshi no Hitokoma" (Shaw and Wickstead--A Scene in the History of British Social Thought), KENKYUNENPO (Dept. of Economics, Kagawa University, Takamatsu), No. 15 (March 1976), pp. 1-54.
[A detailed and well-documented study of Shaw's economics, particularly its process of development in the period of 1882 through 1885 under the overwhelming influence of Henry George, Karl Marx and Philip Wickstead.] [In Japanese.]

2398 Kimura, Masami. "Yakusha Hashigaki" (Translator's Introduction) [Trans of Shaw's "Karl Marx and DAS KAPITAL], KAGAWA DAIGAKU KEIZAI RONSHU (Takamtsu), XLIX (April 1976), 49-51.
Shaw established himself as a confirmed Jevons economist by writing this important review of DAS KAPITAL in 1887, and at the same time he showed that he was the leading economic theorist in the Fabian Society. [In Japanese.]

2399 Kosok, Heinz. "Das Englische Drama und Theater im 18. und 19. Jahrhundert: Eine ausgewählte Bibliographie" (English Drama and Theater in the 18th and 19th Centuries: A Selected Bibliography), DAS ENGLISCHE DRAMA IM 18. UND 19. JAHRHUNDERT. INTERPRETATIONEN (English Drama in the 18th and 19th Centuries. Interpretations), ed by Heinz Kosok (Berlin: Erich Schmidt, 1976), pp. 362-77.
[A useful and selective bibliography. Lists many titles relevant to Shaw researach.] [In German.]

2400 Kosok, Heinz. "Drama und Theater in England:
1700-1900" (Drama and Theater in England: 1700-
1900), DAS ENGLISCHE DRAMA IM 18. UND 19. JAHRHUN-
DERT. INTERPRETATIONEN (English Drama in the 18th
and 19th Centuries. Interpretations) ed by Heinz
Kosok (Berlin: Erich Schmidt, 1976), pp. 7-24.
Shaw's use of conventional forms serves the criticism of
conventional themes. His *Widowers' Houses* is the first
play of the 'new theater' of the turn of the century. [In
German.]

2401 Krause, David. SEAN O'CASEY AND HIS WORLD
(Lond: Thames and Hudson, 1976), pp. 31, 34, 38,
41, 42, 43, 44, 50, 69, 75-76, 77, 89, 92.
[Shaw in the biography of Sean O'Casey.]

2402 Lambert, J. W. "Plays in Performance, London,"
DRAMA, CXXI (Summer 1976), 40-61.
Widowers' Houses is a neat exposure of myopic liberalism.

2403 Lambert, J. W. "Plays in Performance, London,"
DRAMA, CXII (Autumn 1976), 36-55.
[Enthusiastic review of Jack Gold's production of *The
Devil's Disciple*.]

2404 Laurie, Douglas. "Occasional Notes," ISh, XV
(Fall 1976), 14.
Both *The Devil's Disciple* at the Aldwych Theatre and *Arms
and the Man* at the Oxford Playhouse are given first-rate
productions. Roger Butlin, who designed the sets for
Disciple, corrected Shaw's inaccurate visual details.

2405 Leary, Daniel and Judith. "Barnes and Shaw,"
ShawR, XX (Sept 1976), 132-35.
[Survey of the reviews of Clive Barnes in the NYT in which
he consistently dismissed Shaw as a playwright.] New York
directors are influenced by Barne's antipathy to Shaw.
There have been fewer productions than might have been
expected. Perhaps even the phenomenon of the miscast star
is the result of Barnes, for he "only attacks the stars
fitfully."

2406 Ledger, Marshall. "Ring around A CHRISTMAS
GARLAND," AEOLIAN HARPS, ESSAYS IN LITERATURE IN

HONOR OF MAURICE BROWNING CRAMER, ed by Donna G. Fricke and Douglas C. Fricke (Bowling Green, Ohio: Bowling Green UP, 1976), pp. 227-46.
Shaw seems an unlikely contrast to Kipling, but Beerbohm implies a link in his A CHRISTMAS GARLAND. The ego which is repugnant in Kipling's work is praiseworthy in Shaw's plays. The parody of Shaw, A STRAIGHT TALK, lauds Shaw for the qualities Beerbohm himself possesses: the simultaneous presentation of seriousness and fun.

2407 Leland, Charles. "Ibsen, Chesterton and Shaw: A Misunderstanding All Around: A Response to Vincent Balice," CHESTERTON REVIEW, III (Fall-Winter 1976-77), 35-42.
Chesterton can be expected to have a mind of his own, but it is probable that he was aware of Shaw's insights into Ibsen.

2408 Lesley, Cole. REMEMBERED LAUGHTER, THE LIFE OF NOEL COWARD (NY: Alfred A. Knopf, 1976), pp. 56-58, 222, 316.
[Anecdotes; the resemblance of an early Coward play to *You Never Can Tell*; Shaw's kindness to Coward; Coward as King Magnus in *The Apple Cart*.]

2409 Lewis, Felice Flanery. LITERATURE, OBSCENITY, & THE LAW (Carbondale and Edwardsville: Southern Illinois UP; Lond and Amsterdam: Feffer & Simons, 1976), pp. 54-59, 66, 109.
[The banning of *Mrs. Warren's Profession* in New York and New Haven; the withdrawal of *Man and Superman* from the open shelves of the New York Public Library.]

2410 Lin, Yutang. NAN NÜ (Men and Women) (Kowloon: Kong Ming Bookstore, 1976?).
[Not seen.] [In Chinese.]

2411 Littlewood, F. D. "The National Theatre: The Early Story and Some Personal Aspects," CONTEMPORARY REVIEW, CCXXVIII (May 1976), 249-56.
[Shaw and the history of the National Theatre.]

2412 Lossmann, Hans. "Wiener Premieren" (Vienna
First Nights), DIE BüHNE (Vienna), No 214 (July
1976), 4, 6, 8, 10, 16-17.
[A review of a production of *The Doctor's Dilemma* at the
'Theater in der Josefstadt'.] Shaw's play is not very
interesting, and it is out-of-date. [In German.]

2413 Mack, John E. A PRINCE OF DISORDER: THE LIFE
OF T. E. LAWRENCE (Bost and Toronto: Little, Brown,
1976), pp. 21, 51, 213, 228, 229, 303, 312, 322-24,
327-29, 332, 339, 342, 348-49, 352, 354, 365, 370-
72, 375, 378, 384, 386-87, 391-93, 419, 513, 514.
Shaw liked Lawrence's description of Chartres. Shaw never
understood the needs Lawrence's military service
fulfilled. [Shaw's friendship with Lawrence and his
criticism of THE SEVEN PILLARS OF WISDOM and THE MINT.]
Private Meek in *Too True to Be Good* is modelled on
Lawrence, and Lawrence offered advice about military
detail. Lawrence identified himself with Shaw's Saint
Joan.

2414 Meyer, Nicholas. THE WEST END HORROR: A
POSTHUMOUS MEMOIR OF JOHN H. WATSON, M.D./AS EDITED
BY MICHAEL MEYER (NY: E. P. Dutton, 1976).
["An unpublished Sherlock Holmes case," in which Shaw
among other writers figures.]

2415 Moore, Edward M. "Henry Irving's Shakespearean
Productions," THEATRE SURVEY, XVII (Nov 1976), 195-
216.
[Shaw's criticism of Irving used to resolve the
contradiction between the praiseworthy quality of Irving's
voice and his failure to read verse well.]

2416 Motoyama, Mutsuko. "Shaw and Japanese Drama,"
DAI, XXXVI (1976), 3659A. Unpublished dissertation,
University of Washington, 1975.

2417 Nicoll, Allardyce. WORLD DRAMA (Lond: Harrap;
NY: Harper & Row, Barnes and Noble Import Division,
1976), pp. 13, 42, 439, 443, 458, 501, 510, 559,
561, 627-37, 696, 722, 750.
["Revised enlarged and completely re-set" from the 1949
edition.] Shaw and his laughter dominate the annals of
the theater of his time. [A brief survey of Shaw's work.]

2418 Obraztsova, A., and M. Ochikovskaîa. "Na krutykh povorotakh Shoviany: Bernard Shou v zapadnoĭ literature" (On Sharp Turns of Shavians: Bernard Shaw in Western Literature), TEATR (Moscow), No 10 (1976), 95-110.
[Annotated survey of 24 items on Shaw from G. K. Chesterton (1910) to date.] [In Russian.]

2419 Odin, Roger. "A propos d'une source trop négligée de la Jeanne d'Arc de George Bernard Shaw" (The Relevance of a Greatly Neglected Source of the Joan of Arc of George Bernard Shaw), REVUE D'HISTOIRE DU THÉÂTRE, XXVIII (July-Sept 1976), 242-65.
[This article is sub-titled: "Hommage à Mary Hankinson.]
Mary Hankinson, a likeable, middle-aged woman, who ran the Fabian Society Summer School, was one of the models for Shaw's Saint Joan. The traits they share are: 1) a radiant joy, 2) a keen sense of humor, 3) a charming voice, 4) a love of nature and liberty, 5) a straight gaze, 6) musical taste, and 7) leadership. There was no physical resemblance, but both were unwomanly women, neutral in the battle of sex. [Appendix I: Biography of Mary Hankinson; Appendix II: French translations of English texts; letters and a poem by Dover Wilson, "Read at Saas Grund;" photographs.] [In French.]

2420 Ogiso, Masafumi. "Shaw no Warai" (Shaw's Laughter), EIGO EIBUNGAKKAI KENKYUKIYO (Tokyo), No 5 (1976), 54-64.
[Ogiso tries to define the nature of comicality in Shaw's plays, basing his argument chiefly on the following points: paradox; humor and laughter being serious matter to Shaw; function of comedy; Shaw's natural cheerfulness; Aristophanic comedy; intellectual, not farcical, laughter without emotional entanglements.] [In Japanese.]

2421 Ogiso, Masafumi. "Shaw to Shukyo" (Shaw and Religion), JISSEN EIBEIBUNGAKU (Tokyo), No 6/7 (Sept 1976), 31-40.
The gist of Shaw's religion is admiration for the elemental forces that helped to make up Life. The mystical experience of Life is the basis of his religious experience. [In Japanese.]

2422 Oppel, Horst. "George Bernard Shaw: *Widowers' Houses*," DAS ENGLISCHE DRAMA IM 18. UND 19. JAHRHUN-

DERT. IMTERPRETATIONEN (English Drama in the 18th and 19th Centuries. Interpretations) ed by Heinz Kosok (Berlin: Erich Schmidt, 1976), pp. 281-93.
Widowers' Houses serves a political and social program rather than an esthetical intention. As a criticism of the exploitation of the poor in the slums it is a fierce attack against the Conservatives. Several aspects of *Widowers' Houses* recall the plays of Ibsen: its presentation as a play of purpose, the analytical construction, the numerous debates about conventional morals, the characters as illustrations of model cases, the skilled use of the exciting curtain, and the art of destroying ideals. [In German.]

2423 Otten, Kurt. "George Bernard Shaw: *Caesar and Cleopatra*," DAS ENGLISCHE DRAMA IM 18. UND 19. JAHRHUNDERT. INTERPRETATIONEN (English Drama in the 18th and 19th Centuries. Interpretations) ed by Heinz Kosok (Berlin: Erich Schmidt, 1976), pp. 347-61.
[Discusses Shaw's conception of the hero and the five-act structure of *Caesar and Cleopatra*.] Shaw's Caesar is the creative genius of a new world who fails in the old one. *Caesar* breaks the realistic conventions of the drawing-room play. [In German.]

2424 Phillips, Jill M. GEORGE BERNARD SHAW: A REVIEW OF THE LITERATURE (NY: Gordon P, 1976).
"An Annotated bibliography of Shavian biographies and some personal writings by Mr. Shaw together with an additional listing of selected Shaviana and notes by the author."

2425 Remizov, Boris. "Pro p'esu Bernarda Shou *Nerivniĭ shliûb*" (On Shaw's *Misalliance*) VSESVIT (Kiev), no 9 (1976), 175-76.
Under the influence of the russian Revolutionary movement and of Russian emigre members of the Revolutionary movement also, Shaw wrote a satirical-discussion drama, *Misalliance*, depicting the collapse of family life in bourgeois England in the early nineteenth century. He used the ideas of Kropotkin and Perovskaia as models, also the plays of Gorky, especially (*Dachniki*) *Summer-Folk*, with the eccentric Vlas. [In Russian.]

2426 Rodriguez-Seda, Asela. "*Arms and the Man* y EL HÉROE GALOPANTE: la desmitificación (*Arms and the Man* and EL HÉROE GALOPANTE: The Destruction of Heroism) LATIN AMERICAN THEATRE REVIEW (U of Kansas), X (Spring 1976), 63-67.
Nemesio R. Canales, a Puerto Rican essayist, satirist, and journalist began to read Shaw while studying Law in Baltimore early in the twentieth century. Shaw's thought influenced his political thinking and also molded his dramatic abilities. In EL HÉROE GALOPANTE Canales follows *Arms and the Man* in demolishing the conventional ideas of Society about friendship, love, education, courage, marriage, and above all, heroism. [In Spanish.]

2427 Roy, R. N. GEORGE BERNARD SHAW'S HISTORICAL PLAYS (Delhi, Bombay, Calcutta, Madras: Macmillan Company of India Limited, 1976).
Creative Evolution pervades all Shaw's work, and he turned to history for great men in whom life is expressed at a high level. Shaw's genius is in conflict with the scientific view of history, which depends upon natural laws. Shaw is also anti-democratic in his deductions. His history plays are descendants of nineteenth century historical drama with their elaborate spectacle, erotic intrigue and flamboyant histrionics, but they differ in that they use present day attitudes. Shaw took too many liberties with history.

The purpose of *The Man of Destiny* is to show that Napoleon's rise is due to his superior intelligence. Shaw presents Napoleon in a farcical situation that de-romanticizes him; he is a realist, but with streaks of idealism. Though Shaw's Napoleon is fictitious, he is a convincing picture of the man who would become Emperor of Europe.

The purpose of *Caesar and Cleopatra* is to draw a great man in history, possessing absolute disinterestedness, freedom from ambition, and aversion to glory. The Caesar of history was not like this; it is a portrait of Shaw himself.

In *Saint Joan* Shaw is concerned with the fate of individuals in whom Creative Will expresses itself in celibacy and sainthood. *Joan* is excellently constructed; the characters are brilliant; the dialogue is fine. But the Epilogue detracts from the dramatic effect. Shaw does not depart from historical truth in any particular.

With *In Good King Charles's Golden Days*, Shaw sets aside his pugnacity; he postulates questions but offers no final solutions. It is a brilliant, witty Platonic dialogue; it is not a historical romance. Like Caesar, Charles is a realist, guided by self-interest and without principles, but this picture bears no relation to reality. Newton is a great anachronism, though some of his views are presented accurately. Shaw abandoned external truth to reveal the essential truth about Charles and his age.

2428 Rubin, Don (ed). CANADA ON STAGE, CANADIAN THEATRE REVIEW YEARBOOK, 1975 (Downsview, Ontario: CTR Publications, 1976), pp. 29, 53, 64, 123, 199, 251, 261, 264, 266, 287, 345.
Misalliance, Heartbreak House, The Extermination of Jesus Christ adapted from the Preface to *On the Rocks, Arms and the Man, Don Juan in Hell, Pygmalion, Caesar and Cleopatra, Saint Joan,* MY FAIR LADY, and *The Devil's Disciple.* [Illustrated with production photographs.]

2429 Russell, Annie. "George Bernard Shaw at Rehearsals of *Major Barbara*," ShawR, XIX (May 1976), 73-82.
[A talk to the ladies of the St. Ursula Club, New York, on April 28, 1908. Miss Russell stresses Shaw's kindness, patience and good humor during the rehearsals of *Major Barbara* and concludes that Shaw is serious and not a mere jester.]

2430 Scanlon, Leone. "The New Woman in the Literature of 1883-1909," PAPERS IN WOMEN'S STUDIES (University of Michigan), II (1976), 133-59.
Vivie Warren, a new woman, must discover her share of guilt in the unjust society. She is the most aggressively masculine of the new women because of Shaw's comic exaggeration. Frank is feminine for the same comic effect. Because she cannot forgive her mother or accept her own guilt, Vivie gives up feeling. Shaw suggests that in winning independence, Vivie may be gaining only masculine hardness. Ann Whitefield does not defy convention, but she is not a conventional passive woman. She, in fact, exposes the convention, and she controls the situation.

2431 Searle, William. "Part III: Bernard Shaw and the Maid: A Vitalist View," THE SAINT AND THE

SKEPTICS, JOAN OF ARC IN THE WORK OF MARK TWAIN, ANATOLE FRANCE, AND BERNARD SHAW (Detroit: Wayne State UP, 1976), pp. 97-144.
Darwinism, Shaw felt, was irreligious and immoral, and it tended to encourage capitalism. Among the evidence against Darwin is man's irrational, therefore miraculous, heroic commitment, which is far from his will to survive. Joan is such a heroic person, but however much a miracle she may be, she never succeeds in performing one, which points up the difference between her conception of god and Shaw's: God does not intervene in nature. He is dependent upon man. Shaw objected to Christian super-naturalism. Shaw relied for an explanation of Joan's visions on Sir Francis Galton. He identified inspiration and artistic creation with organic process. The clearest exposition of this theory is in Godfrey Kneller's assault on Newton in *In Good King Charles's Golden Days*. [Summary of the Shaw-Catholic controversy and an examination of the Catholic censor's excisions from the Hollywood film script in 1936.] *Saint Joan* is a profoundly anti-Catholic play.

Shaw accepted early the idea that humanity must repudiate ethical training or conscience in favor of benevolent impulses. Man must "protest" against the maintaining of authority by irrationalist methods. Joan is such a protestant. But nationalism need not be materialistic and godless. And Shaw was skeptical about the power of such protestants to induce reform.

In *The Devil's Disciple* Dick Dudgeon acquires his reputation as a diabolist because of his antipathy to self-sacrifice, but Shaw did believe in disinterested service. In *The Shewing-up of Blanco Posnet* he presents a man tempted for his own good. Lavinia in *Androcles and the Lion* is willing to give up her life for motives like those of Dick and Blanco. They are all in the grip of a power that transcends their rational desires. Joan, superficially unlike them, is the same. Shaw is correct to denounce modern despair as a rationalization for cowardice, and he is more successful than either Mark Twain or Anatole France in his treatment of Joan's "martyrdom."

2432 Shawcross, John T. "Shaw's Early Plays: Beyond Apprenticeship," GREYFRIAR, XVII (1976), 20-32.
The view that an author's early work shows his promise does not apply to Shaw. The genre Shaw wrote in was comedy, which was his means of engaging the intellect and keeping it engaged. The generic structures of comedy are

employed in *Arms and the Man* to undercut romantic concepts of war and heroism and sexual liaisons; all the vehicle components aim at engaging thought and an approach to realistic action where war is the issue. In *The Man of Destiny*, Shaw through comedy of the intellect, not of ideas, shows the man of destiny to be he who divorces his mind from his heart. *Captain Brassbound's Conversion* fails because Shaw worked out the plot implausibly, and he sentimentalized the characters. In *Caesar and Cleopatra* Caesar learns to be more truthful with himself, and Cleopatra is revealed as unable to become a force of destiny.

2433 Sheppard, R. Z. "Happy Hooker," TIME, CVII (1 March 1976), 51.
[Review of *Mrs. Warren's Profession*.] Since Shaw was a Socialist though prudish, Vivie can speak to contemporary women about financial independence and job prejudice but not about female sexual needs.

2434 Shinkuma, Kiyoshi. "Bernard Shaw no Pyuritan-teki Kigeki" (Bernard Shaw's Puritanic Comedy), NAGOYA GAKUINDAIGAKU RONSHU (Seto), XIII (Sept 1976), 89-128.
The basic method of Shaw's comedy, whose comic spirit is essentially puritanic, is that of "homeopathic education." [In Japanese.]

2435 Simon, Nancy Lynn. "Henry Irving and Ellen Terry in MACBETH: Lyceum Theatre, 29 December 1888," DAI, XXXVII (1976), 700A. Unpublished dissertation, University of Washington, 1975.

2436 Stockholder, Fred E. "A Schopenhauerian Reading of *Heartbreak House*," ShawR, XIX (Jan 1976), 22-43.
The Schopenhauerian ethical conception of history and his metaphysics take over the whole form of *Heartbreak House*. The residents of Heartbreak House are "dreamers" in the image of the play as the language and the atmosphere of sleeping in the opening make clear. Shaw's dream is analogous to Schopenhauer's two kinds of dreams: first the dream of life as we live it, and second, fantasies. When Shaw's characters lift their romantic dreams, they see, not Schopenhauer's rapacious will, but the Life Force. The mistaken identity of all the characters but

Mangan forces each into self-identification. All the allusions in the play, as well as forcing attention to a Schopenhauer-styled sense of universals, expands the sense of "the infernal repetitiousness of history." When Mangan wakes from his sleep, the others are forced to recognize him as human. "The desired destruction and pain will fall on all, but the man who resists the will-to-live comes off clean even if he is ridiculous." When Mangan tries to strip, forcing a third recognition, there is no tragedy because, although he can feel pain, he can learn nothing from it. The excitement when the bombs fall expresses a celebration of danger and death that competes with Shotover's operation of the will. Shaw is saying "England needs to be destroyed and it needs to be preserved." The "impulse toward death in itself [is] the hope for the future."

2437 Stone, Susan C. "Shaw's Heroic Model in Flux: From Caesar to Charles," ENGLISH STUDIES IN CANADA, II (Fall 1976), 306-13.
Shaw's major history plays, *Caesar and Cleopatra, Saint Joan* and *In Good King Charles's Golden Days,* show a change in his ideas about heroes. His early interest in heroes as inspirational models for the mass of humanity was gradually replaced by the conviction that humanity is unable or unwilling to learn from its heroes, so mankind's only hope lies in the combined efforts of various elements of society. Caesar comes the closest of all Shaw's characters to being a complete, unvanquished hero. In *Joan*, though Joan is given the greatest possible stature, Shaw puts more emphasis on the inability of humanity to profit from her example. *King Charles* divides the attributes of the hero among four characters and suggests that any hope for the future lies in their interaction rather than in the individual hero.

2438 Taylor, George. HISTORY OF THE AMATEUR THEATRE (Melksham, Wiltshire: Colin Venton, White Horse Library; NY: British Book Centre, 1976), pp. 48, 49, 51, 52, 116, 124.
[Shaw and the British Amateur Theater.] *The Shewing-up of Blanco Posnet* was given its first British performance (1912) by the Letchworth Dramatic Society, while it was still under the ban of the censor.

2439 Tetzeli von Rosador, Kurt. DAS ENGLISCHE GESCHICHTSDRAMA SEIT SHAW (English History Drama since Shaw) (Heidelberg: Winter, 1976), pp. 125-60. [Not seen.] [In German.]

2440 Trewin, J[ohn]. C[ourtenay]. THE EDWARDIAN THEATRE (Lond: Basil Blackwell; Totowa, NJ: Rowman & Littlefield, 1976), pp. 1-4, 8, 14, 18-21, 23-25, 29, 32, 41, 46, 55, 59, 62, 64, 68-89, 92-93, 98-99, 101, 117, 121, 125, 132, 144, 148, 151, 152-53, 154, 167, 172-73, 176.
Not all Shaw's plays from the Edwardian period are actor-proof; their narrative power is secondary; thinly spoken they fail to hold attention. But at his richest, Shaw was an extra-special of the English stage. *Candida* is the most compact of the canon. *John Bull's Other Island* in Years's theater would have been another Irish problem. Shaw never wrote anything kinder than *You Never Can Tell*. Perhaps its benignity is the result of Shaw's being in love when he wrote it. *Man and Superman*, once highly regarded, now limps in any average performance. *Major Barbara*, like *Superman*, needs a superlative company. *The Witch of Atlas* is a better title for *Captain Brassbound's Conversion* because Cicely Waynefleet is the center of the play. *The Doctor's Dilemma* can survive any production. *The Philanderer* is a tedious joke. *Caesar and Cleopatra* has never done anything expected of it; Shaw did not visualize its action with his usual clarity. *Getting Married* is remorselessly debating Shaw. In *Misalliance* Shaw's hammer-hammer can be fatiguing. [Brief discussion of *Fanny's First Play, Androcles and the Lion* and *Pygmalion*. History of Edwardian theater and Shaw's role in it. Photographs. Tables.]

2441 Tuohy, Frank. YEATS (NY: Macmillan, 1976), pp. 10, 19, 47, 56-58, 65, 67, 75, 94, 98, 100, 129, 184, 194, 198-99, 221.
[Passing references to Shaw as he relates to Yeats's biography. Photograph.]

2442 Turco, Alfred, Jr. "*The Quintessence of Ibsenism*," TEXAS STUDIES IN LITERATURE AND LANGUAGE, XVII (Winter 1976), 855-79; rptd as Chap 1, SHAW'S MORAL VISION (Ithaca, NY and Lond: Cornell UP, 1976), pp. 23-53.
An ideal according to Shaw is an illusion; and the Shavian idealist is the ordinary person. To the dutiful, self-

sacrificing, reasoning idealist, Shaw opposes the "selfish" realist who follows his own will. Shaw is not so simplistic to use realism to describe the violation of tradition; the realist demands more of himself than his idealist counterpart. Shaw stressed the concrete over the abstract and was not a naive progressive. *Quintessence* is not a polemic in favor of indiscriminate relativism, but a protest against undiscriminating moralism. However, Shaw's failure to make explicit the reliance of all men on certain assumptions raises the objection that the book's ethics are more sophisticated than its epistemological underpinnings. The *Quintessence* is not simply the quintessence of Shaw. The realist is a certain kind of idealist, one whose ideals are not flattering illusions, but necessary illusions. In his analysis of Ibsen's plays, Shaw does not always distinguish between the two kinds of idealism, and in fact exposes the errors of Ibsen's heroic idealists, because the idealists do not pass the pragmatic test. In criticising Ibsen, Shaw intuits that the success of his own reformist goals will depend upon an ability to resist grand designs foredoomed by the nature of the world.

2443 Turco, Alfred, Jr. SHAW'S MORAL VISION (Ithaca, NY and Lond: Cornell UP, 1976). Chapter 1, rptd from "*The Quintessence of Ibsenism*," TEXAS STUDIES IN LITERATURE AND LANGUAGE, XVII (Winter 1977), 855-79; Part of Chapter III rptd from "Ibsen, Wagner, and Shaw's Changing View of 'Idealism,'" ShawR, XVII (May 1974), 78-85. [Abstracted under date of first publication.]

1. "*The Quintessence of Ibsenism.*" 2. Executive Power. The value of a concept to Shaw, as expressed in *Immaturity*, is measured only by the results it produces. [The novels are examined "as preparation for coming to terms with the ethical stance of early Shavian drama."] The novels foreshadow *Quintessence's* advocacy of the primacy of concrete action over abstract principles. In *Widowers' Houses* Shaw betrays a grudging admiration for Sartorius, who understands and acts upon his position in the world. *Mrs. Warren's Profession* is the first example of relating one play to another dialectically. In *Arms and the Man* Shaw concentrates on human foibles instead of crimes and can create a hero who embodies the moral position he had been defining in his previous work. In politics Shaw also emphasized effectiveness, even at the cost of reducing his vision, which explains why he joined the Fabians. At times Shaw's love of efficiency leads to a dangerous idealization of the efficient; i.e., his

flirtations with dictatorship. 3. The Pragmatist as Pilgrim. The conclusion of *Candida* involves a double paradox: 1) the immature boy is stronger than the manly husband, 2) Marchbanks' conviction of his own strength coincides with his apparent renunciation. Dick Dudgeon is also different from the Shavian apostles of survival. Caesar is the archpragmatist whose lack of principle is justified by the results of his actions. Marchbanks, Dudgeon, and Caesar are basically the same character.

4. Dialectic of the Self. Shaw's comments on Ibsen's EMPEROR AND GALILEAN show that he demands a crucial kind of action in which the *perfectly* self-realized person is also advancing the purposes of ultimate reality. Self is the root of all values. This is what makes his position on ethical questions shocking.

5. Don Juan in Heaven. The mistaken view that the characterization of women in *Man and Superman* is both superficial and prejudiced results from their being portrayed as efficient and self-reliant. Don Juan is to Tanner as *The Perfect Wagnerite* is to *Quintessence*; he united practical realism and heroic idealism.

6. *John Bull's Other Island*. *Superman* and *John Bull* and *Major Barbara* deserve to be regarded as a trilogy. When the hypothetical of *Superman* is tested in the actuality of *John Bull*, the world prevents wisdom from being realized.

7. *Major Barbara*. *Barbara* is a magnificient failure. It is a battle of wits between Shaw and his audience. Shaw addressed the problem of *John Bull*: Why the synthesis between the dream and the world was not possible.

8. *Heartbreak House*. *Heartbreak* returns to the themes of *Superman*, *John Bull*, and *Barbara*. The illusions of *Heartbreak* are the ideals of *Quintessence*. Art is not only an instrument of self-knowledge, but also of self-delusion. Shaw's optimism is diminished. Tanner, Keegan, Undershaft, and Shotover are one hero whose advancing age suggests Shaw's maturing vision.

9. Epilogue. After the collapse of the synthesis in *Heartbreak*, Shaw concluded that the only way to preserve the soul from the flesh was to separate them (*Back to Methuselah*). For Joan heaven and earth remain eternally separate. The conclusion to *In Good King Charles's Golden Days* is as pessimistic as the Epilogue to *Saint Joan*. Man's self-division precludes his self-realization.

2444 Vesonder, Timothy George. "Archetypal Patterns in the Plays of Bernard Shaw," DAI, XXXVI (1976), 7448A-7449A. Unpublished dissertation, Pennsylvania State University, 1975.

2445 Wearing, J. P. THE LONDON STAGE 1890-1899: A CALENDAR OF PLAYS AND PLAYERS, 2 vols (Metuchen, NJ: Scarecrow Press, 1976), items 92 & 357; 94.65; 99-204.
[Play bills for *Widower's Houses, Arms and the Man,* and *You Never Can Tell.*]

2446 Weintraub, Stanley. "All Wrong on the Night," TLS, 28 May 1976, p. 634. [Review of T. F. Evans (ed), SHAW, THE CRITICAL HERITAGE (1976).]
Shaw became the captive of his reputation. however well this worked with audiences, it proved counter-productive with critics. Shaw assumed he was educating with each new play critics and audiences for the next one; they could not keep up, thinking each new play was not as good as the last. Shaw thought producing the plays anonymously would prevent preconceived ideas from getting in the way.

2447 Weintraub, Stanley. "Bernard Shaw," ANGLO-IRISH LITERATURE, A REVIEW OF RESEARCH, ed by Richard J. Finneran (NY: Modern Language Association of America, 1976), pp. 167-215.
Shaw is an artist of classical standing. [Survey of research and criticism: I Bibliographies, II Editions, III Biographies and Autobiographies, IV Early Criticisms, V General Critical Evaluations, VI The Novels; and Early Musical, Dramatic and Literary Journalism, VII Criticism of Individual Plays, VIII Influence and Reputation.]

1977

2448 Amalric, Jean-Calude. BERNARD SHAW, DU RÉFORMATEUR VICTORIEN AU PROPHÈTE ÉDOUARDIEN (Bernard Shaw, from Victorian Reformer to Edwardian Prophet) (Paris: Didier, 1977); dissertation, Université de Paris-Sorbonne (1976).

A close examination of the genesis and development of Shaw's ideas in his work as a novelist, a journalist and a critic reveals especially his guiding principles of the Fabian theory of rent and equality of income. Closely linked to his political and economic thought are his ideas on art and the place of the artist in society. When Shaw changes to a concept of life which is more metaphysical and religious, the reformer turns prophet. It is around the theory of the Life Force and the roles of woman and the superman that his doctrine of a mystic and naturalistic vitalism revolves. This line of thought broadens toward a religion of life, in which the will and moral responsibility are emphasized. The double-sided prophet-jester, iconoclast-reformer, artist philosopher sums up Shaw's greatness. [Chronological tables of Shaw's works and activities from 1876-1911, bibliography of Shaw's writings from 1882-1898, extensive bibliography of writing about Shaw. This is a major work on Shaw in French.]

2449 Amalric, Jean-Claude. "Shaw in France in Recent Years," ShawR, XX (Jan 1977), 43-46.
"Owing perhaps to translation, or perhaps some peculiar frame of mind, Shaw and his plays meet with varying success in France."

2450 Anderson Imbert, Enrique. LAS COMEDIAS DE BERNARD SHAW (The Plays of Bernard Shaw) (Mexico: Univ. Nacional Autonoma de México, 1977).
[Not seen.] [In Spanish.]

2451 Astafeeva, M. "Ibsen kak sozdatel' sotsial'noĭ dramy: Shou ob Ibsene" (Ibsen as Founder of Social Drama: Shaw on Ibsen), PROBLEMY ZARUBEZHNOGO TEATRA I TEATROVEDENIIA (Problems of Foreign Theater and Theater Criticism) (Moscow: np, 1977), 161-75.
[Not seen.] [In Russian.]

2452 Barnes, Clive. "A Halo for Lynn Redgrave as *Saint Joan*," NEW YORK POST, 16 Dec 1977.
The main fault with *Saint Joan* is the over-riding inability to resist being cheaply clever. Lynn Redgrave's portrayal has no roots in the tradition, but it is moving.

2453 Barnes, Clive. "Shavian Teamwork," NYT, 16 Feb 1977, III, p. 21.
Man and Superman is probably Shaw's best play. In spite of savage cuts, the production of San Francisco's American Conservatory Theater was a delight largely because of the interplay of the entire company.

2454 Barnes, Clive. "Stage: Shaw's *Caesar and Cleopatra*," NYT, 25 Feb 1977, III, p. 4.
There is probably something for everyone to dislike in *Caesar and Cleopatra*, but Ellis Rabb's production is not all bad.

2455 Baskin, Ken Alexander. "Shaw and Death: A Mythology for Creative Evolution," DAI, XXXVIII (1977), 798A-799A. Unpublished dissertation, University of Maryland, 1976.

2456 Batters, Jean. EDITH EVANS, A PERSONAL MEMOIR (Lond: Hart-Davis MacGibbon, 1977), pp. 27-28, 33, 45, 98, 136, 137.
Shaw tried to stop the broadcast of *The Millionairess* in the middle, because "Edith was ruining the part of Epifania and with it the play."

2457 Berquist, Gordon. THE PEN AND THE SWORD: WAR AND PEACE IN THE PROSE AND PLAYS OF BERNARD SHAW (Salzburg, Austria: Institut für Englische Sprache und Literatur [Poetic Drama and Poetic Theory], 1977).
The Philosophical and Political Background. [General survey of: 1) whether or not war is innate; 2) Militarism; 3) Pacifism; 4) The just war theory; 5) Peace Plans. Shaw shares many of Kant's ideas about peace, but he differs from Kant in supporting some sort of international peace force. Though Shaw disagreed with the hedonist basis for the Utilitarian notion of peace of Jeremy Bentham, he did agree with his general proposition; and 6) The political background.] Shaw accepts war as a fact of human history. He thinks little of the soldier, who is dangerous because he is unmanned by discipline, but Shaw, as a good Socialist, was concerned about the conditions under which the soldier lived. Shaw attacks idealism in *Arms and the Man* and in *The Man of Destiny*. Swindon in *The Devil's Disciple* is the stupid professional soldier. These characters are only precursors to Caesar,

whose single prime quality is his aloofness from ideology, and who represents Shaw's ideals of democracy, discipline, realism. In *Captain Brassbound's Conversion* Cicely is a natural commander. Imperialism is the most relevant expression of things military in *Brassbound*. [Discussion of *Fabianism and Empire* (1900).] Shaw turned his attention to disarmament, which he felt was an impractical myth. In the Preface to *John Bull's Other Island* and elsewhere, he continued to argue against the idiotic military caste system. The Captain in *Androcles and the Lion*, Edstaston in *Great Catherine*, and Devallet in *Fanny's First Play* are all versions of Sergius, good men warped by aristocratic ideals. *Press Cuttings* is a summary of all Shaw's views on the military to that point. Ferrovius in *Androcles* shows that an honest man cannot follow Jesus when the trumpet sounds. The first part of *Common Sense about the War* is a review of the past failures leading to World War I. The second part provides practical conclusions. In the final section he deals with peace and international organization after the war. The chapter headings of the unpublished *More Common Sense about the War* are a good summary of it. *The Playlets of the War* are all insignificant. The *Inca of Perusalem* has as its true subject the false image of the Kaiser held by the British. The theme of these plays is also that of *Heartbreak House*: ineptitude. *Back to Methuselah* is the result of World War I. Shaw's solution was something between the authority of monarchy and the freedom of democracy. *The Intelligent Woman's Guide* is unique in Shaw in that it provides an economic explanation for the war. Cain in *Methuselah* embodies all Shaw's objections to the military man. [Considers the military characters of *Saint Joan*, *Too True to Be Good,* and *Geneva*.] But the idea that reform must begin with domestic reform is a significant theme along with the causes of war, which have not changed. Before and during World War II, Shaw returned to his old themes, but by the end of the war there is the feeling that events passed him by.

2458 Brooks, Harold F. "Shavian Sources in the Notes to QUEEN MAB," ShawR, XX (May 1977), 83-84. Shelley in his Note on QUEEN MAB VI.198 makes the same distinction Shaw's Caesar in *Caesar and Cleopatra* makes between Cleopatra's vengeance on Pothinus and Rufio's slaying of Ftatateeta. Shelley's *reductio ad absurdam* about the existence of God is echoed in Lavinia's faith in an unknown God in *Androcles and the Lion*.

2459 Brophy, Brigid. "A Shavian Night's Entertainment," ISh, XVI (Fall and Winter 1977), 1-4.
The Millionairess is a fairy tale and is more pronouncedly autobiographical than any other play of Shaw's. The magic is Epifania's power to make money. Epifania's test by which she proves herself worthy of the doctor--living alone and unaided on less than £2--is the test Shaw put himself to when he married Charlotte. He proved himself worthy by the £3,000 from the American success of *The Devil's Disciple*. The difference between the monster and the saint, both of whom are bosses by nature, lies in how well society channels their energies, and society can protect itself more easily from millionaires than from tyrants.

2460 Burke, Tom. "They Hope to Heat Up Shaw's *Caesar*," NYT, 2 Jan 1977, II, pp. 1, 7.
[Interviews With Elizabeth Ashley and Rex Harrison before the opening of a revival of *Caesar and Cleopatra*. They discuss their understanding and preparation for the roles.]

2461 Cannon, Betty Jo. "The Dialectic of Shavian Comedy: Shaw's Comic Art Viewed from the Perspective of His Aesthetic and Philosophical Ideas," DAI, XXXVIII (1977), 2771A. Unpublished dissertation, University of Colorado, 1977.

2462 Canovan, Margaret. G. K. CHESTERTON: RADICAL POPULIST (NY and Lond: Harcourt Brace Jovanovich, 1977), pp. 13, 33, 46-47, 64-65, 103.
[Chesterton distinguished from Shaw in his attitude toward social problems.]

2463 Cerf, Bennet. AT RANDOM: THE REMINISCENCES OF BENNET CERF (New York: Random House, 1977), pp. 112-15.
[Anecdotes about Cerf's meetings with Shaw, including how Shaw received twice as much as Eugene O'Neill for permitting *Saint Joan* to appear in THE THEATRE GUILD ANTHOLOGY, a first for any Shaw play. Photograph.]

2464 Chute, Edward Joseph. "Comic Wrestling: A Comparative Analysis of the Comic Agon and Its Dramatic Idea and Form in Selected Comedies of

Aristophanes, Shakespeare, Jonson, Shaw, and Calderon," DAI, XXXVIII (1977), 1367A. Unpublished dissertation, University of Minnesota, 1977.

2465 Clarke, Gerald. "Platonic Exercise," TIME, CIX (7 March 1977), 71.
Caesar and Cleopatra is afflicted by the mummy's curse; it is unworkable. The vigorous pruning of this production by Ellis Rabb makes the plot baffling.

2466 Cohen, M. A. "The 'Shavianization' of Cauchon," ShawR, XX (May 1977), 63-70.
The handling of Cauchon and the Burgundian Church in Saint Joan is largely false because Shaw had to contradict the historical tradition, especially Shakespeare, that portrayed Cauchon as a villain. Shaw wished to attack the English, present the tragic moral that murder of innocents is committed by 'normal' persons, and import Protestantism into the play. The falsity does not matter from an artistic point of view.

2467 Crick, Bernard. "The Transcendental Utilitarian," TLS, 4 March 1977, p. 240.
[Review of Lloyd J. Hubenka (ed), BERNARD SHAW: PRACTICAL POLITICS (1976), and Alfred Turco Jr., SHAW'S MORAL VISION (1976).] The Webbs saw Shaw as their propagandist, and all three thought their aims were consistent, which is true only with qualifications. Historians and students of politics have been shy of Shaw. Shaw was the primal bogyman of the DAILY TELEGRAPH correspondence columns. He did not suddenly turn into a friend of dictators; his despair over the First World War forced him to recognize that "evolution" was not inevitable and that a terrible regression was setting in.

2468 Curnow, D. A. "Modern Shakespeare Offshoots," MOSAIC, X (Spring 1977), 165-70.
[Not seen.]

2469 Curtis, Anthony. "Plays in Performance, London," DRAMA, CXXV (Summer 1977), 46-62.
Eileen Atkins blazed intermittantly in Saint Joan.

2470 Curtis, Anthony. "Plays in Performance, London," DRAMA, CXXVI (Autumn 1977), 45-57.
Harley Granville Barker's THE MADRAS HOUSE and Shaw's *Man and Superman* playing at the same time allow us to see the difference between the lived and the theatrical. *Candida* has in common with *Superman* Shaw's shadow-boxing with the plot-conventions of Victorian drama. [Photograph of *Superman*.]

2471 Curtis, Anthony. "Plays in Performance, London," DRAMA, CXXVII (Winter 1977-78), 45-60.
If Shaw were not so playful, *The Apple Cart* might be regarded as a serious plea for the superiority of persons to institutions.

2472 Davies, Cecil W[illiam]. THE THEATRE FOR THE PEOPLE, THE STORY OF THE VOLKSBÜHNE (Austin: U of Texas P, 1977), pp. 58-59, 70, 92, 94, 156.
[Performances of Shaw by the Volksbühne.]

2473 De Vries, Ella Mae Scales. "Thomas Carlyle and Bernard Shaw as Critics of Religion and Society," DAI, XXXVII (1977), 4365A-4366A. Unpublished dissertation, University of Nebraska (Lincoln), 1976.

2474 Dock, Leslie Anne. "Brigid Brophy, Artist in the Baroque," DAI, XXXVII (1977), 5844A-5845A. Unpublished dissertation, University of Wisconsin (Madison), 1976.

2475 Eagle, Dorothy, and Hilary Carnell. OXFORD LITERARY GUIDE TO THE BRITISH ISLES (Oxford: Clarendon P, 1977), pp. 115b, 164b, 168b, 184b, 207b, 399b.
[A description of places associated with *Widowers' Houses, Mrs. Warren's Profession, Arms and the Man, Candida, The Devil's Disciple, Man and Superman, Major Barbara, Pygmalion,* and *Saint Joan*.]

2476 Eder, Richard. "Shaw Still Has the Power to Captivate," NYT, 4 Sept 1977, II, p. 3.
Bertolt Brecht praised Shaw for his cheerfulness, calling him a good man and a terrorist, a quality almost unique

among the avant-garde today. He disclosed his own limitations without seeming to. *The Millionairess* is so performable that the audience is captivated. *Man and Superman* has greater purpose, but it is too much: "a witty play is interrupted for two hours by a play of wit" [the third act]. Shaw's weakness is his general ideas.

2477 Eder, Richard. "Shaw *Superman* Takes Super Stamina," NYT, 28 July 1977, III, p. 16.
The full version of *Man and Superman* (at Niagara-on-the-Lake) is memorable and exhausting. Shaw's Hell is some-thing like England--his heaven is something like the Fabian Society. Tanner without the Hell scene can be tiresome. Ian Richardson's Tanner is anchored in a kind of discouragement. [Photograph.]

2478 Eder, Richard. "Stage: Lynn Redgrave in *Saint Joan*," NYT, 16 Dec 1977, III, p. 3.
Saint Joan is as close as an artist could come to portraying a saint. Lynn Redgrave is admirable in many ways, but she lacks the irrational contagion.

2479 Edwards, Anne. VIVIEN LEIGH, A BIOGRAPHY (NY: Simon and Schuster, 1977), pp. 66, 133, 135, 137-38, 180, 182-83, 185.
[Anecdotes.]

2480 Eisenbud, Julie. "Possible Sources of Shaw's *Pygmalion*," N&Q, XXIV (Oct 1977), 442-44.
Smollett's PEREGRINE PICKLE, Florence Marryat's OUT OF HIS RECKONING, Henry Sweet, and Shaw's relationship with his mother and his proposal of marriage to Charlotte Payne-Townshend are possible sources for *Pygmalion*.

2481 Evans, Gareth Lloyd. THE LANGUAGE OF MODERN DRAMA (Lond, Melbourne and Toronto: Dent [Every-man's University Library]; Totowa, NJ: Rowman and Littlefield, 1977), pp. 4, 8, 15, 17, 19, 22, 32-64, 65, 73, 79, 80-81, 86, 87, 88, 89, 92, 93, 105, 114, 119, 139, 167, 168, 175, 185, 194, 195.
Shaw is the exception to the notion that the dramatist who deals successfully with contemporary life must use the language of the populace. His plays are in a special sense literary, and he does not attempt an accurate photograph of life. He refined ordinary speech into the

style of public speaking, and he wrote in a way to make any interference on the part of actors impossible. In the preface to *Widowers' Houses*, Shaw proposed a text that fulfilled the requirements of both play and novel. Not Shaw's language but his political and sociological ideas give his plays currency. His name was predominant in the literature and courses for the workers' Educational Association. And the effects of Shaw's language on those who fight the "class struggle" are still working. Shaw's novelist style is most apparent in the descriptive directions of his plays, and there is a discrepancy between these and the technical resources of his theater. There is even an incompatibility for the audience between what it sees and hears. However, the descriptions are helpful to the actor. But for the plays before and including *Heartbreak House*, there is no way they can be satisfactorily represented. Shaw's active-directions bring his dialogue to life. Sometimes his dialogue embodies the directions. Some of his directions are strictly stage directions. Some are mixed stage and active. Some are intended only for readers. A persistent effect of the directions is a static frieze, a deliberate stage design, which is one explanation why the plays seem to be more talk than action. The source of this phenomenon may be the orator in Shaw's make-up, and one may suppose that Shaw desired the effect of music, the right verbal note. The assurance of Shaw's language gives off an air of optimism, except in *Heartbreak*. It makes three demands: 1) the actor must have an unsullied directness of address; 2) the actor must convey confidence and enthusiasm; and 3) the actor must be aware that his dialogue is part of a larger design. Shaw found an echo of his own optimism in John Bunyan's forthright heroics.

2482 Finneran, Richard J., George Mills Harper, and William M. Murphy, eds. LETTERS TO W. B. YEATS, 2 vols, (NY: Columbia UP, 1977), pp. 108, 173, 220, 255, 288, 319-20, 322-23, 389, 408, 481-82, 489, 491, 512, 538, 542, 570-71.
[Letters to Yeats from Shaw and from other correspondents mentioning Shaw.]

2483 Frank, Joseph. "Internal vs. External Combustion: Dickens' BLEAK HOUSE and Shaw's *Major Barbara* and *Heartbreak House*," ShawR, XX (Sept 1977), 126-34.
The basic difference between Dickens's novels and Shaw's plays is Karl Marx. Examining BLEAK HOUSE through the

lenses of *Major Barbara* and *Heartbreak House* shows that
despite theeir antipodal moods, both plays depend upon the
possibility of a better world. BLEAK HOUSE has the
exhuberance of *Barbara* as well as the despair of
Heartbreak. Both Dickens and Shaw were disgusted with
Parliamentary democracy. Both writers have the same views
on poverty, money and exploitation. The difference
between Dickens and Shaw is epitomized by the internal
combustion of Krook and the external combustion of the
German bombs. Dickens is fictional and Shaw is logical
and inevitable. Shaw has a program; Dickens has none.

2484 Friedberg, Maurice. "The Older Anglo-American
'Progressives': Shaw, Dreiser and Others," A DECADE
OF EUPHORIA: WESTERN LITERATURE IN POST-STALIN
RUSSIA, 1954-64 (Bloomington and Lond: Indiana UP,
1977), pp. 219-21, 335.
Shaw was widely performed in the Soviet Union, especially
because the Soviet officialdom favors realistic drama over
"modernist."

2485 Goldberg, Michael. "The Dickens Debate:
G.B.S. vs. G.K.C.," ShawR, XX (Sept 1977), 135-47.
The differences between Chesterton and Shaw were well
defined in their attitudes toward Dickens. Chesterton saw
a fellow mythographer; Shaw saw a fellow social critic.
Chesterton preferred the early novels; Shaw, the late.
But Shaw was haunted by Dickens's ideological innocence.
The battle lines over Dickens are still where Chesterton
and Shaw drew them.

2486 Gomperts, H[enri] A[lbert]. "Gomperts on Shaw:
The View from the Netherlands," trans by James
Brockway, ShawR, XX (Jan 1977), 30-42.
[Reviews of productions of Shaw plays: *Caesar and
Cleopatra*, 1954. *Major Barbara*, 1952. *Pygmalion*, 1957.
Heartbreak House, 1962. *Saint Joan*, 1959. *The Apple
Cart*, 1955.]

2487 Gottfried, Martin. "The Life and Times of
Shaw's *St.* [sic] *Joan*," NYT, 11 Dec 1977, II, pp. 1,
4.
The reaction to *Saint Joan* originally was uncertain. It
is untypical Shaw: a chronicle, humorless, not didactic,
and with a hero rather than anti-hero. Its theme, a

belief in visions, is also unusual and a clue to its endurance.

2488 Gray, Ronald. IBSEN--A DISSENTING VIEW: A STUDY OF THE LAST TWELVE PLAYS (Lond, NY, Melbourne: Cambridge UP, 1977), pp. 1, 22, 53, 60, 83, 201, 205, 224.
[Shaw's criticism of Ibsen and comment on it.]

2489 Green, Martin Burgess. TRANSATLANTIC PATTERNS: CULTURAL COMPARISONS OF ENGLAND WITH AMERICA (NY: Basic Books, 1977), pp. 20, 21, 57-64, 67-69, 71, 76, 84.
Shaw was not a comic genius; he was the most forceful and original inventor of comic situations and effects. One does not respond to Shaw's cleverness but to his delight in his cleverness. [Comparison with Evelyn Waugh.]

2490 Grenfell, Joyce. JOYCE GRENFELL REQUESTS THE PLEASURE (NY: St. Martin's, 1977), pp. 158-61, 179.
[Joyce Grenfell's friendship with Shaw from the age of 15. Photograph.]

2491 Grifsiûtenko, V. J. "Pro ukrains'ki prekladi p'esi B. Shou *Professiîa misis Uorren*" (On the Ukrainian Translation of Shaw's *Mrs. Warren's Profession*), UKRAINS'KE LITERATUROZNAVSTVO (L'viv), No. 29 (1977), 55-64.
Of the two translations of *Mrs. Warren's Profession* into Ukrainian (1932, 1957), the latter preserves to a high degree the artistic function of phraseological units. [In Ukrainian.]

2492 Gruber, W. E. "The Imperfect Action of Comedy," GENRE, X (Spring 1977), 115-29.
Possibly Shaw intended to invoke the perspective of divine unconcern for the future in the Epilogue to *Saint Joan*. But even if it were totally comic, it would not reverse the serious action of the preceding play. It confuses us. Joan's final speech is never reversed, and it is the ultimate confusion. The play is not comedy.

2493 Harmon, Maurice. SELECT BIBLIOGRAPHY FOR THE STUDY OF ANGLO-IRISH LITERATURE AND ITS BACKGROUNDS

(Ontario: P. D. Meany, [Irish Studies Handbook]
1977), pp. 130-31.
[Shaw bibliographies.]

2494 Harris, Edward P. "The Liberation of Flesh
from Stone: Pygmalion in Frank Wedekind's
ERDGEIST," GERMANIC REVIEW, LII (Jan 1977), 44-56.
[Parallels between Shaw's *Pygmalion* and Wedekind's
TRAGÖDIE.]

2495 Harris, Nathaniel. THE SHAWS, THE FAMILY OF
GEORGE BERNARD SHAW, illustrated by Andrew
Farmer (Lond: J. M. Dent [Families in History],
1977).
[It is hard to guess the audience for whom this story of
Shaw's family might be intended. It seems too sophisti-
cated for children, of little interest to adults.]

2496 Hendrick, George. HENRY SALT, HUMANITARIAN
REFORMER AND MAN OF LETTERS (Urbana, Chicago and
Lond: U of Illinois P, 1977), pp. 4, 5, 6, 7, 15-
17, 27-28, 36, 39, 48, 49, 61, 73, 75-77, 82, 95-97,
110, 114, 125, 126, 130, 134-35, 140-62, 166, 168-
70.
[The role of Shaw in the biography of Henry Salt.]

2497 Herr, Linda L. "Dickens' Jaggers and Shaw's
Bohun: A Study of 'Character Lifting,'" ShawR, XX
(Sept 1977), 110-18.
Shaw changed Jaggers's situation externally in
transforming him to Bohun and thereby changed his
disposition. But the two characters look alike, have the
same electrifying effect on others, and speak alike.
Shaw's trick was successful because *You Never Can Tell* was
commercially viable.

2498 Higham, Charles. MARLENE (NY: W. W. Norton,
1977), pp. 74, 75, 307.
[Marlene Dietrich in German productions of *Misalliance*
(Hypatia) and *Back to Methuselah* (Eve).]

2499 Holroyd, Michael. "My God, What Women!" BOOKS
AND BOOKMEN, XXIII (Dec 1977), 28-29.

[Review of FF.] For many feminists there are difficulties in Shaw's work. He confined the role of women in *Man and Superman* to the production of future generations. He almost totally ignored women's suffrage. The new women seem caricatures.

2500 Holroyd, Michael. "Po-faced Shaw," BOOKS AND BOOKMEN, XXII (March 1977), 57-58.
[Review of SHAW'S MORAL VISION: THE SELF AND SALVATION, by Alfred Turco, Jr. (1976).] Shaw's intellectual stimulation combined with his enchanting comic spirit keeps him alive. His plays, though, are in danger of becoming one of the evils of our "prison-school system."

2501 Horowitz, Joseph. "A Shavian Play Becomes Opera That Succeeds," NYT, 7 Nov 1977, p. 43.
[Review of premiere of Joyce Barthelson's Opera, based on *The Devil's Disciple* and performed at the Hoff-Barthelson Music School in Scarsdale on 4 Nov 1977.] Joyce Barthelson's libretto for *The Devil's Disciple* sticks close to Shaw, though the philosophy and wit are not very transferable and the protagonists are softer. The result musically is not bad.

2502 Howlett, Ivan. *"Candida,"* P&P, XXIV (Aug 1977), 25.
Deborah Kerr's flaccid performance reveals *Candida* as dated, sentimental twaddle.

2503 Howlett, Ivan. "Kingship and Conspiracy," P&P, XXV (Oct 1977), 30-31.
The Apple Cart at Chichester is disappointing. [Photograph.]

2504 Jebb, Julian. *"Saint Joan,"* P&P, XXIV (July 1977), 30.
[Review.]

2505 Johnson, Hugo Dean. "The Vocational Argument in Modern Drama: Three Approaches--Dr. Stockman, the Messiah; Undershaft, the Realist; and Vanya, the Fatalist," DAI, XXXVII (1977), 4712A. Unpublished dissertation, University of Colorado (Boulder), 1976.

2506 Johnson, Josephine. "The Making of a Feminist: Shaw and Florence Farr," FF, pp. 194-205.
For Florence Farr, "'feminism' became a life-style after Shaw had encouraged her lofty ambitions to become a new, independent woman." [Traces Farr's development as a feminist and Shaw's role in it.]

2507 Kalem, T. E. "GBS: Holy Terrorist of Iconoclasm," TIME, 8 Aug 1977, p. 46.
As drama critic, Shaw demolished most plays; as dramatist, he demolished society. Today only Tom Stoppard can compare with Shaw as a dramatist of ideas or displayer of language. Shaw's optimism may be his final put-on. [Review of Niagara-on-the-Lake Shaw festival production of *Man and Superman*.]

2508 Kalem, T. E. "Rebel in Arms: *Saint Joan*," TIME, 26 Dec 1977, p. 71.
Saint Joan is a series of lectures labeled "The Protestant Ethic and the Spirit of Nationalism, 1412-1431." Joan as saint is of greater interest to the public than to Shaw.

2509 Kester, Dolores. "The Legal Climate of Shaw's Problem Play," FF, pp. 68-83.
Shaw alone among prominent writers took notice in his novels of parliamentary debate resulting in the Married Women's Property Act of 1882. He returned to the women's issue in the early nineties when Parliament revived the issues. *Mrs. Warren's Profession* was an attempt to revive a juristic tradition of effecting change and thus was fated at the outset to failure, because Parliament ignored the issue of Mrs. Warren's profession. I suspect that Shaw's bout with the censor over *Mrs. Warren* convinced him to moderate his indignation about issues of the day.

2510 Kimura, Masami. "Shaw niokeru Fabian Shakai-shugi no Kakuritsukatei" (The Process of Establishment of Fabian Socialism in Shaw), KAGAWA DAIGAKU KEIZAIRONSO (Takamatsu), L (Oct 1977), 327-57.
[A detailed and well-documented study of Shaw's economics, particularly its development in the period of 1887 through 1889.] [In Japanese.]

2511 Kirillova, L. Ía. "B. Shou i A. Chekhov: o zhanrovo-kompozifsionnykh osobennostíakh" (B. Shaw and A. Chekov: Genre and Compositional Peculiarities), SBORNIK NAUCHNYKH TRUDOV TASHKENTSKOGO UNIVERSITETA, No 577 (1977), 34-45. Both Shaw and Chekov were hostile to existing social conditions. Both regarded the main purpose of their work as enriching the spiritual life of man and liberating him from various forms of social enslavement forced on him by bourgeois morality. Chekov invented a new way to depict reality in lyrical and psychological drama. In *Heartbreak House* and THE CHERRY ORCHARD, both playwrights depicted a stifling atmosphere paralyzing the will of individuals. In both plays, the characters have no means of changing anything. But Shaw's characters are rarely connected with real events and the behavior of people. Chekov's symbols have a psychological motivation and a distinctive spiritual atmosphere. In Shaw the symbols have one meaning, associated with the social ideas of the plays. The tonality of Chekov's plays is defined by the historical prospects of Russia's development and belief in the possibility of attaining humanistic ideals, whereas England gave Shaw no such possibilities. [In Russian.]

2512 Kobler, John. DAMNED IN PARADISE, THE LIFE OF JOHN BARRYMORE (NY: Atheneum, 1977), pp. 89, 196-99, 213.
[Shaw's opinion of John Barrymore's Hamlet.]

2513 Kotsilibas-Davis, James. GREAT TIMES GOOD TIMES, THE ODYSSEY OF MAURICE BARRYMORE (Garden City, NY: Doubleday, 1977), pp. 233, 387, 395, 412, 413-14, 433, 436.
[Maurice Barrymore and Shaw. Barrymore's interest in *Cashel Byron's Profession*, to dramatize it.]

2514 Laurence, Dan H. SHAW: AN EXHIBIT. A CATALOG BY DAN H. LAURENCE FOR AN EXHIBIT SELECTED AND PREPARED WITH LOIS B. GARCIA (Austin: University of Texas Humanities Research Center, 1977).
[Catalog for Shaw exhibit of books, manuscripts, photographs and othrer memorabilia.]

2515 Laurence, Dan H., and Daniel J. Leary. "Introduction" and "Notes and Acknowledgments," Bernard Shaw, *Flyleaves*, ed with an introduction by

Dan H. Laurence and Daniel J. Leary (Austin, Texas: W. Thomas Taylor, 1977), pp. 9-12, 57-62. In straightened circumstances Shaw inscribed with reminiscences the flyleaves of several books from his library. This was designed to make money, but they have proved to be of value largely to scholars. [This volume prints the full texts along with facsimile pages of Shaw's inscriptions.]

2516 Lazenby, Walter. "Love and 'Vitality' in *Candida*," MD, XX (March 1977), 1-19. Throughout Act I and into Act II Candida maneuvers her men efficiently. In Act III her feeling for Marchbanks moves her to appear in a new role: seductress. When Morell returns, she reverts to housewife. She finally throws off both roles and brings each man to a new realization of self; in choosing the *weaker*, she makes a free gift of her love and emancipates herself. Morrell's ordeal purges him of his weaknesses, his illusion about his effectiveness as a minister and his false estimate of his position in marriage, leaving him strong in his knowledge of Candida's love and his productivity as a parson. Marchbanks is initiated into the knowledge that love is an enlightening experience, to be put aside once its work is done. There are nobler things to accomplish than the search for happiness. Each of the characters has been "vitalized."

2517 Lees-Milne, James. PROPHESYING PEACE (Lond: Chatto & Windus; NY: Charles Scribner's Sons, 1977), pp. 19-22, 25, 126-27. [Lees-Milne's meeting with Shaw; an anecdote about a solicitor's devotion to Shaw's bibliography.]

2518 Lindblad, Ishrat. "Bernard Shaw and Scandinavia," ShawR, XX (Jan 1977), 2-16. The only common response of the countries of Scandinavia to Shaw has been their interest in MY FAIR LADY. There is little interest in Iceland. Shaw is performed in Finland, and though there are about ten articles on Shaw, there have been no dissertations. In Denmark the greatest interest was during the fifties and sixties. [Because of Shaw's admiration of Sweden and also his receiving the Nobel Prize, a more detailed study of Shaw and Sweden is included.]

2519 Lorichs, Sonja. "The 'Unwomanly Woman' in Shaw's Drama," FF, pp. 98-111.
Shaw's New Woman he called the "Unwomanly Woman." Vivie Warren is Shaw's first full-length portrait of the Unwomanly Woman. *Mrs. Warren's Profession* attacked prostitution, but his criticism was not very effective. Before *Major Barbara*, the English stage had not seen a heroine who rejected upper-class family life to work as a Salvationist. There are two emancipated women in *Getting Married*. *Fanny's First Play* continues the tradition of strong women with Fanny and her play's heroine, Margaret. Eliza in *Pygmalion* is a portrait of a woman emerging from the slums, and the play preaches the importance of the education of women. Underlying *The Apple Cart* is the implication that career women "could reach the highest possible rank in society." Saint Joan appealed to Shaw as an extremely interesting woman; she is Shaw's most Unwomanly Woman.

2520 Mackenzie, Norman and Jeanne. THE FABIANS (NY: Simon and Schuster, 1977), passim.
[An inclusive and thorough history of the early Fabians. Photographs.]

2521 Maisky, Ivan. "Bernard Shaw," SOVIET LITERATURE, No 11 (1977), 66-72.
[Reminiscences of Shaw, who "had a special attitude to" Russia and Russians. Photograph and facsimile of a letter.]

2522 Mann, Thomas. TAGEBUCHER 1933-1934 (Diaries 1933-1934), ed by Peter de Mendelssohn (Frankfurt/M.: S. Fischer, 1977), pp. 414, 693, 721.
Village Wooing is a good play. *The Shewing-up of Blanco Posnet* seems to be rather cold. [In German.]

2523 Masumoto, Masahiko (trans). "Bernard Shaw in Japan," ISh, XV (Winter and Spring 1977), 17-19.
[Text of dialogue between Shaw and Japanese War Minister Araki in 1933.]

2524 Maver, David. "*Man and Superman*," P&P, XXIV (July 1977), 28.
Richard Pasco gives a star performance as Tanner.

2525 Meyers, Jeffrey. "Bernard and Charlotte Shaw," MARRIED TO GENIUS (NY: Barnes and Noble [Harper & Row Publishers] 1977), pp. 38-57.
Shaw and Charlotte were well suited to each other. Their marriage made few emotional demands and reinforced their personal limitations. Shaw's lack of maternal affection turned him into a bitter selfish man who attracted the compensatory love of women to prove his self worth. Charlotte was a classic Electra. Charlotte's money and Shaw's cold intellectuality drew them together. Shaw was a superficial thinker with a vicarious view of human relationships. [Some discussion of *Getting Married, Bouyant Billions, Man and Superman,* and *Sixteen Self-Sketches.*]

2526 Mikhail, E. H. CONTEMPORARY BRITISH DRAMA: 1950-1976, AN ANNOTATED CRITICAL BIBLIOGRAPHY (Totowa, NJ: Rowman and Littlefield, 1977), passim.
[A bibliography of writing on British drama, briefly annotated. Not indexed.]

2527 Mizuno, Yoshikazu. "G. B. Shaw no Hoshusei--*Major Barbara* no Kigekitekigiko omegutte" (Conversatism of G. B. Shaw--on the Comic Techniques in *Major Barbara*), KIYO (Department of General Education, University of Rissho, Tokyo), No 11 (Dec 1977), 73-83.
In its use of language, character sketch and construction *Major Barbara* is not a "new" play, but a "conservative" play which made a skillful use of the traditional techniques of comedy. Shaw's play is a variant of the comedy of manners in the tradition of Jonson, Congreve, Sheridan and Wilde. [In Japanese.]

2528 Motoyama, Mutsuko. "Shaw in the Japanese Theatre," ShawR, XX (Jan 1977), 49-57.
"The Japanese generally speaking have not found Shaw appealing."

2529 Munzar, Jiří. "Shaw und Ibsen" (Shaw and Ibsen), BRUNNER BEITRÄGE ZUR GERMANISTIK UND NORDISTIK (Brno), I (1977), 137-51.
[An assessment of *The Quintessence of Ibsenism.*] The relationship between Ibsen and Shaw is marked by elective affinities rather than by influences. The works of Ibsen

and Shaw have some essential features in common: a
tendency towards anarchism, a belief in evolution, the
idea of the life-force, a certain irrationalism, the
heritage of romantic individualism. *The Quintessence* is a
book about Shaw and not a discussion of Ibsen. [In
German.]

2530 Nelson, Raymond S. "Shaw's Pre-Raphaelite
Play," PRE-RAPHAELITE REVIEW, I (Nov 1977), 89-94.
Candida is Pre-Raphaelite in its search for moral truth.
Both Marchbanks, the "higher but . . . timider vision,"
and Morell, "bold" but "short-sighted Christian Socialist
idealism," are admirable. Candida cannot make a bad
choice.

2531 Page, H. M. "'A More Seditious Book Than DAS
KAPITAL': Shaw on LITTLE DORRIT," ShawR, XX (Sept
1977), 171-77.
Shaw was a pioneer admirer of LITTLE DORRIT, especially
its political and social aspects. However, he also felt
that Dickens failed to draw the correct revolutionary
conclusions from his own work. Shaw also felt that
Dickens's characters were realistic, that Dickens felt a
gulf between himself and his public, and that Dickens
truly revealed himself in his art.

2532 Pearsall, Ronald. CONAN DOYLE, A BIOGRAPHICAL
SOLUTION (NY: St. Martin's P, 1977), pp. 123, 127-
28, 132, 137, 149.
Shaw infuriated Conan Doyle because he threatened
stability. They quarreled in the press over the blame for
the *Titanic* disaster, Shaw hammering home the basic
undeniable fact that Captain Smith had lost his ship by
steaming at the highest speed into an ice field. During
World War I they disagreed over the use of airplanes, Shaw
arguing that ruling out aerial warfare was unrealistic
nonsense.

2533 Pfister, Manfred. DAS DRAMA. THEORIE UND
ANALYSE (Drama. Theory and Analysis) (Munich:
Wilhelm Fink, 1977), pp. 36, 76, 103, 151, 262, 425.
[An introduction to the poetics of drama with various
references to Shaw, especially the extensive prefaces to
his plays and the discussion scenes.] [In German.]

2534 Pritchard, William H.   SEEING THROUGH EVERY-
THING: ENGLISH WRITERS 1918-1940 (NY: Oxford UP,
1977), pp. 13, 18, 19, 23-24, 28-32, 46, 49, 52,
105, 182-83, 210.
There is no critical accord about postwar Shaw.   Room may
be found for both *Heartbreak House* and THE WASTE LAND as
creations that live through language rather than
apocalyptic visions.   Perhaps *Saint Joan* is so beautifully
engineered that it leaves the audience outside.

2535 Quinn, Martin.   "The Dickensian Presence in
Heartbreak House," ShawR, XX (Sept 1977), 119-25.
Heartbreak House can be compared with BLEAK HOUSE: the
worlds of both totter on the edge of madness.   The comedy
underlying the tragedy of Shaw's play is also Dickensian.
The maritime architecture of Shotover's house is like Sol
Gill's instrument shop in DOMBEY AND SON and Daniel
Peggotty's boat in DAVID COPPERFIELD.   Shotover's
character owes a debt to Peggotty too.   Billy Dunn seems
modeled on Bill Sikes from OLIVER TWIST.   Mr. Merdle in
LITTLE DORRIT is a precursor of Boss Mangan.   Ellie's
rejection of Mangan recalls Louisa's flight in HARD TIMES
from Bounderby.

2536 Rickert, Alfred E.   "George Bernard Shaw and
the Modern Temper," MODERN BRITISH LITERATURE, II
(Spring 1977), 89-97.
The *Weltanshauung* of a playwright determines the choices
he makes in creating a character and then in choosing
among the character's choices.   Shaw is modern in view of
the problem, but pre-modern in his view of the solution.
The essential characteristics of the modern temper are:
1) a break with traditional forms, 2) an experimental
mode, 3) a being at odds with nature, 4) an apocalyptic
vision, 5) alienation, 6) a loss of universal focus, and
7) despair.   Industrialization, urbanization, and democra-
tization have contributed to this development.   In *Major
Barbara* there are clearly delineated characters, but
finally they have no choice but Undershaft's, which Shaw
has arbitrariy established.   No one can believe in Shaw's
panacea.   Shaw is duped by his own Shavianism.   Only
Heartbreak House and *Saint Joan* explore the thrust of the
modern temper to its conclusion.   *Heartbreak* is realistically acceptable, and *Joan* demonstrates vital change and
growth that are "cognizant with general historic fact."

2537 Rodriguez-Seda, Asela. "G. Bernard Shaw y Nemesio Canales: Relaciones e Influencias," (G. Bernard Shaw and Nemesio Canales: Relationships and Influences), SIN NOMBRE (Puerto Rico), VIII (July-Sept 1977), 34-35.
Shaw's thought molded all the ideas and literary works of Nemesio R. Canales, a Puerto Rican lawyer, journalist, and writer. [In Spanish.]

2538 Rogoff, Gordon. "The Last Gentleman-Actor?" SRL, 5 March 1977, pp. 46-47.
[Review of Rex Harrison in *Caesar and Cleopatra*.] Shaw knew what he wanted, and heaven help the director who cannot make it happen. Shaw is not kind to modern actors, or to designers either.

2539 Roll-Hansen, Diderik. "G.B.S. in Norway," ShawR, XX (Jan 1977), 17-29.
Two world wars seem to have been needed to change Norwegian criticism of Shaw from suspicion because of his verbal clowning. [History of Shaw production and criticism in Norway.]

2540 Rosenberg, Edgar. "The Shaw/Dickens File: 1885 to 1950. Two Checklists," ShawR, XX (Sept 1977), 148-70.
[Shaw-Dickens bibliography. Continued in 1978.]

2541 Santos, A. R. "Shaw in Portugal," ShawR, XX (Jan 1977), 47-48.
The past 20 years have little to offer on Shaw.

2542 Sauvageau, David Ronald. "Shaw, Brecht, and Evolution: The Early Plays," DAI, XXXVIII (1977), 1383A. Unpublished dissertation, University of Minnesota, 1977.

2543 Schoeps, Karl-Heinz. BERTOLT BRECHT (NY: Frederick Ungar [World Dramatists], 1977), pp. 17, 94, 151, 159, 248-49, 413.
[Shaw's influence on Brecht.]

2544 Schwartzman, Myron.   "Joyce and Bernard Shaw: With an Unpublished Letter from Joyce to John Quinn," JAMES JOYCE QUARTERLY, XIV (Summer 1977), 483-85.
[Shaw's letter to Sylvia Beach refusing to subscribe to ULYSSES: Joyce's letter to John Quinn enclosing Shaw's letter; comment on Shaw's appearance in ULYSSES as "Disgusted One."]

2545 Seabrook, Alex.   "'Saki'--on Shaw," ISh, XV (Winter and Spring 1977), 20-21.
All Shaw and Saki had in common was their wit. Saki wrote one directly anti-Shaw story, THE INFERNAL PARLIAMENT.

2546 Senart, Philippe.   "La Revue Théâtrale: *Pygmalion*" (Theater Review: *Pygmalion*), NOUVELLE REVUE DES DEUX MONDES (Dec 1977), 685-87.
Pygmalion is very dusty, and the contradictory interpretations of Raymond Gerome as Higgins and Evelyne Buyle as Eliza are unsatisfactory. [In French.]

2547 Seymour-Smith, Martin. WHO'S WHO IN TWENTIETH CENTURY LITERATURE (Lond: Weidenfeld and Nicolson, 1976; NY: McGraw-Hill, 1977), 336.
Shaw exercised little permanent influence. His plays are psychologically empty. His importance is extra-literary.

2548 "Shaw, George Bernard," THEATER-LEXIKON (Encyclopedia of the Theater), ed by Christoph Trilse, Klaus Hammer and Rolf Kabel (Berlin: Henschelverlag Kunst und Gesellschaft, 1977), pp. 496-97.
[A biographical sketch and a survey of Shaw's works from a Marxist point of view.] Shaw unmasks the lies of the capitalistic society. [In German.]

2549 Shawcross, John T.   "You Can't Tell the Characters without an Onomasticon: Shaw's Use of Names," Ish, XVI (Fall and Winter 1977), 10-14.
[Study of Shaw's own name and those of several of his characters from *In Good King Charles's Golden Days, Man and Superman,* and *Widowers' Houses,* considering three classes of names: 1) those of specific persons and places; 2) those used for allusive importance; and 3) those whose etymologies suggest meanings.]

2550 Sherman, Robert. *"Devil's Disciple* Set to Music," NYT, 4 Nov 1977, p. C27.
This is the first instance of a Shaw play set as an opera. The 'interludes' follow the Shaw text, but the songs (arias) have completely new lyrics, written by Joyce Barthelson, the composer.

2551 Shunamee, Gideon. "Melodrama bi-Re'i Akkum (al *Behor Satan* meet G. B. Shaw)" (Melodrama in a Distorted Mirror: On *The Devil's Disciple* of G. B. Shaw), BAMAH, THEATRICAL REVIEW (Jerusalem), No 72 (1977), 28-38.
Shaw saw melodrama as a means of moral education of the masses. In *The Devil's Disciple* Shaw's demands for allegory and idealism are met. [An examination of Eric Bentley on melodrama.] Shaw both parodies melodrama, turning it upside down, and stresses its positive nature.

2552 Shvydkoĭ, M. E. IDEĬNO-KHUDOZHESTVENNYE PROBLEMY ANGLISKOĬ ISTORICHESKOĬ DRAMY XX VEKA: IZBRANNIK SUD'BY, SVATAĬA IOANNA, T͡SEZAR I KLEOPTRA BERNARDA SHOU, UBIĬSTVA V SOBORE T. S. ELIOTA (Ideological and Artistic Problems of the English Historical Drama of the 20th Century: *Man of Destiny, Saint Joan, Caesar and Cleopatra* of Bernard Shaw, MURDER IN THE CATHEDRAL of T. S. Eliot) (Moscow: Institut teatral'nogo iskusstva, 1977).
[Published dissertation. Not seen.] [In Russian.]

2553 Stagg, Louis Charles. "George Bernard Shaw and the Existentialist-Absurdist Theater," TENNESSEE PHILOLOGICAL BULLETIN, XIV (1977), 5-17.
The search for the true self, a major theme of Beckett's and Pinter's plays, is of great consequence in those of Shaw. For Shaw tragedy is knowingly letting yourself be used for base purposes, and he places himself on both sides in a tragedy. Shaw will not tell the viewer what to think; the essence of drama is clear thought. Shaw's characters must face the issues of life directly and resolve them. [Extended examination of *Don Juan in Hell* and *Too True to Be Good* in the light of WAITING FOR GODOT.]

2554 Stewart, Desmond. T. E. LAWRENCE (NY and Lond: Harper & Row, 1977), pp. 209, 235, 246, 252, 271, 288-91, 296, 298, 299, 304.

Lawrence urged Shaw to write a life of Roger Casement.
[Shaw's friendship for Lawrence and his literary influence
on THE SEVEN PILLARS OF WISDOM.] Lawrence called himself
Shaw after Shaw. Part of Shaw's inspiration for *Saint
Joan* he took from Lawrence.

2555 Stone, Susan C. "Whatever Happened to Shaw's
Mother--Genius Portrait?" FF, pp. 130-42.
In the Epistle Dedicatory to *Man and Superman* Shaw admits
the possibility of a cross between the genius-man and the
mother-woman. He envisioned the man and woman in their
Life Force drives as being in conflict, and the internal
struggle of a character possessing both would be an
interesting subject for drama. But when Shaw finally put
the mother-genius in his later plays, she is not at all in
conflict with herself. [Examines Shaw heroines as
sensible women, mother-women, and genius-women.] Eve in
Back to Methuselah is the mother-servant of the Life
Force, and she comes closest to exhibiting a consciousness
of Nature's instinctive purpose, suggesting the
combination of mother and genius. The She-Ancient is
representative of mature womanhood; she combines the
function of mother with that of genius. Lilith even more
clearly combines the mother and genius functions, and
there is no indication of conflict between the two. Yet
she is an abstraction, not a woman. Prola in *The
Simpleton of the Unexpected Isles* suggests an inter-
changeability of man's and woman's roles and at the same
time an almost indefinable superiority of women. Shaw
depicts women on three levels: the social, in which she
is handicapped by biology; interchangeable with men; the
mystical, idealizing her beyond man for her devotion to
life. These three are not incompatible.

2556 Tanzy, Eugene. "Contrasting Views of Man and
the Evolutionary Process: *Back to Methuselah* and
CHILDHOOD'S END," ARTHUR C. CLARKE ed by Joseph D.
Olander and Martin Greenberg (NY: Taplinger Publishing Company, 1977), pp. 172-95.
Both Arthur C. Clarke's CHILDHOOD'S END and *Back to
Methuselah* are developments of the theme of evolution, and
CHILDHOOD'S END might be an addendum to *Methuselah*. The
preface to *Methuselah* is a convincing account of the
devastating impact evolutionary theory had upon late
nineteenth century western thought: there was no hope in
evolution. Shaw could not stand the mechanistic view of
the human condition of Darwinism, so he simply denied it.
Methuselah was a showcase for his Creative Evolution

669

theory. He leaped over Darwin back to Lamarck: "living organisms change because they want to." Individual life for Shaw was just one of the manifestations the original, eternal Life Force takes. This satisfied Shaw the reformer. The new mutant forms survive because they are more fit, or they die off with the bypassed species. This theory also proves that artists (like reformers) are most at one with the Life Force. They lead the way to a better world. The conflict is one between body and thought, because life, for Shaw, is thought, yet it cannot exist without the body. The question of how thought will exist free of material form is possibly answered in CHILDHOOD'S END. [Discussion of CHILDHOOD'S END.]

2557 Tobias, Richard C. "Victorian Bibliography for 1976: Shaw," VICTORIAN STUDIES, XX (Summer 1977), 534-35.
[Very selective bibliography of writing about Shaw for 1976.]

2558 Vesonder, Timothy G. "Eliza's Choice: Transformation Myth and the Ending of *Pygmalion*," in FF, pp. 39-45.
Both actors and audiences are unprepared for and unsatisfied with the feminist ending of *Pygmalion*. The misinterpretations result from the conflicting myths Shaw used. The myth of Pygmalion and Galatea is the most obvious source. But Shaw's play is also a story of transformation. Eliza is not the hero's reward; she has been transformed into a strong and independent woman who is the equal of the hero.

2559 Vogt, Sally Peters. "Ann and Superman: Type and Archetype," FF, pp. 46-65.
Once the presence and the function of the mythic patterns in *Man and Superman* are revealed, Ann's role will be clarified. The surface structure of the play is romantic comedy, especially in Acts I, II and IV. In this aspect, the men are defined by their relationships with women. This inversion is paralleled in the dream symposium which inverts the Don Juan theme. Ann is Queen Goddess of the World, but Tanner does not recognize her. Shaw's portrait of her is consistent with the qualities of the lunar gooddess. "Tanner's metaphorical descent into his unconscious is a journey through the labyrinth of his own disordered thoughts and emotions, as he seeks through his pilgrimage an initiation into 'absolute reality,' what can

670

be called the mystic center of his spirit." The setting
of Act III is the "Sacred Mountain." The promised
marriage becomes a mystic marriage. Ann is archetypal
woman.

2560 Watson, George. POLITICS AND LITERATURE IN
 MODERN BRITAIN (Lond: Macmillan; Totowa, NJ:
 Rowman and Littlefield, 1977), pp. 65, 67, 69, 76,
 94, 96, 107, 176.
[Shaw's role as a political writer.]

2561 Weimer, Michael. *"Press Cuttings*: G.B.S. and
 Women's Suffrage," FF, pp. 84-89.
The historical significance of *Press Cuttings* is clearest
in the light of the struggle for women's suffrage. The
play belongs to the Shavian genre of ideological
conversion that begins with *The Devil's Disciple*, and it
is more interesting than *Disciple* because it relies on
dramatic confrontation and verbal argument rather than
melodramatic devices as the agents of conversion. Shaw
sketched his antisuffragettes to expose the dominance of
women with strong families and position in society.
General Mitchener is persuaded to support suffragism by
recognizing female chauvinism, the harm in the woman-
behind-great-man theory, and the antisuffragist lack of
sympathy for the unenlightened average Englishwoman whose
continued ignorance is a threat to order. The drama's
topicality has not gone stale.

2562 Weintraub, Rodelle. "The Center of Life: An
 Interview with Megan Terry," FF, pp. 214-25.
Terry: I read all of Shaw. Among the few good roles for
women are those written by Shaw. I've seen only one Shaw
production that was halfway good, the Guthrie production
of *Saint Joan.*

2563 Weintraub, Rodelle. "Fabian Feminist," FF, pp.
 1-12.
Shaw refused to be bound by conventional approaches to the
role of women in society. He supported women's freedom,
but he did not reject the traditional domestic role. To
effect equality, Shaw felt, Capitalism had to be
transformed into Fabianism, so that women could not be
exploited economically. He demonstrated his convictions
in his own marriage. In his plays he has created the most
fascinating gallery of women in modern drama. Though many

of the changes Shaw fought for have been reached, there is still a long way to go.

2564 Weintraub, Rodelle (ed). FABIAN FEMINIST, BERNARD SHAW AND WOMEN (University Park and Lond: Pennsylvania State UP, 1977).
Table of contents abstracted separately under year of first publication: Rodelle Weintraub, "Fabian Feminist" (1977); Lisë Pedersen, "Shakespeare's THE TAMING OF THE SHREW vs. Shaw's *Pygmalion*: Male Chauvinism vs. Women's Lib?" ShawR (1974); Janie Caves McCauley, "Kipling on Women: A New Source for Shaw, ShawR (1974); Rhoda B. Nathan, The Shavian Sphinx," ShawR (1974); Timothy G. Vesonder, "Eliza's Choice: Transformation Myth and the Ending of Pygmalion" (1977), Sally Peters Vogt, "Ann and Superman: Type and Archetype" (1977); Dolores Kester, "The Legal Climate of Shaw's Problem Plays" (1977); Michael Weiner," *Press Cuttings*: G.B.S. and Women's Suffrage" (1977); Norbert Greiner, "Mill, Marx and Bebel: Early Influences on Shaw's Characterization of Women," ShawR (1975); Sonja Lorichs, "The 'Unwomanly Woman' in Shaw's Drama" (1977); Barbara Bellow Watson, "The New Woman and the New Comedy," ShawR (1974); Susan C. Stone, "Whatever Happened to Shaw's Mother-Genius Portrait?" (1977); Andrina Gilmartin, "Mr. Shaw's Many Mothers," ShawR (1965); Elsie Adams, "Feminism and Female Stereotypes in Shaw," ShawR (1974); Germaine Greer, "A Whore in Every Home," Program of the National Theatre's production of *Mrs. Warren's Profession* (1970); Marlie Parker Wasserman, "Vivie Warren: A Psychological Study," ShawR (1972); Gladys M. Crane, "Shaw and Women's Lib" (1977); Stanley Weintraub, "Shaw's Lady Cicely and Mary Kingsley" (1977); Josephine Johnson, "The Making of a Feminist: Shaw and Florence Farr" (1977); Rodelle Weintraub "The Gift of Imagination: An Interview with Claire Boothe Luce," ShawR (1974); Rodelle Weintraub, "The Center of Life: An Interview with Megan Terry" (1977); Maud Churton Braby, "G.B.S. and a Suffragist," TRIBUNE (1906); Lucille Kelling Henderson, "A Bibliographical Checklist" enlarged from ShawR (1974).

2565 Weintraub, Stanley. "Editor's Introduction" and "Bibliographical Notes," THE PORTABLE BERNARD SHAW, ed by Stanley Weintraub (Hammondsworth Middlesex, England: Penguin Books; NY: Viking [Viking Portable Library], 1977), pp. 1-26.
[Survey of Shaw's career. Bibliography.]

2566 Weintraub, Stanley. "The Genesis of *Saint Joan*," LITERATUR IN WISSENSCHAFT UND UNTERRICHT (Kiel), X (Dec 1977), 259-74.

Although Shaw utilized Quicherat's transcripts in the 1902 translation by T. Douglas Murray, Joan seems anticipated in *The Perfect Wagnerite*, where he mentions a naive hero upsetting religion, law and order. Joan is mentioned in the prefaces to *Getting Married* and *Androcles and the Lion*. [Further prefigurings of Joan and hints that Shaw is working on a Joan play.] Although tragic, *Joan* suggests an upswing after Shaw's embitterment over the World War. He called it an "Exceptional Play for Exceptional People." The vandalizing of the statue Shaw erected in his garden seems to prove Shaw's point that the world is not yet ready to receive its saints.

2567 Weintraub, Stanley. "Shaw's Lady Cicely and Mary Kingsley," FF, pp. 185-92.

Shaw's reticence in identifying Lady Cicely with Mary Kingsley may have been because she was still alive. [Character and biographical sketch of Kingsley with parallels to Lady Cicely.]

2568 Whitaker, Thomas R. FIELDS OF PLAY IN MODERN DRAMA (Princeton, NJ: Princeton UP, 1977), pp. 5, 9, 37, 79-82, 89-96, 158.

Each character in *Heartbreak House* wears a mask grotesquely at odds with his own face. The set is its own symbol, not nineteenth century British tradition or the whole of Europe on the edge of doom, but Shaw's house. The characters are rhetorical puppets, but each actor is grounding the multiplicity of roles in his and your own protean life. But there is an anxious search for direction in the unmasking. The play is an end to words amid linguistic exhuberance. There is a darkness literally unspeakable. But the characters keep on talking, trying to reach silence. "This present action, no rationalizing in the void, is an undoing of your competence and sophistication . . . shaped by a playful awareness of what such . . . 'self'-destructive laughter allows you to celebrate."

2569 Whitman, Robert F. SHAW AND THE PLAY OF IDEAS (Ithaca and Lond: Cornell UP, 1977).

The antithesis between idealism and realism is the source of the dynamics and conflict in most of Shaw's writing. He was not a doctrinaire Marxist. John Stuart Mill is the father to Shaw's Socialism, but Samuel Butler, Henrik Ibsen, and especially Georg Hegel provided him with a vision beyond Socialism. [A thorough analysis of the Hegelian *element* in Shaw's dialectic follows.] "Seeing Shaw's plays as varied manifestations of the Life Force and of the dialectic principle operating in artistic structure, in the artificial reality of the stage, or in the relationship of the audience to the work of art, is at best a half-truth. But perhaps it is a half-truth that will move us one step closer to the unreachable whole truth. [*Candida, Caesar and Cleopatra, Man and Superman, Major Barbara, The Shewing-up of Blanco, Posnet, Androcles and the Lion, Heartbreak House, Back to Methuselah,* and *Saint Joan.*]

2570 Williams, Raymond. "Social Environment and Theatrical Environment: the Case of English Naturalism," ENGLISH DRAMA: FORMS AND DEVELOPMENT, ed by Marie Axton and Raymond Williams (Lond, NY, Melbourne: Cambridge UP, 1977), pp. 220-21.
Naturalism was limited on the English stage because Shaw in *Widowers' Houses, Mrs. Warren's Profession* and *Heartbreak House* chose to work mainly in old forms.

2571 Williams, Tennessee. "*Candida*: A College Essay," ShawR, XX (May 1977), 60-62.
Shaw is one of the sanest individuals, but this has been his undoing as an artist. *Candida* hasn't a single speech that rings true. I don't understand the point of the play. [An undergraduate essay. Later Williams admits that *Candida* "does play better than it reads."]

2572 Wilson, Edmund. LETTERS ON LITERATURE AND POLITICS, 1912-1972 (NY: Farrar, Straus and Giroux, 1977), passim.
[Wilson's generally approving commentary on Shaw in his letters. Indexed.]

2573 Winkgens, Meinhard. "Shaw und Sternheim, Der Individualismus als Privatmythologie" (Individuality as Private Mythology), ARCADIA, XII (1977), 31-46.
The documented relationship between Sternheim and Shaw is tenuous. There are parallels between them: both were primarily dramatists; both dealt violently with the literary tradition; the reception of both was ambivalent; both are didactic. Their characteristic contribution to

criticism of the ideology of the social order is irrational and takes the form of an individual with a private mythology. The aim of comparing the two is to establish the characteristics of their individual ideas. The contradiction in their plays is the criticism of social ideals and also the presentation of a hero who represents the ideal of what the world requires. There are three questions that need to be asked: 1) What are the social ideals criticized? 2) How are these ideals evaluated? and 3) How do the heroic protagonists criticize the ideals and how do they represent positive values? The solution is the Life Force operating in an individual not corrupted by society, but it is abstract and empty. It has an escapist character. Shaw partly identified with the society he criticized, and supported colonialism and imperialism. He longed for the superman. He was a pseudo-radical who was a victim of the society he criticized. [In German.]

2574 Winkler, Elizabeth Hale. THE CLOWN IN MODERN ANGLO-IRISH DRAMA (Bern: Lang, 1977), pp. 74-95. [Not seen.]

2575 Yarrison, Betsy C. "Marchbanks As 'Albatross': An Interpretation of *Candida*," ShawR, XX (May 1977), 71-82.
In *Candida* Shaw dramatizes the brief impact of a poet's vision on bystanders who have made him their pet. There is a startling affinity between Shaw's depiction of the artist and Baudelaire's in "The Albatross": both are at once romantic and anti-romantic, heroic and mock heroic. The strongest argument in favor of Marchbanks's being Shaw's true poet is his resemblance to Shelley. The existence of his obverse, Henry Apjohn in *How He Lied to Her Husband* is almost as telling. Marchbanks's discovery of his vocation lies in "the coming of age of his ideas." He knows he cannot remain in the world of conventional men.

2576 Yerushalmee, Yosef. "Al G. B. Shaw be-Ivrit: Bibliographia" (On G. B. Shaw in Hebrew: A Bibliography), BAMAH, THEATRICAL REVIEW (Jerusalem), No 72 (1977), 40-46.
[A bibliography of 139 items on Shaw in Hebrew which have not been seen.] [In Hebrew.]

1978

2577 "Adoring Bounder," TLS, 26 May 1978, p. 584.
[Review of THE ACHURCH LETTERS, written and directed by
Don Taylor.] Since the words are mostly Shaw's, they are
worth listening to.

2578 Anikst, A. A. "Shou" (Shaw), B O L'S H A Ī A
SO V ETSK AĪA ENTSIK L OPE DIIĀ (Moscow: Izd. Sovetskaīa
entsiklopediia, 1978), 3 ed., vol 29, pp. 464-5.
Shaw's creative method was apparent in his novels--paradox
as a means for overturning accepted ideologies. Shaw then
established "plays of discussion," in which the collision
of opinions between hostile ideologies depicted the most
urgent problems of society and personal morality. In
Major Barbara, Shaw first expressed the idea that
bourgeois force must be countered by social progress and
justice. In the political extravaganzas, Shaw's idea was
that capitalist society is in an impasse and that
bourgeois democracy is undergoing a serious crisis. He
condemned Fascism. [In Russian.]

2579 Anikst, A. A. "Vstupitel'naīa stat'iā"
(Introductory Essay), POLNOE SOBRANIE P'ES V
SHESTI TOMAKH, I, by Bernard Shaw (Leningrad;
Iskusstvo, 1978) pp. 5-46. (Complete Collected
Plays in Six Volumes)
Shaw scoffed at all questions--religious, philosophical,
moral, political, artistic. He irritated Tolstoi with his
paradoxes, and not only for his unserious way of thinking,
but also because he did not achieve his aims. We should
not forget that Shaw started his activities in conditions
of the rule of lying and prim bourgeois morality, which
refused to see the dark side of life. He soon rejected
Christianity and Schopenhauer's pessimism also, though he
drew on the latter's philosophical ideas. Shaw expressed
his ideas in journalism as well as in artistic form,
though he did not have followers as Tolstoi did.
Archibald Henderson knew much about Shaw but failed to
understand him. Marxists criticise Shaw as a bourgeois
writer, while bourgeois critics accuse him of blind
adherence to Socialism. Although Shaw was a thinker-
playwright, he was not a professional philosopher. As an

artist and thinker, he sought to demonstrate what life ought to be and to show man's struggles for freedom and self-improvement. [In Russian.]

2580 Appasamy, S. P., Dr. "God, Mammon and Bernard Shaw," COMMONWEALTH QUARTERLY, II (1978) 98-112. Socialism was offered as a panacea for social and moral evil both. When Shaw in *Mrs. Warren's Profession* drew attention to the economic necessity behind prostitution, his was not the whole truth. He wished to shock Victorian sentiment. The theme of *Widowers' Houses* is similar. Capitalism turned Christian gentlemen into Jews, that is, usurers. Shaw not only exposes the truth, he also identifies it with capitalism. Shaw identified Jesus with Socialism, but he forgets (in his preference for the virtues of the Life Force over those of Christianity) that many benefactors of society have been poor. The Communist-Socialist experiments without spirituality have failed throughout the world. In *Major Barbara, Saint Joan,* and *Androcles and the Lion,* Shaw himself succumbs to Mammon because he ignores the spirit of mankind.

2581 Armes, Roy. A CRITICAL HISTORY OF THE BRITISH CINEMA (NY: Oxford UP, 1978), pp. 60, 87, 102-3, 163-65, 198, 203-4, 206. [Shaw's plays *Pygmalion, Major Barbara, Caesar and Cleopatra, Androcles and the Lion, The Doctor's Dilemma, The Millionairess* and *Saint Joan,* in movie versions.]

2582 Baker, Stuart E. "Logic and Religion in *Major Barbara*: The Syllogism of St. Andrew Undershaft," MD, XXI (Sept 1978), 241-52. Despite Shaw's denials that his plays were "simply" logical demonstrations, abstract, formal logic is at the foundation of the human story of *Major Barbara*. *Major* and *Barbara* are words with significance in logic. The symbols "S", "P", and "M" are standard references to subject, predicate and middle term. Salvation, Power, and Money are the three principal topics of *Barbara*. The syllogism underlying the play is: "All persons with money are persons in the possession of power; All persons who achieve salvation are persons with money; therefore, All persons who achieve salvation are persons in the possession of power." Barbara and Undershaft are inseparable. "The apparent ambiguities in the Undershaft Syllogism are part of its unambiguous meaning. Spiritual and physical salvation together require both spiritual and physical power. And one cannot *have* power without submitting to it." *Barbara* is neither confused nor contradictory; it is a marvel of logical consistency. Barbara is not its only saint.

2583 Barnes, Clive. *"The Devil's Disciple* at Home in Brooklyn," NEW YORK POST, 9 Feb 1978.
The Devil's Disciple stands up well in the Shaw canon because it is an action rather than a debate.

2584 Barnes, Clive. "Donnelly's Good as Shaw," NEW YORK POST, 19 Jan 1978.
Although Shaw stalks through his plays like an exhibitionist in a hall of mirrors, the real Shaw is best in his guardedly unguarded moments. [Review of MY ASTONISHING SELF.]

2585 Barnes, Clive. "Shavian 'Superman' Surfaces Sans Arch Support," NEW YORK POST, 18 Dec 1978, p. 35.
The most interesting aspect of *Man and Superman* is Don Juan's concept of Heaven and Hell. The play cries for a proscenium arch, though not all the faults of this production can be explained by a lack of one.

2586 Barrick, Mac E. "Though the Ceiling Fall," ShawR, XXI (Jan 1978), 31.
In *Captain Brassbound's Conversion* "Lady Cicely's cognatic translation of the legal maxim *Fiat justitia ruat coelum* as 'Let justice be done though the ceiling fall' has a curious parallel in contemporaneous history."

2587 Baskin, Ken A. "Undershaft's Challenge and the Future of the Race," ShawR, XXI (Sept 1978), 135-51.
To Shaw the paradoxical relationship between man's destructive energies and his civilization is crucial. In *Major Barbara* Shaw furnished the specifications for the Superman. [Robert Ardrey's AFRICAN GENESIS is discussed to illuminate Shaw.] In mythic terms Undershaft is a figure of almost superhuman energy; Lady Brit is the protectress of material being. Barbara is the religious spirit of the race, and Cusins is the humanistic intellect. The play's plot moves to the discovery that intellect is ineffectual without power. The play moves from the hell of the drawing room (hellish because the

warrior energies have reached a dead end) through the
purgatory of the Salvation Army shelter (purgatorial
because the Army is trying to rechannel the destructive
energies of man), to the heaven of the munitions factory
(heavenly because Cusins is given the opportunity to
rechannel weapon-making energy to help save civilization).
Undershaft, Barbara and Cusins together suggest Shaw's
Superman.

2588 Bastable, Adolphus. "A Shavian Notebook,
    London, October, 1978," ISh, XVI (Spring 1978), 31.
The Shaw event of the theatrical season is the National
Theatre production of *The Philanderer.*

2589 Bingham, Madeleine. HENRY IRVING, THE GREATEST
    VICTORIAN ACTOR (NY: Stein and Day, 1978), pp. 80-
    81, 142-43, 211, 247, 249-50, 261-74, 282, 285, 292,
    301, and passim.
Shaw's political and theatrical ideas "proved to be so
much dust blown before the winds of barbarism." He tried
to rescue Ellen Terry from Irving, so that she might play
in dramas of his own. He laid siege to Henry Irving's
Lyceum to cut his own way. Even at Irving's death, Shaw
stung.

2590 Boylan, Henry. A DICTIONARY OF IRISH BIOGRAPHY
    (NY: Barnes & Noble, 1978), pp. 323-25.
[Survey of Life and Works.]

2591 Bringle, Jerald. (ed with assistance of Dan H.
    Laurence). "The St James's Hall Mystery" by Bernard
    Shaw, BULLETIN OF RESEARCH IN THE HUMANITIES, LXXXI
    (1978), 270-96.
It is not Shaw's enlisting characters and their
mentalities from the spirit world that separates *The Saint
James's Hall Mystery* from the work of the other major
writers of his day; "it is his postulation of such a
character as a resurrected and hence ultra-reactionary
Mozart within an openly continued dramatic frame." It
provides a motive and opportunity in a dramatic form to
damn pedantry and to acknowledge excellence, 20 years
before he wrote for the theater. Shaw took the
opportunity "to combine his interest in music and its
criticism, his interest in Mozart and the just dues he
deserved from erratic conductors, and his interest in
fashioning for himself a professional public voice as a

writer." The living performers and members of the audience supply a plausible social context for Mozart's reactions. Mozart appears first as an "unsullied representative" of the self-determining Will that Shaw will later expand upon to embody his own philosophical vitalism. Shaw echoed throughout his life his certainty that his own artfulness and artistic development he owed to Mozart. [Includes the text of *The St. James's Hall Mystery* with an introduction explaining its history and context.]

2592 Britain, I. M. "Bernard Shaw, Ibsen, and the Ethics of English Socialism," VICTORIAN STUDIES, XXI (Spring 1978), 381-401.
A careful analysis of *The Quintessence of Ibsenism*, especially of the draft manuscripts, clears up misconceptions about the attitudes of Shaw and Ibsen toward Socialism and also indicates deep divisions within the English Socialist movement along ethical lines. Although Shaw saw the potential idealism in William Morris and Ibsen, he saw their anti-idealism as more important. He attacked the Social Democratic Federation and the Socialist League for idealism, however, using Ibsen's views as the basis of his critique. Shaw knew Ibsen diverged from the basic tenets of Socialism and did not treat him as though he were a Socialist. Shaw's lecture, though generally well-received, did not evoke universal sympathy in the audience, and the division was largely on the basis of Shaw's questioning the idealist morality of some Socialists. Shaw, in fact, drew on Ibsen's individualist elements to reproach his Socialist colleagues; when this is understood, "his reliability as a critic cannot be so easily impugned."

2593 Brophy, Brigid. "Sidestepping the Life Force," TLS, 22 Sept 1978, p. 1053.
The Philanderer at the Lyttleton is the most topical, funniest, most thoughtful play in town. Shaw believed in causes, and he always wished to belong to some school or movement. Charteris's dodging his role in biological evolution is no longer the sole prerogitive of the male. [Two letters, 29 Sept. p. 1094: Michael Holroyd: The origin of the sexual wrestling match is to be found in Chapter 11 of *The Irrational Knot*. Denis Shaw: The song, "When other lips," like "I dreamt that I dwelt . . . ," is from THE BOHEMIAN GIRL. Only the words to "I dreamt" are unlucky.]

2594 Charney, Maurice. COMEDY HIGH AND LOW: AN INTRODUCTION TO THE EXPERIENCE OF COMEDY (NY: Oxford UP, 1978), pp. 43, 54, 134-35, 153, 189.
"The geniality of satirical comedy is . . . best illustrated by the plays of . . . Shaw."

2595 Crompton, Louis. "Introduction," and "Note on the Selections," THE GREAT COMPOSERS, REVIEWS AND BOMBARDMENTS BY BERNARD SHAW, ed with an introduction by Louis Crompton (Berkeley, Los Angeles and Lond: U of California P, 1978), pp. xi-xxvii.
Music was Shaw's first and longest love. He wrote what is perhaps the most lively and brilliant musical journalism ever penned. His knowledge never congealed into pedantry. His criticism is serious and profound because he possessed a clearly defined set of values. Shaw's aesthetic judgments are intertwined with his social ones; he never posed as impartial. He is conservative and anti-conservative; and he is passionately anti-Mendelssohn, who lacked "depth and dignity," which Shaw found in opera. Although London concert-goers enjoyed Wagner, opera-goers did not. And it was as a composer of opera that Wagner was championed by Shaw. Since the Victorian music world was divided into two camps, Wagner and Brahms, Shaw was naturally anti-Brahmsian. Shaw opposed Walter Pater's view that all art should aspire to the condition of music, believing instead that music itself was greatest when it approached literature. But he changed his mind and supported "absolute music." The music Shaw wrote about is still the staple of our seasons today. His insights into the composer's failings and merits are still pertinent. And he raises what is still the most important critical question: what is musical greatness.

2596 Durbach, Errol. "Pygmalion: Myth and Anti-Myth in the Plays of Ibsen and Shaw," ENGLISH STUDIES IN AFRICA, XXI (March 1978), 23-31.
Despite the promise of its mythical incredients in Act I, Shaw's *Pygmalion* does not recapitulate the incidents of the original myth; Shaw keeps the basic metaphor of metamorphosis, but he removes the mystery. His comment that Pygmalion is godlike and therefore inaccessible suggests a crucial misreading of Ovid. He does not distinguish between man-as-creator and god-as-creator. The most impressive gallery of frozen Galateas in pre-Shavian drama is found in Ibsen's late plays. Though Higgins has much in common with Ibsen's heroes, he is not a destroyer of joy. He is an idealist of the political

life, a reformer of the moral life, and a Socialist of the soul. He is self-sufficient, but not a god. Eliza creates her own self-sufficient woman.

2597 Dyhouse, Carol. "The Condition of England, 1860-1900," THE VICTORIANS, ed by Laurence Lerner (NY: Holmes & Meier, 1978), pp. 79-87.
Widowers' Houses and *Major Barbara* provide a "different" view of economic conditions.

2598 Dyhouse, Carol. "The Role of Women: from Self-sacrifice to Self-awareness," THE VICTORIANS, ed by Laurence Lerner (NY: Holmes & Meier, 1978), pp. 187, 189, 190.
[Shaw and the New Woman: *The Quintessence of Ibsenism, The Philanderer,* and *Getting Married.*]

2599 Eder, Richard. "*Major Barbara* at Shaw Festival," NYT, 21 June 1978, III, 17.
Major Barbara is not one of Shaw's best. Undershaft is a witty paradox, but he is a less complex character than Captain Shotover or John Tarleton. The production at Niagara-on-the-Lake is high-spirited and deft. [Photograph.]

2600 Eder, Richard. "*Man and Superman* at Circle in the Square," NYT, 18 Dec 1978, p. C13.
There is a lot of delight in *Man and Superman*, but some of the ideas time has made familiar. The characters are endlessly engaging. In this production, they get the outsized performance they need.

2601 Eder, Richard. "Stage: *Devil's Disciple* Presented in Brooklyn," NYT, 9 Feb 1978, III, p. 16.
The Devil's Disciple is thinner on ideas than most Shaw plays. General Burgoyne is the most interesting character.

2602 Eder, Richard. "Theater: An Actor Impersonates Shaw," NYT, 19 Jan 1978, III, p. 15.
In Donal Donnelly's re-creation of Shaw, we may never think we are seeing Shaw, but we do feel we are hearing him.

2603 Elsom, John, and Nicholas Tomalin. THE HISTORY OF THE NATIONAL THEATRE (Lond: Jonathan Cape, 1978), pp. 2, 14, 17, 27, 28, 40-48, 53, 57, 58, 61, 63, 64, 66, 68, 71, 74, 75, 76, 80, 82, 83, 96, 109, 120, 131, 138, 145, 215, 255, 256, 269, 278, 284, 285, 326.
[Shaw and the founding and development of the British National Theatre.]

2604 Farr, Diana. GILBERT CANNAN, A GEORGIAN PRODIGY (Lond: Chatto & Windus, 1978), pp. 25, 50, 64, 67, 70, 78-80, 88, 103, 133, 170.
[Shaw and Cannan.]   Shaw caricatured Cannan as Gilbert Gunn the dramatic critic in *Fanny's First Play*.

2605 Fehl, Fred [Photographs] and William Stott with Jane Stott [text]. ON BROADWAY (Austin: U of Texas P [Dan Danciger Publication Series], 1978) pp. 26, 158, 279-84, 384.
The Doctor's Dilemma (1941) with Raymond Massey. *The Devil's Disciple* (1941) with Maurice Evans and Dennis King. MY FAIR LADY (1956). *Too True to Be Good* (1963) with Lillian Gish and Cedric Hardwicke.

2606 Ganz, Margaret.   "Humor's Devaluations in a Modern Idiom: The Don Juan Plays of Shaw, Frisch, and Montherlant," COMEDY: NEW PERSPECTIVES, I (Spring 1978), 117-36.
In Shaw the deadly interaction of Don Juan and the Commander has become amiable and comic.   The whimsy, playfulness and clowning triumph over the defeats of disillusion, loss and abdication.   Shaw anticipates the later devaluations by Frisch (DON JUAN ODER DIE LIEBE ZUR GEOMETRIE) and Montherlant (LA MORT QUI FAIT LE TROTTOIR).

2607 Green, Benny. SHAW'S CHAMPIONS, G.B.S. & PRIZEFIGHTING FROM CASHEL BYRON TO GENE TUNNEY (Lond: Elm Tree Books, 1978).
Shaw was intrigued by prizefighting as a very young man and maintained his interest for the rest of his life; he took lessons in self-defense soon after arriving in London.   [Boxing, *Cashel Byron's Profession*, novel and stage version, Packenham Beatty, James J. Corbett, Jack Dempsey, Georges Carpentier, Eugene Tunney, and other boxers, as they figure in Shaw's life and career.

2608 Grice, Elizabeth. *"Arms and the Man,"* P&P XXV (June 1978), 36.
Arms and the Man seems a light romp now. [Photograph.]

2609 Gussow, Mel. "Giving All 4 Acts of *Man and Superman*," NYT, 24 Nov 1978, p. C4.
George Grizzard, playing Tanner, said the role is like Hamlet and Cyrano in one. Stephen Porter, the director, conceded that *Man and Superman* is discursive and that "whole things" can be cut; the danger lies in keeping a little of everything. It looks forward to *Heartbreak House*; Tanner's drifting in bourgeois society is hell.

2610 Hansen, Richard. "From Social Consciousness to Theatricality," CRESSET, XLI (Sept 1978), 24-27. [Not seen.]

2611 Hark, Ina Rae. "Anti Shavian Satire in *Heartbreak House*," DALHOUSIE REVIEW, LVIII (Winter 1978-79), 661-63.
Shaw justified making light of the sacred cows of his society by appearing to make light of himself, but actually his ideas emerge unscathed. Perhaps in *Heartbreak House* he engages in serious self-criticism. Most of the characters of *Heartbreak* have appeared in previous works about 20 years youngers. The absence of youth suggests a cessation of growth and death. The Heartbreakers take refuge in games to avoid facing the void, refuting evolution through regressive tendencies. Ellie Dunn confronts various Shavian alternatives which formerly promised to lead to a Messianic Age and now lead to dead ends. The Shavian solutions have out-lived their utility. *Heartbreak* still asserts the fundamental core of Shavianism, but it rejects the quasi-utopian outcome. Shaw recovered his optimism to write *Back to Methuselah* where age is an asset.

2612 Harrison, Brian. "Men on Women's Side," TLS, 27 January 1978, p. 87. [Review of Robert F. Whitman, SHAW AND THE PLAY OF IDEAS (1977), and Rodelle Weintraub (ed), FF.]
In two respects Shaw's feminism was more radical than other Edwardian male suffragists. His life demonstrates he acted on his beliefs; he repudiated the male "chivalrous" role. He was elusive as a campaigner, however, possibly because he was humble. He believed he

was more effective in the theater than on the platform.
He also shunned the simplicities of the crusade.

2613 Hart-Davis, Rupert (ed with an intro). THE
LYTTLETON HART-DAVIS LETTERS (Lond: John Murray,
1978), pp. 14, 43, 69, 70, 74, 112, 113, 129, 146,
162, 164, 165, 178, 181, 206.
[References to Shaw and his writing in the Letters of
George Lyttleton and Rupert Hart-Davis.]

2614 Heilman, Robert Bechtold. THE WAYS OF THE
WORLD. COMEDY AND SOCIETY (Seattle and Lond: U of
Washington P, 1978), pp. 20, 22-23, 29-30, 31, 32,
36, 41, 49-50, 51, 55, 56, 58, 59, 73, 91, 104, 148-
50, 153, 175, 176, 184-86, 206n, 210, 211, 238.
[Shaw's plays used as evidence for observations on
comedy.]

2615 Hill, Eldon C. GEORGE BERNARD SHAW (Bost:
Twayne Publishers [TEAS], 1978).
"This survey and critical study is for the reader who
seeks an understanding of Bernard Shaw's life and work.
It is not for Shaw specialists." [Very straightforward
and simple explanation of Shaw's biography and work.]

2616 Hobson, Harold. *"The Philanderer,"* P&P, XXVI
(Nov 1978), 20.
Though *The Philanderer* is funny in parts, what right did
Shaw the self-proclaimed Ibsenite have to make all the
Ibsenites in it fools or cads?

2617 Hodges, Sheila. GOLLANCZ, THE STORY OF A
PUBLISHING HOUSE 1928-1978 (Lond: Victor Gollancz,
1978), pp. 47, 79-88.
[The story of the publication of Frank Harris's LIFE OF
GEORGE BERNARD SHAW (1931): the quarrel over quoting
verbatim from the letters and the "Sex Credo" and Shaw's
re-write. Extensive quotation from the correspondence,
with a facsimile of a Shaw postcard.]

2618 Hogan, Robert. AN UNSOCIAL SOCIALIST, A
DRAMATIZATION OF BERNARD SHAW'S NOVEL IN TWO ACTS
(n.p.: Proscenium P, 1978).
[Exactly what the title says.]

2619 Howlett, Ivan. *"The Man of Destiny/The Dark Lady of the Sonnets*," P&P, XXV (Sept 1978), 24-25. *The Dark Lady of the Sonnets* is a wholesome, outrageous piece of debunking. *The Man of Destiny* does not work in the outdoor setting of Regent's Park; it needs greater intimacy. [Photographs.]

2620 Hughes, Catharine (ed). NEW YORK THEATRE ANNUAL, 1976-77, I (Detroit: Gale Research Company, 1978), 38, 66, 70. *Caesar and Cleopatra* with Elizabeth Ashley and Rex Harrison. MY FAIR LADY. *The Philanderer*. [Photographs and quotations from reviews.]

2621 Irving, John Douglas. "Mary Shaw, Actress, Suffragist, Activist (1854-1929)," DAI, XXXIX (1978), 1932A-1933A. Unpublished dissertation, Columbia University, 1978.

2622 Jewkes, W. T. "The Faust Theme in *Major Barbara*," ShawR, XXI (May 1978), 80-91. *Major Barbara* is more complex than the traditional tragic Faust story with a comic pattern and happy ending. Undershaft is an overwhelming Mephistopheles, and Faust is divided between Cusins and Barbara. Cusins will sell his soul for political and social power, and Barbara, for spiritual power. Like Goethe, Shaw was unsure of his ending, and it may be that Undershaft triumphs and betrays Cusins and Barbara.

2623 Johnston, Denis. "Giants in Those Days of Shaw, DeValera and Sir William Haley," IRISH UNIVERSITY REVIEW, VIII (1978), 68-73. Shaw is the personality on whose shoulders most people of my generation with any thought processes at all are sitting. He is the inspiration of a whole generation of modern dramatists. [Anecdote of how Shaw was persuaded to permit a television film interview to be made.]

2624 Kalem, T. E. "G.B.S. Lives," TIME, 30 Jan 1978, p. 68. [Review of MY ASTONISHING SELF, a one-man show devised by Michael Voysey from Shaw's writings, excluding the plays.]

2625 Kane, Sara W. "The Life Force in Action: The Relationship between Shaw's Theory of Creative Evolution and His Plays," DAI, XXXVIII (1978), 7325A-7326A. Unpublished dissertation, Boston University, 1978.

2626 Kerr, Walter. *"Man and Superman,"* NYT, 24 Dec 1978, p. D3.
Though Act III of *Man and Superman* is not a perfect fit because its characters are not parallel to their doubles, it does put weight on the proceedings.

2627 Kerr, Walter. "Stage View: Taking on G.B.S.," NYT, 29 Jan 1978, II, pp. 3, 32.
Shaw's plays are not all peopled with big and little Shaws. His characters do not all speak in his voice, but they all have his trick of mind of seeing the other side. [Essay on production of MY ASTONISHING SELF, constructed from Shaw's non-dramatic writing.]

2628 Kidd, Timothy J. "James Elroy Flecker and Bernard Shaw," ShawR, XXI (Sept 1978), 124-35.
James Elroy Flecker, who was antagonistic to Shaw, submitted his play DON JUAN to him because Shaw was known to encourage young writers and also as a challenge. Shaw praised the play and wrote a letter of introduction to Herbert Trench of the Haymarket Theatre. [Shaw's slight role in Flecker's writing.] The case for Flecker's HASSAN influencing *Saint Joan* is unproven.

2629 Lago, Mary. "Introduction," MEN AND MEMORIES, RECOLLECTIONS, 1872-1938, by William Rothenstein (Columbia: U of Missouri P, 1978), pp. 20-21.
[This is an abridgement of three earlier books by Rothenstein, MEN AND MEMORIES, 1872-1900 (1931), MEN AND MEMORIES, 1900-1922 (1932), and SINCE FIFTY, MEN AND MEMORIES, 1922-1938 (1939), with references to Shaw on pp. 86-87, 88, 107, 146, 150, 169-70, 191, 217n, 218n, 222n.] Rothenstein responded to Shaw's suggestion in 1940 of a cut-rate system of pricing and selling works of art.

2630 Laufe, Abe. THE WICKED STAGE, A HISTORY OF THEATER CENSORSHIP AND HARASSMENT IN THE UNITED STATES (NY: Frederick Ungar, 1978), pp. 26-27.
[*Mrs. Warren's Profession* and censorship.]

2631 Leary, Daniel J. "Shaw Versus Shakespeare: The Refinishing of CYMBERLINE," ETJ, XXX (March 1978) 5-25.
Using Harold Bloom's studies of influence, *Cymbeline Refinished* can be regarded as a paradigm of Shaw's love-hate struggle with Shakespeare. [Leary demonstrates Shaw's use of Bloom's Six Strategems: 1) Swerve, 2) Partial Completion, 3) Repetition/Discontinuity, 4) Counter Sublime, 5) Purgation, and 6) Return of the Dead, to show that *Cymbeline Refinished* reflects bits and pieces of all Shaw's work.]

2632 Lerner, Alan Jay. THE STREET WHERE I LIVE (NY and Lond: W. W. Norton, 1978), pp. 23, 30-39, 43-50, 52, 61-64, 67, 70, 78, 83, 93, 96, 121-22, 128.
[The Transformation of *Pygmalion* into MY FAIR LADY.]

2633 Loney, Glenn. "Summers of Shaw," THEATRE CRAFTS, XII (May/June 1978), 23, 48, 50-52.
Only Shaw among modern playwrights has the volume to support a summer festival. [Description of Niagara-on-the-Lake Shaw Festival.]

2634 McFadden, Karen Doris. "George Bernard Shaw and the Woman Question," DAI, XXXIX (1978), 2230A. Unpublished dissertation, University of Toronto, 1976.

2635 Matoba, Junko. "The Grotesque as Applied Form for Shaw's Characters," SEISHIN JOSHIDAIGAKU RONSO (Tokyo), No 51 (June 1978), pp. 3-17.
"Exaggeration and strangeness are the words that can explain the basic method of all Shaw's characterization and it tends toward the grotesque, for a salient feature of a character is inflated to the extent of monstrosity with a view to rendering a character either as ridiculous, absurd or repugnant. It is that his characters are grotesque more in the features of their personality than in their physical aspect." This method has a close relationship with an archetypal pattern pointed out by a Russian critic M. Bakhtin in his analysis of Menippean literature.

2636 Meier, Paul. WILLIAM MORRIS: THE MARXIST DREAMER, 2 vols, trans from LA PENSÉE UTOPIQUE (1972) by Frank Gubb (Sussex: Harvester P; NJ: Humanities P, 1978), pp. 17, 23, 24, 30, 161, 172, 197, 202, 205, 211, 212, 221, 281, 284, 299, 335, 435, 437, 478, 504, 509, 535.
[Shaw's role in the life, career, and ideas of William Morris.]

2637 Mosel, Tad, with Gertrude Macy. LEADING LADY: THE WORLD AND THEATRE OF KATHARINE CORNELL (Bost and Toronto: Little, Brown, 1978).
[Shaw anecdotes, production details, and the like, concerning Katharine Cornell's performances in and productions of *Fanny's First Play*, *Candida* (five different productions), *Saint Joan*, *The Doctor's Dilemma*.]

2638 Musil, Robert. KRITIK: LITERATUR - THEATER - KUNST 1912-1930, (Criticism: Literature - Theater - Art 1912-1930) vol IX (Reinbek/Hamburg: Rowohlt, 1978) pp. 1496-98, 1670-73.
[Reprints "*Helden*" (*Arms and the Man*), PRAGER PRESSE, 15 Juhne 1921, and "*Die Heilige Johanna*" (*Saint Joan*), DER MORGEN, 27 Oct 1924, abstracted under date of first publication.] [In German.]

2639 Nathan, Rhoda. "The 'Daimons' of *Heartbreak House*," MD, XXI (Sept 1978), 253-65.
The Greeks believed the daimons lead them from virtue. It is just such an objectification of external, malign forces that Shaw dramatized in Hesione and Ariadne in *Heartbreak House*. He gave them Greek names. These two enchantresses are associated with the sea. Shotover is a literal translation of "hamartia." Like Tiresias, he is unheeded. Hesione comes from a Greek word that means "object of great desire." Ariadne means "hard" or "cruel." Hector means "anchor." The names are clues to an underlying theme. [A detailed examination of the associations of the names to be found in Greek mythology and legend.] Hesione and Ariadne are fit agents for the tragic outcome of this "comedy."

2640 Newby, Richard L. "An Arnoldian Allusion in *Major Barbara*," AMERICAN NOTES & QUERIES, XVI (1978), 68.

Shaw alludes to, and ridicules, an important Arnoldian thesis in CULTURE AND ANARCHY in the exchange between Undershaft and Stephen in Act III of *Major Barbara.*

2641 O'Connor, John, and Lorraine Brown (eds). FREE, ADULT, UNCENSORED. THE LIVING HISTORY OF THE FEDERAL THEATRE PROJECT (Washington, D.C.: New Republic Books, 1978), pp. 14, 18, 32, 150-59.
[Photographs of the cast, set and costume designs, drawings, and posters of Hallie Flanagan's production of *Androcles and the Lion* for Harlem's all black Lafayette unit of the Federal Theatre Project.]

2642 O'Connor, Mary. "Did Bernard Shaw Kill John Davidson? The 'Tragi-Comedy' of a Commissioned Play," ShawR, XXI (Sept 1978), 108-23.
[An account of the relationship between Shaw and John Davidson, especially their disagreement over Davidson's play THE GAME OF LIFE commissioned by Shaw.] Davidson, discouraged by the play's failure to please Shaw and by other set-backs, committed suicide, which Shaw called a "tragi-comedy."

2643 Ogiso, Masafumi. "Shawbungaku no Kaikyu to Ningen" (Classes and Human Beings in Shaw), JISSEN EIBEIBUNGAKU (Tokyo), No 9 (Nov 1978), 1-31.
A distinctive feature of Shaw's understanding of classes is his impartiality. He does not idealize the working class and refused to be sentimental about them. [Surveys the characteristics of the proletarian characters in *Immaturity, An Unsocial Socialist, Widowers' Houses, Mrs. Warren's Profession, Major Barbara,* and *Pygmalion.*] [In Japanese.]

2644 O'Neill, William L. THE LAST ROMANTIC: A LIFE OF MAX EASTMAN (NY: Oxford UP, 1978), pp. 41, 42, 72, 87.
[Shaw's disagreements with Eastman about what should be published in NEW MASSES.]

2645 Platz-Waury, Elke. DRAMA UND THEATER: EINE EINFÜHRUNG (Drama and Theater: An Introduction) (Tübingen: Gunter Narr, 1978), 15, 29, 31, 60, 100.
Shaw's stage-directions tend to check the actor's freedom of acting. [In German.]

2646 Rosenberg, Edgar.   "The Shaw/Dickens File:
1885 to 1950. An Annotated Checklist (continued),"
ShawR, XXI (Jan 1978), 2-19.
[Shaw-Dickens bibliography.]

2647 Rubin, Don (ed).   CANADA ON STAGE, CANADIAN
THEATRE REVIEW YEARBOOK, 1977 (Downsview, Ontario:
CTR Publications, 1978), pp. 40, 64, 71, 90, 91,
143, 147, 267, 295, 306, 308, 309, 338.
Pygmalion (French adaptation), *Village Wooing, Arms and
the Man, Man and Superman, Don Juan in Hell, The
Millionairess, Widowers' Houses, Great Catherine,* and
Androcles and the Lion. [Illustrated with production
photographs.]

2648 Scrimgeour, James R.   SEAN O'CASEY (Bost:
Twayne Publishers [TEAS], 1978), pp. 27, 40, 54, 58,
141.
[Shaw cited in criticism of O'Casey.]

2649 Seidel, Alison P. (comp).   LITERARY CRITICISM
AND AUTHORS' BIOGRAPHIES, AN ANNOTATED INDEX
(Metuchen, NJ and Lond: Scarecrow P, 1978), pp.
159-60.
[Bibliography with brief annotations.]

2650 Sharman, Charles Anthony.   "Bernard Shaw's
Dramatic Theory and Practice: An Examination of
Some Critical Approaches, with Emphasis upon Those
of Shaw Himself," DAI, XXXIX (1978), 1557A-1558A.
Unpublished dissertation, University of Toronto,
1976.

2651 Shimamura, Totaro.   "Courtza niokeru Vedrenne-
Barker Performances" (The Vedrenne-Barker Perform-
ances at the Royal Court Theatre in Sloane Square,
London), UTSUNIMIYA DAIGAKU KYOYOBU KENKYUHO-
KOKU (Utsunomiya), no 11, sec 1 (Dec 1978), 41-54.
[Includes detailed graphic tables of all performances,
based on the original programs.] [In Japanese.]

2652 Simeikina, N. M.   "Bernard Shou i teatral'ne
zhittia Anglii pochatku XX St." (Bernard Shaw and
Theatrical Life of England in the Early Twentieth
Century), RADIIANSKOE LITERATUROZNAVSTVO (Kiev), No.
5, (1978), 73-79.

[Review of PI'SMA by G. B. Shaw, ed by A. G. Obraztŝova (1971) (Not seen.)] Shaw's letters reveal his erudition but also express his artistic and journalistic views, with uncompromising criticism, irony, and penetration into human life. They also reveal his attitude to the October Revolution, 1917. Some of his letters were published in Ukrainian in 1917. English theatrical life of the early twentieth century was marked by the struggle of social and critical realism in the drama, and Shaw was the leader of the struggle, despite the censorship. [In Ukrainian.]

2653 Smith, B. L. O'CASEY'S SATIRIC VISION (n.p.: Kent State UP, 1978), pp. 4, 32, 60, 65, 83, 89, 90, 98, 137, 163, 184, 186, 189.
[Shaw cited in criticism of O'Casey.]

2654 Smith, J. Percy. "Shaw's Own Problem Play: *Major Barbara*," ENGLISH STUDIES IN CANADA, IV (Winter 1978), 450-67.
The origin of *Major Barbara* lies in Shaw's interest in the conflict between the economic and religious views of life. [Survey of the legends of Saint Barbara.] The "source" of Barbara's moral problem is Shaw's own indignation, 20 years earlier, over the acceptance by the Social Democratic Federation of money given by the Tories in order to thwart a Liberal victory. The solution in the third act lets everyone off the hook enigmatically. Because of Shaw's perplexity over the central moral problem of the play, that power tends to corrupt, *Barbara* is not honest and dramatically consistent. Shaw was unable to turn the original tragic material into comedy.

2655 Smith, Warren Sylvester. "The Search for Good Government: *The Apple Cart, On the Rocks,* and *Geneva*," ShawR, XXI (Jan 1978), 20-30.
In his non-dramatic writings, Shaw's politics is largely economics. Finally in *The Apple Cart, On the Rocks,* and *Geneva* Shaw confronted the problem of government itself; his complaints are clear, but his remedies are less so. his most effective though ambiguous statement about government may appear in *Heartbreak House.* "The most important ingredient of good government is competent leadership." Shaw had little faith in self-government. The chief purpose of government is equality of income. Government should be organized with federal legislatures and a central coordinating authority--a benevolent

dictatorship, the dictators to be chosen by examination. Finally he was skeptical of all forms of government.

2656 Sobańska, Anna. *"Androkles i lew"* (*Androcles and the Lion*), TEATR (Warsaw), X (1978), 19-20.
Witkiewicz said of Shaw that "he is an example of a fiendish dramatic talent used for non-artistic purposes." But this remark hardly refers to the grotesque, fairy-tale parable *Androcles and the Lion*, depicting a man's friendship with an animal, or with free Nature. It is an inferior work, dramatizing the Will and conscience of the individual when faced with orders from above, and the problem of choosing the golden mean. But the play is simplified and schematic. The production at the Jelenia Góra Theater (1978) is a colorful spectacle which does not conceal a certain thinness of text. [In Polish.]

2657 Stone-Blackburn, Susan.   "Unity in Diversity: *Androcles and the Lion*," Shaw R, XXI (May 1978), 92-99.
The only legend that satisfied Shaw as he found it was that of Androcles and the Lion. Structurally the legend frames the play. It sets the tone, reminiscent of a mediaeval miracle play, introduces details to be developed later, and provides a symbolic solution to the problems raised in the discussion. One effect of joining the legend to the religious discussion is to raise the question central to Lavinia's religious struggle: to what extent is the story of Christ a legend? The answer is that it is the doctrine and not the man that matters.

2658 Tippett, Sir Michael. *"Back to Methuselah* and THE ICE BREAK," Shaw R, XXI (May 1978), 100-3.
[Michael Tippett's PRIAM, THE MIDSUMMER MARRIAGE and THE KNOT GARDEN owe some debt to *Heartbreak House* and *The Apple Cart*.] *THE ICE BREAK* bears resemblance to *Back to Methuselah*.

2659 Tucholsky, Kurt. DIE Q-TAGEBÜCHER 1934-1935 (The Q-Diaries 1934-1935), ed by Mary Gerold-Tucholsky and Gustav Huonker (Reinbek: Rowohlt, 1978), pp. 55, 158.
Shaw "is not as earnest as he pretends to be in a joking manner." [In German.]

2660 Vesonder, Timothy G. "An Annotated Checklist of Selected Myth Criticism on Shaw's Works," ShawR, XXI (May 1978), 104-49.

2661 Vesonder, Timothy G. "Shaw's Caesar and the Mythic Hero," ShawR, XXI (May 1978), 72-79. Shaw wished to present a full-length portrait of the archetypal hero in *Caesar and Cleopatra*, but he reshaped him to be more realistic and acceptable. Probably his inspiration and support were found in Wagner's RING OF THE NIEBELUNGENS. Shaw's hero is superior to man, yet human, possesses great wit and will, and wishes selflessly to advance the human race.

2662 Vogt, Sally Peters. "*Heartbreak House*, Shaw's Ship of Fools," MD, XXI (Sept 1978), 267-86. *Heartbreak House* is didactically ordered in two metaphors: the ship of state and the ship of fools. The play is a fable, the form Shaw favored in his last 30 years. Sebastian Brant's catalogue of folly in his NARRENSCHIFF reads like a satiric gloss of *Heartbreak*. Shaw used farcical devices, especially mistaken identity, to insure aesthetic distance. The play is pervaded by an implicit religious quality. "The paratactic structure, the final equivalence of all scenes, characters, and themes -- which is separate from their increasing dramatic force -- shapes the drama so that reason and order exist beneath the chaotic structure." "It becomes clear that the ordering structure of *Heartbreak House*, as in all apologues, is rhetorical in nature." "The apologic form, which Shaw perfects in *Heartbreak House*, becomes the predominant form of later Shavian drama."

2663 Webb, Beatrice and Sidney. THE LETTERS OF BEATRICE AND SIDNEY WEBB, 3 vols. ed by Norman Mackenzie (Cambridge, London, NY, Melbourne: Cambridge UP, 1978), passim. [Letters to and about Shaw from the Webbs. Indexed.]

2664 Weintraub, Stanley. "Inscriptions for Sale," ShawR, XXI (Sept 1978), 153-55. [Review of FLYLEAVES, ed by Dan H. Laurence and Daniel J. Leary (1977).] Until 1949 Shaw refused to participate in schemes to create artificial rarities of his own books as well as those of others presented to him. Financial anxieties changed his mind, and he penned substantial inscriptions on the flyleaves of eight presentation copies from his library. They are now all in one place in this volume.

2665 Weintraub, Stanley. "A Passion for Pugilism," TLS, 5 May 1978, p. 495.
[Review of Benny Green, SHAW'S CHAMPIONS (1978).] Shaw, once lured back to his early love of boxing, persisted in his interest. [Letter 3 June, p. 614, John Roe comments on the possible relationship between the advice of Bob Fitzsimmons's wife to hit Jim Corbett "in the slats" and Epifania's admiration for her fiance's solar plexus punch.]

2666 Whitman, Robert F. "The Passion of Dick Dudgeon," Shaw R, XXI (May 1978), 60-71.
Shaw sought the kind of truth shared by myth, legend, and parable, and as he makes clear in the Preface to *Back to Methuselah*, he took the legends from the past, including those from Christianity, and made them parables for a religion of the future. The Manichean polarity between good and evil is reflected in *The Devil's Disciple* but in such a way that raises questions as to their meaning. Dudgeon's diabolism at the beginning is little more than a reaction to his mother's puritanism, but with Anderson as the catalyst, he transcends Judith's romanticism and his mother's selfishness to discover the worth of his life. Shaw's Jesus in *Household of Jesus* [sic?] and in the dialogue between Jesus and Pontius Pilate in the Preface to *On the Rocks* have much in common as rebels. Burgoyne is like Pilate. Both Dudgeon and Burgoyne have much in their natures that is admirable, but Dudgeon is on the side of freedom and the future, and Burgoyne is on the side of the law and the past.

2667 Whittock, Trevor. "*Major Barbara*: Comic Masterpiece," THEORIA (Lund, Sweden), LI (1978), 1-14.
Shaw controlled very diverse material in *Major Barbara* with wit, as defined by Dr. Johnson in his essay on one of the metaphysical poets. Shaw carries his learning lightly, and he deals in real ideas. Shaw's comedy, like Shakespeare's, moves from folly, to disillusion, to discovery. *Barbara* has two interrelated plots: the first is the search for an heir, the second is Barbara's challenge to Undershaft, and his counter-challenge to her. The fundamental issue is that "men must move forward with

the movement of life itself," serving ultimate Creative Energy.

2668 Wilson, Colin. "The Critics Called Them Monsters--Shaw Said They Were Real Women," NYT, 10 Dec 1978, II, pp. 1, 29.
Because Shaw waited so long for recognition, the impact was greater. Shaw's idea of women was derived from his mother and sister. Shaw never resolved the conflict between the mother-woman and the artist-man. *Man and Superman* is Shaw's finest achievement.

1979

2669 Amalric, Jean-Claude. "Modèle actantiel et investissement thématique: quelques remarques sur *Arms and the Man*" (Actantial Model and Thematic Investment: Some Remarks on *Arms and the Man*) CAHIERS VICTORIENS ET ÉDOUARDIENS, No 9/10 (Oct 1979), 87-94.
[An analysis of the structure of *Arms and the Man* with the help of the actantial schema of A. J. Greimas.] In the course of the play, the actantial schema, which seemed to correspond to a traditional, romantic situation, is altered and transformed into an ironical schema, by the use of an ironic Helper/Opponent, Bluntschli. The thematic investment thus discovered enables us to define the actantial schema of the Shavian spectacle of the "conversion." The desired Object can be defined as a conversion to Shavian realism, the Opponent being philistinism and idealism. Most of the dramatic situations in Shaw's comedies of ideas could be explained by this actantial model and this thematic investment.

2670 Anzai, Tetsuo. "Shakespeare to Shaw" (Shakespeare and Shaw), RUNESSANSU TO GENDAI (Rennaissance and the Present Age), ed by Takero Oiji and Peter Milward (Tokyo: Aratake Shuppan, 1979), pp. 71-95.
Shaw's Shakespeare criticism gives us some important clues to illuminate characteristic qualities of the Renaissance and the present age. If we see his Shakespeare criticism in the context of the history of Shakespeare presentation, it is clear that he was strongly supporting the new style

of Shakespeare presentation advocated by Forbes-Robertson,
F. R. Benson, and particularly by W. Poel and Granville-
Barker. Furthermore, viewed from the history of Shakespeare criticism since the sixteenth century, his opinions
will emerge not to be blasphemous nor eccentric but
commonly accepted ones. In fact, his views seem to be
shared by most so-called neo-classicists from Ben Jonson
to Dr. Johnson. [In Japanese.]

2671 Eder, Richard. "Stage: *Heartbreak House* at
the McCarter," N Y T, 12 April 1979, p. C 14.
Heartbreak House was Shaw's Ninth Symphony. In it he is
quintessential Shaw, and still he "took a jump and became
something more." The McCarter Theatre production is fine,
having a "glowing ensemble" and a "wealth of first-rate
performances . . . a rhythm and resonance."

2672 Kimura, Masami. "Shaw, Wilde, Webbfusai -
Rekishi Ishiki omegutte" (Shaw, Wilde and Webbs - on
Their Sense of History), K E N K Y U N E N P O (Dept. of
Economics, Kagawa University, Takamatsu), No 18
(March 1979), 1-61.
It is well-known that Shaw studied Marx's DAS KAPITAL "day
after day for weeks" at the British Museum Reading Room,
and that he read it in Deville's French version. It would
be almost impossible to grasp what Marx really wrote from
reading G. Deville's version; it was also highly probable
that Deville made Shaw's understanding of Marx rather
distorted.

His two contributions in FABIAN ESSAYS IN SOCIALISM reveal
clearly the basic sense of history that he had been
gradually establishing in the '80s and '90s. It is
essentially a composite of ideas held by Marx, Morris and
Webb, not his original one. This sense of history in his
Fabian era shows a gradual development in his dramatist
era in the twentieth century, when these three composite
elements act as antitheses to his groping for wider and
deeper sense of history; his drifting apart from Fabianism
was an inevitable result. [A detailed and well-documented
study; Wilde's and the Webbs' views are also discussed in
comparison with Shaw's.] [In Japanese.]

1980

2673 Kerr, Walter. "Stage: Shaw's *Major Barbara*," NYT, 27 Feb 1980, p. C19.
Stephen Porter's production "is the very model of a modern *Major Barbara*."

2674 Matsumoto, Shinko. MEIJI ENGEKIRONSHI (A History of Japanese Dramatic Theory in the Meiji Era) (Tokyo: Engeki Shuppansha, 1980), pp. 296, 346, 347-48, 390-401, 671, 673, 679, 684, 811, 922, 980, 1015, 1039, 1063, 1064.
[Describes in detail how Shaw was received in Japan in the late 1900's through early 1910's.] [In Japanese.]

2675 Mizuno, Yoshikazu. "Bernard Shaw Hyoden" (Bernard Shaw, a Critical Biography), GENDAI ENGEKI (Tokyo), No 3 (April 1980), 2-17.
We must always bear Shaw's many-sidedness in mind when we consider his life and achievements. [In Japanese.]

2676 Rich, Frank. "Critic's Notebook," NYT, 15 Aug 1980, p. C-3.
Kenneth Tynan's generalization on *Heartbreak House* that "All of Shaw's characters are deficient in human emotion" is often true, but certainly one exception is *Candida*. Blythe Danner as Candida was "the worthy apex of any love triangle."

2677 Shimamura, Totaro. "G. B. Shaw no MSS" (G. B. Shaw's MSS.), GAIKOKUBUNGAKU (Utsunomiya), No 28 (March 1980), 38-47.
[A concise description of Shaw's MSS housed in the British Library, the National Library of Ireland, Universities of Texas (Austin), Harvard and Cornell, and the New York Public Library.] [In Japanese.]

Index

AUTHORS

Included here are authors of articles and books on Shaw, editors and compilers of works in which criticism on Shaw appears. Editors and translators are identified parenthetically: (ed), (trans). Numbers after each name refer to the item(s) in the bibliography where the name occurs.

Applebaum, Stanley (ed):
2347
Aquino, John: 2104
Archer, Peter: 927
Arkadin: 1057
Armand, I. L.: 514
Armes, Roy: 2581
Armstrong, William A.:
832, 1058
Armytage, W. H. Q.: 1185
Arnold, Armin: 928, 1059,
1500
Arnot, R. Page: 236
Ashmore, Basil: 1397
Astafeeva, M.: 2451
Atherton, James S.: 372
Atkinson, Brooks: 3, 135,
136, 237, 238, 239, 240,
373, 602, 603, 697
Auchincloss, Katherine L.:
698
Auden, W. H.: 4, 929
Austin, Don De Forest:
374, 604, 930, 1694
Ausubel, Herman: 375
Axton, Marie (ed): 2570
Ayling, Ronald: 699, 833,
1186, 2348; (ed): 1332,
1333
Ayrton, Michael: 1986
B. T. Y.: 1187
Bab, Julius: 5, 376, 377
Bader, Earl D.: 1612
Bagar, Andrej: 378
Bailey, J. O.: 1987
Bain, Carl E.: 1988
Bain, Kenneth Bruce
Findlater: 1249
Bainbridge, John: 931
Baker, Stuart E.: 2582
Balashov, P. S.: 1613,
1695, 1696
Balch, Jack: 241
Balice, Vincent: 2349
Balint, Stefan (ed): 2206
Ball, John: 2350
Balthasar, Hans U. von:
1989
Bałutowa, Bronisława: 6

Bandyopadhyay, Sarit Kumar:
1614
Bantas, Andrei: 1697
Baquero, Acadio: 1060
Barber, George S.: 7
Barghel, Virginia: 1698
Barker, Dudley: 1990
Barnes, Clive: 1188, 1398,
1399, 1991, 2351, 2452,
2453, 2454, 2583, 2584,
2585
Barnes, John: 1501
Barnes, Kenneth R.: 137
Barnes, T. R.: 515
Barnet, Sylvan (ed): 379,
1189, 2270
Barnett, Gene A.: 1615
Barr, Alan Philip: 834,
1400, 1502, 1992
Barrett, William: 8
Barrick, Mac E.: 2586
Barron, Neil: 2352
Barth, Max: 700
Barzun, Jacques: 701, 2353
Baskin, Ken Alexander:
2455, 2587
Bastable, Adolphus [pseud]:
1061, 1190, 1191, 1192,
1699, 1832, 2588
Bateson, F. W.: 932
Batson, Eric J.: 9, 242,
243, 604, 702, 933
Batters, Jean: 2456
Baugh, Albert C. (ed):
1205
Baxter, Kay M.: 835
Baylen, Joseph O.: 547,
606, 607, 748, 749, 1062
Beard, Harry R.: 1063
Beatty, C. J. P.: 516
Beatty, Jerome, Jr.: 249
Beckson, Karl (ed): 2267
Bedell, Jeanne Fenrick:
2354
Beerbohm, Max: 1503, 1616
Behrman, S. N.: 380, 517,
934
Bender, William: 703
Benedek, Marcell: 381,
704, 705

Brooke, Sylvia, Lady: 1619
Brooks, Cleanth: 842
Brooks, Harold F.: 387,
710, 2458
Brooks, Jean R.: 710
Brophy, Brigid: 1197,
2001, 2459, 2593
Brown, Alison: 612
Brown, Barbara Browning:
2359
Brown, G. E.: 1711
Brown, Geoff: 2211
Brown, Ivor: 843, 937,
938, 1510
Brown, Jack R.: 844
Brown, John Mason: 249
Brown, John, Russell (ed):
637
Brown, Lorraine (ed): 2641
Brown, T. J.: 845
Browne, E. Martin: 1198
Browne, Terry W.: 2212
Brustein, Robert: 250,
613, 939
Bryden, Ronald: 846, 940,
941, 1842, 2109
Budach, Hildegard: 942
Budzinski, Franciszek:
1069
Bühler, Renate: 1070
Bullough, Geoffrey: 251,
614
Bunich-Remizov, B. B.:
1407
Burgaft, E. M.: 615, 1071
Burgess, Anthony: 943,
2110
Burgunder, Bernard F.:
1511
Burke, Tom: 2460
Burns, Edward McNall: 388
Burto, William (ed): 379,
1189, 2270
Burton, H. M.: 252
Burton, Hal (ed): 1219,
1241, 1343, 1344, 1371
Bush, Alfred L.: 1072
Bushko, David Arthur: 2360
Bussmann, Georg: 2310
Butler, Anthony: 1199

Butt, J. (ed): 2075
Büttner, Ludwig: 253
Byers, William Franklin:
711
Byrne, John: 146
Byrom, Michael: 712
C., J.: 398
Cahill, Susan, and Thomas
Cahill: 2003
Calvin, Judith S.: 616
Campbell, Margaret: 2214
Canaris, Volker: 1200
Cannon, Betty Jo: 2461
Canovan, Margaret: 2462
Cantieri, Giovanni: 713
Caputi, Anthony: 1073,
1074; (ed): 1073
Carlson, Marvin: 262, 263,
617
Carmody, Terence F.: 1620
Carnell, Hilary: 2475
Carpenter, Charles Albert,
Jr.: 714, 847, 944,
1025, 1073, 1075, 1076,
1512, 1621, 2215
Carr, Pat M.: 2361
Carrington, Norman Thomas:
15, 147, 148, 1077, 1201
Cary, Richard: 1712
Casper, Vivian C.: 1713
Cassell, Richard A. (ed):
1202
Casserly, C. J.: 16
Cassirer, Peter: 2216
Casson, John: 1843
Castagna, Edwin: 1408
Castello, Giulio Cesare:
618
Cathey, Kenneth Clay: 17
Caute, David: 1844
Cavallini, Graziano: 848
Cavanaugh, Hilayne (ed):
1719, 1720
Cecil, David Max: 849
Çerf, Bennett: 390, 2463
Černy, František, et al.:
2362
Chaillet, Ned: 2363
Chaplin, Charles: 850
Chapman, John: 1203, 1409

Dace, Letitia, and Wallace
Dace: 2011
Daiches, David: 149, 397
Dalmasso, Osvaldo de: 949
Dalrymple, Jean: 2222
Dannenberg, Peter: 1222
Dargan, O. P.: 2119
Darlington, W. A.: 2012
Davidson, J. A.: 528
Davies, Marion: 2223
Davies, Cecil William:
2472
Davies, Robertson: 2120
Davies, Stan Gébler: 2224
Davis, Herbert (ed): 364
Davis, Richard Beale (ed):
582
Davis, Robert B.: 950
Dawick, John: 1721
Deane, Barbara: 2013
Dearden, James S.: 1722
Debnicki, Antoni, and
Ryszard Górski: 22, 150
Delacorte, Valerie: 855
Del Amo, Alvaro: 1223
Demaray, John G.: 719
DeMoss, Virginia: 2225
Dench, Judi: 1723
Denham, Reginald: 151
Denninghaus, Friedhelm:
1724
Dent, Alan: 23, 256, 1224
Dervin, Daniel A.: 1725,
2226
De Selincourt, Aubrey: 398
De Vries, Ella Mae Scales:
2473
Diakonova, Nina: 621
Dickson, Ronald J.: 257
Di Claudio, Giuseppe: 1225
Dieckmann, Jörg: 1226
Dietrich, Richard Farr:
529, 951, 1523, 1850
Dobrev, Chadar: 1414
Dock, Leslie Anne: 2474
Doherty, Brian: 1227, 2121
Dolby, William: 2372
Dolch, Martin: 1624
Dolis, John J., Jr.: 2122
Dombrowski, Eileen: 2227

Donaghy, Henry: 1084,
1228, 1415
Dooley, Roger B.: 1229
Döpfner, Julius: 399
Dorcey, Donal: 1230
Doromby, K.: 720
Dower, Margaret Winifred:
25
Downer, Alan S.: 530,
1231, 1625, 1726
Doyle, P. A.: 1232
Drabble, Margaret: 2123
Drews, Wolfgang: 531
Driver, Tom F.: 258, 1626
DuCann, C. G. L.: 532, 721
Dudek, Louis: 722
Duerksen, Roland A.: 622,
723, 1851
Duffin, Henry Charles: 400
Dukore, Bernard F.: 401,
533, 534, 724, 725, 856,
1085, 1233, 1234, 1727,
1728, 1729, 1852, 2014,
2015, 2016, 2124
Dukore, Bernard F. (ed):
1079, 1416, 2375
Dunbar, Janet: 402, 726
Dunlap, Joseph R.: 403,
535, 536, 727, 952, 1235,
1236, 1237
Dupler, Dorothy: 537
Dupré, Catharine: 2374
Durbach, Errol: 2596
Durbin, James H.: 857
Dyhouse, Carol: 2597, 2598
Dyson, A. E. (ed): 1926,
1934, 1956
Eaton, Peter: 623
Eagle, Dorothy: 2475
Eckstein, Harry: 152
Edel, Leon: 1853; (ed):
2342
Eder, Richard: 2476, 2477,
2478, 2599, 2600, 2601,
2602, 2671
Edwards, Anne: 2479
Edwards, Oliver: 153
Egan, Michael: 1854
Egerton, George
(psued):143

Green, Benny: 2127, 2607
Green, Jonathan (ed): 2027
Green, Martin: 544, 2489
Green, Ronnie Lloyd: 2242
Greenberg, Martin (ed): 2556
Greene, David H. (ed): 647
Greer, Edward G.: 2128
Greer, Germaine: 1633
Gregory, Lady Augusta: 1736
Greiner, Norbert: 2243, 2244
Greiwe, Ulrich (ed): 2107
Grendon, Felix: 42, 43
Grenfell, Joyce: 2490
Grevenius, Herbert: 276, 422
Gribben, John L.: 964
Grice, Elizabeth: 2608
Griffith, Benjamin W.: 1737
Gritsiûtenko, V. J.: 2491
Groshong, James W.: 44, 164
Grossman, Manuel L.: 1265
Gruber, W. E.: 2492
Grunwald, Henry Anatole: 633
Guardia, Alfredo de la: 1634
Gubb, Frank (trans): 2636
Guernsey, Otis L., Jr. (ed): 1266
Guerrero Zamora, Juan: 1267
Gŭlŭbova, S.: 1738
Gupchev, Ivan: 1738
Gurewitch, Morton: 2245
Guseva, E.: 965
Gussow, Mel: 1871, 2609
Guthke, Karl S.: 1091
Guy, Vincent: 1606
Györe, Imre: 966
Hagnell, Viveka: 1092
Hagopian, John V. (ed): 1624
Hales, John: 744
Hamer, Douglas: 1093
Hammer, Klaus (ed): 2548

Han, Tien: 45
Hansen, Richard: 2610
Hardwick, Michael: 1420, 2029, 2030
Hardwick, Mollie: 1420, 2030
Hark, Ina Rae: 2387, 3424
Harmon, Lord Chief Justice Charles: 46
Harmon, Maurice: 2493
Harnsberger, Caroline Thomas (comp): 967
Harper, George Mills (ed): 2482
Harrington, John (ed): 1872
Harris, Bernard (ed): 637
Harris, Edward P.: 2494
Harris, Harold J.: 745
Harris, Nathaniel: 2494
Harrison, Brian: 2612
Harrison, G. B. (ed): 423
Harrison, K. C. (ed): 1204
Harrison, N. J.: 2031
Harrison, Rosina: 2247
Hart, Derek: 1344
Hart, James: 139
Hart-Davis, Rupert (ed): 869, 2613
Hartnoll, Phyllis: 1421, 2248; (ed): 1198
Harvey, Robert C.: 1635
Haskell, John D., Jr.: 1025
Hasler, Jörg (ed): 1562
Hassall, Christopher: 278
Hatcher, Joe Branch: 1535, 1739
Hatlen, Theodore W.: 1268
Häusermann, H. W.: 277
Havighurst, Alfred F.: 2129
Hayman, Ronald: 2249
Hayward, John: 424
Haywood, Charles: 1536, 1537
Hegedus, Geza: 1636
Heidicke, Manfred: 165
Heilman, Robert Bechtold: 2614

707

Heinlein, Robert: 2032
Hellman, Lillian: 2033
Helsztyński, Stanisław:
47, 1740
Henderson, Archibald: 280
Henderson, Leslie M.: 2034
Henderson, Lucile Kelling:
2130
Henderson, Philip: 1269
Henderson, Robert M.: 1873
Hendrick, George: 2496
Henríquez Ureña, Pedro:
281
Henson, Janice: 545
Hentschel, Irene: 870
Hepple, Peter: 968
Hergešić, Branko: 1094
Herman, István: 746
Herr, Linda L.: 2497
Hess, Hans: 2131
Hewes, Henry: 1874
Hewitt, Barnard: 282, 1637
Hibbard, G. R. (ed): 1121
Hibbs, Christopher: 1538
Higgs, Calvin T.: 2388
Higham, Charles: 2250,
2389, 2498
Hildeman, Per-Axel: 546
Hill, Eldon C.: 283, 2615
Hill, John Edward: 2035
Hill, Maureen (ed): 1638
Hiller, Wendy: 1741
Himmelstein, Morgan Yale:
747
Hirota, Norio: 2251
Hirsch, Foster Lance: 1742
Hobsbawm, E. J.: 871
Hobson, Harald: 2616
Hodges, Sheila: 2617
Hogan, Patrick G., Jr.:
547, 607, 748, 749
Hogan, Robert Goode: 425,
969, 1270, 1271, 1272,
1423, 1540, 1640, 2618
Hogg, James: 2325
Holden, David Franklin:
2036
Holland, Norman: 166, 1422
Hollis, Christopher: 1639

Holloway, Joseph: 1273,
1423, 1529, 1640
Holroyd, Michael: 2252,
2390, 2391, 2392, 2499,
2500
Holt, Charles Loyd: 750,
1095, 1096, 1097
Hopkins, Gerard (trans):
311
Hoppe, E. O.: 1743
Hopwood, Alison L.: 1424
Hornby, Richard: 1098,
1274, 1425
Hornby, Richard (comp):
1099
Horowitz, Joseph: 2501
Hortmann, Wilhelm: 970
Houghton, Norris: 1744
Houseman, John: 1875
Houston, Penelope: 48
Hovey, Richard B.: 284
Howard, Leslie Ruth: 285
Howard de Walden,
Margherita: 971
Howlett, Ivan: 2502, 2503,
2619
Hoy, Cyrus: 1745
Hubay, Miklos (ed): 381
Hubenka, Lloyd John: 1100,
2393
Hübner, Walter: 751
Huggett, Richard: 1275,
1540, 1641
Hughes, Catharine: 2394;
(ed): 2620
Hughes, Emrys: 1101
Hugo, Leon B.: 1102, 1276,
1746, 1747, 1896, 1877;
(ed): 1627
Hulban, Horia: 1642, 1878,
2037
Hulse, James W.: 1643
Hummert, Paul A.: 286,
287, 2038
Humphreys, Hubert: 49
Hung, Josephine Huang:
1748
Hunningher, B.: 1749
Huonker, Gustav (ed): 2659
Hurd, Michael: 1277

Kernan, Alvin B.: 1285
Kerr, Alison: 753
Kerr, Walter: 56, 170, 293, 433, 639, 754, 873, 1286, 1886, 1887, 2137, 2626, 2627, 2673
Kesten, Hermann: 294
Kester, Dolores A.: 2047, 2509
Ketels, Violet B.: 1108
Keunen, J.: 550, 1648
Khanna, Savitri: 2048
Kidd, Walter E.: 2049
Kidd, Timothy J.: 2628
Kilty, Jerome: 434
Kim, C. K.: 640
Kimura, Masami: 2397, 2398, 2510, 2672
King, Carlyle: 295
King, Seth S.: 640
King, Walter N.: 296
Kingston, Jeremy: 2265
Kinyon, Frank J.: 1752
Kirillova, L. Ia.: 2511
Kirov, T.: 171, 978
Kissel, Iurii Iakovich: 2266
Klein, John W.: 642
Klein, John X.: 755
Kleinhans, Charles Nelson: 2138
Knappert, Jan: 1287
Knepler, Henry: 1430; (ed): 1202
Knepper, Bill Garton: 1288, 1431, 1547, 1753
Knight, G. Wilson: 643
Knightley, Phillip: 1548
Knorr, Heinz: 57
Knörrich, Otto: 551
Kobler, John: 2512
Kocztur, Gizella: 644, 979, 1109
Kodama, Koichi (ed): 2284
Koffler, Richard: 1617
Kolb, Edward (ed): 1562
Koltai, Ralph: 1549
Komatsu, Motoya: 172, 435, 645, 980, 2050
Kon, Militsa: 1432

Kornbluth, Martin L.: 173, 297
Kornilovaîa, S. (ed): 695
Kosok, Heinz: 2051, 2399, 2400, 2422, 2423
Kostić, Dušan: 756
Kostov, Kiril: 1433
Kotsilibas-Davis, James: 2513
Kudrjavcev, A.: 1434
Kuehne, A. de: 1550
Kovać, Mirko: 757
Kozelka, Paul: 298, 436, 981
Krajewska, Wanda: 1888, 1889
Kranidas, Thomas: 1110
Krasiński, Edward: 437
Krättli, Anton: 1111
Krause, David: 438, 2401; (ed): 2291
Krempel, Daniel: 1207
Kreutzer, Eberhard: 2045
Kristensen, Sven Møller (ed): 11966
Kronenberger, Louis: 439, 1890
Krutch, Joseph Wood: 552
Kulakovskaîa, T.: 440
Kumar, V.: 1289
Kumor, Stanisława: 758, 1754
Kunzins, Kārlis: 759, 1891
Kuosaite, E.: 441
L. T., A.: 553
Laden, Alice: 1755
Lago, Mary M. (ed): 1892, 2267, 2629
Laing, Allan M.: 58, 174, 299, 1435
Lambert, J. W.: 59, 175, 442, 554, 760, 761, 762, 982, 1112, 1113, 1114, 1290, 1436, 1551, 1649, 1650, 1756, 1757, 1758, 1893, 2052, 2139, 2268, 2269, 2401, 2403
Landau, Jacob M.: 176
Langhorne, Elizabeth: 2140

McCann, Sean (ed): 1199, 1230
McCauley, James Caves: 2147
McClean, Robert C. (ed): 1440
McCleary, G. F.: 452
McCollom, William G.: 1764
MacDermott, Norman: 2278
McDermott, William F.: 65
McDonald, David J., Jr.: 1303
McDowell, Frederick P. W.: 66, 67, 303, 453, 559, 560, 768, 875, 991, 1119, 1906, 2059, 2148, 2149
McElderry, B[ruce] R., Jr.: 1440, 1907
McFadden, Karen Doris: 2634
MacGreevy, Thomas: 1120
Machler, Robert (ed): 2334
McIlwaine, Robert S.: 1908
McInerney, John M.: 1765
Mack, John E.: 2413
Mack, Maynard: 1508
McKee, Irving: 304, 579, 876, 1304
Mackenzie, Norman, and Jeanne Mackenzie: 2060, 2520
Mackerness, E. D.: 1121
McKinley, R. D.: 1122
McMillan, Scott: 1123
Macksoud, S. John: 1766
McNicholas, Sister Mary V., OP: 1909
McNulty, Edward: 68
MacOwan, Michael: 1219, 1371
McVeigh, Hugh: 877
Macy, Gertrude: 2637
Mahony, Patrick: 1767
Maiskii, Ivan Mikhailovich: 1305, 1306, 2279, 2521
Makusheva, S. P.: 1910, 2061, 2280
Malcolm, Donald: 305, 306, 307, 308
Malmi, Carol Lea: 2281

Maloney, Henry B.: 769
Mander, Gertrud: 992
Mander, Raymond: 2282
Mann, Thomas: 454, 2522
Manning, Frederick: 654
Manolescu, Ion: 655
Manson, Donald Duane: 1124, 1307
Manvell, Roger: 1441, 2150
Manvell, Roger: 1441, 2150
Marcus, Fred H.: 946
Marek, Jiri: 1308
Martin, Kingsley: 1125, 1442
Martin, Wallace: 1309
Martinez Herrera, A.: 878
Martinez Ruiz, Florencio: 879
Mason, M. A.: 993
Mason, Michael: 770, 2151, 2152
Mason, Philip: 2283
Mason, W. H.: 880
Masumoto, Masahiko: 881, 994, 995, 996, 1126, 1310, 1311, 1312, 1443, 1444, 2284, 2286, 2523
Masur, Gerhard: 561
Mathison, Imogene: 1911
Matignon, M. (trans): 681
Matlaw, Laura T.: 997
Matlaw, Myron: 182, 183, 309, 455, 562, 882
Matoba, Junko: 1768, 1912, 2635
Matsubara, Tadashi: 771, 772
Matsumoto, Shinko: 2674
Matthews, John.: 1556; (ed): 310
Mattson, Mary Catherine: 1557
Mattus, Martha Elizabeth: 2153
Maulnier, Thierry: 883
Maurino, Ferdinando: 1558
Maurois, André: 311
Maver, David: 2524
May, Frederick: 884
May, Robin: 2062

Musil, Robert: 2638
Musulin, Stella: 189
Myers, Charles Robert: 1775
Nadel, Norman: 1564
Nakagawa, Ryoichi: 464, 2286
Nakano, Kii (ed): 1611
Narumi, Hiroshi: 2286
Nathan, George Jean: 465
Nathan, Rhoda B.: 1776, 2158, 2639
Naumov, Nicifor: 1565
Nedich, Borivoje: 891
Neel, Boyd: 1129, 1147
Nelson, Raymond Stanley: 1451, 1566, 1567, 1568, 1569, 1570, 1649, 1660, 1661, 1777, 1778, 1917, 1918, 1919, 1920, 2067, 2287, 2530
Nethercot, Arthur H.: 190, 314, 315, 466, 467, 783, 784, 892, 893, 1130, 1571, 1572, 1662, 1921
Neufeldt, Victoria: 2108
Neukirchen, Alfons: 570
Newby, Richard L.: 2640
Newman, Ernest: 661
Niafied, Uladzimir: 1002
Nichols, Beverley: 191
Nichols, Marie Hochmuth: 785
Nickson, Joseph R.: 192
Nickson, Richard: 316, 318, 1003, 1131, 1327, 1573, 1574, 1779, 2159
Nicoll, Allardyce: 662, 2068, 2417
Nicolson, Harold: 1132
Nicolson, Nigel (ed): 1132
Nikitina, A. I.: 1328
Nolte, William Henry: 318, 894
Norton, Elizabeth Towne: 1025
Nosika, B. (trans): 1101
Novick, Julius: 1452, 1780, 1922, 2069, 2289, 2290

Nowell-Smith, Simon (ed): 895, 1330
Nucete Sarde, J.: 663
Nünning, Josefa: 2024, 2051
Nurmakhanov, Kalzan: 1453
Nyssen, Leo: 1331
Obraztsova, Anna Georgievna: 1004, 1781, 2161, 2418
O'Casey, Eileen: 1782
O'Casey, Sean: 1332, 1333, 2291
Ochikovskaia, M.: 2418
O'Connor, Gary: 2292
O'Connor, John (ed): 2641
O'Connor, Mary: 2642
Odajima, Yushi: 896
Odin, Roger: 2419
O'Donnell, Norbert F.: 75, 76, 193, 319, 664
O'Donovan, John: 786, 1006, 1133
O'Driscoll, Robert (ed): 1808
Ogiso, Masafumi: 1663, 1923, 2420, 2421, 2643
Ohmann, Richard Malin: 468, 665, 1208
Oiji, Takero (ed): 2670
Okazaki, Yoshie (ed): 2079
Okouchi, Toshio: 2070
Okumura, Saburo: 666, 787, 788, 897,m 1134, 1135, 1136, 1334, 1454, 1924, 2162
Olander, Joseph D. (ed): 2556
Oldsey, Bernard S.: 1007
Oliver, William I. (ed): 382
Olivier, Laurence: 1335
Olson, Elder: 1455
Omerov, I. M.: 789, 1137
O'Neill, Michael J.: 321, 1272, 1423, 1540, 1640
O'Neill, William L.: 2644
Oppel, Horst: 77, 790, 791, 794, 2422
O'Riordan, John (ed): 2155

Punch, A. M.: 1463
Purdom, Charles Benjamin:
803; (ed): 83
Purser, John T.: 842
Quartermaine, Leon: 474
Quennell, Peter: 2074
Quigly, Isabel: 84, 326,
327
Quinn, Martin: 2168, 2300,
2301, 2535
Quinn, Michael: 804
Quinton, A. M.: 1934
R., G.: 85
Racheva, Mariîa: 1464
Radford, Frederick Leslie:
1788, 2302
Radin, Nikolaĭ
Mariiûsovich: 1016
Rahill, Frank: 1340
Rakitina, L.: 1667
Raknem, Ingvald: 1789
Rama Rao, Sarvepalli: 2143
Rankin, H. D.: 328
Rao, E. Nageswara: 329
Rattray, Dr. R. F.: 86
Raud, V.: 1935
Rawson, C. J. (ed): 1601
Ray, Gordon N.: 1017, 2169
Reardon, Joan: 1790
Redgrave, Michael: 1342,
1343
Redmond, James: 1791,
1792, 2075, 2170
Reed, Robert R.: 330
Regan, Arthur E.: 1019,
1465
Reichart, Walter A.: 202
Reidinger, Otto: 673
Reinert, Otto: 475, 578,
898
Reitmeir, Rüdiger: 1142
Remizov, Boris: 1466, 2425
Reuben, Elaine: 1668
Riabov, F. G.: 1580
Ricciardi, Joseph: 1793
Rice, Elmer: 87
Rich, Frank: 2676
Richards, Dick (comp):
1018
Richards, Robert F.: 1669

Richardson, Betty Hoyenga:
1936
Richardson, Joanna: 332
Richardson, Ralph: 1344
Rickert, Alfred E.: 2536
Riesner, Dieter (ed): 656,
808, 1769, 1814
Riewald, J. G.: 929, 2171
Rischbieter, Henning: 1345
Rix, Walter Torsten: 1794
Robert, Rudolph: 476
Roberts, Peter: 1346
Roberts, Vera Mowry: 1795
Robinson, Gabrielle Scott:
1938, 2172
Robinson, Marie J.: 477
Robson, William A.: 1347
Roby, Kinley: 1670, 1939,
1940, 2302
Rockman, Robert E.: 88,
1143
Rodale, J. I.: 1144
Rodenbeck, John von Behren,
Jr.: 899, 1581, 1941
Rodgers, W. R.: 1942, 2304
Rodriguez-Seda, Asela:
1796, 2173, 2426, 2537
Rodway, Allan: 2305; (ed):
1121
Rogers, Richard Ernest:
1582
Rogoff, Gordon: 2538
Rojahn, Jobst-Christian
(ed): 2167
Roll-Hansen, Diderik:
1348, 2306, 2539
Rollins, Ronald G.: 1349
Roman, Robert C.: 478
Romm, Anna Sergeevna:
1020, 1145, 1146, 1328,
1671, 1797, 1943
Rose, Clarkson: 89
Rosenberg, Edgar: 2540,
2646
Rosenblood, Norman (ed):
1147, 1148, 1768, 1776,
1798, 1799
Ross, Julian L.: 1467
Ross, Robert: 900
Rosset, B. C.: 901, 902

Roston, Murray: 1468
Rothenstein, John: 1021
Rouby, Jason: 1944
Rouché, Jacques: 204
Rowell, George (ed): 1800
Roy, Emil: 1022, 1672, 1945
Roy, R. N.: 903, 2427
Royall, Walter L.: 1350
Rubin, Don (ed): 2428, 2647
Rudman, Harry W.: 205
Ruff, William: 1469
Russell, Annie: 2429
Russell, Bertrand: 1351, 1470
Rypins, Stanley: 90, 579
Ryšánková, Helena: 1673
Ryskamp, Charles (ed): 1072, 1104
Saffron, John: 1352
Sagittarius: 2076
Sahai, Surendra: 1674
Sainer, Arthur: 674, 805, 904
Saint-Paulien [pseud]: 1353
St. John, Christopher: 334
Salazar Chapela, E.: 675
Salem, James J.: 1471
Salerno, Henry F. (ed): 1472
Salmon, Eric: 2077
Salovac, Ivo: 676
Sal'perina, L. I.: 2307
Santos, A. R.: 2541
Saroyan, William: 807
Sauvageau, David Ronald: 2542
Savchenko, S. V.: 2308
Scally, Robert J.: 2309
Scanlon, Leone: 2430
Schäfer, Jörg (ed): 2334
Scheibe, Fred Karl: 1583
Schellenberger, Johannes: 92
Scherer, Günther: 808
Schlauch, Margaret: 93
Schlegelmilch, Wolfgang: 94

Schneede, Uwe M.: 2310
Schneede-Scesny, Marina: 2310
Schoeps, Karl-Heinz J.: 1946, 2174, 2175, 2543
Schöler-Beinhauer, Monica: 1584
Schonberg, Harold C.: 1585
Schor, Edith: 1023
Schotter, Richard David: 2176
Schrickx, W.: 1586
Schroeder, J. G.: 809
Schuchter, J. D.: 1675
Schultheiss, Thomas: 1354
Schults, Raymond L.: 1947
Schütte, Otto (trans): 574
Schwanitz, Dietrich: 1801
Schwartz, Grace H.: 1149
Schwartzman, Myron: 2544
Scott, Charles: 479
Scott, William: 1024
Scriabine, Vera: 580, 677, 1473, 1587, 1802
Schrimgeour, James R.: 2648
Seabrook, Alexander: 1676, 2545
Searle, William Miner: 1588, 1948, 2431
Seehase, Georg: 1589
Seidel, Alison P. (comp): 2649
Seidel, Christian: 678
Seki, Yoshihiko: 1590
Sekulic, I.: 1150
Selenič, Slobodan: 1151
Sen, Taraknath: 1949
Senart, Philippe: 2311, 2546
Serebriakova, Galina: 1474
Severns, James George: 1803
Seyfarth, Heinz: 1152
Seyfarth, Ingrid: 1041
Seymour-Smith, Martin: 2078, 2547
Shaitanov, I. O.: 2312
Shamshurin, A.: 1950

Sharman, Charles Anthony: 2650

Sharp, Sister M. Corona: 679

Sharp, William: 335

Sharpe, Robert Boies: 336

Shatzky, Joel Lawrence: 1804

Shawcross, John T.: 2432, 2549

Shayon, Robert Lewis: 1355

Shedd, Robert G.: 1025

Shelley, Philip Allison (ed): 692, 693

Shenfield, Margaret: 208, 681

Sheppard, R. Z.: 2433

Sherin, Edwin: 1154

Sherman, Robert: 2550

Shestakov, D.: 1591

Shields, Jean Louise: 209

Shiels, Thomas A.: 1356

Shimada, Kinji: 2079

Shimamura, Totaro: 1592, 2651, 2677

Shinkuma, Kiyoshi: 1593, 1677, 1805, 1806, 1951, 2080, 2434

Shirvell, James: 210

Shrive, Norman: 338

Shunamee, Gideon: 2551

Shvydkoĭ, M. E.: 2552

Sicard, Maurice I.: 1353

Sidhu, Charan Dass: 1807

Sidnell, M. J.: 1478, 1808, 2177

Silver, Arnold: 2314

Silverman, Albert H.: 101, 1155, 1357

Silverstein, Louis: 451

Silverstein, Paul: 1594

Simeikina, N. M.: 2652

Simon, Elliott Martin: 1809

Simon, John: 2081, 2315, 2316, 2317

Simon, Louis: 211

Simon, Nancy Lynn: 2435

Simpson, Colin: 1548

Sinclair, Upton: 480

Sinderman, Peter: 1041

Sirasek, L.: 2082

Skelton, Robin: 1952

Skidelsky, Robert: 2318

Sklar, Sylvia: 2319

Skriletz, Dorothy J.: 1156

Slate Bernice (ed): 718

Slonim, Marc: 481

Slote, Bernice (ed): 1317

Smiley, Sam: 1810, 1953

Smirnov, B. A.: 212

Smith, B. L.: 2653

Smith, J. Percy: 102, 482, 1026, 1811, 2178, 2654

Smith, Thomas W.: 2179

Smith, Warren Sylvester: 103, 483, 811, 812, 814, 1358, 1359, 1360, 1595, 1812, 2320, 2321, 2322, 2655; (ed): 169, 523, 629, 775, 776, 783, 813, 920, 1130, 1170, 1520, 1678

Smoker, Barbara: 104, 105, 106, 107, 108, 109, 213, 214, 215, 339, 340, 341, 484, 485, 581, 815, 1027, 1361

Sobańska, Anna: 2656

Sokoliânskiĭ, M. G.: 1157

Sokolov, Raymond A.: 1954

Solomon, Stanley J.: 682, 907, 908

Somers, John Wilmot: 2180

Soper, Paul: 582

Sos, E.: 216

Speaight, Robert: 486

Speckhard, Robert Riedel: 342, 909, 1028, 1158

Spector, Samuel Hardy: 217

Spencer, Terence James: 110, 343

Spink, Judith B.: 816

Spot, Josef: 1679

Spurling, Hilary: 1362, 1680

Stagg, Louis Charles: 2553

Stambusky, Alan A.: 487

Stamm, Rudolf: 111, 112, 218, 219, 1029

Index

TITLES OF SECONDARY WORKS

Titles of articles in periodicals and chapters in books are in quotation marks; book titles are in upper case; translations of article titles originally appearing in a foreign language are in parentheses, without quotation marks, and in lower case; translations of book titles originally appearing in a foreign language are in parentheses and in upper case. Numbers after each title refer to the item in the bibliography where the title appears.

SHAKESPEARE TO SHAW:
1647
"Actors Company": 2363
THE ACTOR'S WAYS AND MEANS:
1342
"Adam and Eve: Evolving
Archetypes in *Back to
Methuselah*": 556
"Adoring Bounder": 2577
THE ADVENT OF THE BRITISH
LABOR PARTY: 199
"The Adventures of My Fair
Philologist": 1944
AEOLIAN HARPS, ESSAYS IN
LITERATURE IN HONOR OF
MAURICE BROWING CRAMER:
2406
AFTER THE IRISH RENAIS-
SANCE: A CRITICAL
HISTORY OF THE IRISH
DRAMA SINCE *THE PLOUGH
AND THE STARS*: 1270
"After the Revolution":
1054
(The Aftermath of Shaw's
Will: Recent Reflections
on English Spelling):
733
(Afterword): 1696
"The Age of Bernard Shaw":
2229
THE AGE OF CHURCHILL,
HERITAGE AND ADVENTURE:
564
THE AGE OF CONSENT,
VICTORIAN PROSTITUTION
AND ITS ENEMIES: 1928
AGNUS VOLONTARIO: DALLA
"PERSONA" ALLA PERSONA:
2112
"Ako drugite posledvat na
Lenin . . .": 1628
"Akutagawa Ryunosuke to
Eibungaku--Hikakubungaku
koen--": 2079
"Al G. B. Shaw be-Ivrit:
Bibliographia": 2576
ALARMIERENDE BOTSCHAFTEN,
ZUR LAGE DER NATION:
2107

(Alarming Tidings, on the
Situation of the Nation):
2107
(Alexander Hevesi): 2053,
2083
"El Alfabeto de Bernard
Shaw": 675
"All about Shaw": 1610
ALL PEOPLE ARE FAMOUS:
INSTEAD OF AN AUTOBIOGRA-
PHY: 2114
"All Wrong on the Night":
2446
"Alliance and Misalliance:
A Critical Study of
Bernard Shaw's Novels":
899
(Along the Byways of Modern
Drama: The More Recent
History of Drama and the
Shakespearean Tradition):
513
ALVIN LANGDON COBURN,
PHOTOGRAPHEER: AN AUTO-
BIOGRAPHY: 1078
"Ambassadors at Large:
Other Writings": 1007
"An American's Point of
View re The Strange
Triangle of G. B. S.--A
Rebuttal": 72
AMERICA'S TASTE 1851-1959:
THE CULTURAL EVENTS OF A
CENTURY REPORTED BY
CONTEMPORARY OBSERVERS IN
THE PAGES OF THE NEW YORK
TIMES: 451
AMINTIRI: 655
"An Analysis of Selected
Plays of George Bernard
Shaw as Media for the
Examination of 'Closed
Areas' of Contemporary
Society by Secondary-
School Students": 646
"An Analysis of Shaw's
Saint Joan in Preparation
for Directing Scenes IV
and V": 795

INDEX OF TITLES OF SECONDARY WORKS

"George Bernard Shaw": 64, 622, 637, 649, 705, 854, 898, 1285, 1291, 1308, 1681, 2149, 2304

GEORGE BERNARD SHAW: 992, 1020, 1412, 1556, 1711, 2615

GEORGE BERNARD SHAW: A CRITICAL STUDY: 1289

GEORGE BERNARD SHAW: A DRAMATIST OF CONSCIENCE: 1805

(GEORGE BERNARD SHAW, A MEMORIAL ON THE TWENTIETH ANNIVERSARY OF HIS DEATH): 1673, 1679

GEORGE BERNARD SHAW: A REVIEW OF THE LITERATURE: 2424

"George Bernard Shaw als Muziekcriticus": 184

"George Bernard Shaw: an Herbert Wehner": 2107

(George Bernard Shaw and His 'Heroes'): 57

"George Bernard Shaw and Shakespeare's CYMBELINE: 112, 218

"George Bernard Shaw and the Atonement": 1122

"George Bernard Shaw and the Existentialist-Absurdist Theater": 2553

(George Bernard Shaw and the Miracle): 1584

"George Bernard Shaw and the Modern Temper": 2536

"George Bernard Shaw and the Motion Picture": 717

"George Bernard Shaw and the Socialist League": 606

(George Bernard Shaw and the Theater of Social Criticism): 417

"George Bernard Shaw and the Uses of Energy": 1725

"George Bernard Shaw and

the Woman Question": 2634

(GEORGE BERNARD SHAW: ARTISTIC CONSTRUCTION AND DISORDERLY WORLD): 1801

"George Bernard Shaw as a Boy": 68

(George Bernard Shaw as a Music Critic): 184

"George Bernard Shaw: A Selected Bibliography (1945-1955) Part One: Books": 262

"George Bernard Shaw: A Selected Bibliography (1945-1955) Part II: Periodicals": 263

"George Bernard Shaw at Rehearsals of *Major Barbara*: 2429

"George Bernard Shaw: British Fascist?": 316

"George Bernard Shaw: *Caesar and Cleopatra*": 2423

(George Bernard Shaw: *Candida*): 2071

"George Bernard Shaw: Composer": 1040

GEORGE BERNARD SHAW, CREATIVE ARTIST: 780, 831, 1208

"George Bernard Shaw: Critic of Music": 1458

"George Bernard Shaw: *Der Kaiser von Amerika*": 1152

"George Bernard Shaw: *Die Heilige Johanna*": 344

GEORGE BERNARD SHAW. DRAMATIC CRITICISM (1895-1898): A SELECTION: 310

"George Bernard Shaw, du réformateur victorien au prophète édouardien. Formation et évolution de ses idées (1856-1910): 2345

INDEX OF TITLES OF SECONDARY WORKS

INDEX OF TITLES OF SECONDARY WORKS

INDEX OF TITLES OF SECONDARY WORKS

INDEX OF TITLES OF SECONDARY WORKS

Index

PRIMARY TITLES

Included here are all titles by Shaw which occur in titles of articles or books or in the abstracts. Numbers after each title refer to the item in the bibliography where the title appears.

The Admirable Bashville:
329, 696, 1632, 2137
The Adventures of the Black Girl in Her Search for God: 598, 600, 863, 882, 903, 1397, 1437, 1595, 1598, 1602, 1711, 1992, 2050, 2061
Advice to a Young Critic: 844
Aerial Football: 2061, 2184, 2192
Androcles and the Lion: 5, 24, 28, 93, 169, 278, 474, 483, 485, 537, 554, 570, 592, 643, 680, 683, 699, 723, 730, 741, 747, 802, 811, 815, 825, 903, 924, 1028, 1077, 1083, 1120, 1122, 1136, 1158, 1179, 1196, 1197, 1198, 1223, 1242, 1252, 1289, 1295, 1298, 1320, 1324, 1360, 1496, 1564, 1171, 1715, 1730, 1738, 1917, 1920, 1929, 1992, 1994, 2023, 2038, 2294, 2310, 2311, 2362, 2383, 2431, 2440, 2457, 2458, 2566, 2569, 2580, 2641, 2647, 2656, 2657
Androcles and the Lion (film): 478, 2166, 2581
Annajanska: 275, 1250, 2123
The Apple Cart: 42, 75, 134, 176, 196, 275, 303, 382, 394, 484, 491, 529, 643, 660, 773, 903, 963, 1009, 1132, 1152, 1155, 1196, 1210, 1219, 1270, 1281, 1289, 1313, 1324, 1345, 1357, 1379, 1415, 1419, 1494, 1496, 1542, 1599, 1649, 1677, 1695, 1711, 1730, 1746, 1754, 1885, 1899, 1910, 1934, 2038, 2057, 2073, 2088, 2110, 2186, 2408, 2471, 2486, 2503, 2519, 2655, 2658
Are We Heading for War: 623
Arms and the Man: 22, 24, 57, 80, 85, 197, 204, 210, 304, 382, 422, 491, 513, 578, 637, 804, 844, 888, 903, 912, 926, 959,

INDEX OF PRIMARY TITLES

Index

PERIODICALS AND NEWSPAPERS

Included here are periodicals and newspapers for which entries occur in the bibliography. Numbers after each title refer to the number(s) of the item in the bibliography where the title appears.

BOOK COLLECTOR: 424, 623, 845, 1710, 1722
BOOKS AND BOOKMEN: 1743, 1784, 1977, 1978, 2391, 2499, 2500
BORBA: 757, 1151
BOSTON UNIVERSITY STUDIES IN ENGLISH: 67
BRITISH JOURNAL OF AESTHETICS: 1493
BRÜNNER BEITRÄGE ZUR GERMANISTIK UND NORDISTIK: 2529
DIE BÜHNE: 2357, 2412
BULLETIN OF BIBLIOGRAPHY: 292, 431, 432
BULLETIN OF RESEARCH IN THE HUMANITIES: 2591
BULLETIN OF THE NEW YORK PUBLIC LIBRARY: 40, 41, 273, 403, 743, 961, 962, 1232, 1597, 1651
CAHIERS VICTORIENS ET EDOUARDIENS: 2669
CAIRO STUDIES IN ENGLISH: 251
CALCUTTA REVIEW: 1140
CALIFORNIA SHAVIAN: 356, 404, 405, 414, 415, 457, 458, 459, 485, 557, 577, 585, 604, 605, 612, 614, 630, 651, 658, 730, 736, 737, 739, 766, 777, 795, 815, 846, 856, 865, 866, 867, 979, 1065, 1138
ČASOPIS PRO MODERNI FILOLOGII: 223
CEA CRITIC: 1327
CHESTERTON REVIEW: 2349, 2368, 2407
CHRISTIAN CENTURY: 258, 811, 812
CIZÍ JAZYKY VE ŠKOLLE: 1308
CLEARING HOUSE: 769, 1303
COLBY LIBRARY QUARTERLY: 1712
COLLEGE ENGLISH: 629
COLLEGE LITERATURE: 2106

COLUMBIA LIBRARY COLUMNS: 1760
COLORADO QUARTERLY: 408, 1669
COMEDY: NEW PERSPECTIVES: 2606
COMMONWEAL: 33
COMMONWEALTH QUARTERLY: 2580
COMPARATIVE DRAMA: 2259
COMPARATIVE LITERATURE: 740, 1318
CONTEMPORARY REVIEW: 1932, 2287, 2411
CORANTO: 1040, 1375, 1767
CORNELL LIBRARY JOURNAL: 1511
CORNHILL MAGAZINE: 1750
COSTERUS: 1917, 1919, 2066
CRESSET: 2610
CRITICAL QUARTERLY: 804
CRITICISM: 1068
CUADERNOS DEL SUR: 716, 1005
CULTURA PERUANA: 85, 553
D. H. LAWRENCE REVIEW: 1498
DAGENS NYHETER: 512
DAILY MAIL: 133
DAILY NEWS (NY): 1203
DAILY TELEGRAPH: 2012
DALHOUSIE REVIEW: 519, 620, 1081, 1122, 1985
DET DANSKE MAGASIN: 119
DE GOLPE Y PORROZO: 878
DER DEUTSCHUNTERRICHT: 1070
DICKENSIAN: 710, 1655
DIETSCHE WARANDE EN BELFORT: 550, 1648
DISCOURSE: 1456
DIVADLO: 51
DOPOVIDI TA POVIDOMENNÎA L'VIVS'KII DERZH. UNIV.: 521
DRAMA: 59, 142, 175, 510, 554, 642, 708, 755, 843, 870, 982, 1039, 1112, 1113, 1114, 1290, 1437, 1510, 1551, 1756, 1757,

1968, 1972, 1980, 1983,
1987, 1998, 2005, 2007,
2008, 2013, 2015, 2042,
2054, 2065, 2085, 2100,
2104, 2117, 2130, 2141,
2145, 2147, 2158, 2164,
2168, 2172, 2183, 2184,
2186, 2191, 2192, 2203,
2207, 2209, 2256, 2221,
2244, 2263, 2301, 2303,
2306, 2320, 2356, 2358,
2366, 2370, 2380, 2405,
2429, 2436, 2449, 2458,
2466, 2483, 2485, 2486,
2497, 2528, 2531, 2535,
2539, 2540, 2541, 2571,
2575, 2586, 2587, 2622,
2642, 2646, 2655, 2657,
2658, 2660, 2661, 2664,
2666
SHAW SCRIPT: 905
SHIKAI: 1134
SIGHT AND SOUNG: 1057
SIGNUM: 2152
SIN NOMBRE: 2537
SLAVONIC AND EAST EUROPEAN
  REVIEW: 386
SLOBODNA DALMACIJA: 1434
SLOVENSKY POHL'ED: 572
SOUTH ATLANTIC QUARTERLY:
  1044, 2094
SOUTHERN REVIEW: 773, 2021
SOUTHERN SPEECH JOURNAL:
  1265
SOUTHWEST REVIEW: 894
SOUTHWESTERN SOCIAL SCIENCE
  QUARTERLY: 220
SOVIET LITERATURE: 621,
  2239, 2521
SPECTATOR: 84, 167, 326,
  327, 611, 943, 1275,
  1362, 2127, 2199
DER SPIEGEL: 100, 145, 683
SPUTNIK: 1306
STEAUA: 14
STUDIA GERMANICA GANDENSIA:
  1586
STUDIA UNIVERSITATIS BABES-
  BOLYAI: SERIES
  PHILOLOGIA: 1982

STUDIES IN ENGLISH
  LITERATURE, 1500-1900:
  547
SUNDAY TIMES MAGAZINE
  (Lond): 1931
TAMARACK REVIEW: 482
TEATR: 1015, 1055, 1432,
  1486, 1591, 1667, 1883,
  2041, 2073, 2418, 2656
TEATRAL'NAĬA ZHIZN': 440
TEATRO: 82
TEATRUL: 1658
TEATRŬ (SOFIA): 171, 1406,
  1414, 1433, 1786
TELEGRAM: 735
TENNESSEE PHILOLOGICAL
  BULLETIN: 2553
TEXAS QUARTERLY: 544,
  1404, 1490
TEXAS STUDIES IN ENGLISH:
  195, 356
TEXAS STUDIES IN LITERATURE
  AND LANGUAGE: 1644,
  1824, 2442
THEATER DER ZEIT: 118,
  165, 1041, 1338
THEATER HEUTE: 565, 570,
  590, 591, 595, 1200,
  1331, 1345, 1378, 1445
THEATER UND ZEIT: 531
THEATRE ANNUAL: 75
THEATRE ARTS MONTHLY: 69,
  98, 132, 229, 232, 241,
  261, 323, 502, 552
THEATRE CRAFTS: 2633
THEATRE NOTEBOOK: 1250
THEATRE RESEARCH: 1363
THEATRE SURVEY: 657, 1499,
  1609, 2415
THEATRE WORLD: 968, 990,
  1038
THEORIA: 2667
THIS WEEK: 390
THOUGHT: 964
THRESHOLD: 54
TIDSKRIFT FÖR LITTERATUR-
  VETENSKAP: 2216
TIME: 36, 320, 337, 2205,
  2261, 2433, 2465, 2507,
  2508, 2624

Index

FOREIGN LANGUAGES

Included here are the languages in which articles and books listed in the bibliograpahy originally appeared. Numbers under each language refer to items in the bibliography where the foreign-language title is given. English language items are not listed.

Azerbaijani: 789
Bulgarian: 171, 978, 1162, 1406, 1414, 1433, 1464, 1638, 1728, 1786, 2294
Chinese: 2410
Czechoslovak: 34, 51, 223, 224, 378, 572, 733, 1308, 1673, 2329, 2362
Danish: 119, 1196
Dutch: 154, 184, 550, 669, 1648, 1749
Estonian: 1935
French: 24, 27, 204, 518, 681, 883, 887, 926, 1182, 1353, 1475, 1827, 1913, 2103, 2311, 2419, 2448, 2546, 2669
Georgian: 626
German: 5, 28, 29, 35, 57, 70, 77, 92, 100, 111, 118, 145, 159, 165, 180, 184, 189, 219, 222, 253, 277, 294, 313, 344, 376, 377, 399, 417, 454, 531, 548, 551, 561, 565, 570, 656, 678, 683, 686, 700, 706, 751, 790, 791, 794, 808, 860, 928, 942, 970,

992, 1041, 1050, 1059, 1063, 1070, 1111, 1142, 1152, 1200, 1222, 1315, 1331, 1338, 1345, 1378, 1391, 1396, 1418, 1445, 1446, 1447, 1461, 1496, 1500, 1589, 1724, 1770, 1794, 1801, 1814, 1946, 1963, 2024, 2043, 2045, 2050, 2087, 2107, 2176, 2174, 2204, 2310, 2313, 2334, 2346, 2357, 2399, 2400, 2412, 2422, 2423, 2439, 2522, 2529, 2533, 2548, 2573, 2638, 2645, 2659
Hebrew: 2551, 2576
Hungarian: 64, 79, 216, 324, 381, 461, 469, 488, 513, 549, 644, 649, 667, 691, 704, 705, 720, 746, 792, 793, 966, 1086, 1278, 1417, 1636, 1730, 2053, 2083
Italian: 73, 383, 618, 848, 1225, 1427, 1578, 1715, 2112
Japanese: 172, 435, 492,

509, 645, 666, 688, 771,
787, 788, 896, 897, 913,
980, 994, 995, 1008,
1034, 1134, 1135, 1136,
1159, 1168, 1312, 1334,
1444, 1454, 1590, 1592,
1593, 1596, 1611, 1663,
1677, 1806, 1923, 1924,
1951, 2050, 2070, 2079,
2080, 2102, 2162, 2251,
2255, 2284, 2286, 2397,
2398, 2420, 2421, 2434,
2510, 2527, 2643, 2651,
2670, 2672, 2674, 2675,
2676
Korean: 640
Latvian: 441, 1891
Lithuanian: 1101
Macedonian: 752, 774
Polish: 6, 22, 47, 437,
748, 1069, 1457, 1476,
1482, 1622, 1740, 1754,
1888, 1889, 1915, 2656
Portugese: 802
Romanian: 1, 14, 527, 655,
1402, 1658, 1697, 1698,
1826, 1984, 2037, 2206
Russian: 71, 212, 274,
275, 368, 384, 426, 440,
496, 498, 510, 514, 615,
626, 632, 638, 695, 741,
759, 872, 963, 965, 974,
998, 1002, 1004, 1015,
1016, 1020, 1055, 1056,
1071, 1101, 1105, 1106,
1137, 1145, 1146, 1157,
1176, 1177, 1281, 1305,

1328, 1407, 1419, 1428,
1432, 1453, 1460, 1474,
1484, 1485, 1486, 1534,
1542, 1544, 1579, 1580,
1591, 1613, 1632, 1645,
1667, 1671, 1682, 1684,
1695, 1696, 1700, 1751,
1781, 1785, 1797, 1862,
1870, 1881, 1882, 1883,
1943, 1950, 2041, 2044,
2073, 2086, 2111, 2133,
2254, 2266, 2279, 2307,
2312, 2331, 2364, 2365,
2418, 2425, 2451, 2511,
2552, 2578, 2579
Serbo-Croatian: 427, 470,
576, 676, 735, 756, 757,
797, 891, 1049, 1083,
1094, 1141, 1150, 1151,
1434, 1462, 1487, 1514,
1565, 2071, 2082
Slovenian: 566, 1248
Spanish: 2, 39, 82, 85,
187, 281, 371, 410, 553,
568, 663, 675, 716, 779,
782, 796, 806, 809, 810,
822, 878, 879, 889, 925,
949, 1005, 1060, 1223,
1267, 1550, 1634, 1665,
1706, 1828, 1829, 2252,
2426, 2450, 2537
Swedish: 276, 512, 1092,
2216
Ukrainian: 497, 521, 906,
1163, 1466, 1910, 2061,
2280, 2307, 2491, 2652